DORCHESTER.   (210) Roman building in Fordington.
Mosaic pavement (now in D.C.M.)

AN INVENTORY OF
HISTORICAL MONUMENTS
IN THE
COUNTY OF
DORSET

VOLUME TWO
SOUTH-EAST
Part 3

ROYAL COMMISSION ON
HISTORICAL MONUMENTS (ENGLAND)
MCMLXX

SBN 11 700457 X*

Printed in England for Her Majesty's Stationery Office
by Unwin Brothers Limited
Woking and London

TABLE OF CONTENTS

PART 1

PART 2

PART 3

LIST OF PARISHES IN THE INVENTORY
(*see* parish map★ in pocket at end of Part 2)

1 AFFPUDDLE
2 ARNE
3 BERE REGIS
4 BINCOMBE
5 BLOXWORTH
6 BROADMAYNE
7 CHALDON HERRING
8 CHICKERELL
9 CHURCH KNOWLE
10 COOMBE KEYNES
11 CORFE CASTLE
12 CORFE MULLEN
13 DORCHESTER
14 HOLME, EAST
15 KIMMERIDGE
16 KNIGHTON, WEST
17 LANGTON MATRAVERS
18 LULWORTH, EAST
19 LULWORTH, WEST
20 LYTCHETT MATRAVERS
21 LYTCHETT MINSTER
22 MORDEN
23 MORETON
24 OSMINGTON
25 OWERMOIGNE
26 POOLE
27 PORTESHAM

28 PORTLAND
29 POXWELL
30 STAFFORD, WEST
31 STEEPLE
32 STOKE, EAST
33 STUDLAND
34 STURMINSTER MARSHALL
35 SWANAGE
36 TURNERS PUDDLE
37 TYNEHAM
38 WAREHAM LADY ST. MARY
39 WAREHAM ST. MARTIN
40 WARMWELL
41 WATERCOMBE
42 WEYMOUTH
43 WHITCOMBE
44 WINFRITH NEWBURGH
45 WINTERBOURNE ABBAS†
46 WINTERBORNE CAME
47 WINTERBORNE HERRINGSTON
48 WINTERBORNE MONKTON
49 WINTERBORNE ST. MARTIN
50 WINTERBOURNE STEEPLETON†
51 WOODSFORD
52 WOOL
53 WORTH MATRAVERS

★ The parish boundaries shown in red on the map were those in effect when the Inventory was compiled.

† The spelling of 'Winterbourne' here is modern usage; for convenience of reference the alphabetical order of the affixed names is followed in the Inventory.

LIST OF PLATES AND FIGURES

in PART 3

EARTHWORKS (Prehistoric, Roman and undated), other ROMAN REMAINS and ANCIENT FIELDS

For Post-Roman Buildings and Mediaeval and later Earthworks see LIST OF PLATES *etc. in* PARTS 1 *and* 2

PART 1, pp. i–lxx, 1–188; Pls., Frontis., 1–116
PART 2, pp. 189–418; Pls., Frontis., 117–207
PART 3, pp. 419–701; Pls., Frontis., 208–235

(The prefixed numerals in brackets refer to the monument numbers in the Inventory)

EARTHWORKS *continued*

ROMAN REMAINS

ROMAN REMAINS *continued*

ANCIENT FIELDS

ANCIENT FIELDS *continued*

PREHISTORIC, ROMAN AND UNDATED EARTHWORKS, OTHER ROMAN REMAINS AND ANCIENT FIELDS

This part of the Inventory of S.E. Dorset is divided into three sections, arranged as follows:–

Earthworks (pp. 420–519) include those of both the prehistoric and Romano-British periods since it is often impossible, as with settlements, to make a distinction between them; undated earthworks, and stones, are also considered here, but mediaeval or later earthworks are treated above in Parts 1 and 2 in the parish inventories. The monuments are listed by parishes under the following category headings:

Long and Round Barrows, p. 420	Enclosures, p. 502
Mounds, p. 480	Settlements, p. 508
Hill-forts, p. 483	Stones, p. 512
	Dykes, p. 515

Roman Remains (pp. 520–621), other than the earthworks mentioned above, are listed under the following heads:

Roman Roads, p. 528
Roman Dorchester (*Durnovaria*), p. 531
Other Roman Monuments, arranged by parishes, p. 592

Ancient Fields (pp. 622–633) are listed by groups irrespective of the parish arrangement.

An introduction to each section or category discusses distribution, dating and structure, with reference where appropriate to cultural affinities and social implications; explanations of the cultural and chronological terms used, which would have burdened the inventory text unduly, will be found in the Glossary (p. 635). These matters will be more fully considered in a general survey of the whole county to be included in the last Inventory of the Dorset series.

With the exception of the Roman Roads and Ancient Fields, the monuments are identified by numbers continuing from the parish inventories in Parts 1 and 2; within each parish they are described as far as possible from S.W. to N.E. In each entry the first reference in brackets gives the sheet number of the relevant O.S. 6 in. map and is normally followed by the National Grid reference.

EARTHWORKS

LONG AND ROUND BARROWS

The barrows in the Inventory are numbered individually within each parish, generally in the order S.W. to N.E. Each barrow group is described under that parish in which the predominating number of barrows occurs, those in adjacent parishes being cross-referenced thereto; the different parishes are indicated by subheadings in the group entry. All the groups, except those on the Ridgeway, are given reference letters (A, B, AA, AB, etc.) in the order that they are described under parishes in the Inventory; R is reserved for the Ridgeway Group (*see* p. 425), its component groups (R. 1–14) being numbered from W. to E. In addition, groups are given names of local derivation wherever possible. A register of barrow groups is given on pp. 429–30. The titles of round barrows described individually are printed in italics, those of barrows under group headings in ordinary type.

The position of each barrow is given exactly by a grid reference and generally by a topographical description. Relative distances are therefore only given between and within groups and clusters. Measurements between round barrows are from centre to centre, unless they are actually or almost touching when the phrase 'immediately adjacent' is used.

Since most barrows have been damaged, their character and even their identification as barrows may be in doubt. A question-mark is used to mean 'probable' or 'probably': thus 'Barrow (?)' is a mound which is more likely to be a barrow than anything else, as distinct from 'Mound, possible barrow'; a question-mark after a type description means that the doubt is only about the type, *e.g.* 'Bell (?)'. 'Ploughed' implies that the mound has been spread and is therefore lower and of greater diameter than it was formerly. Unless otherwise indicated, the diameter given is that of the mound only; dimensions of other barrow components are also quoted where possible. Heights of mounds on a slope are given as a mean measurement.

Most of the barrows have already been numbered in L. V. Grinsell, *Dorset Barrows* (1959). Correlations with this and other systems of numbering, principally in C. Warne, *Celtic Tumuli of Dorset* (1866), and the E. Cunnington MS. (*c.* 1890) in D.C.M., are given below in concordances (long barrows, p. 433; round barrows, p. 474). References to other main sources occur at the end of individual barrow descriptions and, if it is uncertain exactly which barrows are involved, in the introductions under the parish headings. Omission from this Inventory of examples shown as 'Tumuli' on Ordnance Survey maps or listed in *Dorset Barrows* means that evidence exists that these features are not barrows; some of them are included under Mounds (*see* below, p. 480).

In the statistics quoted below, all numbered barrows, certain, probable and possible, are included. Multiple barrows (*see* p. 422) are treated as single monuments.

LONG BARROWS: INTRODUCTION

There are nine, possibly twelve, long barrows in the *Dorset* II area, all presumably burial mounds of the Neolithic period. They comprise: five earthen long barrows and three more mounds which are probably earthen long barrows; one bank barrow; the Maiden Castle 'long mound' (probably best regarded as a bank barrow); and one chambered long barrow and a second, doubtful, example. Three other long barrows, already described in *Dorset* I, are considered in relation to the huge group of barrows on the

Ridgeway (*see* p. 425); these are the bank barrow Long Bredy (8), and the 'bank barrows' Kingston Russell (6d) and (6i), now reclassified as long barrows. In making this reclassification we are guided by the definition of a bank barrow which requires a length greater than that of the normal long barrow, parallel sides, and parallel side ditches which do not return round the ends.[1]

All the long mounds are situated on chalk, except for Portesham (33), which is on limestone. Their siting varies from 200 ft. above O.D. at Bere Regis (66) to just over 600 ft. at Corfe Castle (181), and most appear to have been deliberately placed just off the highest point in the locality. From a distance therefore they appear in silhouette only from certain directions, though modern features such as hedges often make them less prominent. The bank barrows particularly seem carefully placed for visibility from or towards certain points. It must always be borne in mind, however, that in most cases we can never know for certain how visibility might have been affected by vegetation or artificial structures in the prehistoric period.

Most of the mounds are between 100 ft. and 300 ft. long, the four shorter examples being damaged or doubtful; the bank barrow Broadmayne (19), however, attains 600 ft. and the Maiden Castle 'long mound', Winterborne St. Martin (23), 1790 ft. They vary in width from 40 ft., Corfe Castle (181), to 88 ft., Winterbourne Steepleton (13), the latter being the only true wedge-shaped example. In height they range from $1\frac{1}{4}$ ft., Winterborne Monkton (4), to 9 ft., Church Knowle (34), but the former has been much ploughed and the latter is an unusual, oval type. The majority are between 4 ft. and 7 ft. high and some are higher at one end, always the eastern. In cross-profile they vary from an almost triangular steeply ridged outline at Bincombe (12) to the flat-topped, steep-sided shape of the Broadmayne bank barrow, but ploughing and other destructive activities have often altered the original profile.

Only the 'Hell Stone', Portesham (33), is a certain chambered long barrow, though the existing chamber is a 19th-century reconstruction. With its chamber at the E. end and traces of a peristalith it resembles 'The Grey Mare and her Colts', Long Bredy ((15) in *Dorset* I), less than 2 miles away to the west. Small loose sarsen blocks in the disturbed portions of Bere Regis (66) perhaps indicate that this barrow is related to those with chambers. The stones Portesham (59) and Winterbourne Steepleton (65) cannot be regarded as the undisputed remains of chambered long barrows (*see* Stones *below*).

With two exceptions, Winterborne Monkton (3) and (4), the long barrows are aligned within 45° of an E.-W. line. The significance of this is uncertain, but it seems probable that in some instances they are directed towards local features rather than towards the sun, moon or stars. The long barrow Winterborne Monkton (3), for example, points exactly towards the W. end of the Maiden Castle 'long mound' which is itself apparently placed to be visible from the area of the long barrow. The 'long mound' was built across the ditch of the causewayed camp (*see under* Hill-forts, Winterborne St. Martin (142)), and nine other long barrows are within 6 miles of this monument. This placing of barrows in relation to one another or to other earthworks suggests deliberate siting.

Round barrows, generally later and sometimes much later than the long barrows, were often deliberately placed near them. A round barrow, Broadmayne (20), actually lies over the W. end of the bank barrow, as does another probable barrow over the eastern end of the long barrow Whitcombe (5) (*cf.* also Conquer Barrow, West Stafford (22), built on the bank of a henge monument). The group of round barrows on Ailwood Down is clustered round the long barrow Corfe Castle (181), and in some other groups the lines of round barrows prolong the axes of long barrows, notably the Culliford Tree Group (Plate 209). Visibility from a distance may however have been as important as close proximity and many examples are provided in the remarkable concentration of barrows along and near the South Dorset 'ridgeway' (*Ridgeway Barrow Group*, 'R', *see* pp. 425–9).

The long mounds, Bere Regis (66), Winterbourne Steepleton (13) and, probably, Portesham (33) have been incorporated in 'Celtic' field patterns, the first two at least apparently forming field boundaries. Around Bincombe (12) the negative lynchet on its N. side also suggests a field lay-out earlier than the present one.

---

[1] R. E. M. Wheeler, *Maiden Castle, Dorset*, Soc. Ants. Research Rep. XII (1943), 24.

Round Barrows: Introduction

The round barrows in South-east Dorset have been the subject of much unsystematic study, a situation largely corrected by the publication of L. V. Grinsell's *Dorset Barrows* (1959), which drew in part on the material then unpublished in the Commission's files. Amongst the round barrows listed below are a few not noted by Grinsell under the parishes included in this Volume, and there are differences and additions concerning details such as grid references, dimensions, descriptive observations, earthwork relationships, and interpretation of the evidence from the many particularly ill-recorded barrow excavations (*see* pp. 425, 428). But these differences of detail have not led to any radical revision of the generalisations and lists provided in the first part of *Dorset Barrows*, though recent studies elsewhere of the Middle and Late Bronze Age in general and the so-called 'Deverel-Rimbury culture' in particular have invalidated much of the earlier work collated by Grinsell which sought to explain and date 'post-Wessex culture' Bronze Age material largely on the basis of pottery typology.[1]

Round barrows are predominantly the burial mounds of the Bronze Age, though they were occasionally used, and in a few cases actually built, in the following Early Iron Age, Romano-British and Pagan Saxon times. It can, however, be taken that in the area covered by this Volume all the barrows described, with but a few possible exceptions, were built during the second millennium and first half of the first millennium B.C. Barrows covering primary burials accompanied by bell beakers and long-necked beakers were probably built in the first three centuries after *c.* 2000 B.C., but the great majority probably originated between *c.* 1700 B.C. and *c.* 1000 B.C.

The barrow typology on which the descriptions are based is that now generally accepted.[2] A *bowl* barrow is simply a round mound with or without a ditch (here specified where recognisable) immediately surrounding it. Only one certain example (Winterbourne Steepleton (20)) has a bank outside the ditch. A *bell* barrow is always surrounded by a ditch, separated from the foot of the mound by a flat or sloping ledge called a berm. A *disc* barrow consists of the same elements—mound, berm and ditch—but the mound is small and the berm relatively wide. In addition it is surrounded by a bank, almost invariably outside the ditch. A special type of disc barrow, virtually confined to S.E. Dorset and called by Grinsell the 'Dorset type', has a second ditch outside the bank. It has been suggested that this type takes the place of the *saucer* barrow—a low, broad mound with a ditch and outer bank—of which there are no certain examples in the area. The fifth main type is the *pond* barrow which consists superficially of a circular depression surrounded by a bank, sometimes with a single gap; such monuments were perhaps not primarily burial places. Bell, disc and possibly pond barrows are associated in particular with the Wessex culture of the Early Bronze Age. There are only a few exceptions to this typology, which by its very comprehensiveness isolates the exceptional. Thus, while the term 'bell-disc barrow' is cumbersome, the fact of its use indicates the unusual nature of the barrow and stresses the presence of features of both bell and disc barrows, producing proportions uncharacteristic of either.

Oval barrows are occasionally found. Sometimes they are clearly related to the true long barrow by reason of their ditch arrangements (*e.g.* Church Knowle (34)), but others are on account of their size and detail dealt with here as round barrows (*e.g.* Winterborne St. Martin (28)). Three barrows in square enclosures (Winterbourne Steepleton (24–6)) are seemingly Iron Age or later.

Multiple barrows are also rare. They consist of two or more immediately adjacent mounds apparently forming a single structure, normally surrounded by the same ditch. *Double*, or *twin*, *bowls* are most common (seven examples); Portesham (51) and Winterborne St. Martin (37), both ditchless but with mounds joined by a slight bank, and Tyneham (30), with a common ditch between the mounds, should probably be considered with them. There are four *triple bowls*, two (Bincombe (44) and West Lulworth (35)) apparently ditchless, and two (Winterbourne Abbas (22) and (24)) with a ditch along one side only. In the same Group (AD), Winterbourne Abbas (26–7) perhaps form a *double bell*, and Group AJ contains an

---

[1] *See*, for example, J. B. Calkin, *Arch. J.* CXIX (1962), 1–65; M. A. Smith, *P.P.S.* XXV (1959), 144–87; I. Smith, *Helinium* I (1961), 97–118; J. M. Coles, *Antiquity* XXXV (1961), 63–6; A. M. ApSimon, *P.P.S.* XXVIII (1962), 307–21.

[2] *A.B.M.E.*, fig. 2; *cf.* P. Ashbee, *The Bronze Age Round Barrow in Britain* (1960), 24–9.

apparently unique *quadruple bell* (Winterborne St. Martin (91)). In several other cases (*e.g.* Winterborne Monkton (9–10)), barrows are conjoined but cut or overlap each other, suggesting they are probably successive and therefore not strictly multiple as defined above.

Although the area covered by this Volume is small it nevertheless contains more barrows than the whole of Somerset or of Gloucestershire and Berkshire added together.[1] It is of primary importance for any study of barrows as field monuments, and the results of several excavations, ill-recorded though they may be, have a direct bearing on the nature and chronology of the Bronze Age in Southern England. Our aim in this Volume has been especially to consider the siting and distribution of barrows, particularly in groups. A *group* is defined here as four or more barrows related to one another by proximity, situation or common relationship to some other feature. Three main types of group are distinguished, called respectively *compact*, *linear* and *scattered*. These correspond to the 'nuclear', 'linear' and 'dispersed' types of group recently discussed elsewhere,[2] though 'nuclear' is there used to indicate a particular type of compact group.

Both compact and linear types of group can be subdivided. *Compact* groups, *i.e.* groups of barrows close together, occasionally appear to be related to one specific focal barrow or 'nucleus',[3] and have been called 'nuclear' groups. The *linear* type is subdivided by the distinction between *straight* and *irregular* lines, most straight lines being short whereas irregular lines tend to be strung out over a longer distance. The *scattered* type is simply a rather loose concentration of barrows. Any group may include elements of group-types other than that under which it is classified. Occasionally other, apparently associated, earthworks occur in group areas perhaps to serve as ritual or mortuary enclosures (*see* Enclosures, Winterborne Monkton (11), Winterborne Came (49), and Whitcombe (25)).

Particular interest is given to the area covered in this Volume by the consideration of the South Dorset *Ridgeway Barrow Group* as an entity, consisting of fourteen component groups (R.1 to 14), with 'satellite' groups, together forming one of the most marked concentrations of round barrows in the British Isles.[4] Most of the large groups occur on and near the Ridgeway but there are numerous small groups, particularly of linear type, in the rest of the area.

872 round barrows, a few only tentatively identified, are listed in the following Inventory: 195 form the Ridgeway Group together with 38 barrows already listed in *Dorset* I (the W. end of the Ridgeway Group lies within the parishes of Long Bredy, Kingston Russell and Little Bredy); a further 205 barrows, mostly in groups, lie within the area covered by the Ridgeway map (in pocket), nearly all on spurs projecting northwards from the Ridgeway itself. The concentration of barrows on the Ridgeway and its spurs is emphasised by the fact that half of the barrows listed in the Inventory are grouped there within an area only one-fifth of that covered by the Volume. Allowing for a few unrecognised and some unlocated and destroyed barrows, the total number in the Volume is about half that for the whole of Dorset—some 1800 as estimated by Grinsell[5]—though the area covered is only one quarter that of the county. Even within the Wessex region, therefore, archaeologically characterised by its large number of Bronze Age funerary monuments, this relatively small area in South Dorset was clearly of special importance.

Outside the Ridgeway area there is no comparable concentration within the Volume boundary, though most of the barrows fall within definitely localised scatters (Fig. opp. p. 634). These occur in five main areas: first on the high chalkland, much of it covered by Chaldon Down, between Poxwell and West Lulworth, with the 'Five Marys' (Chaldon Herring (51–6)) on the northern edge overlooking the heathland dropping N. to the river Frome; secondly on the low ridges to the N. of the river Piddle, spanning the junction of the heath and chalk and continuing N. over the Volume boundary; and thirdly on the heath on the northern side of the watershed between the Poole Harbour basin and the valley of the river Stour. The fourth area, with perhaps the densest scatter, is on the heaths to the W., S.W. and S. of

[1] H. E. O'Neil & L. V. Grinsell, *Gloucestershire Barrows* (Bristol and Glos. A.S., *Trans.* LXXIX (1960), Part I), 30.
[2] P. Ashbee, *op. cit.* (n. 2, p. 422), 34.
[3] *cf.* Grinsell's concept of a 'founder barrow', *A.B.M.E.*, 256.
[4] *See* pp. 425–9 and map of South Dorset Ridgeway Area, in pocket, Part 3; *cf.* map showing barrow density in R.C.H.M., *A Matter of Time* (1960), fig. 2.   [5] *Dorset Barrows*, 9.

Wareham; though this land is low-lying, most of the barrows are sited on the local ridges between the streams and on the small knolls rising slightly out of the heath. The fifth is on the high ground, partly down and partly heath, forming the ridge between Swanage and Studland and overlooking Poole Harbour to the N. and the sea to the E. Certain areas, however, were clearly avoided. The most obvious of these is the large stretch of heathland along and near the northern shores of Poole Harbour, an area which has not always been one of heath and which may have been partly cultivated in Bronze Age times.[1] The other area is S. of the Purbeck Hills where the almost entire absence of barrows is particularly striking when compared with the wealth of settlement and burial material of Iron Age and Romano-British times (*see* Figs. opp. p. 634).

Round barrows sometimes occur in apparently significant relationships to long barrows, mostly in groups (*see above*, p. 421; and *below*, p. 426, for discussion of the relationship in the Ridgeway area). Only the *Ailwood Down Group*, Corfe Castle, on the Purbeck Hills, demonstrates this outside the Ridgeway area. It can be regarded as a compact group of nuclear type, with the long barrow as the focal monument, a relationship emphasised by the absence of round barrows from the ridge for some distance to W. and E.

The Ailwood Down Group is one of the two largest groups in the Volume outside the Ridgeway area. The other, also a compact nuclear group, is on *Bloxworth Down* with a large bell-disc barrow apparently as the focal monument.[2] Otherwise most of the groups are on heathland, and a marked characteristic is the frequency with which the whole or part of these groups is based upon straight alignments of barrows. The *Five Barrow Hill Group* (Tyneham) and the *Seven Barrows Group* (Wareham St. Martin) are particularly good examples which also demonstrate how advantage was taken of a local ridge in the heathland to place barrows on sites in low-lying terrain so that the mounds are as clearly visible as those on the more obvious skylines of the chalk downs. The use of these low ridges naturally contributes to the linear nature of some of these heathland groups, but the geometric arrangements are apparently deliberate, since other dispositions could have been made. In addition to these short linear cemeteries, there are a few irregular, spaced-out, linear groups, like the *Corfe Common Group* (Fig. p. 97), as well as a few compact groups; the *Rose Lawn Group*, Poole, is of this last type. Particularly on the heath, barrows outside groups seldom occur singly, being normally in pairs or in clusters or alignments of three. Really low-lying and isolated barrows, like that near Nottington (Weymouth (434)), are extremely rare.

There is a marked discrepancy in the numbers of special or 'fancy' barrows within and outside the Ridgeway area. Whereas 76 special barrows of all types—bell, disc, pond and multiple bowls—occur in the Ridgeway area (29 of them actually in the *Ridgeway Group*), there are only 33 others in the rest of the area covered by the Volume, and all of those are bell barrows except for two double bowls (Tyneham (30) and (37)), a possible triple bowl (West Lulworth (35)), and the 'bell-disc' barrow on Bloxworth Down (Bloxworth (39)). The relative proportion of special barrows to others in the Ridgeway area is about 1 in 6 whereas outside this area it is 1 in 14.

The significance of these special barrows is indicated by some further figures. On average, their overall diameter is nearly twice that of bowl barrows, both ditched and un-ditched. The average overall diameter of a bowl barrow within the strict limits of this Volume is 54 ft. and that of a special barrow is just over 100 ft. The difference is further emphasised by the fact that whereas the largest number of special barrows have diameters of about 100 ft., the majority of the bowl barrows fall within a bracket of 30 ft. to 50 ft. A further quarter have diameters of 30 ft. and less, though some apparently ditched bowls (possibly bells) are over 100 ft. in diameter. The comparison might be made by saying that if all the bowl barrows in *Dorset* II were put side by side in a straight line, they would stretch for about 8 miles. A similar line of special barrows would be just over 1½ miles long.[3]

So many of the barrows have been damaged, particularly by excavation in the 19th century, and by ploughing in the last 25 years, that there is little to be learnt now by a study of heights and profiles. Off

---

[1] *cf.* evidence for early agriculture from beneath the heathland barrow at Chick's Hill, East Stoke (22).
[2] *Dorset Barrows*, fig. 4.
[3] *cf.* this analysis of barrow size by *types* with Grinsell's analysis of size on a cultural and chronological basis, *Dorset Barrows*, 11-15.

the chalk, however, and particularly on the Reading Beds, it is noticeable that many of the barrows have short, fairly steep sides and broad flat tops, apparently as original features. Only some 140 barrows of all those in the Volume are apparently undamaged. About 220—a quarter of the total—appear to have been excavated, judging from disturbance in the top of the barrow mounds, and known excavation accounts can be attached to specific barrows totalling about a quarter of this figure. Nine barrows have been excavated by modern methods (Arne (29), Bincombe (25, 27), Poole (363–5), Portesham (38), Weymouth (416) and Winterbourne Steepleton (46)); otherwise excavation results are almost entirely derived from 19th-century diggings, mostly into barrow centres. In a number of cases, the mound has been shown to consist partly of a turf stack, and in others, particularly in the East Lulworth area, large stones have formed a significant part of the barrow or grave structure (*cf.* Dorchester (169), with a boulder weighing nearly 3 tons, and Bincombe (24) and Poxwell (12) with small internal ring-walls). On the chalk, many of the excavations produced burials in graves, and in one case (Church Knowle (40)) the grave was about 10 ft. deep. In only twelve barrows is it probable that the excavators reached primary burials of Wessex culture date or type, the best-known examples—Clandon (Winterborne St. Martin (134)), Ridgeway 7 (Weymouth (403)), Culliford Tree (Whitcombe (9))—being all secondary deposits. With the exception of 'King's Barrow' (Arne (36)) on Stoborough Heath, all are on the higher ground, and most of them on chalk. It is perhaps instructive that three of these barrows occur in two separate compact groups (*Five Marys* and *Bloxworth Down*), which on other grounds could be regarded as probably having developed from and around a 'focal' barrow.

There is some evidence from S.E. Dorset for the use of barrows for burials subsequent to the Bronze Age. In Bloxworth and Corfe Castle parishes, for example, are barrows which contained several extended inhumations most likely to be of Romano-British date and almost certainly later than the probably Bronze Age type of secondary cremations, accompanied or otherwise, often inserted into the tops or sides of barrow mounds.

There is ample evidence to show that round barrows were used as markers or fixed points in the laying out of 'Celtic' fields and that in general they were deliberately preserved by the farmers of these fields. In Bere Regis, for example, three barrows in the Roke Down area are at 'Celtic' field angles (see *Ancient Field Group* (30)).

THE RIDGEWAY BARROW GROUP (GROUP R)[1]

> 'For sight of barrows, I believe not to be equalled . . .'
>
> Wm. Stukeley, *Itinerarium Curiosum* (1724), 163.

> '. . . notwithstanding the many changes which have taken place since that time [1724], it is certain that every enquiring spectator must be equally struck with this extraordinary district . . . where the adjacent downs or the lofty Ridgeway with its prolonged upland crest, are gracefully undulated with these time-honoured memorials'.
>
> Chas. Warne, *Celtic Tumuli of Dorset* (1866), 4.

South Dorset, particularly north of Weymouth, is dominated by a sharply-defined, 12-mile-long ridge at the southern edge of the chalk downs. This ridge, continued further to the E. by the Purbeck Hills, consists of Upper Chalk, overlaid at points by Clay-with-Flints and Bagshot Beds, dramatically truncated to the S. by the so-called Ridgeway Fault and the escarpment to the Jurassic Beds.

Topographically, where facing S., the ridge resembles a huge rampart, its domed top clearly defined and in places very narrow, notably on Bronkham Hill. It is best shown on the map by the 400 ft. contour, although at several points it rises to over 600 ft. and in one section (on Black Down by the Hardy Monument) to over 700 ft. above O.D. The general run of the ridge is from N.W. to S.E., the higher end being

---

[1] *See* Map of South Dorset Ridgeway Area (in pocket, Part 3), Figs. pp. 458, 460; Plates 209, 210; also *Dorset* I, pp. 38–9, 41–2, 127–9.

on Martin's Down in Long Bredy, from which there is a slight slope down along the top of the ridge towards Osmington in the S.E. This fact is indicated on the map by the 600 ft. ring contours N.W. of Black Down, and their absence to the E.

The rather more gradual rise to the ridge-top from the N. contrasts with the abrupt fall to the S. The chalk uplands have been cut into by small streams, now mostly vanished, resulting in a series of spurs jutting N. from the ridge towards the valley of the South Winterborne, a tributary of the River Frome. The spurs, together creating a rolling landscape, are all slightly lower than the top of the ridge and form a prominent part of the view to the N. from it. Geologically, they are part of the same formation, Upper Chalk. The same is true of the only two spurs S. of the ridge—Bincombe Hill and West Hill.

Most of the ridge-top has at some time been ploughed and only the south-east tip of Bincombe Hill, Came Down, and part of the col to the south of Northdown Barn, are in modern pasture. Bronkham Hill, presumably as a result of its acid soil, has not been ploughed, though it is pitted with solution hollows. Came Wood on the ridge-top, and Big Wood on a spur, are the only sizable plantations. For the rest, the ridge, interrupted only by dry-stone walls and barbed-wire fences, remains a windswept stretch of high ground providing splendid views, both along its own length and over much of S. Dorset and the adjacent English Channel.

Along nine of its twelve miles, between Martin's Down on the W. and the S. tip of Broadmayne to the E., the ridge-top is here regarded as the site of a large barrow group. Of the 233 barrows in the group, all but seven fall naturally into fourteen sub-groups which together make up the *Ridgeway Group (Group R)*. A further 129 barrows in fourteen groups and 76 barrows in clusters or singly, occur, mostly above the 400 ft. contour, on the spurs and slopes related to the ridge-top. Group R includes barrows in the parishes of Long Bredy, Kingston Russell, Little Bredy, Winterbourne Steepleton, Portesham, Winterborne St. Martin, Weymouth, Bincombe, Winterborne Came, Whitcombe, Broadmayne, Poxwell and Osmington. Most of these parishes, plus Winterbourne Abbas, Winterborne Monkton and Winterborne Herringston, also contain barrow groups and barrows related to Group R in ways discussed below. Lack of barrows on the remainder of the ridge suggests that the concentration is due to something more than the existence of any contemporary route that may have run along the top.

The main reason for describing the 233 barrows as part of one huge group is that they constitute a most unusually high concentration clearly associated with the ridge. They are, moreover, contained on one particular stretch between two bank barrows, markedly similar monuments without close parallel in England. Although the ridge itself continues to the S.E. of the Broadmayne bank barrow, apart from the *East Hill Group* (R. 14) ¾ mile from it, there are only two further barrows before the Poxwell Gap and only a scatter of barrows beyond. It might be suggested that the Broadmayne bank barrow is placed where it is, most delicately sited on the exact crest of the ridge, because it is clearly visible from the unusual spurs to the S. as well as from the lower ground to the N. The Martin's Down bank barrow at the W. end is even more dramatically sited at a natural break in the ridge. It can be suggested that the two bank barrows define the ends of a length of ridge-top which was of significance before it became studded with round barrows: its length suggests comparison with the function of the probably contemporary cursuses. There may in fact be a conceptual connection between the linear aspect of long barrows and bank barrows (apparently a local and abnormal development[1]) and of cursuses and, more particularly perhaps, between the ridgeway itself and the ridge-like appearance of the bank barrows. Of the six long barrows in Group R, five are towards the ends of the group as defined by the bank barrows. It may be significant that no henge monuments are known on the Ridgeway. The fact that a large number of round barrows was then apparently related to the demarcated stretch of ridge-top is strongly suggestive of continuity between the Neolithic and Bronze Age periods.

The Ridgeway Group is essentially an irregular linear cemetery because of the nature of the topographical feature on which it is sited; and eight of the groups within it are predominantly linear groups. Six groups

---

[1] Of the only three known monuments in England which can reasonably be described as bank barrows, one is at the W. end and one is at the E. end of the Ridgeway Barrow Group, and the other is within Maiden Castle.

—*e.g.* R.7 on *Ridge Hill*—contain straight alignments and one group just off the ridge-top, that on *West Hill* (R.12) on a southern spur, consists entirely of a straight line of nine barrows. Other groups are compact, or clustered round a 'focal' barrow—*e.g.* the greater (western) part of the *East Hill Group* (R.14) or the *Martin's Down Group* (R.1). Only two groups—R.4 and R.5—are just a scatter with no obvious coherence. The numbers of barrows in groups within Group R varies between five and thirty-eight. The largest group related to the ridge is that on *Winterbourne Abbas Poor Lot* (Group AD) with forty-four barrows down in a valley (although still over 400 ft. above O.D.).

All of the groups, and notably the last-mentioned, both on and off the ridge-top, appear to be deliberately sited so that a complex system of intervisibility is created. Clearly the height, and at times the narrow top, of the ridge make it inevitable that some barrows should be landmarks and intervisible. But many individual barrows and barrow groups are so sited in exactly the right place to achieve a striking effect, to appear on the sky-line when viewed from certain points, and to be seen easily from other barrows and barrow groups, that a considerable degree of control and deliberation must be postulated. The great Ridgeway bell-disc barrow (Winterborne St. Martin (67)), for example, though sited off the ridge-crest and in a dip of the ridge-top so that it is not readily visible when looking along the Ridgeway, is strikingly situated on the sky-line when viewed from the long mound in Maiden Castle, towards which it is tilted.

The topographical advantages of the ridge-top are demonstrated by the length of time it has been used as a burial site. The six long barrows show that the ridge was being used in the Neolithic period, and round barrows were built on the ridge-top between the bank barrows and on related sites by Beaker people. Most of the round barrows were probably erected during the Early and Middle Bronze Ages, but burials continued to be made here intermittently for another thousand years, at least until the Iron Age A burials on *Ridgeway Hill* (R.8) (Bincombe (24)). The ridge's most recent use for the commemoration of a dead personage is represented by the Hardy Monument (Portesham (3)) on its highest point.

There are only two other large areas of comparable barrow density in England and these are both in Wiltshire, around Avebury and around Stonehenge. In the 9 square miles around Avebury, there are about ten barrows per square mile, and in the 12 square miles around Stonehenge, the figure is about twenty-five. Even the whole area shown on the Ridgeway map—some 45 square miles—has an average density of ten barrows per square mile, while an area 1 mile wide based on the Ridgeway and the nearby groups to the N. gives a density of about forty barrows per square mile. Alternatively, the concentration can be emphasised by taking, for example, the arbitrary area within the parish boundary of Winterborne St. Martin which still gives a figure of about twenty-four barrows per square mile. In utter contrast, the Berkshire Downs have two barrows per square mile and the 14 mile long chalk ridge between the Rivers Nadder and Ebble in S. Wiltshire one to two barrows per square mile.[1]

It might be thought that such a relatively high number of barrows in a limited area involved large numbers of people. If, however, most of the barrows were built in the 2nd millennium B.C., as seems likely, then on average only one was built on the Ridgeway every 4 to 5 years. In the whole Ridgeway area, one barrow was built on average every 2 years, and, even if it is accepted that practically all the round barrows were built within the 500 years around 1500 B.C., on average only one barrow was built every year. People were almost certainly attracted from some distance to bury their dead, so even allowing for the probability that only the more important were given barrows and that many barrows held several secondary burials the figures hardly indicate a large population in the Bronze Age.

The main point which these figures suggest is that there was continual sepulchral activity in the Ridgeway area for a very long time, resulting in the relatively coherent pattern we now see. The careful siting within groups of individual barrows, for example, implies direction of labour by persons with a perceptive eye for the lie of the land. This is particularly well illustrated at either end of Group R in the siting both of the bank barrows and of the groups topographically and visually related to them.

---

[1] The sources used in arriving at these barrow densities are: *A.B.M.E.*, figs. 10 & 11; P. Ashbee, *The Bronze Age Round Barrow in Britain* (1960), fig. 6; *V.C.H., Wilts.* I, part i (1957), Map v; S. Piggott in W. F. Grimes (ed.), *Aspects of Archaeology in Britain & Beyond* (1951), fig. 61.

It is, however, difficult to trace the development of Group R, partly because there are few definite earthwork relationships affording relative dates, partly because the excavation records are so defective or non-existent (*see* below).

Six groups on the Ridgeway contain only bowl barrows, which are by far the most frequent type, 205 being recorded. It is likely that excavation would show some of these to be bell barrows, and some of the barrows known only from crop or soil-marks on air photographs, and classified as bowl barrows for lack of other evidence, may also have been bell barrows. The same qualifications must be made for the figure of 153 bowl barrows in the associated area. Such qualifications must not, however, detract from the validity of the total number of barrows in and associated with Group R.

Bell barrows are the next most frequent type, although small in number compared with bowl barrows. There are seventeen in Group R and seventeen (three of which are doubtful) on associated spurs. They occur in only six of the Ridgeway groups, being most numerous on *Bronkham Hill* (R.6), where there are four in a group of thirty, and on *Ridge Hill* (R.7) where there are five in a group of thirty-eight. Three 'bell-disc' barrows also occur, two small examples (Winterbourne Abbas (14–15)) in the *Poor Lot Group* (AD), and the other, with the largest diameter of any in Group R, at the eastern end of the *Ridge Hill Group*. This barrow (Winterborne St. Martin (67)) is, however, quite exceptional and it is probably misleading to classify it.

Disc and pond barrows also occur, though infrequently, in Group R and on associated spurs. Both disc barrows in Group R are on *Black Down* (R.2), while of the possible eleven such barrows related to Group R (two on the Bincombe-Winterborne Herringston boundary being doubtful), six occur in the *Poor Lot Group* and another, a well-preserved example, with an outer but no inner ditch, is in the *Came Down Group* (AG). Pond barrows are slightly more numerous, there being eighteen altogether: seven in Group R, ten in related groups and one, Winterbourne Abbas (32), in the valley bottom near the Broad Stone. Five in Group R are in the *Culliford Tree Group* (R.11), and there are also five in the *Poor Lot Group*. All but two of the others occur singly in different groups. The distribution of both disc and pond barrows shows them to be near either end of Group R, which fact perhaps further suggests that the limits to the group were recognised and thought to be of special significance. Certainly pond barrows seem to be especially related to the Ridgeway Group: there are no other certain examples in the whole of Dorset.

Although about 100 barrows in and related to Group R have been dug into, only seven (three of them pond barrows)[1] have been excavated by modern methods, and only two of those fully published. The value of the bulk of the excavated evidence is limited. Many of the barrows excavated in the 19th century for which excavation records exist have now been identified on the ground, but there remain on the one hand accounts which cannot be related to any one barrow, and on the other barrows which have clearly been dug into but for which there are no recognised records.[2] The latter are noted in the following Inventory, while the former are included in Grinsell's lists and used, for example, in the analysis of barrow structure (*Dorset Barrows*, 46–9), the details of which are not repeated here.

In only a few barrows can it be certain that the primary burial was excavated, and in the majority of excavations it is probable that secondary burials were missed. However, even though dug into by the central hole or trench methods, many excavated barrows have produced more than one secondary burial, and it is quite clear, despite the inadequately recorded evidence, that most of the Ridgeway and related barrows were used many times and over a long period. On the other hand, it is difficult to be certain about the sequence in any given barrow, since stratigraphy was seldom noted, and it is frequently not clear whether the lowest burial found was in fact the primary one. Further, the discovery of burials in the unexcavated, often greater, part of the barrow might alter the interpretation of the excavated evidence at present available. However, Group R and related groups contain some rich deposits, most notable being those from two barrows in Winterborne St. Martin ((134), the 'Clandon' barrow, and (82) in the *Eweleaze Barn Group* (AJ)); from Weymouth (403), better known as Cunnington's 'Ridgeway 7'; and

---

[1] Two of these, in the Poor Lot Group, are in the area covered by *Dorset* I (Kingston Russell (7m, n)): *see* p. 461, *below*.
[2] *See also* J. B. Calkin, Dorset *Procs.* LXXXVIII (1966), 128–48.

from Whitcombe (9), the 'Culliford Tree' barrow. The finds as a whole show the group to have formed during the Beaker period and Early Bronze Age, and to have developed, probably nearly to its full extent, during the Middle Bronze Age.

There is very little evidence for contemporary settlement associated with or adjacent to Group R and its related groups.[1] Earthwork associations occur in several instances between barrows and 'Celtic' fields. The triple bowl barrow on the N. of the *Poor Lot Group*, Winterbourne Abbas (24), is perhaps on top of a 'Celtic' field lynchet; and, within the 'Celtic' field immediately to the E., a small mound (Winterbourne Abbas (25)) is possibly a ploughed-out barrow. 'Celtic' fields probably also impinge on the S.W. edge of the same group. Barrows Winterborne St. Martin (79–80), N. of the W. end of the *Ridge Hill Group*, stand among ancient fields (*Ancient Field Group* (6)); and 'Celtic' field lynchets butt against the southern barrows on Bincombe Hill (*Ancient Field Group* (8)), and against two of the barrows, still preserved in pasture, in the centre of the *Northdown Barn Group* (Weymouth (419–20), *Ancient Field Group* (10)). Numerous barrows, particularly high ones, were used as fixed points for parish boundaries which crossed them, though the continuous line of parish boundaries running E. from the Hardy Monument to Broadmayne (broken now by the reconstituted Bincombe) runs immediately S. of most of the barrows, ignoring them. On the other hand, an unusual small bank and ditch, possibly a boundary line, cuts across the top of barrow Winterborne St. Martin (47) towards the E. end of Bronkham Hill (Fig. p. 519, Plate 209).

REGISTER OF BARROW GROUPS[2]

Abbreviations used in Tables I and II:

Group types (*see* p. 423)   C = compact   *Uncommon barrow types*   db = double bowl
                FC = compact with focal monument   tb = triple bowl
                L = linear, geometric   qb = quadruple bell
                IL = linear, irregular   bd = bell-disc
                S = scattered   bb = bank barrow

TABLE I: BARROW GROUPS IN GROUP R

Group	Parish under which described	Group type	Round Barrows							Long Barrows
			Total	Ditched Bowl	bowl	Bell	Disc	Pond	Others	
R. 1 Martin's Down	Bredy, Long	FC/S	8	5	3					1, 1bb
R. 2 Black Down	Kingston Russell	C/S	12	6	4	2				2
R. 3	Bredy, Little	IL/L	11	10	1					
R. 4 White Hill	Bredy, Little	S	5	5						
R. 5 Black Down	Portesham	S	10	9		1				
R. 6 Bronkham Hill	Winterborne St. Martin	IL	30	19	6	4			1db	
R. 7 Ridge Hill	Winterborne St. Martin	IL/L	38	21	10	5		1	1bd	
R. 8 Ridgeway Hill	Weymouth	IL/L	21	8	12	1				
R. 9 Bincombe Down	Bincombe	S/L	16	14		2				
R.10 Bincombe Hill	Bincombe	IL/L	20	15	3	1			1tb	1
R.11 Culliford Tree	Whitcombe	L/IL/FC	26	12	7	2		5		1, 1bb
R.12 West Hill	Bincombe	L	10	8	1		1			
R.13 Northdown Barn	Weymouth	IL	5	3	2					
R.14 East Hill	Weymouth	FC/IL	14	8	6					

(Braces in the "Parish under which described" column group R.1–R.4 as "Dorset I".)

[1] Neolithic material has been found in pits and in the old land surface beneath barrow Bincombe (27) in the Ridgeway Hill Group (R.8), Weymouth; *cf.* the Neolithic pit near the West Hill Group (R. 12), Bincombe (*see* p. 511).
[2] For positions *see* Fig. opp. p. 634 and map of Ridgeway Area (in pocket).

TABLE II: BARROW GROUPS OTHER THAN GROUP R

Group	Group name	Parish under which described	Group type	Total	Bowl	Ditched bowl	Bell	Disc	Pond	Others	Long Barrows
A	Pallington Heath	Affpuddle	C	8	6	1	1				
B	Worgret Heath	Arne	S	9	3	6					
C	Broomhill	Bere Regis	IL	4	4						
D	Roke Down	Bere Regis	S	6	3	1	2				
E	Bloxworth Down	Bloxworth	FC	15	14					1bd	
F	Chaldon Down	Chaldon Herring	S	5	5						
G	Beaufort Farm	Chaldon Herring	IL	4	4						
H	Five Marys	Chaldon Herring	L	6	1	3	2				
I	Creech Heath	Church Knowle	L	4	3	1					
J	Coombe Beacon	Coombe Keynes	C/S	6	4		2				
K	Corfe Common	Corfe Castle	IL	8	8						
L	Ailwood Down	Corfe Castle	FC/L	17	14	3					1
M		Osmington	L	4	3	1					
N	Canford Heath	Poole	IL	4	2		2				
O	Rose Lawn	Poole	C	8	6		2				
P	Barrow Hill	Poole	L/S	6	1	1	4				
Q	Friar Waddon Hill	Portesham	IL	4	4						
R	(see p. 429)										
S	West Holme Heath	Stoke, East	L	6	6						
T	Farm Heath	Stoke, East	IL	5	4	1					
U	Godlingston Heath	Studland	L	4	1		3				
V	Thorny Barrow	Studland	L	4	3		1				
W	Ballard Down	Swanage	C	5	5						
X	Black Hill	Turners Puddle	L/S	6	6						
Y	Thorn Barrow	Tyneham	L/S	6	6						
Z	Five Barrow Hill	Tyneham	L	6	3		3				
AA	Seven Barrows	Wareham St. Martin	L	8	8						
AB	*	Whitcombe	L	4			4				
AC	Black Knoll	Winfrith Newburgh	IL	5	5						
AD	Poor Lot *	Winterbourne Abbas	FC/IL	44	17	5	7	6	5	2bd, 2tb	
AE	Three Barrow Clump *	Winterbourne Abbas	C	10	2	5	2	1			
AF	Longlands *	Winterbourne Abbas	L	5	3	1	1				1
AG	Came Down *	Winterborne Came	FC	11	6	2	1	1		1db	
AH	Lanceborough *	Winterborne Monkton	C	4	1		3				1
AI	Rew Hill *	Winterborne St. Martin	IL	4	4						
AJ	Eweleaze Barn *	Winterborne St. Martin	IL	10	7	1			1	1qb	
AK	Four Barrow Hill *	Winterborne St. Martin	L	6	4		2				
AL	Ashton *	Winterborne St. Martin	L	4	4						
AM	Rew	Winterborne St. Martin	S/FC	7	6				1		
AN	Third Milestone	Winterborne St. Martin	S	5	5						
AO	Wireless Station	Winterborne St. Martin	S	13	8		4			1db	
AP	Gaythorne *	Winterbourne Steepleton	C	4	4						
AQ	Big Wood *	Winterbourne Steepleton	IL	13	6	5	1	1		1db	
AS	Sheep Down *	Winterbourne Steepleton	C	5	3				1	1db	
AT	Rowden *	Winterbourne Steepleton	S	5	5						
AU	Pound Hill	Winterbourne Steepleton	IL	5	3	1				1db	

* Indicates groups in the Ridgeway area apparently related to Group R.

LONG BARROWS: INVENTORY

BERE REGIS

(66) LONG BARROW, possibly chambered (SY 89 NW; 82989725), lies on Bere Down, about 200 ft. above O.D., just below the crest of a broad chalk ridge, on ground sloping gently to N.W., W. and S.; it is only seen in silhouette at close range from N. and S.

On a bearing of 70°, it is 176 ft. long, 65 ft. wide in the middle where widest, and some 7 ft. high at the E. end and 6 ft. at the W. A slight terrace, some 45 ft. wide, parallel to the barrow on the S., probably marks the site of the ditch. The centre of the mound has been cut into from the S. and the spine hollowed for 114 ft. from the W. end. Five sarsen boulders, none more than 2½ ft. long and 1¼ ft. deep, lie scattered, two on the hollowed spine and three in the S. excavation where there is a large heap of flints. The barrow was used as a 'Celtic' field boundary (see Ancient Field Group (30)), and lynchets run up to it, crossing the line of any ditch that may have existed on the N. The mound has been damaged by rabbits and ploughing.

BINCOMBE

(12) LONG BARROW (SY 68 NE; 68858515; Fig. p. 24), about 520 ft. above O.D., is prominently sited on the crest of a ridge with ground falling from it on all sides but the S.; it forms part of the Bincombe Hill Barrow Group (R. 10).

Almost E.-W. (88°), it is 270 ft. long but formerly extended at both ends beyond the field boundaries, where the hedges still preserve the mound to a height of 3½ ft. Where undisturbed it has a ridged cross-profile and is some 45 ft. wide and about 5 ft. high from the S.; on the N., where ploughing at some time before enclosure has formed a negative lynchet, it is 6 ft. high at the W. end and 8 ft. at the E. Further damage has been caused by modern ploughing on the S. and by tracks at either end.

BROADMAYNE

(19) BANK BARROW (SY 78 NW; 70288533; Fig. p. 458, Plate 209), at the extreme S.W. of the parish was, identified by O. G. S. Crawford (Antiquity XII (1938), 229). It lies at the S.E. end of the Ridgeway Barrow Group (see p. 426), on the summit of the Upper Chalk ridge, about 470 ft. above O.D., with the ground falling from it to N., N.E. and S.

On a bearing of 102°, it is at least 600 ft. long, with flattened top and steep sides; the W. and E. ends are respectively 49 ft. and 57 ft. wide, and 5½ ft. and 7 ft. high above the bottom of the ditch on the S. The ditch here is continuous and about 25 ft. wide, but on the N. constant ploughing has obscured all but a slight depression except adjacent to a round barrow, Broadmayne (21), where a drop of 9 ft. below the crest of the bank barrow apparently represents the original ditch. Another round barrow, Broadmayne (20), seems deliberately placed over the W. end of the bank barrow, and its ditch on the S., where undisturbed, continues the flanking ditch of the latter. At the E. end the bank barrow has been partly destroyed, but it is virtually certain that it never continued to the S. of the modern road. (See profile on map of Ridgeway Area, in pocket.)

CHURCH KNOWLE

(34) OVAL BARROW, long barrow (?) (SY 98 SW; 92348208), 570 ft. above O.D., is prominently sited on Stonehill Down, a narrow steep-sided ridge falling gently E.

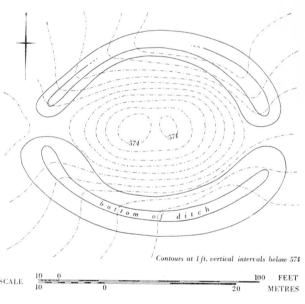

Contours at 1 ft. vertical intervals below 57½

SCALE

Church Knowle (34)

Aligned almost E.-W. (88°), it is 96 ft. long, 64 ft. wide and 9 ft. high from the N. It is very rounded in profile, except for disturbance at the top, and is surrounded by a sloping berm, narrow and indistinct on the sides but well-marked and up to 8 ft. wide at either end. The ditch, at most 1 ft. deep, is 12 ft. wide along the sides and 20 ft. at the ends where it is now interrupted by causeways 11 ft. wide. The E. causeway, on the main E.-W. axis, is clearly original but the western appears to be a later insertion; it dips as it crosses the ditch, which ends irregularly on either side of it.

CORFE CASTLE

(181) LONG BARROW (SY 98 SE; 99588151; Fig. p. 444), is sited about 600 ft. above O.D. on Ailwood Down, adjacent to the round barrows of Group (L). It lies along the contour of the S. shoulder of the chalk ridge of the Purbeck Hills and is only seen in silhouette from the steep slope to the S.

On a bearing of 97°, it is about 112 ft. long, approximately 40 ft. wide, and about 3 ft. high from the N. and 6 ft. from the S. The sides are apparently parallel but are disturbed by old excavations. Slight depressions to E., S. and W. probably mark the original quarry ditches; a small round barrow, Corfe Castle (217), immediately S.E., seems to impinge on the ditch.

PORTESHAM

(33) THE HELL STONE, Neolithic chambered long barrow (SY 68 NW; 60588670; Plate 208), is situated on Portesham Hill, over 600 ft. above O.D., on the summit of the S.-facing limestone escarpment which here forms a flat-topped ridge running N.W.-S.E.; the ground falls steeply on the S.W. to a re-entrant and less steeply on the N.E. to a dry valley. The long mound is aligned along the ridge (130°), with a reconstructed stone chamber exposed at the S.E. end.

The much-damaged mound is at least 88 ft. long and up to 40 ft. wide, tapering slightly to N.W.; it is of rounded cross-profile and rises to a maximum height of 5 ft. near the chamber, but further S.E. it is much disturbed and at most 2 ft. high. The chamber, incorrectly rebuilt in 1866, now consists of nine orthostats, up to 5¾ ft. high and from 1¼ ft. to 1¾ ft. thick, supporting a roughly oval capstone, 10 ft. by 8 ft. and averaging just over 2 ft. thick. Smaller stones embedded in the mound in front of the chamber may represent a former peristalith, probably not continuous. The stones are sarsen of Bagshot age, a hard Tertiary conglomerate containing flint gravel. A drawing of 1790 by S. H. Grimm (B.M. Add. MS. 15538; reproduced on Plate 208) shows the capstone supported by one or two orthostats and tilting to the S., with another orthostat to the N. and recumbent stones to S. and S.W.; Hutchins, who published a similar illustration (II, facing 759), states that the arrangement of the stones was partly due to shepherds who used the chamber as a shelter (1st edn. (1774), I, 554). Nevertheless the stones clearly represent an original chamber, and the Hell Stone is comparable to the 'Grey Mare and her Colts', less than 1½ miles to the W. on the same ridge (S. Piggott, Dorset *Procs.* LXVII (1945), 30–3; *Dorset* I, Long Bredy (15)).

The barrow is now crossed by a stone wall running N.-S., to E. of which it has been disturbed by digging. Ploughing has encroached on the mound, and air photographs (CPE/UK 1824, 3291) suggest that it was used as a 'Celtic' field boundary (*see* Ancient Field Group (5)).

(C. Warne, *Ancient Dorset* (1872), 135 and Pl. XXIII; Dorset *Procs.* XXIX (1908), lxxv-lxxviii.)

WHITCOMBE

(5) LONG BARROW (SY 68 NE; 69978567; Fig. p. 458), 400 yds. N.W. of the bank barrow, Broadmayne (19), is sited about 450 ft. above O.D. just below the shoulder of a broad ridge on ground dipping N.W. On a bearing of 46°, it is about 170 ft. long, 50 ft. wide and about 7 ft. high; at the N.E. end is a sharp rise to an additional mound, probably a later round barrow (Whitcombe (8)), with a total height of 12 ft. (*see* profile, p. 458). Remains of side ditches are obscured by undergrowth and trees. (Hutchins II, 291.)

WINTERBOURNE ABBAS

(13) OVAL BARROW, long barrow(?) (SY 69 SW; 60459006), is sited about 450 ft. above O.D. on a gentle N.E.-facing slope just below the crest of a broad ridge. It has been much ploughed and is now only about 1½ ft. high and measures 70 ft. (E.-W.) by 40 ft. Under plough it showed only earth and flints as in the surrounding field. It lies N.E. of the Longlands Barrow Group (AF).

WINTERBORNE MONKTON

(3) LONG BARROW (?) (SY 68 NE; 66548877; Fig. p. 494), lies 30 yds. due N. of the outer bank of the W. entrance of Maiden Castle, about 350 ft. above O.D. on the E.-facing slope of a chalk ridge. On a bearing of 142°, it is about 90 ft. long, at most about 50 ft. wide, about 5 ft. high from below but almost flat from above with rounded ends returning uphill. At the S. end the plough had exposed a thick spread of heavy flints and there was the remnant of a shallow pit or ditch, over 10 ft. across. Oblique air photographs taken in the 1930's by Major G. W. G. Allen show a narrow mound with unusually tapered ends, possibly sharpened by tracks or ploughing. There has been intensive ploughing since then.

(4) LONG BARROW (SY 68 NE; 66568930; Fig. p. 494), within the Lanceborough Barrow Group (AH), lies over 300 ft. above O.D. on a broad flat-topped chalk rise from which the ground drops gently to N., E. and S. Aligned almost N.-S. (2°), it is 320 ft. long, 45 ft. wide on average, and 3 ins. high above the ditch bottom on the W. and 1¼ ft. on the E. The parallel side ditches have clearly defined ends on the S., but both mound and ditches fade out to the N. The W. ditch shows as a straight dark soil-mark, about 12 ft. wide, along a broad shallow depression; the E. ditch, on an almost level shelf, is less regular. The ditch of a ploughed-out round barrow, Winterborne Monkton (5), almost touches the long barrow ditch on the S.W. The mound has been heavily ploughed and perhaps deliberately levelled.

WINTERBORNE ST. MARTIN

(23) MAIDEN CASTLE LONG MOUND (SY 68 NE; 66608855–67128842; Figs. p. 494, opp. p. 498, Plate 213), is a unique Neolithic burial mound, 1790 ft. long, flanked by parallel side ditches, 60 ft. apart; it is nearly three times as long as bank barrow Broadmayne (19).

It lies within the ramparts of the great hill-fort, Winter-borne St. Martin (142), at 430 ft. above O.D. on a saddle-backed hill forming the W. end of a broad low ridge of Upper Chalk. It is sited to the N. of the crest, and some 600 ft. from its E. end its alignment changes from N.W.-S.E. to W.N.W.-E.S.E. and follows the contour of the hill; it thus seems deliberately placed so as to be wholly visible from the lower ground to the N. (*see* Lanceborough Barrow Group (AH)). The long mound was built over the filled up ditches of the W. side of the causewayed camp (*see under* Hill-forts, Winterborne St. Martin (142)), and has in turn been cut by the ditch of the first-phase hill-fort. A length of 1000 ft. on the W. was apparently destroyed as early as the 1st century A.D., and ploughing from at least the 17th century has reduced it further. It was examined by R. E. M. Wheeler in 1936 and 1937, and in 1951 R. J. C. Atkinson made a small cutting across the W. section.

The W. part of the mound is now barely visible. From immediately N. of the W. entrance of the hill-fort it runs E.S.E. as a very low, rounded scarp for about 1000 ft.; it then continues for 190 ft. as a well-defined mound 60 ft. across and up to 4 ft. high. East of the ditch of the first-phase hill-fort it is over-ridden by the remains of the hill-fort rampart and continues S.E. for a further 500 ft., very spread and rounded and rarely more than 2 ft. high. The flanking ditches do not return round the ends of the mound; the S. ditch is largely undetectable on the ground, and the N. appears as a slight shelf. The W. end of this ditch is covered by the inner rampart of the final hill-fort.

Wheeler's excavations (Fig. opp. p. 498, Plate 213) showed that the ditches were parallel and on average 60 ft. apart except at the change in direction where the distance was rather less. They were mainly regular, steep-sided and flat-bottomed, 5 ft. to 6 ft. deep, 12 ft. to 15 ft. across at the top and 7 ft. to 11 ft. across the bottom. The stratification was fairly uniform. The rapid silt and a black hearth layer overlying it at many points contained sherds of Windmill Hill ware only, with ox bones occurring at the E. ends of both ditches. Above this the filling included Peterborough sherds, and the upper layers contained occupation material associated with Beaker, Rinyo-Clacton and Early Bronze Age wares. A band of clay represented the turf and humus which sealed the ditch between the Early Bronze Age and the Iron Age, and the filling above this was riddled with Iron Age pits. The mound below the hill-fort rampart was preserved to a height of 5 ft. and its 'turf-line' was continuous with that sealing the Early Bronze Age filling of the ditches. Occasional post-holes attributed to the Neolithic period occurred along the inner margin of the ditches, and four post-holes at the extreme E. end of the mound suggested a concave revetment. Immediately W. of this, on the axis of the mound, was an oval pit containing Windmill Hill pottery, limpet-shells and bone fragments. Also on the main axis, 74 ft. from the E. end, was a primary inhumation of a young adult male, the skeleton showing evidence of extensive mutilation, including trepanning, immediately after death; 30 ft. to the S.E. were two crouched inhumations of small children with a small Windmill Hill cup. E. of these, just below the surface, was an intrusive pagan Saxon burial (*see also* p. xlix, *n.* 2).

The cutting by R. J. C. Atkinson across the W. section suggested there had been some destruction during the Iron Age and substantial levelling by the mid 1st century A.D.

(R. E. M. Wheeler, *Maiden Castle* (1943), 18–24, 86–9; R. J. C. Atkinson, Dorset *Procs.* LXXIV (1952), 36–8.)

WINTERBOURNE STEEPLETON

(13) LONG BARROW (SY 68 NW; 60438836; Fig. opp. p. 624), lies on Sheep Down, about 580 ft. above O.D., on the side of a long arable slope falling N.E. from Black Down. On a bearing of 124°, it is 174 ft. long, 70 ft. wide at the N.W. end and 88 ft. at the S.E., where it rises to its maximum height of 6 ft. It was probably incorporated in a 'Celtic' field lay-out (*see* Ancient Field Group (3), p. 624); plough soil is piled against the S. side, and a lynchet meets the E. end at right angles from the S. The whole has been heavily ploughed in recent times.

LONG BARROWS: CONCORDANCE

The parish monument numbers of long barrows in this Inventory are shown in the column headed *R.C.H.M.*. The parish numbers of barrows in L. V. Grinsell, *Dorset Barrows* (1959), and the barrow numbers on the Ordnance Survey *Map of Neolithic Wessex* (1932) are listed respectively under the headings *L.V.G.* and *Neo. Wx.*

	R.C.H.M.	L.V.G.	Neo. Wx.
BERE REGIS	66	I	155
BINCOMBE	12		
BROADMAYNE	19	I	
CHURCH KNOWLE	34	II	
CORFE CASTLE	181	I	185
PORTESHAM	33	II	145
WHITCOMBE	5	I	154
WINTERBOURNE ABBAS	13	I	147
WINTERBORNE MONKTON	3	I	
,, ,,	4		
WINTERBORNE ST. MARTIN	23	I	
WINTERBOURNE STEEPLETON	13	I	146

Other monuments noted as long barrows by Grinsell or the Ordnance Survey will be found elsewhere in the Inventory as follows:—

CHURCH KNOWLE: LVG I, *see* Mounds (51).

PORTESHAM: LVG I and Neo. Wx. 144, *see* Round Barrows (44) and Stones (59).

WINTERBOURNE STEEPLETON: LVG II and Neo. Wx. 148, *see* Stones (65); LVG III and Neo. Wx. 150, *see* Round Barrows (60).

ROUND BARROWS: INVENTORY

AFFPUDDLE

All but three of the twenty barrows in the parish lie on the heathlands rising to the N. of the River Frome. Most have been damaged by recent military activity. Two are probably bells, one within group (A). Barrows (61–3) lie on chalk N. of the River Piddle.

(A) PALLINGTON HEATH GROUP (SY 79 SE). Eight barrows, including one probable bell, immediately S. of Piddle–Frome watershed, near S. edge of broad flat plateau just above 300 ft. contour.

(44) Bowl (78739219) at Pallington Clump. Diam. 70 ft., ht. 7½ ft. Surrounded by tree-clump circle; still prominent with pines.

(45) Mound, possible bowl (78769217), 32 yds. E. of (44). Diam. 20 ft., ht. 2 ft. Damaged.

(46) Bell (?) (78799222) 80 yds. E.N.E. of (44). Diam. 63 ft., including berm on N., ht. 8½ ft., ditch 7 ft. wide and 1 ft. deep.

(47) Bowl (?) (78789223) immediately W.N.W. of (46). Diam. about 20 ft., ht. 1½ ft.

(48) Ditched bowl (78919224) 135 yds. E.N.E. of (46). Diam. 50 ft., ht. 5½ ft. Road cuts N. side.

(49) Bowl (78969222) 50 yds. E.S.E. of (48). Diam. 54 ft., ht. 4½ ft.

(50) Bowl (79089212) 175 yds. S.E. of (49). Diam. 54 ft., ht. 4¾ ft.

(51) Ditched bowl (79109214) 25 yds. N.N.E. of (50). Diam. 37 ft., ht. 4½ ft. Excavated in centre and across E.-W. axis.

(52) Bowl (SY 79 SE; 79709251) in Sares Wood on gentle N. slope just under 300 ft. above O.D. Diam. 43 ft., ht. 3½ ft. Planted with firs.

(53) Bowl (?) (SY 79 SE; 79969226) on edge of plateau just above 300 ft. contour. Diam. 30 ft., ht. 1½ ft. N. half destroyed.

(54) Bowl (SY 89 SW; 80079226) situated as (53) and 125 yds. E. of it. Diam. 26 ft., ht. 1¾ ft. Practically destroyed.

(55) Bell (?) (SY 89 SW; 80539236) on plateau above 200 ft. contour. Diam., including berm, 52 ft., ht. 5½ ft., with ditch 8 ft. wide and 1 ft. deep. Much damaged.

(56) Ditched bowl (SY 89 SW; 80679227) on edge of spur jutting S. from plateau and 175 yds. S.E. of (55). Diam. 45 ft., ht. 5 ft.

(57) Bowl (SY 89 SW; 81399246) on S. edge of plateau 60 yds. S. of Cull-pepper's Dish, a swallow-hole. Diam. about 51 ft., ht. 3 ft. Much damaged.

(58) Bowl (SY 89 SW; 81499243) on S. edge of plateau 100 yds. E.S.E. of (57). Diam. 26 ft., ht. 3 ft. Hollowed on top.

(59) Ditched bowl (SY 89 SW; 81739199) on E. knoll in Starmoor Plantation inside 200 ft. ring contour. Diam. 32 ft., ht. 2½ ft.

(60) Bowl (SY 89 SW; 82499241) in Throop Clump just above 200 ft. contour and on gradual S. slope. Diam. 62 ft., ht. 8½ ft. Damaged.

(61) Double Barrow, bowl (SY 89 SW; 82089453) on 300 ft. contour near W. end of spur. Diam. about 40 ft., ht. about 8 ft. No evidence of contiguous barrow.

(62) Rewbarrow (1811), bowl (?) (SY 89 SW; 81849456). On ground falling S. to 200 ft. contour. Diam. about 30 ft., ht. 5 ft.

(63) Bowl (SY 89 NW; 81899538) below crest of broad S.-facing spur above 200 ft. contour. Diam. 39 ft., ht. 3 ft. In area of very disturbed 'Celtic' fields. Ploughed.

ARNE

Nineteen barrows are scattered irregularly over the parish, all on Tertiary Beds and mostly in heathland. Six, together with three now in Wareham Lady St. Mary, form a group (B) on Worgret Heath, while (42–44) lie very close together on Middlebere Heath. Many are damaged and one (LVG 12), has been destroyed. Three have been excavated: King's Barrow (36) covered a rare example of a tree-trunk coffin burial; one, unidentified, contained an urn cemetery; the third, a small unidentified site near (36), was opened in about 1835 and twenty-five bronze axes, at least two apparently socketed, were found (Hutchins I, 100; Dorset Procs. XX (1899), 159).

(28) Bowl (SY 88 NE; 89658729). Diam. about 55 ft., ht. 4 ft. Ploughed.

(B) WORGRET HEATH GROUP (SY 98 NW), nine barrows, including Wareham Lady St. Mary (82–4) of which (83) is a possible bell. On relatively high ground around the 100 ft. contour, though (31) is below it to the E. One barrow in this area, excavated in c. 1830 by Pennie and later destroyed, contained at least twenty-four Middle or Late Bronze Age urns, some holding cremations. Only one survives, in D.C.M. (Gentleman's Magazine (1838), pt. i, 303; Hutchins I, 108).

(29) Ditched bowl (90028707). Totally excavated 1964 by Dr. G. J. Wainwright for the Ministry of Public Building and Works. Diam. 40 ft., ht. 4 ft., surrounded by a ditch 10 ft. wide. Near the centre of the mound were a biconical urn and a bucket urn but no burial (Dorset Procs. LXXXVII (1965), 119).

(30) Bowl (?) (90258701) 240 yds. E.S.E. of (29). Diam. about 40 ft., ht. about 4 ft. Converted into tree-covered and revetted garden feature.

(31) Ditched bowl (90538709) 330 yds. E.N.E. of (30) on summit of ridge. Diam. 65 ft., ht. 8½ ft. Top flattened and slightly hollowed. Ditch recently widened. Fir-covered.

(32) Ditched bowl (90118720) 175 yds. N.N.E. of (29) on end of spur. Diam. 20 ft., ht. 2½ ft.

(33) Ditched bowl (90128733) 150 yds. N. of (32). Diam. 40 ft., ht. 4½ ft., with ditch 6½ ft. wide and up to 9 ins. deep.

(34) Bowl, possibly ditched (90138736) 38 yds. N.N.E. of (33). Diam. 32 ft., ht. 5 ft. Cut by modern field boundary.

Wareham Lady St. Mary:

(82) Bowl (90238727) 155 yds. S.E. of (34) near edge of slope falling steeply N. Diam. about 50 ft., ht. 5 ft.

(83) Ditched bowl or bell (90308724) 76 yds. E.S.E. of (82). Diam., including possible berm on N., 61 ft., ht. 6½ ft., with ditch 7 ft. wide and 1 ft. deep cut by modern ditch on S. Disturbed on top.

(84) Ditched bowl (90328727) 50 yds. N.E. of (83) at end of spur. Diam. 38 ft., ht. 5½ ft., with ditch 6½ ft. wide and up to 1 ft. deep.

(35) *Ditched bowl* (?) (SY 98 NW; 91648571) in Bartletts Firs. Diam. about 60 ft., ht. 9 ft. Covered in rhododendrons.

(36) *King's Barrow*, bowl (?) (SY 98 NW; 92048572). Now in a garden and covered with trees and shrubs. Diam. uncertain, ht. about 5½ ft. In 1767 said to be 100 ft. in diam., 12 ft. high and apparently constructed of turves. In centre on sandy buried surface was primary inhumation (probably Wessex culture) without skull, wrapped in stitched animal skins, within a hollowed oak tree coffin 10 ft. long by 4 ft. wide by 3 ft. deep orientated N.W.-S.E. Attached to one skin was 'gold lace' 4 ins. by 2½ ins. with 'bits of wire' in it. Near the S.E. end of the coffin was a small cup, now lost, 2 ins. high, at most 3 ins. in diam. at the rim, with sides only ⅛ in. thick, and decorated with incised lines. Though described as of oak, it was more probably made of Kimmeridge shale. (*Salisbury Journal* 9th Mar. 1767; *Gentleman's Magazine* (1767), 53–4; Hutchins I, 100, 563; *W.A.M.* XLIV (1928), 101–5 and 111–17; *P.P.S.* XV (1949), 101–6.)

(37) *Three Lords' Barrow*, bowl (?) (SY 98 SW; 91458475) at junction of four parishes and formerly at junction of three manors. Diam. about 45 ft., ht. 3 ft., on natural knoll with stream to S. and W. A piece of stone window jamb on top presumably serves as boundary mark.

(38) *Bell* (?) (SY 98 SW; 92178469) on slight rise immediately inside modern tree-clump enclosure. Diam. including slight, sloping berm 65 ft., ht. 7 ft. Top flattened and disturbed.

(39) *Bowl* (SY 98 SW; 92988450) on almost level site and crossed by parish boundary with Church Knowle. Diam. 54 ft., ht. 4½ ft. Dug into on top.

(40) *Bowl* (SY 98 SW; 93078466). Diam. 65 ft., ht. 8 ft. Excavation in centre and on E.

(41) *Bowl* (SY 98 SW; 93078481) on almost level site. Diam. 55 ft., ht. 5½ ft.

The *Three Barrows* (SY 98 SW) lie in an E.-W. line within 100 ft. ring contour on S.W. of Middlebere Heath. All are badly damaged.

(42) *Ditched bowl* (93898441). Diam. 84 ft., ht. 6½ ft., with ditch about 10 ft. wide. Possibly contiguous with (43).

(43) *Bowl* (?) (93918441) immediately E. of (42). Ht. about 6 ft.

(44) *Bowl* (?), large (93948441), 25 yds. E. of (43).

(45) *Mound*, possible small bowl (SY 98 NW; 94778514), on O.S. 1811. Crossed by boundary bank.

(46) *Ditched bowl* (SY 98 NE; 96928815) on ridge summit. Diam. 95 ft., ht. 9½ ft., with ditch 14 ft. wide and 1½ ft. deep. An outer bank is possibly a tree-clump enclosure. Damaged.

BERE REGIS

The parish contains fifty barrows, on heathland to the S. and on downland, now largely arable, to the N. The heathland barrows are usually widely spaced; those on the downland are more numerous and often in clusters or groups. The six barrows in the *Roke Down* group include two probable bells; the three clustered in the E. of the parish include one (114) with two concentric ditches. On *Broomhill* is a good example of a small linear group (C). 'Barrow Hill' immediately N. of the village is natural, as are probably the 'tumuli' (LVG 13 and 14) on Lower Hyde Heath.

The parish has an unusual number of named barrows; many, including some now destroyed and forgotten, *e.g.* Muddox barrow (about 852966), are shown on an estate map of 1777 by I. Taylor (in D.C.R.O.).

Confused accounts exist of six 19th-century excavations of barrows in the Roke Down area (*see* Group (D)). Four barrows on 'Kingston Down' were excavated in 1850; the first three were perhaps (107), (106) and (109) since they were probably on Bere Down, not in Winterborne Kingston. The first (Warne, *C.T.D.*, cpf, no. 9) contained an apparently central deposit of two urns, one associated with a piece of green sandstone under burnt matter. Apparently to one side and above this layer were a contracted inhumation and three separate cremations, each burial covered by a flint cairn. In the top of the mound were remains of a large urn with three perforated lugs and immediately below the surface on the S.E. was a probable beaker. Warne's no. 10 (*C.T.D.*, cpf), S.W. of the first, contained a central, probably primary, cremation in an inverted urn, two secondary cremations on the S.E. and a large fragmentary urn on the E. This second urn, with a finger-printed shoulder cordon and horse-shoe handles, contained a bead of rolled sheet bronze like that from the *Roke Down Group*, though much smaller (Abercromby II, 39 and fig. 374; Butler and Smith, 33). The third barrow (Warne, *C.T.D.*, cpf, no. 11) contained, in a small cist covered with flints, a primary cremation in a globular urn. Above was a cremation and in the top of the mound a third cremation in an inverted urn covered by a sandstone slab. Warne's no. 12 (*C.T.D.*, cpf), S.E. of the others and only a very low mound, covered seven extended inhumations, their heads to the E., in a grave cut about 1 ft. into the chalk and covered by a layer of flints. Some of the urns from these barrows are in the B.M. (*Ant. J.* XIII (1933), 443).

(67) *Bowl* (SY 88 NE; 86168926) on South Heath above 100 ft. Diam. 55 ft., ht. 7 ft. Damaged by tanks.

(68) *Bowl* (SY 88 NE; 86208924) 35 yds. S.E. of (67). Diam. 58 ft., ht. 7 ft. Possibly ditched. Damaged by tanks.

(69) *Bowl* (SY 89 SW; 84329102) on flat summit of Gallows Hill above 200 ft. Diam. 58 ft., ht. 5½ ft. Damaged by tanks.

(70) *Bowl*, possibly ditched (SY 89 SE; 85489100) on S.-facing slope of narrow valley above 100 ft. Diam. 46 ft., ht. 3 ft. Hollowed on top.

(71) *Fox Barrow* (1777), ditched bowl (SY 89 SE; 86259228). On Philliols Heath on W. slope of low ridge. Diam. about 54 ft., ht. about 7½ ft. Ditch 7 ft. wide and 2 ft. deep. Thickly overgrown.

(72) *Bowl* (SY 89 SE; 86219290) on W. slope above steep fall, 150 ft. above O.D. Diam. about 30 ft., ht. 3 ft. Thickly overgrown.

(73) *Yon Barrow* (Yarn Barrow, 1777), ditched bowl (SY 89 SE; 86379294). Above 150 ft. on Lockyer's Hill at top of steep W. slope. Diam. 45 ft., ht. 8 ft. Planted with conifers.

(74) *End Barrow*, bowl (SY 89 SW; 84609310). On level ground below 150 ft. Diam. 57 ft., ht. 8½ ft. Thickly overgrown.

(75) *Bell* (?) (SY 89 SW; 84059370) at Blackhill Clump on S. end of ridge above 300 ft. and on parish boundary with Turners Puddle. Diam. of mound 62 ft., ht. 5 ft., with berm (?) and ditch; outer bank 110 ft. in diam., destroyed on S.W., probably a tree-clump enclosure.

(76) *Hundred Barrow*, bowl (SY 89 SW; 84469378). On summit of small spur above 200 ft. Diam. 58 ft., ht. 7 ft. Damaged by rabbits. Perhaps site from which Barrow Hundred named (Fägersten, 166).

(77–8) See BLACK HILL GROUP (X), Turners Puddle, p. 454.

(79) *Bowl* (SY 89 SW; 83539444) on narrow col above 300 ft. Diam. 61 ft., ht. 3½ ft. Damaged by tanks.

(80) *Bowl* (SY 89 SW; 83459448) on crest of narrow ridge 95 yds. N.W. of (79) and on parish boundary with Turners Puddle. Diam. 45 ft., ht. 3 ft. Damaged on E. by boundary bank and ditch.

(81) *Bowl* (SY 89 SW; 83299493) E. of and slightly below summit of ridge S. of Shitterton Wood. Diam. 33 ft., ht. 1½ ft.

(82) *Stand Barrow* (1777), bowl (SY 89 NW; 84289531). On summit of small knoll. Diam. 57 ft., ht. 1 ft. Ploughed.

(83) *Barrow* (?) (SY 89 NE; 85949507) in arable on summit of low wide ridge above 300 ft. Circular soil-mark at least 50 ft. across on vertical air photograph CPE/UK 1934: 4125.

(C) BROOMHILL GROUP (SY 89 NE), four bowls in an irregular line on the crest of a spur jutting E. from Woodbury Hill above 300 ft. All tree-covered and damaged.

(84) (86329508). Diam. 30 ft., ht. 4 ft.

(85) (86359509) 30 yds. E.N.E. of (84). Diam. 40 ft., ht. 5 ft.

(86) (86389509) 35 yds. E. of (85). Diam. 53 ft., ht. 7½ ft.

(87) (86419506) 50 yds. S.E. of (86). Diam. 45 ft., ht. 5 ft.

(88) *Bowl* (SY 89 NE; 86139539) in Bere Wood on level ground. Diam. 56 ft., ht. about 10 ft. Tree-covered.

(89) *Bowl* (SY 89 NW; 82539623) in arable on lower N. slope of ridge above 200 ft. Diam. 72 ft., ht. 3 ft. In Barrow Field (1777). Destroyed.

Bowls (?), three (SY 89 NW), on O.S. (1811), on Roke Down on crest and slopes of low rise above 200 ft. among Ancient Field Group (30). Nearly flattened by modern ploughing.

(90) (81919649). Diam. 55 ft. Apparently at 'Celtic' field angle.

(91) (81969648) 57 yds. E.S.E. of (90). Diam. 36 ft. Apparently at 'Celtic' field angle.

(92) (81999645) 40 yds. S.E. of (91). Diam. 54 ft.

(D) ROKE DOWN GROUP (SY 89 NW), six barrows in two clusters of three, the westernmost including two probable bells. In arable on S. slopes of Down near 200 ft. contour; all except (96) among 'Celtic' fields with (93–5) probably at field angles (*see* Ancient Field Group (30)). All have probably been opened. Accounts exist of six excavations hereabouts but only one can be related with certainty to a specific barrow (97), though the account in Hutchins of even this is confused (Hutchins I, 143–4; Warne, *C.T.D.*, cpf, no. 2 and 17 *n.*; Payne, *Durden Catalogue* (1892), 12–18; Abercromby II, 39 and fig. 375; *Ant. J.* XIII (1933), 443).

A barrow 'on the upper part of Roke Down' (LVG 46a; Warne, *C.T.D.*, cpf, no. 2) contained a cremation, probably primary, in an inverted urn in a grave 3 ft. deep. In the mound near the centre were four cremations in bucket urns, of which three were inverted. Immediately above, three extended inhumations lay E.-W. and a similar inhumation, with a plain urn, came from the S. side of the mound. A sixth cremation, in a very small urn, lay just below the turf on the S.E.

A barrow (LVG 46b) a few yards to the E. contained two primary contracted inhumations. One lay in a grave 6 ft. long, 2 ft. wide and 2 ft. deep, accompanied by a cremation in a small 'drinking cup'. The other was in a grave about 5 ft. away with animal bones. In a layer of soil and charcoal 2 ft. thick at the base of the mound were four more inhumations and two 'drinking cups'. At least seven urns, three of them complete, accompanied or contained cremations higher in the mound. One complete biconical urn with applied horse-shoe handles and perforated lugs contained a bead of rolled sheet bronze; another a small bone pin.

In a third barrow (LVG 46c), a cremation, probably primary, with broken urn lay in a cist, near which were three further cremations and another urn. Four urns lay on the S. side of the mound and on the N.E. was an inhumation in a stone-lined grave. The fourth barrow (LVG 46d) contained three bucket urns, one with perforations on either side of a crack as if to bind it together. Some of the urns from these barrows are in the B.M. Warne also records the opening of a large barrow containing 'great stones ... placed over the urns, similar to those in the Deverel Barrow'.

(93) Bell (?) (82099674). Diam. 80 ft., ht. 1½ ft. Ditch visible as crop-mark 14 ft. from base of mound.

(94) Bell (?) (82279684) 215 yds. N.E. of (93). Diam. 55 ft., ht. 9 ins. Ditch visible as crop-mark around N. half 9 ft. from base of mound.

(95) Ditched bowl (?) (82309674) 120 yds. S.S.E. of (94). Diam. 64 ft., ht. 1½ ft. Ditch visible as crop-mark at base of mound.

(96) Bowl (?) (82639669) 365 yds. E.S.E. of (95). Diam. 91 ft., ht. 2 ft.

(97) Bowl (82659683) 160 yds. N. of (96). A low rise 66 ft. in diam.; almost certainly the barrow excavated in 1840, by Wake Smart and later by Solly, and described as 4 ft. to 5 ft. high. Large sarsen blocks then lay on top; the sarsens now at the field edge were removed from the top of this barrow in about 1914. Primary burial (Wessex interment no. 4): probably cremation under inverted urn with an atypical ogival dagger (ApSimon, Appx. c, 40) and two knife daggers (all destroyed) at bottom of cist over 3 ft. deep. Three urns and 'several glass beads' previously found on E. (Hutchins I, 144; Warne, C.T.D., cpf, no. 21; Ant. J. XIII (1933), 443; ApSimon, 44 and 60.)

(98) Bowl (82709683) 55 yds. E. of (97) on centre of ridge and at 'Celtic' field angle. Diam. 57 ft., ht. 2½ ft.

(99) Bowl (SY 89 NW; 82579728) on E. slope of ridge above 200 ft. and overlooking small valley. Diam. 61 ft., ht. 2 ft. At foot of lynchet of Ancient Field Group (30). Ploughed.

(100) Bowl (SY 89 NW; 82879734) 330 yds. E.N.E. of (99) on opposite slope of valley and 160 yds. N.W. of long barrow Bere Regis (66). Diam. 66 ft., ht. 3 ft.

(101) Bowl (SY 89 NW; 83129714) on W. slope of ridge. Diam. 62 ft., ht. 1½ ft. Ploughed.

Three barrows (SY 89 NW) lie in a line ½ mile S.W. of Bere Down Buildings on the centre of a ridge above 200 ft. All are spread and almost destroyed by ploughing.

(102) Bowl (?) (83399668). Diam. 87 ft., ht. 1 ft.

(103) Bowl (83429662) 70 yds. S.S.E. of (102). Diam. 54 ft., ht. 6 ins.

(104) Bowl (83469659) 50 yds. S.E. of (103). Diam. 60 ft., ht. 6 ins.

(105) Oval mound, possible barrow (SY 89 NW; 83949707) on valley floor below 200 ft.; 60 ft. by 45 ft., ht. 9 ins. Much spread by ploughing.

(106) Bowl (?) (SY 89 NW; 83969724) 187 yds. N.N.E. of (105). Diam. 36 ft., ht. 1 ft. Much spread.

(107) Bowl (?) (SY 89 NW; 83989728) 35 yds. N.E. of (106) above 200 ft. Diam. 36 ft., ht. 1 ft. Much spread.

(108) Barrow (?) (SY 89 NW; 83979748) on gentle rise above 200 ft., 135 yds. N. of (107). Known only from unbroken circular crop-mark about 75 ft. in diam., visible on Cambridge University O.A.P. LR 85.

(109) Bowl (?) (SY 89 NW; 84199734) 240 yds. E.N.E. of (107) on lower slopes of valley between 200 ft. and 300 ft. Diam. 60 ft., ht. 1½ ft. Much spread.

(110) Bowl (?) (SY 89 NW; 84469730) on N.E. edge of Bere Down above 300 ft. and just below 'Celtic' field lynchet of Ancient Field Group (31). Diam. 41 ft., ht. 2½ ft. Much spread.

(111) Bowl (?) (SY 89 NW; 84449717) 145 yds. S.S.W. of (110). Destroyed.

(112) Hawks Barrow (1777), ditched bowl (SY 89 NW; 84349684). On flat-topped spur above 200 ft. contour and just below 'Celtic' field lynchet of Ancient Field Group (32). Diam. 74 ft., ht. 7 ft. Disturbed in centre. A collared urn in D.C.M. apparently came from this barrow (Dorset Procs. LXXXVI (1964), 115).

(113) Rawles Barrow (1777), bowl (?) (SY 89 NE; 85719621). On S.E. slope below 200 ft., adjoining hedge on W. side of road. Now low oval mound 99 ft. by 72 ft., and heavily ploughed.

A cluster of three barrows (SY 89 NE) lies on gentle slope to W. above 200 ft. contour and immediately inside parish boundary with Winterborne Kingston.

(114) Ditched bowl (86129635). Diam. 69 ft., ht. 1 ft. Two concentric ditches visible as crop-marks measure 31 ft. in diam. and 6 ft. wide (inner), and 70 ft. in diam. and 7 ft. wide (outer).

(115) Bolton's Barrow, ditched bowl (86099642), 80 yds. N.N.W. of (114). Diam. 80 ft., ht. 1 ft., with 12 ft. wide ditch visible as crop-mark.

(116) Barrow (?) (86179643) 97 yds. E.N.E. of (115). Visible only as crop-mark circle, diam. 66 ft.

BINCOMBE

All but three (72–4) of the sixty-two barrows in the parish form part of the Ridgeway Group. In the extreme N.W. of the parish, formerly part of Upwey, nine (13–21) form the E. part of the *Ridge Hill Group* (R.7) and about ½ mile S.E. of them a further nine mark the N. and E. edges of the *Ridgeway Hill Group* (R.8). The three groups described within the parish are on *Bincombe Down* (R.9) and *Bincombe Hill* (R.10), both including barrows in Winterborne Came, and on *West Hill* (R.12).

Many barrows certainly or probably in the parish have been excavated but few of the records can be related to visible remains. Conversely, several have clearly been dug into but cannot be related to the barrow diggers' descriptions. A barrow (Warne, C.T.D., tovp, no. 7) opened in 1784 on 'Bincombe

Down on the Ridgeway' or 'on Ridgeway Hill' contained a probably primary cremation in one of two inverted urns, the other containing a three-riveted bronze dagger. Above were an inhumation beneath a flat stone, two urns with cremations, and, 3 ft. from the surface, an extended inhumation lying E.-W. In the same area four (Warne, *C.T.D.*, tovp, no. 65) were opened in 1842: one contained two extended and probably intrusive inhumations and the others only revealed traces of burning. In 1842 a further four were excavated 'on Bincombe Down, on the Ridgeway'. One (Warne, *C.T.D.*, tovp, no. 66), 3 ft. high, contained an (inverted ?) collared urn in the centre and two urns, one an inverted globular urn, side by side 2 ft. below the surface of the mound. In the second (Warne, *C.T.D.*, tovp, no. 67), 'a quantity of bone was found scattered about, with large flat stones' and near the top two inhumations lay E.-W. side by side in a stone-lined cist. The third barrow (Warne, *C.T.D.*, tovp, no. 68) was 12 ft. high and contained a central flint cairn, which was not excavated, and four inhumations near the top. The fourth (Warne, *C.T.D.*, tovp, no. 69) was called a 'twin barrow' by the excavator, but probably only one mound was dug into. It contained two inhumations beside an upright stone and a cremation in an urn also containing a biconical 'incense cup' (for these last eight excavations *see* Cambridge Antiquarian Society, *Procs.* I (1859), 141-5). A small unlocated barrow near (22), excavated by Cunnington (MS., no. 34), contained an inurned cremation.

(13-21) *See* RIDGE HILL GROUP (R.7), Winterborne St. Martin, p. 468.

(22) *Ditched bowl* (SY 68 NE; 67248667). On spur running N.E. from Ridgeway below 400 ft. Ht. 4 ft.; air photograph (V.A.P. CPE/UK 1824: 3290) indicates ditch about 90 ft. diam. Opened by Cunnington in 1881, exposing burnt matter and bone fragments near the centre.

(23-31) *See* RIDGEWAY HILL GROUP (R.8), Weymouth, p. 456.

(32) *Ditched barrow* (?) (SY 68 NE; 67898609) suggested by circular ditch with small external bank about 100 ft. in diam. on air photograph (V.A.P. CPE/UK 1824: 3289).

(33) *Bell* (?) (SY 68 NE; 67918614) 60 yds. N. of (32). Diam. 90 ft., ht. 6 ft. Ditch about 115 ft. in diam. suggested by air photograph (V.A.P. CPE/UK 1824: 3289). Possibly contained a cremation in a chalk-cut cist.

Disc barrows (?), two (SY 68 NE), about 300 yds. N. of the Ridgeway (*Ant. J.* XIII (1933), 443; *Helinium* I (1961), 115).

(34) (68078625). On crest of slope to N., now only an indefinite mound 1 ft. high. It contained a primary cremation under an inverted bucket urn covered by a flat stone.

(35) (68098624) 20 yds. E.S.E. of (34) but now destroyed. It contained a primary cremation with a fragmentary bucket urn.

(R.9) BINCOMBE DOWN GROUP (SY 68 NE). Sixteen barrows, including two bells, partly on heath above the 500 ft. contour and scattered in three clusters. Two of them incorporate short straight alignments, which point towards two separate barrows at the W. end of the group. The top of the Ridgeway bends slightly to the N. at the E. end of the Down so that the Winterborne Came barrows on the S. of Came Down Golf Course lie on the true top of the ridge and directly continue the group. The short straight row (40-43) points towards bell barrow (38) 430 yds. to the W. and is sited on the beginnings of a steep slope to the S. Several barrows have been dug into and (40-3) have been ploughed nearly flat, but some on the Golf Course are relatively well preserved. It was probably into four of these last rather than into those in *Came Down Group* (AG) to the N. that Warne dug. One (*C.T.D.*, mopr, no. 11) contained a central flint cairn over a chalk-filled cist. Close by was a large barrow (*C.T.D.*, mopr, no. 12) over two flint cairns: the lower covered six inhumations, contained an inurned cremation, and was capped by a stone bearing carved concentric circles; the higher cairn was similarly capped. Two smaller, adjacent barrows (*C.T.D.*, mopr, nos. 13 and 14), contained respectively a cremation in a globular urn and an extended inhumation. A barrow (Cunnington MS., no. 57) at the E. end of Bincombe Down contained a primary cremation and a secondary inurned cremation.

(36) Bowl (67838572). Diam. 38 ft., ht. 3 ft. Disturbed in centre.

(37) Bell (67978572) 120 yds. E. of (36). Diam. of flat-topped mound 88 ft., ht. above berm 10½ ft. The berm is 9 ft. wide and 1½ ft. above surrounding ground level within a ditch 23 ft. wide and 2 ft. deep. Much damaged.

(38) Bell (68028570) 75 yds. E.S.E. of (37). Diam. 65 ft., ht. 11 ft., with berm 8 ft. wide and ditch about 15 ft. wide and 1 ft. deep. Ploughed.

(39) Bowl (?) (68158578) 150 yds. N.E. of (38). Now only a slight rise. It probably contained cremations in four inverted Early-Middle Bronze Age collared urns in a cist beneath a cairn. There were two other similar urns, at least one of which was inverted, and two secondary urns (Abercromby II, figs. 5, 5a, 6c; *Ant. J.* XIII (1933), 444; *P.P.S.* XXVII (1961), 294, nos. 17-20).

Winterborne Came:

(10) Bowl (68428583) 307 yds. E.N.E. of the last, immediately above 500 ft. contour on slope to N. Diam. 54 ft., ht. 3 ft. Damaged by bunkers.

(11) Bowl (68468584). On centre of ridge running to N.E., 34 yds. E.N.E. of (10). Diam. 84 ft., ht. 10½ ft. Tree-covered and damaged on E.

(12) Bowl (68408588) 57 yds. N.W. of (11). Slight irregular rise 33 ft. in diam.

(13) Bowl (68438588) 24 yds. E.N.E. of (12). Diam. 33 ft., ht. 9 ins., but spread and cut by small ditch.

(14) Bowl (68468589) 19 yds. E.N.E. of (13). Diam. 39 ft., ht. 9 ins., but spread.

(15) Bowl (68498590) 25 yds. N.E. of (14). Diam. 54 ft., ht. 2 ft. Used as golf green.

(16) Bowl (?) (68578588) 90 yds. E. of (15) and off centre of ridge. Now an oblong mound 2½ ft. high used as tee.

(17) Barrow (68698577) immediately within W. edge of Came Wood 185 yds. S.E. of (16). Much overgrown and disturbed.

Bincombe:

(40) Bowl (?) (68428569). Diam. 60 ft., ht. 4½ ft.

(41) Bowl (?) (68468569). Ploughed flat.

(42) Bowl (?) (68508569). Ploughed flat.

(43) Bowl (?) (68539569). Ploughed flat.

(R. 10) BINCOMBE HILL GROUP (SY 68 SE, NE; Fig. p. 24). Twenty barrows, including a triple bowl and a bell, on one of the only two spurs jutting S. from the Ridgeway. The group is arranged in a rough semi-circle open to the E., curving along the domed top of the spur above the 500 ft. contour, and ending to the N.E. in Came Wood. To the S.E. it ends in a straight line of a triple bowl, a bell and two bowls (44-7), dramatically sited immediately to the S. of the highest point of the spur but visible on the skyline from many points and especially from the Broadmayne bank barrow. They are now preserved under grass among Ancient Field Group (8) (Fig. p. 627) but are damaged by central excavations.

Apart from four outliers, the group can be subdivided into linear cemeteries of seven and eight barrows respectively at the S. and N. ends of the semi-circle, with a long barrow (Bincombe (12)) and a bowl barrow roughly at the centre of the curve in the most westerly position. Most have been damaged by ploughing and now only appear as low, spread rises.

Some of the barrows excavated on the Ridgeway in Bincombe were possibly in this group. Warne's no. 43 (*C.T.D.*, mopr) was probably the largest mound of the triple barrow (44) and his no. 6 (*C.T.D.*, tovp), was almost certainly one of the others near it. In the former a primary cremation lay under an extended inhumation 8 ft. to 9 ft. below the top of the mound; two similar inhumations were about 2 ft. below the top of the mound, all three lying E.-W. in stone-lined graves. The latter contained a primary inurned cremation in a stone cist, above which were three extended inhumations. The group is described from the S. around the semi-circle formed by the barrows.

(44) Triple bowl (69028458) aligned N.W.-S.E. immediately above 500 ft. contour. From W. to E. diams. and hts. of mounds are: 64 ft. and 8½ ft.; 68 ft. and 9 ft.; 67 ft. and 7 ft. There is no sign of a ditch around or between the mounds.

(45) Bowl (68988460) continuing alignment of (44) 25 yds. to the N.W. Diam. 69 ft., ht. 9 ft. Disturbed in centre.

(46) Bell (68948464) 68 yds. N.W. of (45). Diam. 92 ft., ht. 11 ft. Ditch 15 ft. wide and 2 ft. deep destroyed by ? ancient ploughing on S.E. The sloping berm, 9 ft. wide on S. and W., has been partly destroyed. Excavation hollow in centre.

(47) Ditched bowl (68918466) 48 yds. N.W. of (46). Diam. 100 ft., ht. 12½ ft. Ditch 10 ft. wide and 1 ft. deep.

(48) Bowl (69168465) 280 yds. E. of (47) on slight slope to N.E. below 500 ft. contour. Ploughed almost flat.

(49) Bowl (?) (68738493) 325 yds. N.N.W. of (47). Diam. about 65 ft., ht. 1 ft. Ploughed.

(50) Ditched bowl (?) (68748496) 46 yds. N.N.W. of (49). Diam. 90 ft., ht. 4½ ft.

(51) Bowl (?) (68748502) 65 yds. N. of (50). Diam. 90 ft., ht. 4½ ft.

(52) Bowl (?) (68978514) 290 yds. N.E. of (51) and 80 yds. E. of long barrow (12). Ploughed out.

(53) Bowl (?) (68888525) 150 yds. N.W. of (52) and 100 yds. N. of long barrow (12). Diam. 80 ft., ht. 7 ft.

(54) Bowl (?) (68918531) 70 yds. N.E. of (53). Diam 75 ft., ht. 5 ft.

(55) Bowl (?) (68958532) 38 yds. E. of (54). Diam. about 80 ft. Ploughed flat.

(56) Bowl (69008533) 50 yds. N.E. of (55). Diam. about 70 ft., ht. 2 ft.

(57) Bowl (?) (69108536) 120 yds. E.N.E. of (56). Diam. about 60 ft., ht. 1 ft.

(58) Bowl (?) (69198539) 100 yds. N.E. of (57). Diam. about 90 ft., ht. 3 ft.

Winterborne Came:

(18) Bowl (69298547) in Came Wood 145 yds. N.E. of last. Diam. 46 ft., ht. 4 ft. Flattened on top and damaged by excavation.

(19) Ditched bowl (?) (69338549) 50 yds. E.N.E. of (18). Diam. 76 ft., ht. 8 ft.

Bincombe:

(59) Bowl (?) (69208528) 120 yds. S. of (58). Ploughed out.

(60) Bowl (?) (69268528) 60 yds. E. of (59). Diam. about 80 ft., ht. 3 ft.

(61) Bowl (?) (68938546) 300 yds. W.N.W. of (58). Ploughed out. No other barrows lie between it, an outlier of the group, and alignment (40-3) to the W.

(R.12) WEST HILL GROUP (SY 78 SW). Ten barrows, nine of them, including one pond barrow (63), in a straight S.W.-N.E. alignment, lie about ¾ mile E.S.E. of the Bincombe Hill Group on a S.W. spur from the Ridgeway. All are exactly on the spine of the spur and are still visible on the skyline from the Broadmayne bank barrow (19), although seven have been heavily ploughed.

(62) Bowl (?) (70058453). At S.W. end of alignment just above 400 ft. contour. Diam. 54 ft., ht. 5 ft. Overgrown but unploughed.

(63) Pond barrow (70148459) 120 yds. N.E. of (62). Diam. 54 ft., depth 1 ft. within low bank about 25 ft. wide. Almost ploughed out.

(64) Ditched bowl (?) (70198462) 55 yds. N.E. of (63).

Slight rise about 70 ft. in diam., with traces of original ditch on air photograph (V.A.P. cpe/uk 1821: 6444).

(65) Bowl (?) (70268464) 95 yds. N.E. of (64). Diam. 57 ft., ht. 2 ft.

(66) Bowl (?) (70328467) 65 yds. N.E. of (65). Diam. 57 ft., ht. 2 ft.

(67) Bowl (?) (70358468) 30 yds. N.E. of (66). Diam. 60 ft., ht. 2½ ft.

(68) Bowl (?) (70398470) 35 yds. N.E. of (67). Diam. 60 ft., ht. 2½ ft.

(69) Bowl (?) (70478473) 100 yds. N.E. of (68). Diam. 60 ft., ht. about 10 ft. Turf-covered.

(70) Bowl (?) (70528475) 50 yds. N.E. of (69). Almost ploughed out.

(71) Bowl (70588482) 110 yds. N.E. of (70). Diam. 78 ft., ht. 4½ ft.

(72) *Bowl* (?) (sy 68 se; 67538484) in prominent isolated position just above 300 ft. contour on crest of The Knoll. Only slight mound remains.

(73) *Ditched bowl* (sy 68 se; 69488389). Within Chalbury hill-fort (Bincombe (76); Fig. p. 484, Plate 216) above 300 ft. contour. Diam. 66 ft., ht. 5 ft. Probably opened by Warne, who found two inurned cremations in a cairn.

(74) *Bowl* (sy 68 se; 69518384) 50 yds. S.S.E. of (73). Diam. 65 ft., ht. 4 ft.

BLOXWORTH

(E) BLOXWORTH DOWN GROUP (sy 89 ne). Fifteen barrows, including one disc or bell-disc, and comprising all the barrows in the parish, lie on a N. slope at the W. end of a chalk ridge between 170 ft. and 236 ft. above O.D.; (29) is on the highest point in the parish, and ten others cluster N. and E. of it. (40–3) are outliers to the N. Grinsell shows in addition two possible barrows in the group (3a and 7a on fig. 4 in *Dorset Barrows*). Two have been destroyed and all but (29) and (30) are badly damaged by ploughing, as are adjacent 'Celtic' fields (Group 33). (39–40) have been excavated. A third dug by Shipp in 1854 (Hutchins I, 184) might be (41), (42) or a barrow at about 87759595 (on O.S. 1811). It contained an apparently primary cremation with a bone pin 2 ins. long; two secondary cremations under inverted collared urns; a third, near the surface, beneath an inverted urn with a bone needle about 6 ins. long and, near it, six inhumations lying E.-W. The pin and four urns from Bloxworth Down are in the B.M., and a B1 beaker has also been recorded (Abercromby I, 22 and fig. 32).

(29) Bowl (87679619) in Higher Belt Coppice. Marked by trig. point at 236 ft. Diam. 48 ft., ht. 5 ft.

(30) Bowl (87709619) 35 yds. E. of (29). Diam. about 45 ft., ht. about 2½ ft.

(31) Bowl (?) (87699622) 40 yds. N.E. of (29). Diam. 60 ft., ht. 2 ft.

(32) Bowl (87689624) 25 yds. N.W. of (31). Diam. 45 ft., ht. 2 ft.

(33) Bowl (?) (87739623) 40 yds. E.N.E. of (31). Diam. 61 ft., ht. 2½ ft.

(34) Bowl (?) (87719624) 30 yds. N.W. of (33). Diam. about 30 ft., but ploughed almost flat.

(35) Bowl (?) (87699625) 25 yds. N.E. of (32). Diam. about 45 ft., but ploughed almost flat.

(36) Barrow (?) (87619629) 80 yds. N.W. of (35). Diam. about 55 ft., but ploughed almost flat.

(37) Barrow (?) (87649628) 20 yds. E.S.E. of (36). Diam. about 55 ft., but ploughed almost flat.

(38) Bowl (?) (87669626) 30 yds. E. of (37). Diam. about 45 ft., ht. about 1 ft.

(39) Disc or bell-disc (87709629) lying immediately E. of (38) and 50 yds. N.N.E. of (35). Mound formerly about 30 ft. in diam. and 4 ft. high, with berm, ditch and outer bank making total diam. 160 ft. (V.A.P. cpe/uk 1934: 4127); now only visible as slight rise. In c. 1854 Shipp found in a cist a primary cremation under an inverted collared urn also containing bone tweezers, eight amber beads and six or eight segmented faience beads, all now in B.M. (Wessex interment no. 5). In top of mound four inhumations, a woman, two children and a man, lay E.-W. (Hutchins I, 184; Abercromby II, 12 and fig. 49; *Archaeologia* LXXXV (1936), 235).

(40) Bowl (87679638) 110 yds. N.N.W. of (39). In 1854 diam. was 75 ft., ht. 8 ft. but now 1½ ft. Shipp found under a cairn an apparently primary cremation in a bucket urn with horse-shoe handles, now lost (Hutchins I, 184; *Ant. J.* XIII (1933), 444).

(41) Barrow (?) (87769647) 130 yds. N.E. of (40). Entirely destroyed.

(42) Bowl (?) (87529650) almost at foot of N. scarp of Down and 250 yds. W.N.W. of (41). Diam. 100 ft., ht. 5 ft., but badly damaged.

(43) Bowl (?) (87289651) on level site 260 yds. W.N.W. of (42). Diam. 67 ft., ht. 4 ft.

BROADMAYNE

The ten barrows in the parish (20–9) are all on the Ridgeway in *Culliford Tree Group* (R.11), Whitcombe (p. 459), though another possibly existed on the boundary with Bincombe, S. of the group, at 70398513.

CHALDON HERRING

Of the thirty-three barrows and probable barrows, fifteen fall into three small groups, one of them, the *Beaufort Farm Group* (G), very close to the present village. Two barrows, (38) and (39), are earlier than 'Celtic' fields around them (see Ancient Field Group (15), Fig. opp. p. 628).

Bowls, three (sy 78 se), lie S.E. of Hill Barn on almost level summit of ridge overlooking sea.

(25) (77558114). Diam. about 35 ft., ht. about 9 ins. Almost ploughed out.

(26) (77578119) 67 yds. N.E. of (25). Diam. 54 ft., ht. 2½ ft.

(27) (77608116) 45 yds. S.E. of (26). Diam. 54 ft., ht. 2¾ ft.

(28) *Bowl* (SY 78 SE; 77888172) on N. slope below 500 ft. contour. Diam. 80 ft., ht. 2½ ft. Much damaged.

(29) *Bowl* (SY 78 SE; 77918102) on coastal ridge above 500 ft. Diam. 45 ft., ht. 5½ ft. Excavation trench across centre.

(30) *Bowl* (SY 78 SE; 77938102) 23 yds. E. of (29). Diam. 39 ft., ht. 4½ ft. Excavation trench across centre.

(F) CHALDON DOWN GROUP (SY 78 SE). Five bowls on flat summit of E.-W. coastal ridge.

(31) (78318142). Diam. 40 ft., ht. 7 ft. Diam. reduced by ploughing round base.

(32) (78378135) 100 yds. S.E. of (31). Ploughed almost flat.

(33) (78318125) 117 yds. S.W. of (32). Diam. 36 ft., ht. 5 ft. Destroyed W. of hedge crossing mound.

(34) (78388125) 63 yds. E. of (33). Diam. 55 ft., ht. 2 ft. Possible ditch on N.E.

(35) (78448126) 70 yds. E. of (34). Diam. 50 ft., ht. 1½ ft.

(36) *Wardstone Barrow*, bowl (SY 78 SE; 79348133). On N. shoulder of coastal ridge on site prominent from N. Diam. 44 ft., ht. 6 ft., but hollowed by excavation in 1867 which revealed, near the middle and on the original ground surface, a probably primary cremation in a bucket urn, now destroyed, covered by a flat stone (Dorset *Procs.* LXXVII (1955), 127–8). The barrow was probably at the angle of a 'Celtic' field.

(37) *Barrow* (?) (SY 78 SE; 79368133) about 22 yds. E. of (36). Diam. about 40 ft. In arable, and immediately above a 'Celtic' field lynchet.

(38) *Mound*, possible barrow (SY 78 SE; 79288094), on crest of spur falling S. from coastal ridge, some 450 ft. above O.D. Diam. about 21 ft., ht. 1½ ft. Spread, possibly excavated, it lies against the 'Celtic' field lynchet immediately above.

(39) *Bowl* (?) (SY 78 SE; 79278089) in similar position to and 45 yds. S. of (38). Diam. 36 ft., ht. 3½ ft. Earlier than adjacent 'Celtic' field lynchet. Spoil from central excavation thrown to S.

(40) *Barrow* (?) (SY 78 SE; 79638178) now destroyed.

(41) *Barrow* (?) (SY 78 SE; 79858182) now destroyed.

(42) *Bowl* (SY 78 SE; 79958163) on E. slope of ridge. Diam. 43 ft., ht. 5 ft. Much damaged.

(43) *Bush Barrow*, bowl (SY 78 SE; 79958199) on N.E. slope of ridge. Diam. 66 ft., ht. 7 ft. Tree-covered and damaged.

(G) BEAUFORT FARM GROUP (SY 78 SE). Four probable bowls strung along the very narrow spine of a low ridge just above the 300 ft. contour immediately N. of the village. All are in pasture.

(44) (79038358). Oval, 54 ft. (W.-E.) by 33 ft., ht. 4 ft.
(45) (79238358) 220 yds. E. of (44). Diam. 42 ft., ht. 2 ft.
(46) (79288359) 60 yds. E. of (45). Diam. 42 ft., ht. 2 ft.
(47) (79318361) 30 yds. N.E. of (46). Diam. 60 ft., ht. 4 ft.

C

(48) *Lord's Barrow*, bowl (?) (SY 78 SE; 77788412). On crest of ridge 400 ft. above O.D. Diam. 58 ft., ht. 7 ft. Crossed by parish boundary with Owermoigne. Excavated and much damaged.

(49) *Barrow* (?) (SY 78 SE; 77918415) in hedge on parish boundary with Owermoigne 167 yds. E. of (48). Diam. about 36 ft., ht. 1½ ft.

(50) *Bowl* (?) (SY 78 SE; 78698418). Diam. 41 ft., ht. 1½ ft. Disturbed in centre.

(H) THE FIVE MARYS GROUP (SY 78 SE). Six barrows, including two bells, shown as 'Five Meers' (boundary points) on I. Taylor's Map of Dorset, 1765. They lie in an almost straight line along the spine of a narrow W.-E. ridge above the 300 ft. contour some 300 yds. E. of (50). All are under pasture but damaged. Only one has not been dug into. A slight and very small depression with traces of a bank or spoil around it between (51) and (52) has been claimed as a probable pond barrow (LVG 4a). Two, possibly (51) and (53), excavated before 1866 by the exiled Duchess of Berry and suite, covered deep chalk-cut graves, each containing a contracted ('sitting') male inhumation with stag antlers on each shoulder; one also held a female skeleton with antlers similarly placed and the other contained a secondary inurned cremation in the upper part of the mound (Hutchins I, 346).

(51) Ditched bowl (78968421). Diam. 70 ft., ht. 10 ft. Ditch about 20 ft. wide and 3 ft. deep. Damaged by large excavation trench from N. and by hedge banks at base.

(52) Bell (79018421) 50 yds. E. of (51). Diam. 71 ft., ht. 8 ft., with sloping berm only 5 ft. wide and ditch 10 ft. wide and 1 ft. deep. Disturbed on top.

(53) Bell (79038421) adjacent to (52) on E. Diam. 56 ft., ht. 7 ft., with very narrow sloping berm and ditch 10 ft. wide and 1 ft. deep. Damaged by excavation trench from N.

(54) Ditched bowl (79078421) 30 yds. E. of (53). Diam. 56 ft., ht. 4 ft. with very narrow and shallow ditch. Centre of mound dug away and irregular mound immediately to W. is probably resultant spoil.

(55) Bowl (?) (79088421) immediately E. of (54). Diam. 24 ft., ht. 1 ft. Large flints showing in surface.

(56) Ditched bowl (79108420) 35 yds. E. of (54). Diam. 56 ft., ht. 7 ft. Ditch 10 ft. wide and 1 ft. deep. Excavation trench from N. with spoil on sides.

(57) *Bowl* (?) (SY 78 SE; 79288420) on crest of ridge 190 yds. E. of (56). Slight irregular mound about 1 ft. high.

CHURCH KNOWLE

The fifteen barrows in the parish are divided between the chalk ridge of Stonehill Down and Knowle Hill to the S. and the heathlands at its foot to the N. A group of four lies on *Creech Heath*. Four have been excavated: (40) contained a primary contracted inhumation in a deep grave; (41) covered a probably secondary contracted inhumation above a primary cremation with a small dagger.

(35) *Bowl* (?) (SY 97 NW; 93597883) on broad ridge sloping slightly N. Diam. 30 ft., ht. 1½ ft., with many stones visible.

(36) *Ditched bowl* (SY 98 SW; 92108233) on end of spur above 600 ft. contour projecting S. from Creech Barrow hill, and crossed W. of centre by parish boundary bank with Steeple. Diam. 75 ft., ht. about 6 ft. Probably the barrow excavated by Austen, containing three primary contracted inhumations, one with a trepanned roundel from a child's skull, in a flint cairn; and two secondary extended inhumations. (*Purbeck Papers* I, 113–15; *P.P.S.* VI (1940), 112–32.)

(37) *Ditched bowl* (SY 98 SW; 92948226) on Stonehill Down above 400 ft. contour. Diam. 41 ft., ht. 5 ft. Top dug into.

(38) *Bowl* (?) (SY 98 SW; 93038230) on similar site to (37) 117 yds. E.N.E. of it. Diam. 15 ft., ht. 1 ft.

(39) *Bowl* (?) (SY 98 SW; 93168231) on Stonehill Down above steep E. slope below 400 ft. contour and 135 yds. E.N.E. of (38). Diam. 25 ft., ht. 1½ ft.

(40) *Bowl* (SY 98 SW; 94398238) on N. edge of Knowle Hill above 400 ft. contour, crossed by parish boundary with Corfe Castle on N. (Fig. opp. p. 509). Diam. 47 ft., ht. 4½ ft., in arable. Opened 1856 by Austen who found a central primary contracted inhumation in a chalk-cut grave, 8 ft. to 9 ft. in diam. and 9½ ft. deep, with antler, pottery and shale fragments in the chalk packing. Two contracted inhumations in stone cists lay 9 ft. W. and S.E. of centre; 2 ft. below top lay an extended inhumation protected by stones. Apparent overlap with cross-dyke (56e) on W. probably due to excavation spoil. (*Purbeck Papers* I, 110–15; Hutchins I, 595–6.)

(41) *Ditched bowl* (SY 98 SW; 94588236) on Knowle Hill 200 yds. E.S.E. of (40). Diam. 38 ft., ht. 3 ft. Twice opened, in 1861 and in 1934–5. Primary cremation with small two-riveted bronze dagger was in a grave 2½ ft. deep below a small mound. On top of this two inhumations, one contracted, were covered by a larger mound containing Middle and Late Bronze Age pottery within a ditch about 5½ ft. wide and 2 ft. deep. (*Purbeck Papers* II, 55–8; Dorset *Procs.* LXXVI (1954), 51–5.)

(42) *Ditched bowl* (SY 98 SW; 94588233) 40 yds. S. of (41). Diam. 45 ft., ht. 4½ ft. Opened 1861 by Austen who found a probably primary cremation in a cist below much burnt material containing a perforated whetstone now in D.C.M. (*Purbeck Papers* II, 55–8; *Archaeologia* XLIII (1871), 424–5, fig. 116).

(43) *Bowl* (SY 98 SW; 92558310) in Blackhills Plantation at E. end of spur above very steep slopes to N. and E. Diam. 45 ft., ht. 3 ft. (Dorset *Procs.* LXXIV (1952), 93.)

(44) *Ditched bowl* (SY 98 SW; 92768311) in Blackhills Plantation 250 yds. E. of (43) on knoll above steep slopes to N. and N.E. Diam. 75 ft., ht. 9 ft., with flattened top and ditch 9 ft. wide and up to 2½ ft. deep.

(45) *Icen Barrow*, ditched (?) bowl (SY 98 SW; 92188385) on almost level site on Creech Heath. Diam. 56 ft., ht. 5 ft.

Damaged. Bronze Age urn found in it (Dorset *Procs.* LXX (1948), 55).

(I) CREECH HEATH GROUP (SY 98 SW). Four barrows in a short straight W.-E. line above S. slope from slight ridge. Probably one of these, or perhaps (45), was built of turf and contained a probably primary cremation with a small, ruby-coloured object, possibly amber (LVG 5a; Warne, *C.T.D.*, cpf, no. 43).

(46) Bowl (?) (92498402). Diam. about 40 ft., ht. about 3 ft. Almost destroyed.

(47) Bowl (92518402) immediately E. of (46). Diam. 40 ft., ht. 3½ ft. Top dug into.

(48) Ditched bowl (92538402) immediately E. of (47). Diam. 56 ft., ht. 9 ft., with ditch about 7 ft. wide.

(49) Bowl (92598405) on spine of ridge 75 yds. E.N.E. of (48). Diam. 47 ft., ht. 3 ft.

COOMBE KEYNES

All eight barrows lie on heathland about ¾ mile E. of the village; six form the *Coombe Beacon Group*.

(J) COOMBE BEACON GROUP (SY 88 SE). Six barrows, including two probable bells; (13–15) lie in a triangle and (16–18) in an almost straight line.

(13) Bowl (85978435) near summit of knoll 172 ft. above O.D. Diam. 43 ft., ht. 3 ft. Surface irregular.

(14) Bowl (86018436) on slight N.E. slope 45 yds. E. of (13). Diam. about 43 ft., ht. about 2½ ft. but irregular.

(15) Bowl (86008440) in similar position and condition 50 yds. N. of (14). Diam. 62 ft., ht. 3 ft.

(16) Bell (?) (86168446) on almost level ground 183 yds. E.N.E. of (15). Diam. about 64 ft., ht. about 7 ft., with eroded berm and irregular ditch. Top disturbed.

(17) Bell (?) (86158450) on almost level ground 55 yds. N. of (16). Diam. including eroded berm 64 ft., ht. 5½ ft., with ditch 10 ft. wide. Top disturbed.

(18) Bowl (?) (86118454) 60 yds. N.N.W. of (17). Diam. 48 ft., ht. 1 ft.

(19) *Ditched bowl* (SY 88 SE; 86578493) on slight rise on Coombe Heath but below 100 ft. Diam. 56 ft., ht. 4½ ft. Ditch irregular. Top flattened.

(20) *Bowl* (SY 88 NE; 86708507) in similar position 210 yds. N.E. of (19). Diam. 36 ft., ht. 3 ft. Surface irregular.

CORFE CASTLE

There are thirty-eight barrows in the parish. Over half are in two groups, one of eight on Corfe Common S. of the village and the other of seventeen and a long barrow on Ailwood Down E. of the village. (183) and the Afflington Barrow (184) had probable Romano-British as well as earlier burials. A Middle Bronze Age urn, now in the B.M., came from an unlocated barrow on Kingston Down (LVG 25).

(182) *Bowl* (SY 97 NW; 93417846). Set prominently on Swyre Head over 600 ft. above O.D. on spine of ridge with steep slopes to E. and W. Diam. 83 ft., ht. 8 ft. Turf-covered but damaged by paths. Stone base on flattened top of mound.

(183) *Bowl* (SY 97 NE; 96607847). On spur 400 ft. above O.D. above S.E. slope into Coombe Bottom. Diam. 52 ft., ht. 6 ft. In area of 'Celtic' fields (Ancient Field Group (23)). Modern ploughing has exposed several large stones. Austen found an apparently primary cremation in a highly ornamented urn with applied handles (now in D.C.M.), inverted and resting on two flat stones and also surrounded by packing stones. At same level on E. was a bronze, Romano-British, penannular brooch, probably associated with an intrusive inhumation. Two small, probably bucket urns, one inverted and both holding cremations, lay in the stone mound forming centre of barrow. On S. was part of circle of upright stones with signs of burning around. (Austen, *Purbeck Papers* I (1855), 39–40; *Ant. J.* XIII (1933), 444; Dorset *Procs.* LXXXI (1959), 118–19.)

(184) *Afflington Barrow*, bowl (SY 97 NE; 96877880). On E. spur above Coombe Bottom. Diam. 58 ft., ht. 6 ft. Turf-covered. Possibly primary cremation 12 ft. E. of centre. Shale ring and widespread signs of burning lay beneath the mound, in which were a crouched inhumation in a stone grave and, 2 ft. above, nine extended inhumations lying with heads to S.W. in two parallel rows of three and four graves. Five graves were stone-lined, some with cover-stones and one with a bronze finger-ring (in D.C.M.) in filling, but the two at E. each held a double burial, in one case an adult and child covered by a shale slab. A 6-in. stony capping to the mound contained a group of 'apparently Roman' sherds with some bronze belt or strap fittings: of these flat stud, hook, and slider are in D.C.M. (Austen, *Purbeck Papers* I, 40–6, 232; Dorset *Procs.* LXXVII (1955), 149–50.)

(185) *Mound*, possible barrow (SY 98 SW; 94588061). On summit of E.-W. ridge just over 150 ft. above O.D. Diam. about 52 ft., ht. 4 ft. Under turf in arable field. N. side cut into and centre almost dug away.

(K) CORFE COMMON GROUP (SY 98 SE; Fig. p. 97). Eight barrows straggle along the spine of a ridge about 150 ft. above O.D. All but (191) are bracken-covered. LVG 10a-c, between (192) and (193), are unidentifiable.

(186) Bowl (?) (95678097). Diam. 55 ft., ht. 7½ ft. Top flattened but not apparently excavated.
(187) Bowl (?) (95878099) on N.W. slope 230 yds. E. of (186). Diam. 62 ft., ht. 5½ ft.
(188) Bowl, possibly ditched (95918090), 100 yds. S.S.E. of (187). Diam. 38 ft., ht. 2 ft.
(189) Bowl (?) (95958093) 50 yds. N.E. of (188). Diam. 46 ft., ht. 4½ ft. Disturbed on top.
(190) Bowl, possibly ditched (96138090), 210 yds. E.S.E. of (189). Diam. 68 ft., ht. 6½ ft.

(191) Bowl (?) (96328089) 200 yds. E. of (190). Diam. 29 ft., ht. 2½ ft. Turf-covered.
(192) Bowl, possibly ditched (96528084), 220 yds. E.S.E. of (191). Diam. about 67 ft., ht. 5 ft. Irregular surface and flattened top. Area between this and (193) much disturbed.
(193) Bowl (?) (96588082) 60 yds. E.S.E. of (192). Diam. 72 ft., ht. 4 ft.

(194) *Mound*, possible bowl (SY 98 SE; 97148059). Diam. about 61 ft., ht. 3½ ft., though spread and irregular.
(195) *Bowl* (SY 98 SE; 97248112) on tip of slight W.-facing spur. Diam. 50 ft., ht. 2½ ft. Ploughed.
(196) *Bowl* (SY 98 SE; 97268113) 25 yds. E.N.E. of (195). Diam. 25 ft., ht. 2 ft.
(197) *Bowl* (SY 98 SE; 97498093). On spine of slight E.-W. ridge. Diam. about 70 ft., ht. 2 ft. Ploughed.
(198) *Bowl* (?) (SY 98 SE; 95418235; Fig. p. 97) on narrow spine of West Hill. Diam. 63 ft., ht. 3½ ft. Almost level top 43 ft. across, sunken in centre. Base damaged by quarrying on E. Turf-covered.
(199) *Mound*, possible barrow (SY 98 SE; 95468235; Fig. p. 97) 49 yds. E. of (198). Diam. 63 ft., ht. 4 ft. Possibly ditched. Turf-covered but damaged by quarrying.
(200) *Bowl* (SY 98 SE; 96378237; Fig. p. 97) on spine of East Hill. Diam. 40 ft., ht. 2 ft. Turf-covered, though has probably been ploughed. Among Ancient Field Group (27).

(L) AILWOOD DOWN GROUP (SY 98 SE). Seventeen bowl barrows and a long barrow (181) on summit and S. shoulder of part of Purbeck Hills, here over 600 ft. above O.D. Ten form an irregular W.N.W.-E.S.E. line only 250 yds. long on the summit while the rest, including the long barrow, lie on slightly lower ground immediately to S. Only the two highest barrows (208 and 212) have continuous ditches. Some others have quarry pits, probably original. All are under turf. One, unidentified but adjacent, contained a cremation (W. A. Miles, *Deverel Barrow* (1826), 15; Hutchins I, 689).

(201) Bowl (?) (99388159). Diam. 30 ft., ht. 2 ft.
(202) Ditched bowl (99438158) 25 yds. E.S.E. of (201). Diam. 48 ft., ht. 7½ ft. Ditch broken by four causeways, two diametrically opposed on N. and S.
(203) Bowl (99428156) 15 yds. S.S.W. of (202). Diam. 25 ft., ht. 1 ft.
(204) Bowl (99468157) 22 yds. E.S.E. of (202). Diam. 43 ft., ht. 6 ft.
(205) Bowl (99498157) 23 yds. E. of (204). Diam. 55 ft., ht. 5 ft.
(206) Bowl (99518157) immediately S.E. of (205). Diam. 40 ft., ht. 3½ ft.
(207) Bowl (99538156) immediately S.E. of (206). Diam. 40 ft., ht. 3 ft. Probably original quarry pit on S.
(208) Ditched bowl (99568155) 43 yds. E.S.E. of (207). Diam. 90 ft., ht. 10 ft. Ditch, 20 ft. wide and up to 4 ft. deep, cuts that of (212).

(209) Bowl (99548154). The westernmost of three immediately S.W. of ditch of (208). Diam. 27 ft., ht. 2 ft.

(210) Bowl (99558154) 11 yds. S.E. of (209). Diam. 15 ft., ht. 9 ins.

(211) Bowl (99568154) immediately adjacent to (210) on S.E. Diam. 22 ft., ht. 1 ft.

(212) Ditched bowl (99598154) immediately S.E. of (208). Diam. 70 ft., ht. 8 ft., with ditch 10 ft. wide and 1 ft. deep cut on W. by that of (208).

(213) Bowl (99628154) immediately E. of (212), on outer lip of ditch. Diam. 35 ft., ht. 2 ft. Quarry pit on E.

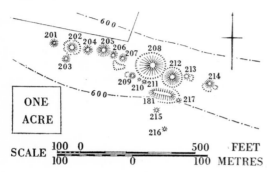

Ailwood Down Group (L), Corfe Castle.

(214) Bowl (99658153) 35 yds. E.S.E. of (213). Diam. 40 ft., ht. 3 ft. Flat-topped, with quarry pits on S.W. and S.E.

(215) Bowl (99578150) 28 yds. S. of W. end of long barrow (181). Diam. 21 ft., ht. 1 ft. Cut by track.

(216) Bowl (99598147) 30 yds. S.S.E. of (215). Diam. 30 ft., ht. 1½ ft.

(217) Bowl (99618151) 47 yds. N.N.E. of (216) and impinging on line of long barrow ditch on S.E. Diam. 27 ft., ht. 1 ft.

(218) Bowl (?) (SY 98 SE; 95718378), possibly ditched. Diam. 45 ft., ht. 4½ ft. Cut on W. by road.

(219) Bowl (SY 98 SE; 98638355). On almost level site on Brenscombe Heath. Diam. 30 ft., ht. 3 ft. Hollowed on top.

DORCHESTER

Three barrows still exist and the position of a fourth is known; possibly six others have been destroyed. One probably lay at present junction of Alington St. and Princes St. beneath the Masonic Hall where a contracted inhumation with a B1 beaker was found in a cist; a ditch was also noted (Dorset Procs. XXIX (1908), 141, no. 111; MS. note with Moule's 25 in. map in D.C.M.; Abercromby I, 87, fig. 30). Two barrows, 'bell-shaped' and only 2 ft. apart, were recorded under the Roman town bank at the E. end of South Walks when levelled in 1864, one containing a possibly primary inurned cremation and several secondary inhumations (Dorset Procs. XVI (1895), 50–1; Cunnington, nos. 1 and 2).

Two barrows, of which no trace remains, may also have existed around 69788990 (Taylor's Map of Dorset (1765); O.S. 1 in. (1811), 6 in. XL SE (1930)). Two small bronze daggers, presumably from a barrow, probably near Fordington, were found with at least six blunt bone implements perforated at one end and up to 3 ins. long (Wessex interment no. 9; Arch. J. V (1848), 322). For bucket urns from Dorchester and area see Dorset Procs. XXIX (1908), 138; Ant. J. XIII (1933), 445. For Conquer Barrow, see under Enclosures, West Stafford (24), p. 504.

(168) Bowl (SY 68 NE; 69708895) on crest of Conygar Hill on Bagshot Sands 280 ft. above O.D. and on parish boundary with Winterborne Herringston. Diam. 75 ft., ht. 11½ ft. Excavated by Cunnington, who found an inhumation lying N.-S. about 4 ft. above the original ground surface, with a nearby cremation.

(169) Bowl (SY 68 NE; 69798893) 105 yds. E. of (168) in similar situation. Diam. 75 ft., ht. 14 ft. Excavated by Cunnington. A primary contracted inhumation with a food-vessel at feet and six barbed-and-tanged flint arrowheads of 'Breton' type[1] at knees (Wessex interment no. 22) lay by a cremation. Above, a block of Portland stone, at depth of 9 ft., measured 7 ft. by 4 ft. by 1½ ft. and weighed nearly 3 tons. Of three secondary cremations, two lay close together 5 ft. from surface and one was in bucket urn 1½ ft. from surface. Food-vessel and arrowheads in D.C.M. (Abercromby I, 95 and fig. 8; Ant. J. VII (1927), 459, and XIII (1933), 445.)

(170) Bowl (?) (SY 69 SE; 68179110; Fig. p. 488) inside Poundbury (Hill-forts, Dorchester (172)) near S. rampart. Diam. 85 ft., ht. 5 ft. Ploughed.

(171) Lawrence Barrow, bowl (SY 69 SE; 68499059). On shoulder of hill 300 ft. above O.D., formerly surrounded by open fields. A borough boundary stone stood on it. Destroyed 1885. Cunnington gives diam. as 35 ft. and ht. as 11 ft. At a depth of 8 ft. was an apparently secondary cremation with grooved copper dagger 8¾ ins. long and a small flat copper knife-dagger 3½ ins. long (Wessex interment no. 10). A typologically early collared urn had previously been found. Finds in D.C.M. (Butler & Smith, 58, no. 16; Archaeometry 4 (1961), 46–7, nos. 21, 36; P.P.S. XXVII (1961), 294, no. 22.)

HOLME, EAST

Two barrows (SY 98 SW), on Holme Mount, lie inside embanked circle 200 ft. in diam. (tree-clump enclosure ?) within 200 ft. ring contour.

(6) Bowl (90698438). Diam. 45 ft., ht. 4½ ft. Bracken-covered.

(7) Bowl (90688442) 45 yds. N.N.W. of (6). Diam. 40 ft., ht. 5 ft.

(8) Mound, possible barrow (SY 98 SW; 90508461) on summit

---

[1] Belonging in Brittany to the first series of Early Bronze Age 'Dagger Graves' (P. R. Giot, Brittany (1960), 131; P.P.S. XVII (1951), 226).

of small knoll and within tree-clump enclosure. Diam. about 90 ft., ht. 10 ft. At least partly artificial.

Three barrows (SY 98 NW) lie above 50 ft. contour just S. of local crest of gravel spur running N. from Battle Plain (*see* Fig. p. 482). All were dug into by Austen in 1860 (*Purbeck Papers* I, 233–8). To N.W. and S. surrounding (9) and (10) is a large group of small mounds, one apparently impinging on (9) (*see* Mounds, E. Holme (12)).

(9) *Bowl* (90648528). Diam. 27 ft., ht. 2½ ft. An inverted urn, probably primary, lay in a cist cut into the sandy subsoil and covered with a sandstone slab. A secondary urn lay 'unprotected' 1½ ft. to the S. and 1 ft. from the surface. Mound (12c) overlaps (9) on W.

(10) *Ditched bowl* (90678529) 40 yds. N.E. of (9). Diam. 36 ft., ht. 4 ft. Probable cremation.

(11) *Bowl* (90698528) 20 yds. E.S.E. of (10). Diam. 36 ft., ht. 4½ ft. Nothing found.

KNIGHTON, WEST

(21) *Bowl* (?) (SY 78 NW; 73528642; Fig. p. 139) on end of small, steep spur just over 200 ft. above O.D. and 230 yds. W.S.W. of Fryer Mayne House, W. Knighton (2). Diam. about 40 ft., ht. about 1½ ft. Overgrown.

(22) *Bowl* (?) (SY 78 NW; 73788924). Virtually destroyed 1890, when diam. 70 ft. Contained probable primary cremation in bucket urn beneath cairn. (*Ant. J.* XIII (1933), 445.)

(23) *Bowl* (?) (SY 78 NW; 74938842) in Knighton Heath Wood at head of gully just over 200 ft. above O.D. Diam. 19 ft., ht. 3 ft. Tree-covered.

(24) *Huck Barrow*, ditched bowl (SY 78 NW; 74958842) on almost level site about 20 yds. E. of (23). Diam. 52 ft., ht. 8 ft., with ditch about 10 ft. wide. Damaged and tree-covered.

LULWORTH, EAST

Of eleven barrows, two (29–30) are on Upper Chalk, the rest on Reading Beds and mostly in heathland. 'Black Barrow' is natural. Sixteen or seventeen barrow excavations have been carried out: eight or nine in 1790 by Milner, seven in the 1820s by Pennie, and one in 1865 by Kendall. Two (29–30) of Milner's excavations were into barrows previously opened and some at least of Pennie's excavations were into barrows opened by Milner. Almost certainly these three diggers opened all the barrows below. One, fairly certainly (32), contained a bucket-urn cremation, probably primary, in a cist lined and covered in stone. Four or five of Milner's excavations, probably among (31–9), produced evidence 'nearly the same' as this. Some of the urns in these barrows were upright, others inverted. An unlocated barrow contained five inhumations, each with an urn (Warne, *C.T.D.*, tovp, no. 12). Probably Pennie opened the two pairs called Water Barrows and Ferny Barrows ((36–7, 38–9): shown on J. Sparrow's

Estate Map of E. Lulworth (1770), in D.C.R.O.), each barrow containing a probably primary inurned cremation within a cairn, apparently in at least three cases a substantial structure of large stones. Nothing in these accounts, poor even for Dorset, suggests that any of the barrows opened is of Early Bronze Age date. The use of stone in or under twelve or thirteen barrows in a small area, even allowing for duplicated records, is particularly striking. (*Gentleman's Magazine* (1790), 897–901; Austen, *Purbeck Papers* I, 35; Hutchins I, 381–4.) All the barrows are on O.S. 6 in. map SY 88 SE.

(29) *Bowl* (85668048). **On** tongue of land projecting W. below Rings Hill at about 150 ft. above O.D. Diam. about 21 ft., ht. 2 ft. Much damaged.

(30) *Bowl* (85688049). In similar situation 26 yds. N.E. of (29). Diam. about 60 ft., ht. 6 ft. Much damaged.

Bowls, three, spread and furze-covered, lie approximately in line on a gravel ridge over 200 ft. above O.D.

(31) (86308149). Diam. 65 ft., ht. 5½ ft.

(32) (86378147) 75 yds. E.S.E. of (31). Diam. 60 ft., ht. 4½ ft.

(33) (86418142) 60 yds. S.E. of (32). Diam. about 70 ft., ht. 2 ft.

(34) *Bowl* (86658129) on summit of Boat Knowl ('Boyt Knowl', 1770). Diam. about 45 ft., ht. about 5 ft. Much disturbed.

(35) *Bowl* (?) (86448195). On local eminence some 240 ft. above O.D. Diam. about 54 ft., ht. 2 ft. Centre disturbed.

The *Water Barrows* (1770), two, lie on almost level site about 220 ft. above O.D.

(36) *Bowl* (86538176). Very irregular; ht. 3½ ft.

(37) *Bell* (?) (86558180) 53 yds. N.N.E. of (36). Diam., including apparent berm on S.E., about 88 ft., ht. 9½ ft., with ditch 12 ft. wide, and 2½ ft. deep on all sides but N. where cut by road. Much disturbed, especially in centre.

The *Ferny Barrows* (1770), two, on summit of slight rise.

(38) *Bowl* (86648165) 180 yds. S.E. of (36). Diam. 48 ft., ht. 5 ft. Disturbed near centre.

(39) *Bowl* (86668161) 40 yds. S.E. of (38). Diam. 75 ft., ht. 6 ft. Damaged on N. and disturbed in centre.

LULWORTH, WEST

There are no concentrations among the eighteen barrows in the parish, not even on Hambury Tout (three (39–41), two of them probably excavated 1790) or Bindon Hill (four possible barrows (42–5)).

(35) *Mound*, possible triple bowl (SY 78 SE; 79958076), partly overlaid on the W. by parish boundary with Chaldon Herring, prominently sited on crest of ridge and aligned at about 8°. Disturbed and very irregular in shape. Total length

114 ft., maximum width 36 ft.; N. crest is flat-topped, 12 ft. across and 4 ft. high, and covered with flints; S. crest is also flat-topped, 4½ ft. across and about 4½ ft. high; the middle crest is very slight and rounded. Shallow scoop at foot of S. mound but no sign of continuous ditch. Lynchets of Ancient Field Group (15) surround it (Fig. opp. p. 628).

(36) *Bowl* (SY 88 SW; 80078112) immediately E. of parish boundary with Chaldon Herring on slight S.E. slope. Diam. about 50 ft., ht. 5 ft. Partly ploughed.

(37) *Bowl* (?) (SY 88 SW; 80508128) near summit of ridge. Ploughed, only slight mound remains. Excavation in 1916 produced a primary (?) cremation in upright bucket-shaped urn in hole beneath flat stone about 5 ft. or 6 ft. W. of assumed centre (Dorset *Procs.* LXXXI (1959), 92–3).

(38) *Bowl* (?) (SY 88 SW; 80638134) 150 yds. E.N.E. of (37). Ploughed almost flat.

(39) *Ditched bowl* (SY 88 SW; 81188043) on spine of ridge sloping to W.N.W. Diam. 46 ft., ht. 4 ft., with ditch about 9 ft. wide. Top of mound markedly flattened but not obviously opened.

(40) *Bell* (SY 88 SW; 81588030) on rounded summit of Hambury Tout 454 ft. above O.D. Diam. 78 ft., ht. 9½ ft., with traces of berm and ditch. Path over top. Probably opened by Milner who found a large heap of ashes under a central cairn, above which was a contracted inhumation with an urn on its chest (*Gentleman's Magazine* (1790), 898; Hutchins I, 383).

(41) *Ditched bowl* (SY 88 SW; 81638030) on E. slope 65 yds. E. of (40). Diam. about 47 ft., ht. 3 ft. Much disturbed. Probably opened by Milner who found bones and urns (*Gentleman's Magazine* (1790), 899; Hutchins I, 383).

(42) *Mound*, possible barrow (SY 88 SW; 82968023), on Bindon Hill. Diam. 14 ft., ht. 1 ft. Abuts on W. side of cross-bank (c) (*see* Hill-forts, W. Lulworth (53), Fig. opp. p. 492).

(43) *Mound*, possible barrow (SY 88 SW; 83548031) about 14 yds. S. of quarry ditch of Early Iron Age rampart (*see* Fig. opp. p. 492). Diam. 30 ft., ht. 3½ ft.

(44) *Mound*, possible barrow (SY 88 SW; 84078026) on spine of Bindon Hill. Diam. 37 ft., ht. 3 ft. Top opened.

(45) *Bowl* (?) (SY 88 SW; 84098026) 23 yds. E. of (44). Diam. 35 ft., ht. 3½ ft. Top opened. Immediately E. is circular depression, 21 ft. in diam. and 1½ ft. deep.

(46) *Barrow* (?) (SY 88 SW; 82588168). Destroyed before 1939 by reservoir.

(47) *Bowl* (?) (SY 88 SW; 83188203) on almost level ground above 400 ft. Diam. about 36 ft., ht. 1 ft.

(48) *Bowl* (?) (SY 88 SW; 83288246) on almost level site near summit of ridge. Diam. about 30 ft., ht. 1 ft. Ploughed.

(49) *Bowl* (?) (SY 88 SW; 83318299) on same ridge as (48). Diam. about 45 ft., ht. 1½ ft. Ploughed.

(50) *Bowl* (?) (SY 88 SW; 83338307) on same ridge as (49), 90 yds. N.N.E. Diam. about 40 ft., ht. 1½ ft. Partly in hedge-row on E. Ploughed.

(51) *Bowl* (SY 88 SW; 83928294) in Burngate Wood on almost flat ground. Diam. about 18 ft., ht. 1 ft.

(52) *Bowl* (SY 88 SW; 83978299) on slight N.E. slope 95 yds. N.E. of (51). Diam. about 41 ft., ht. 2½ ft. Tree-covered.

LYTCHETT MATRAVERS

(37) *Henbury Barrow*, bowl (SY 99 NW; 94899821) in Lower Sandy Coppice above 100 ft. contour on flat-topped spur. Diam. 47 ft., ht. 7 ft. Overgrown.

MORDEN

There are four barrows. A beacon mound (*see* Mounds, Morden (56)) may incorporate another.

(52) *Ditched bowl* (?) (SY 99 SW; 90369338) on almost level ground below 100 ft. Diam. 45 ft., ht. 5 ft. Disturbed on top and tree-covered.

(53) *Cold Barrow*, bowl (?) (SY 99 NW; 90479504), on highest point at N. end of prominent knoll defined by 200 ft. ring contour. Diam. about 21 ft., ht. about 2 ft., with flat top 9 ft. across. Tree-covered.

(54) *Bowl* (?) (SY 89 NE; 89869634) on almost level ground between 100 ft. and 150 ft. above O.D. Diam. about 90 ft., ht. about 2 ft. Under pasture, though probably ploughed.

(55) *White Barrow* (Taylor's Estate Map, 1773), bowl (?) (SY 99 NW; 91029665) on fairly level arable about 140 ft. above O.D. Only broad irregular rise about 2½ ft. high remains, suggesting former large mound.

MORETON

All three barrows, including a bell, are on Old Knowle, a large, prominent, natural knoll, above 100 ft. contour towards S. edge of Moreton Heath (SY 78 NE). They have been damaged by tree-felling. Another (LVG 3) has been claimed in an area now destroyed by quarrying.

(28) *Bell* (79888778). Diam. about 90 ft., ht. 11 ft., with berm about 7 ft. wide. Large tree-clump enclosure lies within and **obscures** original, probably large, ditch. Top hollowed.

(29) *Ditched bowl* (79938779) 55 yds. E. of (28). Diam. 41 ft., ht. 6 ft., with ditch 8 ft. wide.

(30) *Ditched bowl* (?) (79948777) 35 yds. S. of (29). Diam. 13 ft., ht. 2 ft.

OSMINGTON

Although the N. end of the parish runs up to the Ridgeway, only eight barrows occur there including five in the *East Hill Group* ((R.14), Weymouth). Warne excavated two on the Ridgeway (*C.T.D.*, mopr, nos. 5 and 6). No. 5, possibly either (35) or (36), contained a primary cremation in an urn in a chalk-cut cist beneath a flat stone; and two secondary contracted inhumations, one 4 ft. from the top in a flint cairn, the other immediately below the surface with vertical flat stones before and behind the head. No. 6 in the N.E. of the parish contained a bucket urn (no cremation is mentioned) in a cist surrounded by a circle of stones 10 ft. in diam., and a secondary urn was 4 ft. from the top. Coggins Barrow on the cliff edge is natural.

(30–4) *See* EAST HILL GROUP (R.14), Weymouth, p. 457.

(35) *Bowl* (SY 78 SW; 72388421) on crest of ridge. Diam. about 45 ft., ht. 1½ ft.

(36) *Bowl* (SY 78 SW; 72438421) 60 yds. E. of (35). Diam. uncertain, ht. 1 ft. Ploughed.

(37) *Sandy Barrow*, bowl (?) (SY 78 SW; 73028259), on spine of small knoll 367 ft. above O.D. Slight irregular flinty mound, disturbed in centre.

(M) GROUP (SY 78 SW, SE). Four bowls at wide intervals in W.–E. line along spine of ridge above 400 ft. contour. 'Celtic' field lynchets of Ancient Field Group (12) lie 11 yds. to 14 yds. N. of (39–41).

(38) Bowl (74698259). Much damaged by gun emplacement in centre.

(39) Bowl (74928260) 270 yds. E. of (38). Diam. 51 ft., ht. 5 ft., with many flints on surface. Ploughed.

(40) Bowl (75108258) 180 yds. E. of (39). Diam. 51 ft., ht. 4 ft. Ploughed.

(41) Ditched bowl (?) (75208257) 90 yds. E. of (40). Diam. 54 ft., ht. 2½ ft.

OWERMOIGNE

There are twelve barrows. Two, unidentified, 'one on the downs and one on the heath', were opened in the 1890s. Both contained at least one inurned cremation, and from one came two urns, now in D.C.M. (Dorset *Procs.* XVII (1896), xxv–xxvi; XXIX (1908), 136–7; XXX (1909), xlviii.)

(22) *Bowl* (?) (SY 78 SE; 77168142) on ridge top in S.E. of parish. Ploughed almost flat.

(23) *Bowl* (?) (SY 78 SE; 77168152) 98 yds. N. of (22). Only slight mound remains.

(24) *Bowl* (SY 78 SE; 75608362) on Moigns Down. Diam. 35 ft., ht. 4 ft. Top dug into. In pasture.

(25) *Bowl* (SY 78 SE; 75498399) on S. edge of spur which projects N.W. from Moigns Down. Diam. 50 ft., ht. 3 ft. In pasture, but probably ploughed. Among 'Celtic' fields of Ancient Field Group (11).

(26) *Bowl* (?) (SY 78 SE; 76038375) on slope almost at top of S. side of Moigns Down ridge. Oval, about 48 ft. by 54 ft., possibly due to ploughing, and 1½ ft. high. In pasture.

(27) *Ditched bowl* (?) (SY 78 SE; 76078384) on slope to N. Diam. 53 ft., ht. 6 ft.

(28) *Bowl* (SY 78 SE; 76538400) on spine of spur running N.E. Diam. 44 ft., ht. 5½ ft. Overgrown.

(29) *Bowl* (SY 78 NE; 77998595) on small knoll on Galton Heath. Diam. 35 ft., ht. 3 ft.

(30) *Bowl* (SY 78 NE; 77878759). Diam. 51 ft., ht. 5 ft. Tree-covered.

(31) *Tinkers' Barrow*, ditched bowl (SY 78 NE; 77918785). In plantation on top of S. slope. Diam. 44 ft., ht. 4 ft., with ditch 9 ft. wide. Large excavation on top.

(32) *Barrow* (?) (SY 78 NE; 78158783) destroyed by quarrying.

(33) *Tadnoll Barrow*, bowl (?) (SY 78 NE; 79148747). On slight knoll in heathland and cut by parish boundary with Moreton, E. of which road has destroyed two-thirds of site. Diam. about 56 ft., ht. about 5 ft.; around, and 3 ft. from it on W., is a probable tree-clump enclosure, about 75 ft. in diam.

POOLE

Forty-one widely-scattered barrows lie on the heathlands N. of the town, many on ridges or spurs above the 200 ft. contour; seven have now been destroyed. Eighteen occur in three groups: on *Canford Heath* (four); near *Rose Lawn Coppice* (eight); and on *Barrow Hill* (six). The first and last of these contain lines of four barrows and the Barrow Hill Group includes four bells, at least two of which were amongst three barrows opened in the mid 19th century. Although remains of a burial occurred in only one of three modern excavations, all revealed evidence of timber structures with openings to the S.E.; two of these barrows (363–4) had narrow berms, and the other (365) was without a ditch.

(361) *Fern Barrow*, bowl (?) (SZ 09 SE; 06999259), on level site overlooking Bourne valley. Original diam. about 42 ft., ht. about 4½ ft., but much damaged.

(362) *Mound*, barrow (?) (SZ 09 SE; 05429431), on Alderney Heath, now destroyed by gravel digging.

(363) *Bell* (SZ 09 SE; 05689432), built over after complete excavation by H. J. Case in 1949. Overall diam. 43 ft. A central oval sod mound 14 ft. by 12 ft. and 1½ ft. high was edged by revetment of sandy material 22 ft. by 17 ft. and covered with gravel, giving the whole mound diam. of 26 ft. and ht. of about 2½ ft. Berm 3 ft. wide within ditch 5 ft. wide and about 2 ft. deep, interrupted on S.E. by causeway at least 3½ ft. wide. Previous disturbance had destroyed any evidence of burial.

Two small pits containing charcoal were excavated, one 3½ ft. long immediately E. of centre and the other 7½ ft. W. of centre. Beneath mound and on berm were thirty-nine stake-holes, all except four between 1 in. and 4 ins. deep in the Plateau Gravel subsoil. Twelve formed approximate circle 19 ft. in diam., outside, though not concentric with, edge of revetment around central sod mound. The only small finds were 274 struck flints, mostly from top of mound, and many fire-pitted pebbles. Probably Early or Middle Bronze

Age, and possibly later than (364). (*P.P.S.* xviii (1952), 148–59; and xix (1953), 131–3.)

(364) *Bell* (sz 09 se; 05699432) immediately adjacent to (363) on E. and now built over after complete excavation by H. J. Case in 1949. Overall diam. 40 ft. A central mound of sods with vegetation uppermost, 10 ft. in diam. and about 1 ft. high, was covered with gravel to give total diam. of 22 ft. and ht. of 1½ ft. Berm 3 ft. to 5 ft. wide lay within almost perfectly circular ditch 5 ft. wide and 2 ft. to 2½ ft. deep interrupted on S.E. by causeway at least 3½ ft. wide. Beneath sod mound remains of a disturbed central grave 5 ft. long and 6 ins. deep held traces of a presumably primary cremation. Much charcoal, including lumps up to 1 ft. long, lay around the grave; a sample was of oak.

Thirty-two post-holes and twenty-four stake-holes were found. Sixteen post-holes were approximately equidistant on circumference of a circle 28 ft. in diam., around outer edge of berm: ten, associated with the causeway, suggested an entrance structure; and six lay outside the ditch, five of them S.E. of causeway, possibly marking-out posts. They varied between 3 ins. and 15 ins. in depth. Twelve stake-holes, 1 in. to 4 ins. deep, lay beneath sod mound; three, leaning towards the grave, suggested possible temporary structure over it. The others lay at or immediately beyond edge of sod mound, six on an arc from barrow centre. Seventy-nine struck flints, mostly from top of mound, and many fire-pitted pebbles, mostly from sod mound and buried surface, were found. Pollen analysis suggested that forest clearance was well-advanced when the barrow, probably in Early or Middle Bronze Age, was built on land perhaps previously cultivated. (*P.P.S.* xviii (1952), 148–59; and xix (1953), 131–3; *Arch. J.* cxiv (1957), 1–9; P. Ashbee, *The Bronze Age Round Barrow in Britain* (1960), 60–5.)

(365) *Bowl* (sz 09 nw; 04229511) above 200 ft. contour on S. edge of Canford Heath plateau. Destroyed by gravel quarry after complete excavation by P. Ashbee in 1951. The mound, diam. about 30 ft., ht. 3 ft., was of soil and gravel, heaped on site possibly stripped of topsoil. Nineteen post and stake-holes lay about 2¾ ft. apart in a rough arc on the N.E. and E., all but two beneath the mound and all but one 4½ ins. to 5 ins. deep; three were slots about 6 ins. by 4 ins. On W. and S., arc continued as two sections of irregular and shallow trench, linked by three stake-holes and perhaps formed from similar holes by differential weathering. A flanked entrance lay on S.E. No burial occurred in central oval pit, 5 ft. by 4 ft. and a few ins. deep, with pile of gravel to E. presumably dug from it. Immediately S.W., though in body of mound, was about 4 ft. of carbonised hollowed oak tree-trunk. Only other finds were 140 flint flakes and cores over top of mound. (*P.P.S.* xix (1953), 131–3; Dorset *Procs.* lxxvi (1954), 39–50; Ashbee, *op. cit.* in (364), 44, 56, 60–5.)

(366) *Bowl* (?) (sz 09 nw; 02659534) in conspicuous position on Lodge Hill above 200 ft. contour and re-entrant valley to E. Diam. 50 ft., ht. 3½ ft. Slight hollow on top.

(367) *Bowl* (sz 09 nw; 02759534) on opposite side of re-entrant, 100 yds. E of (366). Diam. 22 ft., ht. 3 ft. Much damaged.

(368) *Ditched bowl* (?) (sz 09 nw; 03039530) on S. edge of Canford Heath plateau above 200 ft. Diam. 36 ft., ht. 3½ ft. Hollowed on top and much damaged.

(N) Canford Heath Group (sz 09 nw). Four bowls in slightly irregular W.S.W.-E.N.E. line near W. edge of plateau, above 200 ft. contour and steep W. slope. All much damaged.

(369) Bowl (02279545). Diam. 57 ft., ht. 5 ft.

(370) Ditched bowl (02299545) 20 yds. E.N.E. of (369). Diam. 39 ft., ht. 4½ ft., with ditch about 7 ft. wide.

(371) Bowl (02329545) 30 yds. E. of (370). Diam. 43 ft., ht. 5 ft.

(372) Ditched bowl (02339546) 15 yds. E.N.E. of (371). Diam. 33 ft., ht. 4½ ft., with ditch about 6 ft. wide.

(373) *Bowl* (sz 09 nw; 02439559) on level site above 200 ft., 180 yds. N.E. of (372). Diam. 27 ft., ht. 3½ ft. Much damaged.

(374) *Bell* (?) (sz 09 nw; 01889586) on S. edge of spur, above 200 ft., jutting S. from plateau. Diam. 30 ft., ht. 3 ft., with berm 7 ft. wide about 2 ft. above ground level, and ditch about 10 ft. wide.

(375) *Bowl* (?) (sz 09 nw; 04389591) on Knighton Heath just below 200 ft. on slope to N. Diam. about 20 ft., ht. about 2 ft. Destroyed.

(376) *Bowl* (sz 09 nw; 04699598) in similar position to (375). Diam. 33 ft., ht. 4 ft. Damaged.

(377) *Ditched bowl* (sz 09 nw; 04369618) above small stream on slight ridge between 100 ft. and 150 ft. above O.D. Diam. 32 ft., ht. 3½ ft., with ditch 6 ft. wide. Slight hollow in centre; S. side destroyed by golf tee.

(378) *Bowl* (?) (sz 09 nw; 03439614) on level site above slopes N. and W. to small valley. Diam. 43 ft., ht. 5 ft., but now damaged and isolated in gravel pit. Hollowed on top.

(379) *Bowl* (?) (sz 09 nw; 03459615) 15 yds. N.E. of (378). Diam. about 40 ft., ht. about 4½ ft. Destroyed.

(380) *Ditched bowl* (sz 09 nw; 02589625) on level site within 200 ft. ring contour. Diam. 39 ft., ht. 4 ft. Damaged.

(381) *Ditched bowl* (sz 09 nw; 02539641) in similar position to (380) 185 yds. to N.N.W. Diam. 28 ft., ht. 3 ft., with ditch 4 ft. wide.

(382) *Bowl* (?) (sz 09 nw; 01469655) above 200 ft. contour on tip of spur. Diam. 36 ft., ht. 4 ft. Hollowed on top.

(383) *Bowl* (sz 09 nw; 01899677) in Arrowsmith Coppice at end of low ridge above gentle N. slope. Diam. 54 ft., ht. 5 ft.

(384) *Bowl* (sz 09 nw; 01889679) in similar position 25 yds. N.N.W. of (383). Diam. 30 ft., ht. 3 ft.

(385) *Ditched bowl* (sz 09 nw; 02629690) on fairly level site above steep slopes to W. and N.W. Diam. 40 ft., ht. 5 ft., with ditch about 6 ft. wide. Damaged by gravel digging.

(386) *Ditched bowl* (?) (sz 09 nw; 01999732) in Gravel Hill Plantation. Formed pair with (387). Destroyed by gravel digging.

(387) *Bowl* (SZ 09 NW; 02019732) on edge of ridge above S.E. slope 25 yds. E. of (386). Diam. 45 ft., ht. 5½ ft. Damaged by gravel digging.

(O) ROSE LAWN GROUP (SZ 09 NW). Eight barrows, forming a compact group though with no obvious focus, on and towards N.E. end of broad ridge above 200 ft. contour. Most are on golf course.

(388) Ditched bowl (00579749). Diam. 48 ft., ht. 8 ft., with ditch 12 ft. wide and up to 1 ft. deep. Hollowed on top.

(389) Bowl (00759749) 200 yds. E. of (388). Diam. 21 ft., ht. 1½ ft.

(390) Bowl (00769744) 45 yds. S.S.E. of (389). Diam. 31 ft., ht. 3½ ft.

(391) Bowl (00779754) in Rose Lawn Coppice 115 yds. N. of (29). Diam. 45 ft., ht. 5 ft.

(392) Ditched bowl (?) (00799751) 30 yds. S.E. of (391) and similarly planted. Diam. 51 ft., ht. 7 ft.

(393) Bowl (00939742) 170 yds. S.E. of (392). Diam. 16 ft., ht. 1 ft. Damaged.

(394) Bowl (?) (00939743) 20 yds. N.E. of (393). Diam. about 21 ft., ht. 1½ ft. Damaged and tree-covered.

(395) Barrow (?) (01009743) 70 yds. E. of (394), converted into golf tee. Diam. probably about 60 ft., and ht. over 6 ft.

(P) BARROW HILL GROUP (SY 99 NE). Six barrows, including four bells, on flat-topped ridge above 200 ft. contour. (396–9) form a short S.W.-N.E. alignment. All but (399) have probably been excavated. Three barrows on 'Merley Heath' were excavated by Austen in 1847: two of (396–8) contained unaccompanied cremations beneath a layer of flints; and either (400) or (401) contained a primary cremation in an upright Middle or Late Bronze Age urn, and at least five intrusive inhumations in top of mound (*Ant. J.* XIII (1933), 444).

(396) Ditched bowl (99589745). Diam. 20 ft., ht. 2½ ft.

(397) Bell (99609746) 25 yds. N.E. of (396). Diam. 20 ft., ht. 3 ft., with berm about 6 ft. wide and ditch about 7 ft. wide.

(398) Bell (99669752) 75 yds. N.E. of (397). Diam. about 22 ft., ht. 3½ ft., with berm about 5 ft. wide and ditch about 7½ ft. wide.

(399) Bowl (?) (99699755) 56 yds. N.E. of (398). Diam. 19 ft., ht. 1 ft.

(400) Bell (99599767) 160 yds. N.W. of (399). Diam. about 50 ft., ht. 7½ ft., with traces of berm on S.E. and damaged, irregular ditch about 9 ft. wide.

(401) Bell (99569768) 30 yds. N.W. of (400). Diam. about 40 ft., ht. 7½ ft., with berm about 5 ft. wide and ditch 9 ft. wide and 1 ft. deep.

PORTESHAM

Most of the twenty-two barrows in the parish are scattered in small clusters or singly on the Ridgeway and the lower hills to the S. The scattered *Black Down*

Group (R.5) is on the highest point of the Ridgeway, and two pairs of barrows form part of the *Bronkham Hill* and *Ridge Hill Groups* (R.6 and R.7). On Friar Waddon Hill, S. of the Ridgeway, is a double bowl and a smaller linear group (Q).

(R.5) BLACK DOWN GROUP (SY 68 NW). Ten barrows, including one bell, on gravel-capped heath around Hardy Monument above 700 ft. Five are in Portesham (34–8), the others in Winterbourne Steepleton (16–19) and Little Bredy (*Dorset* I, no. 12).

Little Bredy:
(12) Bowl (60478784). Diam. 46 ft., ht. 5 ft.

Winterbourne Steepleton:
(16) Bowl (60578787) on N.E. slope 107 yds. E.N.E. of last. Diam. 35 ft., ht. 4½ ft. Disturbed.

(17) Bowl (61018787) 480 yds. E. of (16). Diam. 30 ft., ht. 4½ ft.

(18) Bowl (61018779) 70 yds. S. of (17). Diam. 30 ft., ht. 4 ft.

(19) Bowl (61148766) 205 yds. S.E. of (18). Diam. 42 ft., ht. 3 ft. Much damaged by digging, with probable spoil on N.W.

Portesham:
(34) Bowl (?) (61318760) immediately E. of Hardy Monument. Diam. 20 ft., ht. 1 ft.

(35) Bowl (61328761) immediately E. of (34) on edge of steep N.E. slope. Diam. 64 ft., ht. 5 ft. Excavated in centre.

(36) Bowl (61388757) below and 75 yds. S.E. of (35). Diam. 33 ft., ht. 4 ft.

(37) Bowl (61308755) 40 yds. S. of Monument. Diam. 28 ft., ht. 1½ ft.

(38) Bell (61288749) 110 yds. S. of Monument. Overall diam. 110 ft.: mound 80 ft. across and 7 ft. high, and partly removed on W. by gravel pit which revealed a turf core with gravel capping; berm 10 ft. wide and ditch about 8 ft. wide at the lip, 5 ft. deep and narrow at the bottom. Mound possibly examined from this side by Cunnington who in 1878 dug into a damaged barrow about 100 yds. 'north' of the Monument and exposed a pit 6 ft. deep and 5 ft. across with ashes, two whetstones and flint flakes under large stones, all lying beneath a 'very black part' (Cunnington MS. no. 52). Excavation in 1955 (*P.P.S.* XXIII (1957), 124–36) revealed four biconical and sub-biconical Middle Bronze Age urns, three with cremations, near the top of the mound.

(39–40) *See* E. end of BRONKHAM HILL GROUP (R.6), Winterborne St. Martin, p. 467.

(41–2) *See* RIDGE HILL GROUP (R.7), Winterborne St. Martin, p. 467.

(43) *Bowl* (SY 68 NW; 64578646), the only barrow down the slope S. from the Ridgeway. Diam. 70 ft., ht. 8½ ft. Cunnington in 1885 found primary contracted inhumation in cist, and remains of a child inhumation, surrounded by large stones. Above was cremation in large urn with smaller vessel (in D.C.M.); 3 ft. higher, 6 ft. below the top of the mound, lay

two extended inhumations, each with a vessel at its head (one in D.C.M.). Near top of the mound was child inhumation in a grave partly consisting of a Roman roof slab, associated with a Romano-British sherd. Part of a saddle quern was in the body of mound. (Dorset *Procs.* XVI (1895), 177 and XXXVII (1916), 45; *Ant. J.* XIII (1933), 446.)

(44) *Bowl* (?) (SY 58 NE; 59658688). Diam. about 67 ft., ht. 2½ ft. Much ploughed; probably associated with two adjacent stones immediately S. (*see* Stones, Portesham (59)). (Dorset *Procs.* XXIX (1908), lxxiv; O.S. *Map of Neolithic Wessex*, no. 144; *P.C.T.E.W.*, 235.)

(45) *Bowl* (?) (SY 58 NE; 59758645) near summit of Broom Barrow hill. Only much disturbed cairn, 20 ft. in diam., remains.

(46) *Mound*, possible barrow (SY 68 NW; 60488670), on S. shoulder of Portesham Hill 100 yds. W.S.W. of Hell Stone (Long Barrow, Portesham (33)), in area with 'Celtic' fields and later quarrying. Diam. about 42 ft., ht. about 3 ft.

(47) *Bowl* (?) (SY 68 NW; 60658669) 70 yds. E.S.E. of Hell Stone (33). Low elongated mound remains. When excavated by Cunnington in 1894 it measured 48 ft. by 16 ft., was 6 ft. high and had apparently been cut back in making a wall. It covered an inurned cremation (Dorset *Procs.* XVI (1895), 176.)

(48) *Bowl* (?) (SY 68 NW; 61688603) on crest of narrow ridge above 500 ft. Oval, 52 ft. by 21 ft., and 4 ft. high, apparently cut back by strip cultivation (*see* Portesham (32e), p. 246).

(49) *Bowl* (?) (SY 68 NW; 63418557) near E. end of Corton Hill, on spine. Diam. 46 ft., ht. 3 ft.

(50) *Bowl* (?) (SY 68 NW; 64028554) on crest of Friar Waddon Hill. Diam. 20 ft., ht. 1¼ ft.

(51) *Double bowl* (SY 68 NW; 64068550) 56 yds. S.E. of (50). Diams. of mounds 35 ft. and 32 ft., hts. 3½ ft. and 3 ft.; joined by slight bank. Top of S.E. mound flattened, probably by excavation.

(Q) FRIAR WADDON HILL GROUP (SY 68 NW). Four bowls along crest of E. end of hill, one above 400 ft., the others on E. slope.

(52) (64488546). Irregular in plan, 29 ft. by 23 ft., and 2½ ft. high.

(53) (64548545) 65 yds. E. of (52). Diam. 42 ft., ht. 5 ft. Excavated in centre.

(54) (64608540) 80 yds. E.S.E. of (53). Diam. 31 ft., ht. 3 ft.

(55) (64678542) 85 yds. E. of (54). Diam. 25 ft., ht. 2 ft.

PORTLAND

No certain barrows remain but the site of an urnfield within a mound is known. A burial found with a four-handled biconical jar of Armorican type suggests a possible but unlocated barrow on North Common below Verne Hill (*Arch. J.* XXV (1868), 50 (fig.); *Archaeologia* XLIII (1871), 339 and fig. 19; *L'Anthropologie* IV (1951), 432–5).

(96) *Bowl* (?) (SY 67 SE; 68747077). At Suckthumb or Suckton Quarry part of a 'slightly raised mound' surrounded by a ditch was destroyed by quarrying in 1905 when about 160 urns were dug up and nearly all immediately smashed. It was later reported that 'probably 100 to 200' urn burials had been found in the mound, but it is not clear whether this refers to the earlier destruction or to a new group of urns. Some survive in D.C.M. (Dorset *Procs.* XXVI (1905), xxxix; XXIX (1908), cxv; Abercromby II, 42, figs. 419, 419a.)

POXWELL

Warne excavated two unlocated barrows (*C.T.D.*, mopr, nos. 7 and 8) on 'Pokeswell Down, adjoining the Ridgeway'; one of these may be (11), in the *North-down Barn Group* (R.13). Otherwise only two certain barrows are known, emphasising the break in the distribution of barrows on the Ridgeway E. of *East Hill Group* (R.14). A barrow, possibly one of those excavated by Warne, is shown about 715848 on O.S. (1811).

(11) *See* NORTHDOWN BARN GROUP (R.13), Weymouth, p. 457.

(12) *Barrow* (SY 78 SW; 74518357; Plate 211), situated on crest of E.-W. limestone ridge just under 400 ft. Turf-covered mound now oval, about 63 ft. E.-W. and 44 ft. N.-S., with almost flat top, offset to E.; about 2 ft. high. On E. side of top, at probable approximate centre of an original circular mound, is exposed a continuous ring of stones, 14 ft. in diam.

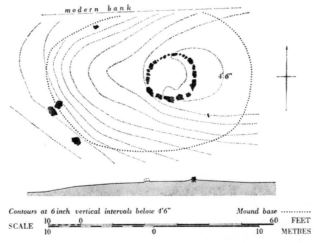

Contours at 6 inch vertical intervals below 4'6"   Mound base ············

SCALE

(cf. Bincombe (24), Group (R.8), Weymouth, p. 456). The stones are a 'recrystallised variety of sarsen' (Arkell, 241). On S. some stand up to 2½ ft. high, while on N. they are virtually flush with the surface. The spaces between all are packed with small limestone rubble. The four stones peripheral to mound on the W. seem more likely to be from this circle than to belong to an outer peristalith. No ditch is visible (but *cf.* Hutchins I, 408; Warne, *Ancient Dorset*, 119–20). A later boundary bank runs along N. side. (Dorset *Procs.* VI (1884), 55–7; *Reliquary*, XI (1870–1), 154–7.)

(13) *Mound*, possible barrow (SY 78 SW; 74728395), 430 ft. above O.D. on almost level site just above S. slope. Height 2 ft. Ploughed.

(14) *Bowl* (?) (SY 78 SW; 74688416) above 400 ft. on N. slope. Now 35 ft. by 29 ft. due to ploughing at base, ht. 4½ ft.

STAFFORD, WEST

(18) *Bowl* (?) (SY 78 NW; 72428904). Near summit of slight ridge over 200 ft., above gentle N.W. slope. Ploughed almost flat.

(19) *Sandy Barrow*, bowl (SY 78 NW; 72788909). On level site above 200 ft. Diam. about 85 ft., ht. about 9 ft. Cut on W. by lane and densely overgrown.

(20) *Bowl* (SY 78 NW; 71518970). On Frome Hill above 200 ft. Diam. about 55 ft., ht. 6 ft. Irregular.

(21) *Bowl* (?) (SY 78 NW; 71478972) 47 yds. N.W. of (20). Ploughed almost flat.

(22) *Conquer Barrow*, barrow (?) SY 70798990, on bank of 'henge' monument, *see* Enclosures, West Stafford (24), p. 504.

(23) *Barrow* (?) (SY 78 NW; 70998995). Near centre of 'henge' monument (24). A 'mound or barrow at the centre' was claimed by R. J. C. Atkinson (*Excavations at Dorchester, Oxon.* (First Report) (1951), 104–5). R.A.F. V.A.P. CPE/UK 1934: 5082–3, suggest former mound here but no clear traces remain on the ground.

STEEPLE

All but one (19) of the seven known barrows are on Grange Heath. One on the heath about ½ mile from Creech Grange—possibly (21)—was said to have been removed in 1854; from it came three secondary inurned cremations. Between the urns was part of an inhumation covered by Purbeck stones, the whole deposit being on a rough flint paving (*Purbeck Papers* I, 238; Hutchins I, 613).

(19) *Bowl* (SY 98 SW; 90158257) on summit of slight rise defined by 200 ft. ring contour just S. of Pomphrey's Plantation. Diam. 43 ft., ht. 4 ft., surrounded by tree-clump enclosure and tree-covered.

(20) *Drinking Barrow*, bowl (SY 98 SW; 90698313) at N. corner of Great Plantation above 200 ft. on small knoll. Oval, 45 ft., E.-W. and about 54 ft. N.-S., ht. 4 ft. No surrounding ditch, that about 6 ft. from base on W. being part of abandoned system of copse banks and ditches, and depression along E. being disused track.

(21) *Ditched barrow* (?) (SY 98 SW; 90728309) 45 yds. S.E. of (20) on slightly lower ground. D-shaped in plan and flat-topped. Diam. about 25 ft., ht. 1 ft. Ditch 6 ft. to 10 ft. wide and 2 ft. deep. Counterscarp bank, spread over about 10 ft. but only 6 ins. high, best-preserved on N. and E. Disturbed by trees.

(22) *Ditched bowl* (SY 98 SW; 90768326) on crest of slight E.-W. ridge about 170 ft. above O.D. and 170 yds. N.E. of (20). Diam. 40 ft., ht. 3 ft. Cut by track.

(23) *Ditched bowl* (SY 98 SW; 90808326) in similar position 46 yds. E. of (22). Diam. 25 ft., ht. 1 ft., with ditch 6 ft. wide and up to 1 ft. deep.

(24) *Ditched bowl* (SY 98 SW; 91128340) on slight S.E. slope, steepening some 20 yds. to S. Diam. 30 ft., ht. 3 ft., with ditch about 4 ft. wide. Tree-covered.

(25) *Bowl* (?) (SY 98 SW; 90668374) about 170 ft. above O.D. towards W. end of slight ridge. Diam. 55 ft., ht. 5 ft., surrounded by tree-clump enclosure. Overgrown.

STOKE, EAST

All twenty-nine barrows lie on heathland to N. and S. of the Frome, eleven in two groups. That on *West Holme Heath* is a good example of a linear group related to only a slight ridge. Many have been damaged by military activity. A completely excavated example on Chick's Hill (22) produced a primary cremation in a globular urn. In another small barrow at Highwood, now unidentifiable but possibly one of (21–5), were three inverted urns with cremations at a depth of 2 ft. (Hutchins I, 413).

(21) *Ditched bowl* (SY 88 NE; 86768559) near end of ridge. Diam. 64 ft., ht. 5 ft. with ditch 9 ft. wide. Excavation in top.

(22) *Ditched bowl* (SY 88 NE; 86878588) on Chick's Hill, a spur S. of the Frome, just over 50 ft. above O.D. Diam. about 28 ft., ht. 3 ft., before partial destruction and excavation in 1955–6. Primary cremation in inverted globular urn lay just above old surface in centre on large flints and immediately above small infilled pit with signs of burning. Some 6 ft. to N.E. was a similar pit containing pine and oak charcoal and burnt flints. The mound had been heaped up in stages with material from slightly irregular flat-bottomed ditch about 5 ft. wide and 3 ft. deep. Some cultivation had probably taken place in the area before the barrow was built. (*Dorset Procs.* LXXX (1958), 146–59.)

Three barrows, including a bell, lie close together on a low rise on Highwood Heath (SY 88 NE).

(23) *Bowl* (?) (86988543). Diam. 20 ft., ht. 2 ft. Trench across centre.

(24) *Ditched bowl* (?) (87018543) 33 yds. E. of (23). Diam. 24 ft., ht. 1 ft. Damaged.

(25) *Bell* (87038539) on summit of rise above 100 ft. contour 46 yds. S.S.E. of (24). Diam. of mound and sloping berm 93 ft., ht. 9 ft., with ditch 10 ft. wide and 2½ ft. deep.

(S) WEST HOLME HEATH GROUP (SY 88 SE). Five, possibly six, barrows lie in an almost straight E.-W. line on a slight ridge in an area devastated by tanks.

(26) Mound, possible barrow (88238460). Diam. about 60 ft., ht. 2 ft. Cut by road on W.

(27) Bowl (88268460) 30 yds. E. of (26). Diam. 54 ft., ht. 4 ft.

(28) Bowl (88298460) 30 yds. E. of (27). Diam. 58 ft., ht. 3½ ft.

(29) Bowl (88328460) 33 yds. E. of (28). Diam. 50 ft., ht. 4 ft. Disturbed in centre.

(30) Bowl (88348460) 23 yds. E.S.E. of (29). Diam. 44 ft., ht. 4½ ft. Disturbed in centre.

(31) Bowl (88378459) 30 yds. E.S.E. of (30). Diam. 56 ft., ht. 4½ ft.

(32) *Bowl* (SY 88 NE; 85838739) on S. end of ridge. Diam. 46 ft., ht. 4 ft.

(33) *Bowl* (?) (SY 88 NE; 88718722) in woodland on South Heath. Diam. about 30 ft., ht. about 4 ft.

(34) *Bowl* (?) (SY 88 NE; 88798723) 92 yds. E. of (33). Diam. about 30 ft., ht. 3 ft.

Three barrows, including a probable bell, form a triangular cluster on top of a ridge at S. edge of South Heath (SY 88 NE).

(35) *Bell* (?) (89388708). Diam. of mound and slight berm about 36 ft., ht. 5 ft., with ditch about 7 ft. wide and 1 ft. deep.

(36) *Ditched bowl* (89408707) 20 yds. S.E. of (35). Diam. 28 ft., ht. 4½ ft.

(37) *Ditched bowl* (89418710) 20 yds. N.N.E. of (36). Diam. 40 ft., ht. 5 ft.

(38) *Ditched bowl* (SY 88 NE; 85998811). Diam. 66 ft., ht. 8 ft. Tank track through centre.

(39) *Ditched bowl* (SY 88 NE; 85848833) on level site. Diam. 70 ft., ht. 6 ft., with ditch 8 ft. wide.

(40) *Ditched bowl* (SY 88 NE; 85958873). Diam. 45 ft., ht. 4 ft. Damaged.

(41) *Bowl* (?) (SY 88 NE; 87238825) on almost level site near top of steep scarp to S. Diam. about 50 ft., ht. 4 ft., but largely destroyed.

(42) *Barrow* (?) (SY 88 NE; 87308816) 130 yds. S.E. of (41), completely destroyed. Possibly only a tree-clump enclosure.

(43) *Barrow* (?) (SY 88 NE; 87468828) 230 yds. N.E. of (42). Destroyed by gravel quarry.

(44) *Ditched bowl* (SY 88 NE; 87648857) on slight N. slope below 100 ft. Diam. 47 ft., ht. 5 ft.

(T) FARM HEATH GROUP (SY 88 NE). Five barrows on slope dropping N. towards River Piddle.

(45) Ditched bowl (88848789) on summit of knoll with steep fall to N. Diam. 46 ft., ht. 8 ft. Much damaged, top excavated.

(46) Bowl (89028783) on flat top of small plateau 220 yds. E.S.E. of (45). Diam. 63 ft., ht. 6 ft. Trench cuts into centre.

(47) Mound, possible barrow (89028794), 133 yds. N. of (46) on top of small knoll. Very disturbed.

(48) Barrow (?) (89158791) 146 yds. E.S.E. of (47). Nothing visible on top of knoll.

(49) Bowl (89288774) above 100 ft. contour 226 yds. S.E. of (48). Diam. 36 ft., ht. 2½ ft. Much disturbed.

STUDLAND

The fourteen barrows include two, probably four, bells. Eight, including the bells, fall within two groups on the N.-facing escarpment overlooking Poole Harbour. A natural knoll, protected by the Agglestone and sometimes thought to be a barrow (Arkell, 224), is excluded, as are three unlocated mounds claimed as possible barrows N. of Dean Hill (Dorset *Procs.* LXXVI (1954), 79). A barrow possibly existed at about 035817 in or beside Cracker Barrow Furlong below Ballard Down (Tithe Map, 1840). A primary crouched inhumation was found in (29).

(29) *Ulwell Barrow*, ditched bowl (SZ 08 SW; 02238132). On nearly level site at lower, W., end of Ballard Down, above steep slopes to S., W. and N. and below gentle rise to E. Diam. 74 ft., ht. 6 ft., with ditch 12 ft. wide. Excavation hollow in top, and cut by hedge-bank from N.; on S., where crossed by parish boundary with Swanage, lies a collapsed obelisk dated 1892 and erected to commemorate 'the introduction of pure water from the chalk formation into Swanage'. In 1857 Austen found a primary contracted inhumation, the skull surrounded by flat stones, in chalk-cut grave 8 ft. by 5 ft. with handled cup of fine red ware; antler fragments occurred in grave filling. In mound near centre were a disarticulated inhumation with urn fragments and, slightly higher, a cremation under a flat stone with more urn fragments. In top of mound were Iron Age and/or Romano-British debris and many flint chippings. (*Purbeck Papers* I, 157–60; *Ant. J.* XIII (1933), 447.)

(30) *Bowl* (?) (SZ 08 SW; 04208132) just S. of spine of ridge. Diam. 20 ft., ht. 1 ft. Hollowed on top.

(U) GODLINGSTON HEATH GROUP (SZ 08 SW). Four barrows, including two, probably three, bells, all relatively undamaged.

(31) Bell (00708193). Diam. 58 ft., ht. 4 ft., with berm up to 8 ft. wide and ditch 11 ft. wide and 1½ ft. deep.

(32) Bell (00728197) adjacent to (31) on N.N.E. Diam. 56 ft., ht. 3 ft., with berm about 12 ft. wide and ditch 12 ft. wide and 1½ ft. deep. Excavation on top.

(33) Bell (?) (00688200) 66 yds. N.W. of (32) and unusually irregular in shape, probably because on small natural knoll. Diam. 52 ft., ht. 4½ ft., with irregular berm 25 ft. wide on N., 15 ft. wide on S. and almost absent on E. Ditch 14 ft. wide, 6 ins. to 2 ft. deep on W. and N. and absent on S. where its line interrupted by (34).

(34) Bowl (?) (00678199) immediately S.S.W. of (33). Diam. 30 ft., ht. 2 ft.

(V) THORNY BARROW GROUP (SZ 08 SW). Four barrows, including a probable bell, in a straight line near S. edge of Godlingston Heath above N. slope. All damaged.

(35) Thorny Barrow, bowl (?) (01438210), on edge of broad ridge but almost unrecognisable owing to encroachment of large sand pit. Diam. about 65 ft., ht. about 8 ft.

(36) Bowl (01648212) 225 yds. E. of (35). Diam. 30 ft., ht. 1½ ft.

(37) Bowl (01658212) immediately E. of (36). Diam. 37 ft., ht. 2 ft.

(38) Fishing Barrow, bell (?) (01818211), 175 yds. E. of (37). Diam. including berm 99 ft., ht. 9 ft., with ditch 12 ft. wide and 1½ ft. deep. Berm largely obscured by slip from mound, which is flattened on top by golf tee.

(39) *Mound*, possible barrow (sz 08 sw; 01798268). On Godlingston Heath above large sand pit to N.W. and steep slope to N.E. Diam. 37 ft., ht. 3 ft., but similar to natural rises in adjacent heath.

(40) *Bowl* (?) (sz 08 sw; 03238306) on natural knoll and merging with it. Diam. about 60 ft., ht. about 2 ft. Hollowed on top.

(41) *Bowl* (?) (sz 08 sw; 03308299) in garden of Studland Bay House 120 yds. S.E. of (40). Diam. 46 ft., ht. 6 ft.; E. half removed and sides revetted.

(42) *King Barrow*, bowl (sz 08 sw; 04618202), on top of natural knoll. Diam. 43 ft., ht. 4 ft. Disturbed.

STURMINSTER MARSHALL

One probable barrow remains. Two other possible examples, one on Barrow Hill and another 145 yds. S. of Newton Peveril Farm, no longer exist; a fourth, from which came two collared urns in the B.M., is unlocated (*Durden Catalogue*, 18–20, nos. 20 and 42).

(46) *The Shapwick Barrow*, bowl (?) (st 90 sw; 93360164), on low-lying and seasonally flooded site 130 yds. S.E. of S. bank of River Stour and 200 yds. N.W. of Badbury Rings–Dorchester Roman road. Diam. 90 ft., ht. 6 ft. Opened in 1838 by Woolls who found a probably primary cremation in other burnt matter with 'a ruby-coloured barrel-shaped glass bead', presumably amber. Flints lay above, and seven more lay in a circle just beneath the surface. There were possibly some secondary interments (*The Barrow Diggers* (1839), 102–5).

SWANAGE

The parish contains eight, possibly ten, barrows. Another (LVG 4) recorded near (81–3) is unlocated. (84–8) are on the high ridge of Ballard Down. Austen opened three in both 1851 and 1857; these included a circular depression, 20 yds. N.E. of (86) at 03988133, 33 ft. across and 3 ft. deep with an irregular bank, in which he found nothing and which is more likely to be a pond than a pond barrow. (89) and (90) covered primary contracted inhumations in chalk-cut graves. (*Purbeck Papers* I, 160–3.)

(81) *Giant's Grave*, barrow (?) (sz 08 sw; 01228106), on steep slope rising to head of re-entrant on S.W. of Godlingston Hill. Diam. about 25 ft., ht. about 2 ft. Irregular and overgrown. Austen found nothing.

(82) *Giant's Trencher*, barrow (?) (sz 08 sw; 01258107), 30 yds. E.N.E. of (81) and similar in situation, condition and size. Austen also found nothing in this.

(83) *Bowl* (?) (sz 08 sw; 01468120) on N.E. spur above steep slopes to N. and S., about 450 ft. above O.D. Formerly larger, now slightly oval in plan: average diam. 48 ft., ht. about 2 ft. Probably opened by Miles, who found a primary cremation between two horizontal stones, and later by Austen, who found nothing (*The Deverel Barrow*, 8; *Purbeck Papers* I, 160).

(W) BALLARD DOWN GROUP (sz 08 sw). Five small bowls close together within 500 ft. ring contour on spine of steep-sided chalk ridge. The area, built on and disturbed in the 1940s and now almost levelled by ploughing, contains numerous slight rises similarly marked by concentrations of stone rubble, making identification of barrows recorded here very difficult. (86–8) are crossed by the parish boundary with Studland. The following are reasonably certain:

(84) Bowl (02738123). Diam. 27 ft., ht. 1 ft.

(85) Bowl (02748123) 16 yds. S.E. of (84). Diam. about 24 ft., ht. 1 ft.

(86) Bowl (?) (02768125) 30 yds. N.E. of (85). Diam. about 30 ft., ht. 1 ft. Boundary stone on top.

(87) Bowl (?) (02798125) 25 yds. E. of (86). Ht. 1 ft.

(88) Bowl (?) (03038127) 260 yds. E. of (87). Diam. 24 ft., ht. 2 ft. Boundary stone on top.

(89) *Bowl* (sz 08 sw; 03978129). Diam. 37 ft., ht. 3 ft. Hollowed on top. Austen found a primary contracted inhumation with antler fragment in grave 5 ft. deep into the chalk; other antler fragments occurred in grave filling. An extended E.-W. inhumation lay 2 ft. beneath top of mound (*Purbeck Papers* I, 161).

(90) *Ditched bowl* (sz 08 sw; 03998129) 20 yds. E. of (89). Diam. 48 ft., ht. 3 ft. Austen found a probably contracted inhumation in chalk-cut grave 3 ft. deep, with urn fragments and human bones in the filling. A child inhumation lay on the chalk at lip of grave and fragments of another occurred near surface of mound (*Purbeck Papers* I, 162–3).

TURNERS PUDDLE

Six (14–19) of the eleven barrows are on rises in the heath S. of the village. Four of the others, with two in Bere Regis, form a small group on *Black Hill*, N.E. of the village. A mound, 60 ft. across, at 83919244 is probably natural.

The following three barrows (sy 89 sw) are on a broad W.-E. ridge.

(14) *Bowl* (?) (82829112). Diam. about 50 ft., ht. 6 ft.

(15) *Bowl* (82929105) 125 yds. S.E. of (14). Diam. 66 ft., ht. 6 ft. Flag-pole on centre. Where cut on S. by road, section showed mound of large heath turves. An ovate flint knife and part of lanceolate flint dagger of Early Bronze Age type were found. Pollen analysis suggested barrow built after

considerable forest clearance. (Dorset *Procs.* LXXV (1953), 34–5.)

(16) *Bowl* (?) (82909096) 100 yds. S. of (15). Diam. 48 ft., ht. 4½ ft. Much damaged.

(17) *Round Barrow*, bowl (SY 89 SW; 83329122) on N. spur from ridge. Diam. 50 ft., ht. 6 ft. Much damaged.

(18) *Bell* (SY 89 SW; 82699179) on prominent hill. Diam. of mound and berm 65 ft., ht. 6½ ft., with ditch about 8 ft. wide. Hollowed in centre and overgrown.

(19) *Ditched bowl* (?) (SY 89 SW; 83239191) on N. spur from ridge. Diam. about 50 ft., ht. 4½ ft.

(X) BLACK HILL GROUP (SY 89 SW). Six bowls, three forming a short straight line on S.W. spur from ridge along which runs parish boundary marked by large standing sarsen stone (*see* Stones, Turners Puddle (25)). All are above the 300 ft. contour, and all but two, in Bere Regis, are damaged.

(20) Bowl (83649401). Diam. 43 ft., ht. 4½ ft. Hollowed in centre.

(21) Bowl (83689403) 50 yds. N.E. of (20). Diam. 50 ft., ht. 4½ ft.

(22) Bowl (83709406) 50 yds. N.E. of (21). Diam. 50 ft., ht. 4½ ft. Hollowed in centre.

(23) Bowl (83789395) 140 yds. S.S.E. of (22). Diam. 57 ft., ht. 4 ft.

Bere Regis:

(77) Bowl (?) (83719411) 85 yds. N.N.E. of (22). Diam. about 45 ft., ht. 3 ft.

(78) Bowl (83999421) on N.E. spur of Black Hill 310 yds. E.N.E. of (77). Diam. 37 ft., ht. 2½ ft.

(24) *Bowl* (?) (SY 89 SW; 82609474) in Piddle Wood on knoll within 300 ft. ring contour. Diam. about 45 ft., ht. 9 ft. at most. Damaged and thickly overgrown.

TYNEHAM

Twenty-four barrows, all but one (14) on Povington Heath, include three bells and two double bowls on the N. part of the Heath and the *Thorn Barrow Group* at its S. end; (14) is very close to the village. At least two other small barrows (LVG 8 and 13) have been claimed on the Heath: military activity makes location and recognition difficult. All but (24) which is very well-preserved have been damaged, some by use as gunnery targets. Two 'large mounds' have been recorded on Worbarrow Cliff (about SY 870800); in one of them, perhaps the 'tumulus' recorded by Miles (*The Deverel Barrow* (1826), 38), was found a Middle/Late Bronze Age pin (Dorset *Procs.* LXXI (1949), 51). (For (14–23) *see* plan of Tyneham Earthworks, in pocket Part 2.)

(14) *Bowl* (?) (SY 88 SE; 87958031) on low spur 235 yds. W.S.W. of Tyneham church about 150 ft. above O.D.

A mound 3 ft. high, probably originally circular but hollowed into horse-shoe shape by excavation, almost certainly contained seven inhumations, possibly Iron Age or later, one with small cup. A detached skull was buried separately (Hutchins I, 628).

(Y) THORN BARROW GROUP (SY 88 SE). Six barrows around 200 ft. contour W. of Povington. Three, possibly four (15–18), are close together in a straight line.

(15) Bowl (?) (87688180). Diam. about 30 ft., ht. about 2 ft.

(16) Bowl (?) (87698181) immediately N.E. of (15). Diam. about 30 ft., ht. about 3 ft.

(17) Bowl (?) (87708182) immediately N.E. of (16). Diam. about 28 ft., ht. 3 ft.

(18) Mound, possible bowl (87728182), 26 yds. N.E. of (17). Slight, possibly natural, rise.

(19) Thorn Barrow, bowl (87698199), on top of slight rise 183 yds. N.N.W. of (18). Diam. 83 ft., ht. 10 ft. Overgrown.

(20) Bowl (87798191) on slight rise 140 yds. S.E. of (19). Diam. 74 ft., ht. about 5½ ft.

(21) *Povington Barrow*, bowl (SY 88 SE; 88058214), above 200 ft. on spur from a knoll. Diam. 56 ft., ht. 7 ft. Cremation in biconical Bronze Age urn, now in D.C.M., found at edge under small flint cairn (Dorset *Procs.* LXX (1948), 55; LXXI (1949), 68–9).

(22) *Bowl* (?) (SY 88 SE; 88008245) on summit of slight rise above 100 ft. Diam. 33 ft., ht. 4 ft.

(23) *Bowl* (?) (SY 88 SE; 88628267) on or incorporating a natural knoll. Diam. about 100 ft., ht. about 16 ft.

(24) *Ditched bowl* (SY 88 SE; 87718272) on fairly level site about 120 ft. above O.D. Diam. 49 ft., ht. 2½ ft., with shallow ditch 8 ft. wide.

(25) *Ditched bowl* (SY 88 SE; 87608281) on summit of slight rise 163 yds. N.W. of (24). Diam. 56 ft., ht. 5½ ft.

(26) *Bowl* (?) (SY 88 SE; 87518323). Diam. about 33 ft., ht. 1½ ft.

(27) *Bowl* (?) (SY 88 SE; 88448311) on a knoll. Diam. about 37 ft., ht. 5 ft.

(28) *Bowl* (?) (SY 88 SE; 88638306) on end of small ridge. Almost destroyed.

(29) *Bowl* (SY 88 SE; 88558372) on small knoll within 100 ft. ring contour. With (30) forms short line of three adjacent mounds. Diam. about 55 ft., ht. about 4 ft. Probably earlier than S. mound of (30).

(30) *Ditched double bowl* (SY 88 SE; 88568374 and 88578376) immediately N.E. of (29). Diams. 62 ft., and 60 ft., ht. of both mounds 8 ft. Surrounding ditches converge into a common ditch between mounds.

(Z) FIVE BARROW HILL GROUP (SY 88 SE). Six barrows including three bells, in an almost straight line along summit of slight ridge which falls gently N.

(31) Bowl (?) (87628390). Diam. about 42 ft., ht. about 4 ft. Destroyed.

(32) Bowl (87638393) 33 yds. N. of (31). Diam. 62 ft., ht. 4½ ft.

(33) Bowl (?) (87638397) 43 yds. N. of (32). Diam. 30 ft., ht. 1 ft.

(34) Bell (87618400) 32 yds. N.N.W. of (33). Diam. of mound and sloping berm 105 ft., ht. 6 ft., with recently recut ditch 12 ft. wide and up to 3½ ft. deep.

(35) Bell (87608405) adjoining (34) on N. Diam. about 100 ft., ht. 7 ft., with berm 12 ft. wide and ditch 12 ft. wide and up to 2½ ft. deep.

(36) Bell (87598410) adjoining (35) on N. Diam. about 90 ft., ht. 5 ft., with berm about 12 ft. wide and ditch 12 ft. wide and up to 2½ ft. deep.

(37) *Ditched double bowl* (SY 88 SE; 88048412) on summit of slight rise. Oval, with two crests in profile; length 105 ft. N.W.-S.E., width 69 ft. and 62 ft. beneath crests, respectively 6 ft. and 7½ ft. high. Ditch about 10 ft. wide surrounds the whole.

WAREHAM LADY ST. MARY

The three bowls (82-4) in the parish, included as a result of a recent boundary change, form part of the WORGRET HEATH GROUP (B), Arne (p. 435).

WAREHAM ST. MARTIN

Eight of the nine barrows are in the *Seven Barrows Group*. Six others have been claimed, but four (LVG 1, 2, 4 and 5) are probably upcast from gravel digging, and nothing remains of the other two.

(AA) SEVEN BARROWS GROUP (SY 98 NW). Eight barrows, all but (13) in a near-straight line S.W.-N.E. on the summit of a small but sharply-defined heathland ridge above the 100 ft. contour. A ninth possibly existed at 91168857 but no trace remains. Probably all but (13) were dug into by Shipp and Durden in 1844 without result (*C.T.D.*, cpf, no. 1).

(8) Bowl (91148864). Diam. 66 ft., ht. 3½ ft. Top markedly flat, apparently an original feature.

(9) Bowl (91168868) 30 yds. N.E. of (8). Diam. 64 ft., ht. 3½ ft. Flat-topped as (8).

(10) Bowl (91188870). 50 yds. N.E. of (9). Diam. about 37 ft., ht. 4½ ft.

(11) Bowl (91188874) 30 yds. N.N.E. of (10). Diam. about 30 ft., ht. about 2 ft.

(12) Bowl (91218878) 60 yds. N.E. of (11). Diam. about 37 ft., ht. 4 ft.

(13) Bowl (?) (91218879) immediately N. of (12). Ploughed almost flat.

(14) Bowl (91238880) 20 yds. N.E. of (12). Diam. about 37 ft., ht. 4 ft.

(15) Bowl (91258883) 45 yds. N.E. of (14). Diam. 42 ft., ht. 4½ ft.

(16) *Bowl* (SY 88 NE; 89168968). On plateau above 100 ft. contour. Diam. about 48 ft., ht. 3 ft. Damaged.

WARMWELL

Only one barrow remains. Three probable bowls in an irregular line at 75878829, 75898822 and 76038805 have been destroyed. Black Hill Clump is a natural knoll with a tree-clump enclosure on top.

(10) *Bowl* (?) (SY 78 NW; 73208530) on top of ridge. Almost ploughed flat.

WEYMOUTH

Most of the forty barrows now within the parish were formerly in Upwey. All are on the Ridgeway except for three (432-4) on the lower ground to the S. Those in the N.W. are part of the *Ridge Hill Group* (R.7), while in the N.E. corner they form parts of the *Northdown Barn* (R.13) and *East Hill* (R.14) *Groups*, themselves part of the complex of groups at the E. end of *Group R* (*see* pp. 425-6, 458).

Many have been dug into: one, not now identifiable, was opened in 1621 (Dorset *Procs.* XIII (1892), 61; *A.B.M.E.*, 111) and from another, also unidentifiable, came an incense cup now in the B.M. The Rimbury urnfield (435), most of the urns from which were broken on discovery, has given its name to part of the so-called Deverel-Rimbury culture.

Six unidentified barrows on the Ridgeway, which may have been in the *Ridgeway Hill Group* (R.8), were, with one exception, described by Warne (*C.T.D.*, tovp, nos. 77-80, *and* mopr, 33 *n.*), four having been excavated by Sydenham (*Archaeologia* XXX (1844), 332, nos. 12, 16, 17 and 18). One on Ridgeway Hill covered a primary inhumation accompanied by an antler and boar's teeth, a collared urn containing burnt animal bones at its feet, two worked flints including an arrowhead, and part of a perforated boar's tusk, all in a central, chalk-cut cist, lined and covered with flat stones. A bell barrow also on the Ridgeway and built of clay produced no finds. Nearby a low flat barrow contained a cremation in a globular urn fitted tightly into a chalk-cut cist covered with several flat stones; and a barrow 8 ft. high covered an empty food-vessel in a central cist lined and covered by six large flat stones and a flint cairn paved with flat stones (Abercromby I, pl. xxix, 1). Another barrow on the Ridgeway covered a circle of stones 2 ft. high around an extended inhumation with an infant inhumation beside it and an inurned cremation between its legs. Four cists also lay within the circle, each about 3½ ft. deep and containing an inhumation, with one of which was 'a small urn or drinking cup'. The sixth barrow, on Ridgeway Hill, was opened *c.* 1818 and contained an urn, part of another and an unburnt human skull (LVG Bincombe 60e).

(396–406) form part of RIDGE HILL GROUP (R.7), Winterborne St. Martin, pp. 467–8.

(R.8) RIDGEWAY HILL GROUP (SY 68 NE). Twenty-one barrows, about 300 yds. S.E. of the E. end of Group R.7, strung irregularly along the broad Ridgeway top here running over and between two rises defined by 500 ft. ring contours. The W. part of the group is in Weymouth, the E. in Bincombe, amongst Ancient Field Group (7). Most of the barrows have been damaged by ploughing and excavation: eleven, opened in the 19th century cannot now be identified, but three of Warne's excavations can probably be located (Weymouth (412–14); *see also Archaeologia* XXX (1844), 333, nos. 13–15). Four barrows have been excavated this century, one by Prideaux in 1922 (Bincombe (24)) and three by Mrs. M. E. Robertson-Mackay for the Ministry of Public Building and Works in 1963 (Weymouth (416), Bincombe (25, 27)).

(407) Ditched bowl (?) (66798604). Diam. 80 ft., ht. 6½ ft. Probably excavated.

(408) Bowl (?) (66828607) 40 yds. N.E. of (407). Ploughed out.

(409) Bowl (?) (66878613) 80 yds. N.E. of (408), forming short alignment with it and (407). Ploughed almost flat.

(410) Ditched bowl (66878599) 110 yds. S.E. of (407). Diam. 60 ft., ht. 1 ft., and heavily ploughed.

(411) Bowl (?) (66908601) 40 yds. N.E. of (410). Diam. about 60 ft. Ploughed out.

(412) Ditched bowl (?) (66928597) 60 yds. S.E. of (410) at S.E. end of short alignment with (407) and (410). Diam. of mound 65 ft., ht. 4½ ft. Overall diam. with ditch about 80 ft. (V.A.P. CPE/UK 1934: 1061). Probably contained primary inurned cremation in a cist, with more than 20 secondary inurned cremations in the mound.

(413) Ditched bowl (66928591) 65 yds. S. of (412). Diam. of mound 63 ft., ht. 5 ft. Overall diam. with ditch about 80 ft. (V.A.P. CPE/UK 1934: 1061). Probably contained primary inhumation in stone-lined cist, and secondary cremation.

(414) Ditched bowl (67018592) 105 yds. E.N.E. of (413). Diam. of mound 84 ft., ht. 6 ft. Overall diam. with ditch about 100 ft. (V.A.P. CPE/UK 1934: 1061). Probably contained two inhumations lying at right angles across each other.

Bincombe:
(23) Ditched bowl (?) (67048599) 55 yds. N.N.E. of Weymouth (414). Circular soil-mark about 70 ft. in diam. on V.A.P. CPE/UK 1934: 1061.

Weymouth:
(415) Bowl (67078590) 70 yds. E. of (414). Diam. 67 ft., ht. 5 ft. Cut on W. by track on line of Roman road.

Bincombe:
(24) Bowl, with internal circle of stones (67208590),

140 yds. E. of last and immediately N. of modern boundary with Weymouth. Diam. 27 ft., ht. 4 ft. Excavated by Prideaux in 1922. The mound covered a circular drystone wall, 25 ft. in diam. and 2 ft.-3 ft. high, enclosing eight inhumations. Two, probably adult males, lay in primary position below buried surface with unusual Beaker bowl; three, a man, a baby and a boy, lay immediately above buried surface, the first two in slab cists and the third with a handled 'A' beaker. Two or three interments were inserted into top of mound, one with Iron Age 'A' jar and broken antler, another with a piece of antler. A second Iron Age 'A' pot was also found. All but two burials were contracted. For stone circle, *cf.* Poxwell (12), and Weymouth (405). (Dorset *Procs.* LXV (1943), 38–52.)

Weymouth:
(416) Ditched bowl (67268580) 130 yds. S.E. of last. Ploughed almost flat. Excavated 1963. Mound built from periphery towards centre. Primary burial robbed; three secondary cremations, two unaccompanied, one in inverted collared urn. Ditch, 6½ ft. wide and 5 ft. deep, with two carbonised timbers about 4 ft. long on primary silt. Overall diam. 59 ft. (Information from excavator; Dorset *Procs.* LXXXVI (1964), 102.)

(417) Bowl (?) (67218572) 98 yds. S.S.W. of (416). Ploughed almost flat.

(418) Ditched bowl (?) (67318580) 60 yds. E. of (416). Ploughed flat but visible on Allen's O.A.P. (Ashmolean Museum No. 154), apparently at 'Celtic' field angle.

Bincombe:
(25) Bell (67398583) 144 yds. E.N.E. of Weymouth (416). Diam. about 90 ft., ht. 6 ft., before excavation in 1963. Central cairn, revetted by drystone wall some 30 ft. in diam. and 2 ft. high, covered three primary burials: a slightly contracted female inhumation, possibly wrapped in shroud fastened at neck by bronze awl, in central cist with short-necked beaker; an unaccompanied child inhumation, perhaps similarly wrapped, in small cist; and an unaccompanied cremation in pit. In cairn were four unaccompanied cremations, and a fifth was contained in large, upright food-vessel. Cairn covered by turf stack capped with chalk. Ditch 6 ft. wide and 4 ft. deep; overall diam. 120 ft. (Information from excavator; Dorset *Procs.* LXXXVI (1964), 102.)

(26) Bowl (?) (67498581) 100 yds. E. of (25). Diam. 95 ft., ht. 7 ft.

(27) Ditched bowl (67558584) 65 yds. N.E. of (26). Diam. 64 ft., ht. 3½ ft., before excavation in 1963. Several Neolithic pits with artifacts of Portland Chert, probably indicating occupation sites, underlay a land surface containing late Neolithic material on which barrow was built. Central cairn was covered by turf stack capped with chalk. Beneath cairn was contracted inhumation with necked beaker in central cist, and unaccompanied contracted child inhumation in cist 2½ ft. long. Six secondary inhumations occurred in a stratigraphical sequence: the first, with food-vessel, was disturbed by the second, slightly contracted and also with food-vessel, inside stone-lined cist; the third, also slightly contracted and with Wessex vase-support, underlay the fourth in same pit; the fifth lay contracted beneath wooden slat, and

Drawing by S. H. Grimm.   1790

Burial chamber, from E.   Reconstructed 1866

PORTESHAM. (33) Hell Stone.

PLATE 209

ROUND BARROWS, etc.

WINTERBORNE ST. MARTIN. Bronkham Hill Barrow Group (R. 6), showing also (145) Dyke, looking S.W.
(Phot.: Min. of Defence, Air Force Dept.)

WHITCOMBE etc. Culliford Tree Barrow Group (R. 11), including bank barrow (Broadmayne 19), looking W.
(Phot.: Camb. Univ.)

PLATE 210

ROUND BARROWS

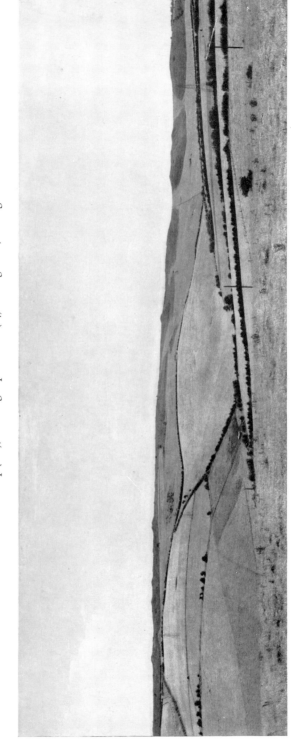

WINTERBOURNE ABBAS. Poor Lot Barrow Group (AD), including triple barrow (24) in foreground, looking S.W.

WINTERBORNE ST. MARTIN. Bronkham Hill Barrow Group (R. 6), looking S.W.

PLATE 211   ROUND BARROW AND STONES

POXWELL. (12) Round barrow with circle of stones, from N.W.

WINTERBOURNE ABBAS. (57) Nine Stones, from E.

the sixth, contracted and in pit, was of a child. Ditch 4 ft. wide and 2½ ft. deep; overall diam. 85 ft. (Information from excavator; Dorset *Procs.* LXXXVI (1964), 103.)

(28) Bowl (?) (67538593) 90 yds. N.N.W. of (27). Diam. about 80 ft., ht. 4 ft. Cut by road and crossed by former parish boundary with Upwey.

(29) Bowl (?) (67608584) 50 yds. E. of (27). Diam. 63 ft., ht. 3 ft.

(30) Bowl (?) (67738585) 150 yds. E. of (29). Diam. 80 ft., ht. 5 ft. At S.W. end of alignment of five barrows on spur running N.E., others being Bincombe (31) and (33) and Winterborne Herringston (3) and (4).

(31) Bowl (?) (67788593) 100 yds. N.N.E. of (30). Ploughed almost flat.

(R.13) NORTHDOWN BARN GROUP (SY 78 SW). Five bowls on the S. side of the Ridgeway along the narrow col between *West Hill* and *East Hill Groups*. A mound (LVG 48) at 70728481 is probably spoil from an adjacent pit. The barrows are in Weymouth and Poxwell.

(419) Ditched bowl (70798474) 80 yds. S.S.E. of Northdown Barn. Diam. 54 ft., ht. 3 ft., with ditch 12 ft. wide and 1 ft. deep. Markedly flat-topped, and probably disturbed. On N. and S., ditch overlain by lynchets butting against mound (Ancient Field Group (10)); and also dug into on S., adding to 'causewayed' appearance.

(420) Ditched bowl (70848479) 60 yds. N.E. of (419). Diam. 76 ft., ht. 10 ft. Warne found cremation with mass of burnt material, 4 ft. in diam., 3 ft. thick, and probably the remains of the funeral pyre. Above was dog's skeleton immediately beneath cremation in handled urn.

(421) Bowl (70968475) 120 yds. E.S.E. of (420). Diam. 57 ft., ht. 10 ft. Disturbed on top.

(422) Bowl (71008475) 60 yds. E. of (421). Diam. 60 ft., ht. 4 ft., before being ploughed almost flat.

Poxwell:

(11) Bowl (71128468) 150 yds. S.E. of last. Diam. 100 ft., ht. 6 ft. Ploughed. Probably one of two together excavated by Warne: one contained primary (?) cremation in globular urn and eight secondary inurned cremations in top of mound; in the other, only dug on E., was a cremation beneath probably inverted urn containing cremation in small vessel (*Ant. J.* XIII (1933), 446).

(R.14) EAST HILL GROUP (SY 78 SW). Fourteen, possibly sixteen, barrows in two compact clusters, the E. one containing a slightly irregular line of seven aligned on Bincombe (69) in R.12. Now mostly ploughed, but some still visible on skyline from *Broadmayne bank barrow* (19). Two barrows (LVG 31a and LVG Osmington 2), one possibly a disc, are untraceable.

One of Osmington (31–3) probably contained a primary inurned cremation in a cist and a fragmentary inhumation near the top.

Weymouth:

(423) Bowl (71118453). Diam. 36 ft., ht. 2½ ft.

(424) Bowl (71148451) 60 yds. S.E. of (423). Diam. 50 ft., ht. 3 ft. Centre dug out.

(425) Ditched bowl (71168452) 30 yds. N.E. of (424). Diam. 53 ft., ht. 5 ft. Excavated.

(426) Ditched bowl (71168455) 40 yds. N. of (425). Diam. 71 ft., ht. 10 ft., with ditch 18 ft. wide and 2 ft. deep. Disturbed on top.

(427) Bowl (71208454) 40 yds. E.S.E. of (426). Diam. 42 ft., ht. 3½ ft. Trigonometrical station on E.

(428) Bowl (71228456) 20 yds. N.E. of (427). Diam. 40 ft., ht. 3 ft.

(429) Bowl (71248454) 33 yds. E. of (427). Diam. 30 ft., ht. 1 ft.

(430) Bowl (71258453) 14 yds. E.S.E. of (429). Diam. 30 ft., ht. 2 ft.

(431) Ditched bowl (71348451) 90 yds. E.S.E. of (430). Diam. 50 ft., ht. 5½ ft.

Osmington:

(30) Ditched bowl (71438450) 100 yds. E. of last. Diam. 65 ft., ht. 8 ft. Ditch about 12 ft. wide.

(31) Ditched bowl (?) (71448453) 33 yds. N. of (30), crossed on W. by parish boundary with Weymouth. Diam. 18 ft., ht. 1½ ft., with ditch 8 ft. wide and 6 ins. deep.

(32) Bowl (?) (71458453) 14 yds. E. of (31). Diam. 45 ft., ht. 1 ft.

(33) Bowl (71468453). 12 yds. E. of (32), possibly making double bowl with it. Diam. 35 ft., ht. 2 ft.

(34) Ditched bowl (71478451) 45 yds. E. of (30). Diam. 30 ft., ditch 12 ft. wide. Ploughed almost flat.

Two barrows on Bayard Hill, a locally prominent rise.

(432) *Bowl* (SY 68 NE; 66418535). Diam. 60 ft., ht. 8 ft. Top flattened and base damaged by ploughing.

(433) *Bowl* (?) (SY 68 NE; 66488537) 85 yds. E.N.E. of (432). Oval, 51 ft., by 35 ft., ht. 9 ft. Damaged.

(434) *Ditched bowl* (SY 68 SE; 66778245), near Nottington, below 100 ft. and on the edge of Plateau Gravel overlying the Oxford Clay. Diam. 65 ft., ht. 4 ft. Excavated 1938. Contained a primary (?) cremation with fragmentary bronze dagger and probable remains of pyre. Destroyed 1947. (Dorset *Procs.* LXXIII (1951), 98.)

(435) *Rimbury Urnfield* (SY 68 SE; 69958336; Fig. p. 24), possibly including barrow(s), on limestone spur S.E. of Chalbury hill-fort (Bincombe (76)). Reservoir now on site. Nearly 100 cremations in mostly upright urns, covered with flat stones, and several probably extended inhumations, some in stone-lined graves, some beneath urns, and at least one in a cist with an inurned cremation, were found during clearance for arable and subsequent excavation. Some urns in D.C.M. and one in Cambridge Univ. Mus. of Arch. and Eth. (*Ant. J.* XIII (1933), 446–7; *P.P.S.* XXVIII (1962), 319–20.)

WHITCOMBE

Eleven of the nineteen barrows are in the *Culliford Tree Group* (R.11), and four in a small Group (AB) on the N. slope from the Ridgeway.

D

(R.11) CULLIFORD TREE GROUP (SY 68 NE, 78 NW; Plate 209). Twenty-six round barrows, with a bank barrow (Broadmayne (19)), a long barrow (Whitcombe (5)) and a small D-shaped enclosure (Whitcombe (25)) closely associated, in the S. of Winterborne Came, Whitcombe and Broadmayne parishes, where they end some 470 ft. above O.D. on top of the Ridgeway. Included in the group are two probable bells, and three, possibly five, pond barrows. A W.-E. line of barrows from (9) to Broadmayne (24), including the bank barrow, is on the exact summit of the narrow but gently defined ridge. (7, 10) virtually share this position but all the others are off the exact summit, long barrow (5) being on a slope about 40 ft. below. Broadmayne (24-9) are on the crest of a spur falling gently N.E.

The bank barrow is earlier than Broadmayne (20), which lies over its W. end (cf. (8) on top of long barrow Whitcombe (5)). It is almost certainly earlier than (9-16), seemingly arranged to continue its alignment to the W. on the crest, and than Broadmayne (21-3),

lying parallel to it on the N. edge of its ditch. Indeed the whole group appears to be related to the bank barrow, from which, also, barrows of *Groups* R.10, R.12, R.13 and R.14 are clearly visible. This concentration of barrows in groups around the bank barrow appears to be the E. end of the *Ridgeway Group*: very few barrows, and certainly no comparable complex, exist along the Ridgeway to the E.

A D-shaped enclosure, now destroyed, lay adjacent to Whitcombe (13) and (14); it was perhaps earlier than (14) and may be directly associated with the barrow alignment (*see* Enclosures, Whitcombe (25)).

All of the barrows are damaged, particularly by ploughing and many are covered by trees or scrub; only one excavation, (9), is certainly located.

Winterborne Came:
(20) Bell (?) (69578548). Diam. about 93 ft., ht. about 12 ft., with ditch about 8 ft. from base of mound.
(21) Bell (?) (69688545) 123 yds. E.S.E. of (20). Diam. 89 ft., ht. 10 ft., with traces of ditch.

CULLIFORD TREE BARROW GROUP
WHITCOMBE, WINTERBORNE CAME & BROADMAYNE

For profile of bank barrow, Broadmayne (19), *see* map of Ridgeway Area (in pocket).

(22) Bowl (?) (69738545) 53 yds. E. of (21). Diam. about 70 ft., ht. about 1½ ft.

(23) Pond barrow (69778543) 52 yds. E. of (22). Central depression, 46 ft. in diam. and about 8 ins. below ground level, is bounded by unbroken bank about 39 ft. wide and over 3 ft. high, with possible traces of external ditch about 20 ft. wide on W. and N. (*see* profile). Thickly overgrown but relatively well-preserved.

(24) Bowl (69828547) 50 yds. N.E. of (23). Diam. 70 ft., ht. 5½ ft.

Whitcombe:
(6) Pond barrow, possible (69838543), 60 yds. S.E. of last. Diam. about 120 ft. and bank up to 20 ft. wide. Cut by parish boundary. Now destroyed.

(7) Bowl (69868553), on parish boundary 105 yds. N.N.E. of (6). Diam. 45 ft., ht. 5 ft.

(8) Barrow (?) (69988567). Diam. 40 ft., ht. 5 ft., on top of N.E. end of long barrow, Whitcombe (5).

(9) Culliford Tree barrow, bowl (69918547), 70 yds. S.E. of (7). Diam. 94 ft., ht. about 13 ft., within tree-clump enclosure, still containing trees, first planted 1740 (Hutchins 1st. ed., I, 419). Large trench on S. and top almost certainly dug 1858 when four secondary extended inhumations, one with necklace of amber and two gold-plated beads, and cremation with incense cup in collared urn, were found (Wessex interment no. 7). Finds lost except for urn-sherd in D.C.M. Barrow became meeting place of Hundred to which it gave its name. (Hutchins II, 485; Abercromby II, 28 and fig. 235.)

(10) Bowl (69958552) 70 yds. N.E. of (9). Diam. 68 ft., ht. 7½ ft. Possibly one of two which yielded skeletons (G. Dugdale, *William Barnes of Dorset* (1953), 167).

(11) Ditched bowl (69978545) 80 yds. E.S.E. of (9). Diam. now 87 ft. but formerly about 100 ft., ht. about 12 ft. with flat top. Spread chalk outside ditch suggests bank.

(12) Pond barrow (69998543), now only slight depression about 65 ft. in diam. immediately S.E. of (11), surrounded by roughly circular chalk bank, about 15 ft. wide (V.A.P. CPE/UK 1821: 6443).

(13) Bowl (70038542) 40 yds. E. of (12). Diam. 72 ft., ht. 4½ ft. On E. probably just touches enclosure (25).

(14) Ditched bowl (70088538). Diam. about 100 ft., ht. 12½ ft., with ditch about 17 ft. wide probably cutting bank of enclosure (25) on N.W.

(15) Bowl (?) (70128538) immediately E. of (14). Diam. about 40 ft., ht. 1 ft. Markedly earthy, with no sign of chalk make-up or ditch.

(16) Ditched bowl (70158537) immediately E. of (15). Diam. now 75 ft., but formerly about 90 ft., ht. 12½ ft., with ditch about 17 ft. wide.

Broadmayne:
(20) Ditched bowl (70198536) overlying W. and smaller end of bank barrow (19) (*see* profile on map of Ridgeway Area (in pocket)). Diam. about 80 ft., ht. 11 ft. above ditch.

(21) Bowl (70268537) on apparent lip of N. ditch of bank barrow. Diam. about 70 ft., ht. about 6 ft.

(22) Bowl (70308535) immediately outside N. ditch of bank barrow and 50 yds. E.S.E. of (21). Diam. 73 ft., ht. 9 ft.

(23) Pond barrow, possible (70338534), 50 yds. S.E. of (22) and immediately outside N. ditch of bank barrow. Roughly circular about 50 ft. by 70 ft. and about 2 ft. deep with broad chalky spread on N.W. only (V.A.P. CPE/UK 1821: 6443).

(24) Ditched bowl (?) (70408528) about 30 yds. E.S.E. of E. end of bank barrow. Diam. 84 ft., ht. 12 ft. with possible ditch about 15 ft. wide.

(25) Pond barrow (70498528) 90 yds. E.N.E. of (24). Diam. about 60 ft., depth about 1½ ft. within unbroken bank about 15 ft. across and at most 6 ins. high.

(26) Bowl (70468533) 40 yds. N.N.W. of (25). Diam. about 84 ft., ht. about 11 ft.

(27) Ditched bowl (70538532) 50 yds. E.N.E. of (25). Overall diam. about 90 ft., ht. 1 ft.

(28) Ditched bowl (?) (70628537) 120 yds. N.E. of (27). Overall diam. about 90 ft. Ploughed almost flat.

(29) Bowl (70708542) 90 yds. N.E. of (28). Diam. about 82 ft., ht. 10 ft.

(AB) GROUP (SY 78 NW). Four barrows, including an oval barrow, in N.W.-S.E. line across S.-facing slope of low ridge running N.N.E. below the Ridgeway. All have been heavily ploughed. The top half of bank barrow Broadmayne (19) and the round barrows continuing its alignment to W. can be seen in silhouette to S.

(17) Ditched bowl (70708626). Diam. about 90 ft., ht. about 5 ft.

(18) Ditched bowl (70748620) 70 yds. S.E. of (17). Diam. 54 ft., ploughed almost flat.

(19) Ditched bowl (70768619) immediately S.E. of (18) and possibly forming double barrow with it. Diam. about 70 ft., ht. about 2 ft.

(20) Ditched oval barrow (70798617) 30 yds. S.E. of (19) and crossed, near E. end, by parish boundary with West Knighton. About 123 ft. long by 80 ft. within apparently continuous ditch; ht. 2½ ft. rising to 5 ft. beneath parish boundary where unploughed.

Four barrows (SY 78 NW), all ploughed, lie on continuation of same low ridge to N.E.

(21) *Bowl* (71078669). Diam. about 70 ft., ht. about 3 ft.
(22) *Bowl* (71008698). Diam. 45 ft., ht. 4½ ft.
(23) *Ditched bowl* (?) (71018701). Diam. 45 ft., ht. 4 ft.
(24) *Bowl* (71668756). Diam. about 72 ft., ht. about 7 ft.

WINFRITH NEWBURGH

Most of the seventeen barrows lie on heathland N. of the village, five forming the *Black Knoll Group* (AC). Another barrow possibly existed at 81938295 (O.S. 1811). Some on Winfrith Down, perhaps including (32), were excavated by Durden but cannot now be identified (*Durden Catalogue*, 9, no. 110; 21, nos. 50–54).

(32) *Bowl* (?) (SY 88 SW; 80378317) on top of broad ridge. Diam. 42 ft., ht. 2 ft. Ploughed. There is now no trace of a second mound (on O.S. 1811) immediately to N.N.E.

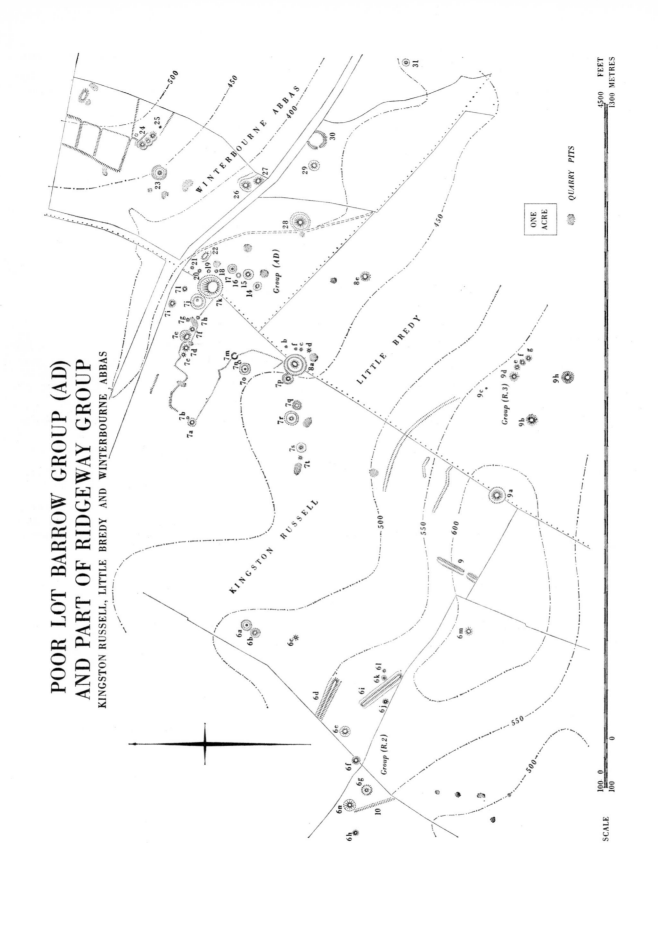

POOR LOT BARROW GROUP (AD)
AND PART OF RIDGEWAY GROUP

KINGSTON RUSSELL, LITTLE BREDY AND WINTERBOURNE ABBAS

ONE ACRE

QUARRY PITS

SCALE

100   0   100

4500   FEET

1300   METRES

WINTERBOURNE ABBAS

LITTLE BREDY

KINGSTON RUSSELL

Group (AD)

Group (R.3)

Group (R.2)

(33) *Bowl* (?) (SY 88 SW; 81508334) on almost level hill top. Diam. about 60 ft., ht. 5 ft., where preserved in hedge bank. Rest ploughed out.

(34) *Bowl* (?) (SY 88 SW; 82298259) on crest of broad ridge. Diam. 72 ft., ht. 1½ ft. Ploughed.

(35) *Bowl* (?) (SY 88 SW; 82298263) 50 yds. N. of (34). Ploughed flat. (O.S. 1811; V.A.P. CPE/UK 1821: 2434.)

(36) *Bowl* (?) (SY 88 SW; 82298292). Ploughed flat. (O.S. 1811; V.A.P. CPE/UK 1821: 2434.)

(37) *Bowl* (?) (SY 88 SW; 82158395) on summit of ridge above slopes to N. and S. Diam. about 60 ft., ht. 1½ ft. Ploughed.

(38) *Bowl* (SY 88 NW; 80238603) on Drove Hill. Diam. 42 ft., ht. 3 ft.

(39) *Bowl* (SY 88 NW; 80368600) on slight knoll. Diam. 42 ft., ht. 2½ ft. Disturbed in centre.

(40) *Mound*, possible barrow (SY 88 NW; 80278623) on end of slight knoll. Diam. 48 ft., ht. 4 ft.

(41) *Ditched bowl* (?) (SY 88 NW; 80158641) on flat top of steep-sided knoll. Diam. 25 ft., ht. 4 ft. Disturbed in centre.

(AC) BLACK KNOLL GROUP (SY 88 NW). Five bowl barrows on knoll rising from undulating heathland to just over 200 ft. above O.D. Much disturbed.

(42) Bowl (80608633). Diam. about 63 ft., ht. 8 ft. Trigonometrical station on top.

(43) Bowl (80628631) 21 yds. S.E. of (42). Diam. 33 ft., ht. 5 ft.

(44) Bowl (80658630) 30 yds. E.S.E. of (43). Diam. about 35 ft., ht. 5½ ft.

(45) Bowl (80668628) 20 yds. S.E. of (44). Diam. 33 ft., ht. 5 ft.

(46) Bowl (?) (80688627) 20 yds. S.E. of (45). Diam. 48 ft., ht. 8 ft.

(47) *Ditched bowl* (?) (SY 88 NW; 80488752) on Whitcombe Hill, a small but steep-sided knoll. Diam. 30 ft., ht. 2½ ft.

(48) *Bowl* (SY 88 NW; 80688747) at top of scarp falling from local plateau in heath. Diam. 30 ft., ht. 3 ft. Disturbed in centre.

WINTERBOURNE ABBAS

The parish contains forty-one barrows including four bell, three disc, one bell-disc and four pond barrows, probably two triple bowls and perhaps one double bell, making it one of the richest of Dorset parishes in special types of barrow. All but six of these barrows are part of, or related to, three groups on the S. of the South Winterborne valley. The largest concentration is in the S.W. corner of the parish, including part of the *Poor Lot Group* (AD) and two smaller groups, *Three Barrow Clump* (AE) and *Longlands* (AF), which lie on spurs projecting N. from the Ridgeway. The five bowls (48–52) scattered N. of the valley emphasise the barrow

concentration to the S., though of all the groups immediately N. of the Ridgeway, the *Poor Lot Group* is the only one partly in a valley bottom. Despite the ploughing and damaging of many barrows, this remains one of the most impressive groups in the county.

(AD) POOR LOT GROUP (SY 59 SE; Fig. p. 460, Plate 210). Forty-four barrows lie around the junction of three parishes. Twenty are in Kingston Russell (*Dorset* I, 129), six in Little Bredy (*ibid.*, 38), and eighteen, described below, in Winterbourne Abbas. Within the group, here considered as a whole, are seven bells, two (26–7) perhaps forming a double barrow, six disc and four, possibly five, pond barrows, two bell-disc barrows, two triple bowls, and twenty-two bowls. It lies nearly ½ mile N. of the Ridgeway on relatively low-lying ground which is, nevertheless, some 450 ft. above O.D., and near the head of a valley winding down to the E. The group includes two irregular but marked alignments (Kingston Russell (7c–k); Kingston Russell (7p–t) and Little Bredy (8a)) strung along the edges of a minor plateau jutting N.E. into the valley bottom from the foot of the Ridgeway. Kingston Russell (7a and b), though separated from these alignments, lie in a similar position on the N.W. edge of the plateau and, like the N. alignment, appear silhouetted on the plateau edge when viewed from the Ridgeway.

From the plateau, which drops sharply on all sides except the S.W., can be seen not only the other barrows in the group, but also the isolated Kingston Russell (6a–c), the two long barrows Kingston Russell (6d) and (6i), and the bank barrow Long Bredy (8) stretched across the end of Group R on Martin's Down, 1 mile to the W. All the barrows in the group, except Kingston Russell (7i) and (7l) and Winterbourne Abbas (20) and (21) on the N.-facing slope, are visible from the Ridgeway at Little Bredy (9a). All those on Fig. p. 460, as well as Long Bredy (8), are visible from the triple barrow (24).

Three barrows of rare types (Kingston Russell (7m, n and o)) are roughly in the centre of the plateau on nearly level ground forming a short alignment pointing in each direction to a disc barrow (Kingston Russell (7j and s)). The two pond barrows (Kingston Russell (7m, n)), excavated in 1952–3 and since almost obliterated, both contained pits and flint paving but no burials (Dorset *Procs.* LXXVI (1954), 89). The E. end of each of the major alignments is marked by a disc barrow, a large bell barrow and a short line of small barrows, mostly bowls, running across the axis of the major alignment. Outside this short line, at the E. end of the N. alignment, is a triple bowl barrow (22) just off the crest of the N.E. slope. A second triple bowl

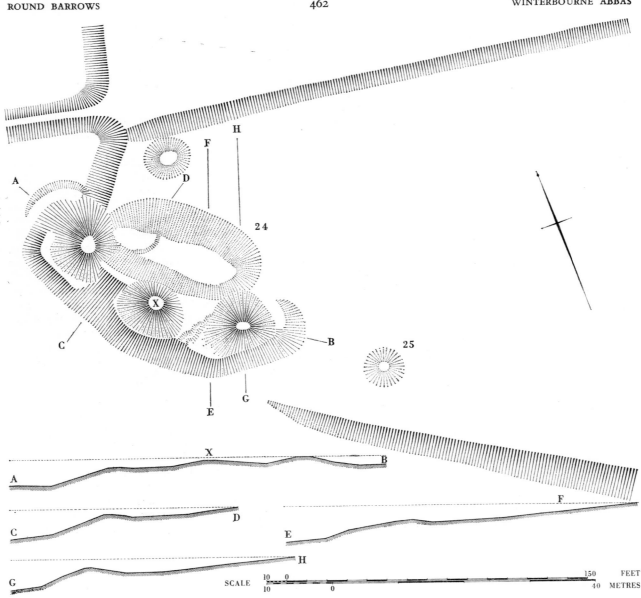

Triple barrow, Winterbourne Abbas (24), and adjacent remains in Poor Lot Barrow Group (AD).

(24) lies, also just off the crest, on the S.W. slope on the other side of the valley. Below it is a disc barrow (23), clearly visible from the valley floor.

On the narrow valley floor four barrows (26–7, 29–30) plausibly form a focus for the group, a suggestion supported by the position of another disc barrow (31) about 300 yds. to the S.E. on a N.W. slope visible from and dropping towards the four 'focal' barrows.

Despite the apparent importance of the group, no finds are recorded from it except a few sherds from Kingston Russell (7n and m), the only excavated barrows. The only certain relative date is that bell barrow Little Bredy (8a) is later than disc barrow Kingston Russell (7p) (*Dorset* I, xxxii, 129). Many of the barrows have now been damaged by ploughing, the smaller ones in particular appearing as flinty mounds. Some mounds were scraped up (*e.g.* (20) and (21)), others were from continuous ditches (*e.g.* (28)) and others were thrown up or down-hill from a ditch on one side or the other (*e.g.* (22)). A mound $2\frac{1}{2}$ ft.

high (LVG 8b) N.E. of (24) is almost certainly spoil from an adjoining pit.

Barrows (14–21) form a short line running roughly N.-S. across the axis of the N. alignment.

(14) Bell-disc (58919064) 97 yds. S. of Kingston Russell (7k). Diam. 31 ft., ht. 2 ft., with berm 6 ft. wide and ditch 12 ft. wide.

(15) Bell-disc (58949065) 34 yds. N.E. of (14). Diam. 24 ft., ht. 3½ ft., with berm 9 ft. wide, ditch 8 ft. wide and 1 ft. deep and outer bank 9 ft. wide.

(16) Pond barrow, possible (58829068), 40 yds. N. of (15). Diam. 33 ft., depth 1 ft., but no outer bank.

(17) Disc (58959069) on crest of E. slope, 19 yds. N.E. of (16). Total diam. about 70 ft. Diam. of central mound 21 ft., ht. 1½ ft., with berm 9 ft. wide, within ditch formerly 8 ft. wide and outer bank about 11 ft. wide.

(18) Bowl (?) (58949072) 35 yds. N. of (17). Diam. about 38 ft., ht. 6 ins.; until recent ploughing appearing as slight circular bank, probably due to unrecorded excavation.

(19) Bowl (?) (58949074) about 15 yds. N. of (18). Formerly about 30 ft. in diam., now destroyed.

(20) Bowl (58949076) 36 yds. N. of (18) on N.E. slope. Diam. 20 ft., ht. 1 ft.

(21) Bowl (58959077) 17 yds. N.N.E. of (20) near foot of slope. Diam. 21 ft., ht. 9 ins.

(22) Ditched triple bowl (58979074) on N.E. slope 38 yds. S.E. of (21). Irregular elongated mound about 70 ft. long, up to 48 ft. broad and 6 ft. high at E., higher, end. Three separate crests show in profile, and ditch 10 ft. wide runs along S.W., uphill, side.

(23) Disc (59159083) across valley from (22) on S.W. slope of 9°. Overall diam. about 100 ft. Diam. of mound 33 ft., ht. 1½ ft. but disturbed. Berm, ditch and outer bank each about 12 ft. wide; ditch 1 ft. deep and bank 1 ft. high. Bank ploughed away on S.E.

(24) Ditched triple bowl (?) (59219085; Plate 210) on false crest of S.W. slope above and 77 yds. N.E. of (23), apparently on lynchet of 'Celtic' field. Appears as undulating and slightly curving bank about 160 ft. long with three arcs in plan on S.W. side and three crests in profile of mounds about 40 ft., 35 ft. and 35 ft. in diam., from N.W. to S.E. Hts. of mounds 6 ft., 7 ft. and 5 ft. respectively, though much greater from downhill side (see profiles). Steep ridge-shaped mound joins W. and central mounds but junction between central and E. mounds much disturbed. On S.W. are remains of possible berm. Shallow elongated depression on N.E. is probably a quarry ditch and has been dug through surface of 'Celtic' field. Ditch about 12 ft. wide also at foot of barrow on N.W.

(25) Mound, possible bowl (59259083) 24 yds. S.E. of E. mound of (24), inside, and presumably later than, 'Celtic' field. Diam. 20 ft., ht. 6 ins.

(26) Bell (59129066) at foot of slope 233 yds. S.S.W. of (24). Diam. 60 ft., ht. 7 ft., with berm and ditch each about 15 ft. wide. Perhaps forms double bell with (27).

(27) Bell (59139064) immediately S.E. of (26). Diam. 60 ft., ht. 7 ft. Apparently shares ditch with (26) on N.E., but disturbed on S. and E.

(28) Bell (59049055) 130 yds. S.W. of (27). Diam. about

90 ft., ht. 11 ft., with berm about 9 ft. wide and ploughed ditch about 12 ft. wide. (28) and (29) are aligned on the entrance of (30).

(29) Ditched bowl (59169053) in woodland 125 yds. E.S.E. of (28). Diam. 52 ft., ht. 6½ ft., with ditch about 10 ft. wide.

(30) Pond barrow (59219052) in woodland 57 yds. E. of (29). Depression 86 ft. in diam., and generally 1 ft. deep; enclosing bank 18 ft. to 24 ft. across, 3½ ft. high from outside and up to 5½ ft. high above centre of interior. Break 12 ft. wide in bank on S.W. is probably original. The N.E. segment of bank, cut away by modern road, shows much flint in section.

(31) Disc (59389033) on N.W. slope tilting towards (30) and 260 yds. S.E. of it, in similar position to (23). Diam. of mound 32 ft., ht. 1 ft., with remains of berm about 5 ft. wide, ditch 10 ft. wide and possible outer bank. Ploughed almost flat.

(32) *Pond barrow* (SY 59 SE; 59579038) on the valley floor like (30) and 25 yds. E. of the Broad Stone (Stones, Winterbourne Abbas (56)). Overall diam. about 96 ft. with slightly sunken interior about 42 ft. in diam. surrounded by flinty bank about 27 ft. wide and 1½ ft. high. Break 12 ft. wide in bank on S.S.W. is probably original. N. half destroyed by road and S. half ploughed.

(AE) THREE BARROW CLUMP GROUP (SY 59 SE). Ten barrows, including one, possibly two, bells and one pond barrow, on the top and N. slope of a spur on S. side of S. Winterborne valley. Most have been damaged.

(33) Ditched bowl (?) (59489003) on ridge top in woodland and crossed by parish boundary with Little Bredy. Diam. about 60 ft., ht. about 5½ ft.

(34) Ditched bowl (?) (59569010) 130 yds. N.E. of (33). Diam. about 40 ft. Ploughed almost flat.

(35) Ditched bowl (?) (59579014) 35 yds. N. of (34). Diam. 15 ft., ht. 9 ins., with ditch 6 ft. wide.

(36) Ditched bowl (59659023) on N. slope 110 yds. N.E. of (35). Diam. 18 ft., ht. 1 ft., with ditch about 6 ft. wide.

(37) Ditched bowl (59729021) 70 yds. E.S.E. of (36). Diam. 62 ft., ht. 7 ft., with berm-like feature, possibly spoil, on S. Ditch 12 ft. wide and 1 ft. deep, filled on N. with spoil from central excavation.

(38) Bowl (59739023) 25 yds. N.E. of (37). Diam. 21 ft., ht. 1½ ft.

(39) Bowl (59749023) immediately adjacent E. of (38). Diam. about 22 ft., ht. 1½ ft.

(40) Bell (?) (59769018) 55 yds. S.E. of (39). Mound quarried away leaving disturbed area surrounded by ditch 85 ft. in diam., 11 ft. wide and 2 ft. deep, itself dug away on E. where probably cut by ditch of (41).

(41) Bell (59809018) immediately adjacent to (40) on E. and probably later than it. Diam. 73 ft., ht. 10 ft., with berm 9 ft. wide and ditch 13 ft. wide and 2 ft. deep.

(42) Pond barrow (59829020) 33 yds. N.E. of (41). Overall diam. 59 ft. Central depression 35 ft. in diam. and 6 ins. deep, surrounded by bank 12 ft. wide and 1 ft. high.

(AF) LONGLANDS GROUP (SY 58 NE, 68 NW). Five barrows, including one possible bell, four in a rough alignment S.W.-N.E. along spine of spur, with possible long barrow (Winterbourne Abbas (13)) at N.E. end. The three S.W. barrows are just above the 500 ft. contour and the others above 400 ft. All damaged. Near foot of steep slope to N. immediately S. of the main road three further barrows at 60449020, 60519025 and 60559018 are shown on O.S. (1811) but there is now no sign of them.

(43) Bowl (?) (59998977) in Dry Wood, now only irregular rise about 9 ins. high.

(44) Bowl (60008978) 25 yds. N.E. of (43) also in Dry Wood. Diam. 48 ft., ht. 3½ ft.

(45) Ditched bowl (60038980) 40 yds. N.E. of (44). About 65 ft. in diam. and 1½ ft. high, within oval ditch about 150 ft. (N.W.-S.E.) by 90 ft. (V.A.P. CPE/UK 1934: 5098). Almost ploughed out.

(46) Bowl (60188993) 220 yds. N.E. of (45). Diam. 52 ft., ht. 14 ft., though base steepened by ploughing.

(47) Bell (?) (60478995) 307 yds. E.N.E. of (46). Diam. about 94 ft., ht. 5 ft., with ditch about 105 ft. in diam., separated from mound by narrow berm (V.A.P. CPE/UK 1934: 5092).

(48) See BIG WOOD GROUP (AQ), Winterbourne Steepleton, p. 472.

(49) Bowl (SY 59 SE; 59629181) in extreme N.W. of parish just off ridge top. Diam. about 54 ft., ht. 4 ft. Ploughed.

(50) Bowl (SY 69 SW; 60109084) near summit of spur on slight S.W. slope. Diam. about 45 ft., ht. 1½ ft. Ploughed.

(51) Bowl (?) (SY 69 SW; 61529162) on summit of ridge above 500 ft. Slightly oval, measuring 38 ft. by 34 ft., ht. 3 ft. Ploughed.

(52) Bowl (SY 69 SW; 61669148) 200 yds. S.E. of (51) on slight S.E. slope. Diam. 25 ft., ht. 2 ft.

(53-4) See POUND HILL GROUP (AU), Winterbourne Steepleton, p. 473.

WINTERBORNE CAME

There are thirty-nine barrows in the parish, fifteen (10-24) in Group R and described under other parishes.

The S. end of the parish also includes the spur where twelve barrows on and near the Golf Course form the Came Down Group (AG). Fourteen others are scattered on the lower slopes to the N., mainly related to a long spur above the 300 ft. contour. Most have been disturbed and damaged.

(10-17) See BINCOMBE DOWN GROUP (R.9), p. 438.

(18-19) See BINCOMBE HILL GROUP (R.10), p. 439.

(20-4) See CULLIFORD TREE GROUP (R.11), Whitcombe, p. 458.

(AG) CAME DOWN GROUP (SY 68 NE). Eleven barrows, including a double bowl, a probable bell and a disc barrow, associated with a 'ring-work', on and near Came Down Golf Course on top of a spur running N.E. from the Ridgeway. The focus of the group is a cluster including the disc, the double bowl, a large bowl barrow and the associated small banked enclosure (see Enclosures, Winterborne Came (49)). Although somewhat altered by the needs of the golf course, the group as a whole is well-preserved and one of the few still under grass (but cf. Dorset Procs. XXIV (1903), pp. xxv and xliii).

Warne recorded the destruction of a barrow 'of immense size' which is probably (35). In it and on its S.E. side were found two inhumations accompanied by parts of antlers some 10 ft. from the surface; 3 ft. to 4 ft. below were two grooved bronze daggers, the longer probably with six rivets, the shorter apparently tanged.

(25) Bowl (68528607) on W. slope of spur. Diam. 72 ft., ht. 5 ft., but spread.

(26) Mound, possible bowl (68398615), 170 yds. N.W. of (25). Perhaps originally elongated, now almost destroyed by bunker.

(27) Bowl (68648616) on slight W. slope 175 yds. N.E. of (25). Diam. 64 ft., ht. 4½ ft. Bunker cuts S. side.

(28) Ditched double bowl (68668621) 25 yds. N.E. of (27). The almost contiguous mounds, 56 ft. in diam. and 4 ft. high, are joined by a broad saddle 1 ft. high. The whole surrounded by oval ditch.

(29) Disc (68718627) on slight W. slope 75 yds. N.E. of N. mound of (28). The oval tump, 30 ft. by 24 ft. and 6 ins. high, is about 6 ft. S. of centre on slightly raised interior 102 ft. in diam., surrounded by bank 26 ft. wide and 1 ft. high and slight external ditch only.

(30) Ditched bowl (68678629) 48 yds. N.W. of (29) on W. slope. Diam. 70 ft., ht. 6½ ft. with ditch 12 ft. wide and 1 ft. deep.

(31) Bowl (68788624) 70 yds. S.E. of (29) on centre of spur. Diam. 79 ft., ht. 4½ ft. Ht. slightly increased for use as tee. Cut on S. by bunker.

(32) Ditched bowl (68818626) immediately E. of centre of spur 50 yds. N.E. of (31). Diam. 101 ft., ht. 9 ft. with ditch 15 ft. wide and 2 ft. deep.

(33) Bowl (68868635) 110 yds. N.N.E. of (32) on N.W. slope. Diam. about 35 ft., ht. 1½ ft. Much spread.

(34) Bowl (?) (69038641) on E. side of Down Wood 270 yds. N.E. of (33). Diam. 42 ft., ht. 1½ ft. Tree-covered.

(35) Bell (?) (69148651) 160 yds. N.E. of (34). Diam. 100 ft., ht. 2 ft., but flattened by ploughing. Probably within ditch about 140 ft. in diam., suggested by air photograph CPE/UK 1934: 1058.

(36) Bowl (SY 68 NE; 68848690) on N. slope near W. parish boundary. Diam. 77 ft., ht. 6 ft.

(37) Bell (SY 68 NE; 68878690) 43 yds. E.S.E. of (36). Diam. 87 ft., ht. 7 ft., with ditch 15 ft. wide, destroyed on E. Berm visible only on S. and perhaps on W. Top of mound used as golf tee. Probably excavated in 1882 by Cunnington who

found a few worked flints and a near-central cremation in a chalk-cut hollow 6 ins. deep, dug apparently beside the pyre (Dorset *Procs.* XXXVII (1916), 43).

Within Cripton Wood about 600 yds. E. of (35) are three barrows roughly in line (SY 68 NE). The westernmost is a bell.

(38) *Bell* (69638657) on slight E. slope at W. end of wood. Diam. 54 ft., ht. 4½ ft., with berm 12 ft. wide and ditch 12 ft. wide and 1 ft. deep.

(39) *Ditched bowl* (69738654) 130 yds. E. of (38). Diam. 33 ft., ht. 3 ft. Damaged by rabbits.

(40) *Bowl* (69758654) 30 yds. E. of (39). Diam. 21 ft., ht. 1½ ft.

(41) *Bowl* (?) (SY 78 NW; 70378648) on W. slope of spur near parish boundary with Whitcombe. Now oval, 55 ft. N.-S. by 80 ft. E.-W., owing to ploughing; ht. 1½ ft.

(42) *Bowl* (?) (SY 78 NW; 70408652) 50 yds. N.E. of (41). Diam. from 82 ft. to 98 ft. owing to ploughing; ht. 2½ ft.

(43) *Bowl* (?) (SY 68 NE; 69498750). Forms a pair with (44) on W. of parish, on W. edge of broad ridge. Diam. 60 ft., ht. 2 ft. Ploughed.

(44) *Bowl* (?) (SY 68 NE; 69538750) 45 yds. E. of (43). Diam. 86 ft., ht. 2½ ft. Ploughed.

(45) *Bowl* (?) (SY 68 NE; 69818703) on col between two combes. Diam. about 58 ft. Ploughed almost flat.

(46) *Bowl* (?) (SY 78 NW; 70128692) on S. slope below 300 ft. contour N.W. of Cripton Barn. Diam. 57 ft. Ploughed almost flat.

(47) *Bowl* (?) (SY 78 NW; 70128685) 75 yds. S. of (46). Diam. 75 ft. Ploughed almost flat.

(48) *Pond barrow*, possible (SY 78 NW; 70178688), 46 yds. N.E. of (47). Regular and slightly oval depression 53 ft. by 57 ft. and 1½ ft. deep. No outer bank.

WINTERBORNE HERRINGSTON

The parish, consisting mainly of relatively low ground N. of the Ridgeway, contains only four barrows. (3) and (4) at the narrow S. end of the parish, where it includes a projecting spur of the Ridgeway, form the N.E. end of a straight alignment 930 yds. long with Bincombe (30–1) and (33).

(3) *Bowl* (?) (SY 68 NE; 68118650). Diam. 61 ft., ht. 1 ft. Ploughed.

(4) *Bowl* (SY 68 NE; 68168659) 100 yds. N.N.E. of (3). Diam. 63 ft., ht. 2½ ft. Ploughed.

(5) *Bowl* (SY 68 NE; 68498843) on W.-E. ridge above 300 ft. Diam. 38 ft., ht. 5½ ft. Slightly flattened on top and crossed by boundary with former parish of Fordington.

(6) *Herringston Barrow*, bowl (?) (SY 68 NE; 68548844), 60 yds. E. of (5). Diam. about 77 ft., ht. 6 ft. Much damaged, and crossed by same boundary as (5). Opened in 1880 by Cunnington who found a primary (?) contracted inhumation under a cairn, in which was possibly a cremation with part of a flint or stone axe.

WINTERBORNE MONKTON

There are six round barrows, three of them in *Lanceborough Group*. The others (including two overlapping disc (?) barrows) point N.N.W. approximately towards the E. end of the Maiden Castle 'long mound'. Two unlocated barrows have been excavated. One in Fordington Field contained a cremation in a small biconical urn covered by a flat stone in a cist (*Arch.* XXX (1844), 334, no. 19; Warne, *C.T.D.*, tovp, no. 81); the other (*C.T.D.*, tovp, no. 62), conceivably (8), contained four inhumations at a depth of 20 ft. towards the centre. A central cist contained an inurned cremation covered by a stone. A perforated boar's tusk was probably with the inhumations and raspberry seeds, allegedly from remains of the stomach of one of them, were subsequently reported as having produced plants and fruit. In the upper part of the barrow were two more inhumations above an inurned cremation with a probable bone pin.

(AH) LANCEBOROUGH GROUP (SY 68 NE; Fig. p. 494). Four barrows including two bells and a possible bell, with a long barrow and a horseshoe-shaped enclosure (Winterborne Monkton (4, 11), lie on a local downland crest about 300 ft. above O.D. some 700 yds. N. of the W. end of the Maiden Castle 'long mound' (Long Barrows, Winterborne St. Martin (23)). A probable small barrow (LVG 1d) towards S. end of dyke (Winterborne Monkton (12)) is not traceable. The adjacent open field furlong was called Lanceborough or Great Barrow Furlong (Tithe Map, 1844), a name probably referring to (6), the largest bell barrow in the area covered by this Volume. All the barrows have been damaged, mostly by ploughing.

Winterborne St. Martin:

(137) Bowl (?) (66508937). Diam. uncertain, ht. 3 ft. Opened by Cunnington who found nothing.

Winterborne Monkton:

(5) Bell, possible (66538924), 110 yds. S.S.E. of last. Diam. about 75 ft., with berm about 15 ft. wide and ditch 10 ft. to 12 ft. wide; on E., ditch almost touches S.W. end of ditch of long barrow (4). Ploughed flat, visible as soil-mark.

(6) Bell (66698928) 160 yds. E. of (5). Diam. about 130 ft., ht. 21 ft., with sloping berm about 20 ft. wide. Ditch about 37 ft. wide and 2 ft.-3½ ft. deep. A stone cist containing an inhumation, probably Roman, with head to E. was found in top of mound (*D.C.C.*, 14 Aug. 1862).

(7) Bell (66778927) 90 yds. E. of (6). Diam. about 76 ft., ht. 5½ ft. Berm about 9 ft. wide and ditch 15 ft. wide.

Three barrows (SY 68 NE; Fig. p. 494; Plate 214), E. of Maiden Castle 'long mound' (Winterborne St. Martin (23)), noted by Skinner in 1829 (B.M. Add. MS. 33715, 2–10) but now virtually destroyed. A fourth, smaller, barrow possibly existed between (8) and the outer bank of Maiden Castle (Cambridge University O.A.P. TC 12).

(8) *Barrow* (?) (67488822) on slope of ridge 450 yds. E.S.E. of E. end of 'long mound'. Circular bank about 60 ft. in diam. Visible only as crop-mark on air photograph.

(9) *Disc* (?) (67528819) about 60 yds. E.S.E. of (8). Central mound about 60 ft. in diam. and 1½ ft. high surrounded by ditch and external bank about 150 ft. in diam. Cut by (10).

(10) *Disc* (?) (67548818) overlapping (9) on E.S.E. Apparently similar in size and type, its ditch and external bank cut bank, ditch and berm of (9).

WINTERBORNE ST. MARTIN

There are 118 round barrows, more than in any other parish in Dorset. The greatest concentration is along the S. edge of the parish where it runs up on to the Ridgeway to include the *Bronkham Hill* and *Ridge Hill Groups* (R.6 and R.7), with further groups – *e.g. Eweleaze Barn* (AJ) and *Four Barrow Hill* (AK) – on spurs projecting N. A scatter of barrows, including *Group* (AM) N. and W. of Rew, lies on the high ground followed by the Roman road running W. from Dorchester in the N. of the parish.

The Bronkham Hill Group, now one of the best-preserved groups in the county, is a good example of the sky-line siting of barrows (Plate 210). The parish includes several remarkable barrows: the huge bell-disc (67) in its S.E. corner; the large and well-preserved bell (75) beside a double bowl (76) on Shorn Hill, and the large Clandon barrow (134). Many have been excavated, chiefly by Warne, Sydenham and E. Cunnington in the 19th century. Finds are particularly rich, including the remarkable series of probably secondary deposits from (134). Flint cairns in barrow mounds are especially a feature of *Groups* (AM–AO). Among excavated barrows impossible to identify is one 'south of Martinstown' from which was ploughed a grooved bronze dagger with three rivets (Dorset *Procs.* LII (1930), xlvii).

(R.6) BRONKHAM HILL GROUP (SY 68 NW; Fig. p. 519, Plates 209–10). Thirty barrows, including four bells and one double bowl, in a mile-long linear cemetery running N.W.–S.E. Nearly all are on top of the Ridgeway, often related to localised small spurs or knolls projecting from the narrow gravel-capped and heath-covered ridge. At least three other small stony mounds on the ridge appear to be artificial and might be barrows. Numerous steep-sided, round-mouthed pits, apparently solution hollows in the gravel capping, lie amongst the barrows, sometimes in their ditches. The group includes Portesham (39–40).

(24) Ditched bowl (?) (62038742) on N.E. slope, 120 yds. S.E. of junction of parish boundary with Winterbourne Steepleton. Diam. 20 ft., ht. 1 ft.

(25) Bowl (62098740) on lip of steep N.E. slope, 70 yds. S.E. of (24). Diam. 27 ft., ht. 3 ft.

(26) Bowl (62128738) on lip of same slope 45 yds. S.E. of (25). Diam. 28 ft., ht. 3 ft.

(27) Bowl (62178736) on edge of short drop to E., 52 yds. S.E. of (26). Diam. 22 ft., ht. 3½ ft.

(28) Bowl (?) (62168730) 70 yds. S. of (27). Oval, 50 ft. (N.-S.) by 36 ft. Ht. 2 ft. Flat-topped.

(29) Bowl (62288731) on top of short S.-N. spur 150 yds. S.E. of (27). Diam. 31 ft., ht. 3 ft. Damaged, showing stony interior. 24 yds. to the N. is small, probably artificial, stony mound 10 ft. in diam. and 6 ins. high.

(30) Ditched bowl (62318724) just off spine of Ridgeway at head of combe running up from N. and 60 yds. S.E. of (29). Diam. 36 ft., ht. 2 ft., with ditch 10 ft. wide and 1 ft. deep. Flat, slightly hollowed, top.

(31) Bowl (62378737) on top of broad spur sloping down to N., 150 yds. N.N.E. of (30). Diam. 42 ft., ht. 2 ft. Much damaged.

(32) Bowl (62398731) 70 yds. S.S.E. of (31) on same spur. Diam. 33 ft., ht. 2½ ft. Much damaged.

(33) Bell (62378717) on small spur sloping down to N., 160 yds. S.E. of (29). Diam. about 70 ft., ht. above berm 7 ft.; berm at most 10 ft. wide, ditch up to 15 ft. wide and 2 ft. deep. Three solution hollows in ditch.

(34) Bowl (62418715) 50 yds. S.E. of (33). Diam. 36 ft., ht. 2 ft. Disturbed.

(35) Bowl (62518708) 130 yds. S.E. of (34). Diam. 18 ft., ht. 1½ ft.

(36) Bowl (62508702) 47 yds. S. of (35). Diam. 28 ft., ht. 1½ ft.

(37) Double bowl (62548703) on flat ground 40 yds. S.E. of (36). Mounds, respectively 25 ft. and 40 ft. in diam., and 2½ ft. and 3½ ft. high, are joined by a slight bank 1 ft. high.

(38) Bowl (?) (62568706) 20 yds. N. of (37). Diam. 18 ft., ht. 1 ft.

(39) Bowl (?) (62628699) 90 yds. S.E. of (37). Oval, 21 ft. (N.-S.) by 17 ft. Ht. 2 ft. Steep-sided.

(40) Bowl (62638694) 50 yds. S.S.E. of (39). Diam. 50 ft., ht. 4 ft. About halfway between it and (39) is small, possibly artificial, stony mound 15 ft. by 10 ft.

(41) Bowl (62648692) 35 yds. S.E. of (40). Diam. 45 ft., ht. 2 ft. Disturbed.

(42) Ditched bowl (62678689) 27 yds. S.E. of (41). Diam. 21 ft., ht. 2 ft. Ditch 3 ft. wide. Steep-sided.

(43) Bell (62708687) 45 yds. S.E. of (42). Diam. 92 ft., ht. now about 14 ft., but originally probably about 10 ft. only. Apparently has two berms, but upper probably result of spoil from N.-S. excavation trench 18 ft. wide through centre of mound. Lower berm 20 ft. wide at most, with stone mound 15 ft. in diam. and 1 ft. high on it on E. Ditch 21 ft. wide and 3 ft. deep.

(44) Ditched bowl (62738703) 176 yds. N.N.E. of (43) and down slope from it at head of combe. Diam. 45 ft., ht. up to 3 ft. Ditch 12 ft. wide, but ploughed.

(45) Bowl (62738684) 60 yds. S.E. of (43). Diam. 45 ft., ht. 4½ ft.

(46) Bowl (62768682; Fig. p. 519) 40 yds. E.S.E. of (45). Diam. 28 ft., ht. 3 ft. Cut on W. by a hedge bank which crosses dyke Winterborne St. Martin (145); (cf. (47)).

(47) Ditched bowl (62798681; Fig. p. 519, Plate 209) on edge of steep drop to N.E., 25 yds. S.E. of (46). Diam. 72 ft., ht. 7 ft. Ditch 12 ft. wide and 2 ft. deep. The dyke, Winterborne St. Martin (145), runs over top of mound.

(48) Bell (62828679) 45 yds. E.S.E. of (47). Diam. 68 ft., ht. 6 ft., with berm 7 ft. wide at most. Ditch up to 9 ft. wide and 1 ft. deep.

(49) Bell (62938674) 135 yds. E.S.E. of (48). Diam. 74 ft., ht. 11 ft., with berm up to 9 ft. wide. Ditch about 18 ft. wide. Damaged, with flattened top.

(50) Ditched bowl (63168665) on slight knoll with steep drop to N., 275 yds. E.S.E. of (49). Diam. 80 ft., ht. 10 ft. Ditch about 8 ft. wide. Disturbed.

(51) Bowl (63258665; Fig. p. 507) at head of steep drop to N., 85 yds. E. of (50). Irregular, with diam. about 22 ft., and ht. 2 ft.

Portesham:

(39) Bowl (?) (63308662; Fig. p. 507) 70 yds. S.E. of last. Irregular, with diam. 33 ft., and ht. 3 ft. Ploughed almost flat. It is within enclosure Winterborne St. Martin (143).

(40) Bowl (?) (63508665) 220 yds. E.N.E. of (39). Oval, flinty mound 39 ft. by 20 ft. and 2 ft. high.

(R.7) RIDGE HILL GROUP (SY 68 NW, NE). Thirty-eight barrows including one bell, four probable bells, one very large bell-disc barrow and one pond barrow, many of them having survived intact in an area extensively covered with 'Celtic' fields (see Ancient Field Group (6), and Fig. p. 626). Ridge Hill continues the Ridgeway to the E. for the next 1¾ miles to the great Ridgeway bell-disc barrow (67). The Ridgeway here is domed on top, and the barrows lie in an irregular line, mostly on the highest ground. The group includes Portesham (41–2), Weymouth (396–406) and Bincombe (13–21). Weymouth (396–404) have all been heavily ploughed and six of them were opened by E. Cunnington between 1884 and 1888, including (403), his 'Ridgeway 7'.

Winterborne St. Martin:

(52) Bell (63818686) 650 yds. E.N.E. of (51). Diam. 74 ft., ht. 12 ft., with berm 12 ft. wide. Ditch about 24 ft. wide and 1 ft. deep. Damaged.

(53) Bowl (63858686) 50 yds. E. of (52). Diam. 34 ft., ht. 3 ft. Depression 24 ft. in diam. and 3 ft. deep lies at foot of mound on N.

(54) Bowl (63958680) 120 yds. E.S.E. of (53). Diam. 90 ft., ht. 8 ft.; N.-S. excavation trench across centre. Half mace-head of palaeozoic quartzite found on mound (*P.P.S.* XVIII (1962), 244, no. 59).

(55) Bowl (64018679) 75 yds. E.S.E. of (54). Diam. 46 ft., ht. 4 ft.

(56) Bowl (64068676) 60 yds. E.S.E. of (55). Diam. 30 ft., ht. 3 ft. Damaged.

(57) Ditched bowl (64248674) 190 yds. E. of (56). Diam. 79 ft., ht. 11 ft. Ditch about 25 ft. wide on E. Excavated in centre.

(58) Ditched bowl (64298674) 50 yds. E. of (57). Diam. 77 ft., ht. 11½ ft. Ditch about 15 ft. wide. N.-S. excavation trench through centre. Bank and ditch run up to it from N.

(59) Ditched bowl (64388674) 100 yds. E. of (58). Diam. 38 ft., ht. 3 ft. Ditch 10 ft. wide. Ploughed.

Portesham:

(41) Bell (?) (64578669) 200 yds. E.S.E. of last. Diam. 71 ft., ht. 10½ ft.

(42) Bell (?) (64598668) 45 yds. E.S.E. of (41). Diam. 62 ft., ht. 10½ ft.

Winterborne St. Martin:

(60) Bowl (64898676) 330 yds. E.N.E. of last on highest point along this stretch of Ridgeway. Diam. 87 ft., ht. 6 ft. Ploughed.

(61) Bowl (65058672) 180 yds. E.S.E. of (60). Diam. about 30 ft. Ploughed flat.

(62) Bowl (65178670) 140 yds. E. of (61). Diam. 37 ft., ht. 4½ ft. Ploughed, and excavated in centre.

Weymouth:

(396) Bowl (?) (65298659) 180 yds. S.E. of last. Completely destroyed.

(397) Bowl (?) (65338658) 40 yds. E.S.E. of (396). Diam. about 60 ft. Ploughed almost flat.

(398) Bowl (65368657) 30 yds. E.S.E. of (397). Diam. 70 ft., ht. 3 ft. Contained a cremation beneath inverted urn in an ash-filled pit, and a secondary cremation.

(399) Bowl (65398657) 30 yds. E. of (398). Diam. 72 ft., ht. 2 ft.

(400) Bowl (65438661) 55 yds. N.E. of (399). Diam. 104 ft., ht. 5½ ft. Contained incomplete inhumation under cairn 8 ft. to 10 ft. in diam. and 3 ft. high, on edge of pre-existing 'pond'. Probably associated were an inverted beaker, a flint scraper and two fragments of saddle querns.

(401) Ditched bowl (?) (65588660) 165 yds. E. of (400). Diam. 75 ft., ht. 3 ft.; probably with ditch about 90 ft. in diam., suggested by V.A.P. CPE/UK 1934: 1062. Contained only ashes and 5 small worked flints.

(402) Bell (?) (65678661) 100 yds. E.N.E. of (401). Diam. about 100 ft., ht. 7 ft. Berm and ditch each about 10 ft. wide suggested by V.A.P. CPE/UK 1934: 1062. Excavation produced evidence of burning but no burial.

(403) Bowl (65748662) 75 yds. E. of (402). Now only an irregular mound 9 ft. high immediately W. of reservoir, in 1885 it was 114 ft. in diam. and 13 ft. high. A primary inhumation in a Portland Stone cist in a pit was covered with a cairn 13 ft. in diam. and 7 ft. high. In and around the cairn were a bone dagger pommel, a bone needle, animal bones, and many flint implements including a flint mace-head, a polished flint axe and part of another, a flint saw, and scrapers. An inhumation with a three-riveted bronze dagger, and a nearby cremation, were in the upper part of the cairn under two layers of stone slabs. In the top of the mound was a secondary cremation with three grooved and riveted daggers —one of copper and two of bronze—gold mountings for a dagger pommel, traces of wooden sheaths and a small flanged copper axe with a small piece of fine cloth adhering to it. This

is Wessex interment no. 20, one of the richest grave groups in Dorset. Surviving finds in D.C.M. (Dorset *Procs.* LVIII (1936), 20–5; *P.P.S.* XVI (1950), 133, pl. XIV, 2; ApSimon 54 and 56, nos. 2, 9, 10; *Archaeometry*, 4 (1961), 47, nos. 37 and 47.)

(404) Bowl (65858661) 130 yds. E. of (403). Diam. 90 ft., ht. 5 ft. Contained burnt material, including bone and several flint scrapers.

Winterborne St. Martin:

(63) Bowl (66038664) on N. slope 190 yds. E. of last. Diam. 60 ft., ht. 3½ ft. Ploughed. Oval depression, 60 ft. (N.-S.) by 45 ft. and 3 ft. deep, touches W. side.

(64) Barrow (?) (66158664) 130 yds. E. of (63) and in direct line between it and (67). Circular ditch about 100 ft. in diam. and 15 ft. wide visible on V.A.P. CPE/UK 1934: 1062. Ploughed flat.

(65) Bowl (66228658) 220 yds. E.S.E. of (63). Diam. about 50 ft. Ploughed flat.

(66) Ditched bowl (66278656) 60 yds. E.S.E. of (65). Diam. 60 ft., ht. 9 ft. Ditch about 9 ft. wide. Damaged.

(67) Bell-disc (66328666) 112 yds. N.N.E. of (66) and crossed by parish boundary. On N. slope just off highest ground, it lies at E. end of line of eleven barrows and is clearly visible on the sky-line from 'long mound' (23) in Maiden Castle. Mound is 79 ft. in diam. and 8 ft. high, with possible surrounding ditch about 10 ft. wide at its foot. Berm varies in width from 51 ft. on N. to 57 ft. on S. Outside an unbroken surrounding ditch 18 ft. wide and 2 ft. deep is a bank 15 ft. wide and 2 ft. high with modern breaks. Total external diam. about 250 ft., though E. third of berm, outer ditch and bank, formerly in Upwey and now in Bincombe, has been ploughed. Top of mound slightly disturbed. The whole monument is exceptional in its size and proportions. On S.E. is an almost straight alignment 230 yds. long formed by (66) and Bincombe (13, 15 and 16) (LVG, plate III).

Bincombe:

(13) Ditched bowl (66368658) 100 yds. S.E. of last. Diam. 96 ft., ht. 12 ft., probably with original chalk capping. Ploughed. (LVG, plate III.)

(14) Ditched bowl (66388662) 33 yds. N.N.E. of (13). Diam. about 40 ft., with ditch about 10 ft. wide, visible on V.A.P. CPE/UK 1934: 1061. Ploughed almost flat. Probably contained primary (?) cremation covered by stone slabs.

(15) Bell (?) (66428660) 45 yds. E. of (14). Diam. about 45 ft., ht. 2½ ft., apparently surrounded by ditch about 80 ft. in diam. visible on V.A.P. CPE/UK 1934: 1061. Now ploughed out. Contained an incomplete primary inhumation in cist under flint layer.

(16) Bowl (66468661) 50 yds. N.E. of (15). Diam. about 50 ft., ht. 2½ ft. Ploughed. Contained cairn of large stones covering primary (?) contracted male inhumation with a cremation near its feet and a bucket urn, now in D.C.M., near its head.

(17) Bowl (66508660) 55 yds. E.S.E. of (16). Diam. about 30 ft. Ploughed out.

(18) Ditched bowl (?) (66518650) 105 yds. S. of (17). Diam. 80 ft., ht. 6 ft. V.A.P. CPE/UK 1934: 1061, suggests ditch about 100 ft. in diam. Ploughed.

(19) Ditched bowl (?) (66568645) 85 yds. S.E. of (18).

Diam. 85 ft., ht. 10 ft., apparently with original chalk capping. V.A.P. CPE/UK 1934: 1061, suggests ditch about 105 ft. in diam. Ploughed.

Weymouth:

(405) Bowl (66498639) 100 yds. S.W. of last. Diam. 60 ft., ht. 2½ ft. Opened in 1884 by Cunnington who found two chalk-cut graves, lined and covered with stones, each containing an inhumation, one with two plain urns. The graves lay within a 'circle' of twenty-two stones, 10 ft. in diam., with a gap 8 ft. wide on the S.E.

(406) Pond barrow (66688633) 220 yds. E.S.E. of (405). Diam. of depression 45 ft., depth about 9 ins. Surrounding bank about 15 ft. wide and 9 ins. high. Ploughed.

Bincombe:

(20) Bowl (66778640) 125 yds. N.E. of last. Diam. 45 ft., ht. 1½ ft.

(21) Bowl (66928645) 170 yds. E.N.E. of (20). Diam. 60 ft., ht. 2½ ft.

(AI) REW HILL GROUP (SY 68 NW). Four probable *bowls* on top of spur running N.E. from Black Down.

(68) (62728847). Ploughed almost flat.

(69) (62808857) 145 yds. N.N.E. of (68). Diam. about 54 ft. Ploughed almost flat.

(70) (62848865) 95 yds. N.N.E. of (69). Diam. about 60 ft. Ploughed almost flat.

(71) (63248887) 490 yds. N.E. of (70). Irregular and ploughed, but ht. still 5 ft.

Bowl barrows, three (SY 68 NW), form a W.-E. line along the crest of Grove Hill about 1200 yds. E. of the *Rew Hill Group* (AI) and about 1 mile N. of the Ridgeway, though visible from it. All have been ploughed and are now of indefinite diameter, though at least 70 ft. Two (72–3) were called 'Sherf Barrows' on I. Taylor's Estate Map of c. 1770 when both lay in an area of former open fields and were surrounded by square enclosures (*cf.* Winterbourne Steepleton (24–6)).

(72) (63888849). Ht. 2½ ft.

(73) (63918849). Immediately adjacent on E.N.E. of (72). Ht. 1½ ft.

(74) (64128852). 230 yds. E. of (73). Ht. 4 ft.

A bell, a double bowl and a bowl lie in a close-packed N.-S. straight line on top of a broad spur on Shorn Hill, about 500 yds. N. of Bronkham Hill (SY 68 NW; Fig. p. 626).

(75) *Bell* (62998721). Mound is steep-sided cone, 90 ft. in diam. and 12 ft. high, with berm 18 ft. wide. Ditch up to 30 ft. wide and 1 ft. deep, ploughed on S. and barely visible on E. Its arc on N. intersects S. end of (76), but there is no ground evidence of their relationship. One of the best-preserved bell barrows in Dorset.

(76) *Double bowl* (62998724) immediately adjacent on N. of (75). Elongated and hour-glass shaped, with N. part 58 ft. in diam. and 6 ft. high and S. part 51 ft. in diam. and 5½ ft. high. N. end cut into by a pond.

(77) *Bowl* (62988728) 50 yds. N. of (76). Diam. about 50 ft., ht. 5 ft. Disturbed and spread.

(78) *Bowl* (?) (SY 68 NW; 63448730) 500 yds. E. of (77) on E. edge of spur. Ploughed almost flat.

(79) *Bowl* (SY 68 NW; 63918704) on Great Hill, the next spur to E. of Shorn Hill. Diam. 74 ft., ht. 9 ft. Disturbed, within Ancient Field Group (6).

(80) *Bowl* (SY 68 NW; 64088720) on crest of N.E. slope of Great Hill 270 yds. N.E. of (79). Diam. 55 ft., ht. 5 ft.

(81) *Ditched double bowl* (?) (SY 68 NW; 64388706) on N. slope of Ridgeway 360 yds. S.E. of (80) across a small combe. Much disturbed, appearing as two mounds 3 ft. apart, each about 27 ft. in diam. W.-E. Whole only 48 ft. long N.-S., and up to 2 ft. high. Ditch on E. about 9 ft. wide, possibly common to both mounds. Not visible from Ridgeway.

(AJ) EWELEAZE BARN GROUP (SY 68 NW). Ten barrows, including a pond barrow (87) and a quadruple bell barrow (91), forming an irregular linear cemetery orientated roughly N.W. to S.E. on top of the second spur E. of Shorn Hill. (92–4) in *Four Barrow Hill Group* are aligned on (87), and many of the Ridgeway barrows between Black Down (Portesham) and Weymouth (403) appear silhouetted on the S. skyline from it. (91) is unique in England. (82), (84), (85) and (87) were excavated by St. George Gray and Prideaux in 1902.

(82) *Ditched bowl* (64658780). Diam. 82 ft., ht. 12 ft. Excavated ditch was flat-bottomed, 10½ ft. wide and 3½ ft. deep, around original turf mound, 64 ft. in diam., 9 ft. high and capped with chalk. N.-S. section across centre revealed crouched male inhumation with handled Beaker bowl in oblong chalk-cut grave, with three child inhumations and smaller jar nearby, all under flint cairn. S. of these but still N. of apparent centre, a ring of stones enclosed a cremation, fragments of incense cup and grooved copper dagger in wooden sheath (Wessex interment no. 12). Many flint implements, cores, and flakes lay in and under mound. (*Dorset Procs.* XXVI (1905), 7–22 and 35–9; Abercromby I, pl. xxii, 299; *P.P.S.* IV (1938), 98–9, 102 and fig. 23, 1 and 1a; Ap-Simon (1954), 57, no. 10; *Archaeometry* 4 (1961), 46, no. 22.)

(83) *Bowl* (64798770) 180 yds. S.E. of (82). Diam. 41 ft., ht. 3 ft. Excavated in centre.

(84) *Bowl* (?) (64808757) 150 yds. S. of (83). Only slight mound remains. Diam. 93 ft., ht. 2¾ ft. before excavation, which revealed two primary crouched male inhumations, one with fragments of food-vessel and infant's bones, and a secondary cremation in woven grass bag under collared urn resting on stone slab. Near centre, circular hole 1¾ ft. in diam. and 1½ ft. deep contained animal bones. Flint implements, cores and flakes and a shale disc were in mound. (*Dorset Procs.* XXVI (1905), 25–35.) Air photograph (Meridian Airmaps 100036, of 1962) shows narrow ditch 65–75 ft. in diam.

(85) *Bowl* (?) (64778746) 120 yds. S.S.W. of (84). Only slight mound remains. Crouched (male ?) inhumation in chalk-cut grave lay under flint cairn including burnt and unburnt human bones, potsherds and flint flakes and a scraper (*Dorset Procs.* XXVI (1905), 23–5).

(86) *Bowl* (?) (64688743) on W. slope 100 yds. W.S.W. of (85). Small, ploughed almost flat.

(87) *Pond barrow* (?) (64738738) 100 yds. S.S.W. of (85). Flint-paved, surrounded by bank 76 ft. in diam. and 4 ft. high above centre of hollow (Dorset *Procs.* XXVI (1905), 23).

(88) *Bowl* (?) (64838639) 100 yds. E. of (87). Diam. 140 ft., ht. 6 ft. Ploughed.

(89) *Bowl* (?) (64868728) 130 yds. S.S.E. of (88). Diam. 45 ft., ht. 3 ft. Ploughed.

(90) *Bowl* (64958721) 100 yds. S.E. of (89). Diam. 115 ft., ht. 15 ft. Excavation trench across centre. Fir-covered.

(91) *Quadruple bell* (?) (65008714) 50 yds. S.E. of (90). Four adjacent mounds, hts. 7 ft. to 8 ft. and diams. N.-S. 84 ft., 67 ft., 62 ft. and 67 ft., along axis of spur in N.W. to S.E. line, surrounded by ditch 15 ft. wide and 1 ft. deep. Overall length of mounds 280 ft. N. mound slightly W. of alignment of others and damaged by excavation. Ploughing has destroyed berm. (*A.B.M.E.* (1953), Pl. IVb.)

(AK) FOUR BARROW HILL GROUP (SY 68 NE). Six barrows, including two probable bells, about ¾ mile N.E. of the *Eweleaze Barn Group* in S.W.-N.E. line on top of a broad spur. (92–4) point towards pond barrow (87), 650 yds. to the S.W. The other barrows are slightly W. of this line. All have been ploughed.

(92) *Bowl* (?) (65078787). Diam. 78 ft., ht. 4½ ft.

(93) *Bowl* (?) (65108793) 60 yds. N.E. of (92). Diam. 93 ft., ht. 5 ft.

(94) *Bell* (?) (65138798) 70 yds. N.E. of (93). Diam. 97 ft., ht. 6 ft. Ditch-circle, about 190 ft. in diam., visible on V.A.P. CPE/UK 1934: 3091.

(95) *Bowl* (?) (65148795) immediately adjacent to (94) on S.E. Ploughed almost flat.

(96) *Bowl* (?) (65148804) 70 yds. N. of (94). Diam. 106 ft., ht. 6 ft. Crossed by hedge.

(97) *Bell* (?) (65188808) 60 yds. N.E. of (96). Ploughed almost flat. Ditch 140 ft. in diam., and apparent berm about 15 ft. wide, visible on V.A.P. CPE/UK 1934: 3091.

Bowls (?), two (SY 68 NE), lie about 1200 yds. S.E. of Four Barrow Hill, above the 400 ft. contour on a spur projecting N. from the Ridgeway.

(98) (65688703). Diam. about 36 ft., ht. 1½ ft. Ploughed.

(99) (65698706) 40 yds. N.N.E. of (98). Diam. about 48 ft. Ploughed almost flat.

(AL) ASHTON GROUP (SY 68 NE). Four barrows about 430 yds. N.E. of (99) in a W.N.W.-E.S.E. line above the 400 ft. contour. All have been ploughed.

(100) *Bowl* (?) (65948720) on slight N.W. slope. Diam. about 50 ft., ht. 1 ft.

(101) *Bowl* (?) (66048718) 120 yds. E.S.E. of (100). Diam. 55 ft., ht. 3 ft.

(102) *Bowl* (66088717) 40 yds. E.S.E. of (101). Diam. 85 ft., ht. 10 ft. Fir-covered.

(103) *Bowl* (?) (66138716) 65 yds. E.S.E. of (102). Almost flat. Fir-covered.

(104) *Bowl* (?) (SY 68 NE; 65788735) 305 yds. N.N.E. of (99) and on ridge of same spur. Diam. 33 ft., ht. 1 ft.

(105) *Bowl* (SY 68 NE; 65628759) near summit of N.E. slope, 313 yds. N.N.W. of (104). Diam. 70 ft., ht. 5 ft. Ploughed.

(106) *Ditched bowl* (SY 68 NE; 65908797) on fairly steep N.E. slope. Diam. 26 ft., ht. 4 ft. Ditch 7 ft. wide.

(AM) REW GROUP (SY 69 SW). Five, possibly seven barrows, including one probable disc barrow, on summit of hill in the extreme N.W. of the parish. Two were probably excavated by Sydenham: his no. 1 contained two primary contracted inhumations and a cremation at bottom of grave beneath a flint cairn. In the cairn was an extended child inhumation with small vessel (in D.C.M.), and at the top was an inurned cremation. On S. of the mound was a cremation in a biconical urn with remains probably of a necklace consisting of cylindrical bone bead, faience quoit-bead, faience star-bead and cowrie shell. Nearby was a fourth inurned cremation, and a fifth cremation lay near the surface with a fragmentary urn. In the top of mound was extended child inhumation (*Archaeologia* XXX (1844), 329–31; *C.T.D.*, tovp, no. 70; Abercromby II, 42; *Ant. J.* XIII (1933), 448; Butler and Smith (1956), 35). A barrow nearby contained a cremation and an extended inhumation (*C.T.D.*, tovp, no. 71).

(107) Bowl (?) (63629013) crossed by parish boundary with Winterbourne Steepleton 170 yds. S.W. of Rew. Diam. about 60 ft., ht. about 5 ft. Ploughed.

(108) Mound, possible bowl (63659029) 180 yds. N.N.E. of (107). Ploughed almost flat.

(109) Mound, possible bowl (63699032) 60 yds. N.E. of (108). Ploughed almost flat.

(110) Bowl (?) (63679034) 30 yds. W.N.W. of (109). Ploughed almost flat.

(111) Disc (?) (63699036) 28 yds. N.E. of (110). Diam. of mound about 40 ft., with ditch-circle about 80 ft. in diam. visible on V.A.P. CPE/UK 1934: 5091. Ploughed almost flat.

(112) Bowl (63699039) adjacent to (111) on N. Diam. 64 ft., ht. 6½ ft. Excavated on top.

(113) Bowl (63669041) 40 yds. N.W. of (112). Diam. 64 ft., ht. 6½ ft. Dug into.

(AN) THIRD MILESTONE GROUP (SY 69 SW). Five barrows in an irregular W.-E. line on the crest of a ridge immediately S. of the Roman road three miles W. of Dorchester. (114) and (115) have probably been excavated twice, by Warne and Sydenham in 1839–40 and Cunnington in 1885, though it is impossible to correlate the accounts. One contained a primary extended inhumation with a chalk-filled urn and an antler in a grave 7 ft. by 4 ft. by 7 ins. deep beneath a flint cairn, above which was a child inhumation with a food-vessel (in D.C.M.) and a cremation beneath an inverted biconical urn. In the top of the mound was an extended inhumation. The other contained three primary inhumations, and two further inhumations

only 1 ft. above them, all in a grave 5 ft. in diam. and nearly 5 ft. deep beneath a flint cairn, above which were two inhumations. (*Archaeologia* XXX, 331, nos. 2 & 3; *C.T.D.*, mopr, nos. 26 & 30.) Of Cunnington's two barrows, both previously disturbed, one contained remains of a large cairn, two inhumations and fragments of three urns, and the other parts of an inhumation in a cairn (MS., nos. 24 & 25).

(114) Bowl (?) (64279035). Diam. 72 ft., ht. 5 ft.

(115) Bowl (?) (64319035) 50 yds. E. of (114). Ploughed almost flat.

(116) Bowl (?) (64389032) 75 yds. E.S.E. of (115), ploughed and only 2½ ft. high.

(117) Bowl (?) (64449032) about 60 yds. E.N.E. of (116). Ploughed flat, but visible on V.A.P. CPE/UK 1934: 5090.

(118) Bowl (?) (64499031) about 60 yds. E.S.E. of (117). Ploughed flat, but visible on V.A.P. CPE/UK 1934: 5091.

(AO) WIRELESS STATION GROUP (SY 68 NW, NE, 69 SW, SE). Thirteen barrows S. of Roman road, all but (130–1) scattered above 400 ft. contour. Most are damaged. Three excavations are recorded (Cunnington MS., nos. 21–23).

(119) Bowl (64689032) 200 yds. E. of (118). Diam. 59 ft., ht. 8 ft. Contained a contracted inhumation in a grave 5½ ft. deep beneath a large flint cairn.

(120) Ditched bowl (?) (64729032) 45 yds. E. of (119). Ploughed almost flat.

(121) Bowl (?) (64759030) 40 yds. E.S.E. of (120). Diam. 60 ft., ht. 3 ft. Ploughed.

(122) Bowl (64809030), surrounded by tree-clump enclosure and still tree-covered, 45 yds. E.S.E. of (121). Diam. 65 ft., ht. 10½ ft.

(123) Bowl (64899024) 120 yds. S.E. of (122). Diam. 60 ft., ht. 7 ft. Large excavation hole on top.

(124) Ditched double bowl (?) (64979023) 75 yds. E.S.E. of (123). Ploughed almost flat. (*cf.* Taylor's Park Farm Estate Map (*c.* 1770), and Air Ministry photo. 5793, dated 1926.)

(125) Ditched bowl (65139036) 230 yds. N.E. of (124) immediately S. of Roman road. Diam. 60 ft., ht. 11 ft. Contained central cairn, above which was cremation near three urns, broken by four intrusive inhumations.

(126) Bowl (?) (65189018) 210 yds. S.S.E. of (125) on S. slope. Diam. 60 ft., ht. 9 ft. Contained cremation with antler, ox bones and flint implements in oval grave 2 ft. long by 1½ ft. deep beneath cairn.

(127) Bowl (?) (64809003) 270 yds. S. of (122). Ploughed almost flat.

(128) Bowl (?) (64808998) 350 yds. S. of (122). Diam. about 50 ft. Ploughed almost flat.

(129) Bowl (64798994) 160 yds. S.S.W. of (127) in small wood on S. slope. Diam. 60 ft., ht. 9 ft. Excavation hollow on top.

(130) Ditched bowl (?) (65068999) 310 yds. E.N.E. of (129) on S.E. slope below 400 ft. Ploughed almost flat.

(131) Ditched bowl (?) (65099000) adjoining (130) on N.E. and possibly forming double barrow with it. Both appear

surrounded by same hour-glass shaped ditch on V.A.P. CPE/UK 1934: 5090. Ploughed almost flat.

(132) *Bowl* (?) (SY 68 NE; 65468978) on slight S. slope. Ploughed almost flat.

(133) *Bowl* (?) (SY 68 NE; 66198978) on S.W. slope tilting towards (134). Diam. 45 ft., ht. 1 ft. Ploughed.

(134) *Clandon Barrow*, bowl (SY 68 NE; 65648900), in prominent position above 300 ft. contour on flat ground at W. end of local ridge. Diam. 90 ft., ht. 18 ft. Markedly conical in profile. Cunnington partly excavated the mound in 1882 without reaching primary burial, the bottom of his pit being probably 9 ft. above original ground surface. About 6 ft. from the top was flint cairn about 1 ft. thick and 8 ft. in diam. Below it, sherds of an incense cup were scattered on a layer of white clay; among the flints were fragments of an amber cup; and on the flints were a grooved copper dagger with traces of a wooden sheath and an attached small bronze ring, a quadrangular gold plate and a shale mace-head with five gold-capped bosses. 1 ft. higher was a cremation in a crushed, typologically early, collared urn on a thin layer of ashes and small flints. 4 ft. higher and 2 ft. from the top of the mound two stone-lined graves, possibly Romano-British, lay E.-W. 4 ft. apart, each with an inhumation on a layer of fine sand. The mound largely consisted of layers of sands, clays and gravels. Finds in D.C.M., Wessex interment no. 6. (Dorset *Procs.* LVIII (1936), 18–25; Abercromby II, pl. LXII, 3; ApSimon (1954), 60, no. 38; *P.P.S.* XXVII (1961), 266, 294, no. 20; *Archaeometry* 4 (1961), 46, no. 33.)

(135) *Ditched bowl* (?) (SY 68 NE; 65748894) 135 yds. S.E. of (134) and ploughed almost flat. V.A.P. CPE/UK 1934: 3089 shows double ring ditches, 80 ft. and 40 ft. in diam. Opened in 1883 by Cunnington who found central cairn covering two inhumations and an 'A' beaker (now in D.C.M.). Cremation in top of cairn and another in broken urn above. About ten inhumations, possibly Romano-British, lay 1 ft. below surface. (Abercromby I, 21, pl. VI, fig. 17.)

(136) *Bowl* (?) (SY 68 NE; 66008848) on slight W. slope. Diam. 50 ft., ht. 3 ft. Disturbed.

(137) *See* LANCEBOROUGH GROUP (AH), Winterborne Monkton, p. 465.

(138) *Bowl* (SY 68 NE; 66278878; Fig. p. 494) 425 yds. N.E. of (136) on N. end of Hog Hill. Diam. 39 ft., ht. 4 ft. Destroyed.

(139) *Bowl* (?) (SY 68 NE; 66438876). Diam. about 50 ft., ht. 2 ft.

(140) *Bowl* (?) (SY 68 NE; 66448870) on summit of col connecting Hog Hill and Maiden Castle. Diam. 50 ft., ht. 1½ ft. Probably covered three inhumations and secondary unaccompanied vessel (*Archaeologia* XXX (1844), 332, and pl. XVII, 7).

Four other barrows, not now identifiable but possibly including (139) above, were excavated by Sydenham and Warne near (140) (*Archaeologia* XXX, 332, nos. 8–11; *C.T.D.*, tovp, nos. 73–6). They contained respectively a primary cremation with a riveted bronze ogival dagger and a flat,

riveted knife-dagger (ApSimon (1954), 57, no. 11); a primary contracted inhumation; a cremation; and a primary and two secondary inhumations.

(141) *Bowl* (SY 68 NE; 66638842; Figs. p. 494, opp. p. 498) inside Maiden Castle (142). Diam. 48 ft., ht. 1 ft. Hollowed on top (Wheeler, *Maiden Castle*, 25 and pl. 1).

WINTERBOURNE STEEPLETON

Most of the forty-nine round barrows form parts of six groups. Four of the southernmost barrows are in the *Black Down Group* (R.5), Portesham; four other groups lie on spurs running N.E. from the Ridgeway above the 400 ft. contour. The *Big Wood* (AQ) and *Sheep Down* (AS) *Groups* each include a pond barrow, of which (46) has been excavated, and double bowls occur in both the *Sheep Down* and *Pound Hill* (AU) *Groups*. The latter is a linear cemetery cut by the parish boundary with Winterbourne Abbas. (24–6) are mounds surrounded by square enclosures. Several barrows were opened in the 19th century: one, un-located, was 36 ft. in diam. and 6 ft. high, covering a central grave about 1 ft. deep which contained a crema-tion and a perforated green-stone battle-axe; fragments of an urn were scattered through the mound (Wessex interment no. 23; *C.T.D.*, mopr, no. 46). Only a pit exists near the E. parish boundary where a barrow (LVG 37) was recorded.

(14) *Bowl* (SY 68 NW; 60088834) crossed by parish boundary with Little Bredy and one of the few isolated barrows on Ridgeway. Diam. about 36 ft., ht. 5½ ft. Disturbed on top.

(15) *Mound*, possibly ditched bowl (SY 68 NW; 60528833). Diam. 42 ft., ht. 2 ft. At corner of 'Celtic' field (Fig. opp. p. 624) in Ancient Field Group (3).

(16–19) form part of the BLACK DOWN GROUP (R.5), Portesham, p. 449.

A cluster of three barrows (SY 68 NW) lies on a knoll above a steep W. slope below and about 500 yds. E.N.E. of Black Down. They are clearly visible from N.

(20) *Ditched bowl* with outer bank (61638776). Diam. 80 ft., ht. 10 ft., with ditch 10 ft. wide and 2 ft. deep and bank up to 18 ft. broad and 2 ft. high on N. Ditch and bank dug away on W. Disturbed by solution hollows.

(21) *Bell*, with mound on top (61688775), on slight S.E. slope 50 yds. E. of (20). Diam. of primary mound 55 ft., ht. 5 ft., with flat top surmounted by mound 24 ft. in diam. and 2 ft. high. On S., where berm absent, slope of upper mound runs into that of lower. Berm 10 ft. wide at most. Ditch 15 ft. wide and up to 2½ ft. deep, disturbed by solution hollows.

(22) *Bowl* (61738770) on slight S.E. slope 50 yds. S.E. of (21). Diam. 33 ft., ht. 4½ ft. Slightly damaged.

(23) *Bowl* (SY 68 NW; 60728861) on Cowleaze above 500 ft. contour. Diam. 50 ft., ht. 6 ft. Disturbed.

Barrows in square enclosures, three (SY 68 NW), lie on a gentle E. slope over Bagshot rubble. Each enclosure is almost square with a bank 1 ft. high and sides approximately orientated. All much disturbed. Probably Iron Age or later, since (26) may be later than boundaries of 'Celtic' field type surrounding it (*see* Ancient Field Group (3), Fig. opp. p. 624), and because in E. Yorkshire smaller barrows tightly surrounded by similarly orientated square ditches (not banks) are of La Tène Iron Age (I. M. Stead, *Ant. J.* XLI (1961), 44–62, for Yorkshire and Continental evidence). The closest parallel, at Leckhampton, Glos., was undated by excavation (Bristol and Glos. A.S. *Trans.* XLVII (1925), 91–101). In Winterborne St. Martin square enclosures around larger barrows in open fields were probably later additions (*see* (72–3)).

(24) (61198857). Diam. about 35 ft., ht. about 2 ft. Enclosure 68 ft. by 66½ ft.

(25) (61268860). Diam. about 35 ft., ht. about 2 ft. Enclosure 64 ft. by 63½ ft.

(26) (61288850). Diam. about 28 ft., ht. about 2 ft. Enclosure 63½ ft. square. Ditch about 9 ft. wide outside bank.

(27) *Bowl* (SY 68 NW; 61638848). Diam. about 40 ft., ht. 4½ ft.

(28) *Bowl* (SY 68 NW; 61658851) 30 yds. N.E. of (27). Oval, 24 ft. by 18 ft., ht. 2 ft. Disturbed.

(AP) GAYTHORNE GROUP (SY 68 NW). Four probable bowls on broad-topped ridge running N.E. from Black Down. The area is naturally hillocky heath, now largely arable, making it uncertain which rises are barrows. (29–31) are under grass. Two 'tumuli' (O.S. 6 in.; LVG 35 and 41) are almost certainly natural.

(29) (62068795). Diam. about 35 ft., ht. 1½ ft. Forms short alignment with (30) and (31).

(30) (62118796) 50 yds. E.N.E. of (29). Elongated and irregular mound about 2 ft. high.

(31) (62138798) 30 yds. E.N.E. of (30). Irregular oval mound 70 ft. by 50 ft. and 2 ft. high.

(32) (62188806) 110 yds. N.N.E. of (31). Ht. 2½ ft. Ploughed.

(AQ) BIG WOOD GROUP (SY 68 NW). Thirteen, possibly fifteen, barrows, including a bell and a pond barrow, lie on W. of parish along the top of a ridge projecting N.E. from the Ridgeway. Neither of the bowls (LVG 6 and 7) E. of (34) is visible, though traces of two possible barrows appear immediately W. of (34) on V.A.P. CPE/UK 1934: 5096, from which some of the following details, particularly of ditches, are taken. (33–7) and (41) have been ploughed over and otherwise all but (43) are damaged; but the group is still visible on the skyline looking N. or N.W. from the Ridgeway.

(33) Ditched bowl (?) (60438943), only a circular crop-mark about 50 ft. in diam.

(34) Ditched bowl (60558945) 130 yds. E. of (33). Diam. 42 ft., ht. 2 ft. Ditch about 60 ft. in diam.

(35) Bowl (60588946) 35 yds. E. of (34). Diam. 60 ft., ht. 1 ft.

(36) Bowl (60618946) 30 yds. E. of (35). Diam. 80 ft., ht. 2 ft.

(37) Bowl (60638947) 30 yds. N.E. of (36). Diam. about 20 ft., ht. 6 ins.

(38) Ditched bowl (60658948) 25 yds. N.E. of (37). Diam. 54 ft., ht. 5 ft., surrounded by wide ditch.

(39) Pond barrow (60718954) 85 yds. N.E. of (38). Circular depression 80 ft. in diam. and 2 ft. deep surrounded by bank 13 ft. wide and up to 2 ft. high. Ploughing, which is clipping the bank, is making it square rather than round.

Winterbourne Abbas:

(48) Ditched bowl (60698956) in Big Wood immediately adjacent to last on N.W. Diam. 86 ft., ht. 10 ft. Ditch, 15 ft. wide, 6 ins. deep, overlaid on S.E. by parish boundary bank; it probably originally cut, or was overlaid by, bank of last (*cf.* (46–7) *below*).

Winterbourne Steepleton:

(40) Bowl (60838957) 130 yds. E.N.E. of (39). Diam. 82 ft., ht. 9 ft.

(41) Bowl (60838964) 70 yds. N. of (40). Diam. 24 ft. Ploughed almost flat.

(42) Bell (60968970) 165 yds. N.E. of (41). Diam. 84 ft., ht. 9 ft. Berm 5 ft. wide and 4 ft. above ditch 15 ft. wide and 1 ft. deep. Excavation hollow on top. Sherds, probably of Bronze Age cinerary urn, on S.E.

(43) Bowl (60988971) 20 yds. N.E. of (42). Diam. 24 ft., ht. 6 ins.

(44) Bowl (61008974) 20 yds. N.E. of (43). Diam. 54 ft., ht. 2½ ft.

(AS) SHEEP DOWN GROUP (SY 68 NW; Fig. opp. p. 624). Five barrows, including a double bowl (47) and a pond barrow (46), lie above apparent limit of 'Celtic' fields on a broad spur running N.E. from the Ridgeway at about 460 ft. above O.D. (*see* Ancient Field Group (3)); they are 500 yds. S. of the *Big Wood Group* (AQ) and divided from it by a shallow combe. (46) has been excavated.

(45) Bowl (60688893) on slight S.E. slope. Diam. 35 ft., ht. 2½ ft. Damaged by excavation.

(46) Pond barrow (60708901) 93 yds. N.N.E. of (45). Central depression, diam. 35 ft., depth 2 ft., surrounded by bank 10 ft. to 12 ft. wide and 5 ins. high. Excavation by H. G. Wakefield for the Commission in 1947–8 and by R. J. C. Atkinson in 1950 showed that a pavement of flints gathered from the top-soil largely covered the depression. Beneath and around the pavement were thirty-five pits cut into the chalk subsoil, in some cases through the pavement. Seventeen pits contained Early Bronze Age urns, two held an urn and an inhumation, one held an urn and a cremation, seven contained only cremations, and eight were filled with soil alone. The whole site had been stripped before the pavement was laid, the pits dug, and the bank built (*Arch. J.* CVIII (1951), 1–24; *P.P.S.* XXVII (1961), 294, nos. 27–33).

(47) Ditched double bowl (60728904) immediately adjacent on N.N.E. of (46). Diams. of mounds 59 ft. and 55 ft., hts. 5 ft. and 4½ ft.; joined by slight bank and surrounded by

hour-glass shaped ditch 12 ft. wide. Partially sectioned during excavation of (46), the ditch was just over 2 ft. deep and probably dug before (46) was constructed. Bronze Age sherds probably of bucket urn found on S.W. of W. mound.

(48) Bowl (?) (60758902) 30 yds. S.E. of E. mound of (47). Diam. 50 ft., ht. 3½ ft.

(49) Bowl (?) (60878907) on summit of spur 130 yds. N.E. of (48). Only slight rise remains.

(50) *Bowl* (?) (SY 68 NW; 60998894) on slight S. slope 190 yds. S.E. of (49). Diam. about 30 ft., ht. 1½ ft. Much disturbed.

(51) *Bowl* (SY 68 NW; 61288898) on slight N.W. slope 330 yds. E.N.E. of (50) across a shallow combe. Diam. 40 ft., ht. 3½ ft. Excavation hollow on top.

(AT) ROWDEN GROUP (SY 68 NW). Five barrows around the 500 ft. contour on W. side of a ridge about 400 yds. E. of (51) across a narrow combe. Of three alleged pond barrows here, one (LVG 25a) is more likely to be a hut platform and the other two (LVG 26a and b) are probable hut circles, all associated with settlement and field remains ploughed in 1962 (*see* Settlements, Winterbourne Steepleton (64) *and* Ancient Field Group (3), Figs. p. 511, opp. p. 624).

(52) Bowl (?) (61698888). Diam. 19 ft., ht. 1 ft.

(53) Bowl (61688892) 50 yds. N.N.W. of (52). Diam. 23 ft., ht. 1½ ft.

(54) Bowl (?) (61698895) at top of W. slope 40 yds. N.N.E. of (53). Diam. 36 ft., ht. 1 ft.

(55) Bowl (61648904) on N.W. slope 125 yds. N.N.W. of (54). Diam. 51 ft., ht. 2½ ft.

(56) Bowl (?) (61708913) 110 yds. N.E. of (55). Almost destroyed.

(57) *Bowl* (SY 68 NW; 62348896) on S.E. slope. Diam. about 80 ft., ht. 5 ft. Much damaged.

(AU) POUND HILL GROUP (SY 69 SW). Five barrows, including a double bowl, lie on either side of the 500 ft. contour, all but Winterbourne Abbas (53) forming a N.W. to S.E. line along the hill crest. Two (53-4) are in Winterbourne Abbas. (58-60) are ploughed almost flat.

Winterbourne Abbas:

(53) Bowl (62309082). Diam. 34 ft., ht. 5½ ft. Disturbed.

(54) Bowl (62329089) 75 yds. N.N.E. of (53). Diam. 60 ft., ht. 10½ ft. Excavation hollow on top.

Winterbourne Steepleton:

(58) Bowl (62399087) 70 yds. S.E. of last. Diam. about 60 ft., ht. 2 ft.

(59) Ditched bowl (?) (62439085) 70 yds. S.E. of (58). Diam. about 70 ft., ht. 1½ ft. Circular soil-mark suggesting a ditch about 100 ft. in diam. appears on V.A.P. CPE/UK 1934: 5093.

(60) Ditched double bowl (62529081) 85 yds. S.E. of (59). Diams. of mounds 72 ft. and 45 ft., hts. 1½ ft. and 1 ft. Both

are surrounded by continuous hour-glass shaped ditch visible on V.A.P. CPE/UK 1934: 5093 (*cf.* LVG III and 48 and O.S. *Neolithic Wessex*, no. 150).

Two barrows (61-2) on the summit of North Hill, a S.E. spur of Pound Hill, were probably opened by Warne. His no. 31 (*C.T.D.*, mopr) consisted almost entirely of a flint cairn in which was an urn surrounded by ashes, directly beneath an unburnt human skull. No. 32 contained a primary inurned cremation in a chalk-cut grave beneath a flat stone (*Archaeologia* XXX (1844), 331-2, nos. 4 and 6; *Ant. J.* XIII (1933), 448). Two other unlocated barrows probably on the same hill produced sherds of a large decorated urn (mentioned under *C.T.D.*, mopr, no. 31), and a cremation and an extended inhumation (*C.T.D.*, tovp, no. 71; *Archaeologia* XXX (1844), 332, no. 5).

(61) *Bowl* (SY 69 SW; 62959001). Diam. 66 ft., ht. 5 ft.

(62) *Bowl* (SY 68 NW; 63028998) 90 yds. S.E. of (61). Diam. 82 ft., ht. 7 ft.

WOODSFORD

Only two probable barrows are known and they are likely to be the mounds dug into by Warne in the 'neighbourhood of Woodsford'. Both are now almost ploughed flat, though showing as soil-marks on V.A.P. CPE/UK 1934: 5074. In one, barely 2 ft. high, were twelve urns, both upright and inverted; three or four were decorated. The other contained four urns immediately below the surface.

(6) *Bowl* (?) (SY 78 NE; 77488949) on gentle slope to S. and E. about 140 ft. above O.D.

(7) *Bowl* (?) (SY 78 NE; 77518948) in similar position 47 yds. S.E. of (6).

WOOL

Five, possibly six, barrows are known, though another (LVG 5) has been claimed between Braytown and Quarr Hill. Coles Barrow on Wool Heath (LVG 7) has not been located but (45) is probably one of two formerly noted S. of Quarr Hill. A biconical urn and a bucket urn, apparently from barrows respectively on Quarr Hill and near Wool, are now in the B.M. and D.C.M. (*Ant. J.* XIII (1933), 448).

(44) *Ditched bowl* (SY 88 NW; 82468630) on level site. Diam. 70 ft., ht. 4 ft. Now ploughed and previously disturbed on top.

(45) *Bowl* (?) (SY 88 NW; 84838573) near S.W. edge of spur. Diam. 72 ft., ht. 4 ft. Trigonometrical station on slightly hollowed top. Probably one of two opened in mid 19th century in 'Young Creech' when several inurned cremations found (Hutchins I, 364; J. Sparrow's Estate Map (1770)).

(46) *Ditched bowl* (SY 88 NW; 81368775) on short heathland spur above 100 ft. contour. Diam. 57 ft., ht. 5 ft. with ditch

E

10 ft. wide and 2 ft. deep. Mound is steep-sided and flat-topped, though hollowed in centre.

(47) *Ditched bowl* (SY 88 NW; 81988750) at N.W. end of heathland plateau dropping sharply to N. and E. Diam. 43 ft., ht. 5 ft. with traces of ditch about 10 ft. wide. Mound markedly steep-sided and flat-topped, though damaged by excavation trench from W. and hollowed in centre.

(48) *Mound*, possible bowl (SY 88 NW; 82218908), now slight, irregular and disturbed in woodland.

(49) *Bowl* (SY 88 NW; 82228912) 50 yds. N.N.E. of (48). Diam. 30 ft., ht. 3 ft. Probably disturbed on top, and tree-covered.

WORTH MATRAVERS

Austen excavated (34), recorded urns from (36) and described a barrow near Renscombe Farm destroyed in the 19th century (*Purbeck Papers* I, 37–8).

(34) *Bowl* (SY 97 NE; 96337597) prominent on edge of almost flat downland. Diam. 41 ft., ht. 5 ft. At corner of a 'Celtic' field of *Ancient Field Group* (24). The barrow was opened in 1850 by Austen. At or about ground level and over a stone-filled pit were seven or eight inhumations, at least three extended. Four skulls lay together over the feet of one. The only associated finds were a round-headed bone pin 3½ ins. long with the four skulls and a 'green glass bead' with a crushed urn, probably a degenerate short-necked beaker, on its side on the chest of one of the apparently extended skeletons. Upright stone slabs, perhaps of an original cist, were associated with the burials. Above was a 6-in. thick layer of stones and, just below the surface, a 2-ft. thick layer of stones and earth included a samian sherd, a 'considerable quantity' of other Romano-British sherds, Kimmeridge shale fragments and five coins (Trajan to Tetricus). (Hutchins I, 704–5.)

(35) *Bowl* (SY 97 NE; 95817649) on Emmett's Hill about 400 ft. above O.D., with gentle slope to E. but precipitous cliff to W. down which greater part has fallen. Diam. about 40 ft., ht. 2¾ ft.

(36) *Bowl* (SY 97 NE; 96287647) about 350 ft. above O.D. on gentle E. slope. Diam. 75 ft., ht. 1½ ft. Ploughed.

ROUND BARROWS: CONCORDANCE

The parish monument numbers of round barrows in this Inventory are shown in the column headed *R.C.H.M.*; a capital letter prefix indicates a barrow group or part of a group (*see* Register, pp. 429–30). The parish numbers of barrows as listed in L. V. Grinsell, *Dorset Barrows* (1959), are given under the heading *L.V.G.*; numbers under the heading *Others* are from earlier works, abbreviated as follows:

m = 'My own personal researches'
f = 'Communications from personal friends' } in C. Warne, *Celtic Tumuli of Dorset* (1866)
v = 'Tumuli opened at various periods'
C = E. Cunnington, MS. in D.C.M.
CR = E. Cunnington, MS. in D.C.M. (Ridgeway barrows)

R.C.H.M.	L.V.G.	Others	R.C.H.M.	L.V.G.	Others	R.C.H.M.	L.V.G.	Others
AFFPUDDLE			AFFPUDDLE (*contd.*)			ARNE (*contd.*)		
44	1		59	17		35	8	
45			60	16		36	19	v4
46	1a		61	14		37 East Holme 6		
A 47			62	13		38	16a	
48	2		63	18		39	21	
49	3					40	17	
50	4					41	18	
51	5		ARNE			42	13	
52	6		28	1		43	14	
53	7		29	8	v58	44	15	
54	8		30	9	C49	45	15a & 20	
55	8a		B 31	10		46	11	
56	9		32	2				
57	10		33	3		BERE REGIS		
58	11		34	4		67	15	

BERE REGIS (contd.)

R.C.H.M.	L.V.G.	Others
68	16	
69	11	
70	23	
71	12	
72	24	
73	29	
74	28	
75	18a	
76	27	
X { 77	21	
78	20	
79	19	
80	22	
81	17	
82	26	
83	18	
C { 84	31	
85	32	
86	33	
87	34	
88	30	
89	41	
90	48b	
91	48a	
92	48	
D { 93	44	
94	45	
95	46	
96	38	
97	39 & 46e	f21
98	40	
99	36	
100	4	
101	37	
102	42	
103	43	
104	43a	
105	1	
106	2	f10 ?
107	3	f9 ?
108	Wint.	
	Kingston 16	
109	5	f11 ?
110	6	
111	7	
112	8	
113		
114	9a	
115	9	
116		

BINCOMBE

R.C.H.M.	L.V.G.	Others
R.7 { 13	50	
(see on) { 14	51	C31, CR3?

BINCOMBE (contd.)

R.C.H.M.	L.V.G.	Others
R.7 { 15	52	C32, CR4
16	53	C30, CR2
17	54	
(contd.) 18	55	
19	56	
20	57	
21	58	
22	59	C33, CR6
R.8 { 23		
24	11	
25	13	
26	14	
27	15	
28	16	
29	17	
30	18	
31	19	
32		
33	1	m41 ?
34	2	m1
35	3	m2
R.9 { 36	6	
37	5a	
38	5	
39	4	m42 ?
40	7	
41	8	
42	9	
43	10	
R.10 { 44	35a–c	m43 ?
45	34	
46	33a	
47	33	
48	35	
49	32	
50	31	
51	30	
52	29	
53	28	
54	27	
55	26a	
56	26	
57	25	
58	22	
59	24	
60	23	
61	21	
R.12 { 62	39	
(see on) 63	39a	
64	40	
65	41	
66	42	
67	43	
68	44	

BINCOMBE (contd.)

R.C.H.M.	L.V.G.	Others
R.12 { 69	45	
(contd.) 70	46	
71	47	
72	20	
73	37	m4
74	38	

BLOXWORTH

R.C.H.M.	L.V.G.	Others
29	11	
30	12	
31	10	
32	9	
33	8	
34	7	
35	6	
E { 36	5b	
37	5a	
38	5	
39	4a	f14
40	4	f15
41	3 }	
42	2 }	f13 ?
43	1	

BROADMAYNE

R.C.H.M.	L.V.G.	Others
20	1	
21	3	
22	4	
23	5	
R.11 { 24	2	
25	8a	
26	6	
27	7	
28		
29	8	

CHALDON HERRING

R.C.H.M.	L.V.G.	Others
25	9	
26	10	
27	11	
28	8	
29	12	
30	13	
F { 31	18	
32	17	
33	14	
34	15	
35	16	
36	19	
37	20	
38		
39		
40	21	
41	22	

R.C.H.M.	L.V.G.	Others
CHALDON HERRING (*contd.*)		
42	23	
43	24	
G ⎰ 44		
45		
46		
47		
48	1	
49	2	
50	3	
H ⎰ 51	4	v82–3 ?
52	4b	
53	4c	v82–3 ?
54	6	
55	6a	
56	32	
57	7	
CHURCH KNOWLE		
35	10	
36	13	v90 ?
37	6	
38	6a	
39		
40	7	v89
41	9	
42	8	
43	12	
44	11	
45	1	
I ⎰ 46	2	
47	3	
48	4	
49	5	
COOMBE KEYNES		
J ⎰ 13	4	
14	5	
15	6	
16	3b	
17	3a	
18	3	
19	2	
20		
CORFE CASTLE		
182	21	
183	22	v87
184	23	v88
185		
K ⎰ 186	5	
187	6	
(see on) 188	10d	
189	7	

R.C.H.M.	L.V.G.	Others
CORFE CASTLE (*contd.*)		
K ⎰ 190	8	
191	8a	
(contd.) 192	9	
193	10	
194	24	
195		
196		
197		
198	2	
199	3	
200	4	
L ⎰ 201	11	
202	12	
203		
204	13	
205	14	
206	15	
207	16	
208	17	
209		
210		
211		
212	18	
213	19	
214	20	
215		
216		
217	20a	
218	25c	
219	1	
DORCHESTER		
168	7	C3
169	8	C4
170	3	
171	4	C7
HOLME, EAST		
6	4	
7	5	
8		
9	3	C ⎱ *Purbeck*
10	1	B ⎰ *Papers* I,
11	2	A ⎰ 233–8
KNIGHTON, WEST		
21	3	
22	1	C28
23	4	
24	Warmwell 6	
LULWORTH, EAST		
29	1	v8
30	2	v9

R.C.H.M.	L.V.G.	Others
LULWORTH, EAST (*contd.*)		
31	5	
32	4	
33	3	v13, 55–7
34	6	
35		
36	7, 5b	v51
37	7a, 5c	v52
38	9, 5d	v53
39	8, 7b	v54
LULWORTH, WEST		
35		
36	1	
37	2	
38	3	
39	14	
40	3a	v10 ?
41	4	v11 ?
42		
43		
44	12	
45	13	
46	5	
47	6	
48	7	
49	8	
50	9	
51	10	
52	11	
LYTCHETT MATRAVERS		
37	2	
MORDEN		
52	3	
53		
54	1	
55	2	
MORETON		
28	2b	
29	1	
30	2	
OSMINGTON		
R.14 ⎰ 30	1	
31		
32		C26 ?
33		
34		
35	3	
36	4	
37	5	

R.C.H.M.	L.V.G.	Others

OSMINGTON (*contd.*)

R.C.H.M.	L.V.G.	Others
M { 38	7	
39	8	
40	9	
41		

OWERMOIGNE

R.C.H.M.	L.V.G.	Others
22	10	
23	11	
24	5	
25	4	
26	6	
27	7	
28	8	
29	9	
30	2	
31	1	
32	3	
33	Moreton 2a	

POOLE

R.C.H.M.	L.V.G.	Others
361	38	
362	35	
363	36	
364	37	
365	32	
366	39	
367	30	
368	31	
N { 369	25	
370	26	
371	27	
372	28	
373	29	
374	24	
375	33	
376	34	
377	23	
378	21	
379	22	
380	20	
381	19	
382	13	
383	16	
384	17	
385	18	
386	14	
387	15	
O { 388	5	
389	7	
390	6	
391	9	
392	8	
393	10	
394	11	
395	12	

POOLE (*contd.*)

R.C.H.M.	L.V.G.	Others
P { 396	1	} f33-4
397	2	
398	3	
399	3a	} f35
400	4	
401	3b	

PORTESHAM

R.C.H.M.	L.V.G.	Others
R.5 { 34	6	
35	3	
36	5	
37	4	
38	2a	C52 ?
R.6 { 39	13	
40	11	
R.7 { 41	7	
42	8	
43	14	C36
44	I & 1	
45	9	
46	10	
47	2	C53
48	6	
49	15	
50	12	
51	16-17	
Q { 52	18	
53	19	
54	20	
55	21	

PORTLAND

R.C.H.M.	L.V.G.	Others
96	1	

POXWELL

R.C.H.M.	L.V.G.	Others
R.13 11	3 & 4	m7 or 8 ?
12	2	C55
13	1a	
14	1	

STAFFORD, WEST

R.C.H.M.	L.V.G.	Others
18	3	
19	4	
20	1	
21	1a	
22	Dorchester 6	
23		

STEEPLE

R.C.H.M.	L.V.G.	Others
19	1	
20	2	
21		
22	3c	

STEEPLE (*contd.*)

R.C.H.M.	L.V.G.	Others
23	3d	
24	3b	
25	3a	

STOKE, EAST

R.C.H.M.	L.V.G.	Others
21	15	
22	15b	
23	17	
24	16	
25	15a	
S { 26	18	
27	19	
28	20	
29	21	
30	22	
31	23	
32	1	
33	7	
34	8	
35	8a	
36	9	
37	10	
38	4	
39	2	
40	3	
41	13	
42	13a	
43	12	
44	11	
T { 45	6	
46	5	
47	6b	
48	6a	
49	14	

STUDLAND

R.C.H.M.	L.V.G.	Others
29	9	v92
30	12	
U { 31	2b	
32	2c	
33	2a	
34	2d	
V { 35	4	
36	1	
37	2	
38	2e	
39	3	
40	6	
41	7	
42	8	

STURMINSTER MARSHALL

R.C.H.M.	L.V.G.	Others
46	1	v63

R.C.H.M.	L.V.G.	Others

SWANAGE

R.C.H.M.	L.V.G.	Others
81	1	
82	2	v93
83	3	
W 84	7	
85	7a	
86	Studland 5	
87	Studland 10	
88	Studland 11	
89	5	v94
90	6	v95

TURNERS PUDDLE

R.C.H.M.	L.V.G.
14	7
15	9
16	8
17	10
18	5
19	6
X 20	4
21	3
22	2
23	1
24	11

TYNEHAM

R.C.H.M.	L.V.G.	Others
14	18	v100
Y 15	15a	
16	15b	
17	15c	
18	15d	
19	16	
20	17	
21	14	
22	14a	
23	11	
24	19	
25	12	
26		
27	9	
28	10	
29	5	
30	7 & 6	
Z 31	4	
32	3	
33	2	
34	1c	
35	1b	
36	1a	
37	4a	

WAREHAM LADY ST. MARY

R.C.H.M.	L.V.G.
B 82	Arne 5
83	Arne 6
84	Arne 7

WAREHAM ST. MARTIN

R.C.H.M.	L.V.G.
AA 8	12
9	11
10	10
11	9
12	8
13	
14	7
15	6
16	3

WARMWELL

R.C.H.M.	L.V.G.
10	5

WEYMOUTH

R.C.H.M.	L.V.G.	Others
R.7 396	1	
397	2	
398	3	C41, CR13
399	4	
400	5	C40, CR12
401	6	C39, CR11
402	7	C37, CR9
403	8	C35, CR7
404	9	C38, CR10
405	10	C29, CR1
406	10a	
R.8 407	13	
408	12	
409	11	
410	14	
411		
412	15	m27 ?
413	16	m28 ?
414	17	m29 ?
415	Bincombe 36	
416	Bincombe 12	
417		
418		
R.13 419	22	
420	23	m3
421	24	
422	25	
R.14 423	26	
424	27	
425	28	
426	29	
427	30	
428	31	
429		
430	32	
431	33	
432	19	
433	18	
434	20	
435	34	m, pp. 7, 58–63

WHITCOMBE

R.C.H.M.	L.V.G.	Others
6	13a	
7	13	
8		
9	1	f22
10	1a	
R.11 11	2	
12	2a	
13	3	
14	4	
15	5	
16	6	
AB 17	7	
18		
19	8	
20	Broadmayne 9	
21	11	
22	9	
23	10	
24	12	

WINFRITH NEWBURGH

R.C.H.M.	L.V.G.
32	11
33	10
34	
35	
36	
37	
38	2
39	3
40	1a
41	1
AC 42	4
43	5
44	6
45	7
46	12
47	8
48	9

WINTERBOURNE ABBAS

R.C.H.M.	L.V.G.
AD 14	28
(see on) 15	27
16	26a
17	25
18	26
19	23c
20	23b
21	23a
22	24a-c
23	20
24	21-3
25	
26	19
27	18

R.C.H.M.	L.V.G.	Others

WINTERBOURNE ABBAS (*contd.*)

R.C.H.M.	L.V.G.	Others
AD (contd.) { 28	15	
29	16	
30	17	
31	8a	
32	35	
AE { 33		
34	8 ?	
35	7	
36	6	
37	5	
38	3	
39	4	
40	2	
41	2b	
42	2a	
AF { 43	29	
44	30	
45	31	
46	33	
47	34	
AQ 48	32	
49	1	
50	11	
51	13	
52	14	
AU { 53	10	
54	9	

WINTERBORNE CAME

R.C.H.M.	L.V.G.	Others
R.9 { 10	18	
11	17	
12	16	
13	15	
14	14	
15	13	
16	12	
17	21	
R.10 { 18	22	
19	23	
R.11 { 20	23a	
21	23b	
22	24	
23	24a	
24	25	
AG (see on) { 25	11	
26	1	
27	10	
28	9 & 8	
29	6	
30	7	
31	4	
32	3	
33	2	

WINTERBORNE CAME (*contd.*)

R.C.H.M.	L.V.G.	Others
AG (contd.) { 34	20	
35	19	m10 ?
36	37	
37	37a	C20 ?
38	26	
39	27	
40	28	
41	30	
42	31	
43	35	
44	36	
45	32	
46	33	
47	34	
48	31a	

WINTERBORNE HERRINGSTON

R.C.H.M.	L.V.G.	Others
3	3	
4	2	
5	1a	
6	1	C6

WINTERBORNE MONKTON

R.C.H.M.	L.V.G.	Others
AH { 5		
6	1b	C17
7	1c	
8	2a	
9	2	} v62 ?
10		

WINTERBORNE ST. MARTIN

R.C.H.M.	L.V.G.	Others
R.6 (see on) { 24	59	
25	60	
26	61	
27	62	
28	63	
29	64	
30	64d	
31	64c	
32	64b	
33	64a	
34	65	
35	66	
36	65a	
37	66a-b, & 67	
38		
39	68	
40	69	
41	70	
42	71	
43	71a	
44	72a	
45	72	

WINTERBORNE ST. MARTIN (*contd.*)

R.C.H.M.	L.V.G.	Others
R.6 (contd.) { 46	73	
47	74	
48	75	
49	75a	
50	76	
51	77	
R.7 { 52	78a	
53	78	
54	79	
55	80	
56	81	
57	82	
58	83	
59	84	
60	85	
61	86	
62	87	
63	88	
64		
65	89	
66	90	
67	Bincombe 60 f	
AI { 68	24	
69	25	
70	26	
71	27	
72	28	
73	29	
74	30	
75	36	
76	35a & b	
77	36a	
78	37	
79	39	
80	38	
81	39a	
AJ { 82	46	
83	45	
84	44	
85	43	
86	42a	
87	41a	
88	42	
89	41	
90	40	
91	40a-d	
AK { 92	47	
93	48	
94	48a	
95	48b	
96	49	
97	50	
98	53	
99	54	

WINTERBORNE ST. MARTIN (contd.)

R.C.H.M.	L.V.G.	Others
AL 100	55	
101	56	
102	57	
103	58	
104	52a	
105	52	
106	51	
AM 107	5	
108	4	
109	3	
110	2	
111	3a	
112	2a	
113	1	
AN 114	6	} m26, 30
115	7	} C24, 25
116	8	
117		
118		
AO 119	9a	C23
120	9	
121	10	
122	11	
123	12	
124	13	
125	16	C21
126	17	C22
127	14	
128	20	
129	15	
130	18	
131	19	
132	21	
133	22	
134	31	C15
135	32	C16
136	34	
AH 137	23	

WINTERBORNE ST. MARTIN (contd.)

R.C.H.M.	L.V.G.	Others
138	33	
139	34a	
140	34b	v72
141	92	

WINTERBOURNE STEEPLETON

R.C.H.M.	L.V.G.	Others
14	Little Bredy 24	
15		
R.5 16	31	
17	32	
18	33	
19	34	
20	38	
21	39	
22	40	
23	21	
24	44	
25	45	
26	46	
27	28	
28	29	
AP 29	30	
30	42	
31	43	
32	36	
AQ 33		
34	5	
35	8	
36	9	
37	10	
38	10b	
39	10a	
40	11	
41	12	
42	13	
43	14	
44	15	

WINTERBOURNE STEEPLETON (contd.)

R.C.H.M.	L.V.G.	Others
AS 45	18	
46	19c	
47	19a & b	
48	20	
49	16	
50	17	
51	22	
AT 52		
53	23	
54	26	
55	24	
56	25	
57	27	
AU 58	2	
59	1	
60	III & 48	
61	3	} m31-2
62	4	

WOODSFORD

R.C.H.M.	L.V.G.	Others
6		} m44-45
7	I	

WOOL

R.C.H.M.	L.V.G.	Others
44	4	
45	6	
46	1a	
47	1	
48	2	
49	3	

WORTH MATRAVERS

R.C.H.M.	L.V.G.	Others
34	3	v86
35	1	
36	2	

MOUNDS

The twenty-seven monuments listed here are mounds, of various forms, but have little else in common. A few might conceivably incorporate, or actually be, barrows,[1] though all those that can certainly or probably be so identified are described above. No purpose can be ascribed to the majority, but known or probable functions include rabbit warrens and windmill and beacon mounds. Some, e.g. the group of small mounds on Battle Plain (East Holme (12)), lack convincing parallels but the 'pillow mounds' (Church Knowle (29), Worth Matravers (32)) are of a kind found widespread over the country (see Sectional Preface, p. lxx).

---

[1] Seven were included by L. V. Grinsell in *Dorset Barrows* (1959); see Concordance, p. 483.

AFFPUDDLE

(64) MOUND (SY 89 SW; 82229165), on parish boundary with Turners Puddle. Possibly originally a small round barrow. Destroyed.

ARNE

(47) MOUND (SY 98 NW; 92328639) on level low-lying ground behind the New Inn, Stoborough. Diam. about 150 ft., ht. 18 ft. with flat top. This is probably a natural hillock scarped and altered in recent times on the N. and E. Early mediaeval pottery has been found here. (T. D. Reed, *The Rise of Wessex* (1947), 332.)

BERE REGIS

(117 a, b) MOUNDS, two (SY 89 SE), probably rabbit warrens, lie on either side of a flat-topped N.W.-S.E. ridge about 150 ft. above O.D. on Warren Heath, 2 miles S.S.E. of St. John the Baptist's Church.

(a) Ditched oval mound (85059130), immediately above steep S. slope 660 yds. W. of Warren House (Bere Regis (53)). Length N.W.-S.E. 140 ft., width 35 ft. Ht. 1½ ft. at N.W. end falling to 9 ins. at S.E. end. Ditch 12 ft. wide and 9 ins. deep along S.W. side and around N.W. end, probably continuing along N.E. side.

(b) Elongated mound with parallel sides (85159142), 165 yds. N.E. of (a) and similarly sited above a steep N.-facing slope. Formerly about 90 ft. long W.-E. and 15 ft. wide, now ploughed almost flat.

BINCOMBE

(75) LONG MOUND (SY 68 SE; 67868491), prominent at about 340 ft. above O.D. on the crest of a narrow ridge ½ mile N.W. of the church. Irregular, roughly wedge-shaped, about 90 ft. long, 40 ft. wide at widest on W., prolonged beyond attenuated E. end by arable scarping which also adds to maximum height of 14 ft. S. of the W. end. On Purbeck Sand; limestone rubble is exposed in places. Formerly amongst strip fields (Bincombe (11), Fig. p. 24).

CHURCH KNOWLE

(50) MOUND (SY 97 NW; 93147957), on S. edge of settlement area on Smedmore Hill (*see* Settlements, Church Knowle (55), Fig. p. 509). Length 22 ft. S.W.-N.E., width 18 ft., ht. 1 ft. Apparently consists of limestone rubble.

(51) MOUND (SY 98 SW; 93538224; Fig. opp. p. 509), on crest of Knowle Hill 665 yds. N.W. of St. Peter's Church. Length 60 ft. W.-E., width 30 ft., ht. 2 ft., with blunt ends. No ditch visible. It is possibly associated with the adjacent Iron Age 'A' settlement (Church Knowle (54)).

(52-3) MOUNDS, two, small and irregular (SY 98 SW; 94608236), about 10 yds. to 15 yds. E. of round barrow Church Knowle (41), at the E. end of Knowle Hill. The more westerly, (52), is crossed by the bank of a slight ditched enclosure, 30 ft. square and probably recent, lying to its N.

Austen described the mounds as barrows but their origin is unknown (*Purbeck Papers* II, 55).

PILLOW MOUNDS, six (SY 98 SW; 929820), between Ridgeway Hill and Knowle Hill, *see* parish inventory, Church Knowle (29), p. 48.

CORFE CASTLE

(220) MOUND (SY 98 SE; 95058035), at Blashenwell, *see* Corfe Castle (175), p. 96.

MOUND, 1½ ft. high, apparently of Romano-British debris, *see* Ancient Field Group (21).

MOUND, associated with limestone debris and Romano-British pottery (95067783), *see* Roman section, Corfe Castle (239).

CORFE MULLEN

(23) MOUNTAIN CLUMP or SOLDIERS' BARROW (SY 99 NE; 97439739) within 200 ft. ring contour, surmounted by trigonometrical station. Oval, 148 ft. W.-E. by 176 ft. N.-S., ht. 25 ft. Part at least appears artificial. Tree-covered.

A mound at SY 99299656 (LVG 2) was excavated in 1964 and found to be natural (Dorset *Procs.* LXXXVI (1964), 109-10).

HOLME, EAST

(12) MOUNDS, small, a large group (SY 98 NW; 90628532–90678531), lie N. of Battle Plain on Holme Heath. Austen (*Purbeck Papers* I, 233–8) described 120 in 1860 though he showed only 107 in his drawing (re-presented here). Forty-five could be plotted with certainty in recent years, lying in approximately parallel rows running from the crest down the S. shoulder of a gravel knoll (*see* introduction to round barrows E. Holme (9–11)). These are close enough to Austen's positions to show that the rest of his plan can be accepted as a rough guide to the lay-out in his day. (Fig. 482.)

Some of the mounds are only 20 ft. apart, centre to centre, but most are more widely spaced. All are very roughly circular and (with one exception, 6 ft. across) vary in diameter from 9 ft. to 15 ft. Twenty-nine are between 9 ft. and 12 ft. Ht. is generally 1 ft. to 1½ ft., though two are 9 ins. high and three are 2 ft. high. All are densely covered in heather and many are disturbed. The plantation banks and ditches shown by Austen, virtually the same as exist today, cut athwart the rows of mounds and one mound, on the S., is sliced.

The whole area was planted in Austen's day, as now, and he says 'the trees which had been planted on them were of much larger size than the generality of those upon the level ground'. He dug into many of the mounds and 'found that they all contained the remains of burned furze in the state of charcoal'.

R.C.H.M. excavated one of the mounds, (a), in 1956. It was found to be built of sods piled direct on an old ground surface. There was no ditch and no internal feature of any sort. The only find, of a rough flint scraper in the body of the mound, had no significance since similar artefacts can be picked

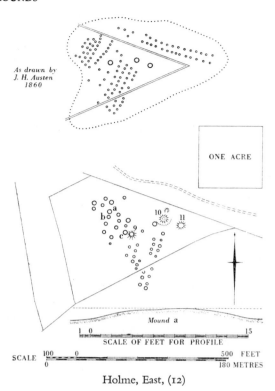

As drawn by
J. H. Austen
1860

ONE ACRE

Mound a

1   0   15
SCALE OF FEET FOR PROFILE

SCALE   100   0   500   FEET
        0   180 METRES

Holme, East, (12)

up on the heath around. There appeared to be the remains of at least four generations of trees. Professor Dimbleby, then of the Commonwealth Forestry Institute, examined pollen samples from a further mound, (b), (also barren of archaeological finds) and concluded that 'the raw humus was buried not later than mediaeval times and not earlier than the Iron Age'. He tended to favour an early place in this bracket. 'The land at that time was dominated by heather.'

Both the date and purpose of these mounds remain obscure. Mound (c) appears to lie over the tail of the Bronze Age barrow (9). A connection with tree planting seems possible but, according to Professor Dimbleby, unlikely.

KNIGHTON, WEST

(25) MOUND, kidney-shaped, irregular (SY 78 NW; 73638780), 460 yds. N.E. of the church and immediately S.E. of Common Plantation in boggy grassland over Reading Beds. Width about 66 ft., ht. about 2 ft.

LANGTON MATRAVERS

(41) WINDMILL MOUND (SZ 07 NW; 00907894), on summit of Coombe Hill, a small W. to E. ridge. Diam. 68 ft., ht. formerly over 3 ft., with slightly-hollowed flat top. Ditch 10 ft. wide and 1 ft. deep, broken by causeway on S. Ploughed.

LYTCHETT MATRAVERS

(38) 'WINDMILL BARROW', probable windmill mound (SY 99 NW; 93729774), on spine of slight ridge about 250 ft. above O.D. Pear-shaped, diams. 107 ft. W.-E. and 94 ft. N.-S. Ht. about 11 ft. Embanked circular depression about 45 ft. in diam. on top of mound, with spur to E.

MORDEN

(56) BEACON MOUND, possibly incorporating a round barrow (SY 99 NW; 90959532), on summit of Beacon Hill about 200 ft. above O.D. and visible from all directions over large area. Diam. about 45 ft., ht. 6 ft., with steep sides and flat top about 18 ft. across. Modern slit trench shows clay earth in section. Noted as beacon by I. Taylor (Estate Map, 1773–7).

OWERMOIGNE

MOUNDS, two (SY 78 NE), near Moigne Court (Owermoigne (2), Fig. p. 186).

(34) (77008573). Approximately rectangular, 40 ft. by 30 ft., with rounded corners, irregular sloping sides, and flat top. Ht. about 3½ ft.

(35) (77008567). Length about 70 ft. N.-S., ht. about 5 ft. Approximately rectangular W. angles, but no clear E. side. Roughly flat top. Much disturbed, formerly in wooded garden.

PORTLAND

(97) MOUND (SY 67 SE; 68357019), on S. slope near bottom of broad gully. Diam. about 110 ft., ht. 15 ft. Flat-topped but irregular, with shelter dug into S.W. Not shown on Tithe Map (1841), when in 'Under Hedge' furlong, though 'Rough Barrow' furlong adjacent on S.

STEEPLE

(26) MOUND (SY 98 SW; 91248090), among settlement remains (Steeple (16), p. 273).

STUDLAND

MOUNDS, thirteen, on S. Haven peninsula associated with earthen circles, see Enclosures, Studland (43).

TYNEHAM

(38) MOUND (SY 88 SE; 88348027), 250 yds. S.E. of St. Mary's Church adjacent to village closes (Tyneham (8), see plan in pocket, Part 2); under 200 ft. above O.D. on ground falling gently W. Square, with sides each 27 ft., ht. 1 ft. Grass-covered but containing stones.

WORTH MATRAVERS

MOUNDS, two (SY 97 NE), on top of broad ridge between Winspit and Seacombe Bottoms in an area formerly covered by strip fields (see Worth Matravers (29), p. 415).

(37) (97907704). Diam. 36 ft., ht. 1½ ft. Turf-covered.

(38) (97977698), 50 yds. S.E. of (37). Diam. 45 ft., ht. 2½ ft., showing many stones, perhaps indicating origin as spoil from field clearance. Overgrown.

PILLOW MOUNDS, three (SY 97 NE; 98427770), at Eastington, see Worth Matravers (32), p. 415.

MOUNDS: CONCORDANCE

Under the heading *L.V.G.* are the parish numbers of mounds as included in L. V. Grinsell, *Dorset Barrows* (1959), and not here considered barrows.

	R.C.H.M.	L.V.G.
AFFPUDDLE	64	12
BERE REGIS	117a	47
CHURCH KNOWLE	51	1
CORFE MULLEN	23	1
KNIGHTON, WEST	25	2
LYTCHETT MATRAVERS	38	1
PORTLAND	97	3

HILL-FORTS

Eight earthworks in the area covered by this Volume are classified as hill-forts. These, with one possible exception, Woolsbarrow, Bloxworth (44), all belong to the Iron Age. Bindon, W. Lulworth (53), is not a true hill-fort but has some comparable features and can be regarded as a gigantic promontory enclosure of the same period. Only Maiden Castle, Winterborne St. Martin (142), has been intensively investigated and even there only a very small proportion of the interior was excavated. Three others have been sampled by excavation and only Woodbury, Bere Regis (118), and Woolsbarrow have never produced significant finds. All these earthworks began as simple enclosures with one main bank and ditch. Such univallate construction with a berm between bank and ditch is mostly attributable to the Iron Age 'A' culture, an attribution confirmed at Bindon, Chalbury (Bincombe (76)), Maiden Castle and Poundbury (Dorchester (172)). Multiplication of the defences by the succeeding 'B' and 'C' cultures was normal. The univallate fort of Bulbury (Lytchett Minster (30)), however, produced a find of La Tène objects probably deposited during the 1st century A.D.; the original construction of the work is undated, but it is the only hill-fort in S.E. Dorset that does not occupy an obviously commanding position.

In size and scale the defences vary from an insignificant ditch surrounding a gravel plateau of only two acres at Woolsbarrow to the multiple ditches, some still 50 ft. deep, and complex entrances at Maiden Castle, 47 acres in internal area and the most massively defended prehistoric earthwork in Britain. The excavator of Maiden Castle thought that the multiplication of ramparts and ditches there and elsewhere was due to the needs of defence in sling warfare. This view perhaps needs to be modified not only because the increased depth improves defence against any sort of attack but because in Gaul large hill-forts of the same period were generally univallate. There is, however, little evidence for archery in the Iron Age and the Chesil Beach was certainly a ready encouragement to the lavish use of sling-stones. The area within the Bindon rampart, about 400 acres, nearly twice that of Ham Hill, Somerset, the largest hill-fort in the British Isles, seems to have been a collecting area for immigrants from the Continent at some early phase of the Iron Age. As such it is perhaps best compared with Hengistbury Head, Hants.

Details of construction and development are best seen at Maiden Castle. The box rampart characteristic of Iron Age 'A' was, however, found in variant form at Chalbury, revetted with stone which was available inside or immediately outside the hill-fort. At Maiden Castle such stone revetment walls occur in a later phase but the stone had to come from at least 2 miles distant. Excavation of the exceptionally complex E. entrance to Maiden Castle demonstrated clearly how archaeological techniques can reveal the evolution of a site and finally link it with a firm historical fact, the Roman invasion of A.D. 43. The entrance to Bindon is the only other example to have been excavated. Its inturned arms are notably long, about 60 ft., though inturns 82 ft. long were alleged by Edward Cunnington to have existed at Bulbury. Outlying defences occur 180 yds. E. of Flower's Barrow (E. Lulworth (40)) where a dyke spans the ridge leading to

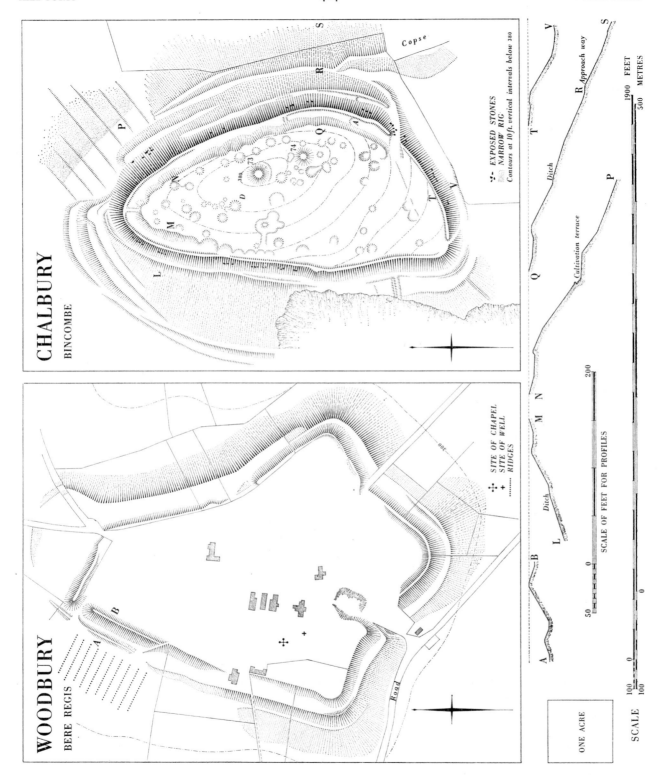

CHALBURY

BINCOMBE

Copse

EXPOSED STONES
NARROW RIG
Contours at 10ft. vertical intervals below 380

WOODBURY

BERE REGIS

SITE OF CHAPEL
SITE OF WELL
RIDGES

Road

V
T
Approach way
R
Ditch
S
Cultivation terrace
Q
P
1900 FEET
500 METRES

B
M N
Ditch
L
A
200
SCALE OF FEET FOR PROFILES
50 0
0

SCALE
100 0 100

ONE ACRE

it. There are probable examples of such cross-ridge dykes covering the approaches to hill-forts elsewhere in Wessex (as at White Sheet Hill, Kilmington, Wilts.) and a number of such dykes facing outwards from an Iron Age 'A' settlement on Knowle Hill (Church Knowle (54, 56)) might easily have been developed into a small hill-fort.

Definite signs of occupation such as hut-platforms and pit sinkings are visible now only in Chalbury and Flower's Barrow. Most have been extensively disturbed by later activities. Ploughing has obliterated surface traces in Maiden Castle but excavation and analogy suggest that its interior would have been full of such remains. That the nature of the occupation was one of permanent settlement was shown by its continuation until c. A.D. 70. At Poundbury, also heavily ploughed, some test excavation produced no sign of interior structures. All the certain houses that have been found were round or polygonal and only exceptionally as much as 30 ft. in diameter. Some stone footings were found in Maiden Castle as well as Chalbury. One such structure (Chalbury, 'D') was built in a quarry pit (cf. Church Knowle (54)). Storage pits at Maiden Castle were occasionally stone-lined. Many were beehive shaped and about 6 ft. deep, suggesting a relationship with those found in the Isle of Portland and known as 'Portland beehives' (see Roman section, p. 606; Geologists' Association, Procs. VIII (1883-4), 404-10). Internal roads were found only in Maiden Castle. One of them led towards the largest of the hut-circles within which had been built, in the late 4th century A.D., a hut associated with a Romano-British temple. One of the three roads in the comparable hill-fort of Hod Hill (Dorset III, forthcoming) led to a structure which Sir Ian Richmond's excavation has shown to have been of pre-eminent importance at the time of the Conquest. No early ponds or wells have been proved and it seems that water, if not fetched from the nearest outside source, was generally collected from eaves drips and the like, though Sir Mortimer Wheeler found water channels leading into pits at Maiden Castle. The only cemetery certainly associated with these hill-forts is at the E. entrance to Maiden Castle.

'Celtic' fields now touch only Bindon and are not necessarily contemporary. Others lie very close to Flower's Barrow (Ancient Field Group (17)). Mediaeval ploughing destroyed any that may have existed near Chalbury or Maiden Castle and those 1 mile N. of the latter (R. E. M. Wheeler, Maiden Castle (1943), Plate LXX) are now known to lie around extensive Romano-British 'open' settlements (Fig. p. 494), though they could well have had Iron Age origins.

It seems certain that some of these forts were centres of political authority and expressed the power of their builders, but there are no clues to the limits of territories ruled from them (cf. Fig. opp. p. 634). The Roman invasion put an end to the power of the rulers of those hill-forts still in use, but not all were immediately or finally abandoned. Within Maiden Castle a Romano-British temple was built in the late 4th century, and in Chalbury and Poundbury scatters of pottery indicate at least casual Romano-British use.

In different ways the forts probably also sheltered men and animals during later periods. A pagan Saxon burial came from the Long Mound in Maiden Castle. Woodbury was the site of a sheep fair. At the time of the Armada Sir John Norris seems to have considered the hill-forts near Dorchester as 'divers old intrenched places which might be made stronger at a small charge but to little purpose' (B.M., Harl. MS. 3324, art. 6, quoted by Hutchins II, 828). Ploughing of the interiors probably began early and was noted at Maiden Castle in about 1610. In two cases damage has been more drastic. Three-quarters of the interior of Woolsbarrow has been quarried away by gravel diggers and at least one third of Flower's Barrow has collapsed seawards, owing to coastal erosion.

BERE REGIS

(118) WOODBURY (SY 89 SE; 856948) is a contour hill-fort which occupies the entire flat top of the gravel-capped spur called Woodbury Hill 360 ft. above O.D., ½ mile E. of the parish church. The area enclosed is about 12 acres.

The defences, though now much broken down, consist of a main inner rampart, at best 40 ft. wide and 19 ft. high above a single ditch, 5 ft. deep and 30 ft. wide, and a relatively massive counterscarp bank up to 26 ft. across, beyond which the ground falls steeply on the E. side and greater part of the S. side. On the N.W. there is a sloping shelf between the ramparts and the steep face of the hill. On this shelf is a series of rather flat-topped parallel ridges 1 ft. high, 10 yds. or so wide and about 50 yds. long, divided by furrows about 4 ft. wide. These are more likely to be connected with the annual sheep fairs once held in the hill-fort (Hutchins I, 135) than with agriculture. To the N. a gently dipping but fairly narrow saddle connects the spur with the main ridge. At this vulnerable point the outer bank seems to have been thrust about 70 yds. forward from the main rampart but the remains have been heavily ploughed. In the lane to the N.E. is a double fall which might mark the line of a ditch but this cannot be confirmed.

The present road in from the S.W. probably follows the line of an original entrance, as possibly does that at the N.E.; but all the other breaks in the defences seem to be secondary. The surface of the interior is uneven in many places but it is impossible to detect anything certainly ancient. The chapel shown on the plan certainly existed in the early 15th century and its footings were still traceable in the late 18th century (Hutchins, *ibid.*). The nearby well was traditionally associated with it.

BINCOMBE

(76) CHALBURY (SY 68 SE; 695838; Plate 216) is a contour hill-fort with single rampart and external ditch, the former augmented by an interior quarry ditch, or line of quarry pits, running inside it for $\frac{3}{5}$ of its length. There is one original entrance at the S.E. The interior, of about $8\frac{1}{2}$ acres, shows extensive signs of occupation. The rampart encloses the domed crest of a knoll, partly Lower Purbeck Limestone and partly Portland Sands, standing prominently at 380 ft. above sea level in a controlling position at the N. end of a ridge (Rimbury) which splits a valley leading inland from Weymouth Bay (Figs. pp. 24, 484). Excavation by Miss M. Whitley in 1939 has shown that it belongs to Iron Age 'A' (*Ant. J.* XXIII (1943), 98–121).

Strip lynchets (Bincombe (11)) run into the defences on the N., and on the N.E. lie at their foot along the steep scarp beneath them; on the E. side are a narrow cultivation terrace and a terraced approach, both of uncertain date. The external ditch running N. from outside the entrance seems to have been converted into a cultivation terrace for much of its length. A large modern quarry bites almost up to the ditch on the W. and it is possible that shallow quarrying of a date later than that of the original occupation might be partly responsible for some of the more irregular sinkings inside the hill-fort. The whole is now pasture. The nearest source of water at present is a spring $\frac{1}{2}$ a mile to the S.

The rampart stands 1 ft. to 3 ft. above the interior except near the centre of the E. side, where it is little more than a scarped edge; its height above the external ditch averages about 21 ft. Where excavated it was seen to have external and internal limestone walls retaining the soil and stone core. Internally there was also, at the S.E., a stone kerb at the tail of the rampart. Externally, convenient stone outcrops were utilised in the structure of the wall and there was a berm 5 ft. to 9 ft. wide. The flat-bottomed ditch was cut into the bed-rock at a variable distance below this. For the greater part the ditch has a terraced appearance. On the E. for 40 yds. N. from the entrance it is rather irregular, some 2 ft. deep.

The internal quarry ditch runs N. from the entrance as a parallel-sided ditch for 115 yds. It was originally about 18 ft.

wide and 5 ft. deep but was allowed to silt up quickly and used as a sheltered occupation area. A 'causeway' blocks this run of ditch and thereafter it is supplanted by a series of quarry pits, broken at the extreme N. by another 'causeway', here found to consist largely of sand. About 100 yds. S.W. of this, the well-marked line of pits gives place to a series of much shallower scalloped depressions which ends abruptly after a further 65 yds. There is, however, no apparent correlation between the size and different treatment of the quarry ditch or pits and the dimensions of the rampart immediately adjacent. A flattened strip, 55 ft. and more wide, lies inside the S. rampart, the slight scarp defining it on the N. side being a continuation of that N. of the entrance.

The entrance is a simple gap with slight hollowing, perhaps partly cut rather than worn, immediately inside. A ramped approach might be original. A track climbing diagonally across the rampart 120 yds. S.W. of the entrance is **not** original.

Two small banks run downhill from outside the ditch. One, from the natural shoulder at the S.W., is 15 ft. wide and 1 ft. high and ends after 33 yds., before reaching the quarry edge. The second, 75 yds. to the N., has a slight ditch on the S. side and is cut by the quarry after 25 yds.

The interior is pocked by numerous roughly circular depressions and weakly-defined platforms. The latter, of which there are 30 or more, appear largely to be ranged around the perimeter, though the hut 'D', built in a shallow Iron Age quarry, was notably high up the slope. Only one platform, 20 yds. S. of the northern 'causeway' across the quarry ditch, had a bank.

The most irregular depressions might be quarries of any date, but if of the Iron Age are likely—as at 'D'—to have been put to some use. The smaller circular depressions up to about 15 ft. across, of which there are at least 20, probably represent original storage pits. There are two main groups, one N. of hut 'D' and one just W. of round barrow Bincombe (74). The only excavated example (in the northern group) was round, 5 ft. in diameter and 4 ft. deep, with straight sides cut into the rock. Both of the Bronze Age barrows (73) and (74), set so prominently on the summit of the hill, were apparently respected.

The excavation of the hill-fort was limited to the following features:—the rampart, ditch and quarry ditch 25 yds. N. of the entrance (site 'A'), the rampart, quarry ditch and causeway across it at the northern tip of the hill-fort (site 'C'), occupation layers with post-holes, probably a hut, in the quarry ditch at site 'A', building 'D', two scooped-out platforms with no signs of structure and few finds, and one storage pit. The building 'D', partly stone-walled, was the only site completely excavated in the interior: it was odd in that, despite abundant evidence of occupation across an internal diameter of 33 ft., it seemed to have neither hearth, entrance nor post-holes.

Apart from a Late Bronze Age layer buried under the rampart at the extreme N., a thin scatter of Romano-British potsherds at site 'D' and a fragment of samian ware in the ditch, the finds were all of Iron Age 'A', exhibiting two phases, the earlier having the finer specimens of haematite pottery. Hut 'A' belonged to the earlier phase and 'D' to the later.

Other finds included a small tanged iron knife, bone 'gouges' (cf. p. 499), a very small annular blue-glass bead, fragments of a bronze ring, a bronze bracelet or ear-ring, bronze binding and rivets, a piece of a saddle-quern, charred wheat (identified as *Triticum vulgare* by Prof. Percival), a spindle-whorl and sling-stones. There were also 11 worked flints, including an end-scraper and borer, of somewhat uncertain date but apparently stratified with the Iron Age material. Scatters of human bones were found, but only a few animal bones—including ox and sheep.

BLOXWORTH

(44) WOOLSBARROW (SY 89 SE; 893925; Plate 212), on Bloxworth Heath and now in a State Forest midway between the Sherford River and a tributary of the Piddle, both ½ mile distant, is the smallest hill-fort in South-east Dorset. Its anomalous form makes its date uncertain.

A single bank with inner ditch surrounds a gravel knoll some 20 ft. below its flat top, enclosing an area of some 2¼ acres. Though the highest point is only 220 ft. above O.D. it domin-ates the surrounding heathland, which falls sharply on all sides except on the S.E., where a simple gap entrance leads to a natural saddle connecting the hilltop with a lower spur.

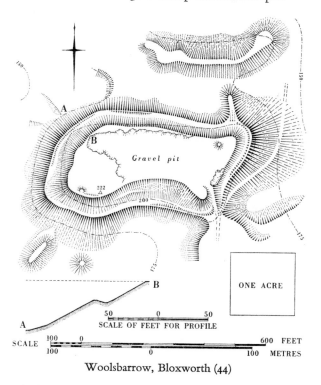

Woolsbarrow, Bloxworth (44)

The whole site has been much disturbed. Most of the interior has been quarried away to a depth of some feet, exposing a well-formed podsol, but there is no evidence that a bank ever stood on the edge of the inner scarp. The mounds in the S.W. and N.E. angles are probably no more than the residue of

quarrying; the N.E. mound was dug by a Mr. Groves of Wareham without result (Warne, *Ancient Dorset*, (1872), 87). Soil slip has largely filled the ditch and the bank, at its most prominent, is about 18 ft. across and only 2½ ft. above the ditch bottom. A modern trackway obscures the original form of the entrance. The 'tumuli' shown on some maps around the site are probably natural, the result of differential erosion (Hutchins I, 181).

DORCHESTER

(172) POUNDBURY (SY 69 SE; 682911; Plate 212), a hill-fort of 13½ acres, lies approximately ⅔ mile W.N.W. of St. Peter's Church, Dorchester, on a bluff of the Upper Chalk at about 300 ft. above O.D. (see Fig. p. 494). Its size and trapezoidal shape are not, apparently, much dependent on its situation. The defences now consist of two banks and two ditches of similar size but variably damaged. Where best preserved, the inner bank is 66 ft. wide and 18 ft. above its ditch. There are only very faint traces of an inner quarry ditch. The interior slopes gently N. and E. but the ground outside falls precipitously to the River Frome on the N., gently away on the S. and E. (where a shallow combe divides the fort from Dorchester), and rises slightly from it on the W. Excavation has shown two main structural phases attributed to Iron Age 'A' and Iron Age 'C' (*Ant. J.* xx (1940), 429–448).

In the Roman period the aqueduct for *Durnovaria* (see Roman section, p. 585) was taken along the outer ditch on the N. and apparently involved the destruction of the outer rampart for part of the E. side. Other activity in the Romano-British period[1] is testified by the considerable spread of 3rd and 4th-century pottery and some of the gaps through the defences on the S., S.W., and N.W. may belong to this period. The earthwork is now used for pasture but has been extensively damaged. In 1855 construction of the railway tunnel defaced the defences on the N. and E.; during the war of 1939–45 a rough wide trench with spoil heaps on its outer side was made along the outer base of the main rampart for most of the W. and S. sides and at the S.E. angle; portions of the summit of the main rampart on W. and S. have been flattened, and the S.E. angle has been cut into from the inside. The interior has been ploughed and this probably involved some prior destruction of the round barrow in the S.W. quarter of the interior (Dorchester (170)). An Early Bronze Age sherd and one of Rinyo-Clacton ware (in D.C.M.) were found in 1947 in slight ditches sealed by a turf line under the main bank near the S.W. corner (Dorset *Procs.* LXXXVI (1964), 106–7).

In 1939 Miss K. M. Richardson dug a single trench through both ramparts and ditches where best preserved, on the W. (just S. of JK on the plan), and further tested details by smaller cuts. These showed two phases of construction. The main rampart had at first been faced by a vertical timber palisade (where shown on her plan not parallel with the existing ditch), set back some 4½ ft. from the lip of a funnel-shaped ditch

---

[1] For Roman remains to E., *see* pp. 570, 583.

29 ft. wide and 14 ft. deep, its bottom a slot little more than 1 ft. wide and 2 ft. deep. There was no indication of any rear revetment to the rampart and the layers all tilted up towards the front. Some of the material seems to have been obtained from an internal quarry ditch.

This primary bank had become grass-covered before being enlarged and converted to glacis form. A second bank (also of glacis form) with external V-shaped ditch was added on the outside. Fresh material, dug largely from a new and deeper internal quarry ditch, was piled in horizontal strata against the inside of the first bank. A mass of chalk blocks capping this was held at the forward edge by a revetment of limestone dry-walling built on the surface of the old bank. An unbroken turf line over the silting of the ditch showed that it had not been

recut. The new, outer, bank was of simple dump construction, its ditch of approximately the same size as the inner one but without the narrow slot at the bottom. In section the vertical height from the crest of the present inner rampart to the old turf line over the silt in the original ditch was approximately the same—22 ft.—as that from the crest of the outer rampart to the bottom of its open ditch. A cut section drawn by the railway surveyor S. of the present tunnel entrance during excavation of its approaches in 1855 showed the aqueduct and other substantial alterations to the outer defences but generally agrees with the above results. 'Ridgeway stone' (probably from the Iron Age 'C' revetment) was also found in the upper fill of the inner ditch (drawing in D.C.M.).

Although no pottery was found in the early filling of the

POUNDBURY
DORCHESTER

ONE ACRE

AREAS SCARPED AGAINST TANK ATTACK IN 1940
+ 4th CENTURY COIN HOARD

SCALE OF FEET FOR PROFILES
10   0   50

SCALE   100   0   1200   FEET
         100   0   300   METRES

BLOXWORTH. (44) Woolsbarrow, from S.W.

DORCHESTER. (172) Poundbury, from N.E.

CHURCH KNOWLE. Knowle Hill, from N.W., with (54) Settlement on summit.

PLATE 213

HILL-FORT, etc.

(*Phot.: G. W. G. Allen*)

WINTERBORNE ST. MARTIN. (142) Maiden Castle and (23) Long Mound, looking E., during excavation 1934–8.

WINTERBORNE ST. MARTIN. (142) Maiden Castle, looking W., showing also, to S.E., cropmarks of round barrows (Winterborne Monkton 9, 10).   (*Phot.: Camb. Univ.*)

PLATE 215   HILL-FORT, etc.

Ground view, from N.

Aerial view, from E., showing also (41) Dyke and 'Celtic' fields of Ancient Field Group (17).

LULWORTH, EAST. (40) Flower's Barrow.   (*Air Phot.: Min. of Defence, Air Force Dept.*)

Ground view, from N.

Aerial view, from E., showing also (11b) Strip fields.   *(Phot.: Camb. Univ.)*

BINCOMBE. (76) Chalbury.

PLATE 217

STONES

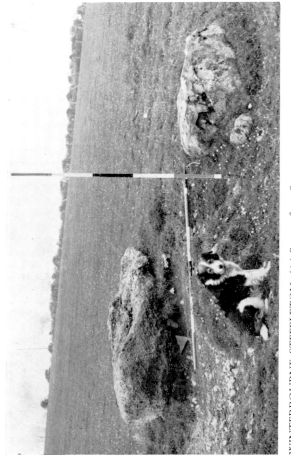

WINTERBOURNE STEEPLETON. (65) Stones, from S.

WINTERBOURNE ABBAS. (56) Broad Stone, from S.E.

STEEPLE. (27) Harpstone, from E.

first ditch it seems likely that the primary defences were uni-vallate and of Iron Age 'A'. The remodelling of the defences probably belongs to Hawkes's Southern Third C culture—sometime after the middle of the 1st century B.C. The excavator's very tentative suggestion that the limestone revetment wall on the forward crest of the inner rampart might reflect a Belgic technique now seems unsupported by the lack of true Belgic pottery. The distribution of 'C' finds in the ditch-fills indicated a long period of usage during this phase, though some 38 trial holes, 3 ft. square, widely distributed over much of the interior, produced no evidence for permanent occupation.

LULWORTH, EAST

(40) FLOWER'S BARROW (SY 88 SE; 864805; Plate 215) is a hill-fort situated between 460 ft. and 567 ft. above O.D. on the cliff edge at the extreme W. end of the Purbeck Hills, known here (because of the hill-fort) as Rings Hill. The subsoil is Upper Chalk with out-cropping sands and clays of the Corallian Beds. Probably a third or more of the original hill-fort has collapsed seaward as a result of coastal erosion, which had already taken place by 1744 (note by Edward Weld in D.C.R.O.). There remain three sides of an enclosure with two main banks and ditches and an original entrance to the S.E. The whole earthwork covers about 15½ acres. Occupation platforms are visible along the N.-facing slope of the interior. The ground falls away very steeply on the W., N. and S.E. but only very gently along the ridge to the E. where, 180 yds. away, a dyke (41) spans three-quarters of the ridge top.

The present earthwork is clearly the product of at least two main phases of construction. The inner enclosure, still 6 acres in area, has a rampart up to 30 ft. wide and in places 30 ft. high above its present ditch bottom and, inside it, a broad quarry ditch which is not, however, continued S. of the entrance. The end of the rampart N. of the original entrance gap is slightly inturned. A counterscarp bank lies immediately beyond the main ditch on the W. and N. but not on the E. At the N.W. angle of the inner enclosure the counterscarp bank is met by the main outer rampart but a later broad track has been cut through at this point. The outer rampart is separated from the counterscarp bank on the N. side by a berm of uneven width averaging 15 ft. to 20 ft., except at the N.E. corner where a bend in the outer rampart reduces it to 6 ft. The space between ramparts increases to 100 ft. on the E. and 180 ft. on the W. Within this area on the E. is a stretch 200 ft. long of low uneven bank following the alignment of the ramparts and situated mid-way between the inner ditch and the outer rampart. It has no visible ditch and its origin is unsure. On the steep slope to the N.W. the outer rampart is scarcely more than a scarp, rising some 33 ft. above its ditch bottom, but on the more level ground to the E. it is a true bank standing 8 ft. above the ground behind it and 20 ft. above the ditch bottom. On the S.E. this rampart curves towards the cliff edge and opposite the inner entrance is a gap, probably a mutilated original entrance, facing S.E.

F

The interior of Flower's Barrow rises gently to the E. and S., on which side nearly half of the remaining area has subsided to a maximum of 12 ft. behind the main cliff fall. A dozen or so roughly elliptical platforms are traceable in the N. half, concentrated towards the E. These have been levelled 2 ft. or 3 ft. into the slope and can probably be regarded as hut sites or working areas (cf. Chalbury, Bincombe (76)). There is now no surface indication of pits but one was excavated in 1939. It lay some 30 yds. inside the entrance and measured about 3 ft. in all directions; it produced bone refuse, a few sling-stones and about 60 sherds 'all probably of Iron Age B' (J. B. Calkin, Dorset Procs. LXX (1948), 44). In the early 19th century a skeleton, said to be of abnormal length, was discovered just beneath the surface of the inner rampart (J. F. Pennie, Tale of a Modern Genius (1827), II, 85).

The remains suggest a development from a simple univallate fort to a larger and stronger structure. The Phase I fort comprised either (a) the present inner rampart on the W. and E. and the outer rampart on the N. or (b) the present inner rampart on the E. and the outer on the N. and W. Both theories depend on the bend in the N. side of the outer rampart near its N.E. corner and the corresponding very sharp angle of the N.E. corner of the inner rampart. That the original rampart probably became part of the present outer rampart on the N. side is explained by the very steep slope here. For the possible relationship of the hill-fort to 'Celtic' fields see Ancient Field Group (17).

Cross-ridge dyke (41), on the ridge 180 yds. E. of the hill-fort, is probably an outwork. It runs parallel to the E. ramparts for nearly 300 ft. beginning a little below the edge of the steep slope on the S. but ending some 80 ft. short of the edge of the less steep N. slope, with no indication that it ever continued farther N. As it is unbroken by any original cut, traffic must have passed round it on the N. side where there is now a terraced approach track. Where best preserved the bank of the dyke is 20 ft. wide at its base and stands 2½ ft. above the ground on the W. and 5 ft. above its ditch, which is approximately 15 ft. wide at the lip. (R.A.F. V.A.P. CPE/UK, 1821: 5427.)

LULWORTH, WEST

(53) IRON AGE EARTHWORKS, on Bindon Hill and near West Lulworth village (SY 87 NW, 88 SW; 82227992–84808021). The main defences, a bank and ditch facing N., 1⅜ miles long, were apparently intended to enclose an area of about 400 acres including Lulworth Cove, the coastal shelf and the hog-backed chalk hill, 560 ft. high. At a later stage a N. to S. bank (c) was commenced which, with a terrace above Lulworth Cove probably indicating an incomplete ditch, enclosed the western 24 acres of Bindon Hill. Thirdly a cross-ridge dyke (b) was made to cut off 12 acres at the W. tip of the hill. Both the main defences and these subsidiary earthworks are probably unfinished. Their form suggests that different gangs worked simultaneously. There is little doubt that all were built by people of the Iron Age 'A' culture, although only small portions have been excavated (for

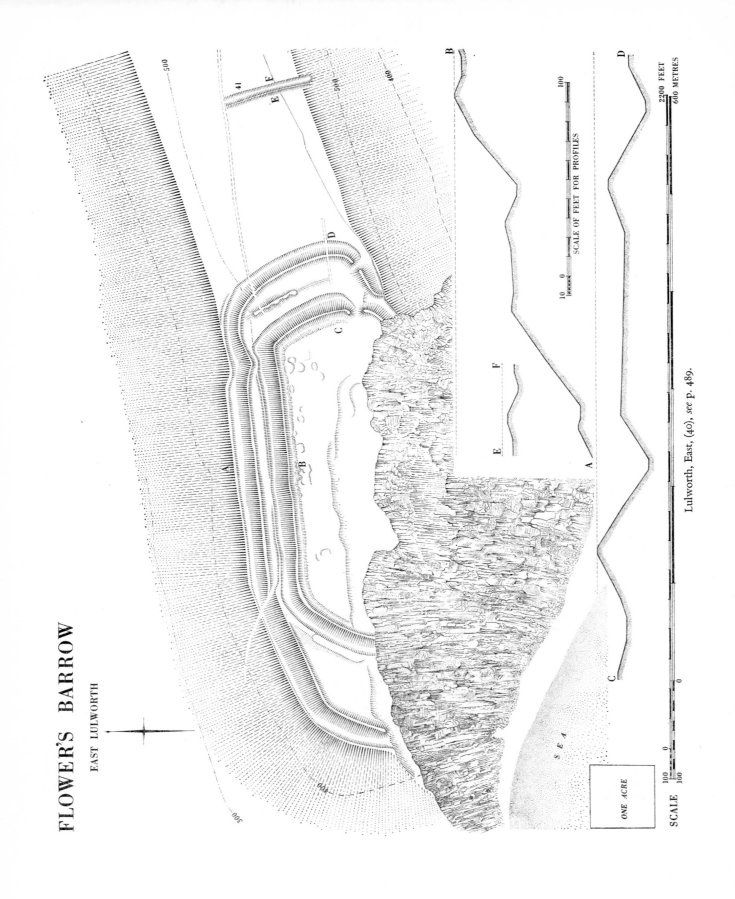

FLOWER'S BARROW

EAST LULWORTH

ONE ACRE

SCALE

SCALE OF FEET FOR PROFILES

2200 FEET
600 METRES

Lulworth, East, (40), see p. 489.

R.C.H.M. in 1950, *see* R. E. M. Wheeler, *Ant. J.* XXXIII (1953), 1–13).

The situation and arrangement of the earthworks suggest that they were the work of immigrants. The main defences, which have an entrance like that of a hill-fort, face inland covering the good natural harbour of Lulworth Cove. A stream runs into the Cove from the W. through a sheltered valley, and the undulating coastal shelf E. of the Cove is fertile. 'Celtic' fields of Ancient Field Group (16), on the N. slope of Bindon Hill, are probably later than the earthworks, which they only adjoin at one point W. of the entrance. The hill-fort of Flower's Barrow (E. Lulworth (40)) is 1 mile to the E. but there is no evidence that the Bindon earthworks were ever linked to it, as suggested by Warne (*Ancient Dorset*, 41–2, 64). Between the two, on the cliff edge 1170 yds. E. of Cockpit Head, is a slight terrace, possibly a length of ditch, but even if this is ancient it is much more likely to have been related to an independent enclosure.

In the 13th century A.D. both the 'dike of Julius Caesar' on Bindon Hill and the 'dike to Starhole (Stairhole)' were recognised as boundaries (P.R.O., *Calendar of Charter Rolls*, II, 2116–7). In 1770 hedges apparently ran along the cross-dyke, and along the main rampart between the cross-dyke and the entrance and for almost ¼ mile E. of the entrance to a point from which there are traces of a bank running S. (J. Sparrow, Map of Weld Estate (1770), in D.C.R.O.). All the earthworks are now under grass and the eastern two-thirds of Bindon Hill is in a firing range. Only 4 acres of the ridge-top immediately E. of the cross-dyke seem ever to have been ploughed, but on the coastal shelf any traces of Iron Age occupation or fields have been obliterated by ploughing, much of it in the 19th century.

The main defences. At the extreme W. a bank and ditch runs N.N.E. for 300 ft. from a crumbled area on the cliff edge above Stairhole. The bank, about 35 ft. wide and 2 ft. high, is separated by a very marked berm 18 ft. across from the ditch which is 35 ft. wide and 3 ft. deep. The berm perhaps indicates lack of finish. This stretch is much disturbed on the miniature golf course.

N.E. of the village a bank and ditch continues the same line up the steep slope of as much as 25°. The ditch is larger than in the previous length and there is no berm (*see* profile FF). Complete breaks in the line indicate that the work is unfinished, especially N.E. of FF (*cf.* cross-dyke (b)), and it ends in an isolated mound-like fragment (a).

From this point irregular earthworks run N. and then E. along the hill-top to the cross-dyke. They seem to belong to a univallate defence, apparently unfinished. This is clearly shown at the N.W. angle and further E. (profiles GG, HH), where a small bank rises above a scarp and a small ditch. In places the bank is set back leaving a berm while the ditch is interrupted by several original causeways. Behind the bank is

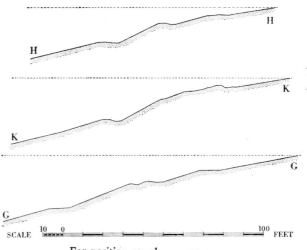

For position *see* plan, opp. p. 492.

a series of dumps forming a very irregular inner bank which is met by the cross-dyke at a point where a hedge (shown on the 1770 map) crosses the earthwork from the N. Irregular quarrying occurs uphill from the line of dumps.

Between the cross-dyke and the inturned entrance the irregular inner bank is smaller and set a little farther northwards. Its inside face is very steep and outside it is a shelf, in some places with a berm instead of an outer bank (profile KK). The ditch varies in form and size. Cross-bank (c) butts against the inner bank, crossing the small quarry pits behind it.

The entrance is a gap 50 ft. wide between banks projecting internally for 60 ft. and converging slightly at their S. ends. Although these do not look unfinished, excavation produced no sign of a gate and only an incomplete pattern of post-holes. A terrace-way which approaches the entrance from the N.E. and cuts through its N.W. angle is unlikely to be original.

The defences to the E. of the entrance at first appear smoother and less disjointed, although the bank is small and varies in height, while a berm is only visible in places. Further E., however, there are considerable variations for long stretches. Near round barrow W. Lulworth (43) sporadic inner quarry pits are replaced by a sharply-defined, flat-bottomed inner 'ditch', 10 ft. across, behind a bank only 10 ft. wide set on the lip of the outer ditch. Along the bottom of the 'ditch' runs a slight bank and ditch which could be a marking-out feature. S. of the 'ditch' a scarp rises at most 2 ft. to a very slight inner bank. For about ¼ mile E. of barrow (43) there are fairly continuous quarry pits and, 216 yds. further E., the outer ditch comes to a positive end N.N.E. of barrow (45). Thereafter for the final 750 yds. to Cockpit Head there is only a slight bank with an inner 'ditch' and occasional quarry pits on either side.

Structural and dating evidence mainly came from a cutting across the defences 50 ft. E. of the entrance at (BIN 2). A palisade trench 2 ft. wide dug 2 ft. deep into the chalk 20 ft. N. of the present outer crest of the rampart had been deliberately re-filled and was sealed with turves, presumably before the other defences were constructed. A very small marking-out bank about 11 ft. behind this was followed, approximately, by a line of post-holes, each about 5 ins. across, irregularly placed but clearly representing the principals of a revetment (of which a section was experimentally reconstructed by the excavator). This was probably the outer face of a rampart no more than 12 ft. across (from the position of the slight quarry ditch behind it) and perhaps 6 ft. high in a final stage. The general aspect of the bank as a whole is unfinished, the two 'peaks' in the excavated section perhaps comparable with those in surface profiles GG, HH. The excavator suggested an uncompleted intention to build a typical Iron Age 'A' boxed rampart a further 12 ft. across in front of this, to be contained by another revetment rising from the palisade trench. Alternatively this palisade was free-standing and preceded a hill-fort type structure. A sharp scarp drops immediately from outside the palisade trench for some 9 ft. to a ditch only 3 ft. in total depth from the top of the present slight grass-covered counterscarp bank.

The dating material, all pottery, comprised numerous sherds found in and beneath the present bank. Most were from 'coarse situlate pots with finger-tip decoration round the rim and/or shoulder'. The firmness of the shoulder was thought to indicate an early phase in the development of this Iron Age 'A' style. There were also occasional fragments of 'bowls with S-profile'. There was no haematite coating. Wheeler suggested a comparison with pottery from Scarborough (now Hawkes's Eastern First A) but regional distinctions and the relatively drab range of finds make close attribution virtually impossible.

Interior earthworks. At the W. end of the hill unfinished defences run S.E. from (a) and were perhaps connected with similar remains running W. from the S. end of (c). They consist of a terrace about 12 ft. wide with small quarry scoops to the N. and a scarp about 1½ ft. high to the S.

The cross-ridge dyke (b) is 220 yds. long and relatively massive. Its bank is up to 5 ft. high and the ditch to the E. is 5 ft. deep, both irregular and demonstrably unfinished. A low marking-out bank 10 ft. across lies on the intervening berm, and one break in it, corresponding with the southern of three gaps in the dyke, suggests the position of an entrance. The dyke is marked out to the present cliff edge above Lulworth Cove.

The cross-bank (c) is 180 yds. long and very disturbed. It is 35 ft. wide and very low with no apparent ditch, although there are signs of hollowing on both sides. It is broken by a gap N. of barrow (42), and at the S. it ends slightly beyond the point where a terrace runs up to it from the W. leaving a narrow original gap. This terrace is comparable with that farther W. and is perhaps a part of the same scheme.

Of other earthworks detectable in the interior, only a probable hut-platform (d), circular and about 20 ft. across, on the N. shoulder of the ridge 800 yds. E. of the entrance, is likely to be contemporary. The round barrows, West Lulworth (42–45), are all earlier than the Iron Age, and enclosure (e), which butts against the rampart 500 ft. E. of the entrance, is probably fairly recent. It is rectangular, 170 ft. by 150 ft., with a very slight bank and an external ditch which has been recently recut; there are fragments of brick inside it. A low bank of indeterminate age runs W. for 150 yds. from the cross-ridge dyke, S. of EE. It is 10 ft. across and 1 ft. high with a ditch 4 ft. wide and 9 ins. deep to the S.

LYTCHETT MINSTER

(30) BULBURY (SY 99 SW; 929942), a very disturbed, single-banked enclosure of 8½ acres interior area, lies in an unusual situation between the 100 ft. and 200 ft. contours on a local rise on ground which generally falls S.E. towards Lytchett Bay in Poole Harbour, 2 miles distant. The subsoil is London Clay. A notable chance find from the interior, made in the late 19th century, included objects which are unlikely to be much earlier than the date of the Roman conquest.

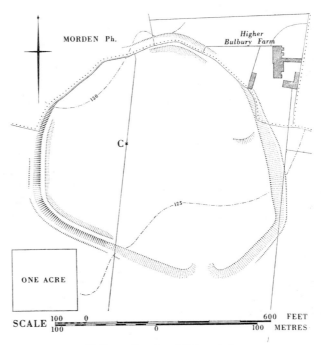

Bulbury, Lytchett Minster (30)

The earthwork spans a falling tongue of land flanked on the W. by a sharp drop into a shallow gully with a stream, and by another, less marked, gully on the E. Higher Bulbury Farm impinges on the N.E. To the S. a narrow gully runs some distance into the earthwork; there is now water in this gully 50 yds. outside the enclosure. On the N. side the ground rises gently at first, then more steeply, to a ridge about ½ m. distant. There is a clear view to N. and S., but the site itself—although wetter conditions may have increased its defensive potential—is much less commanding than that of any other hill-fort in S.E. Dorset.

On the N. the defences are much defaced with a scarp falling 4½ ft. to the N. The external ditch has been largely filled. The parish boundary with Morden follows this side. On E. and W. the bank is in places about 6 ft. high above the ditch bottom with a fall of, at most, 1½ ft. to the interior. On the S.E., where early O.S. large-scale maps seem to mark the rampart well inside the true line, it has now been almost entirely flattened by the ploughing which has long continued over all except the N. bank. According to E. Cunnington, whose indicated measurements agree with those shown on the plan, the bank at the N. was 10 ft. above the ditch and 'the breadth of the vallum was 41 ft. . . .' (*Archaeologia* XLVIII (1884), 115–20). He drew opposed entrances with unusually long inturns (80 ft.) at E. and W. and plain gaps, also opposed exactly, at N. and S. It is now impossible to say which of these was original. The scarp, 4 ft. high, curling W. from the inside of the E. side, is approximately where Cunnington envisaged an entrance.

The finds recorded by Cunnington suggest that the hill-fort was used in the 1st century A.D. They were 'all found together . . . from 2 ft. to 3 ft. underground while draining the camp', about 120 ft. W.N.W. of centre (C on plan). The following survive in D.C.M.: part of a collared mirror handle and a fragment of decorated mirror plate 'characteristic of very late British mirror art', two bronze rings from a snaffle bit, a fragment of an iron sword hilt of Piggott's Group IV A, a piece of unclassified bronze chape, a unique tankard handle like Fox's Type III B mirror handles, eight glass annular beads, four bronze mounts for a chariot yoke, two iron sledge-hammers (one unfinished or a 'waster'), a long narrow iron axe, andiron fragments and an iron anchor 4½ ft. long together with an iron chain (*Arch. Camb.* C (1948), 40; *P.P.S.* XVI (1950), 27; XVIII (1952), 94; C. Fox, *Pattern and Purpose* (1958), 73). Also recorded by Cunnington but not preserved were iron nails 6 ins. to 7 ins. long, 'thick as a thumb', 2 or 3 'rounded flat pieces of iron, which may be timber clamps', 'half of a good quern of very hard sandstone', 'a piece of fine bronze chain', 'a piece of bronze with iron ribs for strengthening it', '3 small bronze rings', and 'fragments of black well-burnt pottery'.

WINTERBORNE ST. MARTIN

(142) MAIDEN CASTLE (SY 68 NE; 669885; Fig. opp. p. 498; Plates 213–4), an Iron Age hill-fort of great complexity lying 2 miles S.W. of Dorchester, was excavated by R. E. M. Wheeler in 1934–8 (*Maiden Castle, Dorset* (1943)). It is probably 'the city of Dunium' referred to by Ptolemy (*Geographia*, I, 103, ed. C. Müller (1883)) and must have been an important centre of the Durotriges. Part of the hill-fort lies on the site of a Neolithic causewayed camp and it also contains within its bounds a unique 'long mound' (Long Barrows, Winterborne St. Martin (23)) of the same period, a Bronze Age round barrow (141) and the foundations of a Romano-British temple and accompanying buildings (*see* p. 499). It takes in the two knolls of a saddle-backed spur of Upper Chalk, though in the Neolithic phases and in Iron Age phase I only the E. knoll was enclosed. The highest point is about 440 ft. above O.D. The defences enclose 47 acres and consist of three banks and two ditches with an additional bank inserted along most of the S. side where the defences are 20% wider than on the N., including wide

berms (*see* profiles YY, ZZ). There are two entrances, at the E. and at the W., each with double openings elaborately defended by outworks (*see* profile XX). In the interior the W. rampart of the first phase hill-fort is still visible up to 5 ft. high above its ditch.

'Celtic' fields of Ancient Field Group (2) with associated settlements known only from the Roman period lie 1 mile to the N. The South Winterborne runs ¼ mile to the S. and the South Dorset Ridgeway is ¾ mile further S. Since the Roman period the site has been used for various purposes. A long brick and timber barn identified at the E. entrance is evidence for agricultural activity in the 16th century (Wheeler, 78). Ploughing of the interior was noted in 1611 and intermittently until some time within the century before 1865 (J. Speed, *The Theatre of the Empire of Great Britain* (1611), Book I, 17; Wheeler, 7). Traces of 'narrow rig' can be clearly seen on Allen's air photographs. Such a history explains the total lack of surface remains of Iron Age occupation. In the 1860s a square pond was built; a circular hollow 10 ft. deep shown on some maps as 'well', 125 yds. S.W. of the pond, was already noted as of doubtful nature in the early 19th century (Rev. J. Skinner, B.M. Add. MS. 33715, 10). The site is a guardianship monument of the Ministry of Public Building and Works.[1]

THE NEOLITHIC CAUSEWAYED CAMP

The causewayed camp lies between 380 ft. and 430 ft. above O.D. with fairly steep slopes down on all sides except the W. where there is only a gentle dip before the ground rises to the W. knoll. Where located it comprised two concentric lines of causewayed ditch lying under and completely masked by the rampart of the Phase I hill-fort which it probably resembled in plan. It was examined at two points only, on the E. and W., involving a total of about 250 ft. of ditch. The camp is of the Windmill Hill culture and may have been constructed soon after 3000 B.C. The long mound (Winterborne St. Martin (23)) was built across its W. side when the ditches were almost completely filled up. The ditches were irregular, flat bottomed and steep-sided, situated 50 ft. apart. At the western entrance of the Phase I hill-fort the inner ditch was 8 ft. to 12 ft. wide and 5 ft. deep and the outer about 7 ft. wide and 5 ft. deep. A causeway 20 ft. wide interrupted the latter. Under the E. entrance of the fort the inner ditch had been largely destroyed but the outer was of similar dimensions as before and showed traces of a slight interruption. No significant portion of Neolithic bank was discovered in the excavations and recently it has been suggested that the banks had been deliberately thrown back into the ditches (*Windmill Hill and Avebury*, ed. I. F. Smith (1965), 17). The overall area of the camp was probably about 20 acres.

The inner ditch was by far the more productive and in every case the lower half of the filling contained remains exclusively of the Windmill Hill culture, the pottery being of south-

---

[1] Since going to press, air photographs have indicated a pattern of rectangular enclosures, (a) on Fig. p. 494, 600 yds. N. of Maiden Castle. This is probably Romano-British.

MAIDEN CASTLE AND AREA
DIAGRAM SHOWING IRON AGE AND ROMANO-BRITISH SETTLEMENT

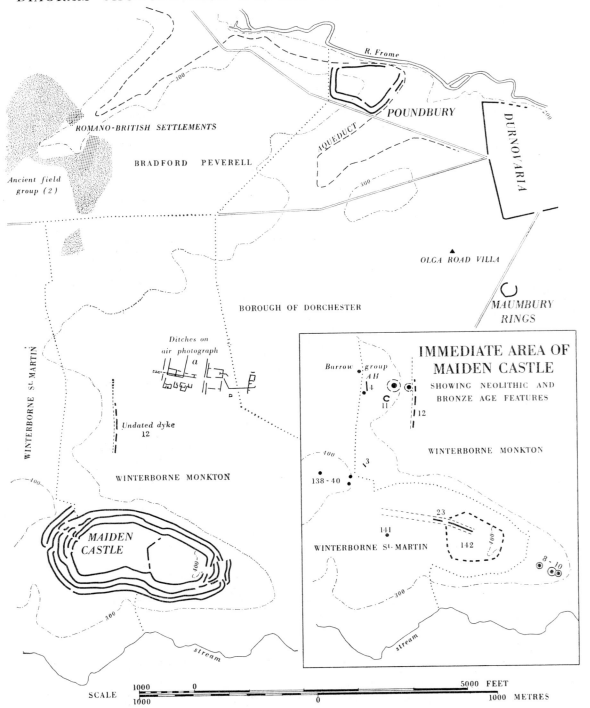

R. Frome

POUNDBURY

DURNOVARIA

ROMANO-BRITISH SETTLEMENTS

AQUEDUCT

BRADFORD PEVERELL

Ancient field group (2)

OLGA ROAD VILLA

BOROUGH OF DORCHESTER

MAUMBURY RINGS

Ditches on air photograph

WINTERBORNE S.ᵗ MARTIN

Undated dyke 12

WINTERBORNE MONKTON

MAIDEN CASTLE

stream

IMMEDIATE AREA OF MAIDEN CASTLE
SHOWING NEOLITHIC AND BRONZE AGE FEATURES

Barrow group A H

C

11

12

WINTERBORNE MONKTON

138 - 40

23

141

142

WINTERBORNE S.ᵗ MARTIN

8 - 10

stream

SCALE

1000   0   5000 FEET

1000   0   1000 METRES

western or Hembury type. The filling of this ditch at first by the rapid weathering of the sides and later by the addition of occupation and bank material had reduced it to a broad shallow depression, little more than a quarter of its original depth, before the first sherds of early Peterborough (Ebbsfleet) pottery appeared. The final upper filling included sherds of later Peterborough and Rinyo-Clacton ware, beakers and early collared urns. Before the appearance of any Peterborough pottery, however, the camp had apparently fallen out of use and the 'long mound' been built across its filled up western ditches.

Additional occupation evidence came mainly from pits; no hut structures were found. Between the ditches of the camp, two cooking pits contained Windmill Hill pottery, leaf-shaped arrowheads, scrapers and flint flakes. Beyond this, among the Iron Age outworks, were a further eight pits varying in diameter from 2 ft. to 8 ft. and in depth from just under 2 ft. to 4 ft. All but one contained Windmill Hill pottery. Other finds included flint axes, scrapers, arrowheads, and waste flakes (*P.P.S.* xxvii (1962), 247), saddle querns, a chalk figurine, an unfinished shale bead and skeletons of two dogs. Within the camp on the summit of the knoll a number of shallow pits and scrapings were found under the long mound. These, together with a thin layer of occupation debris containing flint implements and flakes and some Windmill Hill sherds, were sealed by a turf layer before the mound was built.

HISTORY OF THE IRON AGE DEFENCES (*see* Fig. p. 496 and Wheeler, fig. 3; *also* Wheeler, figs. 4, 5, 8 and 9)

Note on cultural sequence and chronology. Since the Maiden Castle report was published in 1943 new discoveries elsewhere have made it possible for a revised chronology of the British Iron Age to be postulated. The system propounded by Professor C. F. C. Hawkes (*Antiquity* xxxiii (1959), 170–82, with some amendments subsequently supplied by him) involves a new terminology and modification of the excavator's account in the following ways:

(i) Iron Age 'A1' and 'A2' (later thought by Wheeler to be not properly divisible) become Hawkes's Southern Second A culture. Wheeler's initial date for it, *c.* 300 B.C., though repeated by Hawkes in 1959, should now be placed somewhat before 350 B.C. as indicated by its association with the earliest Second A cultures of S.E. England rather than with those of inland Wessex.

(ii) The dating of the introduction of Iron Age 'B' is raised from *c.* 56 B.C. to *c.* 150 B.C. or not much later. It can no longer be associated with an immigration of Venetic refugees in 56 B.C. Wheeler's 'early' and 'developed B' are both embraced by Hawkes's Southern Third B, a culture that flourished in the assumed tribal area of the Durotriges.

(iii) Iron Age 'C' (Southern Third C) is now taken to begin about the middle of the 1st century B.C. It is a development of the Durotrigian culture of Southern Third B, with new elements including a silver coinage modelled on Belgic gold coinages previously circulating E. of the region but leading to base silver and ultimately to cast bronze types. In the developed form in which it is at present recognized

at Maiden Castle, the culture is typified by modified hand-made pottery styles in which some degree of Belgic and perhaps Armorican influence may be traced.

Structural Phase I: Iron Age 'A' (Southern Second A), probably towards 350 B.C. The first defences consisted of a single rampart, of a Continental type with external ditch beyond a berm, enclosing 16 acres of the eastern knoll. This hill-fort, roughly hexagonal in plan with entrances at E. and W., seems to have coincided approximately with the causewayed camp, though the entrances did not correspond.

The rampart was a wall of earth and chalk 12 ft. wide, with vertical faces retained front and back by timbering anchored to tall posts 10 ins. across set at about 5 ft. intervals. It was originally 10 ft. to 12 ft. high and reinforced at the rear by a low bank 4½ ft. high. In front, a berm 6 ft. to 10 ft. wide separated it from the ditch which at best was 50 ft. wide and 20 ft. deep.

The W. entrance had been much mutilated when it fell out of use but was marked by a 47 ft. wide 'causeway' of natural chalk and by evidence for a double gate barring a passage 19 ft. wide between the timber-revetted ends of the ramparts. From the beginning the E. entrance comprised two separate portals— a feature so far without parallel—about 50 ft. apart. They were at this stage blocked by gates 14 ft. to 15 ft. wide and lined with massive palisades. Outside the gates, whether from the start or added later, was a wide area of flint-metalled paving extending for 300 ft. or so. Timber pens had been built on this paving (possibly for extra-mural markets).

Before the metalling had become badly worn a claw-like barbican was built which extended 160 ft. over it in front of the original gates, funnelling all traffic into two passages, almost 240 ft. long but without gates (Wheeler, fig. 5). The triangular flanking enclosures so formed were about ⅒ acre each and had entrances at their inner corners. They were bounded externally by ramparts originally up to 8 ft. high, the outer face retained by dry-walling of limestone from Upwey, over 2 miles to the S. The berm was some 7 ft. wide and the associated ditch was about 23 ft. across and 12 ft. deep. The passages, too, were lined by timber and limestone walling and were separated from each other by ramparts without ditches set back to back. Whether this construction took place before or at the time of the western extension of the hill-fort (Phase II) is uncertain.

Structural Phase II: Iron Age 'A' (Southern Second A), probably in the second half of the 3rd century B.C. The defences were now extended to take in the western knoll and thus enclose a total of about 47 acres. The fort remained a single-banked and ditched enclosure but the Phase I wall-and-berm rampart (now generally ruinous except perhaps along the face of the E. barbican) was continued from the S.W. and N.W. angles by a heaped bank of chalk rubble and earth, the outer slope of which continued the inner slope of the accompanying ditch in 'glacis' fashion. On the S. side under the extension rampart where it departed from the original was a human (? foundation) burial in a pit contemporary with the extension.

The W. entrance was not investigated in detail but it seems, like the E. entrance, to have had a barbican through which two roads passed between ramparts revetted with thin limestones (Wheeler, fig. 24). The twin portals, over 200 ft. apart, through the main rampart were certainly original but it was

W. knoll   E. knoll   Long Mound

Working Floor   Settlement   Round Barrow

Pits

NEOLITHIC   Phase I   Phase II

IRON AGE   Phase I   Phase II

Phase III   Phase IV

SCALE   1000   0   5000   FEET
         100   0   1700   METRES

MAIDEN CASTLE. Diagram showing structural sequence (*after R. E. M. Wheeler*).

uncertain whether the outwork existed from the first. It covered a considerably larger area than that at the E.

Structural Phase III: Iron Age 'B' (Southern Third B), from c. 150 B.C. or not much later. The main rampart, now in a decrepit condition, was rebuilt on twice its original scale—producing a steep scarp 80 ft. long from crest of bank to bottom of ditch, 50 ft. high vertically—and reinforced at the back by internal walls of chalk and limestone and by an exposed limestone revetment along the inner side of the summit. Most of the material was obtained from a quarry ditch 70 ft. wide and 8 ft. to 9 ft. deep immediately behind the rampart. (These defences are positively related to the 'B' culture by the latter's pottery present in the lowest levels of the filling of the quarry ditch, although the sherds recovered from the new rampart were still of Iron Age 'A'.) The main ditch was enlarged and the material from it used chiefly for the construction of a counterscarp bank which in places was given a berm between its inner face and the main ditch. At the same time additional lines of defence were built, two on the S. and one on the N. side of the fort.

At the E. entrance the Iron Age 'A' barbican was retained but on its S. side the enlargement of the main ditch and the new counterscarp bank were not carried right up to the causeway but ceased at a point just overlapping the barbican. The first of the new lines of defence on the S. side of the fort, a ditch 20 ft. wide and 10 ft. deep, was cut along the outer margin of the counterscarp bank, providing it with extra material; this ditch, with a smaller rampart derived solely from it, continued beyond the counterscarp bank, curving round as far as the flank of the approach to the S. portal. A similar lay-out existed on the N. side of the entrance. A further bank and ditch along the S. side of the fort ran parallel to the ditch just described. A hornwork of flattened 'Y' form was added to protect the entrance and to continue its twofold division. It consisted of a median ditch (probably with banks on both sides) which extended eastwards from the central 'double-rampart' of the Iron Age 'A' barbican and, after 180 ft. or so, forked S. and N. to screen the two approaches (Wheeler, fig. 8). It was probably during this phase that the portals of both entrances were repaired partly with big blocks of chalk inviting comparison with the large unwieldy stones that the excavator took to be a characteristic of the developed 'B' culture.

In the interior, because of the shelter they afforded, the floors of the quarry ditches were soon filled with hearths and hut floors and the layers contained mixed 'A' and 'B' pottery from the beginning.

Structural Phase IV: Iron Age 'B' (Southern Third B), beginning *c.* 75 or perhaps as early as 100 B.C. This phase represents the final remodelling of the site as a whole. In it the ditches and ramparts added during Structural Phase III were refashioned on the same extremely massive scale as the inner rampart and ditch, while the entrances were developed to the degree of intricacy reflected by the surviving remains.

At the E. entrance the outer (Phase III) barrier (the arms of the 'Y' ditch) was retained and strengthened by the deepening of its ditch and the raising of a further bank beyond it (Wheeler, fig. 9). The revetted banks lining the entrance ways were removed and a middle barrier of glacis type constructed over the Phase I barbican. This blocked the latter's central exits and necessitated the construction of new approach ways through the old barbican defences near their junction at N. and S. with the main inner defences. This barrier was strengthened on the inside by two internal chalk or limestone walls, and its summit revetted on its western side by an exposed limestone wall. Opposite the S. portal this wall expanded westwards to form a platform (or low tower) and probably did likewise opposite the N. portal. The northern and southern extremities of this work, now detached by the cutting of the new flanking entrances, were also converted into platforms by masonry revetment. Yet another feature of this type flanked the N. portal of the outermost barrier. They were probably for slingers. There were also stone footings of two small 'sentry-boxes' on the inner flanks of the southern portal and, immediately adjacent to them, a shallow pit 11 ft. by 10 ft. containing a stock of 22,260 sling-stones. The extensive use of vehicles is indicated by the ruts in the worn entrance ways pointing to a wheel-gauge of 4½ ft. to 5 ft. The small Phase III rampart immediately outside the Phase I barbican survived in part on the S. side but its ditch had been filled in; a little further to the S.W. however the ditch had actually been re-cut.

The lay-out of the W. entrance, though but slightly explored, suggests a similar evolution to that of the E. entrance. Two fragments of Mediterranean amphorae were incorporated

in work of this structural phase, evidence already of a wine trade from southern Gaul.

There appears to be a rough ratio between the natural slope and the spread of the defences. On the N. side where the slope is about 14° the overall distance across the ramparts is 100 yds., but on the S., where the average slope is only 9°, the distance is 140 yds. It has been held that the multiplication of defences during Iron Age 'B' at Maiden Castle and elsewhere was due to the increased use of the sling, facilitated here by the profuse natural supplies 8 miles away on Chesil Beach. While the span of the defences was probably sufficient to enable defenders on the superior elevation of the inner rampart to engage attackers on the outermost without effective return so long as no penetration was attempted, the main advantage of a complex system was probably to delay attackers and break up a concerted rush. Doubts have been expressed elsewhere upon a causative relationship between the sling and multiple ramparts (*cf.* A. L. F. Rivet, in S. S. Frere (ed.), *Problems of the Iron Age in Southern Britain* (1960), 31–2).

Iron Age 'C' (Southern Third C), beginning after *c.* 60 B.C. The inner rampart, in a state of disrepair, was covered with a thick layer of earth and chalk and the stone revetment was replaced by a line of posts, probably linked by wattles, along its inner crest. Pottery of a developed phase of the culture came from the heightened rampart (Wheeler, 100, 103: 'sherds showing Belgic . . . influence'); thus the repair cannot be a primary feature of Iron Age 'C' in the region as a whole. The hollow-worn E. gateways and streets were re-metalled with pebbles and the metalling several times renewed, the earliest work dating from *c.* 25 B.C. or later, as amongst several earlier Durotrigian coins it contained one of Allen's reverse type 5 (Wheeler, 332, no. 9; S. S. Frere (ed.), *Problems of the Iron Age in Southern Britain* (1960), 112).

About A.D. 44 the *Legio II Augusta* under its legate Vespasian stormed the hill-fort, as indicated by Suetonius and by remains at the E. entrance. The British victims of the assault were buried behind the 'middle barrier' hornwork, and the gates and flanking walls of the E. portals, and probably also the timber palisade, were slighted. Native occupation was allowed to continue (*see* pp. 499–500).

THE INTERIOR IN THE IRON AGE

The excavation was devoted mainly to the elucidation of structural phases in the defences and information gained about interior features was largely incidental to this, to the tracing of the 'long mound', and to the stripping of the area of the Romano-British buildings, the earlier investigation of which had suggested to Edward Cunnington that the whole earthwork was Roman (Dorset *Procs.* XXIV (1903), xxxiv–viii; Wheeler, 7).

The fact that most cuts revealed occupational evidence suggests that virtually the whole of the interior was at some time occupied but details of the development are uncertain; for example site 'L' was almost entirely devoid of finds of Iron Age 'B' (Wheeler, 126). Apart from small finds, the evidence of occupation depends on post-holes, wall footings, floors of chalk, clay, gravel or limestones, clay ovens, pits and ditches. The post-holes are sometimes arranged in patterns indicating hut remains—with which hearths, floors and pits are occasionally associated. While some of the disturbed alignments which the excavator suggested were those of rectilinear huts might now be suspected to relate to granaries, drying racks, or the like, one complete plan of a building about 27 ft. by 13 ft. is claimed; there is no other structural evidence for huts in the Iron Age 'A' phase (Wheeler, 36).

In the Iron Age 'B' and 'C' phases all the 11 huts recorded were circular, oval or polygonal, but it was often impossible in this 'honeycombed site' to establish more than a portion of their outline (Wheeler, 55). Two circular huts were bounded by wall footings of chalk rubble (DB 2 on site 'D') or chalk and limestone (site 'L'). The first was 22 ft. in diameter, had an inner ring of post-holes cut into a levelled floor dug into a local patch of clay, and included a pit as well as the remains of three small circular clay ovens, a central hearth and another near the wall. The much-disturbed second hut was the largest to be excavated, being some 31 ft. in diameter (Wheeler, Pl. XX, though the account, p. 127, says 15 ft.). One of the two roads running into the site from the East Gate led up to it and the excavator noted that its 'prominent position suggests . . . a building of some distinction' (Wheeler, 76). A Roman hut, perhaps a shrine associated with the adjacent 4th-century temple, was later built directly over its site, but there was no positive evidence for sacred use at this earlier date.

Huts were also identified outside the main portals of the E. entrance and between them and the 'middle barrier' hornwork. One of the five of which the plan was partially recoverable had, in the Iron Age 'C' phase, been rebuilt on the site of an Iron Age 'B' structure. It had a rough line of rubble at the base of its wall giving an interior diameter of 16 ft. and had been used in connection with iron smelting (Wheeler, 118). The other huts identified, lined inside the 'middle barrier', varied in diameter from 10 ft. to 16 ft. A thick layer of ash covered the hut-sites and the spaces between them, and it was assumed that all had been burned down simultaneously. The graves of the 'war cemetery', roughly cut into the ground here and all filled with ash, suggest the circumstances and the date (c. A.D. 44). Twelve of the skeletons bore wounds. It seems, however, that a regular 'peace-time' cemetery, also 'flat', lay just to the S. (Wheeler, 347–56).

Very many gullies or ditches were found, being 'perhaps the most remarkable feature' of site 'B' (Wheeler, 91). The larger were probably originally accompanied by banks. Some were probably associated with compounds or other divisions but numbers are said to have run into pits, notably B 9, which was 7 ft. deep and 4½ ft. across, and may have held a water-butt. No Iron Age ponds were identified. Of more than 200 pits recorded about 40 were 3 ft. or less in depth. Some were irregular or notably wider than they were deep, e.g. R 8, 23 ft. by 7 ft. by 1 ft. deep, pear-shaped and linked with another irregular pit 3¾ ft. deep. Such a description recalls 'working-hollows' of the type defined by Bersu at Little Woodbury, Wilts. (P.P.S. VI (1940), 311). G 10 may be another. It seems that about half of the pits were 4 ft. or more deep and most of these appear to have been for storage. They were generally circular, roughly flat-bottomed and often narrowing to the top in 'beehive' fashion. This was sometimes very pronounced in the deeper pits. It seems likely that their tops and margins were carefully protected from weather and wear. Altogether, 22

pits were 8 ft. or more deep. Of these, five were 10 ft. or more deep and the deepest was 11 ft. 10 ins. Pits deeper than 5 ft. usually had mouths at least 4 ft. across and frequently 5 ft. to 7 ft. In contrast a few 7 ft. to 8 ft. deep had mouths 4 ft. or rather less across pointing perhaps to a specialised type, e.g. L 4 or B 12.

Pit B 12 held 4,000 sling-stones and since such objects cannot be regarded as rubbish this could be a proper usage for such a pit; two further pits in site B held sling-stone 'hoards' (cf. the huge piles at the E. entrance). It is an example of grouping which can be otherwise detected: e.g. in this same area there was a noticeably high proportion of pits (7 out of 50) about 8 ft. or more deep. Whether most pits were used for corn storage is uncertain. Pits were quite often dug partly into the fill of old pits (probably levelled so effectively that their position was lost, insufficient time having passed for subsidence to mark them). Some of these were not lined or revetted. In contrast, some of the lined pits were apparently dug into solid chalk. These were revetted and occasionally paved with limestone (Wheeler, Pl. CX). Such revetment was perhaps for a special purpose, e.g. storage of the more perishable foods. The floor of one pit (B 1) was ringed with mutton bones and a few had had fires lit in them, but it is not now considered that they could have been lived in even for short periods. Almost all had been deliberately filled with domestic rubbish. In one, however, an adult female was buried on the floor (Q 4).

Some pits appear to have been built into the floors of huts but most were probably outside under their own covers. A few had scoops impinging on their lips and the excavator suggested that these might represent side openings. There seems little to distinguish pits of any one phase. They were in full use in Iron Age 'A' and 'B'. It is not clear whether pits were used here in Iron Age 'C', still less that they were deliberately filled 'by general order' (Wheeler, 58); characteristic 'C' pottery appears, however, to have been scarce in their fillings.

FINDS OF THE IRON AGE

Finds were too numerous to be detailed here. Since, however, the excavations produced important stratified series and there have been certain re-interpretations in the last 20 years, the following summary may be useful. (The finds are in D.C.M. and the Institute of Archaeology, London.)

Pottery—Iron Age 'A': Wheeler noted that it was later than the earliest Iron Age phase, e.g. at All Cannings Cross, and it now becomes Hawkes's Southern Second A. Pottery consisted of situlate jars, rarely angular and with very little finger-tip ornament, none on the rim. Bowls in early levels had bodies rounded or carinated with flaring rim and omphaloid bases. A haematite slip was plentifully used on these. Some jars had attached handles pierced horizontally or vertically, Pedestal bases were found.

Iron Age 'B': 'B' features and types appeared 'for some time subordinate to the continuing A tradition'. Haematite finish was occasionally found. New types included bead-rims (found in stratified sequence on site 'D'), countersunk-handled jars, flat-rimmed and other large jars (essentially derived from 'A'), a few imported decorated wares mainly of 'Glastonbury' type, and local imitations. Two Mediterranean amphora sherds occurred in latest levels.

Iron Age 'C': 'B' forms persisted or were developed, and some distinctive types emerged, notably the 'war cemetery bowl'. The vessels were more smoothly finished or burnished than in 'B', but were rarely or never wheel-thrown, although they may betray familiarity with wheel-thrown forms perhaps of Belgic or Armorican origin. The main types have been listed by Brailsford and called 'Durotrigian' (*P.P.S.* XXIV (1958), 101–119). Imported wares included amphorae and 'Glastonbury' ware as in the later 'B' phase, a little Belgic and imitation Gallo-Belgic ware, and a very few fragments of vessels derived from the wheel-thrown Armorican 'Hengistbury Class B' forms of Iron Age 'B'. Arretine ware was not found.

Brooches: these included seven of La Tène I, including one from a 'B' layer (the earlier dating of the 'B' levels now generally recognised makes this association less surprising, *cf. Arch. J.* CX (1953), 89); also one unusual La Tène II example and another, coral-studded, found in 1907. There were numerous La Tène III types. Eight penannular brooches included two typologically characteristic of the Iron Age (E. Fowler, Types Aa and B, *P.P.S.* XXVI (1960), 172).

Other metal objects—Iron Age 'A': these were very scarce indeed apart from six iron ring-headed pins.

Iron Age 'B' and 'C': in these phases bronze was notably scarce and iron sometimes used in its place, *e.g.* iron mirror fragments and an iron linch-pin. Weapons included a tanged iron arrowhead from site 'H' (a 'B ii' layer), a bronze chape-end and seven unclassifiable fragments of swords or daggers (*P.P.S.* XVI (1950), 28), all Iron Age 'C' (two from the E. entrance, four from site 'L'), and spears. Implements included three tangential sickles, knives, a chisel and saws. There was a bronze chariot horn-cap (C. Fox, *A find of the Early Iron Age from Llyn Cerrig Bach* (1946), 15). Only one fragment of currency bar was found. Personal ornaments included iron bracelets and a dozen rings of bronze ribbon (some found as toe-rings in the 'war cemetery'). There was one bronze ring-headed pin (Iron Age 'C'). Four crucibles were evidence for metal working which, at least in the later phase, was carried on extensively outside the E. portals where copious slag came from 'puddled wrought iron'. A dozen *ballista* bolts and socketed arrows were relics of the Roman assault of *c.* A.D. 44.

Sling-stones: vast numbers were found, mostly in great dumps amongst the eastern defences (54,000 counted) and in pits on site 'L' (*cf.* finds of swords). The proportion of Iron Age 'A' finds to those of Iron Age 'B'/'C' was 1 to 30 or 40. A few clay sling-bullets were found.

Beads, etc., included glass (plain and inlaid, Iron Age 'A'–'C'), bone, *Porosphaera* and precious coral (one, Iron Age 'A').

Implements associated with spinning and weaving included spindle whorls, weaving combs (bone and antler), and loom weights, preponderantly of chalk. Some, very heavy, may have been roof weights.

Bone 'gouges': these were probably weavers' 'beaters' (*Antiquity* XIX (1945), 157–8), mostly from leg bones of sheep or goats. Iron Age 'A' examples generally had the butt at the distal end and those from 'B'/'C' phases at the proximal end of the bone.

Other bone or antler implements included horse-bit cheek pieces of antler and oblong bone dice. There were no antler picks in the Iron Age levels.

Kimmeridge shale was perhaps worked locally in 'A' and 'B' phases, but less probably in 'C' since only one turned armlet core was found, of Calkin's class A (Wheeler, fig. 111, no. 22, described as a spindle-whorl; *cf.* Dorset *Procs.* LXXVII (1955), 45–71). Armlets occurred throughout, in the 'C' phase sometimes lathe-turned. Part of a large lathe-turned jar and fragments of other vessels were found in 'C' contexts.

Quern-stones comprised seven saddle querns (Neolithic and Iron Age 'A') and 56 rotary quern-stones, none prior to 'B', including 21 of 'Wessex' or 'beehive' type typical of 'B' and 'C', and seven of flatter form in latest 'B' and 'C' phases.

Small clay ovens and perforated girdles were used for cooking.

Grain: the remains found were chiefly of Spelt and some other wheats (Emmer and Bread) with smaller quantities of Hulled Barley (*P.P.S.* XVIII (1952), 228–9). Part of a small carbonized wheaten loaf was found.

Coins: of 19 Celtic coins recorded (all of Durotrigian types save three 'Armorican', one 'British L' and one fragment), 15 were found by Wheeler in 'C' or early Roman contexts, mostly in street metalling. The Durotrigian coins include early types, similar to those in the Le Catillon (Jersey) hoard of *c.* 56–51 B.C., probably originating *c.* 60 B.C. as silver versions of the gold types known as 'British A' and 'British O' previously centred on W. Sussex and Hampshire: the Durotrigian series is, however, also linked with 'British B' gold believed to have circulated mainly in the area of the Durotriges between *c.* 75 and 60 B.C. (D. F. Allen, in S. S. Frere (ed.), *Problems of the Iron Age in Southern Britain* (1960), 105–7, 112–3, 119–120). Such silver coins have not been found in Iron Age 'B' contexts, and are the best evidence for the revised initial dating of Iron Age 'C' in the region. The coins from Maiden Castle include several struck bronze issues of the 1st century A.D.

Bone evidence: human, includes one adult Iron Age 'A' skeleton and over 50 skeletons of 'B' and 'C' indicating a small, light-boned, short-lived people. Only infants and exceptional burials were found in the interior. A cemetery existed outside the E. portals and was used before, and probably after, the 'war' phase. Burials were generally flexed. There were no certain grave goods before the 'C' phase. Thereafter pots, missiles, an axe-head and knife, personal ornaments including a Roman 'ear-scoop', and bones of sheep, pig and ox were found, mostly in the 'war' cemetery.

THE ROMAN PHASE

A temple of the late 4th century A.D. with associated building and hut-shrine (?), a road and inhumation burials have been excavated at about 420 ft. above sea level in the E. part of the hill-fort, which is believed to have reverted to pasture and tillage after cessation of native occupation *c.* A.D. 70. The partly restored foundations of the temple and adjoining building are exposed to view.

Fresh road metal laid directly over the debris of the Roman

slighting of the E. gateways, but without new gates, incorporated samian and coarse pottery and indicated continued occupation by disarmed natives until *c.* 70, as did pottery on the summit of the E. knoll where Iron Age 'C' occupation passed without structural division into early Roman. Slighting, perhaps *c.* 70 and possibly of ceremonial character, of the Iron Age stone-faced platform or 'bastion' on the W. flank of the southern causeway (Wheeler, fig. 9) was not followed by a reopening of the road to the S. portal, and soil accumulated over the early Roman road through the N. portal.

Only 20 coins and 38 samian sherds were found to span the following century and a half, while the total of at least 266 coins dated between *c.* 235 and 350 includes many coins deposited during the late 4th-century occupation. The Neolithic 'long mound', still at its E. end a sufficient obstacle to occupation in Iron Age 'C', had been reduced presumably by ploughing to an average height of 1 ft. by perhaps *c.* 340 or 350, after which a road presumably to be identified with the late metalling in the N. portal of the E. entrance (*see below*) was laid across it. This road (Wheeler, Pl. IV), passing 15 yds. S. of the oval hut of the temple complex, and continuing W. apparently across the filling of the W. ditch of the Phase I hill-fort, may imply undiscovered buildings of earlier date than the temple complex; a hoard of 70 bronze coins formed soon after *c.* 345 and buried thereafter in a coarse ware jar on the road surface S. of the temple (in Wheeler's view *c.* 350, which seems too early), implies however that the metalled surface soon fell out of use, at least beyond this point. The existence of two parallel square-cut Roman drains running N., the western one beneath the E. foundations of the temple (*Ant. J.* xv (1935), 270–1; Wheeler, Pl. VII), and of lumps of mosaic and building debris used in the construction of its primary floor, also suggests earlier buildings.

The temple precinct. The surviving rampart of the original Phase I hill-fort seems to have formed the wall of the temple precinct or *temenos*, much as at Lydney of similar date (T. V. and R. E. M. Wheeler, *Lydney Park, Gloucs.* (1932), 57–9). Masonry screen-walls (Wheeler, Pl. XVII) blocking the two portals of the E. entrance, the northern one provided with a 10 ft. wide double-leaved gate and a new road surface showing wheel-ruts of 3½ ft. gauge, were built not earlier than *c.* 340, or 350 if, as seems likely, road and walls were of the same date. A contemporary oblong foundation, 4 ft. by 3 ft., obstructing the N. half of the road 15 ft. within the entrance, was possibly for an altar or inscription. Wheeler associated these features with the building of the temple after 367, although the road found in the interior by-passes the complex and could be slightly earlier in origin.

The temple (67118846), excavated by E. Cunnington in 1882–4 and by Wheeler in 1934, was of Romano-Celtic type, 43½ ft. by 40½ ft. externally, and terraced into the gentle northerly slope. The cella, 20 ft. by 19½ ft., or 16 ft. square internally, was slightly W. of centre and surrounded by a passage or verandah. A paved approach indicated a central E. entrance, and post-sockets on E. and W. perhaps imply a fence.

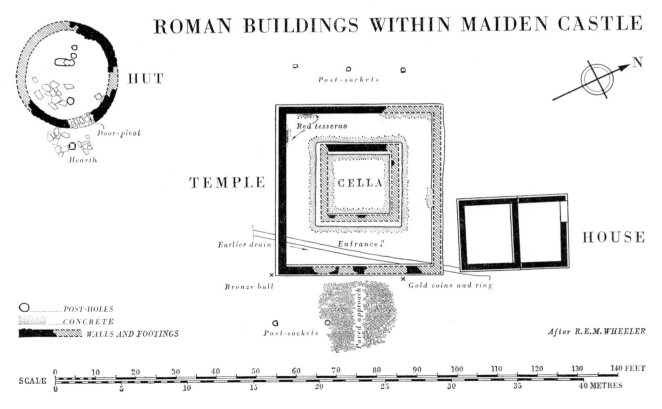

ROMAN BUILDINGS WITHIN MAIDEN CASTLE

HUT
Door-pivot
Hearth

Post-sockets

Red tesserae

TEMPLE

CELLA

HOUSE

Earlier drain

Entrance?

Bronze bull

Gold coins and ring

Post-sockets

Paved approach

After R.E.M. WHEELER

○ .... POST-HOLES
.... CONCRETE
.... WALLS AND FOOTINGS

SCALE   0   10   20   30   40   50   60   70   80   90   100   110   120   130   140 FEET
        0   5   10   15   20   25   30   35   40 METRES

The walls, largely robbed but uniformly some 2 ft. wide, were of coursed herring-bone flintwork above a levelling course or courses of Purbeck limestone on chalk rubble footings; the external wall survived to 3 ft. on S., but evidence is lacking for use of columns here or elsewhere. The walls were probably plastered on both sides. Plaster of the outer S. wall, originally yellow outside with a basal panel or border of oblique red splashes, had been renewed three times. The W. cella wall had remains inside of mortar rendering with 'roughly stuck' false joints; loose fragments within indicated panels of blue-green, dark red and white, on a mainly terra-cotta ground, while one piece in yellow and black showed two renewals.

No remains survived in 1934 of the 'small portion of black and white tessellated pavement' reported by Cunnington or of his mass of masonry 9 ft. by 6 ft., both apparently *in situ* in the cella. Cement foundations for such a floor remained, however, over rubble and cement make-up which contained debris and lumps of black and white mosaic border from an earlier building; the surround or verandah had been floored wholly or partly with coarse red tesserae. Both these floors had been largely replaced by reused stone roof-slabs which had possibly formed the original roof of the building, which was probably covered with clay tiles in the second phase.

122 coins were found in and near the building, all save 11 of the 4th century. Several sealed below the floors and paved approach dated the original construction at earliest to 367, and the reconstruction to 379 or later; further occupation was represented by eight Theodosian issues and a hoard of four gold coins of Arcadius and Honorius of *c.* 405 found with a gold ring beside the outer wall.

A rectangular building (the 'priest's house'; Wheeler, Pl. CXV), 26 ft. by 18 ft. overall and roughly aligned with the temple, lay immediately N.; it consisted of two rooms stepped down the slope, with an entrance in the N. end. The walls 1½ ft. wide were of herring-bone flintwork, levelled with and partly based on limestone courses; it had no surviving floor-surface or wall-plaster. The building contained 4th-century pottery but no coins.

An oval building (67098844; Wheeler, Pl. CXVI) lay on the local hill-crest 12 yds. S.W. of the temple. It was 23 ft. by 21 ft. internally, with rough drystone wall; holes and debris suggested a clay-tiled roof on axial posts. The floor was of limestone roof-tiles and slabs, and had been levelled into that of the largest Iron Age 'C' hut found at Maiden Castle (Wheeler, Pl. XX). A pivot-stone showed the position of a S.E. doorway, outside which was rough paving containing a tile-lined pit-hearth filled with wood ash. As well as cult objects listed below, the hut contained 171 coins mostly of 4th century down to Honorius (393–423); a preponderance of issues of *c.* 350–360 suggested a slightly earlier period of use than that of the temple.

Discussion. The date of the temple aligns it with others built or restored in Britain in the late 4th century in response to a widespread revival of paganism. Its dedication is unknown, and the small private *ex voto* objects frequently found on such sites are lacking; nevertheless several objects of dedicatory or cult significance show signs of the syncretism of Roman and native religion. From the temple itself came a fragment of a near life-size bronze statue, a feather-shaped bronze plaque with repoussée figure of Minerva with traces of an inscription (Wheeler, Pl. XXXIX B), and in 1934 a figurine of tinned bronze probably representing the Celtic three-horned bull surmounted by three human busts with bird-like bodies, thought probably all female (*ibid.*, Pl. XXXI B). This figure, and another, in private hands, from Waddon Hill, Stoke Abbot, have been further discussed by F. Jenkins (Dorset *Procs.* LXXXII (1960), 104–8, fig. 9). From the oval hut came a bronze pedestal for a standing statuette (Wheeler, fig. 97) and the base of another in Italian marble with the feet presumably of Diana and a hound (*ibid.*, Pl. XXXI A).

The objects found in the hut, as well as the quantity of coins, may be cited in support of the view that it served as a shrine, perhaps consciously archaic and continuing a local cult of Iron Age origin, despite the apparent discontinuity of occupation; the importance of the Iron Age 'C' hut which underlay it is evident both from its size and its situation astride or at the head of an Iron Age main street leading from the E. gate (Wheeler, Pl. I), although there is no direct evidence of religious use. If this view is correct, parallels are offered by the 'rotunda' near the temple at Frilford, Berks., overlying an Iron Age penannular ditch (*Oxoniensia* IV (1939), 11–15), and the polygonal shrine at Brigstock, Northants., in a similar association (*Ant. J.* XLIII (1963), 235–8). The identification of the small rectangular building as a priest's house, although without obvious parallel, is supported by its division into two small rooms, and by the absence of coins and cult objects.

The inhumation burials. An irregular line of four extended burials (one male, three female) was partly excavated about 150 yds. W. of the temple, overlying the S. ditch of the 'long mound' and close within the original W. rampart, here supposed to form the precinct wall (66988847; Wheeler, Pls. III, V). All were orientated E.–W. with head W., and one at least was not earlier than the 4th century A.D. Fragmentary remains of a child were in the same stratum.

Of earlier burials, in addition to 38 male and female skeletons in the war cemetery of *c.* 44, 18 inhumations are referred to the Iron Age 'C'/Roman phase, mostly within the outworks of the E. entrance. Some (*e.g.* T 3–6) were in orderly lines; heads were normally towards N.E., E., or S.E. All save one had limbs flexed or slightly bent, in plain graves accompanied in some cases by vessels or food. The exception was a female fully extended with head S. and hob-nails at feet, accompanied by the headless skeleton of a lamb, in a coffin indicated by iron nails, and with a young dog probably outside the coffin. Interments in the war cemetery, despite evidence of haste, indicated a substantially similar ritual of burial.

ENCLOSURES

This category embraces earthworks of very diverse form and date. It includes two 'henge' monuments (Dorchester (228) and W. Stafford (24)), three small Bronze Age enclosures, possibly for ritual (Whitcombe (25), Winterborne Came (49) and Winterborne Monkton (11)), and eight small, somewhat angular enclosures, probably prehistoric or Romano-British occupation or stock enclosures. In addition there are three enclosures of possibly later date (Arne (48a), Portesham (56) and W. Lulworth (53e)) and a concentration of seventy-seven circles of unknown date and function (Studland (43)). One enclosure (Portland (98)) has been long destroyed. Some of these enclosures might prove to be settlements, though all certain settlements are discussed under that category. Enclosures of known mediaeval date are described in the parish inventories. Excavation has provided conclusive results only for Maumbury Rings, Dorchester (228).

ARNE

ENCLOSURE, *see* Dykes, Arne (48a).

CHALDON HERRING

(58) THE ROUND POUND (SY 78 SE; 79638168), lies at about 480 ft. above O.D. on Chaldon Down, part of an undulating E. to W. chalk ridge here covered by angular flint gravel. The earthwork is on a knoll but with a rise to the S.W. blocking any view towards Portland. Visibility is otherwise extremely good and extends from the Hardy Monument in the W., to Bindon Hill, Flower's Barrow and St. Aldhelm's Head in the E. and to the limits of the chalk downs on the N. The date is unknown; the only evidence is a single sherd of Iron Age 'A' ware with finger-tip decoration found by R.C.H.M. staff scraped from the body of the bank at the W. corner.

A single defensive bank about 36 ft. across at its base and at most 5½ ft. high above the rather dished interior and 10 ft. above an external ditch about 25 ft. wide encloses an irregular, roughly square area of about ⅙ acre with sides 80 ft. to 110 ft. long. The interior ground level is somewhat higher than the outside. The rounded corners at the N. and W. are notably higher than the general run of the sides. The only possible entrance is a dip in the crest of the bank for about 10 ft. immediately S. of the very rounded E. corner. This depression is not certainly original, however, since the scarp of the bank falls for some 4 ft. below it to the outside and perhaps 3 ft. to the inside. The earthwork has been much disturbed and to the E. the ditch, elsewhere almost filled, has been completely obscured.

DORCHESTER

MAUMBURY RINGS, 'henge' monument, *see* Roman section, Dorchester (228).

LULWORTH, WEST

ENCLOSURE, butting against bank of dyke on Bindon Hill, *see* Hill-forts, W. Lulworth (53e).

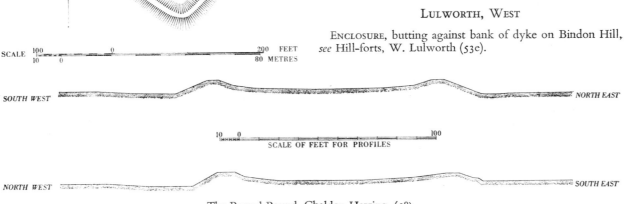

SCALE
100 0 200 FEET
10 0 80 METRES

SOUTH WEST — NORTH EAST

10 0 100
SCALE OF FEET FOR PROFILES

NORTH WEST — SOUTH EAST

The Round Pound, Chaldon Herring (58)

OSMINGTON

(42) ENCLOSURE, trapezoidal (SY 78 SE; 75058282), of about ½ acre, sharply angular, with three sides of 140 ft. and one of 170 ft. It lies, almost ploughed out, near Ringstead Barn at about 250 ft. above O.D. on a gentle N.-facing slope, dipping on the W. into a small gully. It is below 'Celtic' fields of Group (12), but remains undated. (R.A.F. V.A.P. CPE/UK 1821: 4442–3.)

OWERMOIGNE

(36) ENCLOSURE, near-rectangular (SY 78 NE; 769880), partly survives in Bowley's Plantation at 200 ft. above O.D. on a plateau (Reading Beds) with ferruginous gravels and sandy clays. The W. part, outside the plantation, has been destroyed by ploughing, but the area enclosed was originally about ½ acre. On the E. is an outer bank, 16 ft. across and 4½ ft. high above a ditch of similar width, with an inner bank, 15 ft. wide and 1 ft. high above the interior. The single causewayed entrance, 10 ft. wide, is slightly S. of centre on the E. side.

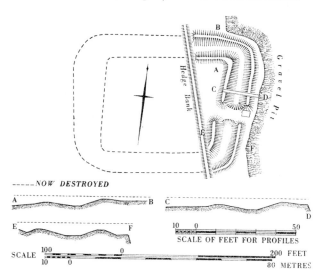

----- NOW DESTROYED

SCALE OF FEET FOR PROFILES

SCALE

Excavation by Mr. N. H. Field at C–D (Dorset *Procs.* LXXXI (1959), 102–3; LXXXII (1960), 85) showed the ditch to be V-shaped and 6 ft. deep below the outer bank. Sherds from a bowl in the primary silting were comparable in date with complete Durotrigian jars found upright in shallow pits immediately E. of the bank outside this point. Pollen analysis by Professor Dimbleby suggested open land when the earthwork was constructed and thus a mediaeval or later date. Its form is without any close parallel in the area to give further guidance on the date.

PORTESHAM

(56) ENCLOSURE, square, possibly mediaeval or later (SY 68 SW; 64358423), lies on the N.-falling slope of Hewish Hill, a limestone ridge just above 100 ft. A shallow unbroken ditch

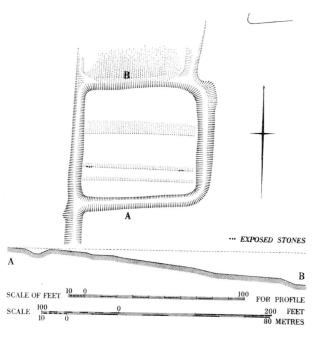

··· EXPOSED STONES

A   B

SCALE OF FEET   10   0   100   FOR PROFILE

SCALE   100   0   200   FEET
        10   0   80 METRES

11 ft. to 21 ft. wide with no trace of an inner or outer bank bounds an area of just under ½ acre. A drainage ditch running N. to S. continues the line of the W. side and another runs N. from the N. side near the N.E. angle. This angle juts prominently above the level of the ground outside, giving a platform-like effect. Slight scarps run E. to W. across the interior and some small limestone blocks appear in one, to the S., which edges a shallow platform 12 ft. wide. The site is probably that noted in 1923 (Dorset *Procs.* XLIV (1923), lxix).

(57) ENCLOSURE, angular (SY 68 NW; 61578700), lies S. of Benecke Wood on a gentle S.-facing slope. Only two sides and part of a third remain, consisting of a low bank about

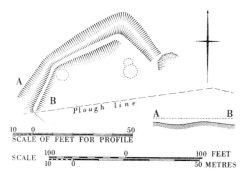

SCALE OF FEET FOR PROFILE

SCALE   100   0   100 FEET
        10   0   50 METRES

20 ft. across with an outer ditch, all disturbed by gravel digging and solution hollows. The S. part has been destroyed by ploughing. The enclosure might have been connected with ancient fields of Group (5) to the S.

PORTLAND

(98) ENCLOSURE, oval, now destroyed (SY 67 SE; 68987354), lay on the Verne at about 440 ft. above O.D. near the highest point of the Isle of Portland. An unbroken bank with an outer ditch and indications of a counterscarp bank enclosed an area of about ⅓ acre. The defences were best preserved on the W. and external measurements were about 250 ft. by 150 ft. On the S. and W. two terraces continued for some distance northwards and eastwards along the edge of the steep scarp of the hill. To a local antiquary, J. Medhurst, these seemed earlier than the enclosure (C. King Warry, *Old Portland Traditions* (*c.* 1908), 15–16). The enclosure was noted as well preserved from the 17th century until its destruction during the building of the fort in *c.* 1860 when inhumation burials, probably Romano-British, were found in the interior and a flint axe and a ball of chert were discovered in the bank on the S.W. Iron Age and Roman finds have been made nearby to the E. and a hoard of '2,000 slingstones the size of cricket balls' came from the area in 1936. (Hutchins II, 817–18; C. Warne, *Illustrations to the History of Dorset*, MS. in D.C.M., 251, with plan; Tithe Map of Portland (1839); Dorset *Procs.* XXXVII (1918), 246; XLIV (1923), 34; *Portland Official Guide* (1947), 21.)

STAFFORD, WEST

(24) ENCLOSURE, oval, probably a Neolithic 'henge' monument (SY 78 NW; 710899), lies across a low hill called Mount Pleasant with gentle slopes on all but the N. where the fall, to the R. Frome, is steeper. The enclosing bank only remains on the S. side and the whole site has been heavily ploughed except for the coppice around Conquer Barrow, a large, much disturbed, mound apparently built on the bank at the W.

The bank is of loosely-packed chalk and earth, spread over a width of 50 ft. or more, and, where best preserved, stood about 5 ft. above the old ground surface. Within the bank was a shallow ditch generally 50 ft. to 60 ft. wide. The simple causewayed entrance at the S.E. is certainly original.

Air photographs indicate that when complete the enclosure measured internally about 1150 ft. (E. to W.) by 1000 ft. and covered 12 acres. The area and the position of the existing entrance suggest that it was probably a 'henge' of Atkinson's Class II and would therefore have had an opposed entrance at the N.W., but there are no indications of such an entrance. Warne called it 'Vespasian's Camp' and recorded the finding of 'a sword and a few ancient relics' (*Ancient Dorset*, 150–1, 242).

Conquer Barrow (22) is about 90 ft. in diameter and lies on the W. bank of the enclosure at the highest point of the hill (*see* plan). It has a flat top 24 ft. across and on the E. is 7 ft. high above a shelf 24 ft. wide, possibly representing part of the original top of the bank, from which there is another drop to a 'berm' immediately above the inner ditch. On the W. the mound falls 15 ft. without a break to a very disturbed sloping shelf up to 30 ft. wide. A bank 2 ft. high and 10 ft. across runs up to the outer edge of this from the S. This shelf could be due to interference, perhaps deliberate remodelling connected with the name 'Mount Pleasant'. Conquer Barrow is probably a

Bronze Age round barrow since its situation on the bank of a Neolithic earthwork has parallels (*e.g.* Robin Hood's Ball, Shrewton, Wilts.). It is shown without the 'henge' on I. Taylor's one inch map of Dorset (1765). It has been suggested that another barrow (23) existed at the centre of the enclosure but the traces are very slight (R. J. C. Atkinson etc., *Excavations at Dorchester, Oxon.* (*First Report*) (1951), 94, 95; S. and C. M. Piggott, *Antiquity* XIII (1939), 158; R.A.F. V.A.P. CPE/UK 1934: 5081–3; 58/271: 5128–30).

STUDLAND

(43) CIRCLES (SZ 08 NW, SW; Fig. p. 506), occur S.E. of Poole Harbour in two groups: seventy-one on the heath of South Haven peninsula W. of the ferry road (025855 to 029860) and six 1000 yds. S.S.W., just W. of the base of the peninsula (021845). Traces of others, totally destroyed, formerly appeared on air photographs at about 017842 (R.A.F. V.A.P. CPE/UK 1821: 4396 and 6388). They all lie on Bagshot Beds, which at surface levels include sands above an iron-pan, and clays, up to a height of 32 ft. above O.D. Most have single banks about 1 ft. high and 9 ft. to 27 ft. across forming rather irregular circles; the interiors are slightly dished but are all almost horizontal, being built up downhill and cut back uphill if on the slight slope to the Harbour. Diameters between crests vary from 36 ft. to 125 ft. Ten banks have narrow gaps in them, one gap being known from excavation to be original. Many held rainwater for short periods, displaying a wet bog flora; others are heather-covered. One or two circles with relatively deep-cut interiors may have been ponds but the function of the others is quite unknown and their date only fixed between the Iron Age and *c.* A.D. 1700. The northern group are associated with thirteen low sandy mounds but these have also defied explanation. In the centre of the peninsula is a straight line of five regularly placed stones, originally standing upright, with a sixth N.W. of the N. end of the line. (*Antiquity* XXXVII (1963), 220–3; R.A.F. V.A.P. 540/723: 5040–1 and CPE/UK 1821: 6385–8.)

WHITCOMBE

(25) ENCLOSURE, D-shaped (SY 78 NW; 70078542; Fig. p. 458, Plate 209), about 100 ft. by 80 ft. with bank and inner ditch each about 13 ft. across, visible on air photographs only. It lies among barrows of the Culliford Tree Group and is apparently cut by ditch of round barrow Whitcombe (14); it is therefore probably of the Bronze Age at latest.

WINTERBOURNE ABBAS

(55) ENCLOSURE, irregular and now flattened (SY 69 SW; 60359175), lies near Lankham Eweleaze on the W. shoulder of a spur falling gently to the 600 ft. contour. The subsoil is thick Clay-with-Flints. The enclosure (Figs. p. 507, opp. p. 623) was built over 'Celtic' fields of Ancient Field Group (1), and the N., W. and S. sides are lynchets, low on the S., 5 ft. to 8 ft.

high on the W. and built up into a slight bank on the N. The S. part of the bowed E. side had a bank 30 ft. wide and 4 ft. high above a wide external ditch. A later, very slight, bank and ditch run up on to the S.E. corner. In the interior a slight scarp, possibly an earlier lynchet, runs E. to W.; its ends correspond with changes in the form of the E. and W. sides. A very slight scarp runs W.S.W. away from the N. side. The earthwork may be unfinished and is possibly a settlement area of the Romano-British period. Broad ridge-and-furrow, probably mediaeval, lies N., E. and probably S. of it.

EARTHWORKS AND BARROW ON MOUNT PLEASANT
WEST STAFFORD

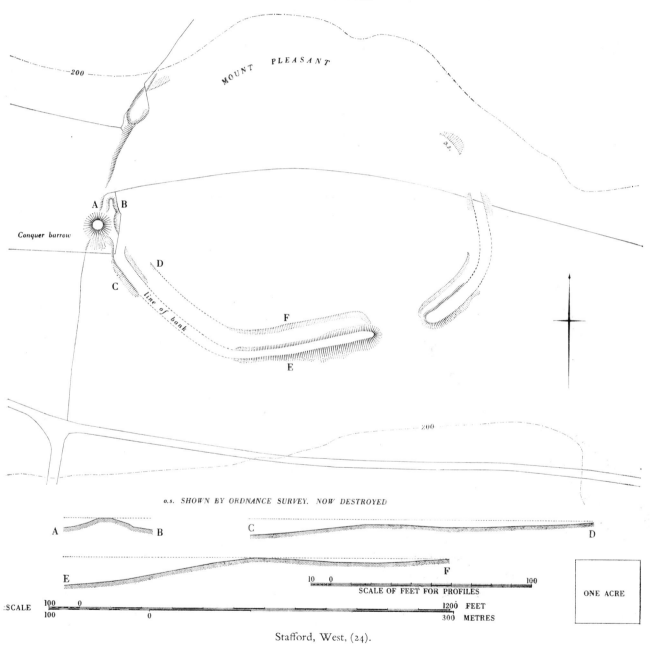

o.s. SHOWN BY ORDNANCE SURVEY. NOW DESTROYED

ONE ACRE

SCALE OF FEET FOR PROFILES

Stafford, West, (24).

G

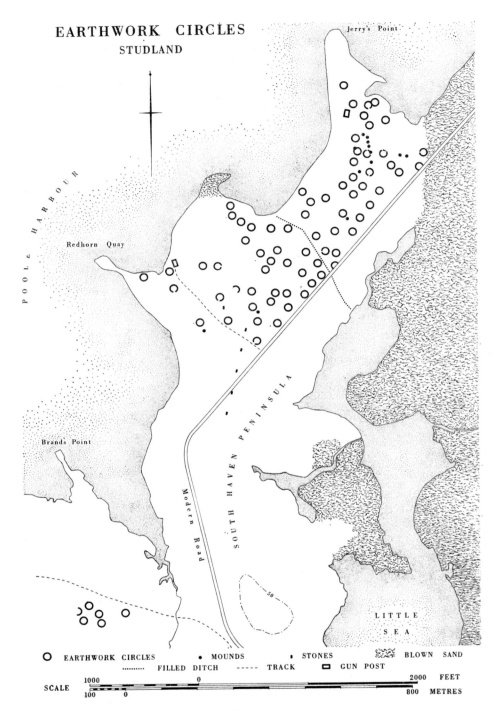

EARTHWORK CIRCLES
STUDLAND

Jerry's Point

POOLE HARBOUR

Redhorn Quay

Brands Point

SOUTH HAVEN PENINSULA

Modern Road

50

LITTLE
SEA

○ EARTHWORK CIRCLES   • MOUNDS   ▪ STONES   ░ BLOWN SAND

.... FILLED DITCH   ----- TRACK   ▭ GUN POST

SCALE

1000   0   2000 FEET
100   0   800 METRES

Studland (43), *see* p. 504.

WINTERBORNE CAME

(49) RING-WORK (SY 68 NE; 68728621), 45 yds. E. of the N.E. mound of round barrow Winterborne Came (28). A depression 41 ft. in diam. and 2 ft. deep in centre is surrounded by a bank 25 ft. wide and 1¾ ft. high broken on S.E. by a gap 15 ft. wide, perhaps an original entrance. An external ditch 22 ft. to 28 ft. wide and 9 ins. deep was recently filled on E. with soil from Dorchester containing Roman and later material. Whether the ditch continues across the gap in the bank is unknown. The form and position of the work, within a close-packed barrow group ((AG) Came Down Group, Winterborne Came), suggest kinship with pond barrows or 'henge' monuments.

WINTERBORNE MONKTON

(11) ENCLOSURE, horseshoe-shaped (SY 68 NE; 66658920), associated with Lanceborough Group of barrows (AH) (Fig. p. 494). It measures overall about 105 ft. E.–W. and about 93 ft. N.–S. The bank, apparently of chalk rubble, is broken by an entrance on the E. There is no sign of an external ditch but the site has been heavily ploughed.

WINTERBORNE ST. MARTIN

(143) ENCLOSURE (?), irregular (SY 68 NW; 63308664), spans the parish boundary with Portesham, just below 600 ft. above O.D., on the gravel-capped Bronkham Hill where it begins to dip E. and falls sharply N. immediately outside the earthwork. Only the N. and part of the W. side survive, forming an 'angle-ditch'. On the N. the bank is downhill, 6 ft. across and 1½ ft. high above the silted ditch, 4 ft. across. On the W. the bank is about 17 ft. across, inside and 3 ft. high above a ditch of similar width. Round barrow Portesham (39) (p. 467) and two solution hollows lie inside this 'angle-ditch', which is probably prehistoric.

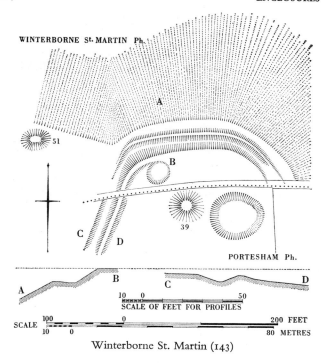

Winterborne St. Martin (143)

(144) ENCLOSURE, rectangular (SY 68 NW; 62508734), lies on the E. side and near the S. end of a gully 120 yds. N.E. of round barrow Winterborne St. Martin (32) on Bronkham Hill (Group R.6) and at about 550 ft. above O.D. It is defined by scarps on the N. and W., up to 3 ft. high at the N.W. angle, by a vestigial scarp on the S. and by the steep gully side on the E. The interior, about ⅕ acre in area, falls gently N. In the

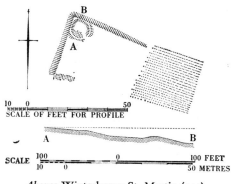

Above: Winterborne St. Martin (144)

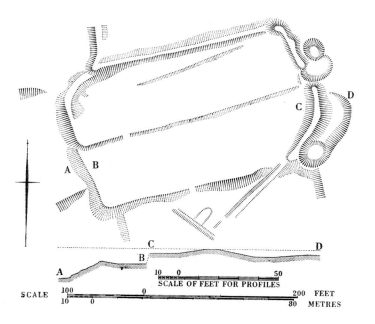

Left: Winterbourne Abbas (55), *see* pp. 504–5

N.W. angle is an apparent hut-circle with an almost level floor about 15 ft. across and sunk some 3 ft. below the scarp which marks it uphill; it has an entrance 6 ft. wide at the S.E.

The enclosure is probably prehistoric. Immediately to the N.E. are fragmentary, very low, rounded lynchets. (R.A.F. V.A.P. CPE/UK 1934: 1066 etc.)

WINTERBOURNE STEEPLETON

(63) ENCLOSURE, sub-rectangular (SY 68 NW; 60338807), lies 300 yds. N. of the summit of Black Down some 650 ft. above O.D. and within the N.W. angle of the cross-roads (Fig. opp. p. 624). It lies on a gentle slope on pebble gravel of the Bagshot Beds. A bank about 14 ft. across rises some 1½ ft. above the interior and about 4 ft. above an outer ditch some 14 ft. wide with traces of a counterscarp bank. The interior is flat, ¼ acre in extent, and may have been subdivided. The simple gap and causeway entrance is midway along the E. side.

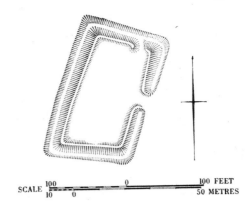

ENCLOSURES

SCALE 100 — 0 — 100 FEET
10 — 0 — 50 METRES

Winterbourne Steepleton (63)

SETTLEMENTS

The sites described in this section are open or unenclosed settlements, probably prehistoric or Romano-British, with earthwork remains in the form of hut-sites, closes, terrace-ways, etc. Other less well-defined settlements or settlement areas, closely associated with 'Celtic' fields, are noted here but are described under the Ancient Field Groups. Additional evidence of settlement comes from finds of occupation material unassociated with earthwork remains: most of these sites were occupied in the Roman period and are listed in the Roman section; those with prehistoric material only are listed on pp. 511–12. Known mediaeval settlement remains are described in the parish inventories.

Within the area covered by this volume only five certain settlements have survived to be recorded as earthworks, of which one, Winterbourne Steepleton (64), has since been destroyed. Only Church Knowle (54) and Winterbourne Steepleton (64) lie on chalk. The former, shown by test excavation to be Iron Age 'A', consists of a series of poorly-defined, shallow scoops on the N. brow of Knowle Hill in an area confined within cross-dykes. Finds and the absence of 'Celtic' fields suggest that it may have been a predominantly pastoral settlement. The latter comprises a group of circular hut-platforms and poorly defined irregular enclosures lying within an area of 'Celtic' fields, though not clearly related to them. Circular hut-platforms, either singly or in groups, among 'Celtic' fields are found chiefly in W. Dorset and beyond. Such settlements are in the native tradition and are probably Iron Age in origin rather than later. The remaining settlements are on limestone in the Isle of Purbeck. Corfe Castle (221) and (222) are small settlements, probably no more than farms, side by side within the same group of limestone-walled 'Celtic' fields; Church Knowle (55) is of unusual form, comprising a block of small, platformed enclosures.

The known distribution of settlement for the Iron Age and Romano-British periods is shown, together with the known areas of 'Celtic' fields, on the half-inch physical background map (opp. p. 634). This distribution is the product of chance survival and probably bears only a very limited resemblance to the original distribution of Iron Age and Romano-British occupation. Settlements have survived for the most part in areas remote, or well away from, mediaeval and later settlements, generally on the higher ground where arable activity over the past one and a half millennia has been negligible. On the lower ground, especially around modern settlements, permanent cultivation, from at least the early mediaeval period onwards, has largely destroyed the remains of earlier occupation. Two points are, however, clear from the distribution map: the high density of settlement, especially in the Roman period, in the Isle of Purbeck, and the almost complete absence of settlement from the poorer soils of the Tertiary sands and gravels, today largely covered by heath and woodland.

Detailed knowledge of the economy of Iron Age and Romano-British rural settlements is wanting, but in Wessex generally a mixed farming economy almost certainly predominated. Settlements devoted solely or largely to specific activities such as shale or salt working would have formed but a minority. The relative importance of arable to pastoral farming, either generally or on any one site, remains unknown; and large areas of 'Celtic' fields associated with settlements need not imply an economy almost entirely dependent on arable farming. Trackways leading from enclosures and 'open spaces' around settlements outwards through arable fields suggest the movement of stock, while the considerable quantities of pottery, particularly Romano-British pottery, found scattered over 'Celtic' fields and usually thought to have been spread with manure, imply the existence of numerous domesticated animals.

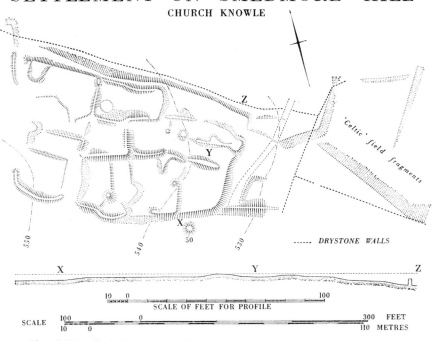

SETTLEMENT ON SMEDMORE HILL
CHURCH KNOWLE

Church Knowle (55), *see* p. 510. (Shown at larger scale than other settlements.)

BERE REGIS

Probable SETTLEMENT, *see* Ancient Field Group (30a).
Probable SETTLEMENT, near Elderton Clump, *see* Ancient Field Group (31).

CHALDON HERRING

Possible SETTLEMENT AREAS, associated with 'Celtic' fields, *see* Ancient Field Group (15).

CHURCH KNOWLE

(54) SETTLEMENT, of Iron Age 'A', on Knowle Hill (SY 98 SW; 93568224; Plate 212), lay within an area of 4½ acres between cross-ridge dykes on the summit and N.

shoulder of the chalk ridge about 470 ft. above O.D. (*see* Dykes, Church Knowle (56c,d)). Extensions of the dykes towards each other on the N. suggest an unfulfilled intention to enclose the whole area, but the arrangement of the two parts of dyke (d), with the ditch on different sides, can be matched in a settlement on Muston Down, Winterborne Kingston (*Dorset* III, forthcoming).

Ill-defined scoops are found over one acre only, on the N shoulder, but excavation of the clearest and largest of these, (x), showed that occupational material had been washed into it from the crest of the hill above. Abundant finds here indicated an economy dependent upon cattle, though there was also much evidence for the working of Kimmeridge shale. (Dorset *Procs.*, LXXIX (1957), 106–7.) The arrangement of dykes (56a, b, e), to E. and W. of those enclosing the settlement, suggests pastoral usage as does the absence of 'Celtic' fields. A mound, Church Knowle (51), might be associated with the settlement. Ditched banks, up to 24 ft. across and 2 ft. high, running up the N. side of the ridge on a slope of up to 26°, are undated and of uncertain purpose though such banks are occasionally found in a similar relationship to hill-forts (*cf.* Chalbury, Bincombe (76)).

(x), a roughly circular area about 24 ft. across, was dug during the Iron Age into a natural N. slope of 9°. Whatever its origins, it eventually had a flat floor about 11 ft. across 3½ ft. below the surface on the uphill side. In this floor were four post-holes, 9 ins. in diameter and arranged in a square with sides of 8 ft., that probably held roof supports. The pottery is all coarse with relatively little finger-tip decoration but no sign of Iron Age 'B' influences.

(55) SETTLEMENT, probably prehistoric and Romano-British (SY 97 NW; 931796; Fig. p. 509), in Ancient Field Group (20), covers just over 1 acre at about 540 ft. above O.D. on a gentle N. slope of Smedmore Hill, a limestone ridge, where the main fall is E. towards a valley-head. The settlement consists of a block of small enclosures unlike any other in Dorset. These enclosures are platformed, bounded by scarps or banks up to 2½ ft. high; some seem to contain limestone rubble. A mound just S. (*see* Mounds, Church Knowle (50)) may be connected with the settlement but any extension on this side has been obliterated by ploughing in narrow rig. Iron Age 'A' and Romano-British pottery, samian to late coarse ware, came from a pipe trench (Dorset *Procs.* LXXVIII (1956), 76) at the extreme E. of the settlement where it seems to be linked to 'Celtic' fields. The short, straight lengths of scarp along the N. side of the settlement further suggest that 'Celtic' fields ran up to it. (R.A.F. V.A.P. CPE/UK 1821: 5415.)

CORFE CASTLE

Note: The two settlements, (221–2) *below*, lie in close relationship on Kingston Down within Ancient Field Group (23) (Fig. p. 631). They are so integrated with the fields that their precise limits are uncertain.

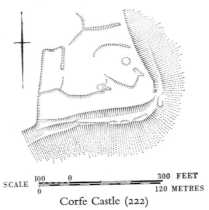

SCALE 100 0 300 FEET
0 120 METRES

Corfe Castle (222)

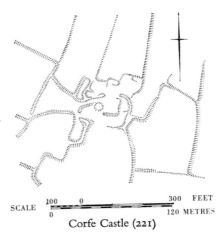

SCALE 100 0 300 FEET
0 120 METRES

Corfe Castle (221)

(221) SETTLEMENT, prehistoric or Romano-British (SY 97 NE; 957781; Plate 235), covers up to 6 acres just over 400 ft. above O.D. on the almost flat, exposed top of the limestone coastal plateau. It comprises a series of closes marked by low turf-covered banks and includes at least two hut-circles, one embanked and 17 ft. across with an entrance on the E., and another, slightly sunken, 20 ft. across. Between the hut-circles a stretch of track runs for 30 yds. E.–W. and opens into a close.

(222) SETTLEMENT, prehistoric or Romano-British (SY 97 NE; 960779; Plate 235), covers 3 acres or more about 250 yds. S.E. of (221), on the same limestone plateau. The ground falls steeply S. and E. from it. Two shallow circular depressions about 22 ft. and 27 ft. across lie 120 ft. apart in an area of disturbed closes, some with curved sides, defined by low banks. Iron Age 'C' or Romano-British sherds were found on the surface. Two tracks lead from it: one W.S.W. to the S. tip of the plateau, where rough platforming suggests a further possible area of settlement, and a second S.W. diagonally downhill for 250 yds. between 'Celtic' fields before being lost in an area of landslip.

LULWORTH, WEST

Possible SETTLEMENT AREAS associated with 'Celtic' fields, *see* Ancient Field Group (15).

OWERMOIGNE

Possible SETTLEMENT AREA associated with 'Celtic' fields, *see* Ancient Field Group (11).

WINFRITH NEWBURGH

Probable SETTLEMENT AREA associated with 'Celtic' fields, *see* Ancient Field Group (15).

WINTERBOURNE STEEPLETON

(64) SETTLEMENT, probably prehistoric (SY 68 NW; 61538937–61668904), lay in Ancient Field Group (3) (Fig. opp. p. 624) and covered 8 acres of former downland called 'Rowden', which divided two blocks of open

fields (Winterbourne Steepleton (12), p. 396); it was examined before destruction in 1962. The features were not necessarily contemporary but all except (e) appeared to be linked by tracks. They lay at around 500 ft. above O.D. facing W. on the brow above a dry valley in the chalk. (R.A.F. V.A.P. CPE/UK 1934: 3095–6.)

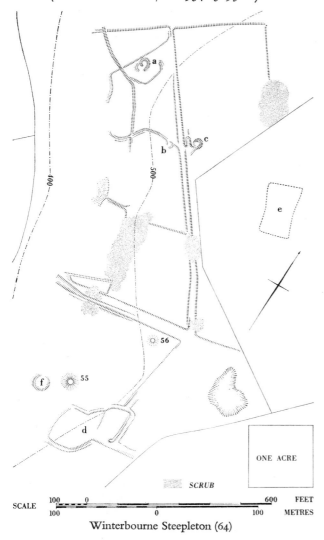

ONE ACRE

SCRUB

SCALE   100   0   600   FEET
         100   0   100   METRES

Winterbourne Steepleton (64)

From the N. the complex comprised: (a) a hut-circle 14 ft. across within an incomplete angular enclosure of ⅙ acre, itself apparently set within an irregular enclosure of 1½ acres; (b) 80 yds. S.E., a circular hut-platform 20 ft. across set against the E. end of the S. bank of the last-named enclosure; (c) a hut-platform 15 ft. across, to the N.E. of (b); (d) 300 yds. further S., an angular enclosure of ⅗ acre; and (e) 100 yds. E. of (c), the soil-mark of an irregular oblong enclosure, long ploughed flat, about ⅖ acre in area. A large circular platform (f), with almost flat floor 36 ft. across levelled into

the slope, was more likely to be a hut-circle and part of the settlement than a pond barrow.

A terrace-way 10 ft. to 15 ft. wide ran from due E. of (a) S.E. for about 280 yds. to a disturbed junction of tracks. A broad slightly sunken way 45 ft. wide ran downhill W. from this junction, its lower end hollowed on the S. side by later usage. Traces of a track ran S. from the junction towards (d), from which a track extended N. to meet it. This last led round the E. side of (d) to an entrance where it was met by a further track from the E.

Slight lynchets and banks within the area indicated cultivation but there were no certain contacts with 'Celtic' fields. The nature of the remains and the existence of at least six barrows around (d) suggest that this area never bore 'Celtic' fields and was reserved early for settlement.

For further possible settlement areas see Ancient Field Group (3).

FINDS INDICATING SETTLEMENT

At the sites listed below there are no earthworks but finds indicating probable prehistoric settlement have been made. For other sites where finds indicate probable continuity into the Roman period, see the Roman section, pp. 520–621. Within each parish the sites are listed in order of probable date. Unless otherwise stated, references are to *Proceedings* of the Dorset Natural History and Archaeological Society.

BINCOMBE

West Hill SY 70398476	Neolithic bowl of Windmill Hill ware with flint and chert flakes in pit (LXXIX (1957), 112–3, under Sutton Poyntz)
Ridgeway Hill SY 67558584	Pits containing Neolithic implements of Portland chert; sherds of Beaker coarse wares and other late Neolithic material in overlying land surface, immediately beneath round barrow Bincombe (27) (see p. 456 above)

CHICKERELL

Littlesea SY 650782	Flint and chert implements, probably Mesolithic (LXXXIII (1961), 97; LXXXIV (1962), 101; LXXXV (1963), 109)

CORFE CASTLE

Blashenwell SY 95108052	Mesolithic implements and flint flakes with bones of pig, deer and ox sealed by tufa deposit and dated by C 14 method to 4490 ± 150 B.C. (LXXXIII (1961), 94–5)

CORFE MULLEN

Beaucroft SY 977977	Mesolithic flints (LXXXIII (1961), 96)
Crumpets SY 964964	Mesolithic flints (*ibid.*)
Draglen's SY 979980	Mesolithic flints, including microlithic cores (*ibid.*)

East End
SY 992983

Neolithic hut site in gravel pit; an oval hollow 7 ft. by 4 ft. and 3 ft. deep with pottery and flint flakes (LX (1938), 73–4)

Sleight
SY 985981

Iron Age pottery, charcoal and burnt flints (LII (1930), xl–xli; LXXXVI (1964), 120–2)

LANGTON MATRAVERS

Lynchard
SY 99207965

Early Bronze Age cist with shale button, flint knife and whetstone (LXXXI (1959), 116–7)

POOLE

Plainfield Farm
SZ 012951

Mesolithic flints (LXXXIII (1961), 96)

PORTLAND

Portland Bill
SY 681690

Mesolithic working-floor, with numerous picks (LXXXVIII (1966), 102).

SWANAGE

Ulwell
SZ 02058098

Mesolithic implements, bones and shells in small pits (LXXIV (1952), 48–9)

TYNEHAM

Whiteway Farm
SY 87758170

Iron Age occupation (W. H. C. Frend, note on O.S. 6 in. map, LV NE, in D.C.M.)

WEYMOUTH

Wyke Regis
SY 657769

Chert cores and implements, probably Mesolithic (LXXXIII (1961), 97; LXXXV (1963), 109, 115)

The Nothe
SY 685786

Middens with shells, fish bones, charcoal and pottery, perhaps Neolithic (R. Damon, *Geology of the Weymouth Area* (1884), 164)

Wyke Regis
SY 65697695

Iron Age salters' hearth with burnt shale and pottery (LXXXIV (1962), 132–6, 143–4)

WORTH MATRAVERS

Gallows Gore
SY 97907899

Floor with flint flakes and Bronze Age food-vessel (LXXXI (1959), 117, 118, fig. 2(2))

Sheepsleights
SY 96887827
SY 96917836

Late Bronze/Early Iron Age pottery, querns, worked flint and shale, bronze razor, bones and grain (spelt) in pits (LXX (1948), 30–2; LXXIV (1952), 50–1; LXXXI (1959), 117)

STONES

Both single stones and multiple arrangements of stones, of varied date and purpose, occur in South-east Dorset. Some are clearly mediaeval or later, but others, even if on parish boundaries, are of uncertain date and are therefore described in this section.

Single stones: most of the uninscribed, unshaped stones can be regarded as markers; some like Portesham (60–1) may be relatively recent, but others like the 'Harpstone', Steeple (27), apparently old enough to have given a name to the mediaeval manor, may be Saxon or prehistoric. The very numerous mere or boundary stones, particularly in the limestone areas, are all post-mediaeval. All the surviving examples associated with strip fields are described in the parish inventories (Corfe Castle (177), Kimmeridge (15), Portland (95), Swanage (79)) as are representative examples of those marking parish boundaries (Church Knowle (26)) or manor and estate boundaries (Studland (26)).

Multiple arrangements: the earliest are undoubtedly the circles, Winterbourne Abbas (57) and Corfe Castle (223), composed of well spaced standing stones. The first of these, the 'Nine Stones', is of particular interest since two of its stones, exceptionally massive compared with the other seven, can be paralleled by the Late Neolithic/Early Bronze Age 'A' and 'B' stones of the Kennet Avenue in the complex at Avebury, Wiltshire, and suggest both deliberate selection of such stones, and also a close link between the smallest and largest of stone arrangements. The Rempstone circle has a diameter three times that of the 'Nine Stones' and might have been connected with a possible avenue, now destroyed. Its low situation is akin to that of the 'Nine Stones' but its size resembles that of the circle in Kingston Russell (4) (*Dorset* I), which is probably of similar date but sited on high downland. Recent excavation has shown that the original circle on Portesham Hill, Portesham (58), was slightly smaller than the 'Nine Stones'. The Poxwell circle (12), likely to be of similar or rather later date, differs radically from the free-standing stone circles since there is little doubt that it was an integral part of a burial mound, now almost destroyed, and was originally a continuous stone wall. There is no pointer to the relationship between free-standing circles and barrows.

Big sarsens occur naturally in certain areas, *e.g.* the Valley of Stones (Ancient Field Group (3)), around Little Mayne, West Knighton (20), and in Portesham village (Arkell (1947), 241).

AFFPUDDLE

(65) DEAD WOMAN'S STONE (SY 89 SW; 82209164), shown by O.S., cannot be traced in heathland now devastated by tanks.

CHURCH KNOWLE

BOUNDARY STONE, see Church Knowle (26), p. 47.

CORFE CASTLE

(223) REMPSTONE[1] STONE CIRCLE (SY 98 SE; 99468207; Fig. p. 514), now incomplete, lies in a wood just S. of the Corfe Castle to Studland road at 278 ft. above O.D. on a gentle W.-facing slope near the foot of Nine Barrow Down. The wet site is cut by pools and ditches, owing largely to clay workings shown on a map of 1772 (in the possession of Major D. C. D. Ryder, Rempstone Hall).

The stones are irregularly-shaped boulders of hard gritstone from the local Bagshot Beds. Those surviving form an arc suggesting a circle originally about 80 ft. in diameter. Of the 12 on or near their original setting five still stand to heights varying from 2 ft. to 3¾ ft.; seven are prone and some of these have clearly been moved. The largest visible stone is 6½ ft. long, 2¾ ft. wide and 2 ft. out of the ground. Nine other stones are piled 80 ft. to the E.

The circle was first noted in 1908 and probably belongs to the Early Bronze Age (Dorset *Procs.* XXIX (1908), liii and Pl. facing liv; see also *Antiquity* XIII (1939), 148). In 1957 J. B. Calkin described two parallel rows of stones about 9 ft. apart ½ mile W. of the circle but aligned to a point some 12° N. of it. The stones, again of local sandstone, averaged 2½ ft. by 1 ft. by 6 ins. in size. It was suggested that they might have formed part of a processional way leading to the circle (Dorset *Procs.* LXXXI (1959), 114–6). The circle is No. 184 on the O.S. *Map of Neolithic Wessex* but early editions wrongly describe the Holdenhurst long barrow against this number.

MERE-STONES, see Corfe Castle (177), p. 98.

KIMMERIDGE

BOUNDARY STONE, see Kimmeridge (15), p. 135.

KNIGHTON, WEST

Some 50 recumbent sarsens (SY 78 NW; 72148707, 72288717, 72388705) are scattered around Little Mayne Farm. They are a natural phenomenon and form no coherent plan, despite alleged arrangements in one or more circles or avenues (one of which is certainly a mediaeval road). Most have been moved. (R. Gale: notes made April 1728, printed in Surtees Soc. II (1883), 127; C. Warne, *Illustrations of the History of Dorset* (1847 MS. in D.C.M.), 232; Dorset *Procs.* XXX (1909), xlvi; Arkell (1947), 241; see also Knighton, West (20), p. 140.)

---

[1] The name apparently refers to a family, not to stones (Fägersten, 120).

PORTESHAM

THE HELL STONE, see Long Barrows, Portesham (33).

(58) STONE CIRCLE (SY 58 NE; 59628650), on Portesham Hill, stands 550 yds. S.E. of Hampton Barn on a level site about 680 ft. above O.D. (Fig. p. 514). Excavations in 1965, by Dr. G. J. Wainwright of the Ministry of Public Building and Works, established that the surviving stones were not bedded and that there had been an earlier circle. This circle, represented by the sockets of stones, lay under and to the W. of the field bank which crosses the site. It was 18 ft. to 20 ft. in internal diameter and was composed of nine stones, set in two arcs to N. and S.; the E. and W. sides were defined by narrow V-sectioned ditches. A hollowed track, running up to the circle on the N., was revetted on its W. side by small flat stones, and three stake-holes were found on the perimeter of the circle immediately to the W. A low bank of clay had been constructed between the track and the stones in the N.W. quarter and the S. edge of the socket on the E. side of the track was also built up with clay and stones. The circle had been disturbed before or by the building of the field bank with its side ditches. Stones have now been placed in the excavated holes. (Information from Dr. G. J. Wainwright; Dorset *Procs.* XXIX (1908), lxxviii (with photograph of later circle), 250; LXXXVIII (1966), 122–7; *Antiquity* XIII (1939), 142, fig. 2; O.S. *Map of Neolithic Wessex*, no. 143; R. D'O. Good, *Weyland* (1945), 32.)

(59) STONES (SY 58 NE; 59658688), two recumbent and partially buried sarsens, lie 5 yds. apart 350 yds. W. of Hampton Barn on top of Portesham Hill at 650 ft. above O.D. and on gentle slopes down to N. and E. They measure 10½ ft. by 4 ft. and 7½ ft. by 3 ft., the larger lying to the N. These two stones are probably the only remains of the 'collapsed dolmen' illustrated in Dorset *Procs.* XXIX (1908), lxxiv. The photograph, in which four or five stones are visible, suggests a collapsed chamber with a large tilted capstone. Crawford listed this as a long barrow orientated N.W. to S.E., with the two stones presumably as the remains of a chamber at the S.E. end, but there is now no evidence for this. Just to the N. is a probable round barrow, Portesham (44). (LVG I; O.S. *Map of Neolithic Wessex*, no. 144; G. E. Daniel, *P.C.T.E.W.* (1949), 235.)

(60) STONE (SY 68 NW; 61508664), irregular, of sarsen, stands 1600 yds. N.E. of Portesham Church. It is slab-like and about 3 ft. high with numerous shallow horizontal grooves, all but one apparently natural, on the N. face. The stone was probably erected in its present position in relatively recent times. Sarsens are natural in this area.

(61) STONE (SY 68 SW; 62758412), irregular, of limestone, stands in a hollow 220 yds. S. of East Shilvinghampton just N. of and slightly below the crest of an E. to W. ridge at about 230 ft. above O.D. It may mark the S. limit of shallow quarrying extending to E. and W.

PORTLAND

MERE-STONES, see Portland (95), p. 259.

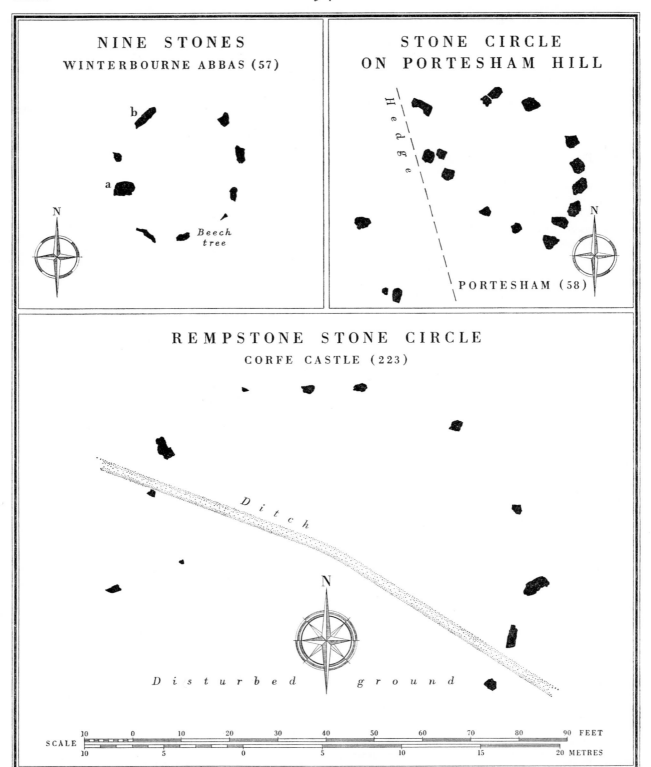

NINE STONES
WINTERBOURNE ABBAS (57)

STONE CIRCLE
ON PORTESHAM HILL

PORTESHAM (58)

REMPSTONE STONE CIRCLE
CORFE CASTLE (223)

Portesham (58) shown as before excavation in 1965 (*see* p. 513).

POXWELL

'STONE CIRCLE', *see* Round Barrows, Poxwell (12).

STEEPLE

(27) THE HARPSTONE (SY 98 SW; 92168058; Plate 217), monolith, of limestone, stands 1,180 yds. E.S.E. of St. Michael's Church, on the bank of a small stream and just inside the W. edge of Hurpston Coppice on ground falling gently N. to the Corfe River in the marshy valley bottom. It is 7¼ ft. high with a jagged and uneven top and has a maximum width of 3¾ ft. E.-W. and 3 ft. N.-S. The four faces are largely disfigured by vertical grooves and hollows, the result of weathering. Its origin is unknown. The place-name *Herpston* (1340) may refer to the stone, which stands on the bank between Herpston and Hyde manors and flanks the ancient road from Creech to Kimmeridge. (Hutchins I, 609; Fägersten, 136.)

STUDLAND

BOUNDARY STONES, *see* Studland (26), p. 282.

SWANAGE

MERE-STONES, *see* Swanage (79), p. 287.

TURNERS PUDDLE

(25) STONE (SY 89 SW; 83749403) of sarsen, stands 1000 yds. N.E. of Holy Trinity Church on Black Hill and on the parish boundary with Bere Regis. It is 11 ft. high, 4 ft. in circumference and very much weathered.

WINTERBOURNE ABBAS

(56) THE BROAD STONE (SY 59 SE; 59549040; Plate 217), a large sarsen boulder, lies half-buried in the scarp falling from the S. verge of the Bridport Road 2530 yds. W. of Winterbourne Abbas Church. It is approximately 9 ft. long, 4 ft. wide and 2 ft. thick with the long axis E. to W. and a pointed E. end. All markings appear to be natural. (Hutchins II, 196.)

(57) THE NINE STONES stone circle (SY 69 SW; 61079043; Fig. p. 514, Plate 211), stands immediately S. of the Bridport road 850 yds. W. of the church in an enclosure just inside Nine Stone Wood. The site is level at 345 ft. above O.D. on the S. edge of a narrow valley floor. The subsoil is apparently river gravel with Upper Chalk adjacent to the S.

The stones, all sarsens, are arranged in a rough circle with internal diameters of about 27½ ft. (N. to S.) and 23½ ft. (W. to E.). Though they are irregularly spaced, a gap to the N. is almost twice as wide as any other gap. Seven of the stones are small and low, from about 1 ft. to 2½ ft. high. Two are more massive: (a) is 7 ft. high and its elongated form recalls the 'A' stones in the Kennet Avenue near Avebury, Wilts.; (b), a large slab, 6 ft. high and 6 ft. across at the base, is like the 'B' stones in the same Avenue (*cf. Antiquity* X (1936), 420).

Aubrey recorded only nine stones, as did Hutchins in 1768; but Warne alleged traces of a tenth to the N.E., presumably in the wide gap. Stukeley's drawing of 1723 shows the circle in the same state as at present and nothing could be seen of any additional stone in 1936. (S. and C. M. Piggott, *Antiquity* XIII (1939), 146, with facsimile of Aubrey's MS. notes as pl. I; J. Hutchins, *History of Dorset* II, 196, and *Gentleman's Magazine* (1768), 112–3, letter signed J. H.; C. Warne, *Ancient Dorset* (1872), 117–8; J. Stukeley, *Itinerarium Curiosum* II (1724), *tab.* 92, which has been wrongly identified as showing a site in Winterbourne Monkton, Wilts.) The site is a guardianship monument of the Ministry of Public Building and Works and is No. 149 on the O.S. *Map of Neolithic Wessex*.

WINTERBOURNE STEEPLETON

(65) STONES, possibly remains of chambered long barrow (SY 68 NW; 61408968; marked 'cromlech' on some maps; Plate 217), lie 1630 yds. W.S.W. of the church at 400 ft. above O.D. on a steep S.E.-facing slope, now in pasture. One large sarsen, an irregular oblong 8 ft. by 4¾ ft. and 1¼ ft. above ground, lies in the shoulder of a rounded scarp some 2 ft. high. A second sarsen, 4 ft. across and 1 ft. 8 ins. deep, projects from the scarp 5 ft. to the E. Three small boulders can be seen between these large stones. Warne listed this site among 'destroyed cromlechs' describing 'one large stone apparently the capstone with two or three others . . . in a confused heap' (*Ancient Dorset* (1872), 136). The stones may not be *in situ* since the area was once part of the arable fields of Winterbourne Steepleton (Monument (12)), and the scarp is in part a lynchet ploughed down since enclosure. (LVG II; O.S. *Map of Neolithic Wessex*, no. 148.)

DYKES

The dykes described in this Volume are classified as linear dykes or cross-ridge dykes. The former are generally longer and more irregular than the latter which run approximately at right angles across a ridge or spur.

Linear Dykes: four of the nine examples are clustered together on Worgret Heath (Arne (48)). Another, mostly outside the Volume boundary (Winterbourne Steepleton (66)), is the only one to be dated even approximately: it appears from an R.C.H.M. excavation to be of the Late Bronze Age. Attached to it is a small enclosure recalling a similar relationship of this period on Boscombe Down East, Wilts.[1] This is the only example which warrants any comparison with the linear ditches of N.E. Dorset and beyond, and even so, seems to form no part of a large enclosure as would be usual with a 'ranch boundary'. Doubtful analogy suggests that the only multiple examples, amongst the Worgret Dykes, are Romano-British. Battery Bank (E. Stoke (50)) by its possible length of over 3 miles suggests comparison with boundary works like Comb's Ditch 4 miles S.W. of Blandford (to be described in *Dorset* III) or the late Roman but much bigger Bokerley Dyke. None of the single banks and ditches exceeds 53 ft. in maximum overall span (Battery Bank) and only one has a depth, from crest of bank, approaching 8 ft. Most are much less, the very curious Winterborne St. Martin (145) being the smallest.

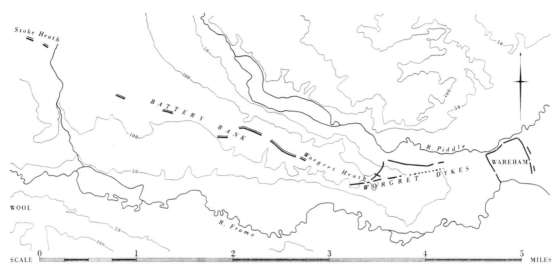

Linear Dykes W. of Wareham. Arne (48), East Stoke (50).

Cross-ridge Dykes: all ten are on chalk and eight are probably Iron Age. Five, on Knowle Hill (Church Knowle (56)), are arranged in a coherent pattern around a proved Iron Age 'A' settlement, which strongly suggests that they could have been developed into a small hill-fort with outlying dykes. The hill-fort of Flower's Barrow actually has such an outlier (E. Lulworth (41)). This is considerably smaller than the relatively massive dyke, Weymouth (436), that may have converted the Windsbatch spur into a promontory fort, rather as W. Lulworth (53b) cut off the W. end of Bindon Hill.

Winterborne Monkton (12) is anomalous in that, although it crosses a spur from combe to combe, the even and gentle fall of the spur and the presence of barrows on one side and former open field on the other leave its function and date quite uncertain. Portesham (62) could be recent.

ARNE

(48) LINEAR DYKES, four, on Worgret Heath and Wareham Common, partly in the parish of Wareham Lady St. Mary (SY 88 NE, 98 NW; 89638705 to 91218745). This complex lies on gravels and sands, now mostly heath and poorly drained, between the rivers Piddle and Frome (Fig. above). The W. end is 1½ miles due W. of Wareham and about 750 yds. S.E. of the first of a series of discontinuous lengths of dyke, all facing N.,

known collectively as Battery Bank (*see* East Stoke (50)). There seems to be no necessary connection between these two sets of earthworks.

The dykes are of different forms but their siting is nowhere tactical and they appear to be boundaries forming barriers to movement, possibly of cattle, rather than defences. Alignment (c) differs from (a) and (b) in situation, however, while only (b) has double ditches. The fragmentary bank-and-ditch (d) cuts through (b) and may conceivably be connected, from its alignment, with Battery Bank. The line of earthworks shown on

---

[1] *W.A.M.* XLVII (1936) 466–89.

DYKES ON WORGRET HEATH AND WAREHAM COMMON
ARNE AND WAREHAM LADY St. MARY

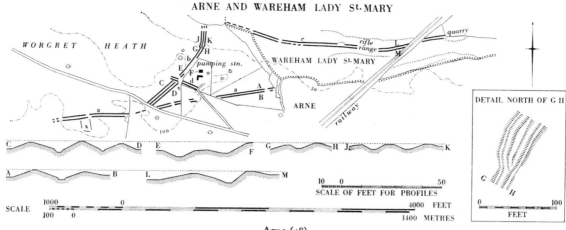

Arne (48).

O.S. maps N. of the W. end of (a) appears to be the result of gravel digging.

The date of the dykes is uncertain. The nearest possible analogy for the variably multiple form is on the chalkland of Cranborne Chase, where the dykes are possibly Romano-British (D. W. Harding, Dorset *Procs.* LXXXI (1959), 110–13). If (d) can be connected with Battery Bank, then (b) would have gone out of use when Battery Bank was built.

(a) consists of two banks, some $1\frac{1}{2}$ ft. high, on either side of a narrow-bottomed ditch 4 ft. deep; the overall width is 45 ft. It runs N.E. for about 1000 yds. from a re-entrant gully and is now broken by two wide gaps. There are faint traces at the N.E. end of a link with the present Arne-Wareham parish boundary which continues the alignment for $\frac{4}{5}$ mile. Near the S.W. end, on a plateau 100 ft. above O.D., discontinuous banks about 1 ft. high, double on the E., spring from the S. side and might have formed a trapezoidal enclosure (x), measuring some 120 ft. (E.) by 225 ft. (N.).

(b) is of varied form: for the first 200 yds. triple banks contain two ditches, the whole being 62 ft. wide, but after being cut by (d), there are first two ditches and two banks, then one bank between two ditches, then one ditch between two banks and finally three banks and two ditches, 50 ft. overall (for junction between these last two forms, *see* detail on plan). It runs N.E. and then N. for about 400 yds. from the modern road near a gap in (a) to a scarp 10 ft. high falling to the flood plain of the river Piddle.

(c) consists of double banks with a ditch between them, the whole varying in width from 45 ft. to 55 ft. In places the ditch is up to $5\frac{3}{4}$ ft. deep below the banks but recent excavation of a field drain along part of it may point to similar scourings in the past. A recent cut near the rifle butts suggested the possibility of a flat bottom 7 ft. below the top of the banks (Dorset *Procs.* LXXVIII (1956), 78). The dyke follows the low-lying terrace approximately parallel to the river Piddle for 860 yds. from a point 200 yds. E. of the N. end of (b) and

may have continued further W. on the line of the Arne-Wareham parish boundary. The rifle butts and much of the length E. of them have recently been destroyed (Dorset *Procs.* LXXXI (1959), 108); a large field bank continued the line further E. towards the N.W. angle of Wareham defences.

(d) is a bank 3 ft. high with a ditch and counterscarp bank on the N., about 30 ft. wide overall, and cuts (b) at right angles. It projects only a few feet to the N.W. but traces exist to the S.E. for about 100 yds.

BERE REGIS

(119) LINEAR DYKE (SY 89 NW; 81389644–81889701) runs along the parish boundary with Milborne St. Andrew, down the sides and across the bottom of the small dry valley followed by the Bere Regis–Milborne road. To S.W., it begins about 610 yds. S. of the road, in the centre it is broken for about 25 yds. either side of the road, and it apparently ends about 230 yds. N. of the road. The ends are ill-defined, owing to an overlying (manorial?) boundary bank, which continues the line to the S.W. The dimensions vary along the dyke's length, but at most it is 23 ft. wide and 6 ft. high; throughout, it is higher above present ground level on the W. than the E., suggesting a ditch on the W. and uphill side. Towards its S.W. end, the bank is crossed by a double-lynchet track running past the probable settlement in Ancient Field Group (30). (Warne, *C.T.D.*, cpf, barrow no. 2.)

CHURCH KNOWLE

(56) CROSS-RIDGE DYKES, five, on Knowle Hill (SY 98 SW; Fig. opp. p. 509, Plate 212), are of varying form; (c) and (d) are complex. Some or all are likely to be contemporary with the Iron Age 'A' settlement, Church Knowle (54), which lies between (c) and (d), the ditches of all the dykes being on the side distant from it. The apparently unfinished works along the N. shoulder

between (c) and (d) suggest that there may have been an intention to enclose this area.

(a) (93088211) is much disturbed by a quarry on the S. but runs 100 ft. to the edge of the ridge on the N. The bank is about 15 ft. across and now up to 3 ft. high above its ditch, 10 ft. wide. A slighter bank, 12 ft. wide and 1 ft. high, also with a ditch on the W., joins the dyke at the N. and bends slightly W. before running down to the foot of the steep slope. Burials, probably Roman, were found to the E. (Roman section, Church Knowle 59).

(b) (932821), 130 yds. E. of (a), is 150 ft. long, rising diagonally across the ridge from a broken edge on a quarry at the S. to the shoulder above the steep slope on the N. The bank is 23 ft. across and about $2\frac{1}{2}$ ft. above the ditch, 13 ft. wide. The modern ridgeway track crosses it. 55 yds. to the E. a sharply defined shelf crossing the ridge is modern.

(c) (93378217), 200 yds. E. of (b), two banks with a ditch between, about 160 ft. long, span the hilltop where it is still rising to the settlement area (54). A gap in the banks 100 ft. from the S. end corresponds with an original causeway. The ditch is here 22 ft. wide, notably wider than elsewhere and 8 ft. below the E. bank. The W. bank, about 25 ft. wide and nearly 3 ft. high from the W., is bowed markedly W. At the N. end the outer scarp swings sharply E. and is continued as a terrace about 10 ft. wide, possibly the first stages of ditch construction, for 400 ft.[1] The E. bank is about 28 ft. wide.

(d) (93658228), 320 yds. E. of (c), spans the hilltop and is bowed to the E. The bank is $3\frac{1}{2}$ ft. high from the W. and $4\frac{1}{2}$ ft. above E. ditch, but probing suggests the ditch is at least 3 ft. deeper than this. The present break in the dyke is secondary; uninscribed mere-stones formerly lay on either side of it. The dyke seems to end about 50 ft. short of the edge of the really steep slope to the S. but on the N. ran up to the edge, making a junction (obscured by the later hedge bank) with another length of dyke, its ditch on the uphill side, which then runs W. for 200 ft., oddly veering away from the edge.

(e) (94398235), 810 yds. E. of (d), is 270 ft. long with an original gap near the centre, now widened. It has long been ploughed but its dimensions were probably similar to (d): there is an apparent constriction of the ditch 60 ft. S. of the entrance. A round barrow (Church Knowle (40)), immediately E., appears to extend into the ditch but the excavator's note that he threw soil to the W. may explain this (*Purbeck Papers* I, 110–15). The dyke ends on the shoulder of the steep slope to the N., but 200 ft. short of the corresponding edge to the S.

LULWORTH, EAST

(41) CROSS-RIDGE DYKE, E. of Flower's Barrow (SY 88 SE; 868806) and partly in Tyneham parish, *see* Hill-forts, East Lulworth (40).

LULWORTH, WEST

CROSS-RIDGE DYKE, on Bindon Hill (SY 88 SW; 82688020), *see* Hill-forts, West Lulworth (53b).

---

[1] Tested by Mr. J. Forde-Johnston in 1961 and found to be an artificial terrace.

OWERMOIGNE

(37) LINEAR DYKE, on Owermoigne Heath (SY 78 NE; 78138790–?78058769). In an area scarred by gravel quarrying a bank and ditch are aligned N.-S. along the W. edge of a low plateau sloping gently southwards at about 150 ft. above O.D. The subsoil is Bagshot Beds, now with a thick scrub cover. The dyke is 270 ft. long, with a modern break near the centre: its ditch, on the W. side, is 14 ft. across, its bank 18 ft., rising from 6 ft. to 8 ft. above the ditch bottom. The S. end has been destroyed by quarrying but in a field immediately S. of this, and ploughed almost flat, are traces of a bank and ditch, the ditch on the W. side, extending S.S.E. for about 250 ft.

PORTESHAM

(62) CROSS-RIDGE DYKE, on Friar Waddon Hill (SY 68 NW; 64258542), a bank and ditch about 70 yds. long, is aligned N.-S. across the axis of the limestone ridge at about 400 ft. above O.D. It lies on a gentle S.-facing slope and extends from the edge of the steep S. face of the ridge to its summit. The bank is 14 ft. across and 1 ft. high, the ditch, to its E., 14 ft. across and about $1\frac{1}{2}$ ft. deep; 3 yds. beyond the N. end of the bank is an irregular mound, not a barrow, 20 ft. across and $2\frac{1}{2}$ ft. high. Level with the N. end of the bank the ditch is shallower and turns sharply eastwards for some 20 yds., running under a stone field wall before being lost in very disturbed ground. It may be related to the 'Celtic' fields of which faint traces are discernible all over the hill-top, but there is no visible connection.

LINEAR DYKE, on Bronkham Hill, *see* Winterborne St. Martin (145).

STOKE, EAST

(50) BATTERY BANK, a series of discontinuous stretches of dyke (SY 88 NW, NE; 844894–891874), runs S.E. towards Wareham along a heathland ridge 150 ft. above O.D. (plan p. 516). At the S.E. end the earthwork is on the ridge crest but at the N.W. it is on the S. slopes. The remains consist of a bank 20 ft. to 33 ft. wide and 1 ft. to 2 ft. high with a ditch on the N. 18 ft. to 20 ft. wide and 1 ft. to $1\frac{1}{2}$ ft. deep. The surviving lengths, possibly once continuous over $3\frac{1}{5}$ miles, have been much damaged, especially by gravel quarrying; none of the gaps is certainly original. There is no certain connection between this boundary dyke and the complex on Worgret Heath (Arne (48)) commencing 750 yds. from its S.E. end.

The lengths are as follows: (a) of 300 yds., very slight and mostly only traceable on air photographs (R.A.F. V.A.P. CPE/UK 1934: 5063), runs from about 84438941 to 84658929; (b) of 200 yds. from 85788863 to 85948853; (c) of 230 yds. curving from 86558831 to 86768828; (d) of 220 yds. from 87478787 to 87688787; and (e) of 1500 yds. from 87828800 to 89068743.

Wareham Lady St. Mary

Linear Dykes, on Wareham Common, *see* Arne (48).

Weymouth

(436) Cross-ridge Dyke, on Windsbatch (SY 68 NE; 65748504 to 65778517), a bank 30 ft. across and some 8 ft. above a W. ditch 30 ft. wide, is bowed slightly E.

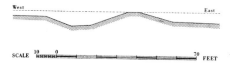

and virtually cuts off the E. end of the limestone ridge. Its S. end is on the 300 ft. contour, at the edge of a very steep slope (an apparent continuation downhill is a small boundary bank of later date built in the ditch and continuing its line); 240 ft. to the N. is a gap, probably original, 16 ft. across. A less clear length of bank running for some 90 ft. N. of this gap ends a little way down the rounded shoulder of the hill where there is much old quarry disturbance. The N. slope is only notably steep E. of the dyke, which is therefore defensive in situation as well as size. There are slight banks and scarps in the 8 acres of ridge top to the E. but the area is very disturbed. Immediately N. of the ridge are faint traces of 'Celtic' fields broken down by strip ploughing before the whole area was flattened by more recent cultivation.

Winterborne Monkton

(12) Cross-ridge Dyke, traces of bank and ditch (SY 68 NE; 66808932 to 66798902; Fig. p. 494), lies between 200 ft. and 300 ft. above O.D., spanning the forward slope of a low broad spur between two gullies; the bank with a ditch on its W. side, now in arable land and almost totally flattened, ran approximately N.-S. for 1620 ft. The northern 630 ft. is visible on air photographs only (R.A.F. V.A.P. CPE/UK 1934: 3089). A portion of mutilated bank measured before ploughing was 18 ft. across and 1½ ft. high; when later seen spread in plough-land the bank was about 36 ft. across and the ditch was 18 ft. across.

Date and purpose are both unknown. The dyke changes direction as it passes a round barrow (Winterborne Monkton (7)) and is probably later than it. The form, with a ditch uphill, is unusual in this area but has affinities with cross-ridge dykes elsewhere, *e.g.* in Sussex, associated with 'Celtic' fields. Immediately N. of it was 'Ditch End Furlong' of Fordington open field (Tithe map 1844). It was conceivably built to bound arable fields and to preserve the barrows (Lanceborough group) on the spur, whether in the mediaeval period or earlier.

Winterborne St. Martin

(145) Linear Dyke, on Bronkham Hill (SY 68 NW; 62558680 to 62948675; Plate 209). Running athwart the Ridgeway and cutting over round barrow Winterborne St. Martin (47)

is a single bank, at most 14 ft. across and 1½ ft. high, with a ditch on the N. Short erratic stretches link solution hollows—but do not run down into them as do later banks—from a point about 230 yds. W. of barrow (47) to about 185 yds. E. of it. The dyke climbs the S. face of the ridge (in the parish of Portesham), and is crossed by the present stone wall on the

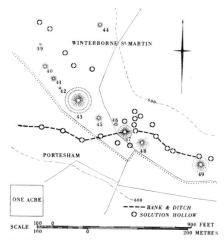

Dyke, Winterborne St. Martin (145), with part of Bronkham Hill Barrow Group (R. 6).

Winterborne St. Martin boundary and by another running up to the boundary. The bank appears to consist solely of the gravel of the underlying Bagshot Beds. The barrow is the only feature which clearly ante-dates it, and the fact that it mutilates the barrow strongly suggests a Romano-British or, probably, later origin, while its disregard for the parish boundary could point to a date before the formation of the parishes.

Winterbourne Steepleton

(66) Linear Dyke, on Black Down (SY 68 NW; 60078795 to 60568793), within Ancient Field Group (3), runs E.-W. for 530 yds. from just below 700 ft. to about 575 ft. O.D. (Fig. opp. p. 624). To the W. it passes into Little Bredy parish where a small enclosure (*Dorset* I, Little Bredy (6)) is attached to it. W. of the enclosure it extends downhill along the N.-facing slope of a re-entrant valley, first as a ditch with a bank on the S. side, then as a soil-mark, then as a depression 15 ft. wide, and finally as a narrow sloping terrace which fades into the hillside below a 'Celtic' field scarp. E. of the enclosure after a 14 yd. gap, perhaps due to quarrying, the dyke continues uphill, first as a depression then, E. of the parish boundary, as a ditch with a bank on its N. side.

Small-scale excavations on the dyke where it forms part of the enclosure (by R.C.H.M. in 1956) showed that the bank was 12 ft. across and only 1 ft. high, while the ditch was 9 ft. across the top, 2 ft. across the bottom and 3 ft. deep. A few coarse undecorated sherds from the ditch filling might indicate a date in the Late Bronze Age.

ROMAN REMAINS

The Roman roads and the Roman town of Dorchester (*Durnovaria*) receive separate treatment in the first part of this section of the Inventory; otherwise the remains of the Roman period in the area, being less usefully classifiable, are described in a succeeding gazetteer; in this the monuments are arranged topographically in alphabetical order of parishes.

Where appropriate, a prefatory note to the parish includes the following: cross-references to monuments described in the Earthworks section of the Inventory which are known to have a Roman phase; sites discovered subsequent to the preparation of the Inventory; discoveries of Roman objects that do not necessarily indicate occupation; sites of which the position is insufficiently known, unless they can be reasonably associated with listed monuments.

Evidence for the prehistoric origin of sites of Roman date, other than those described in the Earthworks section, is considered here; purely prehistoric sites with no earthwork remains, and prehistoric phases of Roman sites where there is apparent discontinuity, are listed elsewhere (pp. 511–12). Maumbury Rings, although an earthwork of Neolithic origin, is described under Roman Dorchester, since its adaptation as an amphitheatre was mainly responsible for its present appearance.

Museum accession numbers are given only for more significant finds where difficulty may arise in identification. For the occasional use of ten-figure map references, *see* p. 540b, *n.* 1. In the Introduction that follows, attention is directed mainly to monuments other than those of the Roman town, which has its own Introduction (p. 531).

INTRODUCTION

THE area described in this volume fell in Roman times within the territory of the Durotriges who were with little doubt one of the two unnamed tribes that offered a stubborn resistance to the 2nd legion under Vespasian in *c.* A.D. 44. Evidence for the campaign, and for the subsequent military occupation of short but uncertain duration, comes mainly from the hill-fort of Maiden Castle considered above (Winterborne St. Martin (142), pp. 493–501), the Roman forts at Hod Hill and Waddon Hill, and the Lake Farm site.[1] The existence of early military sites has been suggested at Dorchester and at Hamworthy on Poole Harbour, and may be suspected at Weymouth, the two latter as links in a coastal series extending from Fishbourne near Chichester perhaps to Topsham near Exeter.[2] There is little direct evidence for Weymouth either in the site at the head of the Radipole inlet (Weymouth (437)) or in the solitary legionary belt-plate from 'Greenhill' (p. 614) but the alignment of Approach Road 2 at Dorchester may have been a relic of the military phase (p. 533). Military equipment has not yet been found at Hamworthy and the early Roman objects from the known site there (Poole (402)) could perhaps be explained by continuance of the long-established trade attested there by pre-Roman imports, and perhaps also in the hinterland if the Greek coins listed by Milne can be relied upon.[3] That a military site remains to be located nearby, perhaps closer to the mouth of the Holes Bay channel,[4] seems certain however from the behaviour, near

---

[1] For Hod Hill *see Dorset* III, forthcoming, and Sir Ian Richmond, *Hod Hill* II (1968); for Waddon, *see* Dorset *Procs.* LXXXII (1960), 88–108, and LXXXVI (1964), 135–49; for Lake Farm *see* below, p. 529.

[2] *Arch. J.* CXV (1958), 57, 95; G. Webster and D. R. Dudley, *The Roman Conquest of Britain* (1965), 103–4, 109.

[3] J. G. Milne, *Finds of Greek Coins in the British Isles* (1948).

[4] It could alternatively have been sited near the Wareham Channel on the S. side of the peninsula, in which connection *see* p. 531, *n.* 1.

Badbury Rings, of the road linking the peninsula with the main road from Old Sarum which it seems was first surveyed to run to Poole Harbour rather than Dorchester (*see* Fig. p. 529).[1] The military character of the route is confirmed by the presence near it of a Claudian kiln at Corfe Mullen (pp. 525–6) probably making pottery for the army, and of the extensive military site of like date newly discovered beside it in the Stour valley at Lake Farm (*see* p. 529). The large mill from Hamworthy and part of a donkey-mill of Pompeian type from the Corfe Mullen site, both imports from the Rhineland, are antiquities of the highest rarity in Britain and in their context hardly allow an alternative explanation.

The fort at Hod Hill was evacuated by A.D. 51 at the latest, but military control of the district no doubt continued until the granting of self-government to the *civitas*, centred on *Durnovaria* (Dorchester), most probably *c.* 70 when native occupation of Maiden Castle seems to have ended (*see* p. 533). Thereafter we find little to indicate political conditions in the region,[2] although the main tendencies distinguishable in the civil zone of Roman Britain in urban and in rural development, at least in the few known villas, are evident. Mosaic floors in the latter, and at Dorchester in some profusion, are probably largely referable to the 4th century and imply prosperity in the late Roman period at least among landed and perhaps official classes. Two coin hoards of the mid 3rd century, however, at Sterte (Poole (404)) and Jordan Hill (Weymouth (445)), and others at Jordan Hill, Maiden Castle and Dorchester of *c.* 400, may reflect economic or political insecurity.

Standards of Romanization do not seem to have been high outside the capital and the villas; minor urban centres are lacking unless there was one at Wareham (p. 614),[3] and although the roads shown on the distribution map facing p. 634 can represent only those sufficiently important to be solidly constructed with agger and metalling, and perhaps not all of these,[4] few settlements show any close relationship to the system of through roads. Local networks of roads associated with a particular settlement, as at Town Hill (Ancient Field Group (1)), may however have been connected with them. As will be seen in the following review of rural settlement, the distribution remained in essence a prehistoric one; such changes as can be discerned, at least in the direction of industrial expansion, seem already in process before the Roman period. The reason may lie in the political, economic and cultural conservatism manifest in what we know of regional history in the preceding five or six centuries, but which it would be inappropriate to enlarge upon here.

Rural settlement. The area of the present survey includes parts of all three major ecological regions of Dorset as defined by Good,[5] namely (i) a large part of the Poole Basin consisting of Tertiary clays, sands and gravels,[6] (ii) a relatively small part of the Chalk, mainly to W. and S. of (i), and (iii) most of the Southern Vales sub-region, consisting of older and more varied formations around Weymouth and in Portland and S. Purbeck. The distribution of visible remains of prehistoric and Romano-British settlement, treated in the Earthworks section, is largely an upland one, strikingly in favour of the Chalk and of the limestone areas in S. Purbeck, and almost wholly ignoring the Poole Basin. The pattern is doubtless incomplete and arguably misleading since the uplands have been least subject to destructive agencies, but in the main it is supported by the buried sites treated in this section. These may be considered complementary in that they frequently owe their discovery, directly or indirectly, to the same agencies of destruction.

The distribution of these sites, a third of them perhaps with roots in the pre-Roman Iron Age, does however show that settlement in the valleys was greater than has been supposed;[7] of 119 sites,[8] no fewer

---

[1] A contrary view is discussed below (p. 528).

[2] For indications of a division of the tribe, at least in the 3rd or 4th century, between Dorchester and Ilchester, the only other walled town of the Durotriges, *see* pp. 531–2.

[3] There is evidence for the survival of a British community in this area in the early Christian inscriptions at the church of Lady St. Mary (*see* p. xlix).

[4] A road connecting Dorchester with the Isle of Purbeck is the most obvious omission.

[5] R. Good, *A Geographical Handbook of the Dorset Flora* (1948), 9–12.

[6] The region is slightly more extensive than the area of surviving heath indicated in the distribution map facing p. 634.

[7] The suggestion has been made for other regions of 'Wessex'; *see* Charles Thomas (ed.), *Rural Settlement in Roman Britain* (C.B.A. Research Report no. 7, 1966), 54–6.

[8] The total includes the Olga Road 'villa', Dorchester (p. 570), the temple complex at Maiden Castle (pp. 500–1) and a newly discovered site at Broadmayne (p. 594). If some 23 sites indicated solely by burials are excluded the ratios are not significantly affected.

H

than thirty-nine fall within the Poole Basin, while of the forty in S. Purbeck, fifteen lie off the limestone plateau on Wealden Beds and Kimmeridge Clay. The extent to which this should be seen as a development preceding the Roman conquest, and how far it should be associated with industry or hunting and fishing rather than with farming, is not wholly clear, but the evidence implies that it was under way in Iron Age 'A' times[1] around Poole Harbour, e.g. at Wareham, as well as in the Wealden valley and the lower Kimmeridge Clay slopes of S. Purbeck.[2] The peripheral distribution of sites on Bagshot Beds in the Poole Basin, where ancient field remains are absent despite good conditions for survival, and where the collection of shell-fish and industrial activities such as salt-boiling are evident, suggests that agriculture was desultory in much of this area. Settlements indicated by finds alongside the river Frome, however, can have profited from the more fertile alluvial soils, if adequately drained,[3] while a number fringing the S. margin of the heathland probably cultivated the strip of downwashed soils at the foot of the Chalk. In S. Purbeck however both Kimmeridge Clay slopes and the Wealden valley show traces of fields (Ancient Field Groups (22, 25–6)).

It will be seen from the distribution map that not many field systems are accompanied by earthworks of settlements, and it is likely that some of these establishments are to be recognized in the sites considered in this section, whether on the uplands as at Bagwood (Bere Regis (120)) near Ancient Field Group (32), or in the valleys. If this should be true of a site like Wilkswood (Langton Matravers (42)) below Field Group (28), we have an indication of the participation of a Romano-British agricultural community in the working perhaps of both shale and Purbeck marble, and we need not regard the many settlements in Purbeck showing evidence of the former as of purely or even mainly industrial character. Evidence from one of the few sites yet excavated systematically, at Eldon Seat (Corfe Castle (240)) near Field Group (22), points in the same direction although it refers largely to Iron Age 'A'.[4]

The buried sites offer most of the information at present available for a more particular dating of rural settlement in the region; about forty-one can lay some claim to an origin at least as early as Iron Age 'C', and of these at least fourteen can be placed certainly or probably in Iron Age 'A'. There is no reason to doubt continuity on these sites, although pottery characteristic of the regional 'B' phase is uncommon and stratified 'B' deposits are unknown in our area outside the hill-fort of Maiden Castle.[5] Thereafter most sites not indicated solely by burials seem to range over all or most of the Roman period, but the only examples to show positive signs of late 4th-century occupation are those at West Hill (Corfe Castle (232)), Wareham (85), Jordan Hill (Weymouth (445)), the temple at Maiden Castle (p. 501), and perhaps Whitcombe (26). The settlement at Bagwood (Bere Regis (120)) may have come to an end c. 350.

Imperfectly as they are known some of these sites yield direct evidence for agriculture in the shape of storage-pits for grain, as at Corfe Mullen. The stone-lined 'bee-hive' chambers, peculiar to the limestone of Portland and a sign perhaps of an insularity that has persisted to the present day, call for notice in this connection; carbonized grain was recovered from one of a series at King Barrow (Portland (101)) and their form suggests that they were intended for storage under sealed conditions. Instances of laterally and vertically conjoined pairs at King Barrow (Fig. p. 606) and of a subterranean passage leading to a chamber at Coombefield (105) imply storage of other commodities. They are presumably pre-Roman in origin.

There is little evidence in the area for the high farming associated with villa estates; only five recorded

---

[1] Bronze Age settlement on the heaths, although largely in different areas, is suggested above (p. xxxvi). Two sites of Iron Age 'A' in S. Purbeck show pottery with Late Bronze Age antecedents (Eldon Seat, Corfe Castle (240), and Sheepsleights, Worth Matravers (p. 512), the former on Kimmeridge Clay).

[2] At sites where the earliest known material is in the Durotrigian tradition of Iron Age 'C' the evidence is often insufficient to determine a date before rather than after the Roman conquest.

[3] The same should be true of the Stour valley (the storage of Spelt wheat is attested at East End (Corfe Mullen (24)) on Valley Gravel).

[4] Cf. Sheepsleights, Worth Matravers (p. 512), where occupation involving grain-storage and shale-working seems, however, to have ceased before Roman times.

[5] Iron Age 'C' occupation has been assumed, unless there are reasons to the contrary, wherever sites of native character appear to have existed already in the early Roman period; for Iron Age 'A', only sites with stratified levels or with unambiguous 'A' pottery have been included. For the currently accepted dating of Iron Age cultural phases in the region, see p. 495.

buildings can be regarded as villas, and their plans and history are largely unknown. One on the Chalk at Olga Road, Dorchester (212), lay unusually close to the Roman town; two near Weymouth (439, 447) suggest increased exploitation of clayey soils in the vales. The two remaining examples, at E. Creech (Church Knowle (57)) and Brenscombe Farm (Corfe Castle (229)), were situated some three miles apart on Bagshot Beds at the S. edge of the Purbeck heaths, and here the closely adjacent parts of the Chalk ridge, where conditions for survival have been excellent, show no trace of ancient cultivation. If these areas were within the domains of the villas they were probably used for pasture; the villas' arable will have been the narrow strip of downwashed soils at the foot of the Chalk worked by the existing farms.[1] The fact that these villas seem to turn their backs on soils preferred by early farmers suggests that their owners were interested in the industrial potential of the heathlands in pottery and salt, while the Creech villa, like a few other heathland sites, may have been concerned in the shale industry.

Apart from the villas the most romanized settlement yet known, at Woodhouse Hill (Studland (46)), lies towards the broader E. end of this arable strip, about half a mile N. of Ancient Field Group (29). The site is highly complex with little stratification and with its earlier phases much disturbed by later building. Its interpretation in detail is open to doubt, but the community, established in round hut perhaps shortly before the Roman conquest, seems to have practised mixed farming and to have formed by the 4th century a hamlet or small group of rectangular cottages in which a workshop and perhaps quarters for a few favoured animals could be housed under the same roof as the human occupants. Rectangular buildings of less certain use are known or implied at a few sites by rough footings of local stone or remains of floors, most clearly at Encombe (Corfe Castle (235)) where a small building seems to have stood alone and out of conformity with the 'Celtic' fields in which it lay. At Fitzworth (Corfe Castle (226)) a small round hut seems to have been occupied as late as the 4th century.

Industries. The notable concentration of sites in Portland and S. Purbeck suggests that the presence of raw materials enabled these areas to support a larger population than might have subsisted by farming alone, although modern exploitation of both these regions, frequently disclosing antiquities, and in Purbeck a long tradition of archaeological fieldwork, doubtless overstress the contrast. Of the industries involved—stone, Kimmeridge shale, pottery and salt—the first three at least were of more than regional importance.

No Roman stone-workings are known, but quarrying of outcrops rather than collection of weathered stone began in Portland probably by the first half of the 2nd century A.D., on the evidence of an undated sarcophagus of hewn stone found in a cemetery apparently of that date at N. Common (Portland (99)). Quarrying of Portland stone may be assumed to have continued into the late 3rd or 4th century from like evidence at Poundbury (Dorchester (225e) and p. 537), but its place in the economic history of Roman Britain is difficult to estimate since stone of this type is not peculiar to Portland; it does not seem to have been preferred to Ham Hill stone at Dorchester.[2] Purbeck stone was probably quarried extensively at Upwey for the walls of *Durnovaria* (see p. 543) but the outcrop extends from Portesham on the W. to Durlston Bay, Swanage, and it is not possible to determine the exact source lithologically. The thin bands of the so-called marble of the Upper Purbeck, however, are distinctive and outcrop in a narrow belt on the lower slopes from Peveril Point to Worbarrow Tout, Tyneham, beyond which there are only negligible traces at Lulworth. This fossiliferous limestone was highly valued for monumental inscriptions, architectural veneers and decoration found as far N. as Chester and Lincoln,[3] and was used most notably in the pre-Flavian or early Flavian Cogidubnus inscription at Chichester and for the dedication slab of the forum at *Verulamium* in 79. Its use at *Camulodunum* before A.D. 60 indicates a promptness of exploitation all the more remarkable in that there appears to have been no pre-Roman industry to attract attention. Early prospecting, perhaps official, might well explain the relatively sophisticated pottery at Wilkswood

---

[1] *Cf.* L. E. Tavener, *Report of the Land Utilization Survey of Britain*, part 88, *Dorset* (1940), 283.

[2] The use of other local stones, and of Ham Hill stone from Somerset, is discussed on pp. xxxix–xl.

[3] The industry has been studied by G. C. Dunning who has kindly made his distribution map available (*see Archaeological News Letter* I, no. 11 (1949), 14–15).

(Langton Matravers (42)), situated on the marble outcrop and furnishing the only instance of worked marble of Roman date yet found in Purbeck. Other sites within yards of the outcrop, besides one newly discovered at Dunshay (p. 620b) and another unlocated at Lynch (p. 596b), are at Blashenwell (Corfe Castle (234)), and Worbarrow Bay (Tyneham (40)); this site has yielded an unfinished mortar of 'burr-stone' from the Broken Shell Limestone stratum closely associated with the marble, but in this sector the latter is perhaps too thin to be usefully worked. Dunning has suggested[1] that the latest evidence for the industry is to be found in the small, lugged mortars in marble or 'burr-stone', with straight sides, dated to the 4th century and reaching Corbridge (Northumberland); the column capital from Jordan Hill (Weymouth (445)), however, if not reused, should indicate that the industry was still capable of supplying stone for major monuments at this late date.

The manufacture of armlets from the bituminous Kimmeridge shale in the Iron Age and Roman periods has been studied by J. B. Calkin,[2] who has shown that the material, though liable to fracture, was very tough and intractable when freshly quarried, and better worked on the lathe with hafted flint chisels than with metal tools; the ornaments were finished by grinding and perhaps polished with wax to resemble jet. Sites of the earlier hand-cut armlet industry, originating apparently in Iron Age 'A',[3] are betrayed mainly by the presence of roughed-out rings and discs, and unspecialized or semi-specialized flint flakes; those of the later lathe-turning industry mainly by specialized flint flakes and waste shale cores, of several well-defined types, formerly known as 'coal-money'.[4] It is evident that usually two armlets of different sizes were turned from each prepared piece of shale.

Armlets from Maiden Castle, and from Glastonbury, Meare and Cheddar in Somerset, suggest that the origin of the lathe industry should be sought in Iron Age 'B' or 'C', although no lathe-working of certainly pre-Roman age has yet been identified in Purbeck or elsewhere. Prototypes of the standardized flint lathe-tools, however, have been found at Green Island (Corfe Castle (224)) in association with a typologically early and rare variety of lathe-core (class A), which may belong there and at Gallows Gore (Worth Matravers (40)) to Iron Age 'C'. Turned armlets, moreover, appear at Wilkswood (Langton Matravers (42)) in an early post-conquest deposit. Survival of the older technique in some places in the 'C' phase is suggested by waste showing use of iron chisels, as at Green Island, while the essential continuity of the industry is shown by the number of sites where both rough-outs in the Iron Age 'A' tradition and lathe-cores occur. The growth of the industry in the Roman period, especially perhaps from the early 2nd century, is marked by the vast preponderance of lathe-cores of class C, and it clearly lasted into the 4th century at least, together with its specialized flint industry.

There is little evidence for the organization and equipment of the workshops, although, as has been remarked above, there is reason to suppose that shale-working was not the sole activity of the communities involved. At Gallows Gore in the Roman period low stone blocks and perhaps also lengths of drystone wall may have served as bases for pole-lathes, while at Kimmeridge Bay ('Gaulter', Steeple (31)) similar walls were found in a secondary Iron Age 'A' horizon, although less certainly associated with shale; at Encombe (Corfe Castle (235)) a rectangular 'cottage' standing amidst 'Celtic' fields seems to have been occupied by shale-workers. There is no sign of any substantial return in the form of money or imperishable luxuries. The sites yielding waste from the armlet industry, of which over thirty are now known,[5] are not confined to the vicinity of the outcrop, and include Green Island and Hamworthy (Poole (402)) in Poole Harbour, as well as a number of sites on the S. fringe of the Tertiary heaths where, as has been suggested, it is likely that villa owners were to some extent concerned with the industry. The raw material

---

[1] B. W. Cunliffe (ed.), *Richborough* V (1968), 110–11.   [2] Dorset *Procs.* LXX (1948), 37–40, 55; LXXV (1953), 43–71; LXXXVIII (1966), 114–15.
[3] The shale was also used for ornaments in the Neolithic and Bronze Ages.
[4] The latter could be hoarded, perhaps for supposed talismanic qualities held in common with jet and other substances, and are not alone sufficient to prove manufacture on the site. Old records of the ritual use of shale in Purbeck lack confirmation.
[5] Several have been added to Calkin's appendix I in Dorset *Procs.* LXXV: the settlement on Knowle Hill (Earthworks, Settlements, Church Knowle (54)), where working in Iron Age 'A' is proved, Corfe Castle (238–9) and Worth Matravers (42–3). Hamworthy (Poole (402)) and E. Creech (Church Knowle (57)) should probably be included; Calkin's site 15, Whitecliff Farm, Swanage, where evidence for ancient occupation seems unfounded, should be omitted.

in block or roughed-out form may well have been exported to be worked up further afield, as perhaps at Maiden Castle, Hengistbury Head (Hants.), Glastonbury and Meare. It has been assumed that the best 'coal' or 'blackstone', outcropping as a thin layer only in the cliffs near Kimmeridge Bay, was alone exploited, but it is likely that lower quality Kimmeridge shale occurring there and formerly accessible at Portland was also used; characteristic flint lathe-tools, though not the shale, have recently been found at Abbotsbury in W. Dorset.[1] Other superficially similar materials, such as lignite and cannel-coal, were also widely used in Britain in Roman and earlier times, and increase the difficulty of assessing the full importance of the Purbeck industry for the Roman province, at least in satisfying the demand for ornaments and spindle-whorls.

Other less well known products of the shale industry may have been equally important. The occurrence in S.E. England[2] of the graceful Belgic lathe-turned pedestal urns presumed to be of Kimmeridge shale may show export of the raw material, since neither they nor their equivalent in pottery are known in Dorset, but fragments of turned shale bowls or dishes, rarely figured in the literature, are common in Roman deposits in the region. Shale furniture has been better studied in the whole or fragmentary carved table legs found mostly in and near Dorchester but also as far away as *Verulamium*, Rothley (Leics.) and Caerleon.[3] The distribution of these objects, and of the bevelled oblong plaques or tablets incised with geometric decoration at centre and edges, and sometimes identified as wall or furniture panels,[4] entitles us to assume that the material thus widely valued was shale from the Kimmeridge formation. The sites of manufacture have not been traced, although Norden (Corfe Castle (230)) was perhaps one. There was also a limited use of shale, if not exactly for building at least for lining or covering graves, for mosaic cubes, and square floor-tiles as at the Preston villa (Weymouth (447)) and Bignor (Sussex).

The pottery and salt industries are to some extent related. Site finds suggest that the regional pottery industry was concerned to a very large extent with the production of vessels of black burnished heat-resistant kitchen ware.[5] Only two kilns are known, at East End (Corfe Mullen (24)) and near Cleavel Point, Ower (Corfe Castle (227)), the latter of unusual horizontal-draught type. Pottery-making, however, is possible or likely at several other known sites on Bagshot Beds in the parishes of Arne and Corfe Castle, especially perhaps at Stoborough (Arne (50)) where indications, in addition to what may be a clay-puddling basin, seem extensive.[6] The sites now visible are known mainly from surface debris consisting of oxidized brown or reddish sherds from vessels of burnished kitchen ware intended to be reduced in firing to a black colour; the sherds are regarded therefore as probably belonging to wasters, although, like those from the known kiln at Corfe Mullen, which are also oxidized, they do not seem to include the contorted or fused examples often found beside kilns. Several of these sites, however, also yield evidence for salt-boiling, implying combustion on a large scale probably in open conditions, which could have caused oxidization of sherds of domestic vessels lying about in the vicinity; the distribution map therefore acknowledges only proven kilns, although it is clear that at Ower, as in some Romano-British saltings outside the county, both activities were carried on.

Although there is evidence nearby for the production of black burnished vessels in the late 3rd or 4th centuries, the kiln at Corfe Mullen belongs to the mid 1st century A.D. It is anomalous in that its products fit only partially into the conspectus of regional wares. The flagons and mortaria are romanized types while the vessels of Durotrigian shape (classes C and E) are small, relatively delicate wheel-thrown or wheel-

---

[1] Dorset *Procs.* LXXXIX (1967), 121–3.

[2] As at Old Warden, Bedfordshire (*Later Prehistoric Antiquities of the British Isles* (B.M., 1953), 71, pl. XXIII, 3).

[3] J. Liversidge, *Furniture in Roman Britain* (1955), 37–47, 51. A curved slab of Kimmeridge shale from Bagber, Milton Abbas, in D.C.M., is doubtless part of the circular top of one of these three-legged tables.

[4] Fragments occur at rural sites such as Bagwood (Bere Regis (120)), as well as in more romanized centres (*e.g.* in London). They are known to have served as trays for vessels in burials at Jordan Hill (Weymouth (445)) and Winchester (*Ant. J.* XLVII (1967), 230–4, 248–50, where they are called trenchers).

[5] Some early types must be regarded as at least the progenitors of one of the most important strains of kitchen ware in Roman Britain, most fully studied on northern military sites in deposits dating from *c.* 120 by J. P. Gillam (*Arch. Ael.* XXXV (1957), 180–251; *Procs. Society of Antiquaries of Scotland* XCIV (1960–1), 126–9).

[6] One formerly accepted kiln site, Hamworthy (Poole (402)), has had to be removed from this category.

finished versions of the native types. The kiln was doubtless worked by a native potter, but it is probable that production was instigated by the army during the early years of the conquest; it stood by an early military route, and its products have not been identified on occupation sites save one evidently of military character recently discovered near by at Lake Farm (*see* p. 529). The Ower kiln produced vessels of normal black burnished fabric, but since types in the Durotrigian Iron Age 'C' tradition were stratified here and in the surrounding area with types current in the 2nd and 3rd centuries and even the 4th century, it is likely that more than one kiln was involved. The absence of any indication of manufacture nearer Dorchester is remarkable, although there is indirect evidence there for a tile-kiln (*see* p. 537).

Evidence of the crystallization of salt from sea-water in prehistoric and Roman Dorset comes entirely from coastal areas within the region studied in the present volume, and has been more fully discussed elsewhere.[1] The sites, indicated by the presence of 'briquetage' (hand-moulded clay props and pieces of crudely made containers, the latter necessarily fired before use), occur (i) on the Tertiary heaths around Poole Harbour, and (ii) as a small group, mainly on Kimmeridge Clay, from Kimmeridge Bay to Tyneham Cap, in which shale was used for fuel. One site, which probably used shale from Portland, is known further W. on the Fleet at Wyke Regis (p. 512), and two more are suspected, at Jordan Hill near Weymouth, and Osmington. There are no mounds of burnt earth such as are elsewhere associated with saltings, but mounds of shale and ash are known at two adjoining sites in Tyneham parish (41–2).

In view of the presence of a pottery-kiln at the salting in the Ower peninsula, Corfe Castle, evidence for structures of burnt or fired clay in connection with the industry has to be treated with caution, but a floor of fired or fire-hardened clay at Shipstal (Arne (54)) and rounded ovens at Hamworthy, of Roman date, may belong to it. A narrow rectangular stone-lined hearth below present high water mark on the foreshore of the Fleet, Wyke Regis, seems to show salt-boiling with shale fuel late in Iron Age 'B' or early in the 'C' phase. A small quantity of 'briquetage' was found, but domestic jars of a uniform type may have been used as containers for drying and marketing.[2] Elsewhere the only positive evidence for the pre-Roman industry is at Gaulter, Kimmeridge Bay (Steeple (31)), where it belonged to Iron Age 'A' and was associated with small semi-cylindrical clay troughs and small bowls. Some of the Romano-British saltings may nevertheless have had their origin in Iron Age 'C'. Here the evidence is for two mutually exclusive varieties of container: heavy sub-rectangular flat trays, confined with the exception of Hamworthy to the Kimmeridge group, and what seem to have been large thin-walled semi-cylindrical troughs, peculiar to the heathland group; hand-moulded props are common to both.

The sites on Kimmeridge Clay, though coastal, are nearly all on the cliffs at 50 ft. or more above sea level. The heathland sites are near the water's edge, except at Godlingston Heath (Studland (45)), 1½ miles inland at 300 ft.; here the most reasonable explanation would be the manufacture of boiling-vessels, or perhaps the refining of impure salt by boiling in fresh water.

Temples, shrines and cemeteries. The persistence of native tradition apparent in material aspects of life is no less so in religious and burial ritual, as far as these can be revealed archaeologically. The late 4th-century pagan temple at Maiden Castle, and the building of like date interpreted as another temple at Jordan Hill (Weymouth (445)), share with the villas an architecture of competent provincial type; but at Maiden Castle the 4th-century round hut, built within the largest prehistoric hut known there and reasonably interpreted by Wheeler as a primitive shrine, suggests the continuity of a pre-Roman cult despite an apparent gap of three centuries. Jordan Hill affords a prime example of the ritual shaft or pit common amongst the Celts[3] and associated there either with the supposed temple or the cemetery; a like significance may be suspected for simpler pits and cists containing animal bones and ashes in this cemetery, and in others at The Grove (Portland (102)) and Dorchester (218b, d). Devotions of a more Roman kind, presumably at domestic shrines, are implied by the niche in the town house at Colliton Park (Dorchester

---

[1] Dorset *Procs.* LXXXIV (1962), 137–144. Turlin Moor (Poole (403)) may perhaps be added to the sites listed therein, while new evidence from Gallows Gore (Worth Matravers (39)) suggests at least trade in salt.
[2] *Ibid.* 132–6.   [3] *Cf.* Anne Ross, *Pagan Celtic Britain* (1967), 24–8.

(182)) and perhaps by a small uninscribed altar of Purbeck stone ploughed up at Kingston (Corfe Castle (238)). The relief from Whitcombe (26), however, if not a tombstone, would suggest an E. European pagan cult of the mounted hero or demigod, acclimatized in its rendering in Portland stone but not otherwise very clearly attested in Britain. Evidence for Christianity in the region here surveyed is confined to Dorchester (p. 536).

The regional burial rite in the Iron Age was inhumation, and this continued scarcely affected by Belgic or Roman practice of cremation, even in the capital; a cremation at Cogdean (Corfe Mullen (25)), the sole instance in our area outside Dorchester, where too it was exceedingly rare,[1] was probably of the early military phase. Known burials of Iron Age 'A' and 'B' are too few to determine a rule, but, as in the 'C' phase, the body seems normally to have been placed on its side in an oval grave, with limbs contracted or flexed. Practice in Iron Age 'C' is best shown, despite the special circumstances, in the 'war cemetery' of c. A.D. 44 at Maiden Castle, where food offerings and vessels of Durotrigian black burnished ware accompanied the dead. In the Roman period the body was usually fully extended on the back, with arms crossed or by the sides, but flexed posture was not uncommon and at Weymouth (438) and (441) could apparently be late in the period. Personal possessions are not often recorded,[2] and imperishable grave-goods, where present, consist normally of one or occasionally several black ware vessels. In the 1st century at least these would mostly be standard Durotrigian types[3] and will not alone suffice to fix a date before or after the Roman conquest, as the graves at Whitcombe (26) most clearly show. The rarity of 3rd and 4th-century vessels with burials must imply a decline in offerings. Unaccompanied burials in extended posture, occurring so often amongst known Roman graves, have been treated as Roman in the Inventory; some few may be Saxon, before burial in churchyards became normal, but doubtless more really belong to British communities spanning the period of some 250 years between the end of Roman rule and the Saxon settlement of the region in the 7th century.

Wooden coffins, doubtless introduced in the Roman period, are quite common; the earliest known, at Maiden Castle, with a female skeleton with hob-nails at feet, was probably buried before c. A.D. 70.[4] Cist graves, lined and covered with stone slabs or occasionally shale, could enclose wooden coffins and are common except on the Chalk, where graves could be cut in the rock; they need not therefore reflect a distinct tradition. It is reasonable to suppose that short cists containing flexed skeletons can be pre-Roman, but there are no proven examples here, either short or long, for the Iron Age. Sarcophagi, of Portland stone with ridged lids, occur in Portland and at Dorchester and neighbourhood where, however, most are flat-lidded and of Ham Hill stone; they may contain wooden or plain lead coffins but none is reliably reported as having grave goods.

There is no evidence for walled cemeteries except possibly at Jordan Hill (Weymouth (445)). Groups of burials rarely display system, although there are exceptions at Bare Cross (Church Knowle (59)), Charborough Park (Morden (57)) and Afflington (Corfe Castle, p. 443), as well as at Dorchester;[1] the Afflington Barrow furnished one of several examples of intrusive burials of the period in Bronze Age barrows. Orientation of individual graves in an E.-W. direction seems to occur in about two cases in every three, with head as often at one end as at the other; a few graves contain more than one individual, usually side by side, and the heads could be at opposite ends. Notable instances of the careful interment of bodies with lower jaw or whole skull removed and placed separately are recorded at Kimmeridge (Steeple (31)) and St. Nicholas's Church (Studland (47)).

---

[1] For an analysis of burials in the town cemeteries, see p. 571.

[2] Notable exceptions are at Weymouth (446), and at Whitcombe (26) where the armed warrior must surely have been buried before the Roman occupation.

[3] The commoner types are listed by J. W. Brailsford, P.P.S. XXIV (1958), 103.

[4] Similar indications of footwear are not common but have a wide distribution in the region.

ROMAN ROADS

Four Roman roads fall wholly or partly within the area of the present volume: the main road from London to Exeter *via* Badbury Rings and Dorchester, the roads from Dorchester to Ilchester and Radipole (Weymouth), and the road from Hamworthy (Poole) to Badbury. Descriptions of the first two, except where they approach Dorchester (*see* Approach Roads, p. 539), are reserved for treatment in *Dorset* V; the others are described here.[1]

ROAD I. *Dorchester to Radipole, Weymouth* (SY 68 NE, SE).

The road (Margary's no. 48) running S.W. from the S. exit of Dorchester has been recognized as Roman since the 17th century (Coker, 67); the only monumental remains are on Ridgeway Hill. The distance of six miles was covered in one minor alignment of 600 yds. to Maumbury Rings and perhaps two major alignments of almost equal length, laid out from the crest of Ridgeway Hill, to what would then have been a tidal creek at Radipole. Alternatively the route S. of Ridgeway Hill may have been in three alignments, following more nearly the line of the modern road through Broadwey.

The first alignment, represented by if not necessarily coinciding with Weymouth Avenue, is discussed below (*see* Dorchester, Approach Roads, 2). Thereafter from Maumbury Rings the elevated Weymouth road (A 354) is impressively straight and must be on the line almost to the summit of Ridgeway Hill where the present road bends southwards. Here the Roman agger continues the line for nearly 70 yds. to the crest; it was some 27 ft. wide and 3 ft. high above ditch bottom in 1953, but has been under plough. The W. side-ditch has probably been enlarged by erosion or use as a hollow-way, while the E. ditch is obliterated by a metalled track (SY 67078602; Bincombe parish). From the crest the new Roman alignment ran almost due S.; if the change was made in a curve the lane and the former parish boundary[2] may preserve the line, as they clearly do further downhill until it is lost in the old quarries. From Elwell the main road (A 354) follows the line as far as the corner of Stottingway Street.

The remainder of the route is uncertain. An unaltered alignment is perfectly feasible and would touch the known Roman site on Spa Hill (Weymouth (437)) before the final descent to Radipole Lake, but no positive remains are known although Hatcher's observations in 1802, recorded by Warne, seem to confirm it as far as Broadwey village. Alternatively the modern road diverging through Broadwey may indicate two Roman alignments, the second of which, followed in part by a former parish boundary as far as Redlands, would also touch the Spa Hill site. Roman burials at Broadwey (*see* Weymouth (443)) are doubtless associated with the road but cannot be said to favour either route decisively. Margary follows Codrington in suggesting that there was a final alignment from Redlands S.S.W. to reach the creek by the gentler incline, but the evidence is unsatisfactory. (Dorset *Procs.* LXXIII (1951), 97–9; I. D. Margary, *Roman Roads in Britain* (2nd edn. 1967), 112–13; T. Codrington, *Roman Roads in Britain* (revised edn. 1918), 256–7.)

ROAD II. *Badbury Rings, Shapwick, to Hamworthy, Poole* (ST 90 SE, SY 99 NE, SE, SZ 09 SW; Figs. pp. 529, 530).

The road (Margary's 4d) linked the settlement at Hamworthy, Poole, probably a port of the early conquest phase, with the Roman road from London to Exeter at a point N.E. of the Iron Age hill-fort of Badbury Rings.[1] The distance of nearly seven miles was covered in two major and three minor alignments, of which the first was a direct continuation of the line of the London road for some 400 yds. beyond the latter's branch S.W. towards Dorchester. The London road has thus been plausibly claimed as laid out in the first instance to pass E. of the Rings to Hamworthy, with the Dorchester line as a subsequent although doubtless very early development.[2] Another road (Margary's 46)

---

[1] Remains of a road connecting the New Forest region with the Hamworthy road have been claimed S.W. of Wimborne near Lake Farm and E. of Wimborne near Park Farm (*see* p. 530). There is also some slight evidence at Norden for the road that must surely have linked the important industrial region of Purbeck with the hinterland of Dorset *via* the Corfe gap and perhaps Wareham (*see* Corfe Castle (230) and p. 539).

[2] Shown on the older O.S. 6 in. maps.

[1] The whole course of the road is described here, although the first half lies outside the volume area in the parishes of Pamphill and Shapwick.

[2] Codrington, *op. cit.*, 253; Margary, *op. cit.*, 105–6, and 1st edn. (1955), I, pl. viii; J. K. S. St. Joseph, *J.R.S.* XLIII (1953), 93, pl. xiv (2). The continuation, now most clearly seen on the R.A.F. aerial photographs noted on p. 531, was first observed by Hutchins as a band of small pebbles—doubtless from the local Tertiary cap (Reading Beds)—and by Colt Hoare as a low agger. Its connexion with the Hamworthy road, hitherto believed to branch from the main S.W. road near More Crichel, was first appreciated by Wake Smart in 1847, and its appearance on O.S. maps followed the publication of his observations in Warne's *Ancient Dorset* (1872), 180–1 (*see also* Dorset *Procs.* XI (1890), 22–3). A contrary view expressed by Sir Ian Richmond and published posthumously (*Hod Hill* II (1968), 1, 2) was withdrawn by him some months before his death in a letter dated 2nd June, 1964 (R.C.H.M. records).

Sir Ian retained his belief in the priority in date, however slight, of the road towards Bath over that to Dorchester; the former's association with the Hamworthy road, and the interruption of its ditches by those of the Dorchester road, apparent in the aerial photographs by Dr. St. Joseph, seem to confirm this, but factors indicating the remaking

ran N.N.W. towards Bath from the bend or angle made by Road II outside the E. ramparts of Badbury in turning S.E. towards Poole Harbour.

A road from Winchester *via* Nursling and the New Forest (Margary's 422) seems to have joined Road II somewhere S.W. of Wimborne. Warne's and Wake Smart's claim to detect the beginning of a branch from Corfe Hills towards Christchurch is not substantiated.

The road is now accurately marked on the O.S. maps throughout most of its course, but its termination in the Hamworthy peninsula, where it may have thrown off a branch touching the known settlement (Poole (402)) on the S. shore of Holes Bay, is uncertain. Aerial photographs give the clearest indication of the junctions at Badbury and of the route in the N. sector, but an agger remains in several places between Lodge Farm, N. of Kingston Lacy, and the Stour backwater at Lake, perhaps the original main stream,[1] and is exceptionally fine in lengths on Barrow Hill and Corfe Hills, S. of the by-road between Sleight and Merley, where part of it is scheduled as an ancient monument. Where best preserved in this sector the agger is nearly 3 ft. high and 25 ft. wide, between side-ditches 82 ft. or more apart, but elsewhere spreads up to about 45 ft. wide. It has been fully sectioned only behind Almer Road on Ham Common, but the road metal appears to have been of local gravels and, in the Hamworthy peninsula, of beach shingle.

The route was undoubtedly an early one; in addition to the Claudian occupation at Hamworthy, a pottery kiln of like date probably serving military needs is known by the road at East End (Corfe Mullen (24)), and a camp or stores base adjacent to it is currently under investigation a half mile beyond in the Stour valley at Lake Farm.[2] The constructional details, however, need not be those of the original road.

Badbury Rings to Eye Mead, Pamphill (alignments 1 and 2). The agger of the London–Exeter road branches S.W. from the Harley Down–King Down alignment about 370 yds. beyond King Down Farm, Pamphill, but although no ridge remains it is clear that Road II, partly under the modern lane, continues without deflection (alignment 1) to the Shapwick parish boundary.[3] Immediately beyond the hedge a turn S.E.

into alignment 2 is masked by a spinney, although the curving agger shown on O.S. maps since 1887 is now, at least, no more than a slight scarp falling eastwards; a road towards Bath strikes off N.N.W. from the curve. Some trace of the agger of Road II is discernible immediately beyond the bend

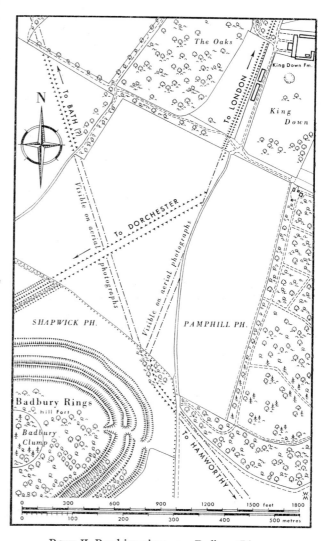

ROAD II. Road junctions near Badbury Rings.

where turf-stripping in 1953 uncovered small Tertiary pebbles, presumably metalling rather than exposed cap; a width of 84 ft. centre to centre between side-ditches was indicated when the field beyond the parish boundary was under plough (Dorset *Procs.* LXXXV (1963), 106).

Remains of the agger by Lodge Farm, on Upper Chalk, are now negligible but 170 yds. are preserved in fair state through Abbott Street Copse as far as the lane; there are no appreciable

---

of the main S.W. road near Bokerly Dyke in Cranborne Chase (*cf. Arch. J.* CXVIII (1961), 75) warn us that these ditches at Badbury and the great agger between them need not be early features.

[1] It is in part a parish boundary and the road changed direction on crossing it.

[2] Dorset *Procs.* LXXXVII (1965), 99–101, LXXXVIII (1966), 115, LXXXIX (1967), 143; S. S. Frere, *Britannia* (1967), 74. The site lies partly in Poole parish but extends into the parish of Pamphill to N., and will be described in *Dorset* V.

[3] Aerial photographs show side-ditches similar to those of the London road. The continuation was first noted by Hutchins, as a band of small pebbles—doubtless from the local Tertiary cap (Reading Beds).

remains in Grove Wood nor alongside the earthwork[1] at Cowgrove where it was formerly traced. Beyond Cowgrove Road the line crosses Valley Gravel presumably across a bridge across what is now the main stream of the Stour, midway between Eye Bridge Ford and Old Ford, and reappears intermittently as a distinct agger dead on course across the alluvial flats of Eye Mead. Its condition there implies that, beside the river, the agger has been destroyed rather than buried below silt; the clearest exposure (the N. bank) shows no trace of the road in section nor of approaches to a ford. The agger in Eye Mead is interrupted by old flood channels but is almost continuous for some 370 yds. as it nears the Stour backwater; at best it is 30 ft. wide with crest 1 ft. above the alluvium.

Lake Farm to Ham Common, Poole (alignments 3 and 4). Near Lake Farm the road swung S.S.W. as the low terrace of Valley Gravel was reached some 45 yds. beyond the backwater; the bend and general direction established by Smith (*op. cit.* below, 1943), in a number of test holes of which details are unknown, has been further defined (i) in an exposure of gravel (SY 99809910) in 1962 in a drainage trench dug along the N. side of the main road (A 31); (ii) by the location of the E. ditch in 1966 at 99709903 immediately E. of the former railway crossing where the road enters the parish of Corfe Mullen.[2] (Information from Mr. N. H. Field.)

A low ridge, spreading to about 80 ft. wide and clearly marked for some 460 yds. in the arable fields beside the former railway to E., seems to head straight for the bend made by Road II at the backwater (*see* Fig.; R.A.F. V.A.P. CPE/UK 1934: 5192). It coincides with a former field boundary (Tithe Map, Great Canford, 1843) but may be part of a road identified as Roman by C. D. Drew near Park Farm, Colehill (SZ 02679948 to 03529984) and thought to come from the New Forest (Margary's 422; Somerset and Dorset *Notes and Queries* XIX (1927–9), 170–1; H. P. Smith, *op. cit.* 1948, 85–7); excavations on both sides of the cattle-way crossing the old railway to Lake Farm have, however, failed to reveal convincing traces of road metal or side-ditches, while a direct prolongation E. involves difficulties with the course of the Stour S. of Wimborne (Dorset *Procs.* LXXXVII (1965), 99–101).

Smith's observations may be accepted for the course of Road II for 750 yds. beyond the old railway; they imply a substantially straight alignment of half a mile between the Lake Farm bend and the crest of the Plateau Gravel at East End,[3] where the road's second major alignment begins its course almost due S. to Ham Common. There are few traces of the new line until Barrow Hill is reached, except at the foot of Happy Bottom, in which the agger, where least disturbed, is 45 ft. wide and 2½ ft. high but has no visible ditches; such

---

[1] This feature, on Reading Beds, is locally reputed to be an old clay-pit; it was discussed in 1919 by H. Sumner (*Local Papers* (1931), 36–40).

[2] The E. ditch here lies beside buried ditches thought to belong to a Claudian military site (Dorset *Procs.* LXXXVIII (1966), 115; LXXXIX (1967), 143.

[3] Parched grass is often visible in summer on the line immediately E. of the present road below Lamb's Green. For a Claudian pottery kiln and other remains by the Roman road in this sector, *see* Corfe Mullen (24–5) and p. 600. An oven was found near the W. side of the road (99619885; Dorset *Procs.* LXXXVIII (1966), 115).

ROAD II. Alignments 2 and 3 near Lake Farm.

traces as exist of a much wider agger affirmed by Smith seem due to splay as the ridge runs into the N. slope. From Higher Merley Lane an old heathland road formerly known as Old Bound Lane follows the line across Bagshot Beds and Plateau Gravel for 2½ miles with the parish boundary on its W. margin; the lane is now viable mainly as a cart track or bridle path which crosses and recrosses the agger or follows its crest. Substantial lengths of the Roman road, in places up to 3 ft. high and 25 ft. wide, remain on Barrow Hill and Corfe Hills above the 200 ft. contour; the finest sectors are 300 yds. N. and 500 yds. S. of Rushcombe Bottom, where shallow side-ditches, over 6 ft. wide and between 82 ft. and 85 ft. apart, centre to centre, fall outside the bounds of the lane. Thereafter remains are negligible between the houses and gardens of Broadstone and past Upton Heath, but suggest that the crest of the agger lay generally towards the E. margin of the lane; W.

of Ty-coed Cottages the agger survives for 70 yds. as a broad low ridge altogether E. of the lane. A coin of Commodus (A.D. 180–192) was found nearby in 1942. At Broadstone, Codrington noted a section in a gravel-pit (SY 99319595) where 1½ ft. of gravel metalling, 18 ft. wide at base, overlay the old heath soil. At Ty-coed the lane diverges at last, but the parish boundary continues straight into the grounds of Upton House; there are no traces of the road, but beyond the railway a ridge, 40 ft. wide and 2½ ft. high W. of Vineyard Copse (formerly a parish boundary), shows that the line was maintained across the main road (Blandford Road, A 350) to the verge of Ham Common.

Ham Common to Hamworthy (alignment 5). The remainder of the route has been accurately traced by Smith, who sectioned the agger, on Bagshot Sands, by the cottages in Almer Road where it is still plain (SY 99049144; Smith, *op. cit.*, 1932). The metalling consisted of sandy gravel on beach shingle, over 26 ft. wide and 1½ ft. thick, on a 4 in. bedding of clayey sand laid on cut heath vegetation. A ditch was found on the W., 16 ft. from the centre of the ridge.

At the edge of the common,[1] on Plateau Gravel, the line swings S.E. from the local crest into the final or last known alignment,[2] crossing Lake Road and passing S. of St. Michael's Church near which Roman remains are said to have been found (*see* Poole, p. 603). It recrosses the main road E. of the Rectory (99429101)[3] and passes immediately in front of the new school, where gravel, mainly beach shingle, was noted

in 1947 up to 1 ft. thick. Some of the surface signs recorded by Smith in this sector have now disappeared, but 10 ins. of beach shingle metalling were found behind the house renumbered 134 Blandford Road (99979048). The last indications on this alignment were at the houses renumbered 128 and 126, and reputedly under the Coronation Room (SZ 00079038) which is about 150 yds. W.S.W. of the occupation site on Holes Bay (*see* Poole (402)). Smith considered that the road would have terminated in a more easterly alignment bringing it to the deep water of the Holes Bay channel, and suggested that this was the function of a supposed branch road, over early 'huts', located along the S. side of the known settlement area at Carter's Tile Works from 00229039 to 00269037 (Dorset *Procs.* LII (1930), 102, fig. 5); 10 ins. of compact shingle metalling contained fragments of amphora and samian ware.

(H. P. Smith, Dorset *Procs.* LIV (1932), 5–14, LXV (1943), 53–9, *History of Poole* I (1948), 78–85; I. D. Margary, *Roman Roads in Britain* (2nd edn. 1967), 105–6; T. Codrington, *Roman Roads in Britain* (revised edn. 1918), 253–4; T. W. Wake Smart, Dorset *Procs.* XI (1890), 20–5; C. Warne, *Ancient Dorset* (1872), 180–3; Hutchins (1st edn. 1774), I, xiv, 2; R. C. Hoare, *Ancient Wiltshire*, II (1821), Roman Aera 34–5. Aerial photographs: R.A.F. V.A.P. CPE/UK 1893: 3096–7; CPE/UK 1934: 5192–3; J. K. S. St. Joseph O.A.P. UL 2, UL 9, LL 24.)

ROMAN DORCHESTER (*DURNOVARIA*)

(O.S. 6 in. sheets SY 68 NE, 69 SE, 78 NW, 79 SW)[4]

INTRODUCTION

The site of the Roman town is a Chalk plateau rising to the W. and bordered on the N. and N.E. by the River Frome flowing south-eastwards to Wareham and Poole Harbour. The highest point (Top o' Town) on the W. is 255 ft. above sea level.

The name *Durnovaria*, though hallowed by long usage, is only known from one variant reading in manuscripts of the Antonine Itinerary which otherwise give *Durnonovaria*, but the latter seems less likely in view of the 9th-century forms *Dornwaraceaster* and *Dornuuarana-ceaster* and Welsh *Durngueir*.[5] The town was on the Roman trunk road from London to Exeter *via* Old Sarum (*Sorviodunum*), and although the true distance between the latter and Dorchester is 43 Roman miles against 20 in the Itinerary (*Sorviodunum—Vindocladia* xii, *Vindocladia—Durnonovaria* viii), the discrepancy is substantially resolved if one supposes scribal omission of a numeral x from each section, with *Vindocladia* at the Roman road junction at Badbury Rings.

Although the name is not recorded with a tribal suffix, *Durnovaria*, which, by the middle of the 2nd century covered an area of some 70 or 80 acres, must be presumed from its size and position to have been the cantonal capital of the Durotriges. A division of the canton, at least in the 3rd or 4th century, has

---

[1] O. G. S. Crawford claimed remains of alignment 4 continuing across Ham Common towards the Wareham Channel at Lake (MS. notes, O.S. 6 in. sheet Dorset XLIII S.E., in National Monuments Record). This line, adopted in the map revision of 1925, was subsequently abandoned in favour of Smith's, and little can be found to substantiate it except perhaps in the gardens N. of Hoyal Road, and just short of the railway at Lake. Late Roman pottery has, however, been found at Branksea Avenue by the end of the line (*see* Poole, p. 603).

[2] A ridge can be traced on the curve but is probably upcast from a sunken track or ditch running into the adjacent clay-pit.

[3] A Durotrigian silver stater (Mack's type 317) was found at the Rectory (H. P. Smith, *op. cit.* 1948, 56–8).

[4] The prefix SY, common to all Dorchester map references, is not repeated in the text.

[5] O. Cuntz, *Itineraria Romana* I (1929), 483, 486; A. Fägersten, *Place Names of Dorset* (1933), 1–2.

however been suggested,[1] based upon *Durnovaria* and *Lindinis* or *Lendiniae* (Ilchester, Som.), which, of some 30 acres, is the only other walled town known in the assumed tribal area. The extent of the latter is inferred largely from the distribution of the pre-Roman coins and of pottery, especially types of bead-rimmed bowls and countersunk-handled jars. These suggest an area defined on the W. by the Axe, on the N.W. by the Somerset marshes,[2] on the N. by the headwaters of the Stour and by the Ebble or the Nadder,

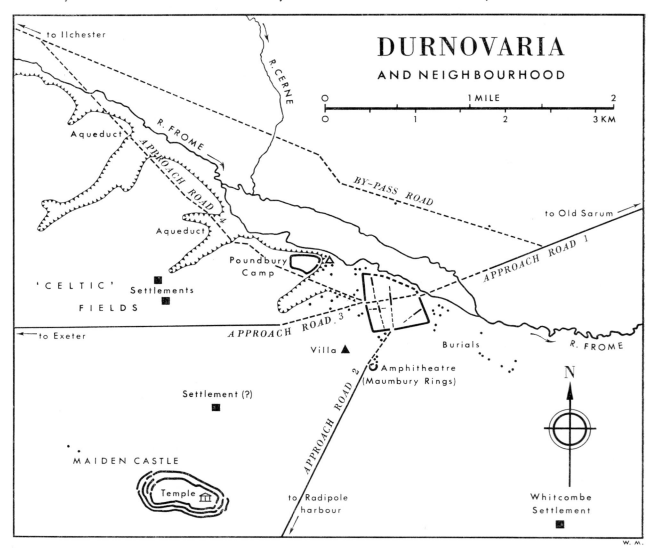

and on the E. by the Hampshire Avon. A division between the two centres could have coincided with Blackmore Forest.[3]

The origins of the Roman settlement are still obscure. The claims of the Iron Age hill-fort of Poundbury, about half a mile to the N.W. on the neighbouring plateau, and of Maiden Castle, some 2 miles S.W., to be

---

[1] C. E. Stevens, in Somerset Arch. and Nat. Hist. Soc., *Procs.* XCVI (1952), 188; I. A. Richmond, *Roman Britain* (1955), 79; A. L. F. Rivet in J. S. Wacher (ed.), *The Civitas Capitals of Roman Britain* (1966), 109.
[2] There may have been an outlet to the Bristol Channel near Bridgwater.
[3] A. L. F. Rivet, *Town and Country in Roman Britain* (1958), 50, 155–6, 175; *P.P.S.* XX (1954), 12–15, XXIV (1958), 101–19; S. S. Frere (ed.), *Problems of the Iron Age in Southern Britain* (1960), 239–46.

its native predecessor, have been discussed by Wheeler.[1] Of pre-Roman occupation on the site of the Roman town there seems no trace, other than a few coins and brooches which may well relate to the early Roman period, although Fordington Hill has yielded what may have been remains of an Iron Age chariot burial (216 d).

It has been suggested more than once that a camp or fort of the early conquest phase may have occupied the site to guard a ford or bridge over the Frome, and to the items of military or probable military equipment, recently studied by Webster,[2] there may now be added a bronze harness ring, a decorated bronze mount, and part of a handle of a skillet or mess-tin, found W. of Somerleigh Road and in Cornhill, as well as Claudian pottery and brooches (see Monuments (179a, 189c, 190, 196, 200)). Although the Roman road system as we know it need not be very early, it is not likely to have departed much from the lines of early advance and supply, and Dorchester is a nodal point in this system, and one that would have attracted settlement whether or not a military site had existed of sufficient permanence to provoke it. Sufficient early samian and imported coarse ware is moreover now known from the town to justify the assumption that there was pre-Flavian if not indeed Claudian occupation of some sort, and although the incidence of Claudian coins, including the copies of supposed military origin, has been exaggerated,[3] the percentage of early issues (p. 538) is not unlike that of Roman Silchester, the Claudian origin of which is not in doubt.

Frere has reasonably suggested that the headquarters and base of *Legio II Augusta* may have been set up at Dorchester or divided between it and Exeter, until the regrouping of the legions following the departure of *Legio XIV* from Britain in A.D. 67;[4] both towns were linked with harbours thought to have been used in the south-western advance of *Legio II* under the future emperor Vespasian. No structural remains of early date or military type have, however, been identified at Dorchester, and the early finds are too widespread to suggest a site. The right angle formed by the S.W. defences of the later town, and the alignment of the road from the harbour at Radipole W. of Maumbury instead of E. (see Approach Roads, 2), may point to the S.W. quarter as the most likely site for an establishment of this sort if it was located within the area of the future town; if so, the possibility that the street (176) sealed below the town rampart at Lee Motors was the *intervallum* road of a fort deserves to be considered.[5]

The likelihood of an occupation in the first few years of the conquest involves reassessment of Wheeler's view that the town was founded *c*. A.D. 70 (*op. cit.*, 66–8). This depended on the evidence for a complementary evacuation of Maiden Castle about that date, which there is no need to question (see Hill-forts, Winterborne St. Martin (142), pp. 499–500), and on an analysis in 1936 by T. Davies Pryce of 75 vessels or sherds of samian ware from Dorchester, of which no more than three or four need have been pre-Flavian. Pryce's unpublished list (in D.C.M.), however, reveals that of this small quantity no fewer than 54 pieces came from one site (194 a), so its statistical value is negligible. On the other hand, Wheeler was doubtless correct in assuming that 'Maiden Castle . . . must have contributed largely to the population of the new Roman town . . .'(*op. cit.*, 12). Although little is known of the nature or extent of the native occupation there in the years following the slighting of *c*. A.D. 44, there is no reason to suppose that any British nobles who had collaborated with or submitted to the conquerors would have taken up their abode in the *canabae* or licensed civil lines attached to a fort, or in a trading settlement at a Roman road junction, if that is what the pre-Flavian finds represent. Such authority as they and their fellows may have been permitted to retain under military supervision from Dorchester or elsewhere is more likely to have been exercised from such traditional centres of the tribe as were allowed to remain, of which Maiden Castle, unlike Hod Hill near Blandford, was patently one. The abandonment—perhaps the ceremonial abandonment, as

---

[1] R. E. M. Wheeler, *Maiden Castle, Dorset* (1943), 12. It may be significant that the Roman cemetery (225) at Poundbury seems wholly without early burials.

[2] *Arch. J.* xcv (1958), 79; G. Webster and D. R. Dudley, *The Roman Conquest of Britain* (1965), 108 and pl. 28. The sword grip was found at the Post Office, South Street, the belt plate W. of Weymouth Avenue outside the defences (see Monument (211)), and the key at the Gasworks (203).

[3] The copies were contemporary although not all authorities agree that they were of military origin. The seven imitations in D.C.M. said to form some 25% of the 'fair number of Claudian coins' from the town (C. H. V. Sutherland, *Romano-British Imitations of Bronze Coins of Claudius I* (1935), 7) are in fact of unknown provenance, and neither extant records nor collections substantiate the implied number of regular issues. Only eight coins of Claudius I are genuinely known from Dorchester; five of these are certainly or probably imitation *asses*, three from Maumbury (1893, 1908–10) and two from Colliton Park (1938, 1963).

[4] S. S. Frere, *Britannia* (1967), 74–5, 79, 93.   [5] There is need for careful excavation of the front of the rampart in Bowling Alley Walk.

Wheeler inferred—of the former tribal stronghold may thus have symbolized the grant of self-government to an existing but augmented community, rather than the deliberate creation of a new town. The settlement at Dorchester would thus, *c.* A.D. 70, have become the centre of the *civitas peregrina* of the Durotriges, or of those Durotriges who were not, perhaps, dependent on Ilchester.

Growing evidence shows that such a development would not have been exceptional under the Flavian governors. It will have involved the establishment of an *ordo* or senate of leading members of the tribe, modelled on those of the *coloniae* and *municipia* of the Roman provinces, and will have been accompanied or soon followed by the construction of a centrally located Forum and Basilica to replace the existing market or bazaar and provide the appropriate setting for the exercise of the judicial and administrative functions allowed to the *civitas*.[1] No traces of these or other public buildings such as baths and temples have yet been identified within the walls, unless the gravelled yard and flanking walls observed in and W. of Cornhill do in fact belong to the Forum (*see* Monument (196)).

The presence of public baths is with little doubt implied by the existence of the aqueduct (227a), constructed perhaps in or after the last decade of the 1st century, although first call upon it would have been the supply of public fountains; the only known distributing channel, in Colliton Park, was probably a spillway (227b) which seems to have gone out of use in the 4th century if not before. The aqueduct itself, the longest example of a type in military and civil use elsewhere in the province, was an open leat cut in the Chalk and following the contours of the Frome valley for some 12 miles from an intake probably at Notton 6 miles from Dorchester. Domestic needs were doubtless wholly or largely met by wells, examples of which are known at Colliton Park and elsewhere.

The public amusements afforded by the amphitheatre may have been available at an early date, since Maumbury Rings (228), a quarter of a mile outside the S. gate, was built as a Neolithic henge monument and seems to have needed few alterations to fit it for its new purpose. There is no direct evidence, however, that it was in use before the 2nd century. St. George Gray's plan of the Roman entrance revealed in the excavations of 1908–12 is here published for the first time (Plate 227), while the plan (Fig. p. 591) indicates the main features of the three principal phases of its life from its inception as a single-entranced circular bank with a deep inner ditch dug as a series of coalescing shafts. The Roman phase involved lowering the floor, filling the ditch and heightening the bank to form an oval earthwork some 330 ft. long. A timbered gangway around the arena, a beast pen at one end and chambers for performers (or perhaps shrines) at the sides are known, but seating arrangements were not revealed; the smaller stone-faced legionary amphitheatre at Caerleon was estimated to hold 6,000 spectators,[2] but the peculiar origin of the Dorchester amphitheatre shows that its magnitude need not indicate the size of audience expected.

Few of the streets are yet known, but it is clear that they were planned as a grid on an axis slightly W. of N. and corresponded roughly with the line of the W. and S. ramparts; civic policy seems to have been to remake streets rather than add successive metallings. The date of this plan is unknown but, if the supposed street (176) was part of it, it would antedate the construction of the earthwork defences referred probably to the latter part of the 2nd century. It is impossible to determine the standard of insula width between the normal extremes of 250 ft. and 450 ft., but the excessive distance of about 480 ft. between the two N. to S. streets (178) and (179) suggests the lower figure, as also does the distance of about 300 ft. between the lateral street (177) and the line proposed for the main street between the E. and W. gates. The eccentric alignment of street (175) in the S.E. quarter may be early in origin, perhaps reflecting military or other arrangements before the assumed Flavian expansion of the town (*see* p. 551); alternatively it can have defined the side of some special enclosure such as a temple area.

The defences enclosed an area of between 70 and 80 acres[3] and are notable for their original size rather

[1] Collingwood's suggestion that Carinus, whose Roman citizenship is attested, in the reading hitherto generally accepted, by his superbly lettered grave slab at Fordington ((216d), Plate 226), was a 'resident' entrusted with the furtherance of romanization, deserves to be considered, but there is no indication that he held any official position (Somerset and Dorset *Notes and Queries* XVIII (1926), 31–3). An alternative reading, however, deprives him of this status (*see* p. 574n.).
[2] *Archaeologia* LXXVIII (1928), 111–218.
[3] The uncertainty is due to lack of evidence for the course in the northern sector between Colliton Park and the foot of High East Street.

than for the visible remains, which are slight. An earthen bank and ditch (174), the latter ultimately if not from the first of multiple form, were constructed after c. A.D. 130 and may well be referred to an official policy of civil defence which, it has been suggested, was instituted in the latter part of the 2nd century.[1] The stone wall (173), of which one portion of the robbed core remains above ground in Albert Road, was certainly a later feature added to the front of the bank, which then became a ramped approach and reinforcement. The dating evidence, although by no means secure, suggests that this change was made little if at all before c. A.D. 300, somewhat later than has been proposed for the stone walls of other towns of similar status.[2] There is no evidence for projecting wall-towers.

It is not known how fully the area within the walls was occupied by buildings. The apparent spaciousness of development at Colliton Park (182–8) may be misleading since the conditions of observation in much of the area have not facilitated recognition of traces of timber foundations, but it is clear that there was little if any construction in more substantial materials in this N.W. corner of the Roman town until the 3rd or 4th century, and it seems doubtful whether the street grid was ever complete in this sector. It is also noteworthy that no structural remains and few other finds of any kind have been recorded along High East Street or in the area N. of it. On the other hand the extinction, when the primary rampart was raised, of the E. to W. street (176) adjoining Bowling Alley Walk, suggests that the grid may elsewhere have been planned on too ambitious a scale, unless it can be shown that this street belonged instead to an early fort (see p. 533).[3] If there is some evidence for ribbon development along the E. and S.W. approach roads (see p. 569 and Monument (210)), there is no reason to suppose that this was due to internal pressure.

The recorded remains tell us little of the size or type of the town houses of *Durnovaria*, although the best preserved and still largely exposed building (182) at Colliton Park is an example of unusual development of residential rooms away from the sides of the courtyard or quadrangle, and has made a distinct contribution to knowledge of window design. So far as their fragmentary state allows interpretation, the remains of building (186) suggest a more regular courtyard plan, although on no grand scale. The small but neat building (185) to the S.W., however, was no more than a cottage; its porch shows that it was not an outbuilding or shop. Building (187), of aisled plan, may have been a warehouse or even a barn, while (184) was of awkward, elongated plan, also suggesting commercial or light industrial rather than purely domestic use, although its large ovens or furnaces were not original features. Building (183) seems also to have enclosed an industrial area. The association of such establishments with relatively opulent and at least partly contemporary dwellings is curious, unless it reflects the presence in the 4th century of a different class of owner from the members of the landed tribal nobility who are believed to have built such town houses and taken office as decurions in earlier centuries.

Outside Colliton Park, where conditions may have been exceptional, there is little to be learnt of house plans. Where their orientation is known there seems, with some exceptions, to have been a more or less close correspondence with the street grid, and perhaps also with the unconforming street (175) in the S.E. The tessellated pavements, most of them patterned mosaics, of which there are records of about 50,[4] testify however to a profusion of wealthy dwellings. Evidence of date comes largely from inadequate 19th-century records and from study of the mosaics, which, however, can have replaced earlier floors; no substantial building remains can in fact be dated with any certainty before the 3rd century.

Allowing for this imbalance, the evidence for prosperity in the 4th century, and at Colliton Park even into its second half, is still impressive, although the coin evidence (p. 538) may be held to imply a less favourable situation than at the other major centre of the tribe, Ilchester, which must be supposed to have reached its peak in the late 4th century as a result of the proliferation of exceptionally rich villas around it.[5] The coin list from Dorchester is virtually a list from one corner of the town[6] and has to be treated with

---

[1] S. S. Frere, *Britannia* (1967), 251.   [2] *Ibid.* 252.
[3] The apparent absence of burials other than those of infants and young children within the walled area suggests that the boundaries of the town were determined at an early date.
[4] The total includes two at Fordington (210) immediately outside the walls.
[5] The contrast was first pointed out, in correspondence, by A. L. F. Rivet.
[6] Colliton Park (1937–9, 1961–3); about 170 coins, excluding hoards, are listed from other areas.

reserve. Only one coin, however, other than some in the silver hoard from Somerleigh Court (*see* p. 562) can be dated later than A.D. 395, a pattern that is repeated elsewhere in Britain, save in a few exceptional cases, and one that doubtless signifies the general decline of a money economy[1] and not the extinction of corporate life, which must have continued in Dorchester in the 5th century as long as the economy of the region was capable of supporting it. In any case the percentage of latest issues compares with that of Exeter and *Verulamium*, where the existence of 5th-century communities need not be questioned.[2]

The decline was certainly gradual. Although a wrecked mosaic (198) may now perhaps be added to the instances of deliberate or wanton destruction observed during the excavations at Colliton Park (182), where evidence was also held to show neglect of civilized standards, it would be easy to exaggerate the importance of isolated instances of which the date is uncertain. The sporadic presence of early Saxon raiders or settlers in the region is attested only by the single warrior's grave at Hardown Hill (R.C.H.M., *Dorset* I, 265),[3] and Dorchester shows no more signs of a violent end than do other Roman towns in more vulnerable areas. The survival of some kind of community, however little it may have merited the name of town, into the 6th or even the 7th century, when the area was at last incorporated into the kingdom of Wessex, may be guessed from the survival of the Roman name, almost unchanged, in the Saxon *Dornwaraceaster* and its variants.

The standard of material Roman civilization attained is best exemplified by the number and, at Fordington at least (Monument (210)), the quality of the mosaics. Indeed the existence has been suggested of a 'school' of mosaicists centred on *Durnovaria* in the 4th century, of which the pavements at Fordington and Durngate Street (202) are probable examples. On the other hand the town is poor in monumental sculptures or inscriptions, which are represented only by the early tombstone of Carinus at Fordington (Plate 226), unless the Whitcombe cavalier (Whitcombe (26); Plate 228), and a military dedication to Jupiter found in 1964 re-used in Godmanston church,[4] can be considered as objects removed from the town. A certain degree of literacy is indicated by Latin graffiti on wall-plaster at Wollaston Field (205) and Colliton Park (182), but it is uncertain to what social level these should be attributed. In burial customs (pp. 571–2) the inhabitants shared with their fellow Durotriges a conservatism that allowed little change in regional Iron Age tradition other than a more regularly extended posture or the provision of a wooden coffin; cremations and what might pass for rich grave goods are virtually unknown, while stone sarcophagi and lead coffins have been found only in the cemetery at Poundbury (225) where they appear to be late and quite often associated with the use—otherwise best known at York—of plaster or gypsum packed round the body. A possibility that this cemetery was largely or exclusively Christian is discussed below (p. 572). The presence of a Christian community in *Durnovaria* in the late 4th century is implied by the Somerleigh Court silver hoard of over 50 *siliquae* concealed *c.* A.D. 400 with five spoons and a pronged *ligula* (Fig. p. 563).[5] The inscription AVGVSTINE VIVAS on the bowl of one spoon and the fish inscribed on another, together with the *ligula*, suggest a liturgical use, as does a similar group of objects found at Canterbury in 1962, where the *ligula* was inscribed with a *chi-rho* monogram.[6]

There is little evidence for Roman and native cults other than the Jupiter Optimus Maximus of the aforementioned Godmanston inscription. A bronze statuette of Mercury, in D.C.M., was found in 1747 in the old Grammar School garden (197), while three grotesque heads in relief, carved or perhaps adapted as keystones and re-used in the 18th-century structure of Colliton House, have been supposed ancient and thought to represent the Romano-Celtic horned deity, Cernunnos.[7] Small votive objects are uncommon

---

[1] *Cf* Frere, *Britannia* (1967), 370–2. [2] *Ibid.* 376–8.

[3] The grave at Maiden Castle belongs probably to the 7th century A.D. (*see* p. xlix, *n.* 2).

[4] Dorset *Procs.* LXXXVI (1964), 104–6; *J.R.S.* LV (1965), 220–1.

[5] *See* Monument (190). The objects are now in the D.C.M. It is also noteworthy that two of the mosaics of the 'Durnovarian school', at Frampton (R.C.H.M. *Dorset* I, 150) and Hinton St. Mary (*J.R.S.* LIV (1964), 7–14; *Dorset* III, forthcoming), include Christian symbols.

[6] *Cf. J.B.A.A.* XVI (1953), 21–2, and, for Canterbury, XXVIII (1965), 1–15. *See also* under *cuiller* in *Dictionnaire d'archéologie chrétienne et de liturgie*, III, 2 (1914), 3172–83.

[7] J. M. C. Toynbee, *Art in Britain under the Romans* (1964), 180. The proposal was first made by T. Dayrell Reed. One, comparatively featureless, remains as a keystone in a chimneystack visible from Glyde Path Road. Of the others, now in D.C.M. and both of Portland stone, one with short animal ears and gaping mouth served as keystone in the door of an outhouse demolished in 1947. The other was built into the E. wall of Colliton Park facing the road; the face, with protruding animal ears, is fringed with a beard and crowned with voluted ornament or stylized antlers. The

but include part of a Rhenish pipeclay figurine of Venus from the 2nd-century filling of the well at Wollaston Field (205); a fine wheel-cut Rhenish glass bowl from Colliton Park (184) depicts Bacchic dancers.[1] The niche in room 2 of the house (182) probably marks a household shrine (Plate 220).

There is some evidence for industry and commerce, although the main function of the town, other than as administrative centre and staging post in the imperial courier system, was doubtless as a market serving the surrounding countryside. The presence apparently of a villa less than a quarter of a mile from the walls, at Olga Road (212), may argue a more direct participation in agriculture than is usually apparent in the towns of Roman Britain. None of the late ovens of buildings III and IIIA at Colliton Park (184), however, were obviously for drying corn; two of them may have been for some process involving ash and beach shingle. The curious stone-lined, corbelled pit adjoining the house (182) has, however, a more obvious resemblance to the 'beehive' chambers of Portland, probably for storing grain (Fig. p. 606), than to other known structures.

Lead and iron-working on a small scale are indicated respectively by a hearth in South Street (196) and a late forge at Colliton Park (183), where an industrial or commercial use has already been suggested for some of the buildings exposed in 1937–9 (see p. 535). There is some slight evidence at Poundbury (214) for the finishing of flat-lidded sarcophagi of Ham Hill stone from Somerset. The provision of this mellow brown stone for this and to some extent for general building purposes, as at Colliton Park (182, 187), indicates an overland trade in heavy materials with the Durotriges of the Ilchester region; the ridge-lidded sarcophagus at Poundbury came, doubtless more readily, from Portland. Much Purbeck stone was employed, as in the town wall, but it can have come from nearer beds between Dorchester and Radipole; the so-called marble can only have come from Purbeck, and the Carinus tombstone (Plate 226) is a prime example of its early use.

Much of the trade with Purbeck was doubtless in articles of Kimmeridge shale and pottery. The shale trade was mainly in armlets, but a carved leg with claw-foot and griffin's head from a three-legged round table, found in a pit at Colliton Park (182), and fragments of three from South Street and one from Princes Street, show that furniture was included;[2] although it is likely, there is nothing to prove that any of these objects were made in the town rather than in Purbeck (see p. 525). No pottery-kiln has been recorded near Dorchester, and it is at least clear that there was no considerable coarse ware industry nearer than Purbeck; finer wares, other than Gaulish samian, are uncommon, but were imported from the Rhineland and the Nene Valley or similar potteries in E. Britain until the New Forest industry reached its apogee in the 4th century with *Durnovaria* probably as its major market. The existence of a local tilery, however, is suggested by the distribution of a number of terracotta antefixes, all but one from the same mould (Plate 228; Appendix II, p. 538).

The most notable find made in Dorchester is the mid 3rd-century coin hoard of over 22,000 *antoniniani* found, with a few *denarii*, at Marks and Spencer's, South Street, in 1936 (Plate 230; see Monument (194)).[3] Of the containers the bronze jug at least (Fig. p. 565) was a foreign import, already old when the hoard was deposited in A.D. 257 or soon afterwards. The coins probably represent a consignment of cash not yet in general circulation. Little is known of a Constantinian hoard lost in or deposited near the River Frome N. of Grey's Bridge (see Approach Roads, 1), but a hoard of over 100 bronze coins concealed c. A.D. 353 at Poundbury (see Monument 214)) included both official issues of Constantius II and Gallus and die-struck copies made from them, no doubt here or at Dorchester. This local striking of small change is probably exemplified for the 3rd century in five die-duplicate copies of a radiate coin of Tetricus I, found in the E. room of the cottage (185) at Colliton Park.[4]

---

three carvings are much more weathered than the Portland stone facings of the house but there is no evidence when they were set in position. Differences in style suggest that they never formed part of a single monument, and keystones are otherwise unknown in a Romano-Celtic religious context. (*See also* Dorchester (23), p. 118.)

[1] Dorset *Procs.* LX (1938), 55–6 and pl. iii.
[2] *Antiquity* XXIV (1950), 25–9; *Ant. J.* XXXI (1951), 193–4, XL (1960), 72–3; J. Liversidge, *Furniture in Roman Britain* (1955), 37–47.
[3] The silver hoard of Honorius has been noted above (p. 536).
[4] Information from R. A. G. Carson.

APPENDIX I: COIN SERIES FROM ROMANO-BRITISH TOWNS

Town	Pre-Claudian	Claudius	Nero to Nerva	Trajan to Pius	Aurelius to Commodus	Severus to Valerian	Gallienus to Numerian	First Tetrarchy	Constantine I to 330	330 to 364	364 to 383	After 383	Total
Dorchester ..	1·0	0·5	0·8	3·0	1·6	1·3	37·3	3·6	3·8	35·5	6·5	4·6	1730
Colchester ..	2·5	4·1	8·7	10·3	5·0	8·1	27·5	5·6	5·0	15·5	3·8	3·0	7570
Exeter	1·3	7·7	15·7	11·1	2·5	3·7	13·5	6·4	6·5	20·2	5·9	2·9	1108
Ilchester		0·8	1·8	5·4	2·2	1·9	24·5	6·7	6·5	32·5	10·2	6·3	714
Leicester	1·1	0·7	6·8	8·3	1·7	2·2	28·4	4·4	8·8	23·1	8·8	4·3	696
Silchester ..	0·5	0·8	2·7	4·3	1·9	2·3	30·9	6·0	16·9	14·3	12·8	6·6	6367
Verulamium ..	1·4	2·4	6·5	5·2	1·7	2·5	45·2	7·3	2·9	14·5	5·4	2·5	3192

Note: The numbers of coins of the different periods are expressed as percentages of the total number identified from each town; only the single coin closing the series has been counted from hoards, where these are distinguishable (as they invariably are in Dorchester). Pre-Claudian coins include native British; owing to differences in the sources it has been found impracticable to separate Neronian from Flavian issues.[1]

APPENDIX II: ANTEFIXES

Five antefixes of red tile-clay (in D.C.M.) come from Dorchester and neighbourhood. Similar objects are known in this country from Caerleon, Chester, Silchester, York, and from the legionary workshop at Holt, Denbighshire, but they are not common and were probably reserved for use as finials in conjunction with ridge-tiles, or for the eaves of public buildings. The most complete example, from High East Street, is illustrated (Plate 228), but lacks the original frame which was probably semicircular, or rectangular with gabled crest. All five are casual finds, three from widely separated points within the Roman town (10 South Street, High East Street, H.M. Prison), one from Cattistock 8 miles to the N.W., and the fifth perhaps from Preston 5 miles to the S. (*see* Weymouth (447), p. 618b). All but the last are from the same mould, with minor differences due to trimming and handling before firing, and are therefore likely to come from a local tilery. The series is without precise parallel although very similar to that in gritty grey clay at Silchester, Hants., also from a single mould.[2]

The examples from Dorchester and Cattistock show a head in relief with straight forelocks and beard framing the face; wings, feathered below but with traces of the upper hair above, sprout from the centre of the forehead. The reverses show traces of attachment to *imbrex* tiles by luting. In the Silchester series, rectangular with gabled crest containing a debased palmette, the face is beardless with prominent ears, and has perhaps twining snakes or a bow[3] tied below the chin; the wings, unfeathered but otherwise identical with the Dorchester type, have been interpreted as horns.[4] The worn fragment from Preston (?) is not of the Silchester mould or clay, but the wings may also have been unfeathered.

Both series are clearly versions of the same type and derive ultimately from the common classical terracotta antefix with Gorgon's mask or other mythological subject, frequently combined with the anthemion or palmette.

[1] The analysis of coins from Dorchester has been made possible by the reports, in D.C.M., on the series from Colliton Park by C. H. V. Sutherland (1939), revised and completed for this volume by R. A. G. Carson (1963). Acknowledgement is also due to Mrs. G. M. Aitken for further lists from Colliton Park, to J. Stevens Cox for the series from Ilchester, and to S. S. Frere for supplementary figures from the post-war excavations at *Verulamium*. The remainder has been compiled from published sources. Attention is drawn to the fact stated above (p. 535) that the Dorchester series is very largely derived from one corner of the town.

[2] G. C. Boon, *Roman Silchester* (1957), 135, 148. The only evidence for date there is given by a fragment recovered from debris of an early 2nd-century building.

[3] *Cf.* the *gorgoneion* on the gold cuirassed bust of Marcus Aurelius at Avenches, Switzerland: E. Esperandieu (R. Lantier), *Recueil général des bas-reliefs . . . de la Gaule Romaine*, XIV (1955), 51.

[4] See Boon, *op. cit.*, 135; J. M. C. Toynbee, *Art in Britain under the Romans* (1964), 430–1, accepts them as wings but prefers to regard the crest as depicting 'elaborate horns'.

APPROACH ROADS

Four Roman roads approach Dorchester (Fig. p. 532). Those from London, Radipole (Weymouth) and Exeter entered the town by the main E., S. and W. gates respectively; the fourth, from Ilchester, also seems to have entered by the W. gate, *via* Poundbury, although there is good evidence for a branch by-passing the Roman town to the N. to join the London road one mile E. of Dorchester. This by-pass was first recognized by O. G. S. Crawford[1] and incorporated in the 2nd edition of the O.S. *Map of Roman Britain* (1928) to the exclusion of the Poundbury route, but the 3rd edition (1956) returned to the situation shown in the edition of 1924. I. D. Margary is probably right in accepting both (*Roman Roads in Britain* (2nd edn., 1967), 111). The alignments of the first three roads are well enough known outside the borough boundaries but none can be precisely located within it; this uncertainty may well remain until the problem of the gates is resolved (*see* pp. 549–51).

The evidence for a fifth road in the direction of Wareham and Purbeck is entirely circumstantial. That there was direct communication by land between the capital and the major industrial region in the tribal area can hardly be doubted, and the coincidence of burials with such a line, for over half a mile out of Dorchester, is far more striking than in the case of the recognized roads. This coincidence, and the slight evidence for a gate at Gallows Hill (p. 550), point to a southerly route such as is followed by the present main road (A 352), tending towards the Chalk downs. If this existed as a metalled route, as seems probable, it could be seen as a valleyward version of the native ridgeways of the S. Dorset Downs leading to Swanage and Studland Bays. Grinsell (*Archaeology of Wessex* (1958), map v), favours a different route, running N.W. from Wareham across the heathland to reach the Roman trunk road (Approach Road 1) between Puddletown Heath and Dorchester, much as G. B. Grundy suggested (*Arch.J.* xcv (1938), 215–7). Hutchins's claims for an agger crossing the heath were, however, doubted by Warne (*Ancient Dorset* (1872), 195–7), and no other signs of a made road have been recorded; such ways, if they existed, were doubtless native tracks continuing in use as pack-horse routes.

A route of similar character has been suggested by Margary (*loc. cit.*) as connecting Dorchester at the W. gate with settlements around Cerne Abbas to N. and with the aforesaid native ridgeways at Came Down to S. Again there is no question of a made road, although the suggestion is consistent with the distribution of

Roman burials (226) W. of the Grove (*see* p. 571b), and could explain the behaviour of the supposed Roman by-pass in the sector S.E. of Charminster (p. 541b).

There are several ambiguous records of metalling below modern streets on the E. and S.E. sides of Dorchester, the first two of which, at least, have been considered Roman. (i) A layer of grouted flints $1\frac{1}{2}$ to 2 ft. thick at a depth of 5 ft. below surface, lying on black (burnt?) soil, was traced in 1892 for some 70 yds. under the N. side of High Street, Fordington, between the main Foundry building (itself the site, it is believed, of a plain tessellated pavement) and the extra-mural mosaic (210) under the Foundry Yard; this was believed to point towards Holloway Road rather than Fordington Hill. It was seen again *c.* 1903 below the projecting crane of the Foundry (69599073; information from O. C. Vidler). (Dorset *Procs.* xiv (1893), 52; xvi (1895) 152–3; xlix (1928), 90; Moule, 30–1; Moule MS., 14–15; Dorset Album II, f.44A, in D.C.M.) (ii) Similar metalling was later seen under Holloway Road opposite the school (69759070; Dorset *Procs.* xx (1899), 131). (iii) A paving of 'hand laid' black flints at a depth of 3 ft., direction N.E. to S.W., was noted in 1926 by C. D. Drew on a 25 in. O.S. plan in the D.C.M., at the junction of Prince of Wales Road and Alington Road (70049015), with 'the same kind of road' under Standfast (now King's) Road (70029053) near Prince's Bridge. The coincidence of these exposures with the modern network of suburban streets argues for earlier but not Roman routes, issuing from the ford much used both before and after the opening of Grey's Bridge in 1748 (*see* p. 550a, and *cf.* William Simpson's map of the manor of Fordington, 1779, in the offices of the Duchy of Cornwall).[1] On the other hand, no remains have been recorded outside the town to support the suggestion made below (p. 551a) that the street (175), apparently crossing the S.E. quarter of the Roman town at Wollaston Field, was the relic of an earlier through route from the E.

The evidence for the four known approach roads is detailed below; the further course of Approach Road 2 outside the borough is described above under Roman Roads (p. 528). The branch or by-pass road, although lying wholly outside the area of the present volume,[2] is most conveniently discussed as an appendix to the description of Approach Road 4.

APPROACH ROAD 1. The road approaching Dorchester from the E.N.E., from London *via* Old Sarum and Badbury Rings,

---

[1] Hutchins recognized the portion W. of Charminster as part of a route supposedly reaching Dorchester from Wolfeton (Hutchins I, vii).

[1] Deeply buried metalling apparently of similar nature but certainly later than *c.* 1740 has been noted within the town at the foot of High East Street and in Wollaston Field (Dorset *Procs.* lxxvii (1955), 130–2).

[2] The parishes involved are Stinsford and Charminster, in the area of Volume III (forthcoming), and Stratton in Volume I where, however, the Roman roads are not discussed.

apparently crossed the Frome and entered the borough about 100 yds. N. of Grey's Bridge. With Approach Road 3 it formed part of the Roman trunk road to Exeter (Margary's route 4, *op. cit.*, 108–10). The last or last known alignment, heading for the centre of the town and still well preserved in Kingston Park, is straight for more than 1½ miles as far as Stinsford Hill, about 1600 yds. from the approximate line of the E. wall, where a ploughed ridge some 60 ft. wide and 2 ft. high can be traced, S. of the road junction, for 100 yds. (70959130).[1] Then the modern road down Stinsford Hill is approximately on the line nearly to the foot of Slyer's Lane where it diverges S.W., but the road before 1746 evidently maintained the Roman alignment for a further 290 yds. or so beyond the lane, before swinging more sharply S.S.W. to cross the Frome by the 'Old Bridge' or 'Stocken Bridge' about 120 yds. downstream from Grey's Bridge (*see also* p. 550a; Dorset *Procs.* XIV (1893), 51; XXXVIII (1917), 31–2). There is little room for doubt that the Roman road continued straight across the meadows, where the metalling probably remains below the flood-plain silt, although the alignment, as far as can be judged, points rather S. of the foot of High East Street where the E. gate would be expected.

The only place where a Roman road on this line could have been encountered in making the new London road in 1746–8 was in East Parade S. of the close (now built up) then known as Segar's Orchard (69609080; Glover's Close in Simpson's map, 1779, Grey's Orchard in the Tithe Map of Fordington, 1843). Hutchins, however, states that 'on making the new way, a very little E. of Segar's orchard at the entrance into Dorchester, the Icening Way was discovered and crossed',[2] and elsewhere that it was nearly parallel with the new road, 'paved with flints and stone, under which was a layer of chalk, near the east end of Dorchester, coming from Stinsford Lane. It pointed thence to the back of the old gaol, the north side of St. Peter's, and through Trinity Church' (Hutchins I, vi).[3] The ambiguity is such as to throw doubt on the relevance of the discovery; more acceptable, however, is Warne's record of the site of a Roman ford (or bridge?) about 100 yds. N. of Grey's Bridge, which is precisely where it would be expected if the straight alignment was preserved.[4] The site was marked by compacted debris in the river bed including several hundred coins, probably votive offerings or a hoard (untraced), of which the latest recorded coin was of Maximinus II (A.D. 305–14).

APPROACH ROAD 2. The road from Radipole (Weymouth) approaching Dorchester from the S.S.W. crosses the borough boundary at Maiden Castle Cottages (Margary's route 48, *op.*

cit., 112–3). The present Weymouth Road preserves the straight alignment from Ridgeway Hill for some 1100 yds. more, to pass W. of the amphitheatre (Maumbury Rings), where a new north-easterly alignment, for the remaining 600 yds. or so, was evidently struck out from the local crest to reach the Roman town at a point nearer the centre of the S. rampart. This last alignment has also been held to coincide with the modern road, Weymouth Avenue, and may well do so although a line tending more truly N.E. is by no means impossible (*see* p. 550b). Hutchins wrote, 'It has a high broad ridge paved with flint, and was very perfect between Mambury and Winterborne Monkton, before that enemy to antiquity called a turnpike road was made' (Hutchins I, viii); a ridge is not shown, however, between Maumbury and the town in Newton's engraving of the amphitheatre (1755; Dorset *Procs.* XXXVIII (1918), 29).

Two discoveries of gravelled surfaces may be remains of the road and, if so, confirm the substantial identification with Weymouth Avenue. The first, made in 1960 in the former garden of Mentone Lodge after cutting back the corner between Weymouth Avenue and Great Western Road, consisted of an uncambered layer of flint gravel some 3 ins. thick resting on natural Chalk (plan, opp. p. 584). It was slightly higher than the present surface of Weymouth Avenue. Pottery including metallic-lustred New Forest ware, lying on the flints, implied use in the 4th century and also a late date for overlying deposits probably to be identified as remains of a counterscarp bank of the defences (*see* (174 i), p. 549). The extent of the gravelled area is unknown and the direction uncertain, but at its S. exposure, in the trench for the new front wall of the garden, it reached at least to the pavement of Weymouth Avenue and was clearly not less than 23 ft. wide; in the northerly exposures about 15 yds. to N.E. it was at least 17 ft. wide but was not traced closer than 9 ft. from the pavement. A ditch, roughly V-shaped and 10 ft. wide by 4 ft. deep at the point where it was sectioned (69148:90298),[1] ran parallel with Weymouth Avenue along the N.W. side of the feature, and seems to have been filled sometime between the mid 2nd century and the close of the 3rd century. It may have been a roadside ditch, but there are difficulties. Opposite the burial (219b) found in its filling, the flint gravel continued for at least 1½ ft. beyond its N.W. side. Indications towards the corner angle between the two modern roads suggested that the ditch was bending E. to cross the line of Weymouth Avenue, and a connection is possible with one of two E.-W. ditches of rather similar width, found side by side 30 yds. away under the E. pavement of the avenue, W. of Rowan House (69184:90309; information from Mr. C. J. Green). Thirdly, the evidence shows that the gravel, so far as it was exposed, was covered by the supposed counterscarp bank (R.C.H.M. records). A choice would presumably lie between interpretation of this feature as a local hard standing of some kind, or a road metalling superseded in late Roman times.

The second discovery, in 1965, 60 yds. to N.N.E. under the

---

[1] At this point about one Roman mile from the town and within the area of Volume III, an upright stone resembling a Roman milestone but uninscribed has been re-erected at least twice beside the present road; its claim to a Roman origin is unsubstantiated (Dorset *Procs.* LXXIX (1957), 110–2).

[2] 1st edn. (1774), I, 575; *see also* Vertue, *Minutes of Soc. Antiquaries* V, 128. A 'hypocaust' was found on the S. side of the supposed road on this occasion (*see* p. 569).

[3] The old gaol was at the N. foot of High East Street.

[4] *Ancient Dorset* (1872), 173; Hutchins I, vii, note a; Moule in Fordington St. George's *Parish Magazine*, May 1885, and in Dorset *Procs.* XIV (1893), 52, where, however, he mistakes Old Rod Mead for Old Road Mead.

---

[1] National Grid map references are normally given in eight figures, to the nearest 10 metres; the latest edition of the O.S. 1 : 2500 plan for Dorchester, however, makes it possible to give ten-figure references, to the nearest metre, and these are used where a more precise location is required.

kerb towards the E. foot of Trinity Street (69178:90350) and hardly, if at all, outside the estimated line of the town wall, consisted of a thin layer of flints 1 ft. below surface and at least 12 ft. wide. It rested on loamy soil, over the natural Chalk 2 ft. below surface. The W. side was not exposed, but the feature was judged to run rather E. of N. and to represent remains of the approach road. On the E. the Chalk continued level for some 10 ft. before falling steeply to at least 6 ft. below surface.[1] (Information from Mr. C. J. Green.) The evidence is thus not inconsistent with a causeway carrying the approach road across the town ditch, but there seems no other evidence for a gate so far W. (see pp. 550, 551).

APPROACH ROAD 3. The road approaching Dorchester from the W. from Exeter via Bridport (Margary's route 4, op. cit., 113–6) enters the borough near the first milestone S.E. of Poundbury Farm. The alignment, aimed at the S.W. quarter of the town, was the last but one of a series of straight lengths following the ridge from Eggardon; it was described in 1709 as 'a raised causeway coming directly from the west' (Warne, Ancient Dorset (1872), 221), and is plainly represented by the present Bridport Road which masks any remains of Roman construction. In 1774 it was said to be 'in perfection, high and broad, paved with flint and stone', from the W. end of Dorchester (Hutchins I, vi).

A final E.N.E. alignment of some 1100 yds., required to bring the road in by the W. gate, is doubtless also masked by the modern road, although, as with Approach Road 2, a certain latitude is possible. Reasons are given below (p. 550) for suggesting that the W. gate was not quite at the head of High West Street, and may have been a few yards to the S. In 1965, however, a single thin layer of flinty gravel 27 ft. wide, resting on what was supposed to be natural Chalk, was seen in a cable trench dug N. to S. across the top of High West Street at a distance of some 10 ft. E. of the traffic island (as enlarged subsequent to the 1956 edition of the O.S. plan SY 6890). The exposure was thus slightly outside the line of the town wall and could be the remains of the approach road (Dorset Procs. LXXXIX (1967), 144). There were signs suggesting the presence of the inner lip of the ditch both N. and S. of the supposed metalling, corresponding with the exposure a few feet to the N. in 1955 (Dorset Procs. LXXVII (1955), 129; see also Defences (174 h)). If correctly interpreted, these discoveries imply a causeway across the ditch, and a Roman gateway at the traditional site, but a made causeway could have been of more recent date.

APPROACH ROAD 4. The road from the N.W. connecting Dorchester with Ilchester (Lendiniae(?)) is clear beyond Stratton about 3 miles from the W. gate (Margary's route 47, op. cit., 110–2). No positive traces are recognizable between these points, but there seems no reason to reject the route proposed by Hutchins and followed by the present road from Bradford Peverell, which enters the borough a few yards outside the S.W. corner of Poundbury Camp. A road hereabouts is strongly supported by the presence of the Roman cemetery (225) on the E. slopes of Poundbury. Hutchins stated that it left the main Roman road at the W. end of Dorchester 'at an acute angle, its dorsum broad and high, paved with flints. It is the present road to Bradford Peverel, and is very perfect in some places, especially near Bradford; and at the higher end of that village it crosses several branches of the Frome, and is visible in the meadows . . .'. In 1829 the Rev. James Skinner sketched the line as it appeared to him across the water-meadows between Stratton and Bradford (B.M. Add. MS. 33715, 12, 15), while Margary (op. cit., 111) has noted a gravel spread which he thought confirmed a route northwards across the meadows to Stratton, to join the branch route there.[1]

The present road from Poundbury eastwards, while not exactly straight, suggests an alignment towards the traditional site of the W. gate at Top o' Town, or slightly to the S.; the line crosses the re-entrant, formerly Sheald's Bottom, where the Aqueduct (227 a) must have been crossed at least once, and gains the crest of the ridge to join Approach Road 3 near the W. gate. A deposit of gravel, 12 to 14 ft. wide and about 3 ins. thick, seen in 1931 alongside the paint shop in the Corporation Yard, close to a burial (223 a), was believed to be a metalled road pointing towards Top o' Town (information from Mr. W. Yard, 1951). It would certainly be on the line, but the diversion of the present road immediately E. of the Depot Barracks is relatively modern;[2] the metalling, if such it was, need not then be Roman.

APPENDIX: A road by-passing Durnovaria to the N. and connecting the London road (Approach Road 1) at Stinsford with the Ilchester road at Stratton, is accepted by Margary (route 470, op. cit., 111) but omitted from the O.S. Map of Roman Britain (3rd edition, 1956). From Stinsford Hill a footpath and minor road, including a short length of the Charminster–Stinsford parish boundary, indicate a possible line, while, N.E. of Frome Whitfield House, remains perhaps of an agger 2 ft. high can be seen inside the N. verge of Pond Close (693916) for about 230 yds. E. of North Lodge; traces remain for some 180 yds. further E. Burials in stone cists at Pond Close and in a stone sarcophagus at Slyer's Lane (about 703915), all probably of Roman date,[3] support this suggested line. The supposed alignment W. of Charminster village is parallel but some 300 yds. to N., and Margary proposes a linking alignment making use of part of a native ridgeway now represented by the upper road from Dorchester to Charminster (see p. 539). There are no likely traces of Roman work in this sector, but it may be significant that the village of Stratton,[4]

---

[1] Acland noted a flat bottom to the Chalk, 8 ft. to 9 ft. below surface, at a point (69187:90347) only some 7 ft. S.S.E. of this scarp and it was here that he recorded a narrow trench, cut N. to S. mainly in the fill, which he regarded as post-Roman and possibly the beginning of a Civil War communication trench to Maumbury Rings (Dorset Procs. XXXVI (1915), 2–3).

[1] Similar gravel, however, is exposed frequently in this area where the banks of the stream are sufficiently trampled by cattle. An alternative course in this sector, running obliquely across the meadows and probably to be identified with that claimed by Hutchins, is now marked on the latest edition of the O.S. 6 in. map SY 69 SE.

[2] cf. Military map of the Encampment at Dorchester, 1757 (B.M. Add. MS. 15532), which shows the road running through.

[3] Hutchins II, 739, footnote; Gentleman's Mag. (1841), pt. ii, 393; the sarcophagus is untraced.

[4] A. Fägersten, Place Names of Dorset (1933), 185–6, Stratton; 'farm by the (Roman) road'.

named from its position on the 'street', has developed along the line towards Charminster.

DEFENCES

The defences of *Durnovaria* (173–4), so far as they are known, consisted of an earthen bank and ditch system constructed not earlier than *c.* A.D.130 and more probably during the second half of the 2nd century, and a stone wall, added to the front of this bank after an uncertain but appreciable interval, perhaps as late as the 4th century. No evidence has yet been found for turrets or projecting towers, or for the number and exact position of the gates, although the main gates probably corresponded approximately with the present exits to London, Weymouth, Exeter and perhaps also to Wareham. No traces of any earlier system of defences, either military or civil, have been identified.[1]

Although the exact position of the wall is only known at two places in the W. rampart, in Albert Road (173a), where 28 ft. of the rubble core still stand 10 ft. high above the foundations, and under Colliton Walk (173b), where these were exposed in 1938, the perimeter of the Roman town is defined with tolerable accuracy by visible or recorded traces of the earthworks, or by indications in the modern topography, save in the N.E. sector between Friary Hill and the foot of High East Street where no Roman features of any kind have been recorded (Fig. opp. p. 584). The area of between 70 and 80 acres so enclosed may be regarded as a quadrant, the N.E. side probably laid out in a series of straight traverses, or a combination of traverse and curve, to take in all or most of the firm ground falling to the meadows of the Frome, then doubtless a marshy flood-plain. The W. and S. sides, meeting at a right-angle and respectively some 740 yds. and perhaps 720 yds. long, were each probably formed by two distinct but nearly aligned traverses set off from the gates; there is, however, some doubt as to the nature of the S.E. corner at Gallows Hill.

It is clear that the walls were not kept in repair in the Middle Ages, and indeed by the beginning of the 17th century little more could be seen of them than is apparent today.[2] The works of the vanished Castle and Friary on the N., and the development of the suburb of Fordington at the E. exit of the town, had probably contributed to the complete destruction of surface remains in those sectors before the age of topographical and antiquarian records. The survival elsewhere of traces of the earthworks may be attributed to their having formed an economically valuable if sometimes contentious[3] boundary between the property of the

burgesses and the tenants of Fordington, and they were considerable enough, with the addition of bulwarks and outworks at the exits, to form the basis of defensive measures against the Royalists in 1642–3.[1] The banks were partly landscaped in laying out and planting the Walks between 1702 and 1743.

The rear of the bank survives, with some later accretion, as a gentle scarp of varying height and width, behind Colliton Walk and North Walk—sufficient evidence of an intention, sometimes doubted, to fortify the bluff overlooking the meadows—and also behind West Walk, Bowling Alley Walk and South Walk, and behind Salisbury Walk on the E. The short but relatively steep forward scarps below the several Walks are probably the result of the 18th-century levelling, and afford no precise indication of the margin of bank or ditch. The latter may be traced, however, as a wide depression, (i) N. of the W. exit, to Bridport, occupied by The Grove (the Sherborne road) and the buildings to W., descending to the meadows; (ii) W. of the South Street exit, occupied by Great Western Road and the buildings to N.; (iii) E. of South Street, occupied by South Walks Road, where a grassy scarp between Rothesay House (69409034) and the grounds of South Court (69549037) probably masks the undisturbed counterscarp of the ancient ditch. Elsewhere, as in the Borough Gardens on the W. and Salisbury Field on the E., it has been filled or levelled by ploughing.

For a fuller account of the later history of the defences and of the excavation of the wall in Albert Road, *see* Dorset *Procs.* LXXV (1953), 72–83; some results of subsequent observation are noted in *ibid.* LXXVI (1954), 74–5, LXXVII (1955), 129, 132, LXXXIII (1961), 89–90, LXXXIV (1962), 102–3, 112–3, LXXXV (1963), 96, and LXXXVIII (1966), 119. The excavation of the defences at Colliton Park was summarily described in *ibid.* LX (1938), 63; the original site notebooks and section drawings have, however, been used for the present account.

(173) THE WALL. References to the walls, or the 'greene walles', in the borough records of the late 14th and 15th centuries clearly apply to earthworks; none implies repairs to masonry. Camden, in 1586, ascribed the ruin of the walls to the Danes, and in 1607 the boundary claimed by the manor of Fordington in part followed 'the Topp or Crest of the banckes called the Walles which doe circuitt and bound in the towne and groundes of the town of Dorchester'; only where the wall is still visible in Albert Road did the survey mention 'a peece of Wall on the southside of West Yate' (*see* Dorset *Procs.* LXXV, *loc. cit.*, for this and other authorities). Speed, however, seems to imply that some

---

[1] *See*, however, p. 533.
[2] John Speed, *Theatre of the Empire of Great Britaine* (1611), 17.
[3] C. H. Mayo, *The Municipal Records of Dorchester* (1908), 469–70.

[1] A. R. Bayley, *The Civil War in Dorset* (1910), 98–9.

part of the S. wall also remained in 1611, while in 1668 objection was made on antiquarian grounds to the destruction of 'a parcell of the old towne wall' at least 6 ft. wide and nearly 36 ft. long at Colliton Park in the N.W. sector. The Rev. Conyers Place (1709) and Stukeley (1724) clearly knew only the W. sector, incorporating the present remains, to which all later records of destruction refer. Hutchins recorded the demolition c. 1764 of 85 ft., leaving 77 ft. standing, and E. Cunnington recorded the disappearance c. 1840 of 48 ft. more, evidently S. of the present remains, where private garages now stand.

Construction. The wall, originally some 8 ft. or 9 ft. wide at base and probably between 20 ft. and 25 ft. high with its parapet, was built of well-grouted courses of limestone rubble on a foundation of unmortared flints. There were bonding or lacing courses of flat slabs at irregular vertical intervals, and the rubble core would have been faced on both sides, externally doubtless with ashlar, and probably reduced in width internally at bonding course level, although no evidence survives. Stukeley described the remains as still 12 ft. high on his visit in 1723, with rubble courses generally laid in herring-bone fashion between triple lacing courses, but his width, also of 12 ft., was an inaccuracy corrected in 1774 by Hutchins who quoted 6 ft. for the visible remains (*cf.* (a) below). There is no sign now of Stukeley's herring-bone work except in the footings below ground level, although the rubble stones are often pitched obliquely; two double bonding courses, however, survive, and traces of a third single course above, at a closer vertical interval than appears in a sketch by the Rev. J. Skinner in 1829 (B.M. Add. MSS. 33715, f.12, 319).

Stukeley observed the footings in a saw-pit, laid on the 'solid chalk', but in Albert Road, and in Colliton Walk where they were exposed in 1938, they rested on consolidated chalk rubble of the earthen rampart; their relatively higher position in this rubble at Colliton suggests that the wall was climbing gradually to assume a more secure position on the crest rather than on the forward slope of the rampart at the steep N.W. corner of the town overlooking the Frome valley.

Date. The structural relationship of wall to rampart shows that, as in many comparable town defences in Roman Britain, it was an addition to the original scheme, and one that can hardly have been envisaged when the rampart was built some time after c. A.D. 130, as shown by pottery found in the bank at Lee Motors (174 b). On the assumption that the construction of civil defences was controlled consistently and effectively by Imperial edict,[1] the addition might be dated to the closing years of the 2nd century at earliest and more probably to the first half of the 3rd century, to which much of the evidence from comparable towns currently points. On the other hand a later date in the 3rd century seems likely for the walls of Canterbury and perhaps of Caerwent, as well as of several lesser towns,[2] while some towns of economic if not also

administrative importance such as Great Chesterford[1] and Cambridge[2] are not yet known to have had defences of any kind until the 4th century. There is some evidence to suggest a late date for the walls of Dorchester. Both the exceptional width of the earth bank and the presence, best shown in the W. Rampart Cut at Colliton Park ((174a), Fig. p. 546), of what seems to be a secondary capping over the rear of the bank, suggest a substantial enlargement of the earthwork which it would be natural to associate with the addition of the wall. The chalk rubble of this supposed capping, some 20 yds. to N. where it was cut by the 4th-century 'West Ditch', yielded a sherd of a flanged bowl of Gillam's type 228, dated in the N. to c. A.D. 300 or thereafter;[3] another was found in what seems to be an equivalent deposit in N. Rampart Cut A (Fig. p. 546), where a thick deposit of loam ('brown clay') appears to represent the secondary make-up (G. E. Kirk, MS. analyses of pottery from the 'West Ditch' and N. Rampart, in D.C.M.). These scraps of evidence thus suggest a date not much earlier than c. 300 as a *terminus post quem* for the stone wall of Dorchester.

Structural remains. (a) A fragment of the rubble core, 28 ft. long and at most 8 ft. high above external ground level, forms part of a brick garden wall on the E. side of Albert Road; it has belonged to the borough since 1886 and is scheduled as an Ancient Monument (68949063; Fig. p. 544; Plate 221; *see* also Wheeler, *Maiden Castle* (1943), pl. cxv).

The footings were examined in 1879 and again in 1951 (Dorset *Procs.* LXXV (1953), 77–83). The wall was found to survive to a maximum height of 10 ft. above the footings (9 ft. in Fig.), and below ground level to a width of nearly 6 ft., the inner side being severely robbed. The footings, here 9 ft. wide and 1½ ft. thick, more nearly indicating the original width of the wall, consisted of four courses of flints in puddled chalk and sand, pitched aslant, the upper two in herring-bone fashion.[4] A thin bed of mortar separated them from the grouted rubble core almost wholly of limestones often pitched aslant, and apparently without reused material except a very few small lumps of brick. A double course of flat bonding slabs seems to have run through the core some 7½ ft. above the footings, with another double course 8 ins. above; a third, single course is visible 6 ins. higher, in the highest part of the inner face. The limestone was probably obtained from the Upwey area, on the Roman road from Radipole, and the flints, in the main, directly from the Chalk.

Layers of chalk, varying in consistency and containing some flints at base, survived over the old turf line on natural Chalk to a thickness of 1 ft. or more below and 3½ ft. behind the

---

[1] *Cf.* S. S. Frere, *Britannia* (1967), 250.
[2] The walls of Canterbury are dated after c. 270 and perhaps before c. 290 (Frere, *op. cit.*, 252; Frere, *Roman Canterbury* (1957), 10).

[1] V.C.H., *Essex* III (1963), 75–6.
[2] *J.R.S.* LV (1965), 213.
[3] *Arch. Ael.* XXXV (1957); see also discussion in *Arch. Camb.* CXII (1963), 63–4. Caution is needed, however, in applying evidence derived from the military establishments of Wales and the North, although these appear to have obtained their vessels very largely from potteries in the civil zone. The Durotrigian region was, from pre-Roman times, in the mainstream of the development of the black-burnished cooking vessels of which these bowls were a late class, and a somewhat earlier origin and local distribution may be suspected at the kilns producing them, wherever these may prove to be.
[4] The loose flints in front of the wall were disturbed but sufficiently regular to be regarded as part of the footings.

footings; these were remains of the original rampart cut back to accommodate the wall. The deposits immediately behind the core were of modern origin, although it may be that part of the foundation trench for the wall remains below the recent brick wall. Both footings and bonding courses show a pronounced forward tilt, and the whole mass may perhaps be presumed to have shifted from the vertical rather than to have been built on some kind of stepped foundation. Immediately

The footings had been laid in a trench dug in the chalk rubble of the earth rampart a few feet forward of what seems from the tip-lines shown in the excavators' pl. viii[1] to have been the original apex of a work constructed in two phases (see (174a)); the base was $3\frac{1}{2}$ ft. above the natural Chalk, a higher relative position than the footings at (a) to which they were otherwise similar. If a flat berm was made in the forward slope of the earth rampart between wall and ditch, all trace was subse-

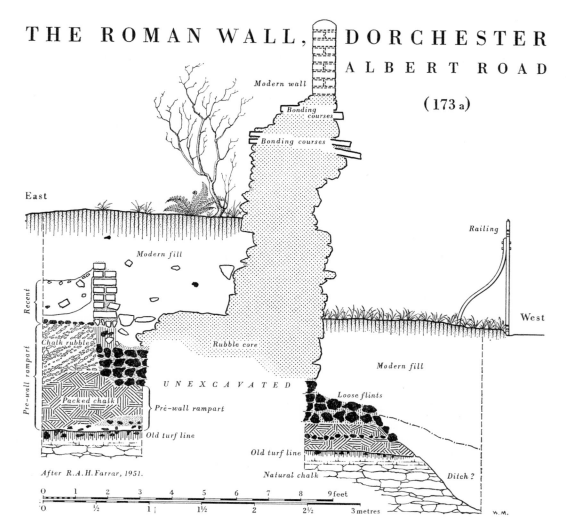

THE ROMAN WALL, DORCHESTER
ALBERT ROAD
(173 a)

East
Modern wall
Bonding courses
Bonding courses
Railing
West
Modern fill
Recent
Chalk rubble
Rubble core
Modern fill
Pre-wall rampart
Packed chalk
Loose flints
Pré-wall rampart
U N E X C A V A T E D
Old turf line
Old turf line
After R.A.H.Farrar, 1951.
Natural chalk
Ditch?
0 1 2 3 4 5 6 7 8 9feet
0 ½ 1 1½ 2 2½ 3 metres
W.M.

outside the footings the regular scarp of a depression may belong to the town ditch; it contained 17th or 18th-century material and may not coincide with the Roman inner lip, where a berm would have been normal between ditch and wall.

(b) A section of the wall footings, $8\frac{1}{4}$ ft. wide, of three courses of flints below a spread of yellow mortar, was exposed in 1938 under the footpath of Colliton Walk W. of building (183) (68919088; W. Rampart Cut, Figs. pp. 546, 554).

quently swept away and replaced by debris presumably from ruin or dilapidation of the wall.

No certain remains of the wall were found in further sections dug at Colliton Park in 1938, at the N.W. corner (Cut B), where a tower was looked for, and about 60 yds. to E. (Cut

---

[1] These, however, are not shown in the MS. section drawings, except as between separate deposits or pronounced textural changes, and then only in the region behind the park wall.

A, Fig. p. 546),[1] and it was doubted whether the town was walled on the N. side. In Cut A, however, a distance of 13 ft. under and N. of the park wall in North Walk was apparently unexcavated, while the rampart deposits again suggest two phases of construction consistent with the addition of a wall. In Cut B, it is tempting to associate a disturbed setting of limestone blocks, about 3 ft. below the footpath, with a robbed wall, although the excavators made light of the possibility. Alternatively, the configuration of the N. and N.W. sections is not inconsistent with a view that there may have been some erosion or removal of the front of the scarp here since Roman times, which could have carried away remains of the wall. (Dorset *Procs.* LX (1938), 63; Colliton Park site notebook V and section drawings, in D.C.M.)[2]

(174) THE EARTHWORKS. The earthen defences of Dorchester were unusually large and elaborate. The bank still remains some 80 ft. wide overall where best preserved. In the first phase it would have been furnished with a timbered breastwork and presumably with appropriate gates and turrets. It seems to have been initially at least 50 ft. wide at base, if the primary phase is correctly identified in the rampart cuttings at Colliton Park, and some 65 ft. in its secondary phase, as a backing bank or ramped approach to the stone wall. The ditch system was correspondingly large, perhaps varying from about 125 ft. to 155 ft. overall excluding a counterscarp bank, or glacis, for which there is some evidence on the S.; its multiple character, involving two intermediate ridges where it is best known on the S., near the Great Western Hotel, may have been part of the original design. It was probably interrupted by causeways rather than spanned by bridges and was presumably omitted on the N., where the natural or perhaps artificially steepened scarp falls to the Frome meadows.[3]

With or without a counterscarp bank, these defences with their triple ditch were of a scale unequalled amongst civil settlements in Roman Britain, as far as these are known.[4] Amongst the major towns, double ditches supposedly belonging to an initial earthen system of defences are known at Wroxeter, Caerwent, Caistor-by-Norwich and Cirencester, and similar arrangements are known at several of the lesser towns.[5]

At one of these smaller towns, Great Casterton (Rutland), where, however, the rampart was fronted with a stone wall from the outset, at least two and probably three or even four small ditches, doubtless individually embanked, guarded the easier N. approaches; the total span would have been about 107 ft.[1] At some other towns, however, the presence of more than one ditch has been shown to be due to modification, as at Silchester where an earlier ditch was filled on the addition of the stone wall.[2] More commonly, however, the replacement or recutting of an earlier ditch system seems to have been associated with the addition of projecting wall-towers in the 4th century, under the influence of late 3rd-century military architecture.[3] This development seems generally to have involved the digging of a new and broader ditch, further from the foot of the wall and capable of being commanded by fire from heavy *ballistae* or catapults mounted on the wall-towers, and may also have involved the obliteration or partial obliteration of earlier defences, as at Great Casterton. Evidence for an evaluation is almost wholly lacking at Dorchester, where neither the stratification of the multiple ditch nor the composition of the corresponding portion of the rampart is known, and where the existence of wall-towers, although unlikely as at Silchester, is not disproved. Some pointers exist, however. On the one hand the quantity of relatively clean chalk rubble and loam, forming what is here suggested as a secondary capping, would seem to imply the digging of a new or supplementary ditch when the stone wall was added. On the other, the regular profile of the multiple ditch, and the arrangement implicit in the close spacing of the intervening ridges in the Chalk, whereby the excavated spoil, if not wholly absorbed by the bank, must have been disposed as a bank or glacis beyond the furthest counterscarp, argues for a single conception. The force of this argument is strengthened rather than weakened by the apparent uniqueness of this arrangement, since the ditch supposedly of W-profile at Wroxeter (*loc. cit.*, 30–1) has been shown to be due to recutting following the silting of an earlier ditch. It is possible to reconcile the two propositions, if one supposes a primary ditch incorporated or obliterated in the creation of a more elaborate system.

The composition of the bank was demonstrated in the excavation of the W. wall (173a) in Albert Road in 1951, in the three sections cut through the N. and W.

---

[1] The W. face of the section is here shown in reverse, to simplify comparison with the W. Rampart Cut.

[2] It is possible that remains of the S. wall were seen in 1956 in 'stone foundations' observed in two stanchion pits dug for a new front to Tilley's cycle showrooms between Trinity Street and South Street (69199035; R.C.H.M. records).

[3] The river channel at its foot, at least in its present form as a mill-stream, may be post-Roman (Hutchins II, 337).

[4] *Cf.* J. S. Wacher (ed.), *The Civitas Capitals of Roman Britain* (1966), 60.

[5] Wroxeter: Birmingham Arch. Soc., *Trans.* LXXVIII (1962), 31–2; Caerwent: *Archaeologia* LXXX (1930), 269–70, *Arch. Camb.* LXXXVI (1931), 212–5; Caistor: *J.R.S.* LI (1961), 132; Cirencester: *Ant. J.* XLIII (1963), 22, XLIV (1964), 17, *Arch. J.* CXIX (1962), 104–5.

---

[1] P. Corder, *The Roman Town and Villa at Great Casterton, Third Report* (1961), 15, 30.

[2] G. C. Boon, *Roman Silchester* (1957), 75, 85.

[3] *Arch. J.* CXII (1955), 35–6. Earlier defences, whether or not they were equipped with internal turrets of timber or stone, were presumably defended mainly by the use of personal weapons and perhaps light artillery.

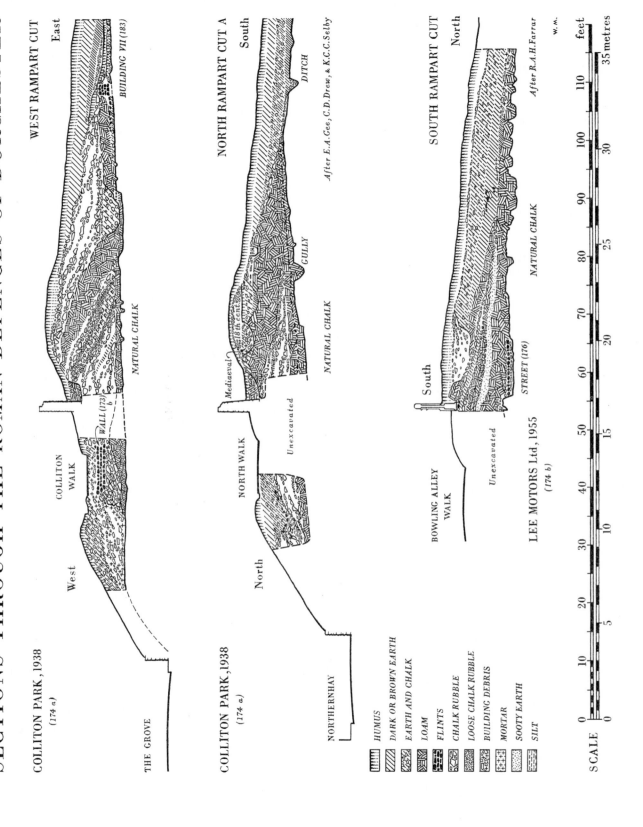

SECTIONS THROUGH THE ROMAN DEFENCES OF DORCHESTER

WEST RAMPART CUT
COLLITON PARK, 1938
(174 a)

West — COLLITON WALK — East

BUILDING VII (183)

WALL (173 b)

NATURAL CHALK

THE GROVE

NORTH RAMPART CUT A
COLLITON PARK, 1938
(174 a)

North — NORTH WALK — South

Mediaeval

18th cent.

DITCH

GULLY

Unexcavated

NATURAL CHALK

NORTHERNHAY

After E.A.Gee, C.D.Drew, & K.C.C.Selby

SOUTH RAMPART CUT
LEE MOTORS Ltd, 1955
(174 b)

South — BOWLING ALLEY WALK — North

STREET (176)

Unexcavated

NATURAL CHALK

w.m.

After R.A.H.Farrar

Legend
- HUMUS
- DARK OR BROWN EARTH
- EARTH AND CHALK
- LOAM
- FLINTS
- CHALK RUBBLE
- LOOSE CHALK RUBBLE
- BUILDING DEBRIS
- MORTAR
- SOOTY EARTH
- SILT

SCALE

feet: 0 10 20 30 40 50 60 70 80 90 100 110
metres: 0 5 10 15 20 25 30 35 metres

rampart at Colliton Park in 1938 (a), and in the S. rampart behind Bowling Alley Walk in an extension to Lee Motors in 1955 (b). The ditch system was almost completely sectioned in a drainage trench dug in 1896 from the Borough Gardens to the centre of Great Western Road (d), and partially in 1892–3 in building South Court at the opposite end of the S. ditch (f). Minor exposures elsewhere, some of them unpublished, have been taken into account in the plan (opp. p. 584); only the more significant are discussed below (c, e, h, i).

The Bank. Remains of the earth rampart in Albert Road have already been noticed (*see* (173a), pp. 543–4).

(a) The bank on the N. and W. sides of Colliton Park (Figs. pp. 546, 554) consists of alternate deposits of chalk rubble and loam ('clay'); the crest remaining on the N. was probably formed when the park wall was built in the 18th century, but on much of the W. side the upper levels have been removed since the excavations of 1938. These excavations showed that the Roman work survived to maximum heights of $8\frac{1}{2}$ ft. above the Chalk in N. Cut A, $11\frac{1}{2}$ ft. in the W. Cut where it remained $7\frac{1}{2}$ ft. above the level of the Roman wall footings, and 18 ft. at the corner in N. Cut B where the greater depth is explained by a fall in the level of bedrock. The width at base was some 80 ft. overall, considerably increased in the corner cutting where, however, the complete section was not excavated. (Dorset *Procs.* LX (1938), 63; MS. section drawings in D.C.M.)

The W. Cut best illustrates the secondary character of the wall also apparent in Albert Road, and gives grounds for supposing a primary rampart of loam and chalk some 50 ft. wide, with a secondary capping of similar materials remaining only at the rear and increasing the width to about 65 ft. behind the Roman wall footings (*see also* (173b)). Alternatively, the secondary capping may have consisted only of the upper chalk rubble, between which and the underlying loam a rearward depression containing building debris suggests some interval of time between the two deposits. The N. and N.W. sections are consistent, but none affords proof in the shape of a buried land surface or turf line between the deposits. The tail of the supposed secondary bank lay over the footings of building (183) on the W.[1] but had been covered in part by ashes from a forge of presumed 4th-century date; on the N.W. in Cut B, 72 ft. behind the park wall, it sealed a substantial U-shaped ditch or pit, 12 ft. wide and 8 ft. deep, aligned N.N.E. and containing mixed rubble and some ash. The scanty material for dating belongs entirely to the supposed second phase and is considered above (p. 543); it may be significant that the deposits supposedly associated with the first phase were uniformly sterile.

(b) In Bowling Alley Walk, the clearance of 84 ft. of the rearward scarp of the S. rampart for the extension of the garage of Lee Motor Works in 1955 exposed a long-axial section and two transverse sections, of which the westernmost is illustrated (69129035; Fig. p. 546; Dorset *Procs.* LXXVII (1955), 129). A foundation $9\frac{1}{2}$ ft. wide, consisting of three layers of flints capped and interleaved with chalk,[2] was traced eastward across the site on an alignment diverging slightly from the axis of the S. defences; although resembling the footings of the town wall at Colliton Park, it was sealed by the layers forming the back of the rampart, and was interpreted as the foundation metalling of a street (176) buried when the rampart was made.[1] The rampart was composed of layers containing occupation debris as well as relatively clean loam and chalk, and both its width, no more than 35 ft., and the inclination of its tip-lines suggest that the footings of the wall should be sought some yards further S. in Bowling Alley Walk. A Roman building (191) lay a few yards to the N. and the rear of the bank may have been curtailed or cut away accordingly. The tail, formed of chalk rubble under loam, was provisionally identified by Mr. C. J. Green towards the foot of Trinity Street to E. (69179036), where a more normal width is implied of at least 50 ft. behind the estimated line of the town wall; its relationship with deposits believed to indicate streets is discussed below (p. 551 (ii, iii)).

The rampart deposits at Lee Motors yielded over 20 sherds of samian ware, identified by Mr. B. R. Hartley as mainly of the 1st century but including four of the 2nd century, one of which, from the lower loam deposit and perhaps by the potter Docilis of Lezoux, is unlikely to be earlier than *c.* A.D. 130 and may be as late as *c.* 150. The first of these dates is thus the earliest possible date for the earthwork defences of *Durnovaria* as known to us, although the real date probably lies appreciably after 150 in the context of the military and political disturbances of the later 2nd century. The dating of the coarse pottery is consistent with that of the samian, including nothing characteristic of the 3rd or 4th centuries.

Mollusca collected from the Roman horizon by the British Museum (Natural History) indicated a climate similar to that of modern Dorset; the assemblage lacked woodland forms and was characteristic of rather damp grassland, probably with some scrub (information from Mr. M. P. Kerney).

(c) Exposures E. of South Street—at the foot of Charles Street (69289038) and in Icen Way outside Culliford House (69609047)—showed chalk rubble backed and evidently covered by loamy soil, both rising towards the modern surface (information from Mr. C. J. Green). If these were rampart deposits, as seems likely, they suggest, in the former instance, a tail about 75 ft. behind the estimated line of the town wall and, in the latter, one about 110 ft. behind the N. wall of South Walk. The last figure is excessive if one supposes an unaltered alignment, but would be consistent with other evidence (f) for a N.E. change in direction of the defences at Gallows Hill, whereby a sharp angle was avoided and an appropriate setting provided perhaps for a gate. That the rampart adhered to the South Walk line as far E. as Culliford House is clear from the record of the destruction of the 'vallum' in 1864–5 between Acland Road and Gallows Hill (Cunnington MS. in D.C.M., 129–31, and Dorset *Procs.* XVI (1895), 50–1). This feature was present in 1596 when it was plainly referred to as '. . . the east greene walles on the west parte of the gallows . . .', so although it was said to overlie metalling of a

---

[1] Dorset *Procs.* LXXV (1953), 75.
[2] The feature is atypical where it appears in Fig. p. 546.

[1] *See* Introduction, p. 533, where it is suggested that this may have been the *intervallum* road of a fort. The curious irregularities in the surface of the Chalk, here seen in section, are undoubtedly natural solution hollows, and do not permit of interpretation as building slots of dismantled military hutments.

street or pathway believed Roman (p. 551), it is evident that it was not solely, if at all, a Civil War work as Moule and others suggested (Mayo, *Municipal Records of Dorchester* (1908), xxxiii; Moule, 30; Dorset *Procs.* XIV (1893), 47; *Arch. J.* XXII (1865), 348–9). There is no independent record of the two incorporated barrows (*see* Round Barrows, Dorchester (p. 444)) claimed by E. Cunnington as visible in the long-axial section of this 'vallum'.

The Ditch. (d) A section through the S. ditch drawn by the Borough Surveyor in 1896 from Bowling Alley Walk across the garden (now car park) of the Great Western Hotel, shows its multiple character (Figs. below and opp. p. 584; Dorset Album I, p. ii, f.26B, in D.C.M.; *D.C.C.* 5 Mar. 1896, 4; Dorset *Procs.* XVIII (1897), xxvi). The section, nearly enough square to the defences, indicates a total width of probably about 155 ft. Two ridges, 12 ft. and 10 ft. high respectively, remained in the

N. of Rowan House (69200:90323), and exposures in 1960 in setting back the garden walls of the same and of Southfield House to E. (69193:90314; 69222:90321), seemed to show natural Chalk near the modern surface where the ditch could otherwise be expected (R.C.H.M. records). The situation could also be complicated here by Civil War outworks protecting the 17th-century exit and by the communication trench believed to connect the latter with the emplacement at Maumbury Rings (228) (*see also* p. 541*n.*).

(f) The situation near the S.E. corner of the town is comparable with that at the Great Western Hotel (d). Sections at South Court, particularly in excavation for the stable wall in Culliford Road, were sketched by Moule in 1892–3 (Dorset Album I, part ii, f. 26A; Moule, 23). At the foot of a 40 ft. wide counterscarp sloping at 15° to 9 ft. below the surface level of the Chalk, a ridge with sharp apex rose 6 ft. high and was

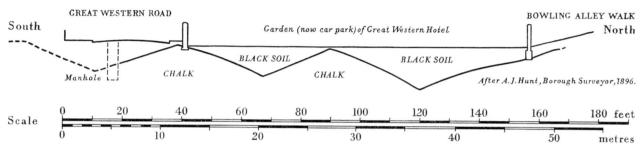

Dorchester (174d). Section through ditch system on S. side of town.

natural Chalk, forming in effect three ditches each some 50 ft. wide and about 13 ft. deep. Nothing is known of the ditch filling except that it consisted mainly of black earth with a 'sandy gritty soil' likened by Moule to material seen in the ditch at South Court and elsewhere (*in lit.* to F. Haverfield, in Ashmolean Museum; Dorset *Procs.* LXXV (1953), 73, note 7). The profile at the N. end probably implies that the ditch was turning.

(e) A comparable situation has been shown to exist near the S.E. corner of the town (f), but between that point and (d) the arrangement is less clear. In 1965 the apex of a ridge in the Chalk under the N. side of South Walks Road was uncovered in a telephone-cable trench opposite the N.W. corner of Southfield House (69231:90344;[1] information from Mr. C. J. Green). About 1940, a ditch believed to be at least of W-section was seen in a trench between South Walks Road and Great Western Road (information from C. D. Drew). Both these exposures suggest a multiple ditch. In a trench dug in 1912 for surface-water drainage of the Walks, a slope of about 35° in the Chalk, seen under the pavement at the W. foot of South Street (69196:90349), was identified by J. E. Acland as the inner scarp of the ditch (Dorset Album I, part ii, f. 26A; Dorset *Procs.* XXXVI (1915), 2). The last two observations, particularly the former, would suggest a continuous ditch outside the traditional site of the S. gate; on the other hand, an exposure in 1965, seen by Mr. C. J. Green under the pavement

perhaps 15 ft. wide; its N. foot and the inner half of the ditch under South Walks Road were not exposed, but there was room for a second ridge of similar or perhaps somewhat larger size. The inner scarp of the ditch was identified by Acland in a slope of about 30° in the Chalk seen here to the N. under South Walk in the 1912 drain trench (Dorset Album, *loc. cit.;* Dorset *Procs.* XXXVI (1915), 2). These records imply an overall width of about 125 ft. This reduced width, compared with that at (d), accords with the smaller size of the ridge or ridges here, and is consistent with the position of the 6 ft. high slope still to be seen in the paddock between the grounds of South Court and Rothesay House to W., which can thus be recognized as the remains of the counterscarp. The reduction can be traced at least as far W. as the Conservative Club (former surgery), immediately E. of which the lip of the counterscarp was exposed in laying gas pipes in 1965, 70 ft. from the wall of South Walks Road (69329033; information from Mr. C. J. Green). The inner scarp had not been seen opposite this point in the 1912 drain trench dug along the centre of South Walk, and its margin may be supposed to lie nearer the wall of the properties to N. in Longmans Road. The available evidence suggests no substantial increase in width until after the line reaches Great Western Road.

The behaviour of the defences at the S.E. or Gallows Hill corner is obscure. Although the ditch was traced, as has been seen, as far as the stables of South Court in Culliford Road, the foundations and associated drain trenches of the house 'Robin's Garth' less than 30 yds. to E. showed undisturbed Chalk at

---

[1] For ten-figure grid references, *see* p. 540*n.*

$1\frac{1}{2}$ ft. below surface in 1955 (R.C.H.M. records). Unless the ditch was interrupted, perhaps for a gate, the inference must be drawn that it had already begun to turn, in which case a curving S.E. corner or straight traverse between two obtuse angles may be proposed for the defences instead of the acute S.E. angle suggested by the modern topography. The apparent behaviour of the rampart opposite ((c) *above*) lends itself to the suggestion.

(g) There is no evidence for the character of the E. ditch, already filled when Stukeley visited Dorchester in 1723, but the extra-mural mosaic (210) at Fordington, probably of the 4th century, lay no more than 150 ft. outside the estimated line of the town wall, while the position of the mosaic (202) in Durngate Street, also of late date, may imply a narrower bank behind the wall than can be shown elsewhere.

(h) The W. ditch seems to have been multiple. Traces of double 'valla' or banks outside the wall, first noted by Conyers Place in 1709, remained in the N. part of the area now occupied by the Borough Gardens until *c.* 1850 (Dorset *Procs.* LXXV (1953), 74). A superficial exposure in 1955 at the top of High West Street, on the N. side, suggested a ditch 33 ft. wide, separated from a second ditch of unknown width by a flat-topped ridge of Chalk 2 ft. below the road surface and 15 ft. wide; the evidence seems to have been against a third ditch here (*ibid.* LXXVII (1955), 129; LXXXVIII (1966), 119; LXXXIX (1967), 144; *see also* Approach Road 3). There was no evidence of the date of these features, which can equally well have belonged to works connected with the platform for ordnance made at the W. gate in 1642–3, but they could fall in quite well with indications forthcoming from exposures near by to the N., which suggest a ditch system narrower than surface signs might suggest.[1] A fall of 20° in the Chalk, noted before 1928 by C.S. Prideaux in a 13 ft. exposure running E. as far as the pavement at the garage N. of Top o' Town House (68909073), suggests a ditch or ditches at least 60 ft. wide overall (*addendum* to Moule MS., 12). Observations a few yards further down The Grove in 1962 had ambiguous results but are not obviously inconsistent with a ditch system up to about 125 ft. wide, in which internal features could have been altered or destroyed (Dorset *Procs.* LXXXIV (1962), 102–3). N. of School Lane, however, the ditch seems to have been more than 125 ft. wide and probably multiple. A ridge of Chalk was exposed in 1967 about 100 ft. W. of the top of the scarp at Colliton Walk (68873:90929); the outer scarp was not seen (information from Mr. C. J. Green). The ditch presumably ran out into the meadows at the foot of The Grove, where Roman burials (226b) have been found.

(i) Evidence exists on the S. for a glacis, or counterscarp bank, outside the ditch. So it seemed to Moule, at South Court near the S.E. corner of the defences (f); in 1892 layers of redeposited surface soil and chalk, $2\frac{1}{2}$ ft. thick, were noted by him at the outer edge of the ditch on the old land surface above the Chalk, here 10 ft. below ground level (Dorset Album, I, pt. ii, f. 26A).

Both Cunnington and Hogg referred to the 'vallum', pre-sumably a counterscarp bank although its composition was not described, in recording Roman burials (219a) found in the Chalk at Beggar's Knap when the counterscarp was cut back to build the terraced houses in Great Western Road in the 1880s. Some appear to have lain under this bank, but whether they preceded it or were intrusive is not clear, although one or more of Cunnington's were probably of the 4th century. Miss Whitley's observations when the garden in front of Mentone Lodge was levelled in 1960 confirm that, as at South Court, there was a considerable overburden outside the ditch in this sector, consisting, at base, of deposits of loamy character about $2\frac{1}{2}$ ft. thick, similar to those of the rampart proper, below some 3 ft. of recent or disturbed deposits. Burials noted by her, above the Chalk, were evidently intrusive, but another recorded by R.C.H.M. was in a narrow ditch filled probably in the late 2nd century or 3rd century but evidently sealed below the loamy deposits of the supposed counterscarp bank (*see* Burials (219b)). A late date for this feature, here if not necessarily elsewhere, is suggested by the fact that it overlay a gravelled surface part of which, at least, was in use in the 4th century (*see* p. 540b).

Some of the chalk-cut graves found at Beggar's Knap were certainly in the counterscarp itself and were therefore later than the construction of the defences, whether or not they imply their neglect as Moule supposed (Moule, 47); these graves were matched by others (222b) found in the W. counterscarp immediately N. of the Borough Gardens, but too imprecisely recorded to permit an evaluation of the width of the W. ditch.

THE GATES. There is no reliable evidence of the discovery of structural remains of the gates of the Roman town. The road system, however, indicates the approximate position of three main gates on the E., S. and W., and it can hardly be doubted that there would have been a minor gate or gates to the meadows and river on the N. The distribution of burials S.E. of the town (Fig. p. 532) argues strongly for a road towards Wareham and Purbeck, but this might have issued from the E. or London Gate equally well as from some point in the S.E. sector.

The survival of the Roman routes to the W. and S.W., if not so clearly to the E., and the massive ditch system, whether crossed by causeways or by bridges, is likely to have ensured the retention of the Roman exits when the late Saxon and mediaeval town took shape, though there is no reason to suppose that the Roman gate structures survived long enough to determine the precise position of their successors. Late 14th and 15th-century documents[1] locate the E., W. and S. gates at

_____

[1] The scarp falling E. from the long walls W. of The Grove, although masked or interrupted by cottages now (1967) in process of demolition, has suggested a W. ditch as much as 170 ft. wide.

[1] The references are to properties in these streets: '. . . alta strata que ducit ad portam orientalem . . .' 1410; '. . . in occidentali vico prope portam . . .' 1410; '. . . ad portam australem in vico australi . . .' 1402; '. . . ad portam borialem et ex parte orientali vici ibidem inter clausum dominii de ffordyngton in parte boriali et burgagium W. Fouler . . .' 1440; '. . . a lane which leads from South Street towards la Durne-gate . . .' 1395 (Mayo, *op. cit.*, xxxiv, 119, 151, 187–8, 286; Dorset *Procs.* XI (1890), 41, XIV (1893), 53).

the appropriate ends of the High Street and at the foot of South Street, the N. gate in Glyde Path Hill, and a 'Durnegate' evidently at the foot of Durngate Street.[1] Speed's plan, inset in his map of Dorsetshire (1610), showing what is very largely the present street plan and in all probability essentially that of the mediaeval town, adds another N. exit in Friary Hill, two more S. exits at Gallows Hill and Charles Street, and another W. exit at the top of Princes Street. The Gallows Hill exit is, perhaps, the only one of the minor gates for which a Roman origin can be argued.

West Gate. The Roman roads from Exeter and Ilchester (Approach Roads 3, 4) indicate a W. gate at or near the top of High West Street (Top o' Town). It cannot be doubted that this was the main if not the only Roman gate on this side. There is no firm evidence, however, for the metalling of either approach road, and nothing to substantiate Miles Barnes's statement that the foundations of the gate were observed here where they are marked on the Ordnance map (Dorset *Procs.* XII (1891), 142). The presence of a tessellated pavement (206) under High West Street within 50 yds. of this spot, surely implying that the principal street, or *decumanus maximus*, ran either to the N. or S. of the present roadway, cannot easily be reconciled with a site directly at its head. On the reasonable assumptions that the *decumanus* ran straight between E. and W. gates and conformed with normal closeness to the street grid, if the latter was not in fact set out from it, a W. gate rather to the S. of the present roadway at Top o' Town seems probable.

East Gate. The line so postulated for the *decumanus* can be reconciled with an E. gate at the foot of High East Street, although the precise line of the Roman defences here is uncertain. Prolongation of the Stinsford alignment of the Roman road (Approach Road 1; plan opp. p. 584), which was apparently maintained without substantial alteration, if any, points distinctly S. of the foot of the street, but an error of no more than one degree in estimating the alignment over the lost mile could involve a difference of some 25 yds. in the supposed point of entry. The antiquity of the High East Street exit is shown by the relationship to it of the village of Fordington; moreover it remained the London gate although, before the opening in 1748 of Grey's Bridge and the new London Road, traffic had to take the circuitous route *via* Holloway Road, the ford below Fordington mill, and Stocken or Old Bridge.[2]

Durnegate. The other mediaeval E. gate, the Durnegate, may owe its importance if not its origin to the need for a more convenient exit to Fordington; a minor gate hereabouts could have served the Roman cemetery (216), which seems unrelated

to the London road across the Frome valley, but that it was not at the foot of Durngate Street seems clear from the incidence of Roman buildings (200–2) either certainly or probably under the street. The direction of street (175) across Wollaston Field may point to a gate beyond the gasholders, about 100 yds. S. of the mediaeval Durnegate, although the back of the rampart is said to have been seen here uninterrupted, in alterations made in 1965 (Dorset *Procs.* LXXXIX (1967), 143–4).

Gallows Hill. The local antiquary E. Cunnington claimed that the foundations of what he called the E. gate had been exposed and destroyed 'between the south east angle of the walks—where Culliford House now stands—and the south end of Woolaston Terrace' (*c.* 1856–60; Cunnington MS., 95; Moule, 23–4; Dorset *Procs.* XI (1890), 40–1, referring to 'gateway jambs'; XIV (1893), 50; XV (1894), xliv). Whatever these remains were—and they were presumably substantial— their evident position about the end of Linden Avenue shows that they were too far behind the S.E. corner to have belonged to a gate in the defences known to us, despite the suggestion (*see* (174 f)) that these may have been foreshortened at this corner. However, although a road towards the industrially important area of Purbeck is as likely to have proceeded from the E. or London gate, there is nothing improbable in the idea of a Roman predecessor to the Gallows Hill gate, even if it could hardly conform to the known street grid. The only evidence for a street leading to it is to be found in the narrow road of doubtful date at Culliford House (p. 551), but the possibility has been noted above of an interruption in the town ditch E. of Culliford Road (174f), which would be consistent with the existence of a Roman gate.

South Gate. A S. gate W. of centre is implied by the alignment of the road from the harbour at Radipole, which could seemingly have been engineered just as easily to pass E. instead of W. of Maumbury Rings, so reaching the town at what was, ultimately at least, a central point in the S. side, without the need for the apparent adjustment of the final 600 yds. Whilst the Roman character of the $2\frac{1}{2}$-mile straight alignment of the present road from Ridgeway Hill to Maumbury cannot be doubted (p. 528), the correspondence thereafter with Weymouth Avenue need not be so exact. There is, however, some evidence tending to show that it is substantially correct, but without positively indicating a site for the gate; this evidence consists of records pointing perhaps to a street of the regular grid at the foot of South Street (p. 551) and implying a gate at the traditional site, and of gravel exposures perhaps indicating the line of the approach road running by the W. side of the present road (p. 540) and implying a gate at the E. foot of Trinity Street, some 25 yds. W. of the former. For what it is worth, J. E. Acland's recognition of the S. gate in 'some rough courses of stones without mortar, but presenting the appearance of foundations', which he saw in the 1912 drainage trench evidently close to the E. side of South Street, is reconcilable, if at all, only with the nearer of these alternatives. Consideration must also be given to the possibility that there was a S. gate, perhaps a main or even a sole S. gate, some 70 yds. E. of the area so far envisaged, although still W. of centre; this could be indicated by the possible convergence at the S. rampart of the well-attested alignment of street (179) which

---

[1] The Durnegate (*cf.* Winchester and Northampton) was the only gate with a proper name; the Oxford English Dictionary gives the meaning of *dern* as '. . . lying out of the way, dark, etc.' but also *durn* or *dern* as a 'door-post, when made of solid wood; usually in *pl.* The framework of a doorway'. There seems no need to follow Moule (Dorset *Procs.* XIV (1893), 50–1) in supposing that the Durnegate was the gate at Gallows Hill.

[2] Dorset *Procs.* XIV (1893), 51; XXXVIII (1917), 31–2. No route appears in Speed's plan answering to the new London Road; this was in effect an unwitting reconstitution of the direct Roman route although somewhat to the S.

may be the main N. to S. street (*cardo maximus*) of *Durnovaria*, with that of street (175), the unique south-westerly direction of which may indicate a route originally laid out prior to the imposition of the grid (*see below*). Such a conclusion need not involve rejection of the route supposedly preserved in Weymouth Avenue, assuming there was more than one gate in the S. defences.

North Gate. The only evidence for a route directly northwards from *Durnovaria* has no bearing on the location of a N. gate (*see* p. 539), and it is probable that any gates on this side were simple exits giving access to the river Frome, which cannot have been more than locally navigable for small craft.

STREETS

It may be accepted that High East Street and High West Street approximate to the main Roman street (*decumanus maximus*) between the E. and W. gates, but the degree of correspondence is uncertain since neither gate has been recognized and remains of Roman buildings have been shown to underlie High West Street (*see* Monument (206) and p. 550). Roman metalling has not been identified on the line except perhaps immediately outside the line of the W. wall at Top o' Town (68933:90683)[1] where, if correctly identified, it may more properly be referred to the road from Exeter (*see* Approach Road 3). Remains of at least eight other streets (175–181) have, however, been found, of which all save two are components of an essentially rectangular grid in approximate conformity with the W. and S. ramparts. Of the exceptions, street (181) at Colliton Park may have been a private path; the other (175), in the S.E. quarter, ran N.E. to S.W. and might be thought to aim for a S. gate somewhat E. of the traditional site at the foot of South Street (*see* p. 550). The course beyond Wollaston Road is, however, unconfirmed and metalling was not seen crossing the foot of Charles Street on the postulated line further S.W. in a partial exposure of the base of the S. rampart in *c.* 1965 (69289038; information from Mr. C. J. Green). If it did lead to the S. gate, wherever this was sited, it might be interpreted as a survival of an early route of the branch road to Radipole harbour prior to the development of the town.

Two exposures in direct alignment (179 a, b) must represent an important N. to S. street, perhaps even the *cardo maximus*, which ran through the centre of the Roman town, skirting the W. side of a gravelled area, possibly extensive and suggesting perhaps the site of the Forum (*see* Monument (196)). This street could also indicate a S. gate E. (by some 70 yds.) of its traditional site in South Street. On the other hand the distance of some 160 yds. between this street and its westerly

neighbour (178) passing southwards by the County Hospital, is abnormally large for a single insula and argues for an intermediate street, which would have reached the town wall on or near the traditional site of the gate. The evidence for the course here of the road from Radipole (*see* Approach Road 2), although not free from ambiguity, favours a gate in this area, and some grounds can be found for claiming traces of the intermediate street in question. Remains of flint 'metalling,' 8 ins. thick, believed to run approximately N. to S., were seen in 1965 at a depth of about $3\frac{1}{2}$ ft. below the E. side of Trinity Street about 15 yds. S. of the New Street corner (69189047; information from Mr. C. J. Green), while a piece of 'solid, grouted road', thought to be Roman and to tend northwards in the direction of Trinity Street, was seen in drain excavations *c.* 1895 outside the Carriage Works at the foot of South Street, now Tilley's cycle showrooms (69209036; Moule MS., 14; Moule, 31).

Other remains possibly belonging to Roman streets have been recorded. In *c.* 1865 a 'very hard, smooth, cemented roadway, about 3 yards wide', believed Roman, was traced and cleared away across the garden of Culliford House, Icen Way (Moule, 30). The 25-in. plan attached to the Moule MS. in D.C.M. shows it for some 65 yds., running W.N.W. from the S.W. corner of the house (69589045); prolongation E.S.E. would bring it out at the Gallows Hill exit. It was said to run under the 'vallum' on the N. side of South Walk, evidently the remains, since removed, of the Roman rampart. It conforms in no way, however, with what is known of the Roman street pattern, while deeply buried cemented metalling in Dorchester can be as late as the 18th century (Dorset *Procs.* LXXVII (1955), 131–2; *see also* Defences, pp. 547, 550).

The following remains were noted by Mr. C. J. Green in 1965. (i) A deposit of gravel, nature and extent unknown, was exposed at a depth of about 1 ft. below the pavement outside the Printing Works, Durngate Street (69319065). (ii) Two cambered layers of 'metalling' separated by 'clay' and based on a chalk deposit, some 20 ins. thick in all, were cut through at a depth of about 3 ft. by a telephone-cable trench alongside the E. kerb towards the foot of Trinity Street (69179036); the S. edge was not exposed but the width was at least 21 ft. The direction was thought to be slightly S. of due W. Overlying deposits of chalk and loam were believed to be the base of the Roman town rampart, but the 'metalling' was some 8 yds. too far N. to coincide with the line of the sub-rampart metalling of different construction, at Lee Motors some 30 yds. to the W. (*see* Defences (174b) and Street (176)). (iii) Immediately N. of (ii), and marginally overlying it, more cambered

---

[1] For ten-figure grid references, *see* p. 540 *n.*

'metalling', 9 ins. thick and 12 ft. wide, was believed to diverge W.N.W. Unlike (ii), it was later than the supposed rampart. It may have been widened on the S., up the tail of the latter, before being covered by an ash deposit and superseded by a thin cambered spread of chalk thought to represent a crude remetalling at the original width of 12 ft. Sherds of New Forest type lay on the upper surface at a depth of about 2½ ft. An upright monolith 3 ft. high marked the N. edge of the feature (69179037).

The character of the streets, so far as it is indicated by the remains listed below, calls for little comment. They are generally some 15 ft. to 20 ft. wide, occasionally narrower at about 10 ft., and none shows evidence of more than one side ditch or gutter. The metalling, consisting in the main of rammed or mortared flints and gravel of local origin, frequently shows signs of repair or, at Colliton Park (180), of replacement following the submergence of the former surface under rubble or mud. The thickness, usually less than 2 ft. including the bottoming, suggests that those responsible for repairs preferred to remake the surface rather than to add successive layers.

(175) STREET, sectioned in four places in 1947–50 in Wollaston Field (69479054). It was about 16 ft. wide and was traced for 150 ft. from S.W. to N.E. (52°). The original metalling, about 1 ft. thick at the centre of the camber, was cemented flint gravel on a foundation of large flints in sandy loam over the natural Chalk. Remains of cemented finer yellow gravel on top, some 3 ins. thick, probably represent a general repair. At the S. edge a flat-bottomed gutter some 3 ft. wide had been re-cut after silting to form a gutter of rounded profile, about 1 ft. wide, associated with local repairs to the street. The absence of recognizable 4th-century pottery in the silt of both gutters suggests repairs before c. 300 and subsequent neglect. A worn coin of Tetricus I (A.D. 270–3) was found on the street surface. (Dorset *Procs.* LXX (1948), 61; LXXI (1949), 64–5; LXXIV (1952), 97–8.)

(176) STREET, sectioned in building construction and excavated in 1955 on Lee Motors' premises, Trinity Street, was sealed by the S. rampart of the Roman defences (69139035; Fig. p. 546). The remains, some 9½ ft. wide, ran from W. to E. (80°) for at least 85 ft., consisting of a trench-laid foundation, 14 ins. thick, of alternate layers of flints and rammed or puddled chalk; the section illustrated was not typical. The smooth chalk capping, flush with the natural Chalk, may imply removal of the original surface metalling, before the construction of the rampart some time after c. A.D. 130–150 (*see* p. 547). There may have been an intermittent gutter on the N. side. The street is at a right angle with street (179). The possibility that this was the *intervallum* road of an early fort is noted above (p. 533). (Dorset *Procs.* LXXVII (1955), 129; R.C.H.M. records.)

(177) STREET, sectioned in 1963 by foundation and drainage trenches for the Children's Ward of the Dorset County Hospital, Somerleigh Road (69049058). The remains, traced for 60 ft. from W.S.W. to E.N.E. (approximately 75°), consisted of a cambered layer of cobbles surfaced with small flints, 10 ft. wide, on foundation layers of 'brown clay' and rammed chalk, the whole 18 ins. thick. The subsoil was loam over Chalk. A gutter of rounded profile 3 to 4 ft. wide and 1½ ft. deep adjoined the metalling on the N. The street presumably joined a continuation of the N. to S. street (178) some 50 ft. to the E. (Information from Mr. C. J. Green.)

(178) STREET, sectioned in 1949 in foundation trenches for an annexe to the S. wing of the County Hospital, Somerleigh Road (69079058). It was traced for 50 ft. from S.S.E. to N.N.W. (approximately 345°), with a northerly rise of 1 in 25. The cambered metalling, some 20 ft. wide and 1 ft. thick, consisted of a layer of gravel and flints over two layers of flints bedded in loam and separated by a thin chalk layer. The whole rested on 5 ins. of chalk rubble, perhaps weathered rock. A shallow gutter of rounded profile at the E. edge had been filled before the street was remetalled with 3 ins. of loose flints and gravel. This remetalling, sealing holes in the original surface, was dated to c. A.D. 330 or later. The remains were more or less in line with those of street (180) in Colliton Park. (Dorset *Procs.* LXXI (1949), 63–4; R.C.H.M. records.)

(179) STREET, two exposures on the same alignment of about 350°.

(a) Observed in 1965 in building work behind Messrs. Boots, South Street (69219066). The metalling, at least 16 ft. wide, was traced northwards for some 21 ft., and was without doubt continuous with (b) some 130 yds. to the N. The end of the handle of a bronze skillet, perhaps a military mess-tin, was found below the metalling (*cf.* J.W. Brailsford, *Hod Hill* I (1962), fig. 5, A 134). (Information from Mr. C. J. Green.)

(b) Observed in 1937 in building an extension to Skyrme's workshops in the garden behind No. 64, High West Street (69199078). It was thought by C. D. Drew to point towards the S. exit of the town, and its alignment of approximately 350° has been confirmed by the subsequent discovery at Boots (a). The metalling, damaged on the W. side, was 18 ft. wide but was probably formerly at least 21 ft. An old turf line over the natural Chalk was covered by a thin layer of chalk; above this about 2 ft. of loose flints, steeply cambered and capped by three thin layers of chalk, sand, and gravel appear to be remains of original metalling. Further irregular deposits of gravel, sand and mixed debris, thickest at the sides, were probably later repairs levelling the camber. There were ruts or holes in the remetalled surface. Damage on both sides prevents an estimate of the ultimate width of the street. (*Dorset Daily Echo*, 15th May, 1937; Dorset *Procs.* LX (1938), 64; field notebook, photograph, in D.C.M.)

(180) STREET, traced at Colliton Park in 1938 by C. D. Drew and K. C. C. Selby for some 90 yds. (69029080 to 69009089; Fig. p. 554). No remains survived to the N., where it could have been joined by the paths leading E. from the 4th-century house (182). The alignment of 349° suggests that, although of inferior construction, it was a continuation of street (178). It was perhaps about 15 ft. wide but the metalling, consisting of a thin skin of unmortared flints and small stones laid carelessly on the natural Chalk or over the fillings of earlier

Head, perhaps of Spring or Flora.

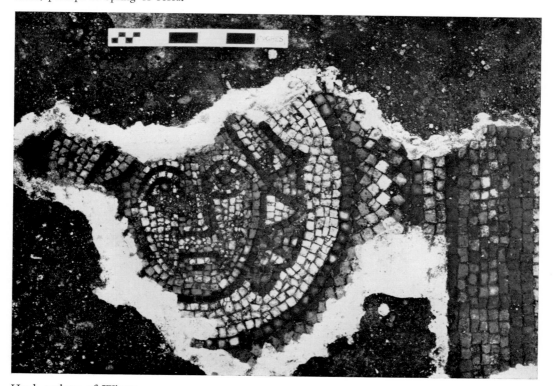

Head, perhaps of Winter.

DORCHESTER. (182) House, Building I in Colliton Park. Details of mosaic in Room 15.

PLATE 219

ROMAN

Room 17, from W., showing hypocaust.

Timber building 19, with overlying cobbled path, from W. *(Phot.: D.C.M.)*

Room 13, from N.

Room 18, S.E. corner, from W.

DORCHESTER. (182) House, Building I in Colliton Park.

PLATE 220

ROMAN

Room 7, S. range, from S., showing hypocaust.

Room 10, from N., showing collapsed window jamb.

Room 2, S. range, from N., showing niche.

Room 8, mosaic floor.

DORCHESTER. (182) House, Building I in Colliton Park.

PLATE 221

ROMAN

(182) House, Building I in Colliton Park, from N.E.   (*Phot.: D.C.M.*)   (173a) Town wall, in Albert Road, from N.W.

(227a) Aqueduct, in Fordington Bottom, looking E.N.E.

DORCHESTER.

PLATE 222

ROMAN

(184) Building IIIA, from W.

(184) Building III, from N.

(185) Building IV, from E.

(186) Building VI, S. room, showing mosaic.

DORCHESTER.   Colliton Park.

(Phots.: D.C.M., except IIIA)

PLATE 223

ROMAN

(202) Building, in Durngate Street, from S.

(212) Building, in Olga Road, central room, from S.

DORCHESTER. Mosaic pavements.

(*Phots.: D.C.M.*)

PLATE 224

ROMAN

H.M. Prison. (209a) Building, W. room. Now in Dorset County Museum.
(Phot.: D.C.M)

Colliton Park. (186) Building VI, N. room, from E.
(Phot.: V. F. M. Oliver)

DORCHESTER. Mosaic Pavements.

PLATE 225   ROMAN

DORCHESTER. (210) Building, in Fordington. Head of Oceanus, mosaic detail, now in Dorset County Museum.

WEYMOUTH. (447) Preston villa, mosaic pavement.   (*After G. R. Crickmay*)

features, was nowhere found complete. A later metalling of similar character and condition was laid above it, over deposits of earth and debris. Monuments (186) and (187) encroached on the original line, and the remetalling was substantially reduced in width between them. To the S. the street, represented by a single metalling, crossed the filling of a disused water conduit, Monument (227b), which, according to MS. lists in D.C.M., here contained 4th-century sherds. If the conduit was originally covered or bridged, the street may have been part of the earlier town plan despite the evident lateness of the metalling here. (Dorset *Procs.* LX (1938), 64, pls. ix and x; site notebooks, section drawings, in D.C.M.)

(181) STREET, excavated for about 45 ft. in 1963 by Mrs. G. M. Aitken in Colliton Park 10 ft. E. of the rear scarp of the Roman town rampart (68959075; Fig. p. 554). A gravelled walk was noted between the rampart and the street. The street ran N. on a bearing of some 4° for some 33 ft., but seemed to veer eastwards a further 8° in the remaining 12 ft. exposed. The metalling, of small flints and gravel cemented with chalk or lime, was about 8 ft. wide and 9 ins. thick where best preserved. Several ruts cutting into the natural Chalk had been repaired with gravel; one contained a coin of Faustina I (d. 140). The street was subsequently blocked by a 4th-century timber building (*see* Monument (188)). (Dorset *Procs.* LXXXV (1963), 96; R.C.H.M. records.)

Excavation in 1965 for the N.W. corner of the County Library appeared to show that the bend in this street was in fact continued for at least 45 ft. to bear N.E. or E. (Information and photographs from Mr. C. J. Green.)

BUILDINGS WITHIN THE WALLS

In addition to the sites listed below as monuments there are two that cannot be precisely located. Part of a mosaic pavement apparently with coarse white surround, found in 1841 in a field occupied by Mr. H. Barnes 'near the south-western angle of the town', measured 14 ft. by 8 ft. but of the design only part of the guilloche border with an outer border of spiral and circular patterns remained. A 'zotheca' (alcove) with floor 'of a very favourite pattern in such pavements' was divided from the main floor by a lozenge-patterned strip. Colours used were black, blue, red, light brown and white. (*Gentleman's Magazine* (1841), pt. ii, 413; Hutchins II, 396–7.) An undated note on Whitehead's plan of Dorchester (1854) in the office of the Borough Surveyor assigns to Mr. Barnes a field or garden now occupied by Whetstone's Almshouses (69029040). In 1852 a very fine tessellated pavement had 'lately been discovered in a garden behind a house, in one of the back streets towards the south-east' (Dorset *Procs.* XLIV (1923), 98) but seems otherwise unrecorded, unless it is a garbled reference to (204b).

A small mosaic square 'from Dorchester', presented in 1920 by J. E. Acland, Curator of the Museum, to the City Museum, Plymouth, and consisting of a single knot in black, white and red, is unrecorded and may have

been made up from spare tesserae in imitation of a motif of the Olga Road mosaic (212).

Monuments (182–187), in Colliton Park, now occupied by the County Council offices, were excavated in 1937-9 by C. D. Drew and K. C. C. Selby. Interim reports appeared in Dorset *Procs.* LIX (1937), 1–14, and LX (1938), 51–65. Where the following accounts differ from these reports they are based on unpublished finds and site notebooks in D.C.M., and on a re-examination of the visible remains including the re-exposure in 1959 of the floors of rooms 14 and 18 of Monument (182). For the street and water conduit also excavated by Drew and Selby, *see* Monuments (180) and (227b).

(182) HOUSE, in the N.W. corner of the town (68959096; Building I in *op. cit.* (1937); Figs. pp. 554, 556; Plates 218–21). The wall footings and hypocausts, and the mosaic of room 8, are on view under the care of the County Council, and are scheduled as an Ancient Monument. There were two separate ranges, never directly intercommunicating, aligned respectively N.—S. and approximately E.—W. parallel with the town defences, each involving extensions to an earlier nucleus. The basically L-shaped plan embracing a small courtyard is anomalous in that extension of the main residential wing was largely to the W. instead of around the remaining sides of the yard. These sides were however occupied by timber buildings, perhaps until the cobbled path was made apparently in the late 4th century. These timber buildings may have supplemented the limited service accommodation available until the S. range was extended.

The site does not appear to have been built on previously, and material of the 1st and 2nd centuries was scarce. The nucleus of the W. range, rooms 10, 13 and 14, probably belongs to the early 4th century; of its extensions room 15 at least seems to have been added after *c.* 341. The S. range consisted of three rooms, 2, 3 and 6, built probably after *c.* 307 and extended, probably after *c.* 341, by the addition of a heated room to W., a corridor on the N., and a kitchen or bakehouse to the E. perhaps replacing an equivalent timbered room, 19, to the N. If coins are a reliable guide, civilized occupation would not appear to have continued long after *c.* 375, although it is to this phase that the neatly cobbled path seems to belong. There was, however, evidence for deliberate wrecking in both ranges, and for occupation of slum character even after collapse of some of the walls, though this may have happened in the 5th century.

The walls of both ranges, 2 ft. thick and laid on natural Chalk, were largely of roughly knapped flints often laid in herring-bone courses; limestone was also

K

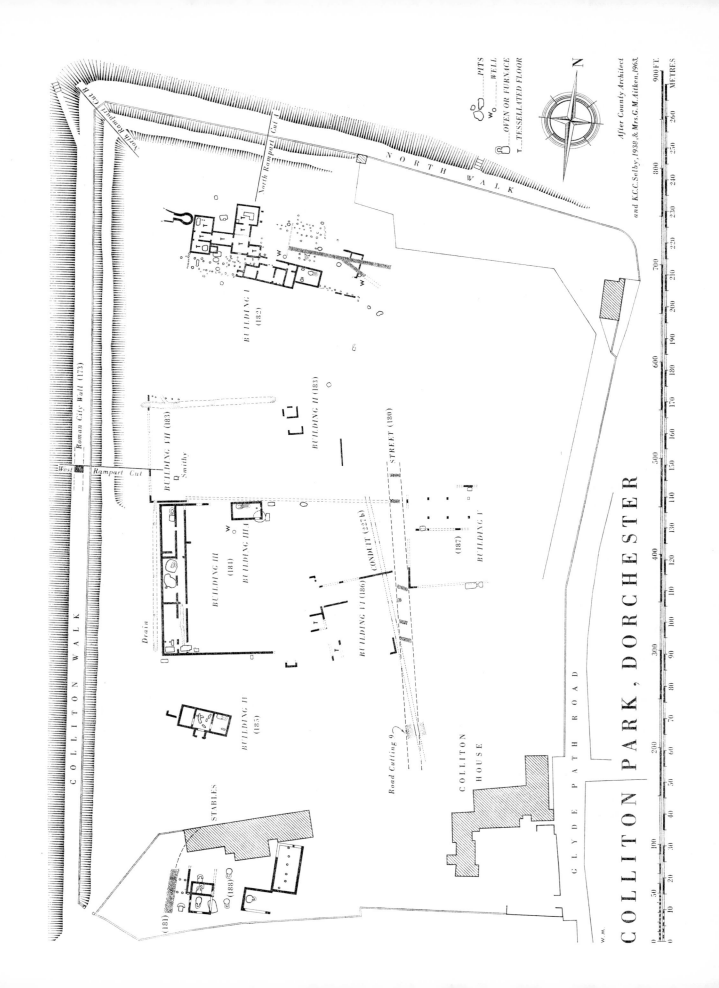

COLLITON PARK, DORCHESTER

*After County Architect
and K.C.C.Selby,1938,& Mrs.G. M.Aitken,1963.*

PITS
WELL
OVEN OR FURNACE
T. TESSELLATED FLOOR

N

METRES
900 FT.

COLLITON WALK

Roman City Wall (173)

West Rampart Cut

North Rampart Cut B

North Rampart Cut 1

NORTH WALK

BUILDING I
(182)

BUILDING VII (188)

Smithy

Drain

BUILDING III
(181)

BUILDING IIIA

W

BUILDING II (183)

BUILDING II (185)

STREET (180)

CONDUIT (227 b)

BUILDING I (186)

(187)
BUILDING I

Road Cutting 9

COLLITON
HOUSE

STABLES

(181)

(188)

GLYDE PATH ROAD

W.M.

employed, normally for quoins and bonding courses. The walls were generally plastered on both sides and painted a Pompeian red externally; inner faces were predominantly red or white with evidence for geometric and floral patterns. Impressions of laths and reeds on plaster fragments imply timbered upper walls even in the heated rooms, although room 15 was wholly of masonry and possibly of two storeys. All rooms of the W. range were tessellated, normally with a thin mortar bedding on the natural chalk; those of the S. range were concreted or stone-flagged. At the junction of walls and floors quarter-round fillets were normal, and in the W. range the floor levels of rooms 15, 14/10 and 13 were lowered progressively, with imbrex-tile drains through the walls to facilitate washing the mosaics. Room 14 afforded a rare example of a collapsed window embrasure, now rebuilt. Roofs were of hexagonal limestone slabs, except for the two external stokeholes, which were apparently roofed with red tiles.

The *West Range*. In the W. wing of the range the N. room, 18, measuring 16½ ft. by 15 ft. internally, had a mosaic floor in red on a white ground, of which only parts of the borders survived, a swastika pattern within chevrons, with a dentil pattern to the E. (Plate 219). A stone amongst several flagstones over a pit in the N.W. corner was roughly inscribed VAL (R. G. Collingwood and R. P. Wright, *The Roman Inscriptions of Britain*, I (1965), no.190; *J.R.S.* XXIX (1939), 227). There was a door near the S.W. corner leading into a room or passage, 16, measuring 16½ ft. by 6 ft. Here traces remained of a coarse red and white tessellated pavement apparently of diagonal lattice pattern, as well as of a later floor of flagstones, which overlay a mosaic panel in the threshold of the doorway to E.

Room 17 to the S. (Plate 219), 16½ ft. long by 10½ ft., was heated by a hypocaust 3 ft. deep with 11 channels circulating between engaged piers of masonry or of stone-faced natural chalk; the brick-lined, stone-capped furnace was served from a stokehole against the E. wall. The irregular plan of the channels, leading to box-tile flues in the walls, suggests the existence of a window in the centre of the S. wall. The mosaic floor, with its mortar foundation 5 ins. thick over stone slabs, had been deliberately smashed; its red and white border was of rectangular panels between swastikas, while the centre had included circular medallions with guilloche and chevron borders in blue-grey, red and white. The painted wall plaster on the S. wall had a dark red border at the base, 1½ ft. high, above which were remains of a white ground with two narrow horizontal lines. Fallen fragments included panels and traces of a floral pattern with a blue flower and green leaf. One fragment bore the cursive graffito PATERNVS SCRIPSIT ('Paternus wrote this'). A shale table leg was found in the filling of an earlier pit in the E. part of the room; sherds of metallic-lustred New Forest pottery in its lower filling and in a pit underlying the stokehole, 17a, may imply a date after *c.* 330 for the W. extension of the range.[1]

---

[1] B. Cunliffe has drawn attention to instances of this ware in late 3rd-century contexts (Hampshire Field Club, *Procs.* XXIII (1965), 44–5).

Room 13, linking the two wings of the range and entered from the E. by a step of limestone blocks, measured 20½ ft. by 11 ft. but straight joints in the walls 3 ft. from the W. end showed that it had been extended when rooms 16–18 were added. The mosaic floor (Plate 219), a secondary feature appropriate to the enlarged room, had a border of red and white chequers around an overall swastika pattern in coarse red and white tesserae partly covered by a later floor of packed chalk. A drain at floor level through the N. wall led by a gully to a stone-lined sump, as in rooms 14 and 18. A small coin hoard of A.D. 317 or later was buried near the E. door.

In the E. wing, room 15, 19½ ft. by 17½ ft., had walls of solid masonry at least 15 ft. high perhaps supported to the E. by two piers or buttresses. This height, indicated by the outward collapse of the E. and W. walls, the former in mass, suggests an upper storey, and the piers may have carried instead an external wooden stair. The latest coin below the collapsed wall was an issue of Constans of 341–6; a rough limestone floor laid over it during the slum phase sealed several coins, the latest an issue of 367–75 of Gratian. The fragmentary mosaic pavement, once the finest in the house, had an outer border of red and white chevrons and a wide inner swastika border enclosing rectangular panels of 2 and 4-strand guilloche and chequers. Within this, bands of 2-strand guilloche flanked two circular medallions (Plate 218) at the centre of the W. and N. sides, containing respectively a female head with long ringlets and a flower on either side of the face, perhaps Spring or Flora, and a head with parti-coloured hood, perhaps Winter. The tesserae were in four sizes from ¼ in. to 1 in. square, and colours used were white, red, dark and medium grey, pinkish brown and yellow, with blue, brown, green and light yellow in the faces. Straight joints showed that this room was an addition to the original plan; two Constantinian coins in the underlying level imply that it was not made before *c.* 341. An infant burial lay under the eaves to the N. (*see* Burials (215c)).

A doorway in the centre of the S. wall of room 15 led down a Purbeck stone step to the main part of the original nucleus, a room 28 ft. by 14 ft. divided by a wooden or plaster partition into a N. part 10 ft. long (room 14) with a coarse tessellated floor of broad red and grey stripes and a S. part (room 10) with a much damaged mosaic pavement (Plate 220). The border was of swastikas in red on white between square chequered panels, with a rectangular panel of two-strand guilloche in the centre of the S. side. The central design had probably consisted of twelve octagonal panels of which six and part of a seventh remained. In each of these, formed by guilloche borders, a guilloche or a fret-bordered circle enclosed a rosette pattern. Colours used were dark grey, red, yellow and white. At the S. end a fallen portion of wall, rebuilt in 1950, included the splayed opening of a window with rebates for a wooden frame still clear in the plaster (D. B. Harden, in E. M. Jope (ed.), *Studies in Building History* (1961), 49–50, pl. vi). The sill had been about 2½ ft. above the floor, some 4 ft. wide internally narrowing to some 3 ft. Fragments of window glass were found in this and other rooms. The main entrance to the house, 5 ft. wide, was in the E. wall at the N. end of room 10; two post-holes perhaps indicate an external porch. The wall plaster of this room seems to have had a rectangular panelled design with curvilinear

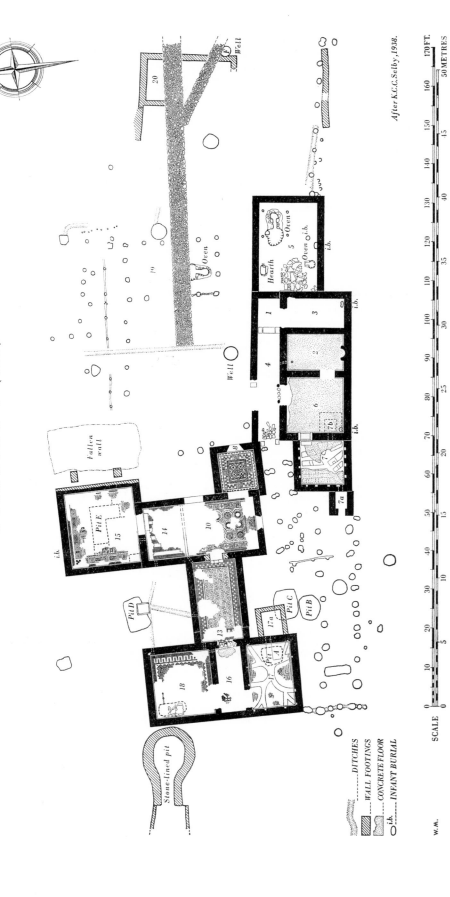

COLLITON PARK, DORCHESTER

BUILDING I (182)

N

Well

20

Oven

19

Well

Hearth

Oven

Oven

i.b.

5

i.b.

1

3

0

i.b.

4

2

6

7b

i.b.

7

7a

Fallen wall

8

i.b.

15

Pit E

14

10

Pit D

Stone-lined pit

13

Pit C

Pit B

17a

18

16

17

Pit A

Pit

After K.C.C.Selby, 1938.

SCALE

w.m.

DITCHES
WALL FOOTINGS
CONCRETE FLOOR
i.b. INFANT BURIAL

170 FT.

50 METRES

elements; that on the window splay showed remains of a panel in red with traces of blue and grey, while loose fragments bore bands and lines of red, white, blue, green, purple, yellow and shades of brown, mainly on a red or white ground.

Room 8, 10¾ ft. by 9¼ ft., regarded as an addition on account of its awkward position, was reached by a doorway near the S.E. angle of room 10. Its well-executed mosaic floor was substantially complete when uncovered (Plate 220), and is now on view under a protective cover. A coarse border in red on a white ground, consisting of chevrons outside a chequer pattern with a central swastika in each side, enclosed a rect-angular panel of smaller tesserae. In this panel, borders of two-strand guilloche, doubled at each end, framed a central circle containing a rosette, four semicircles tangential to it, and four quarter-circles in the corners. The intervening spaces contained knots. Colours used were three shades of grey, red, white and yellow. A rough window sill of flint remained in the centre of the E. wall about 2½ ft. above the floor. Fragments of plaster in panelled design in black, blue, brown, green, red and white presumably came from the walls.

The *South Range* in its final form was a block of five rooms 77 ft. long overall with a corridor along part of the N. side. The W. room (7), 11 ft. square with channelled hypocaust 3 ft. deep and concrete floor carried on massive flagstones (Plate 220), had been added to room 6, as shown principally by its disalignment with the nucleus and the failure to carry the foundation of the W. wall of room 6 to the basement of the hypocaust. The exposed chalk face had been in part protected by clay tiles, secured by T-shaped nails. These tiles had blocked the upper part of the brick-lined, stone-capped furnace channel leading from an original stokehole 7b in room 6. The disposition of the masonry piers implies a com-plete remodelling of the hypocaust when the external stone-lined furnace 7a was made, while a narrow channel alongside the walls, and shallow transverse slots in the tops of the piers, were required to serve the flues of the W. wall. Both walls and piers, including the slots, appear to have been plaster-rendered. Plaster debris from the room above indicated a panelled design, perhaps foliate, in white and red, with green and brown lines. A Portland stone step led up to room 6 through a doorway in the E. wall and the well-worn threshold was a block of Ham Hill stone slotted for a door frame.

Room 6 with concrete floor 14 ft. square, was entered from the N. between two pedestals or pillars. It had probably been a fuel-store and wash-kitchen before the remodelling, since stokehole 7b had stone bearers in the sides evidently for a hot-water tank. There was an infant burial (215c) in the S.W. corner. The concrete floor may have been first laid rather than patched when the stokehole was filled; a coin of Constans of 341–6, found in a gully somewhere beneath the floor, may therefore be taken to give an earliest possible date for the reconstruction rather than for the initial building.

A doorway in the E. wall led to room 2 (Plate 220) which was at a slightly higher level and measured 14 ft. by 10½ ft. It was notable for its well-preserved concrete floor with quarter-round moulding, a plastered semicircular niche partly recessed into the centre of the S. wall, and an outfall pipe in the N. wall above floor level. The niche, probably an original

feature since it was recessed into the wall, was possibly for a domestic shrine, with which the provision for water may have been connected. Room 3, entered from the N., was 14 ft. by 7½ ft. and apparently had walls painted with a green leaf pattern on red; there were no remains of flooring. An infant skeleton (215c) with bird bones in the S.E. corner belonged to a late stage. A coin of Licinius I (307–24) in the E. wall of 3, and a sherd of coarse pottery (*cf.* Gillam, *Arch. Ael.* xxxv (1957), type 228) in the S. wall, suggest a date in the early 4th century for the construction of the nucleus.

The corridor (4), 5½ ft. wide, had a rough chalk floor lower than the floors to the S., and during its construction the adjacent wall of room 2 had had to be underpinned with a

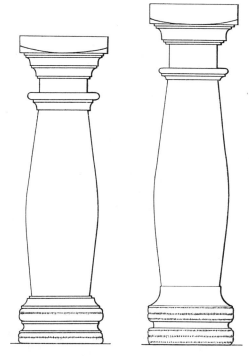

(182) Colliton Park, Building I, columns. (¹⁄₁₂)

mass of herring-bone masonry made up of broken limestone roofing slabs. The N. wall, as now suggested in a rebuilt portion, was almost certainly a dwarf wall carrying a lean-to roof on small Portland stone columns, roughly carved and varying in detail but about 3¼ ft. high and 9 ins. in maximum diameter (*see* Fig.); parts of nine columns were found in the well to the N. and part of another in the hypocaust of room 7. There was a doorway in this wall opposite that of room 6 and another at the W. end flanked by stone jambs or pedestals with a patch of rough limestone paving to the E. A step flanked by pedestals, probably for small columns, cut off the E. end of the corridor to form a small chalk-floored lobby (room 1).

Room 5, 23 ft. by 14½ ft., with straight joints in the masonry at the W. end, had clearly been added when 3 and 1, from which it was entered, already existed. The walls were apparently unplastered. Several coins, the latest of 341–6, give an earliest possible date for a floor of limestone slabs at the W. end, if not for the addition of the room itself. A kerb at the N. edge of these slabs possibly indicated a partition in line with the S. wall of the corridor. In the N.E. corner was a stone-lined oven, perhaps roofed, and near the N. wall a rough hearth of tiles and roofing slabs. There was a small oven S. of the paving and two infant burials (215c) near the S. wall. A line of post-holes extending E. from the S. wall of the room was backed in part by remains of a dry-stone wall.

Other features. A well 3½ ft. in diameter and 33½ ft. deep lay N. of the S. range and contained much debris including the dwarf columns and two hexagonal bases. A neat cobbled path 4½ ft. wide ran E. for at least 100 ft. from a point where a small gully ran N. from the well and perhaps delimited a contracted courtyard in front of the house. The path was aligned on the entrance to the W. wing and its interruption implies the existence in the yard of stone flagging later removed. A coin of Valentinian I of 367–75 beneath the cobbles suggests a late 4th-century date for the feature. A narrower path branched S.E. from the main one 60 ft. from its W. end and partly sealed a well (F), 27¾ ft. deep, containing 4th-century pottery.

To the W. of the S. range parallel lines of post-holes, some of them renewed, indicated two long, narrow rectangular sheds with chalk floors, perhaps erected after *c.* 330. They may have served as fuel-stores for the hypocausts. A series of more regular post-holes on the N. and E. sides of the courtyard apparently supported a more substantial L-shaped building (19) of two rooms set at right-angles (Plate 219). The S. room, with an oven at its S. end, was sunk about 1 ft. below the surface of the natural chalk and perhaps served as kitchen or bakehouse before the construction of room 5. The building had been demolished and its site levelled on or before construction of the cobbled path. Rubble footings of a small rectangular stone building (20), apparently of the 4th century, were also found under the cobbled paths.

Immediately W. of room 18 of the W. range, a stone-lined pit of key-hole plan, 14 ft. across and 16 ft. deep, evidently had a corbelled roof; it had a basin-shaped hollow in the centre, 4 ft. deep, into which ran a narrow channel cut in the floor of a passage leading into a roughly square stone-lined chamber of neater build. There was some ash and many of the lining stones of the circular chamber had been reddened by fire. It was filled with rubble some time after A.D. 270 and before room 18 was built. Of several other pits and gullies the most notable was a system of chalk-cut channels about 2 ft. wide just N. of room 18, presumably for drainage, and a storm-water gully for the W. range cut across the filling of the stone-lined pit. For a boundary ditch to the S., *see* Monument (183). A stone-lined oven 75 ft. S.E. of room 5 has been relaid near the cobbled path.

(183) BUILDING, much damaged, 120 ft. S. of the S. range of (182) (68979091; Buildings II and VII in interim report, Drew and Selby, *op. cit.* on p. 553 (1938); Figs. pp. 554, 559).

Fragmentary wall footings enclosed two rectangular rooms but no floors survived; a small oven was said to have been found by contractors some yards to the S.E. An E. to W. ditch (the 'West Ditch') 130 ft. long and 5 ft. wide, with some post-holes on the N. side, apparently bounded the property to the N. (182) and cut into the rear chalk capping of the town rampart; its filling throughout included New Forest pottery, consistent with its attribution to the 4th-century house (182). Walls to the W. and S., 'Building VII', probably with an isolated length to the E., evidently formed a rectangular enclosure about 192 ft. by at least 110 ft., which had been contracted on the N. when the 'West Ditch' was dug. Its alignment conforms quite well with that of the street (180) to the E. The W. wall footings were covered by the extreme tail of the Roman town rampart, in the second phase proposed in this volume, after *c.* A.D. 300 (*see* p. 543); the fresh state of the footings suggested no great interval of time between the constructions.

Towards the S.W. angle of the enclosure was a forge consisting of a low kerbed platform of limestone slabs, shield-shaped in plan and 4 ft. long E. to W. by some 3 ft. wide at most. Short extensions of the kerb splayed out at the narrow E. end, and upright settings of slabs and of animal shin-bones, parallel with the end splay and apparently without functional purpose, flanked both sides. The W. end of the platform was heavily burnt, and ashes spread over the whole area, sealing the tail of the town rampart and including many short iron rods, in some cases drawn out to form small spearheads. A similar platform, unburnt and 4 ft. to the N.E. but not on the plan, is dated by New Forest ware below it to the 4th century.

(184) BUILDING, parallel with and only 1½ ft. S. of the wall of the enclosure, *see* (183), and likewise nearly in conformity with the street (180) (Buildings III and IIIA in interim report, Drew and Selby, *op. cit.* (1938); Figs. pp. 554, 559, Plate 222). It consisted of a N. to S. range (68949085) on the W. side of a slightly sunken courtyard, apparently open but extending 85 ft. to the E., with a detached single room on the N. side (68969087). It appears to have been used, at least ultimately, for industrial purposes; there is little evidence for its date, except that it was in use during the 4th century.

The main range, 158 ft. long by 25 ft. wide overall, probably thatched and with little sign of regular flooring, was divided into three narrow rooms each 12 ft. wide, entered from a corridor on the E., 6½ ft. wide. The N. room, 47½ ft. long, had an oven near the N. end built on the footings of the corridor wall after its collapse or demolition. A small apartment at the S. end, 3 ft. 2 ins. wide, may have contained stores or a staircase. The central room, 47 ft. long, also had a late oven in similar relationship to the corridor wall, and near it a large shallow pit filled with ashes and beach shingle. The S. room was 51 ft. long; a coin of Gallienus of 260–8 underlay its chalk floor and there were late pits at the S. end. In the corridor, also divided into three parts, the only apparent outer doorway was 3 ft. 7 ins. wide; a notable Rhenish glass bowl of the 4th

BUILDING VII (183)

DITCH

Oven

1

1a

Oven
Pit N

Pit O

2

Door

3

Pit Q

Pit R

Pit S

Pit U

Pit T

BUILDING IIIA

Furnace

Pit K

Pit L

Pit J

Well

N

COLLITON PARK
BUILDING III (184)

SCALE

| 0 | 10 | 20 | 30 | 40 | 50 | 60 | 70 | 80 | 90 FEET |
| 0 | | 5 | | 10 | | 15 | | 20 | 25 METRES |

Pit

After K.C.C. Selby, 1939.

DRAIN

century engraved with Bacchic dancers was found in a sump pit at the S. end.

'Building IIIA', about 31 ft. by 18½ ft. overall with its N. wall on the line of the courtyard wall, was built more neatly with flints set herring-bone fashion with limestone quoins, and was probably unplastered. There was a door in the S. wall and the floor was of packed chalk over dark earth. A large oven or furnace with a flue 6 ft. long lay against the N. wall; its filling contained ash and beach shingle similar to that in the central room of the main range. No dating material came from a pit underlying the S.E. corner of the building, but a tangential pit (J) was of the 4th century. Of several pits to the W., not shown in plan, two were 18 ft. deep. A well to the S., over 52 ft. deep, had a limestone coping. There were some remains of a small building on a similar alignment outside the courtyard to the S.E.

(185) BUILDING, probably a small house, S. of (184) and on exactly the same alignment as the S. range of (182), was a well-preserved rectangular block of three rooms, entered by a central porch to the S. The significance of a length of wall to the W. is uncertain. (68959081; Building IV in interim report, Drew and Selby, *op. cit.* (1938); Figs. below and p. 554, Plate 222.)

COLLITON PARK

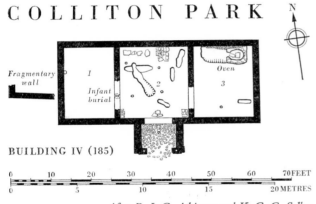

BUILDING IV (185)

After R. J. C. Atkinson and K. C. C. Selby.

The building measured 51 ft. by 21½ ft. overall. Its main walls, surviving, except in the porch, to an even height of 2½ ft., perhaps the original height for a timber frame, were neatly constructed, mainly of herring-bone flint courses with limestone quoins, and were probably not plastered; the S. wall was faced externally with limestone. The floors, however, were poor, consisting largely of packed chalk. In the S. angles of the central room two small platforms of stone slabs showed signs of burning, as did the adjacent wall; a larger platform against the N. wall was unburnt. Both this room and the E. room overlay earlier pits, some containing shale(?) ash, and under the E. room was an oven, the stokehole of which accommodated some of the footings of the N. wall; the significance of post-holes here and in the porch is not discussed. The rooms communicated by doorways near the S. wall. An infant burial with a coarse ware pot of *c.* 250 or later underlay the W.

dividing wall where it carried under the doorway (*see* Burial 215e). The porch, robbed more thoroughly or perhaps dismantled before abandonment of the building, was 8½ ft. wide internally and projected about 7½ ft. with dowel holes for a wooden door-frame set in limestone blocks 6¼ ft. apart. The building was thought to have been built in the 3rd century and to have been used until the end of the 4th century.

(186) BUILDING, probably a house on at least two sides of a small courtyard E. of the yard of Monument (184), was poorly preserved (69009084; Building VI in interim report, Drew and Selby, *op. cit.* (1938); Fig. p. 554, Plates 222, 224).

Two rooms with mosaic floors were found to the W. of the courtyard. The northerly room, 14½ ft. from N. to S., had the remains of a pavement with coarse white surround 3½ ft. wide; the design was apparently an oblong some 10 ft. long, with panels of two-strand guilloche to E. and W. of a square pattern with semicircular panels on the sides and quadrants in the angles, as in room 8 of Monument (182). The S. semicircle with a voluted *pelta*, the S.W. quadrant with a lotus blossom, and part of the W. guilloche remained (Plate 224); removed to the site of Monument (182), the piece was subsequently destroyed by vandals. A room 15 ft. to the S., 8 ft. by over 18 ft., had a floor with coarse white surround at least 2 ft. wide on the S. and probably some 10 ins. at the sides. The decorated portion, in white, red and dark blue-grey, was a panel 6¼ ft. wide and over 13½ ft. long consisting of a single strip of intersecting octagons with alternate knot and triangle centres, within a tripartite border of linked triangles, two-strand guilloche and chevrons. It is said to have been lifted but is untraced. To N.E. this building overlay the filling (here undated) of the conduit (227b). It also encroached on the earlier metalling of the street (180), and was associated with the later metalling; this part of the building, at least, was therefore probably of the 4th century.

(187) BUILDING N.E. of (186), fronting on the E. side of the street (180) with which it was approximately aligned, was also poorly preserved (69029089; Building V in interim report, Drew and Selby, *op. cit.* (1938); Fig. p. 554).

The most certain remains consisted of nearly parallel E.–W. walls of an aisled building some 45 ft. wide and over 65 ft. long, with two rows of three bases for wooden posts between them. The bases, of Ham Hill stone about 2 ft. square and 1 ft. high, formed bays averaging 20 ft. wide, and the building was probably a warehouse or barn. A pit with late 1st-century pottery, an iron wheel-tyre and hub bands, underlay the S. wall. An angle of walling on the same alignment, although associated with some loose tesserae, probably indicates a yard attached to the building on the S.; it overlay an earlier metalling of the street (180) and a pit to the E. containing 4th-century pottery.

(188) BUILDINGS, in Colliton Park S. of (185), excavated in 1961–3 by Mrs. G. M. Aitken (68979076; Fig. p. 554).

A rectangular building 50 ft. by 26 ft., aligned due N. to S., had walls of mortared flint and limestone 2 ft. thick, perhaps with a door in the N. end, a puddled chalk floor, and a line of five post-holes down the centre for a roof probably of stone slabs. The W. wall footings had shifted where they overlay pits containing 1st and early 2nd-century samian ware and coins; a layer accumulated after disuse of the building contained 3rd-century coins. A second building or room, 24 ft. wide, and 30 ft. long if post-holes to the E. belonged to an E. wall of timber, had been added on the S.W.; its chalk and earth floor sealed an oven. There was a cobbled yard in the angle between these buildings; stone slabs sealing a roofed oven to the W., containing a coin of Victorinus (A.D. 267–70), were probably part of this paving.

On a parallel alignment to the W. was another building 28 ft. wide and over 26 ft. long, with well-built herring-bone limestone walls 1¾ ft. thick, possibly plastered in red on the inside, and with doorways in the W. and S. sides. Its floor of puddled chalk sealed an unused oven in the centre of the building; there were apparently a timber lean-to on the W. and a drainage gully outside the E. wall, while to the S. a large rectangular storage pit and an oven W. of it may have been in contemporary use. The pit, 15 ft. deep and flat-bottomed, contained debris including coins from 253 to 278 and wheat, bean and vetch seeds. A layer of debris on the floor of the building had not accumulated before A.D. 270. Another rectangular building similarly orientated and measuring 32 ft. by 23 ft. was erected in the 4th century over its S. end. The wall footings had holes for a timber superstructure and there was a doorway in the S. wall; an oven towards the N. end was built in the flue of an earlier oven against the N. wall. The date of this building is given by a coin of Claudius II (A.D. 268–70) below its floor of puddled chalk, and one of the early 4th century in the filling of the pit below the S.E. corner. Two parallel rows of post-holes running W. at right angles to the W. wall apparently indicated a fifth building, of timber, 23 ft. by 17 ft., with three successive chalk floors, the earliest sealing New Forest pottery. This structure overlay remains of a narrow, rutted street or path (181), of similar alignment to the buildings but curving N.E. and perhaps not one of the public streets of the town. (Dorset *Procs.* LXXXIV (1962), 101; LXXXV (1963), 96; Somerset and Dorset *Notes and Queries* XXVIII (1964), 189–91; information from Mrs. G. M. Aitken.)

Indications of two walls were seen to the N. in a drain trench dug northwards from the new County Library in 1965; one of them (68969079), running rather E. of N., had fallen wall plaster to the E.; the other (68969078), below the footpath beside the Library, ran E. to W. (information from Mr. C. J. Green). They are not shown on the plan. The street or path (181) seems, however, to have turned north-eastwards to run between these remains and those excavated by Mrs. Aitken.

(189) BUILDING REMAINS with fragmentary mosaic and tessellated pavements have been found at Somerleigh Court, now the Maternity Wing of the County General Hospital, during building operations since 1862. They may belong to a large house or several houses, probably fronting on a street (178) to the E.

(a) A much damaged mosaic pavement was uncovered at the foot of the garden terrace S. of the house in 1862 or 1863 and subsequently reburied (69069048). A drawing, apparently of a corner of the decorated portion, shows a band of inter-secting circles about 3½ ft. in diameter with geometrical and leaf motifs in the spaces, separated by a narrow strip of linked triangles from a running *pelta* panel. At least seven colours were used, mainly black, white, red, grey and blue. The design may have had a plain centre according to Moule. (Letters from Sir Robert Edgecumbe (1900) and sketch in D.C.M.; Moule, 33–6; Moule MS., 2; *D.C.C.*, 23rd Apr., 24th Sept. 1863.) This is with little doubt the pavement 'almost Gothic in character' of which a photograph, untraced but probably by J. Pouncy, was exhibited in 1864 (*J.B.A.A.* XX (1864), 201).

(b) Part of a red tessellated pavement, at least 15 ft. E. to W. by 5 ft., bounded by walls on the N. and E., the latter probably continuing the northward line of the W. wall of (c), was observed in 1963 immediately E. of the presumed site of (a), to which it may have belonged (69079048). At one point the pavement overlay a length of E. to W. wall parallel with and 4 ft. S. of the N. wall of the room, associated with a chalk floor on which was 2nd-century pottery. (Information from Mr. C. J. Green.)

(c) A room 13½ ft. E. to W. by 9½ ft., floored in part with a coarse red and grey tessellated pavement of chessboard pattern flanked by alternating strips of the same colours, was excavated in 1963 immediately S.E. of (b) (69089048). The flint walls, 2 ft. thick and at least 4 ft. high, evidently with timbered superstructure, had been plastered in a painted panel design; there was a door in the S. wall and, in its E. end, a relieving arch of bricks and stone tiles in the wall face over the filling of an earlier pit. Some small pieces of wall plaster *in situ* well below the level of the tessellated floor suggested that the latter was an insertion; the excavators considered that there had been two earlier floors, the lower possibly of flagstones forming an original basement room. The E. end of the room was much disturbed, but there was no evidence that it had been tessellated. Both the S. wall and a parallel wall 2½ ft. to the S. had corbelled overhangs suggesting an original arched passage some 5 ft. high. Its filling contained 1st or early 2nd-century pottery thought to have been contemporary with the original construction, and some small sherds of 4th-century New Forest ware, regarded as intrusive. The gap was sealed over by fallen masonry, which with little doubt serves to identify the remains with those seen in 1875 when a flint wall said to be 6 ft. thick was found E. of (a) adjoining a coarse red and white tessellated pavement. Part of a concrete floor adjoining the chamber, to the W., showed that the W. wall was a party wall; the relationship of this floor to the tessellated pavement (b) seen later 7 ft. to the N. is unknown. (Moule, 34; Dorset *Procs.* LXXXVI (1964), 155–7.)

Further observation in 1963 suggested that the building also extended to the N. The most significant remains were of a thin cement floor believed to extend for some 30 ft. in both directions on the N. side of the tessellated room, overlying remains of an E. to W. wall of Ham Hill stone and a deposit assigned to the later 2nd century. To the N.E. a stone wellhead of hexagonal plan with a circular shaft 2 ft. in diameter contained late Roman material in its partially excavated upper filling (69099050). (Information from Mr. C. J. Green.)

From this area and from (d) came several sherds of Claudian type, including Belgic *terra nigra* and *terra rubra*. A bronze harness ring, from below the cement floor, and a rectangular bronze platelet perhaps originally decorated in niello and attached to leather, from a 2 ft. wide gully running N. to S., 6 yds. E. of the tessellated room, may be early military equipment.

(d) Immediately S. and S.E. of (c), on a similar alignment but without obvious connection, remains were observed in 1963 of an oblong building or perhaps a small yard, 11 ft. wide and over 25 ft. long E. to W. (69089047). A parallel wall 6½ ft. to the S., with a cement floor between, suggested a corridor which on the W. may have met a wall apparently running N. to S. from near the S.W. corner of the tessellated room (c). The corridor may have turned at the E. end where there were further remains of a cement floor extending for some 40 ft. northwards. Evidence for date was a samian sherd of the mid 2nd century below the cement floor, and 4th-century pottery upon it. There were signs of further walls to the S. and of two successive chalk floors close to the S. wall of the corridor, the lower sealing 1st-century pottery. (Information from Mr. C. J. Green.)

(e) A damaged mosaic, apparently over a hypocaust, was found in 1889 in a manhole a few feet W. of the porch of Somerleigh Court (69079050). A portion some 8 ft. by 5 ft. was relaid diagonally in the porch with a made-up border. Two panels 2 ft. square, one with an endless knot pattern, the other with a design of squares and triangles within a circle of two-strand guilloche, were enclosed by a black swastika pattern on a white ground. Other colours used were grey, blue-grey and red. The pavement lay 3 ins. above 'some beautifully constructed heating flues, about 4 ins. deep and 8 ins. wide', and a red plastered wall adjoined it to the E. It may have formed part of (f). (Letters from Sir R. Edgecumbe (1900) in D.C.M.; Moule, 34–6; Moule MS., 2, 11; D.C.C., 1st Aug. 1889; Dorset Procs. XXVII (1906), 247.)

(f) A damaged mosaic, apparently with the same design as (e) and possibly part of the same, was found 20 ft. to the W. in 1889 in foundation trenches, 10 ft. apart, for a small closet in the angle between the main building and the N. wing (69069050; for references, see (e)).

(g) Fragments of a coarse black and white tessellated pavement were seen about 1890 when the clock-house (69089051) was being built about 10 yds. N.E. of the porch (Moule MS., 18). Remains of walls were seen about 1950 under the road immediately to the N. (information from Mr. A. Y. Nother). In laying drains by the N. wall of the Court 10 ft. S. of the clock-house in 1963, a small part of a grey tessellated pavement interspersed irregularly with red tesserae was exposed, bounded on the S. by a wall running E. on an alignment similar to those of (b) and (c) (information from Mr. P. Whatmore; Dorset Procs. LXXXVII (1965), 109).

(190) BUILDING REMAINS observed in 1963 to the N.W. of Somerleigh Court on the site of the new Children's Ward of the County Hospital and at the new Mortuary consisted, at the former, of two pits, building debris, and a gravelled area (69059058) attached to the side of an E. to W. street (177), and extending at least 13 ft. to the S. One pit, to the N. of the street, had 4th-century pottery and tesserae in its filling (69049058); the other to the S. (69049056) contained clinker. At the Mortuary, S. of the Chest Clinic, a ditch some 3 ft. wide running N. to S. for over 20 ft. was noted in drain and foundation trenches (69029054); two post-holes in line E. to W., the nearer about 20 ft. from the ditch, may have been associated with post-holes at the N. end of the Boiler House (69059055; Dorset Procs. LXXX (1958), 102). A pit W. of the ditch (69019054) contained much good quality painted wall plaster with patterns of grapes and foliage; a brooch near by was probably of Claudian date. A tinned bronze brooch of 'Hod Hill' type and sherds of white flagons from the area (69039054) were also probably of the mid 1st century. To the S. of the site (69049053) a stone-lined and covered drain was traced for 7 ft. (information from Mr. C. J. Green).

A chalk floor was sectioned in an extension to the main building of the County Hospital in 1949, E. of the Roman street (178). (69099058; R.C.H.M. records; Dorset Procs. LXXI (1949), 64.) The late 4th-century hoard of silver coins and spoons (Fig. p. 563; see also p. 536) was found in 1898–9 in building the stables, now ambulance garages, fronting on Princes Street to the N.W. (69049063; Ant. J. II (1922), 89–92; Num. Chron. II (1922), 134–9; letter from T. Lynes, D.C.M. correspondence (1920–2)).

(191) BUILDING, adjoining the Roman town rampart, excavated in 1938–9 by G. E. Kirk on Lee Motors' premises in the angle between Trinity Street and Bowling Alley Walk (69139037).

A room 18 ft. by 14 ft. internally, apparently the N. end of a building aligned slightly E. of N., was defined by flint footings 2 ft. wide bearing on the S. a limestone wall, laid partly in herring-bone pattern and probably unplastered. The floor, in which two infants (215b), were buried, was partly paved with limestone roofing slabs and there was a hearth against the S. wall. An adjoining room to the S. was largely unexcavated but had a hearth in the N.W. corner; there was no doorway in the dividing wall and access was probably from the W. where there were remains of a stone-flagged yard or path. Debris suggested that the walls stood about 9 ft. high with a stone slab roof. The building was dated to the mid 3rd century, but a few pieces of New Forest ware and of cooking vessels of types not securely attested before the 4th century, in deposits below the floor, suggest that it was not built before c. A.D. 300. The debris from its decay included a coin of Valentinian II (375–92). Of two phases of occupation prior to its construction, represented by a gully, two pits, an oven, a fireplace and a number of post-holes, only the post-holes have a sound claim to a date before the 4th century. (Dorset Procs. LXI (1939), 48–59; full typescript report in D.C.M.) Remains apparently of a street were found in 1955 on the same premises some 45 ft. to the S. (see Monument (176)).

(192) BUILDING, mosaic pavement only, found in 1925 under Tilley's Garage, 26 Trinity Street, about 90 ft. from the street and 30 ft. S. of the passage to Somerleigh Road (69149051).

The largest of three disconnected portions thought to have belonged to one pavement was said to have been several feet long and to have been of 'black and white mosaic squares with a centre piece of red and white squares'; another, under one of the garage walls, was 'an elongated triangle in black and white', and the third, an oblong panel, had 'a red and white design down the centre on a black background with a bordering in white and black'. Portions of Roman pavement had been found earlier some 20 yds. away. (*D.C.C.*, 25th June 1925, 5; Moule MS., 8.) A tracing by O. C. Vidler, in D.C.M., of a mosaic fragment in black, white and red said to be from this site, shows a border of two-strand guilloche, parti-coloured squares and a lozenge, and may relate to the earlier discovery. For an arched passage, said to have been found in or about 1925, *see* Monument (227 c).

design, in black, white, red and grey ½ in. tesserae, was a panel 8 ft. square bordered with two-strand guilloche enclosing quadrants at the corners and containing an eight-pointed star formed by two intersecting squares, also of two-strand guilloche. The destroyed centre was almost certainly a circular medallion with quatrefoil, as in two late 4th-century mosaics, one of them almost identical in design, in ancillary buildings of the temple at Lydney (R. E. M. and T. V. Wheeler, *Lydney*

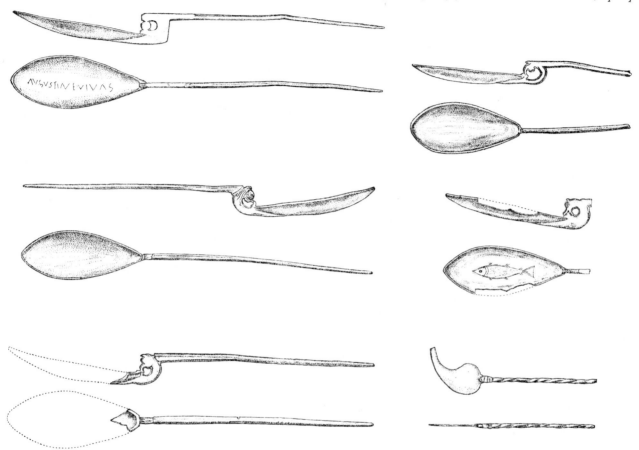

Dorchester (190). Silver spoons and ligula from Somerleigh Court. (½)

Part of another mosaic, of four (?) colours, probably belonging to a passage 7 ft. wide running E.-W., was found in 1967 about 30 ft. back from the building frontage (69169052). The lower walls appeared to have been plastered to simulate marble (information from R. N. R. Peers and C. J. Green).

(193) BUILDING, mosaic pavement only, found in 1905 about 40 ft. from Trinity Street nearly opposite the passage to Somerleigh Road, in building Tilley's Motor Salerooms, 45 South Street (69209053).

The whole pavement, including a surround of coarse grey tesserae varied with a narrow band or bands of red and with finer white tesserae on the inside, was some 14 ft. square. The

Park, Gloucestershire (1932), pl. xxi). Two coins of Constans (A.D. 333–50) were found on the pavement. Flooring in the porch of the D.C.M. was made up in 1908 of tesserae from this site; further parts of the surround were destroyed in 1912. (Moule MS., 48; photograph, and sketch plan by J. E. Acland, in D.C.M.) Remains seen in 1964 suggested that the building had continued to the S. (69219052; Dorset *Procs.* LXXXVIII (1966), 110–11).

(194) BUILDINGS with mosaic pavements have been found at various times between South Street and Trinity Street in the area formerly known as Cedar Park, and to the W. of Trinity Street. They may belong

to a large house W. of the street (179) running S. in the centre of the town.

(a) In foundation trenching in 1936 for Marks and Spencer's Store, 48 South Street (69199056), a limestone wall nearly 3 ft. wide was noted 17 ft. E. of the pavement of Trinity Street running N. to S. for over 45 ft. with a turn W. for over 11 ft. at the N. end. Close to its N.E. angle were traces apparently of a S.E. angle of another building, well faced in stone.

Other disconnected lengths of wall between the long wall and Trinity Street were associated with cement floors and apparently belonged to at least two periods. The long wall seems to have been associated with a concrete floor with a soling of mortared flints, at one point at least directly overlying an earlier cement floor containing a worn coin of A.D. 87. The earlier floor had a flint wall (I) underlying the long wall (II), and remains of another cement floor outside it. A tessellated pavement ignoring the earlier division overlay wall II and a debris layer beside it, and almost certainly belongs to a fragmentary floor of coarse tesserae at least 20 ft. long by at least 16 ft. wide running W. to E. from beneath the pavement of Trinity Street. No walls can be associated with it, but an unpublished plan shows a wide swastika pattern in red on white probably bordering rectangular panels to the S. Another fragmentary tessellated pavement, not placed but probably to the N., measured at least 18 ft. by 12 ft. with a simple red on white pattern of concentric rectangles. To the E. of wall II were traces of wall footings on a slightly different alignment, pits, an infant cremation in a jar of the 1st or 2nd century (215a), and a silver coin hoard (69209056), probably a 'bank' hoard, deposited in or soon after A.D. 257 (Plate 230). The hoard, of over 22,000 antoniniani and 16 denarii, including so many die identities as to suggest that the money had not been in normal circulation, was contained in a bronze jug, a plain bronze bowl, and a box or keg, apparently cylindrical with bronze-bound staves of yew wood; records suggest that the latter was about 10 ins. in diameter and 8 ins. high. The jug (Fig. p. 565), doubtless of foreign workmanship, had three blister feet, soldered but now detached; the handle, decorated with a conventional vine branch, is attached to the rim by duck's head arms and to the body by a soldering plate with mask of Silenus. His eyes and those of the ducks are inlaid with silver; so also are the band of his coronet and the volute centres and 'grapes' of the stem. The blister feet are unusual but the jug is of Wheeler's type B1 or B2 probably of the 1st century or early 2nd century (London Museum Catalogue no. 3, *London in Roman Times* (1930), 114). The objects are in D.C.M.; the coin hoard was broken up for sale after retention of collections by the British Museum, D.C.M., and Portland Museum. (MS. plans and section drawings of the site in D.C.M.; *J.R.S.* XXVII (1937), 243; *Num. Chron.* XIX (1939), 21–61.)

(b) A fragment of a coarse mosaic pavement was found in 1895 against the S. wall of Cedar Park on a site E. of (a), now covered by the same store (69219055). The remains running approximately N. to S. measured 8 ft. by 5 ft. with a red lattice pattern on a grey background within a border of four alternating red and grey bands. The piece was relaid in D.C.M., without the outermost band. (Moule, 37–8; Moule MS., 3;

D.C.C., 21st Feb. 1895, 9; *Southern Times*, 23rd Feb. 1895; photograph, Dorset Album I, part i, f. 14, in D.C.M.)

(c) A fragment of mosaic pavement with a similar pattern to (b), and probably part of the same floor, was found in 1898 on a site to the S., now occupied by Woolworth's Store, 47 South Street (*D.C.C.*, 12th May 1898, 4; Dorset *Procs.* LXXXIII (1961), 90). A length of 'subway' running parallel with the road was also seen (Moule, 28; *see* Monuments (195) and (227c)).

(d) A piece of coarse tessellated pavement in red and white, of which about 7 ft. were said to have been taken up, was found in 1932 on the site of the Plaza Cinema, 32 Trinity Street, continuing under the latter (69179057). This is nearly opposite (a) and probably part of the same building. (*D.C.C.*, 12th May 1932.) Part of the same or another pavement in red and white was noted by C. D. Drew on 20th Sept. 1932 (MS. note in D.C.M.).

(e) A damaged mosaic pavement was found in *c.* 1725 in Mr. Templeman's garden occupying the later Cedar Park and perhaps an equivalent area to the N., between South Street and Trinity Street. The pavement may originally have measured about 14 ft. by 12 ft. The design within a plain border was a swastika pattern on a white ground enclosing at least six panels 2 ft. square, in echelon, containing rosettes with at one end a band of lozenges. (Hutchins II, 394, (fig.) 692; *Notes and Queries* XVII (1921–3), 112, 147.)

(195) BUILDING, mosaic pavement only, found in December 1899 on the site of the Devon and Cornwall Bank (now National Provincial), 50 South Street (69239061).

Large fragments remained of a neat floor apparently with a white surround and a border, of which a specimen is framed in D.C.M., of superior two-strand guilloche of circular twists ending, probably at each corner, in a panel 2 ft. square enclosing a rosette. Colours used were black, white, red, brown, and grey (mostly Purbeck marble judging from the specimen). *The Builder* refers to a photograph (untraced) and states that there was 'an octagon centre panel with a circular centre'. A length of 'subway' (*see* Monument (227 c)) was found several feet beneath the floor. (Moule, 28, 38; Moule MS., 3; *The Builder* LXXVII (1899), 602.) It is uncertain whether the remains were E. or W. of the Roman street (179). A length of N. to S. walling, with remains of a floor to the W., was seen under the pavement outside the bank in *c.* 1964 (information from Mr. C. J. Green).

(196) BUILDING REMAINS, walls, floors, etc., observed during 1963–5 in trenches dug in the N. end of South Street (Cornhill) and behind premises on the W. side.

Three trenches in gardens S.W. of Lloyds Bank, 2 High West Street (69229069, 69239070, 69239069), exposed a flint-gravelled floor or floors some 2½ ft. below surface, laid on chalk rubble overlying a brown loam, probably of natural origin, on the surface of the Chalk. This gravel may have been continuous with similar flooring noted 30 yds. to the N.E. in Cornhill S. of the Town Pump (69269070). Gravel was also found under the pavement outside the Midland Bank (69259069); a lead-worker's hearth was found some 10 ft. to S. Late Roman pottery was recovered from the surface of these gravel exposures, and in 1955 sherds perhaps as early as the mid 1st century A.D. had been found in the top of the underlying

Dorchester (194a). Bronze jug found with coin hoard. (½)

loam at one point (Lloyds, 69239070). Sherds of the mid 1st century were found on similar loam N.E. of the Town Pump (69269071). Remains of walls conforming with the street grid, some of them perhaps substantial, were seen in the exposures in Cornhill. The observer suggests a gravelled area spreading some 125 ft. E.-W., representing the site of the Forum. (Information from Mr. C. J. Green.)

(197) BUILDING DEBRIS, probably of a hypocaust, found in c. 1865 at the old Grammar School, South Street (about 69279046). Two masses of tiles mortared together were noted (Moule, 44; cf. J.B.A.A. XII (1865), 25). A bronze statuette of Mercury, in the D.C.M., was found here in 1747 (Hutchins II, 394).

Substantial remains of wall plaster found in 1963 some 40 yds. to the N.E. (69289050) included imitation marbling of black and white flecks on a red ground and a curved design in blue and red on a white ground, perhaps a medallion. Some showed impressions of reed bundles on the reverse. (Dorset Procs. LXXXVIII (1966), 112.)

(198) BUILDING, hypocaust and walls, excavated by A. L. Parke in 1955–6 in Greyhound Yard, E. of South Street (69309062).

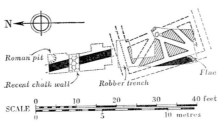

The W. part of a room was found, orientated N.N.W. to S.S.E. and measuring about 20 ft. by over 10 ft. Within it free-standing hypocaust piers of limestone and flints laid in herring-bone fashion, triangular in plan and some 3 ft. high, had supported a mosaic floor, totally destroyed, of dark grey, light grey and red tesserae, the red of tile and the greys probably derived from rocks of the Jurassic series of Gloucs. and Wilts. The plastered W. wall of the basement, 1¾ ft. thick, had a flue channel passing diagonally through it in the S.W. corner of the room, probably to an external stokehole. In the 4th century or later the floor had been destroyed and the channels filled with debris including clay roof-tiles and wall plaster, applied to bundles of reeds instead of laths, with traces of panel designs on a white ground in black, brown, green, red and pink. A poorly built flint wall 2 ft. thick, running N. for at least 16 ft. on a slightly different alignment, may not have been contemporary. (MS. report by A. L. Parke in D.C.M.; R.C.H.M. records; Dorset Procs. LXXVIII (1956), 79; LXXIX (1957), 116.)

(199) BUILDING, tessellated pavement only, exposed in c. 1875 in digging foundations for the Wesleyan Methodist Chapel at the junction of Durngate Street and South Street (69269064). Large light grey tesserae were set in a mortar bed 2 ins. thick; a small fragment is in D.C.M. (Moule, 18; Moule MS., 1.)

(200) BUILDING REMAINS found in 1883 during sewer excavations near the centre of Durngate Street opposite the former entrance to Wollaston House (69389066). A deposit of 'chalk and broken brick', perhaps a secondary floor, separated by some 3 ins. of soil from a floor of 'rubble stone in mortar', was bounded on E. and W. by walls respectively 1¾ ft. and 2¼ ft. thick and 18 ft. apart. The W. wall retained three courses of tiles on stone footings 3½ ft. high. (Cunnington MS., 101–3; Moule, 38; section drawing in D.C.M.) Partial exposures in 1964–5 also revealed the N. wall and established the alignment of the building as some 345°, as well as revealing a spread of gravel for at least 94 ft. E., and some pre-Flavian pottery. A fragment of N. to S. walling of clay roof-tiles set and faced in pink concrete was observed some 25 yds. to the W. at the junction with Acland Road (69359066); signs of a wall running N.E. to S.W. was also seen 80 yds. to the S. on the W. side of Acland Road (69369058; information on all recent exposures from Mr. C. J. Green, mostly since published in Dorset Procs. LXXXVIII (1966), 112; LXXXIX (1967), 127–32).

(201) BUILDING, mosaic pavement only, noted in 1898 at a depth of 7 ft. or 8 ft. during the building of All Saints' Church House at the junction of Durngate Street and Icen Way, was thought to run under the street (69459067). The fragment, given to D.C.M. but untraced, had a guilloche design in black, two shades of grey, and white. (Moule, 38; Moule MS., 3–4; D.C.C., 24th Mar. 1898, 4; Dorset Procs. XIX (1898), liv; letter from Moule, 19th Mar. 1898, in Haverfield Library, Ashmolean Museum.)

(202) BUILDING, mosaic pavement only, found in 1905 3½ ft. below surface during erection of a school attached to the Primitive Methodist Chapel (now the Salvation Army Hall), Durngate Street (69539068; Plate 223). It was relaid in the D.C.M.

The pavement, measuring 21 ft. by 12½ ft., was aligned N.N.W. to S.S.E. reaching the present footpath to the N. The design, within a narrow surround of coarse red tesserae, was a square between rectangular panels to N. and S. In the square a two-strand guilloche border enclosed a circle, also of two-strand guilloche, with a cantharus in each spandrel. Within the circle an eight-pointed star formed of two interlaced squares of two-strand guilloche enclosed a central roundel consisting of a four-petalled flower framed in fret and three-strand guilloche. From two of the canthari emerged two crested snakes; from a third two sprays of foliage; the fourth, empty, had two leaves springing from the base. The rectangular panel at the S. end was a broad swastika pattern bordered with three-strand guilloche; the N. panel had a wreath border around a narrower swastika pattern enclosing two small panels, one of two-strand guilloche, the other of knots. The materials used were black, dark and light grey limestone (including Purbeck marble), red tile and white chalk. The design has been compared by D. J. Smith with pavements of the 'Durnovarian school' of the 4th century. (Moule MS., 8; D.C.C., 6th July 1905, 4; Dorset Procs. XXVII (1906), 239, 246–7; D. J. Smith, 'Three Fourth-Century Schools of Mosaic in Roman Britain', La Mosaïque Gréco-Romaine, Colloques Internationaux du Centre National de la Recherche Scientifique, Paris (1963), 104.)

(203) BUILDING, mosaic pavement only, found in 1902 in the

Gasworks E. of Icen Way, formerly Bell Street (69559058). The design included a guilloche pattern. A few red, white and grey tesserae remain in D.C.M. In *c.* 1896 a floor of mortar or concrete, possibly belonging to the same building, had been found in constructing the large gasholder (69579060) adjoining Salisbury Walk (Moule MS., 4–5; *The Antiquary*, XXXVIII (1902), 108; letter from Moule, 26th Feb. 1902, in Haverfield Library, Ashmolean Museum). A bronze key of military type from the former site is described in *Arch. J.*, CXV (1958), 79. Signs of two N. to S. walls, with a floor to the W. of the E. wall, were noted in 1965 N.W. of the Gasworks on opposite sides of IcenWay (69469064, 69489063; Dorset *Procs.* LXXXVIII (1966), 112–3).

(204) BUILDING REMAINS, mosaic pavements and floors, exposed before *c.* 1908 in and near All Saints' Road, were at a higher level than the foregoing remains to the N. and may have belonged to a single house.

(a) A rectangular mosaic 20 ft. by 10 ft., with an attached tessellated corridor to the N.E., was revealed in 1897 and 1901 when All Saints' Road was made (69559052). The pavement, lying N.W. to S.E. across the road at the junction with Icen Way, was a red and light grey chessboard pattern of coarse tesserae with a blue-grey surround. The corridor, with a floor some 3 ft. wide of light grey tesserae apparently varied with a band or bands of red along the sides, ran from the N.E. angle of the mosaic for some 60 ft. alongside the N. pavement of the road. A lump of the corridor floor is in D.C.M., but most of the mosaic tesserae were relaid in the High School, Dorchester, Massachusetts, and a few made up into a pattern in the porch of All Saints' Rectory. (Plan, Dorset Album I, part ii, f. 14, in D.C.M.; Moule, 37; Moule MS., 4–5; *D.C.C.*, 14th May 1903; Dorset *Procs.* XXIV (1903), xliii.)

(b) A square mosaic of small black, red and white tesserae was in use *c.* 1850 as a kitchen floor in a cottage on the site of 18 Icen Way (69539054). Scattered tesserae were found in the adjoining gardens. (Moule, 36–7; Moule MS., 4; W. Barnes, *Guide to Dorchester* (1864?), 5.)

(c) A floor, probably of mosaic, was found and reburied or destroyed *c.* 1908 when 'Hambledon' and 'Ranston' were built on the N. side of All Saints' Road (69559054; MS. note by R. G. Bartelot in Moule, 37, in D.C.M. library).

(d) A wall of mortared flints running approximately E. to W. was seen in 1963 crossing an electricity-cable trench dug in the W. pavement of Icen Way N. of Culliford House (69589048; information from Mr. C. J. Green).

(205) BUILDING REMAINS, consisting of a wall, gully and well, excavated in 1947–8 in the S.E. corner of Wollaston Field (69479055).

A wall of dressed limestone blocks 2 ft. thick and 3½ ft. high, based on the natural Chalk and running E.N.E. to W.S.W., may have been the S. end wall of a building ruined or destroyed in the 4th century; 5 ft. to the N., a 6 ft. wide clay-lined gully, probably a water conduit, was presumed to be a secondary feature. The side of a circular shaft, probably a well some 6 ft. in diameter, was noted 24 ft. S. of the wall at the base of a flat-bottomed emplacement some 9 ft. deep in the Chalk. A stack of poorly mortared clay roofing-tiles, still 3¾ ft. high, revetted one side of the emplacement, which may have

accommodated a pump or winding gear. The filling contained debris, including a piece of wall plaster with the graffito MOLIRI, suggesting disuse some time after *c.* A.D. 125. A street (*see* Monument 175) was found 16 ft. S. of the shaft, and 2 ft. S. of this were fragmentary wall footings. Debris suggested that in the 4th century the area was waste or gardens. (Dorset *Procs.* LXX (1948), 61–2; (graffito) *J.R.S.* XXXIX (1949), 115.)

(206) BUILDING REMAINS, tessellated pavements and a wall, observed in 1937 at the Handicrafts Shop, 34A High West Street, and under the street (68979068).

Remains of a coarse tessellated pavement 1¼ ft. below surface, with a cement foundation 8 ins. thick, were traced for 16 ft. N. of the E. shop front. The section drawing is not clear, but apparently 3 ft. S. of the front, a small fragment of another floor lay 1 ft. deeper, probably connecting with a thin chalk floor directly underlying the cement foundation of the upper floor. The tesserae of the lower floor appear to have sunk 4 ins. over the filling of a ditch or pit some 9 ft. wide. In the top of this filling, it would seem some 5½ ft. S. of the shop front, wall footings 1½ ft. wide were probably associated with the lower tessellated floor, if not with both. A chalk and earth floor covering the wall footings and the adjacent area to the S., with a post-hole cut in it, was the latest feature in the sequence. The tesserae of both floors appear to have been of light grey limestone. (Field notebook, in D.C.M.; Dorset *Procs.* LIX (1937), xxx; V. L. Oliver MS., 15, in D.C.M.; *Salisbury Times*, 19 Mar. 1937).

A wall was seen before 1895 during pipe-laying in High West Street at its junction with Trinity Street (69169072). The foundations ran diagonally or at right angles across the road. (Moule MS., 11; Dorset *Procs.* XVI (1895), 153.)

(207) BUILDING REMAINS, including fragments of tessellated pavements and perhaps a hypocaust, in the area of Glyde Path Road.

(a) A small piece of mosaic in six colours and part of a red tessellated floor or border were found in 1957 behind 37 Glyde Path Road (69099076). The former, about 2½ ft. long on more extensive remains of its cement bedding, seems to have belonged to a floor with a series of circular medallions, about 2 ft. in diameter, closely set in echelon. Of two medallions surviving in part, on a white ground, one, probably in an octagonal frame, contained a wreath, the other a heart-shaped leaf within a fret border. The tesserae were of red brick, white and blue chalk, brown oolitic limestone probably from Portland, yellow Dolomitic limestone and black Liassic (?) marl, both probably from the Jurassic belt. Traces of an E. wall 2 ft. thick, of flints, aligned slightly W. of N., showed that the room had been more than 17 ft. wide. Against the E. face of the wall, which had red plaster and a convex moulding at the base, a strip of red tessellated pavement 9 ft. by 2 ft. may have belonged to a plain floor or a mosaic border. A well, 5 ft. in diameter, lined with unmortared flint and limestone, lying within a room to the N., was presumably not contemporary and may be post-Roman. The fragment of mosaic is in the D.C.M. (R.C.H.M. records; Dorset *Procs.* LXXXI (1959), 97–9.)

(b) A pit 18 ft. deep was found in 1937 on the site of the Clinic about 30 yds. W. of (a) (69069077). The filling, mostly of mixed building debris, included a fragment of tessellated floor, loose tesserae and coloured wall plaster (Colliton Park site notebook III, 7, in D.C.M.).

(c) Clay tiles were found and a hypocaust was suspected in about 1882 at the stables behind Stratton Manor, now the Agricultural Hall, High West Street, about 30 yds. N.N.E. of (a) (69109079; note by Moule in MS. catalogue in D.C.M.).

(208) BUILDING, with tessellated pavements, between Glyde Path Road and H.M. Prison to the E.

(a) Remains first found c. 1830 were excavated in 1880 by B. A. Hogg in a garden E. of Colliton Park (69109088). Foundations 1½ ft. thick and about 2 ft. high indicated a range of buildings 16 ft. wide and over 43 ft. long aligned E.N.E. to W.S.W. A cross wall at the E. end formed a small room of 16 ft. by 7½ ft. A wall continued the approximate line of the E. wall to the S., separated from it by a gap 2¼ ft. wide. Red-painted wall plaster was also noted. A strip of coarse floor 6¾ ft. wide, possibly a corridor on the same alignment as the building, was traced from a point 11 yds. E. of the latter for 13 ft. to out-houses formerly existing against the garden wall of H.M. Prison (69129088). It was composed of five alternate bands of red and white tesserae. A well 2½ ft. in diameter 3 ft. N. of the building was apparently Roman. (D.C.C., 7th Oct. 1880, 3; Archaeological Review IV (1889), 298; Moule, 33; Moule MS., 1, 24; plan by B. A. Hogg in Dorset Album II, 35, in D.C.M.) Substantial remains of this floor and other pavements were observed in 1966 in exploratory excavation prior to building (information from Miss E. Watkins).

(b) Another E. to W. tessellated corridor of simple pattern was exposed c. 1809 'in digging the foundation for a garden wall belonging to the New Gaol', W. of the main prison wall near (a) and probably part of the same building (about 69139088). The mosaic, 4½ ft. wide and over 10 ft. long, was of 'blue' tesserae on a white ground arranged in a series of double rectangles (i.e. one within the other) enclosed, alternately singly and in pairs, within a third rectangle, the whole set between two plain parallel bands. (Archaeologia XVII (1814), 330–1; MS. plan by the Rev. Thomas Rackett, Society of Antiquaries of London, red portfolio.)

The following remains were found in the precincts of H.M. Prison. In addition, a worn as of Domitian of A.D. 87 (in D.C.M.) was found in 1885 in a cavity between two stones cemented together with 'remains of parchment' (Moule, 24); a terracotta antefix was found in the prison grounds in 1890 (see above p. 538).

(209) BUILDINGS with mosaic pavements in the E. part of the Prison area.

(a) In 1841 part of a mosaic, a lozenge pattern in rather large red, 'blue' and white tesserae, was seen in the burial ground near the S.E. corner of the prison (69229085), some 20 yds. from another portion seen some years previously. These were probably the 'other two pavements . . . extending into the neighbouring garden on the South of the Castle Yard', mentioned in D.C.C., 23rd Sept. 1858.

In 1858, following the disclosure of another mosaic in the graves of Martha Brown (1856) and James Seal (1858),

Governor J. V. D. Lawrance excavated the N. end of what was probably a range of rooms running N.E. to S.W., with wall footings 1½ ft. or more in width, against the E. side of which had been added a structure, probably a yard, and two stone-lined pits. The orientation of these remains is established, but their position on the plan (opp. p. 584) is approximate. Three rooms floored with mosaics were exposed. The two at the N., each about 20 ft. square, had a central connecting doorway with step. The mosaic in the W. room of this pair, which had been found in Seal's grave and was damaged in one corner by earlier burials, had a coarse surround striped in white, red and grey, which was left in situ and marked by a stone which now stands at the S.W. corner of the burial ground. The decorated portion (Plate 224), 10½ ft. square, of ¾ in. tesserae in black, grey, red and white, consisted of an elaborate border of chevron, coloured bands, fret, and vari-coloured chequers, enclosing a central panel, 4¾ ft. square. This, framed in thin black lines with triangles in the corners, contained a similarly-framed 8-pointed star formed of two intersecting squares, enclosing an octagonal space layered in the four colours around a central circular medallion with chevron border. In the medallion were placed two outwardly-pointing hearts or heart-shaped leaves, one on a grey, the other on a white ground. The decorated portion, originally in the Prison Chapel, was removed to the D.C.M. in 1885 after further damage. The foundation of this pavement was 2 ft. thick of alternate layers of flints and mortar.

The fragmentary mosaic of the E. room, on a foundation, 3 ft. thick, of mortared flints, was thought to have been of circular medallions bordered with two-strand guilloche; a portion removed to the Chapel is untraced. Lawrance's plan suggests that the N. side of this room was altered to form an apse. The room to the S., 38 ft. wide by at least 17 ft., had traces of a mosaic with a two-strand guilloche border, of which a piece is in the D.C.M., and a plain circular centre of 'stone-coloured' tesserae.

Painted wall plaster included fragments of pale green with a maroon border and, from the S. room, red, bordered with black, and white, edged with black and red. Hexagonal stone roof-slabs and a coin of Constantine I (A.D. 306–337) came from the floor of the W. room.

The structure to the E. was apparently added when the W. range was in use since an entrance 3½ ft. wide was left clear between the two. Walls some 2½ ft. to 3½ ft. thick enclosed what seems to have been a yard 19 ft. square open to the N., with, at its centre, a stone-lined pit with rounded corners, 4¾ ft. square and 5 ft. deep. To the W. another pit, roughly but more substantially stone-lined, 6½ ft. square and 9 ft. deep, cut into the N.E. corner of the earlier E. room. Both pits contained domestic refuse, but their original function is obscure. A length of wall 3 ft. to the N. ran approximately parallel with these remains, overlying a square chalk-cut pit containing 4th-century pottery of New Forest type. (J. V. D. Lawrance, MS. account and plan in D.C.M., cf. Hutchins II, 394–6, and Arch. J. XVI (1859), 82, 183–6, which contains some errors; D.C.C., 7th Jan. 1841, 4; 12th Aug. 1858, 23; 23rd Sept. 1858, 144; 30th Sept. 1858, 163; 21st Oct. 1858, 223; 3rd Feb. 1859, 523–4; Moule, 32–3; carbon photograph of mosaic by J. Pouncy, in D.C.M.)

(b) Remains of a mosaic with a two-strand guilloche border

in red, black and white were found in 1854 in building the former Lodge and prison workshops W. of the entrance from North Square (69259083). A length of the border is in the D.C.M. (*D.C.C.*, 17th Aug. 1854, 20; 23rd Sept. 1858, 144.)

(c) An inferior tessellated floor was found in 1856 in building the N. block of warders' houses on Friary Hill (69289088; *D.C.C.*, 23rd Sept. 1858, 144; note by J. V. D. Lawrance, in D.C.M.).

EXTRA-MURAL SETTLEMENT

Two buildings, with elaborate mosaic pavements probably of the 4th century, have been found outside the walled area. One of them (210), close to the E. defences, probably indicates ribbon development alongside the main road outside the E. gate; the other (212) at Olga Road, some 400 yds. from the S.W. angle of the Roman town, was probably the headquarters of a villa estate.

Other discoveries outside the walled area may indicate settlement. In addition to Monuments (211), (213) and (214), the first suggesting ribbon development on the road to Radipole harbour, occupation debris has been recorded on all sides save in the low-lying meadows to the N. At the Depot Barracks (687907) late Roman sherds and a key now in D.C.M. were found in 1936, and, before 1884, two pottery candlestick bases, also in D.C.M. A pit 'near Queen's Avenue' (685898) yielded animal bones, coarse ware and pieces of roofing and flue-tile, in D.C.M. A concrete floor was reported between Bridport Road and Damers Road (Moule MS., 8); another with coins of Constantine I and II was reported on South or Castle Farm (680890; Moule, 39; R. G. Bartelot, *History of Fordington* (1915), 25 *n*.). An octagonal roof-tile and crop-marks (observed from the ground) of a building on Middle Farm (675901) could also be Roman (information from the late O. C. Vidler).[1] An occupation deposit containing a brooch of *Aucissa* type (in D.C.M.) was found N. of the Grammar School in 1939 (69728989; Dorset *Procs.* LXXI (1949), 64); on Conygar Hill, half a mile to S., a coarse ware sherd and piece of flue-tile were found in topsoil of a barrow (69798893) opened by E. Cunnington in 1880 (Round Barrows, Dorchester (169); Cunnington MS., 139). At Wareham House (702900) there were signs of occupation that need not have been directly associated with the cemetery but are described thereunder (218a,b). Similarly, building remains or debris beyond what might be expected in a cemetery were found at St. George's, Fordington (216d). In 1746 'foundations of buildings' thought to be a hypocaust, with thick fragments of glass and flue-tiles, some of the

latter burnt, were discovered on the S. side of the Roman road (*see* Approach Road 1) in making the new London road 'a very little E. of Segar's orchard' (69609080; Hutchins II, 375, 797; letter from George Vertue, *Minutes of Soc. Antiquaries*, V, 128).

(210) BUILDING, mosaic pavement only, found in 1903 and uncovered in 1927, 3 to 4 ft. below the footpath and Foundry Yard between Nos. 12 and 14 on the S. side of High Street, Fordington (69589073; Frontispiece and Plate 225). It would have been within 50 yds. of the Roman town wall to W.

The pavement, relaid in D.C.M., was mainly of tesserae $\frac{1}{2}$ in. or less, some being as fine as $\frac{1}{8}$ in., and was of eight colours; dark and light red, dark and light yellow, blue, grey, black and white. It consisted of an approximately rectangular floor over 15 ft. or 16 ft. long by 15 ft. 7 ins. wide, on an axis some 12° W. of true N., leading into a horseshoe-shaped apse to S., 13 ft. 7 ins. wide by 10 ft. 6 ins. deep. The whole pavement had a white surround, continuous but varied in width, of $\frac{1}{2}$-in. tesserae, bordered with coarse red tesserae probably covered by the wall plaster.

The rectangular pattern consisted of a square panel with a narrow oblong panel at the N. balancing a similar but wider panel in the entrance to the apse. The square was divided by 2-strand guilloche borders into nine octagonal panels containing circular medallions with central rosettes, except for the central medallion, which had borne an individual design, possibly figured, within an octagonal frame; this had been damaged or defaced, probably in antiquity. Four pairs of border and rosette motifs, each pair similar save for minor variations in colour, were used for the eight circular medallions; a consistent sequence of arrangement is apparent if viewed diagonally from N.W. to S.E. or *vice versa*. The borders were of banded circle, wreath, and 2-strand and 3-strand guilloche pattern. The spaces between the octagonal panels were filled appropriately with square and triangular motifs, varied by single *peltae* in the end triangles.

The oblong panel at the N. end consisted of a row of twelve conventional ivy leaves in ovals united by chevrons; the S. oblong panel, at the chord of the apse, had running scrolls issuing from the base of a central *cantharus* and bearing pomegranates and ivy leaves, with stylized trumpet-shaped flowers between the spirals.

The main design of the apse was contained in a triple bordered lunette, struck off as arcs from three different centres and using the same three cabled motifs employed in the medallion borders of the square floor. It consisted of an exceptionally finely executed head of Oceanus as if emerging from the sea, flanked by two dolphins and two fish (Plate 225); the god's hair and beard were of sea-weed, while two tendrils springing from the crown of his head have been likened to the legs or claws of a sea creature. A comparison with the Neptune mosaic at Frampton (*Dorset* I, 150) has suggested that the floor was a work of the 'Durnovarian school' (*cf.* (202)).

The tesserae had been bedded in $1\frac{1}{2}$ ins. of fine mortar on a foundation of 9 to 12 ins. of heavy mortared flints, with a

---

[1] For crop-marks, probably Romano-British, extending E. for $\frac{3}{8}$ mile from 670895, 600 yds. N. of Maiden Castle, *see* p. 493 and Fig. p. 494. The site yields Roman tile and sherds (Oct. 1968).

L

bottoming of smaller rammed flints. Two sherds of samian ware, believed to be of the 1st century, were recovered from the foundation, but the pavement is now regarded as of 4th-century date like the apsidal pavement at Bignor, Sussex. The walls of the room had been robbed to below floor level but appeared to have been of flints and oolitic limestone probably from near Weymouth; the tesserae included examples of Purbeck marble, Portland stone, red and brown tile, and some made from samian sherds. Debris on the pavement included flints and fragments of clay roof-tiles but was said to consist mainly of wall and ceiling plaster of which Pompeian red was the dominant colour, with designs in dark red, yellow, blue, green, black and white. The upper walls and ceiling were thought to have been plastered largely in white. Some objects are in D.C.M. (Dorset *Procs.* XLIX (1928), 89–100; *Ant. J.* VIII (1928), 237–8; *J.R.S.* XVII (1927), 207.)

A plain tessellated pavement was said to have been found under the Foundry opposite (*c.* 69589074; information from the late O. C. Vidler).

(211) BUILDING(s), mortar floor and perhaps tessellated pavement only, at the corner of the fair ground, now Cattle Market, adjoining 'The Elms', Weymouth Avenue (*c.* 69129024).

'A well-made Roman mortar floor' was seen by E. Cunnington in or before 1878, and an enamelled bronze military belt plate (in D.C.M.) and pottery were found. (Dorset *Procs.* II (1878), 109–11; *Arch. J.* CXV (1958), 79; G. Webster and D. R. Dudley, *The Roman Conquest of Britain* (1965), 108, pl. 28; Cunnington MS., 103, in D.C.M.)

A small portion of a 'coloured tessellated pavement' was seen *c.* 1935 in a trench dug in the Market (information from Mr. P. J. Dear).

(212) BUILDING, mosaic pavements only, found in 1899 at a depth of about 2 ft. at the rear of No. 21 (formerly 9) Olga Road, some 400 yds. from the S.W. corner of the Roman town (68709010; Plate 223). Its situation suggests that it was a villa rather than a town house.

The floors, excavated by the owner and subsequently relaid in D.C.M. without most of the coarse border, indicate three intercommunicating rooms on an axis of about 5° E. of N., apparently some 26 ft. wide (Moule), and considerably over 40 ft. long overall. No information was recorded as to the outer walls; the two partition walls appear to have been robbed to below floor level. Each room, with long axis E. to W., had a plain surround of coarse red brick tesserae, interspersed with a few of grey stone, arranged so as to preserve an uninterrupted patterned surface from room to room. The colours used for the patterns, in ½-in. cubes, were red, black, white, brown-grey and blue-grey.

The central and presumably largest room, probably 26 ft. by 18 ft. internally, had a rectangular pattern measuring some 17 ft. by 12½ ft., with a small rectangle attached centrally to both N. and S. sides interrupting the coarse surround and continuing into the thresholds of both adjoining rooms. The large rectangle had a wide border of swastikas varied by contained panels of 2-strand guilloche or lozenges set with leaves placed

base to base. An inner border of 3-strand guilloche surrounded a rectangle divided into a large central square flanked on both E. and W. by a pair of smaller squares separated by a narrow panel of leaves branching from an undulating stem. The N.W. and S.E. squares contained endless knots, the other two an 8-petalled rosette in a square bordered with 2-strand guilloche. The large central square contained an octagon, bordered with 3-strand guilloche, enclosing a 16-petalled rosette with a single knot at centre. The spaces around the octagon held leaf and spiral *pelta* motifs.

The two rectangular panels in the N. and S. sides of this room each measured some 7½ ft. by 5 ft.; continuing into the thresholds, they linked the three rooms, which were presumably divided, if at all, only by hangings. The designs, both bordered with 3-strand guilloche, were variations of a single theme—an inwardly facing *cantharus* between oblong panels divided into right-angled triangles in black and white; the northern vessel was within a plain rectangle, the southern in a circle contained within a square with triangular fillings in the spandrels.

The floor of the N. room, damaged in the centre, but apparently roughly patched with flagstones, had a pattern of some 14½ ft. by 8 ft., with coarse surround on the three outer sides. A 2-strand guilloche border probably enclosed two squares separated by a narrow band of some kind and each bordered with a band composed of lozenges between isosceles triangles with inwardly projecting apices. The squares each contained a rosette within a double circle with twin leaf and campanula (?) motifs in the spandrels.

Little remained of the floor of the S. room, of which the central design was some 9 ft. square, again with coarse surround on three sides. Borders of chevrons and 2-strand guilloche seem to have contained a central guilloche-framed medallion. Twin leaves, similar to those in the lozenges of the central room, appear between the circle and the guilloche border to the S. (Somerset and Dorset *Notes and Queries* VII (1899), 47–9, 192; *The Builder* LXXVII (1899), 484–5, reproducing most of the drawing, in D.C.M., made *in situ* by Messrs. Jennings and Goater; Moule, 40–2; Dorset *Procs.* XXI (1900), 162; XXII (1901), xxviii–ix; *The Antiquary* XXXV (1899), 289, 364; photographs by W. Pouncy, in D.C.M.)

According to a letter from Moule, 23rd Oct. 1899, in the Haverfield Library, Ashmolean Museum, excavation for foundations on all sides except S., showed no signs of floors; buildings were suspected further S., and a wall was found some 200 to 300 yds. in that direction. *See*, however, Monument (213); for adjacent burials, *see* (221).

(213) BUILDING, tessellated pavement only, found in 1899 in making Dagmar Road (68709020).

The site is marked on Moule's plan, and he states it was struck on both sides of the roadway; this would be less than 100 yds. N. of (212) and may belong to the same establishment. (Moule MS., in D.C.M.)

(214) BUILDING(s), partly excavated in 1966–7 outside the N. end of the E. rampart of Poundbury Camp (*see* Hill-forts, Dorchester (172)).

Three supposed sections of wall, 20 yds. apart and indicated by robber-trenches some 2 ft. wide, suggest a complex of buildings of approximately E. to W. alignment, roofed in stone and lying close to the outer ditch of the Iron Age defences, here filled in Roman times with spoil obtained from levelling and digging the aqueduct (227a). The southerly exposure (68499113) was the W. end of a building some 10 ft. wide internally and seemingly already ruined when an inhumation burial was laid E. to W. within it. Chips of Ham Hill stone on the natural Chalk floor, some with chisel marks, and one piece probably from a sarcophagus lid, suggest that this building was either a workshop or a mausoleum. Of the other two exposures, of straight E. to W. lengths of robber-trench, one 20 yds. to N.W. (68489114) was probably robbed after c. A.D. 350; the excavator found evidence suggesting that the small bronze bowl and votive axe-head found in 1943 (Dorset *Procs.* LXXIV (1952), 98–9) was a foundation deposit below this wall rather than a burial deposit. The third exposure, 20 yds. E.N.E. of the first (68499115), had apparently been cut by a grave containing a Ham Hill stone sarcophagus. *See also* Burials (225g). (Information from Mr. C. J. Green, who has since published some details of these and further finds suggesting timber structures, in Dorset *Procs.* LXXXVIII (1966), 110; LXXXIX (1967), 133–5.)

Previously, Moule had recorded (i) a loose fragment of mosaic of fine white ¼ in. cubes (in D.C.M.) found by a bather below Poundbury, and a coin of Faustina II, also from the river; (ii) a crop-mark some 100 yds. S.E. of the barrow (170), seen after an exceptional drought and thought to show a building of some 20 ft. by 12 ft. (c. 68249105). Scattered finds of 4th-century pottery in the ditches and interior in the excavations of 1939 suggested 'some sort of activity in or near Poundbury' at that date, and a coin hoard (in D.C.M.) consisting of mid 4th-century official issues and their copies was concealed in or not long after A.D. 353 in the W. inner ditch (68089120; Plan, p. 488). (Moule, 39, 42; *Ant. J.* xx (1940), 431, 434, 445–6; *Num. Chron.* 6th ser. XI (1952), 87–95.)

BURIALS

Roman cemeteries have been found on all sides of the town except the N. and N.E. The law applicable to Roman chartered towns and evidently adopted by others of lesser status, that burials should be outside the urban perimeter, seems to have been punctiliously observed save for a few of young children (215), but the normal grouping along the approach roads is perhaps not so marked here. No known burials can be associated with the main road to London crossing marshy ground from its exit from the E. gate. Burials to the S.E. (216–218), beginning with what seems to have been numerically the largest cemetery, on Fordington Hill, are strung out further than usual and are the only tangible evidence for a road in that direction, perhaps also issuing from the E. gate, towards Wareham and the Isle of Purbeck. To the S.W., groups of burials (219–220) flanked the road to the harbour at Radipole at least as far as the amphitheatre. Sporadically recorded graves (222–224), including perhaps some considerable groups, range from the area of the W. gate mainly to N. of the main

road to Exeter (*Isca Dumnoniorum*). Some of these could as well be referred to the N.W. road to Ilchester (*Lendiniae* (?)) if the route S. of Poundbury Camp to the well-attested road beyond Stratton is accepted. An otherwise strangely situated cemetery (226) at the foot of The Grove, near the river, is consistent with I. D. Margary's supposition of continued use of a pre-Roman trackway from the N.[1]

Records before the present century provide little information as to posture and orientation. At Fordington Hill (216a), orientation N. to S. was said to be the rule amongst some 200 graves found in 1747; juxtaposition, in the form of the letter 'T' was, somewhat improbably, claimed between earlier burials lying N.E. to S.W. and later burials N.W. to S.E., amongst some fifty found in 1838–9 (216c). Otherwise a comparative consistency in major cemeteries is recognizable only in those near Weymouth Avenue (220) and Poundbury (225). Of forty-nine Dorchester burials for which more adequate information is available, thirty-eight were approximately E. to W. and eleven approximately N. to S. Of those lying E. to W., five out of six had heads to W.;[2] of those lying N. to S. the proportion was about equal. With posture we are on surer ground. Extended burial, supine, was normal, but instances are frequent of burial on the side with legs more or less flexed; this mode of interment may be suspected in some records of 'sitting' or 'upright' posture in connection with burials of the period in the borough of Dorchester and elsewhere.[3]

The Chalk subsoil evidently dispensed with the need for slab-lined graves, although at least two such cists have been recorded here (220f; 224h), while the burial richest in grave-goods (216c) was under a corbelled stone cairn; stone sarcophagi, uninscribed and ostensibly without grave-goods, and nearly all of Ham Hill stone, are known in Dorchester only at the Poundbury cemetery (225), where there is some evidence that they were made or more probably finished. Wooden coffins were often used and there are three instances of a lead coffin or lining (one decorated?), again at Poundbury. Most bodies, however, seem to have been interred in shallow graves without protection other than, perhaps, a shroud or other vestments, of which indications were preserved in the gypsum or plaster moulds formed round two bodies in stone sarcophagi at Poundbury (225e, g), and probably also in a child's burial at Colliton Park (215d) and in the arrangement of brooches on the brow of skeletons at Thomas Hardy's house, Max Gate (218d). The six known 'gypsum' burials are the only

---

[1] *Roman Roads in Britain* (2nd edn., 1967), 111.
[2] The disproportion results largely from discoveries at Poundbury since 1964.
[3] *See* (216b; 220a, b; 224i); *cf.* J. F. S. Stone, *W.A.M.* XLV (1932), 572, 575.

instances in the region of a practice commonly revealed amongst the richer of the Roman burials at York (R.C.H.M., *Eburacum* (1962), 79 etc.) and occasionally in cemeteries elsewhere, as at London. 'Gypsum' burials do not seem to be reliably attested before the late 3rd century. The tombstone of Carinus at Fordington Hill (216d) is otherwise the clearest testimony to a burial in other than native style, unless the horseman sculpture (Whitcombe, Monument (26), Plate 228) is in fact sepulchral and referable ultimately to *Durnovaria* rather than to the site of its discovery.

The rarity of cremation, more striking in the highly romanized cantonal capital than it would be elsewhere, also points to regional conservatism in burial custom, although it is true that inhumation already had respectable adherents in the Roman world before the 1st century A.D. The region appears to have had little or no tradition of sumptuous burial in the Iron Age, and a corollary may well be the comparative poverty of the graves of the Roman period, although the horse-bit at Fordington Hill (Plate 230), and perhaps an iron collar at Northernhay (226a), which has not survived, faintly echo the panoply of wealthier or more Belgicized regions. Hobnails at the feet occasionally indicate the wearing of stout boots; a shale spindle-whorl may occasionally show the domestic occupation of the spinster or housewife; finery, where it is to be found, is confined in the main to bronze or shale bangles, necklets of twisted wire, brooches, pins, or a bone comb. Weapons seem only to have occurred in graves of which we owe our knowledge to the scanty reports of the earlier antiquaries, and there is nothing else that might hint at the employment of Teutonic warriors before or after the cessation of Imperial rule in the early 5th century.

The vessels chosen to accompany the dead are nearly always of black-burnished coarse pottery rather than of fine table ware, the lead-glazed jar from Icen Way (Plate 228; Fig. p. 576, *no. 6*) being a notable exception, and are often nothing more than cooking-pots. The Iron Age forms and fabric so frequently found amongst them reflect the conservative tradition of potting in the Roman canton of the Durotriges even into the 3rd century, and should not be regarded as consciously archaic in the sense that objects of ritual or sepulchral association have sometimes seemed to be. It is clear, however, that most graves furnished with vessels, and perhaps with other grave-goods, are to be assigned to the 1st and 2nd centuries; those of later date must have been more often unaccompanied, at least by imperishables. The occurrence of similarly unaccompanied Durotrigian graves in certainly early contexts, as at Maiden Castle (p. 501), however, does not permit an un-qualified correlation here between an observed increase of inhumation without grave-goods and the spread of Christianity. On the other hand, the incidence at Poundbury of burials consistently, it would seem, aligned E.-W. with feet to E., in a cemetery as remarkable for the almost total absence of recorded grave-goods as for the comparative wealth displayed in the provision of containers for the bodies of the departed, prompts the question whether this cemetery was partly or wholly Christian. The stone sarcophagi and lead coffins are widely distributed in the area at present known to have been occupied by graves.

In the following account, separate monument numbers are given to each major group of burials without necessarily implying individuality as cemeteries; sub-divisions (a, b, etc.) are based on topographical sequence where this is apparent or are in order of discovery. References as (1846.2.15) are to the Dorset County Museum collection; vessels illustrated on pp. 576, 577, 579, are indicated by numbers in italics (*nos. 1–44*). Unless otherwise stated the pottery vessels described are of black or grey coarse ware sometimes discoloured brown by oxidization in firing; the term Durotrigian applied to pottery indicates types of vessel of Iron Age 'B' or 'C' origin unromanized in form or fabric, and the class numbers are those suggested by J. W. Brailsford in *P.P.S.* XXIV (1958).

(215) WITHIN THE DEFENCES

(a) Cremation of infant found in 1936 in a jar of the later 1st or 2nd century (Fig. p. 576, *no. 1*; 1936.50), in a pit 7 ft. N. of the 3rd-century coin-hoard near Roman building (194 a) at 48 South Street (69209056; plan by C. D. Drew, in D.C.M.).

(b) Inhumations, two, of infants in shallow graves cut into the floor of the N. room of the 4th-century building, Trinity Street (191). Both had legs slightly flexed; one lay E. to W. (head E.), the other N. to S. (head S.). They were contemporary with the occupation of the room. (Dorset *Procs.* LXI (1939), 50, fig. 3; full typescript report and site notebook in D.C.M.)

(c) Inhumations, five, of infants mostly in shallow holes in the floors of building (182), Colliton Park (Fig. p. 556). One was under the eaves of the N. wall of room 15, an extension dated after *c.* 341; one was in room 3, two in room 5, and one in room 6, of the service wing; they are therefore all of the 4th century. No objects were found other than bird bones with the infant in room 3, and a sherd of amphora with one in room 5. (Dorset *Procs.* LIX (1937), 11–12; site notebook I, in D.C.M.)

(d) Inhumation of a child of about 5 years, extended N. to S. (head S., facing E.) in a grave carefully cut in the Chalk, with remains of a wooden coffin, about 30 yds. S.E. of building (182), Colliton Park (68999093). It had apparently been wrapped in a shroud done up with bronze pins, of which several were found, mainly on the chest; on the left wrist was a cord or hair bangle. Parallel with the grave and adjoining its W. side, a shallow elongated pit contained a bronze ring, an iron blade, a fragment of glass, and animal bones. (Objects in D.C.M., untraced, Colliton Park 1622c–1629c; site notebook IV, 12.)

(e) Inhumation of an infant under the W. partition wall of building (185), Colliton Park (Fig. p. 560). The body, contracted on its left side, lay E. to W. (head), and was evidently in the doorway, so burial need not have been earlier than the 3rd or 4th-century occupation; a black-burnished jar (1937.70) with lattice decoration not earlier than c. 250 was near by. (Dorset Procs. LX (1938), 58.)

(f) Two probable cremations found in 1856 at a depth of 2 ft. in laying sewers in Colliton Street near the Unitarian Chapel, later Holles Hall (69189081). The County Chronicle records two oval urns of black ware in the possession of Mr. Gould, 'one large and one small, the larger containing the remains of bones. The contents of the smaller are supposed to be the ashes of a heart'. (D.C.C., 6 Nov. 1856, 265; Gentleman's Magazine (1856), pt. ii, 755.)

(216) FORDINGTON HILL

(a) Inhumations found in 1747 near the Manor Pound, now occupied by the Moule Institute (69799063). Over 200 burials lay 4 to 5 ft. below surface, mostly orientated N. to S. with 'some inclined E. and W.'; one is said to have had a sword blade over 2½ ft. long by the side. They were reburied on the site and in St. George's churchyard. (Hutchins II, 793.)

(b) Several inhumations found in 1788 in demolishing cottages W. of the Pound included one 'in a sitting posture, another as if thrown in neck and heels tied together, also a sword, and one or two different weapons beside, all now lost'. (Hutchins II, 793.)

(c) Inhumations, and perhaps two cremations, found in 1838–9 in lowering 200 yds. of Fordington High Street between the former Pound (69799063) and a point some 75 yds. W. of the junction with Holloway Road. Over 50 complete skeletons of adults and children were noted in the Chalk, at depths of a few inches to six feet, in the winter relief work sponsored by the Rev. H. Moule, vicar of Fordington; several were examined by him. A number of accounts exist, all of which differ in particulars; the principal authorities are the antiquary John Sydenham (1839), H. Moule (1846), C. Roach Smith (1854, derived from H. Moule), and H. J. Moule (1901, 2nd edn. 1906), curator of the museum from 1881, who was to some extent associated with his father in the work. H. Moule's account of the principal finds, for which he was responsible, is to be preferred.

The cremations consisted of an urn containing burnt human bones, and fragments of another said to show evidence of similar use. About 30 of the inhumations were judged from nails with adherent wood (some in D.C.M.) to have been enclosed in wooden coffins; about half the graves were said by Sydenham to have been orientated N.E. to S.W., the rest, at a higher level, N.W. to S.E., the heads 'placed indifferently'. Two lay face downwards. Finds without particular association included sherds of brown, red and black ware, with one probably of New Forest ware; hob-nails, with several burials; a heap of small beach pebbles between the legs of another; an iron knife; an armlet of twisted bronze wires (1846.2.26); a bronze buckle on the breast of a skeleton, with traces of leather; a coin of Postumus (A.D. 259–68; 1846.2.27). The only other coin, an issue of A.D. 317–20 of Constantine I (1846.2.25), was from the mouth of a male skeleton by the roadside close to the garden door of the former Vicarage (69749063). Three female skeletons were examined by H. Moule on the other side of the road opposite the Vicarage. The first, with head to N. and nails indicating a wooden coffin, had a necklace of which there survive one annular bead of amber, six brown or blue glass beads (onion-shaped, biconical, or roughly made from a wound coil), and about eleven links mostly of flat bronze wire, as well as a fragment of transversely moulded bronze tube, presumably from the clasp; also a notched shale armlet and plain shale spindle-whorl, both turned (Plate 230; 1846.2.12, 23–4). On either side of the skull were a globular black jar and a red flask (Fig. p. 576, nos. 2–3; 1846.2.10–11).

The second female was under a corbelled stone cairn according to Sydenham. She wore a necklace of which 168 unlinked beads were recovered, six of amber, one of stone or chalk, two of bone, and the rest of glass; under the skull were seven pins of dark blue and pale green glass with tapered or swelling shanks, some headless or otherwise imperfect (Plate 230; 1846.2.15–22). There is no evidence as to the precise function or arrangement of these pins, of which the largest was 71 mm. (2⅝ ins.) long. The arrangement of the necklace is wholly conjectural. The most distinctive beads are the amber pendant, the cushion-shaped blue bead of polished and bevelled glass adjoining, and five segmented glass beads of pearly appearance probably due to decomposition. Most are biconical (57) or globular (55), with a fair number (19) of irregularly shaped, transversely laminated beads made from wound coils of glass; the remaining 22 glass beads are annular, tubular, onion-shaped, oblong, or roughly square. The colours are brown, dark blue, light blue, green and 'pearl'; two of the blue beads are opaque. The third female possessed a plain shale armlet and a grooved shale spindle-whorl, both turned (Plate 230; 1846.2. 13–14); the spindle-whorl is neater and more nearly spherical than that described above.

Sydenham's account mainly differs in divorcing the glass pins from the necklace, in transposing the spindle-whorls (in which he is supported by the County Chronicle and perhaps by William Barnes), and in assigning the globular jar to a fourth burial where it was allegedly associated with another vessel. There need be no doubt, however, that two if not all three female burials were approximately contemporary, in virtue of their apparently close grouping and the unusual character, regionally, of the principal ornaments. Their date depends upon the pottery, of which the flask, wheel-thrown but of extremely poor brick-like ware with no trace of slip-coating, cannot be dated at all closely within the Roman period. The globular vessel, while not indisputably associated with the group, belongs to a local class of jar of which a very large example, of storage-jar proportions, was in use in the 4th-century house (182) at Colliton Park. It is not yet known, however, when the class was first developed. There is no sound evidence to attribute to the site any other vessels (e.g. 1902.1.42) preserved in D.C.M. (D.C.C., 27 Dec. 1838, 4; 28 Mar. 1839, 4; Gentleman's Magazine (1839), pt. i, 114 (Barnes), 196, 528–31

(Sydenham[1]); H. Moule, *Scraps of Sacred Verse* (1846), 40–1; C. R. Smith, *Collectanea Antiqua* III (1854), 33–4; H. J. Moule, *Dorchester Antiquities* (2nd edn., 1906), 46–8, 57–8, 62–3, 70; Hutchins II, 793–5.)

(d) Inhumations, a burial of a horse with an undecorated two-link snaffle-bit of later Iron Age type, and an inscribed tombstone, found in 1840 and 1907–8 at the parish church of St. George, Fordington, about 100 yds. S.E. of (c). The remains of the horse were found under the old N. wall of the church in making the Harvey family vault N. of the W. end of the chancel (69859056). The bit, taken from the mouth, is of two iron links plated with bronze, engaging bronze cheek-rings, and was apparently accompanied by two small bronze rings of unequal size (Plate 230; 1846.2.9,8,10); the type is the south-western or two-link variety of bit occurring relatively late in the Iron Age, but might indicate a pre-Roman chariot-burial on the hill. (*Gentleman's Magazine* (1841), pt. i, 81–2; Hutchins II, 795; Moule, 46, 72; R. G. Bartelot, *History of Fordington* (1915), 71.)

In renovations in 1907–8 'a human skull and horse bones' were found built into the base of a S. pier of the nave; the front wall of the porch was found to be built over graves, and 'several very old graves' were found lying N. to S. in the Chalk near the old N. wall of the church. The latter at least, from their orientation, are likely to have been pre-Christian. In underpinning the porch, 'British' pottery, flints, and a large quantity of animal bones, some worked and many burnt, were found; in lowering the nave, the westernmost Norman pillar was found to rest on what was described by Bartelot as the base of a Roman column. Many Roman bricks, clay and stone roof-tiles, painted plaster, coins, buckles, glass, samian ware, etc., were also found, of which a few relics survive in the vicar's possession.

In the same work the major part of an inscribed tombstone of Purbeck marble (Plate 226) was found face downwards serving as a foundation of the S.E. corner of the extended porch. It is 2 ft. 11 ins. by 2 ft. 4½ ins., and at least 5 ins. thick but now cemented to a backing in the church. The inscription, of the 1st or more probably the 2nd century A.D., has lettering decreasing in size from top to bottom by rather more than ¼ in. per line:

[D M . . . . . .]
CARINO
CIVI · [R]OM
ANN L
RVFINVS · ET
[C]ARINA · ET
AVITA · FILI · EIVS
E [T · R]OMANA · VXOR
[F C]

[*D(is*) *M*(*anibus*) . . . . . .]/*Carino*/*civi* [*R*]*om*(*ano*)/*ann*(*orum*) L/ *Rufinus et*/ [*C*]*arina et*/ *Avita fili eius*/ *e*[*t R*]*omana uxor*/ [*f*(*aciendum*) *c*(*uraverunt*)]

'To the spirits of the departed: for . . Carinus, Roman citizen,

aged 50; Rufinus and Carina and Avita, his children, and Romana, his wife, had this set up.'[1]

Another stone, untraced, of similar size and presumably also of Purbeck marble, is said to have been secured, 'on which from exposure the writing has entirely perished'. It was thought to contain the rest of the inscription, but the latter is so nearly complete that if the second stone was inscribed it must have belonged to another. (Bartelot, *op. cit.*, 20–1, 71–2; Dorset *Procs.* XXIX (1908), xl–xli and plate; XXX (1909), 166–7 and plan; *Ephemeris Epigraphica* IX (1913), no. 983; Somerset and Dorset *Notes and Queries* XVIII (1926), 31–3 and plate; R. G. Collingwood and R. P. Wright, *The Roman Inscriptions of Britain* I (1965), no. 188.)

(e) Inhumations and cremations found in 1810, probably at the W. corner of Fordington Green. According to Robert Bryer, the burials were found in excavating an area 92 ft. by 43 ft. in the N.W. slope to a depth of up to 13 ft., prior to building in a garden belonging to William Bower 'about 50 yards East from the corner of the Walk, called the Walls'. Bartelot is probably right in identifying the site with the new brewhouse and cellar, now the Old Court House cellar adjoining Greenhill House (69759053), although this is some 100 yds. E. of the Walk. 'Certainly not less than an hundred' skeletons lay in different directions, interred 'from four feet to nearly the depth opened'. The closeness of interment in the Chalk, and absence of nails and traces of wood, were held to indicate burial without coffins, but the record of several metal rings of 2 in. diameter suggests ring-bolts like those from Poundbury (225e); 'small iron knobs like nail-heads' were probably hob-nails. The only coin found, on the sternum of a skeleton, was a 'second brass' of Hadrian (A.D. 117–38) apparently wrapped in a perishable substance. Many vessels were broken by treasure-hunters, but about 70 were preserved by Bower, of which a few were given to Bryer. Drawings accompanying Bryer's letter to Taylor Coombe are untraced, and the only extant vessel from the site is a black ware bowl of the 1st century probably derived from samian or Belgic platters (*no. 4*; 1902.1.41, Hall collection), although other vessels from the Hall collection supposedly marked 1839 and 1840 (*sic*) could have come from here and from (c) (Dorset *Procs.* XXXV (1914), li). Bryer describes them as urns and *paterae* (dishes) of red, reddish-brown and black earthenware, with lattice, diagonal or wavy lines, and also refers to what appear to have been large, handled flasks. The smaller urns were generally at the heads of the skeletons. 'Many' larger urns, one of them covered with a black *patera* full of charcoal, contained sifted human bones or burnt bones and charcoal, and some were surrounded with ash—more positive evidence of a substantial element of cremation burial than appears elsewhere. The remains were reburied in a cask in an adjoining garden. (*Minutes* of the Society of Antiquaries, 24 Feb. 1814,

---

[1] Contribution signed J. S.; W. Bonser, *A Romano-British Bibliography* (1964), 199, wrongly ascribes the initials to James Savage (*cf.* Hutchins, *loc. cit.*).

[1] Professor S. S. Frere, in consultation with Professor E. B. Birley, has commented on the apparent lack of room for the *praenomen* and *nomen* of a Roman citizen following the formula D.M., and prefers the reading CIVI DOM once proposed as an alternative by Haverfield (*Eph. Epig.*). In Professor Birley's view the use of the dative case for the name of the deceased can hardly be expected before *c.* A.D. 150, and the 1st-century date hitherto proposed on stylistic grounds has been qualified accordingly. *See also* p. 534 *n*.

CARINO
CIVI·ROM
ANNL
RVFINVS·ET
CARINA·ET
AVITA·FILI·EIVS
ET·ROMANA·VXOR

PLATE 226

DORCHESTER. (216d) Tombstone of Carinus, in Fordington church. One quarter full size.

Note: The surface of the stone is such that neither rubbing nor photograph would show the inscription satisfactorily, but both have been used in preparing the drawing here reproduced. Surviving incisions, however slight, are shown naturalistically as V-cuts; the convention of plain white is used for incisions eroded or lost. An alternative reading CIVI · DOM has been proposed for the second line.

letter to Taylor Coombe, Director; *Archaeologia* XVIII (1817), 421–4; Hutchins II, 793; R. G. Bartelot, *History of Fordington* (1915), 27–9.)

(f) Inhumation, one or more, found in 1894 in Salisbury Field (c. 69659060), at least 90 yds. W. of (c). A black ware jar 8 ins. high of 1st or early 2nd-century type, with diagonally tooled body decoration, and a saucer or lid of a smaller vessel (*no. 5*; 1894.5.2), were found, it was believed, with human bones. The jar (1894.5.1) is untraced but sketched in D.C.M. card index. (Moule, 46–7; Moule MS., 22.)

(217) ICEN WAY

(a) Inhumations found in 1886 on the N.E. side of Icen Way, S.E. of Gallows Hill. It appears from B. A. Hogg's annotated sketch that the burials, 'in various postures', were found in the 1880s (the last digit is omitted) in the bottom of a wide trench in the Chalk, in digging cellars of new houses above Icen Cottage; evidently the semi-detached pair 'Devon Lodge' and 'Calder' (69719040) approved by the Borough Surveyor in 1886. A blue-glazed 'melon' bead and about 30 hob-nails (1886.9.136) from Icen Way, given by Hogg, are probably from the site, as are also two black ware vessels—a 4th-century bowl with flanged rim, of Gillam's type 228,[1] and a cooking-pot, undecorated but similar to *no. 41* from Victoria Park (1886.9.5 and 49; Hogg collection). The most notable object is an olive-green lead-glazed jar of the 1st or early 2nd century with seven irregularly spaced groups of repoussé bosses; the sandy body is dark grey to brown in fracture (*no. 6*; Plate 228; 1886.9.19, Hogg collection). Further discoveries, probably in the houses at the foot of Duke's Avenue, are indicated by the coffin angle-iron found in Gallows Hill in 1895 'with an amphora and other Roman relics', and a fractured, healed femur (in D.C.M.) from a Roman grave, both given by A. Groves. (Dorset Album II, f. 44A, in D.C.M.; Moule, 51, 56, 85–6.)

(b) Inhumations, two in one grave, found in the early 1930s in making a sunken rockery (69699033) on the S.W. side of Icen Way. The skeletons, of individuals said to be girls about 7 and 12 years old, were extended side by side E. to W. (heads E.). Nails with adherent wood at 7 in. intervals on either side indicated wooden coffins, and one burial had a small dark grey bowl of the 3rd century (*no. 7*) and three grotesque flint nodules. The remains were reburied *in situ* under a mound in the rockery. (Information from the finder, O. C. Vidler, who kept the objects.)

(218) ALINGTON AVENUE

(a) Inhumations, and other remains found N.E. of the Wareham road (Alington Avenue) in 1846 and 1884 in making and widening the S.W. Railway cutting (c. 702901). Of many human bones and much black pottery from the work in 1846, two bowls of Durotrigian class 1, given by the Rev. H. Moule, survive (*nos. 8–9*; 1846.2.6–7). Some of the discoveries of 1846 came from a trench or ditch 7 ft. to 8 ft. deep containing much pottery, animal bones and some human teeth; this feature, running apparently N.W. to S.E., was seen again in 1884 in both faces of the widened cutting, and later at Ware-

ham House to E. (b). The discoveries of 1884 included several 'remarkable circular pits' (Hogg), filled with chalk, 4 ft. in diameter and 5 ft. deep with concave base. One had a levelled floor of baked clay perforated with $\frac{3}{8}$ in. holes, and in the centre a storage-jar of Durotrigian class 12, burnt inside, with its base on a flat stone marked round with soot (*no. 10*; 1886.9.65). Some of these details are suggestive of a pottery-kiln. There were said to be no other traces of fire in these pits, although H. J. Moule claimed 'a slight indication of smoke' on the upper part of this one. Another, according to Hogg, had a 'clay heater' 10 ins. by $5\frac{1}{4}$ ins. 'with a hole on each side for drawing it out of the fire'. A 1st-century segmental strip brooch of Collingwood's Group K and part of a bronze tubular bracelet filled with composition (1886.9.180–1) also came from a pit, according to Moule. Hogg mentioned a nearby grave 'containing a skeleton and three specimens of well finished grey-black ware' given to the Museum with the 'heater' and a piece of the perforated floor (untraced); these vessels are doubtless his hemispherical bowl (*no. 11*) similar to *no. 4* from Fordington Green, the globular Durotrigian bowl, (*no. 12*), and probably the incomplete bowl (*no. 13*) with cordoned shoulder, perhaps derived from a 'Hengistbury Class B' type of Hawkes' 'South-western Third B' culture (1886.9.4, 1884.10.6, 1886.9.28, Hogg collection). A fourth jar from the same collection (*no. 14*; 1884.10.7), of Durotrigian class 4, may not be from this cemetery. None of the remains from the railway cutting need be later than the end of the 1st century. (Moule, 45–6, 82; B. A. Hogg, MS. note in D.C.M.; Moule MS., 22; *D.C.C.*, 21 May 1846, 4; 28 May 1846, 4; Dorset *Procs.* XXI (1908), 108.)

(b) Inhumations, nine or more, and other remains, found in the garden of Wareham House immediately to S. of (a) in 1892 (702900). At least six burials were found, closely fitted into graves cut 2 ft. or so into the Chalk, in clearing an area 40 ft. by 10 ft. for cucumber frames, evidently near the railway cutting. All 'faced the N.E.' and seemed to have been arranged systematically, three in particular being 'in line'; two were on their sides, the rest extended. The ages of two were estimated as 26 and 60. An iron nail and knife blade (in D.C.M.) were 'embedded in the left arm of one'; the knife was between radius and ulna according to the old label. Further burials found in planting apple trees included one unique in 'facing south', one of a young person with a double-sided bone comb probably of the 4th century, and a third with two ear-rings of silver wire and four beads of blue, green and yellow glass near the neck; the yellow bead was threaded on an ear-ring (1888.1.2–6). Several pits were found, some filled with a black material like charcoal. One, 'elliptical', 2 ft. wide and 4 ft. deep, perhaps for rubbish, contained animal bones including dog, and many minute shells of carnivorous snails; another was filled with red earth and contained an antler pick (in D.C.M.). Sherds (1938.10) in the topsoil included samian ware, but none of the burials had vessels. The ditch found in the railway cutting (a) had earlier been encountered across the garden, cleared and refilled with chalk. (Dorset *Procs.* XIV (1893), xxxviii–ix, 105–7; XV (1894), xxiv; XXI (1900), 108; Moule MS., 22; Moule, 56; R. G. Bartelot, *History of Fordington* (1915), 29.)

(c) Inhumations, probably four in number, found in 1960 in

---

[1] *Arch. Ael.*, XXXV (1957).

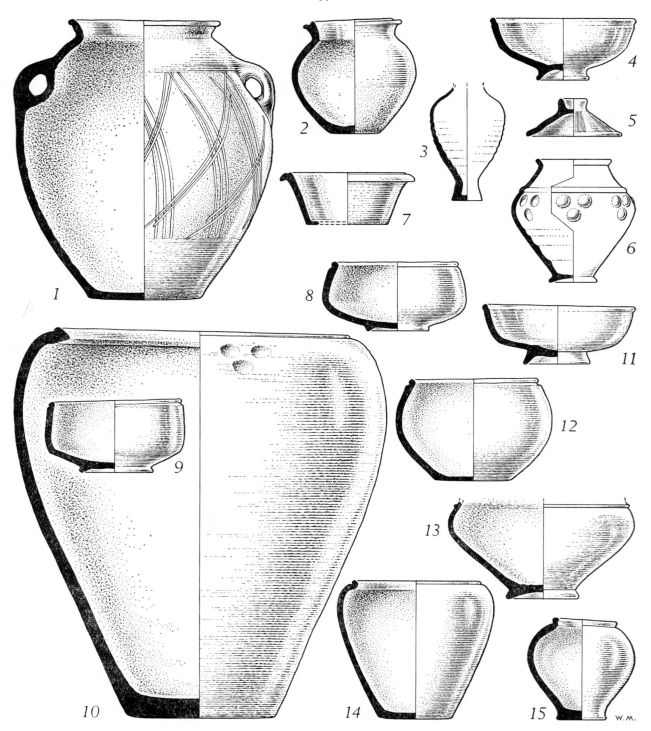

Dorchester. Pottery from burials: *No. 1*, (215a) Within the defences; *nos. 2–5*, (216c, e, f) Fordington Hill; *nos. 6, 7*, (217a, b) Icen Way; *nos. 8–15*, (218a, c) Alington Avenue. (¼)

trenching for water-mains about 50 yds. E. and S.E. of Wareham House. A burial of a powerfully built man extended E. to W. (head W. but tilted forwards towards the feet) was cut through some 44 yds. from the Wareham road (70308999). The grave of rounded cross-section cut into Chalk contained a few sherds of coarse pottery and samian but no apparent grave-goods. Human bones were seen at two places respectively 35 yds. and 53 yds. N.N.E. (70319002, 70329004); 6½ ft. beyond the latter, human bones, of which a broken mandible was preserved, were found near a small 1st-century jar of Durotrigian class 7 (no. 15; 1960.44). The jaw was of a

other had four vessels by the breast, also nearly upright but touching each other; two were of 'ordinary' size, two small. The burial less completely known to Hardy had 'two other urns of like description', and, it would seem, a second fibula. Two yards S. of these graves a circular pit, 2 ft. by 5 ft. deep, packed with flints, had a flagstone at bottom and above it an ox horn, with ox bones and teeth and pieces of bituminous matter. Some tile, Roman brick and glass were found in the area. Hardy's further discoveries, presumably also on the site of the house, are noted by Moule. Of many other skeletons, some were extended, some on their sides, with no consistent

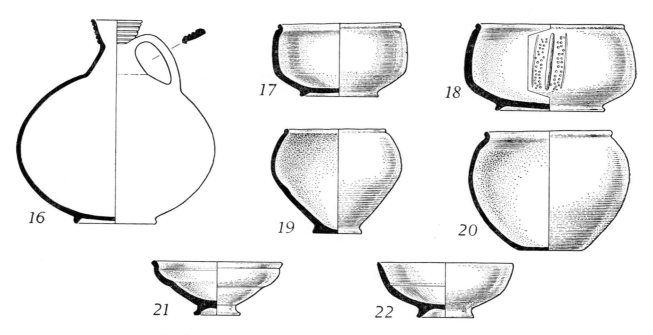

Dorchester. Pottery from burials. *Nos. 16–22*, (218d) Max Gate. (¼)

male aged at least 40 with parodontal disease (pyorrhoea). At least seven shallow depressions mostly saucer-shaped in section, apparently carrying across the 2 ft. wide trench, were also observed in the Chalk between the burials. (R.C.H.M. records; information from Mr. R. N. R. Peers and Mr. C. J. Bailey.) No remains were found when 'Loud's Piece' was built for C. D. Drew, between these burials and those at Max Gate about 170 yds. S.E. (information from C. D. Drew).

(d) Inhumations found in 1884 by Thomas Hardy, during building excavations for his house, Max Gate (70448991), about ⅓ mile S.E. of the Roman town. Of three burials apparently close together in 'elliptical' graves 4 ft. by 2½ ft., cut vertically in the Chalk, with heads W., E., and probably S.W., at least two were contracted on their right sides with hands touching the ankles. One of the latter had a bronze fibula (untraced) on the skull between forehead and crown, probably securing a shroud, a flask (no. 16; 1926.3.1) by the breast, and two similar black or 'grey ware' urns touching the shins, with a half only of another urn beside them. The

orientation. A large stone, 'set up at Max Gate as a menhir', covered one; from the brow of another Hardy took two bronze penannular brooches linked by an elaborately decorated bronze fibula of 'Maiden Castle' type with iron hinge-pin[1] (1936.9.4, a–c; Fig. p. 578). A large pit contained remains of a horse, much ash, and an iron spear-head (1936.1). (Dorset *Procs.* XI (1890), 78–81; Moule MS., 23; Moule, 46, 48, 75–6.)

The ring-neck flask of cream-coloured ware (no. 16) is comparable with Claudian examples from the Corfe Mullen kiln (Corfe Mullen (24)), but it may well have been prized for a generation or more before its consignment to the grave. Since the six black ware vessels preserved from the site are of early types not necessarily later than the 1st century A.D., it is of less consequence that none can be assigned to a particular burial. Three are bowls of Durotrigian classes 1 (no. 17), 1a (no. 18; 1936.9.3) and 2 (no. 19; 1936.9.2); one is a globular Durotrigian bowl (no. 20; 1936.9.1). The other two, which, like no. 17,

[1] It is dated by M. R. Hull as pre-Claudian to Neronian.

are without accession number and came to D.C.M. with other contents of Hardy's private study, are small bowls or lids of less common native types—one, unburnished inside, perhaps influenced by the samian form 27, the other by form 18 or Belgic platters (*nos. 21–2; cf.* also *nos. 4* and *11*). In D.C.M. are also an iron pruning hook and knife, and, from the garden of

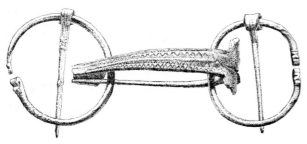

(218d) Brooches from burial, Max Gate. (¼)

Max Gate, some figured samian sherds of the late 1st to mid 2nd century and a sherd of late slip-coated ware (1936.1.11, 14–15, 17).

(e) Inhumations, five, found since 1951 in building the Came View Estate about 100 yds. E. of Max Gate. The known burials fall into two groups, near the N.W. and S.W. bends in Casterbridge Road. In the N.W. group, human remains were noted in 1951 in a pit 5 ft. deep behind the present No. 15 Casterbridge Road (*c.* 70608996); about 25 yds. N.N.W., a burial of a male aged 30–40 extended W.S.W. (head) to E.N.E. was cut through and partly salvaged in 1958 about 6 ft. N. of No. 17 (70608999).

In the S.W. group, a burial extended E.N.E. (head) to W.S.W. in a shallow grave 2 ft. wide cut in the Chalk was found in 1955 in a cable trench 51 ft. from the front of No. 26 Came View Road (70558986). The lower part of the skeleton was left *in situ* under the pavement at the bend in the road. The burial was of a female of 22–3 with one carious tooth among the 14 recovered; a 4th-century sherd probably came from the filling. Another burial in a similar grave, extended W.N.W. (head) to E.S.E., was found in 1957 about 30 yds. to N. in making the garage drive of No. 4 Casterbridge Road (70558988). The skull faced S. and the arms were folded over the chest; there were no grave-goods. A coin of Constantine I issued between 317 and 320 was found in the garden. The remains (1958.46) proved to be those of an elderly male of muscular build with general periarticular ossification of the fibrous tissues, possibly limiting movement of joints and certainly of the spine; there were signs of parodontal disease in both jaws, and a malpositioned healing of the fractured neck of the left femur. About 30 yds. E. of the last, a burial said to have been extended N. to S. was found in 1957 about the centre of No. 1 Casterbridge Road (70578988). The grave was in a trench or fissure 5 ft. wide and here at least 14 ft. deep, also said to have been seen at two points to W.S.W.—at No. 2 Casterbridge Road (70548987) and close to Syward Road (70498986)—and again to E.S.E. at No. 9 Came View Road (70658984) where a worn *sestertius* of Antoninus Pius (A.D. 138–61) was said to have been found in it. With the skeleton

(destroyed) were substantial parts of three Durotrigian vessels (1957.33) with fractures mostly fresh: a bowl of class 1 (*no. 23*) and a small example of class 2 (*cf. no. 19* from Max Gate), and a variant of class 2 with a true pedestal base (*no. 24*). Parts of a human mandible, of a male (?) aged between 25 and 30, were found a yard away. (Dorset *Procs.* LXXIII (1951), 100; LXXIV (1952), 85; LXXVII (1955), 133; LXXIX (1957), 116; LXXXI (1959), 107; R.C.H.M. records.)

(f) Inhumations of uncertain date, found *c.* 1925 in building one of five blocks of houses on the N. side of St. George's Road between Ackerman Road and Red Cow Dairy, about 300 yds. N. of Wareham House (*c.* 70219031). Of about three skeletons, one was on the back with knees drawn up, the others fragmentary. Some ancient sherds were noted in the soil. (Information from Mr. W. G. Lee, Director of the Dorchester Building Guild, 1951.)

(219) BEGGAR'S KNAP (GREAT WESTERN ROAD)

(a) Inhumations, and one child's cremation, found in the 1880s in building houses on Beggar's Knap or Nap along the S. side of Great Western Road. Hogg refers to an unstated number of burials found in 1881 'all in the chalk, of which the ramparts were formed, and the graves thus varied in depth from three to nine feet, according to their position on the vallum or the fosse'. The feet were invariably E., and the heads usually resting on a stone. Several urns and a *patera* were found with them, and also a child's cremation 'carefully placed in an urn, and covered by a well chiselled stone which measured two cubic feet'. Cunnington clearly refers to the same locality in recording three skeletons found in December 1881 in digging a cellar near Mentone Lodge (in the counterscarp of the ditch according to Moule), 'two feet under the original chalk, and five feet of the Roman vallum over that again'; two close together were with three pieces of black ware (in D.C.M., with a skull; one is a flanged rim of the 4th century). The cellar will be that of No. 5 or 6 Great Western Road (69069026).

Seven vessels from Beggar's Knap are in the Hogg collection in D.C.M. The *patera*, found with a bronze penannular brooch (old no. Br. 106, untraced), is a small dish probably of the mid 3rd century (*no. 25; 1886.9.144*). A cooking-pot with tooled lattice, of the 1st century or first half of the 2nd, was, according to Moule, with a handled mug of ordinary coarse ware (*nos. 26–7; 1886.9.47* and 8). The latter is a local imitation of a type common in the 2nd century, also represented here by a wheel-thrown example in hard orange-brown clay, apparently 'Glevum' ware[1] (*no. 28; 1886.9.11*). Three cooking-pots of rather weak profile, with essentially similar tooled lattice decoration, may reasonably be referred to the mid 2nd to mid 3rd century (*nos. 29–31; 1886.9.12–14*). Remains of at least three angle-irons, ½ in. wide, and two wider hooked fittings (in D.C.M.) indicate a coffined burial or burials. The cemetery seems to have been in use in the 2nd and 3rd centuries, and although the apparent position of the graves, or some of them, in the ditch or counterscarp bank of the rampart is anomalous, it is consistent with the dating of the latter not before *c.* A.D. 130 at earliest. (B. A. Hogg, MS. note in D.C.M.;

---

[1] *J.R.S.* XXXIII (1943), 15-16.

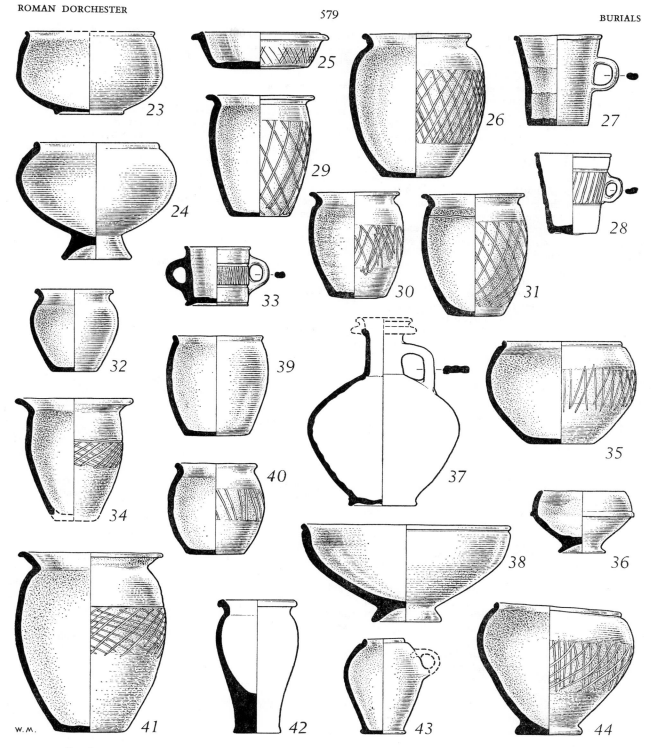

Dorchester. Pottery from burials: *Nos. 23–4*, (218e) Came View Estate; *nos. 25–31*, (219a) Beggar's Knap; *nos. 32–8*, (220c, e, f) Weymouth Avenue; *nos. 39–40*, (220h) Maumbury Rings; *no. 41*, (221) Victoria Park; *no. 42*, (222b) Borough Gardens; *no. 43*, (225b) Poundbury; *no. 44*, (226b) The Grove. ($\frac{1}{4}$)

Cunnington MS., 103–5, in D.C.M.; Moule MS., 22; Moule, 47, 86; Dorset *Procs.* XXI (1900), 73.)

(b) Inhumation, one or more, found in 1960 after the levelling of part of the garden in front of Mentone Lodge for traffic improvement. A skeleton (69148:90298),[1] without gravegoods unless they were beyond the head, lay N.E. to S.W. (head), at a depth of 2½ ft. in the filling of a ditch cut 10 ft. wide and 4 ft. deep in the Chalk and either adjoining or cutting through a gravel floor or metalling to S. (*see* Approach Road 2). The body, of a woman aged 20–30, had been buried or thrown in the ditch on its left side, legs flexed and forearms crossed, and the head appears to have been already dislocated so as to face S.W. instead of N.W. The ditch was probably filled between the mid 2nd century and the end of the 3rd century and must have been covered by the deposit interpreted below as a counterscarp bank. (R.C.H.M. records.)

A pit or grave (69140: 90294) noted by Miss M. Whitley at the angle in the new garden wall in front of Mentone Lodge was said by workmen to have held remains of two skeletons; it had been dug from upper levels into the loamy soil overlying the natural Chalk, possibly to be interpreted as remains of a counterscarp bank outside the town ditch. Other remains suggested a 'hurried burial' in a similar but shallower pit 10 ft. to W., and there was a skull in disturbed upper levels 12 ft. from the wall of Weymouth Avenue. (Information and section drawing from Miss M. Whitley; R.C.H.M. records; *see also* Defences, p. 549.)

(220) WEYMOUTH AVENUE

(a) Inhumation found *c.* 1930 in trenching for water-mains in the Cattle Market. The remains, with a pot, were at the E. edge of the concrete apron between the old Butter Shed and the N.E. exit to Weymouth Avenue (69099021; information from Mr. W. A. Dare, who believed that the body was buried sitting upright with the pot between the knees—*see also* (224, i)).

(b) Inhumations, five, found in 1859 when building the County Police Station (690900). The skeletons were said to be in a pit in an 'upright' position with three pottery vessels 'superimposed' on them. Two of the pots, said to be in D.C.M., had necks and one was cup-shaped; a handle was missing from one. (*D.C.C.*, 17 Mar. 1859, 643; 28 Apr. 1859, 763.)

(c) Inhumations, eight or more, one certainly recent, found in 1893 in building the existing S.W. precinct wall of the Police Station. Five steep-sided cuttings in the Chalk, evidently running approximately at right angles to the wall trench, were sketched by Miles Barnes at points measured from the railing of Weymouth Avenue (his A). The first cutting (B) had a narrow funnel of unknown depth in the bottom (69023: 89993); (c) was a 'probable interment' (69026: 89991); (D) had human bones with head N. (69047: 89978). Cutting (E) was the 10 ft. wide sunken way to Maumbury Rings, probably of 1642 (69050: 89977); *see* Monument (228). Cutting (F) contained a small Romano-British jar and mug (69053: 89975). At the S.E. corner of the precinct wall (69056: 89973), a recent pit (G) disturbed a grave (H) a few feet to N. with skeleton 6 ft. deep;

some 18 ft. N. of the corner a grave (J), containing a skeleton with 'rapier' or 'foil' laid upon it (of 18th century according to Moule), may have been aligned N. to S.;[1] at (K) where the 1893 work ended against the old S.E. corner of the precinct, three skeletons lay close together (69057: 89980). The two vessels at (F) (*nos. 32–3; 1893.2.2–3*) were accompanied by two coins and there were also coffin fittings (in D.C.M.) consisting of flat iron straps 1 in. wide with substantial rivets with heads 1 in. in diameter indicating coffin-boards ¾ in. thick, and a broken angle-iron, of Poundbury type (*see* Fig. p. 584), fixed at right angles to the grain of the timber. The coins (1893.2.5,4) are a provincial imitation *as* of Claudius (A.D. 41–54) and a much worn *sestertius* of Hadrian (117–38) implying a date in or after the mid 2nd century, with which the small jar and two-handled mug of grey ware are consistent. Barnes stated that more burials were found in widening the trench from the railing of Weymouth Avenue. A 4th-century jar from the Police Station (*no. 34; 1886.9.16*, Hogg collection) probably came from these works. (W. Miles Barnes, Dorset Album I, part ii, f. 27 b; Moule, 48–9, 85; Moule MS., 22; Dorset *Procs.* XXXIII (1912), xi.)

(d) A complete bowl of Durotrigian class I (1933.15.1; *cf. no. 23* from Came View Estate) was found in 1905 under the same precinct wall in a building extension, evidently that at about 70 ft. from the railing of Weymouth Avenue (69018: 89996); it was doubtless part of a burial deposit of the 1st or early 2nd century. (D.C.M. accessions book, Nov. 1933.)

(e) A globular Durotrigian jar and a cordoned cup (*nos. 35–6; 1946.10.1–2*) were found in 1939 on the site of the garage (69055: 89985), or perhaps the cycle sheds adjoining to N.W. (Information from C. D. Drew.)

(f) Inhumations, five, in chalk-cut graves, and remains of a burial group of vessels, found in 1952 in rebuilding work S.W. of the single men's quarters. Two, extended N.N.E. to S.S.W., parallel but not quite abreast with heads at opposite ends, were found in removing a passage (69036: 89999). Another a few feet to S. was in a partly covered stone cist similarly aligned, with head S. (69037: 89997). A fourth, already partly destroyed by the passage wall, lay approximately at right angles to the others, on its right side and perhaps with legs flexed, with head E.S.E. 1 ft. S.S.W. of the cist. The fifth, about 5 yds. to S.S.W. (69035: 89991), was extended E.N.E. to W.S.W. (head). Most of the bones were removed by workmen, but the cranium and mandible remained, with some teeth carious and some lost through parodontal disease. A detached humerus of a muscular male of at least middle age lay under the skull and presumably belonged to the same person; it was in contact above the wrist with a bronze brooch of Hull's 'applied hook' type of Flavian or earlier date; the pin was replaced in antiquity and the hook is missing. A second brooch, of pre-Flavian 'Polden Hill' type, with pierced catch-plate, was probably associated with it (*see* Fig. p. 581; 1952.27.1–2). About 30 ft. to E.S.E. (69043: 89987), substantial remains of a group of vessels, probably undamaged when discovered, point to another burial, probably of the late 1st or first half of the 2nd century. A red ware flask with creamy slip-coating and a

---

[1] For ten-figure map references, *see* p. 540 *n.*

[1] For burials of the 17th century (?) at Maumbury, *see* Dorset *Procs.* XXXI (1910), 252–3.

hemispherical Durotrigian bowl are illustrated (*nos. 37–8; 1952.28.1–2*); the other pieces were of a white rough-cast beaker with red slip and a Durotrigian jar or bowl with foot-ring, perhaps a small example of class 1 (Dorset *Procs.* LXXIV (1952), 97; LXXVII (1955), 132–3; R.C.H.M. records).

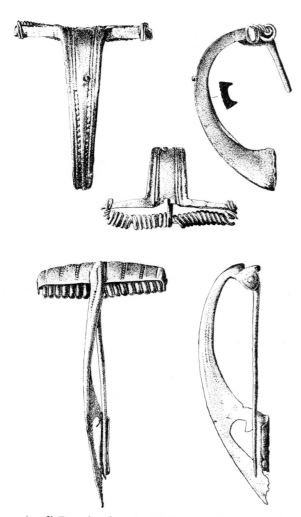

(220f) Brooches from burial, Weymouth Avenue. (¼)

(g) Inhumations, four or more extended in chalk-cut graves, found in 1955 and 1960 near the S.E. corner of the precinct, close to some of those found in 1893 (c). One, beside the kennels, lay N.N.E. to S.S.W., with head, 'raised', at the latter end, and arms crossed over the pelvis, in a coffin indicated by nails with traces of wood (69054 : 89980); the remains were of a robust male of about 5 ft. 5½ ins. aged between 40 and 50 (Dorset *Procs.* LXXVII (1955), 132). Three others lay N.N.E. (head) to S.S.W. about 3½ ft. below surface; two sets of foot bones with hob-nails, and long nails with adherent wood, found in a trench extending the line of the precinct wall (69058 :

89971), indicated parallel coffined burials 6 ft. apart (objects in D.C.M.). Of the third, 12 ft. to N.E. (69061 : 89975), few traces survived mechanical excavation. Two narrow cuttings in the Chalk, seen in the S. face of the trench that exposed the first two, may belong to graves; one adjoined the easterly skeleton, the other was 7 ft. further S.E. A substantial ditch, apparently running N. and perhaps 35 ft. wide but of unknown depth, was seen in the same trench, its centre (69073 : 89963) some 65 ft. S.E. of the former corner of the precinct. (Information from Mr. R. N. R. Peers.)

(h) Inhumations, three, found in 1910 and 1912 in the excavation of Maumbury Rings by H. St. George Gray. Two were in the chalk-cut passage descending to the Roman arena. The first, probably a female of about 4 ft. 7½ ins., lay N. to S. (head) in an irregular oval chalk-cut grave, against and at a slight angle to the W. wall of the passage (69037 : 89958); it is unknown whether silt had accumulated on the passage floor before interment. The skeleton was on the right side with legs flexed and arms bent. Part of a pig's jaw was behind the skull and there were two flint flakes; a provincial imitation *as* of Claudius (A.D. 41–54), in D.C.M., was found 3½ ft. to S., 2 ins. above the passage floor. The second, some 13 ft. to S.W., a powerful middle-aged male of about 5 ft. 7¼ ins., lay N.N.E. to S.S.W. (head) against and parallel with the W. chalk wall of the passage, but rested on about a foot of passage silt; the skeleton was on its left side with legs more tightly flexed than the last (69034 : 89956). Besides over 70 flint flakes in the grave, remains of a small jar (*no. 39; 1908.29.19*) were near the right hand; a tooled lattice pattern claimed by Gray cannot be distinguished, but the vessel is probably of the 2nd century A.D., comparable with an example found in a grave at Portland with a samian dish (form 18) of Secundus (*see* Portland, Monument (99)). The burial, evidently later than the cutting of the passage, affords the only direct evidence for the date of construction of the amphitheatre (*see* plan p. 591).

The third burial, some 20 yds. W.N.W. of these two (69027 : 89974), was of another powerfully built male, about 6 ft. 1 in. tall, lying E. to W. (head E.), extended as far as possible in an irregular chalk-cut grave only 5 ft. 2½ ins. long, both legs being drawn up at the knees; the head faced S.S.W. A few flint flakes were in the grave, but a subsidiary cavity in the Chalk beyond the head, some 3½ ft. long, contained at the far end an upright jar (*no. 40; 1908.29.20*) probably of the 2nd century, and near by a group of 2½ in. iron nails with adherent wood, suggesting an oaken object, perhaps a box. (Dorset *Procs.* XXXI (1910), 238–41; XXXIV (1913), 93–4 and plate.)

(221) VICTORIA PARK

Inhumations and cremations found in 1899 at the building, probably a villa, in Olga Road (68709010; Monument (212)), and probably to be associated with it rather than with the town cemetery. 'Some large flat stones, such as were used for sepulchral purposes', 'three cinerary urns of black un-glazed ware . . . filled with calcined bones', and also unburnt human bones 'together with decayed horns of some animals', were found on the E. side of the building at a spot 'over which the tesselation in all likelihood originally extended.' (*D.C.C.*, 31 Aug. 1899.) Graves found earlier in the area are implied by a coffin-fitting and nails (in D.C.M.) given by J. Paine in 1897. Several complete vessels are probably from burials: two 1st or early 2nd-century bowls of Durotrigian classes 1 and 1a (0.139.1, 0.140.1), and two lattice-decorated cooking-pots, one (0.155.1; *cf. no. 31* from Beggar's Knap) probably of the mid 2nd to mid 3rd century, the other (*no. 41;* 1886.9.48) of the later 3rd or 4th century. (*D.C.C.,* 3 Feb. 1898, 5; Moule, 86.)

(222) BOROUGH GARDENS AREA

(a) Inhumations found in the Borough Gardens between 1895 and 1942. In Dec. 1895 two or more skeletons were discovered in the earth above the Chalk, one apparently face downwards; amongst several bronze objects, including a nail-cleaner, an armlet and brooch seem to have been associated with one burial. Numerous human bones had been seen. A human skull believed Roman was found in 1921, and a newspaper report of 1942 states that human remains were found when the tennis courts (689903) were laid out (between the O.S. revisions of 1901 and 1928). In making a static-water tank to N. (68889053) in 1942, over a dozen fragmentary skeletons were found, some within 1 ft. of the surface, with no attempt at orderly burial; others deeper were apparently in confusion. Mr. W. Yard, a council employee known to be a reliable informant, has however estimated (in 1951) a total of about 50 skeletons on this occasion, some of children, extended in different directions with no observed grave-goods or signs of coffins. Some of the remains could be of more recent plague victims, but the diffusion is in favour of regular burial, and the Roman age of some is unquestioned. (Moule, letter 4 Dec. 1895, in Haverfield Library, Ashmolean Museum; *D.C.C.,* 7 Dec. 1921; 17 Sept. 1942.)

(b) Inhumations, several, and perhaps some cremations, found in 1896 in laying drains in Albert Road along the N. side of the Gardens, and near by in Cornwall Road to W. Opposite 'West Grange', No. 8 Albert Road (68909057), the skeleton was found of a man buried with an expanding bronze bracelet (Moule, fig. 29) clasping the thigh just above the knee. A jar 13½ ins. high (untraced), found near by above a skull, was thought to have been used for a cremation. The top of another large vessel with flanged rim (also untraced, but *cf.,* for shape, *no. 2* from Fordington) was found in Cornwall Road in the same works and ascribed to a like purpose. The skeleton of a woman in Albert Road had an armlet on each wrist of 4-ply twisted bronze wire with hook and eye terminals (Moule, 78, fig. 32), and another burial found in the same road in 1898 had one armlet. Other finds suggesting burials in Albert Road include a 2½ in. iron ring, two bronze penannular armlets (one strip-like, one of solid ¼ in. section with grooved terminals), and two identical wheel-thrown jars of hard black-surfaced ware, unparalleled but ostensibly of Roman date (*no. 42,* 1886.9.18; 1886.9.17; Hogg collection). From Cornwall Road comes a brooch with a narrow, flat, gently curved bow. Objects are in D.C.M. According to Moule, some of the burials were, as at Beggar's Knap (219), in the 'counterscarp of the fossa', and under 6 ft. of black earth, but there is no other indication of the stratification. (Moule, letters 28 Feb., 19 and 30 Mar. 1896, in Haverfield Library, Ashmolean Museum;

D.C.C., 19 Mar. 1896, 4; Dorset *Procs.* XVIII (1897), xxiii–vii; XXI (1900), xxii, 65, 69–71, 84, 92; Moule, 47, 49–50, 78–80, 82–3; Moule MS., 21, in D.C.M.; Moule, MS. list of Roman pottery in D.C.M.; Somerset Archaeological and Nat. Hist. Soc., *Procs.* LVII (1911), ii, 94–5, illustrating the expanding bracelet.)

(223) WEST GATE AREA

(a) Inhumation found in the Corporation Yard, Poundbury Road, in 1931 (68819069). The skeleton was extended E. to W. (head E.), 3½ ft. below surface, lying without obvious signs of a grave in a wide ditch probably running N. to S., possibly the Aqueduct (227a) or a branch from it. The right arm, across the breast, had an armlet (1901.4.1) of 3-ply twisted bronze wire with soldered hook terminals, 4 ins. above the wrist. Five nails recovered with wood adhering suggested a coffin, and the burial may be accepted as a regular one, almost certainly later than the ditch filling. (O. C. Vidler, letter, 9 May 1931, R.C.H.M. records; Dorset *Procs.* LIV (1932), xxix–xxx; information of location from Mr. W. Yard, 1951.)

(b) Inhumations, about 30, found *c.* 1920 in making the former Women's Institute tennis courts (68849078) about 100 yds. N.E. of (a). No objects were recovered, and the burials, about 2½ ft. deep in marly soil, seemed to have been disturbed, as many of the skulls were broken. (Information, 1951, from Mr. Slade, builder.) Two more were seen some 30 ft. apart in building development of the site in 1965. Both were extended approximately E.-W. (one with head W.) in graves cut a foot or less into the Chalk. They lay on either side of a pair of parallel ditches running N.W. to S.E. (*see* the Aqueduct (227 a), p. 588); Romano-British sherds were found in the topsoil. (68819080; information from Mr. C. J. Green.)

(224) BRIDPORT ROAD AREA

(a) Inhumations, number unspecified, found *c.* 1938 in laying drains between the married quarters of the Depot Barracks (68639076; information from C. D. Drew).

(b) Inhumations, about six, found in 1940 in digging air-raid trenches in the Depot Barracks about 10 yds. from Poundbury Road, S.W. of the main entrance to Marabout Barracks opposite (68669076). The skeletons were spaced out, but no objects were noted. (Information from A. Y. Nother.) Roman pottery and a key have come from the Depot Barracks (*see* p. 569).

(c) Inhumations, one or two, found in 1962 in laying water-mains along the E. side of St. Thomas Road (68589066). A skeleton, only partly excavated, was found extended N.W. to S.E. with skull dislodged, in a chalk-cut grave about 4½ ft. deep. There were signs perhaps of a parallel grave in the E. face of the trench. (Dorset *Procs.* LXXXV (1963), 100.)

(d) Inhumations, number unknown, found between 1886 and *c.* 1921 at the E. end of Mountain Ash Road, some 40 yds. N.W. of the last. Human skulls and bones were found on the site of the E. house of the S. row built between the 1886 and 1901 surveys (68559069; information from a resident, Mr. H. Short). Two burials, supposedly in stone 'coffins', probably slab-lined cists, were found *c.* 1921 in the road close to the railway cutting (information from Mr. A. E. Rossiter, County Police, 1950).

(e) Inhumations, number unknown, found in Prospect Road in c. 1910 and c. 1955 about 100 yds. N.W. of the last (684907). A number of skeletons buried in chalk-cut graves, some with 'brown pots' near the head, were found in drain-laying along the N. side of the road shortly before the 1914–18 war. Some nails with wood adhering were noted (information from Mr. Stone, 1951). An employee of the Water Works stated that many burials were seen c. 1955 in a trench in Prospect Road (information from Mr. R. N. R. Peers).

(f) Inhumations, number unknown, found in the 1880s in building houses on both sides of Bridport Road. The houses will be those on the S. side E. of the railway cutting (formerly Bridport Terrace, built in 1885; 687906) and those on the N. side W. of the cutting (formerly Sydney Terrace; 685905). (Moule MS., 21; Moule, 47.) Part of a metallic-lustred beaker of 4th-century New Forest ware (1852.3.1) was found in the railway cutting in 1854.

(g) Inhumation found in 1965 at Hawthorn Lodge, N. of Sydney Terrace (68509062). The skeleton, extended E. to W. (head) with hands over the pelvis, lay in a grave cut $1\frac{1}{2}$ ft. into the Chalk; the filling contained a sherd of black ware, probably Roman. (Dorset *Procs.* LXXXVII (1965), 110.)

(h) Inhumation found c. 1940 in building the tall chimney at the Steam Laundry, Bridport Road (68459060). The burial, broken up before inspection, had evidently been in a stone cist. (Information from O. C. Vidler.)

(i) Inhumation found c. 1943 at the Water Works, Bridport Road (68339066). The skeleton, the remains of which are said to have been left *in situ*, was found in cutting back and concreting the face of a N.-sloping scarp W. of a small building used as a chlorinating room. Two observers state independently that the body had been buried sitting upright. (*See also* (220 a); information, 1951, from Mr. H. W. Morris, foreman engineer, and Mr. W. Yard, who adds that cooking vessels placed between the knees were taken away soon after discovery; a third observer recollects only a burial on its side with knees drawn up.)

(225) POUNDBURY

(a) Sarcophagus of Ham Hill stone found c. 1855 in excavating the railway cutting E. of the Poundbury tunnel (c. 68409105). The sarcophagus, in D.C.M., has sides 9 ins. thick and a hole bored through the bottom; it measures 7 ft. 2 ins long, by 2 ft. 9 ins. to 2 ft. 4 ins.; height 1 ft. 3 ins. There is no lid. Barnes states that Roman coffins of Ham Hill stone were found near the N.E. corner of Poundbury. An iron sword (in D.C.M., Moule, fig. 34), with tang $3\frac{1}{2}$ ins. and blade $1\frac{1}{2}$ ft. long, tapering from sloping shoulders $1\frac{3}{4}$ in. wide, was found in the same works. (Moule, 50, 84; W. Barnes, *Guide to Dorchester* (1864?), 4; D.C.M. correspondence 1914–16.) A discoloured reddish-grey jar $9\frac{1}{2}$ or 10 ins. high, with a deep zone of tooled lattice pattern, found in 1855 and given to D.C.M. by Canon Bingham, is untraced (Moule, MS. list of Roman pottery in D.C.M.). It was almost certainly a type earlier than the mid 3rd century.

(b) Inhumation, remains of, found with a handled beaker in

the railway cutting, 1854. According to the original label with the vessel (*no. 43;* 1854.1.1), it was 'found together with the frontal bones of a child, at a depth of 7 or 8 ft. beneath the surface in the Railway Cutting through Whitfield . . . .'. Moule evidently did not construe the latter name as referring the discovery to Whitfield Farm W. of Poundbury Camp rather than to the known cemetery to E. The vessel is of a type believed to have a wide range of date from the 2nd to the 4th century. (Moule, 50.)

(c) Inhumations, number unknown but including two in stone sarcophagi, and a lead coffin or lining, found in 1914–18 at the prisoners-of-war camp E. of Poundbury. In making a road and laying surface water drains in 1915 'between the lines of huts nearest to Poundbury, about 150 yards N.E. of the railway cutting' (c. 68489117; *Notes and Queries*), a sarcophagus of Ham Hill stone with an anciently broken cover was found 2 ft. below surface. It was 7 ft. long, 2 ft. 7 ins. wide, and about 2 ft. high including cover. The skeleton had head W.; no grave-goods were found. A second sarcophagus, of which details are lacking, was found near by, but both were left *in situ* to await proper examination. A lead 'coffin' found shortly afterwards was broken up, but rescued pieces (in D.C.M.) appeared to be the top and bottom portions 6 ft. long and 17 ins. wide, and fragments of the joints. Many traces of ancient burials were found in the construction work. One of these was the skull of a child buried with a Romano-British necklet of twisted 3-ply bronze wire (1908.29.57); another was a skull and other bones found in the bottom of a V-shaped cutting showing 50 yds. from the tunnel entrance in the E. face of the railway cutting widened in 1918. (Somerset and Dorset *Notes and Queries* XV (1917), 91–2; *Procs. Soc. Antiquaries* XXVIII (1916), 201–2; Dorset *Procs.* XLI (1920), xliv; D.C.M. correspondence (M. Jones) 1914–16, (W. H. Cozens) 1917–19.) A half-dozen or more of these burials, said to be evenly spaced and in line abreast, were seen, it is believed, some 50 yds. W. of the military hospital of the R.H.A. (now Marabout) Barracks (c. 68549100; information from Mr. W. G. Lee, 1951). These would be well to the S.E. of burials otherwise recorded in this cemetery.

(d) Inhumation, 4th-century, excavated in 1939 in the filling of the Iron Age inner ditch at the N.E. corner of Poundbury (68449120). The skeleton, of a man aged about 30 and 5 ft. 2 ins. tall, was extended in a shallow grave roughly E. to W. (285°, head W. resting on right cheek), with right hand on pelvis and left flexed over the abdomen. There were no signs of disease; a few teeth were lost or carious. Iron nails showed burial in a wooden coffin. (*Ant. J.* XX (1940), 431, 446–8.)

(e) Inhumations, three, in stone sarcophagi, found within 100 yds. of each other in Jan. and Mar. 1940 in making roads and hut foundations on the E. slopes of Poundbury in the army camp N.E. of the railway cutting. A sarcophagus of Portland stone (Plate 229; 1940.3.1), with ridge-roofed lid mended with iron cramps leaded into dowel holes, and containing a fragile skeleton broken up by workmen, was found on 5 Jan. in digging hut foundations. It is obliquely tooled, with overall dimensions of 6 ft. 4 ins. by 1 ft. 11 ins., and 2 ft. 4 ins. high.

Another of Ham Hill stone found on 11 Jan., with a flat lid of approximately the same depth, lay E. to W. in a chalk-cut grave 4 ft. below modern surface (Plate 229). A fragmentary skeleton of a man 5 ft. 9 ins. tall, head E., was enclosed except for face and shoulders in a preservative packing of plaster of Paris or raw gypsum (obtainable in outcrops in the Purbeck cliffs). The hands were crossed on the lower part of the trunk. Ring-bolts and ornamental angle-irons, and nails with remains of wood, enabled C. D. Drew to reconstruct the design of an inner coffin of oaken boards 1 in. thick with neatly fitted butt

Camp. The first (68499113), about 15 yds. N.W. of (f), lay some 5 ft. deep in a grave dug through fallen roof-tiles inside the W. end of a building, already in ruins, which may earlier have been connected with the finishing of Ham Hill stone sarcophagi; the filling contained sherds suggesting a date for the burial after c. 250. The cranium showed signs of disease. The second, of like date and 17 yds. to N. (68499114), was a

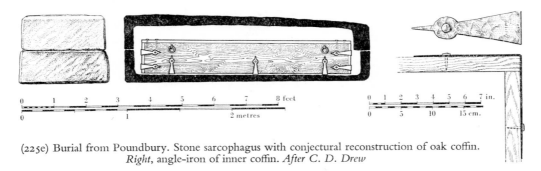

(225e) Burial from Poundbury. Stone sarcophagus with conjectural reconstruction of oak coffin. *Right*, angle-iron of inner coffin. *After C. D. Drew*

joints (Fig.). The gypsum or plaster mould had collapsed but seemed to retain, in the head area, the impression of a shroud; it was free from lead, traces of which were unaccountably found, on chemical analysis, to be present in the wood. The sarcophagus had been roughly dressed with a bull-nosed axe; the angles of sides and top were bevelled. The external dimensions are 7 ft. 9 ins. by 2 ft. 8 ins. narrowing to 2 ft. 3 ins.; height 2 ft. 2 ins. Sarcophagus and fittings in D.C.M. (1940.4. 1–3).

The third sarcophagus, of Ham Hill stone with shallow flat lid broken in two, was found in laying a water-main at or very near the site of the fire hydrant (68469109) in the turning-circle 60 yds. from the entrance to the Iron Age Camp. The orientation was E.S.E. to W.N.W. (head), but the skeleton was fragmentary. The sarcophagus, with 9-in. sides, length 7 ft. 7 ins., width 2 ft. 6 ins., height 2 ft. 8 ins., is now at the Roman house, Colliton Park (182). (Notes by C. D. Drew in D.C.M.; *J.R.S.* xxx (1940), 176; information from C. D. Drew.) A small bowl and model axe-head of bronze, in D.C.M., found in 1943 in trenching between the railway and the river, were possibly grave-goods of a burial (Dorset *Procs.* LXXIV (1952), 98–9; *see*, however, Monument (214)).

Burials at (f)—(h) have been found since 1964 in light industrial development of the former army camp.

(f) Inhumations, five, in four graves aligned W.N.W.– E.S.E., mostly excavated by R. N. R. Peers in 1966 at new premises for Messrs. Rossiter, some 45 yds. N.E. of the last-mentioned burial. Two graves were end to end (68509112); a third 7 yds. S.W. contained remains of an adult and child (68499111). The fourth grave, excavated by Mr. P. F. Kear about 7 yds. S.E. of the last, contained an adult skeleton extended with head W.; nails indicated a wooden coffin. (Dorset *Procs.* LXXXVIII (1966), 109; LXXXIX (1967), 144.)

(g) Inhumations, three, aligned approximately E.–W., two extended with head W. and one similarly placed in a stone sarcophagus, found in 1966 in excavating Roman building remains (214) some 60 yds. outside the N.E. corner of Poundbury

young man in a wooden coffin indicated by nails; there were no grave-goods other than an object beside the left leg represented by small pieces of carbonized matter, and a large iron stud between the knees. The third burial, 10 yds. E.N.E. of the last (68499115), consisted of a roughly finished sarcophagus of Ham Hill stone with flat lid broken in antiquity, apparently laid on the site of a robbed wall. The sarcophagus was opened in 1967 revealing poorly preserved bones of an adult and traces of 'gypsum'. Further excavation in 1967 disclosed two burials adjacent to this one—(i) a better finished sarcophagus of Ham Hill stone containing a skeleton, perhaps female, with remains of a bone comb and 'gypsum' retaining cloth impressions; (ii) an inhumation of a juvenile in a coffin indicated by nails and angle-irons, earlier than the burials in sarcophagi. Five more extended inhumations, probably all in wooden coffins indicated by nails, were found dispersed in an area some 40 yds. S.S.W. (68489112, not shown in the plan opposite); one of these, largely destroyed but evidently of a child, was apparently decapitated and was exceptional in having feet to W. All ten graves listed in this section were aligned approximately E.–W. (Dorset *Procs.* LXXXVIII (1966), 110; LXXXIX (1967), 133–5.)

(h) Inhumations, seven, found in 1964 in building Wyvern Fireplaces' factory; they include three 'gypsum' burials, two in lead coffins and one in a stone sarcophagus, and are the easternmost graves yet known in this cemetery. All the burials were extended E.S.E.–W.N.W. in graves cut into the Chalk to a depth of some 5 ft. or 6 ft. below the modern surface. Remains of a compact group of three immediately outside the N.W. corner of the factory (68559112), about 60 yds. E.S.E. of the last-mentioned burial at (g), consisted of (i) the poorly preserved remains of an adult (?), packed in 'gypsum' inside a wooden coffin contained in an outer coffin of lead sheeting soldered at the edges; (ii) an adult, head W., immediately to N. and parallel with (i), in a wooden coffin probably not earlier than the 4th century judging by nails and a sherd in the filling; (iii) an adult, mostly destroyed by the workmen, also evidently in a wooden coffin, at the E. end of (ii) and in line with it. At the N.E. corner of the factory building (68579111), 28 yds. E.S.E. of (iii), traces of another skeleton packed in 'gypsum' lay apparently in a wooden coffin inside an outer coffin of lead sheeting; sherds in the filling indicate a date after *c.* 250. Of the remaining three burials, one, packed in 'gypsum' and poorly preserved but with foot bones at the E. end, lay 25 yds. S. of (i) in a sarcophagus of Ham Hill stone with flat lid freshly broken (68549110); it was 6 ft. 5 ins. long, 2 ft. 6 ins. wide at head by 1 ft. 11 ins. at foot, and 2 ft. high including lid. There were no grave-goods within, and it is not known whether there were traces of a wooden coffin. Some 9 yds. W. by S. (68549110), the W. end of a grave otherwise destroyed by the builders had the skull of an elderly individual. About 27 yds. E. by S. of the sarcophagus, at the road verge E. of the factory (68579110), the S.W. corner of a grave was seen, apparently aligned with the others, with skull W.; no traces of coffin were seen, but a sherd in the grave filling implied a date after *c.* 250. Objects are in D.C.M., except the stone sarcophagus at Wyvern Fireplaces Ltd. (Information from Mr. C. J. Green; Dorset *Procs.* LXXXVIII (1966), 109.) One of the lead coffins is understood to have some decorative beading.

(226) THE GROVE

(a) Inhumations, two or more, found in chalk-cut graves in 1841 in levelling a meadow, evidently Northernhay, between the river and the North Walk (689910). One had an iron collar round the neck fastening behind with a spring. Near another were three small undecorated jars; the two larger, given probably in error as 2 ins. high, were of polished black and matt brown ware, the other of fine light red ware and 'of the Graeco-Roman character'. (*Gentleman's Magazine* (1841), pt. ii, 303; Hutchins II, 397.)

(b) Inhumations, 17 or more, found in 1903 and 1963–4 in building works W. of the foot of The Grove. Two extended skeletons 'in different directions' were found in clearing the ground for the New Compasses Inn (68869106). With them were two restorable vessels, one a bowl of Durotrigian class 2 (*no. 44; 1907.3.8*) datable to the 1st century or first half of the 2nd century. The other, of brownish ware, 3 ins. high by 2⅝ ins. in maximum girth, does not seem to have reached the Museum. Moule thought the site lay within the Roman town ditch. (Moule MS., 20–1; Moule, letter 9 Nov. 1903, in Haverfield Library, Ashmolean Museum; Dorset *Procs.* XXVII (1906), xxviii.)

The disclosure in 1963 of a skeleton, apparently lying E. to W. without grave-goods, some 40 yds. W.S.W. of the Inn, was followed by the discovery of about 14 more within an area some 15 yds. square (68829104). The burials, variously orientated but all apparently extended, were in chalk-cut graves some 6 or 7 ft. below the former surface, under soil and chalk rubble. (Dorset *Procs.* LXXXV (1963), 100.)

(c) Inhumations, one or more, partly exposed in 1964–5 in building works about 45 yds. S. of the last, on the line of the garden wall running E. from School Lane. One, about 25 yds. from the lane, lay approximately N.–S. with the feet, with hob-nails, to the N. (68829100); the presence of two more, of similar alignment, was suggested by excavations resembling

graves some 15 yds. to the W. (68819100). (Information from Mr. C. J. Green.)

WATER SUPPLY

(227) AQUEDUCT and CONDUITS: (a) an open chalk-cut channel apparently tapping the R. Frome and doubtless intended to supply fountains and public baths of the Roman town; (b) a conduit found at Colliton Park within the town ramparts, presumably fed from (a); (c) other works, doubtfully Roman.

(a) Aqueduct (Fig. p. 586, Plate 221) is traceable as earthworks, or in aerial photographs, at a number of places along the nearer or eastern two-thirds of its estimated length of about 12 miles from near Notton Mill (609958). The course runs through the parishes of Maiden Newton, Frampton, Bradford Peverell and Dorchester, and follows the S. side of the Frome valley, making sharp bends in the re-entrants. The remains are noteworthy in Bradford Peverell in the re-entrant S. of Stratton, in both re-entrants W. of Whitfield Farm below Fordington Down, and along the scarp E. to the mouth of the railway tunnel at Poundbury Camp (*see* Hill-forts, Dorchester (172)). Parts are scheduled as Ancient Monuments.

The remains were first recognized as belonging to an aqueduct by Major J. N. Coates, R.A., in 1900. The revised course for the western half, postulated in 1922 by Major P. Foster, R.A., who assumed an intake in the area of Notton Mill, Maiden Newton, is supported by subsequent readings of the surface levels and may be accepted, although it has never been confirmed; an intake 10 miles from Dorchester is, however, not impossible, in the Steps Farm[1] re-entrant S. of Frampton Court, the only such valley on the course possessing a stream.

The assumed course from Notton to the highest point of the Roman town, *i.e.* the area of the W. gate, measures some 12 miles. The present level of the stream bed at the bridge (60929598) N. of Notton Mill is approximately 275 ft. above O.D. and the bottom of the aqueduct channel at No. 22 Poundbury Crescent (67969064), ⅔ mile from the W. gate, is approximately 250 ft., a decline of some 25 ft. in about 11⅓ miles (1 : 2400 or 0·04%). Intermediate readings, at points where the depth of the channel below present ground level is known, show considerable variation, but corroboration is afforded in the results achieved in surface levelling by the Royal Engineers in *c.* 1925, based on Liverpool datum. There is no evidence whether such variation is due to imprecise cutting rather than to cleaning or natural scouring of the channel.

---

[1] Formerly Steps Barn.

M

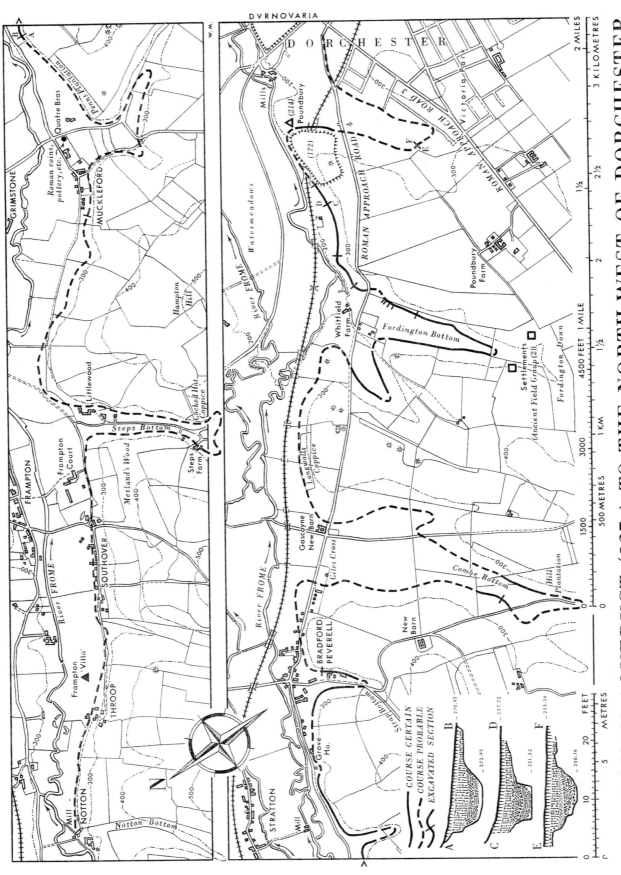

DVRNOVARIA

THE ROMAN AQUEDUCT (227a), TO THE NORTH-WEST OF DORCHESTER

Figures can be given for the level of the channel bottom at four points: from W. to E. these are (i) Bradford Peverell, 1939 (64789333), 272·95; (ii) Poundbury, section F, 1938 (68009127), 251·52; (iii) Poundbury, section E, 1938 (68139125), 250·90; (iv) 22 Poundbury Crescent, 1956 (67969064), N. section, 250·09, S. section, 250·16. Nos. (i)–(iii) are calculated from levels of datum lines supplied by the late W. Thorneycroft, no. (iv) from a temporary bench mark of the Borough Surveyor, by R.C.H.M. Approximate distances are: nos. (i)–(ii), 6¼ miles; (ii)–(iii), 140 yds.; (iii)–(iv), ⅔ mile.

The aqueduct has been sectioned between 1855 and 1956 at 14 points, for most of which drawings, photographs or notes are available. These disclose variations in profile but suggest that the channel was dug as a flat-bottomed ditch with steep sides in ratio of 2 : 1, in some instances at least in a flat terrace prepared in the slope of the natural Chalk. The excavated spoil formed an outer bank, still well marked near Whitfield Farm. The bottom, between 2½ ft. and 3 ft. below the Chalk surface, is generally some 5 ft. wide, between recorded extremes of 3 ft. and 6 ft. 2 ins.; the upper sides are eroded, but the channel was probably 7 ft. or 8 ft. wide at the chalk shoulders. Assuming a depth of water of 2 ft. the section would have been 12 sq. ft., which at a declination of 1 : 2400 gives a velocity of 2 ft. per second, and a maximum discharge of 24·06 cubic ft. per second, or 12,958,000 imperial gallons per day; for the formula used, see *Bulletin of the Board of Celtic Studies* XIX (1960), 78–9.

There is no evidence that the channel was covered or lined. Where it was cut into the filling of the Iron Age outer ditch, near the N.W. corner of Poundbury Camp, its outer or N. side was built up in clay; elsewhere clay found in the bottom was probably a natural deposit. A tank or tanks, undetected but presumably situated in the elevated region of the W. gate of the Roman town, would have been required for storage if not also for settling. Whatever the method of controlling the flow at source, the readiest means of regulation would have been an overflow from the reservoir itself to the river; the lined conduit at Colliton Park (*see* (b) below) may have been a spillway for this purpose, since no installation was found there to justify the provision of a water supply of this order to what seems to have been a private sector of the town.

Little evidence exists for the date of the aqueduct. Samian sherds of the 1st or 2nd century A.D. have been recovered from the channel at Poundbury and Fordington Bottom, while there is no record of later material. If, as seems reasonable, it is to be associated with the conduit at Colliton Park, the latter's date of construction in or after the last decade of the 1st century

may be relevant; but the disuse of the conduit, whether in the 2nd century, as has been claimed, or later, has no necessary implication for the major work. It is to be noted that the building with 4th-century mosaics near Frampton (61599529) lies beside the aqueduct and hardly more than half a mile from its assumed intake (*Dorset* I (1952), 150; *Dorset Procs.* LXXVIII (1956), 81-3). Occupation sites are also recorded near it at Muckleford (*ibid.* LXXVII (1955), 133-4), Fordington Bottom (*ibid.* LXXVIII (1956), 80-1), and E. of Poundbury Camp (*see* Monument (214)). In Fordington Bottom it seems to have cut across 'Celtic' fields (*see* Ancient Field Group (2)), and there and elsewhere would have been crossed six times by the Roman road from Dorchester to Ilchester if the course of this road between Dorchester and Stratton has been correctly postulated (*see above*, Approach Roads, 4).

Description. Notton to Muckleford (SY 69 NW, SW). There are no visible remains certainly attributable W. of Quatre Bras near Muckleford, some 4 miles along the supposed course from Notton and 8 from Dorchester. From Notton the course should correspond approximately with the footpath and road close to the meadows of the Frome through Throop and Southover, and S. of Frampton Court would have followed the re-entrant to Steps Barn, below the lower edges of Metland's Wood and Cocked Hat Coppice; indications of the terrace claimed here by Foster are ambiguous in view of the terraced lynchets of strip cultivation following the contours on both sides of the combe, but he was probably correct in placing it below the lowest lynchet on the E. side. E. of Littlewood the course should run some 60 to 80 yds. N. of the 300 ft. contour.

At Muckleford, a section cut in 1939 across a terrace claimed by Foster as aqueduct, along the S.W. side of Marsh's orchard (63729368), produced Romano-British pottery but seems not to have exposed the channel, although the cut was extended first below and then above the terrace; but records and recollections of those concerned are incomplete (field notebook, and some objects, in D.C.M.; information from K.C.C. Selby and W. Thorneycroft). A terrace, not on O.S., at about the same level S. of the Mission Room, resumes as a single scarp on the W. side of the Muckleford re-entrant, where it is in fact the lowest scarp of a series of strip lynchets; a corresponding scarp in the plantation on the E. side was surveyed by O.S. in 1958 and accepted as remains of the aqueduct. These scarps, and others like them, have probably been affected by pre-Enclosure cultivation if they are not solely the result of it; disclosure of the buried channel can alone determine the relationship.

Muckleford to Whitfield Farm (SY 69 SW, SE). E. of Quatre Bras a slight terrace at the foot of Penn's Plantation grows more distinct in the belt of trees to E. and emerges as a distinct work in what was formerly Quatre Bras Eweleaze, within the re-entrant and on both its shoulders. On the W. shoulder the terrace was about 30 ft. wide in 1955 including a slight outer bank, but both here and elsewhere ploughing is altering its character; it was sectioned in 1939 by K. C. C. Selby and G. E. Kirk at 64789333 (Fig. p. 586; field notebook, and some objects, in D.C.M.; *J.R.S.* XXX (1940), 175-6; information from Selby, section drawing and levels from W. Thorney-croft). A section was also cut by H. Colley March and H. B. Middleton in 1902, probably on the E. shoulder where a cultivation lynchet remained immediately below the aqueduct terrace. E. of the re-entrant, traces of the terrace remain as far as Grove House, and it is again well marked on both sides of Strap Bottom, S. of St. Mary's Church, Bradford Peverell, where the channel was exposed but not excavated by W. Miles Barnes in 1901 (c. 65849289).

The line is lost in the village but is recognizable again near the head of its greatest detour, in Combe Bottom. On the N. side of the combe, in the field W. and N. of Hill Plantation, where it was sectioned by Barnes in 1901 (c. 65589182), it now shows best as a soil-mark in aerial photographs (R.A.F. V.A.P. CPE/UK 2431 : 4263–4); on the S. it is barely visible alongside the edge of Hill Plantation but is well marked running for about 100 yds. across the N. neck of the plantation. Thereafter major scarps in the copse at Gascoyne New Barn and at the foot of the older W. half of Longwalls Coppice, surveyed in 1958 and accepted as remains of the aqueduct by O.S., may well mask rather than represent the Roman work.

Whitfield Farm to Dorchester (SY 69 SE). Despite renewed ploughing the aqueduct remains at its most impressive in the two adjoining combes in Fordington Down, W. of Whitfield or Whitewell Farm (Plate 221; R.A.F. V.A.P. CPE/UK 2431: 4260–1). The upcast bank is often present, standing to 3½ ft. or 4 ft. above the channel filling. Towards its S. exit from Fordington Bottom the seeming descent of the aqueduct terrace some 16 ft. below the level of the succeeding stretch to Poundbury was explained in a series of five cuts made in 1902 by Colley March, which showed that the terrace had parted company with the buried channel some 150 yds. short of the road by Whitfield Farm. The aqueduct terrace, serving as a lyncheted arable strip—one of several still discernible in the valley bottom and shown on the Tithe Map of Fordington (1844) as part of Whitewall or Whitewell Bottom Furlong—had been diverted as a gentle ramp to permit exit from the strip. At this point the original terrace may have already been buried by soil-creep from the hill-slope above. The buried channel, probably commencing a slight re-entrant bend to E. in conformity with the natural contour, was found behind the foot of the upper scarp, maintaining its own gradient until in Colley March's Cut B (c. 67359132) it was found below the surface at the top of the upper scarp, immediately N.W. of the iron fence. Fragments of samian ware (D.C.M. 1898.4.2) were found in the channel bottom in his Cut E (c. 67189122; some photographs, annotated sketches of all his aqueduct sections, in D.C.M.).

N. of the road the channel was sectioned by Barnes in 1901 at the bend (c. 67529142) and further E. in 1902 by Colley March (67739140). The substantial terrace approaching Poundbury is best viewed from the Sherborne road. The channel was sectioned W. and N. of Poundbury Camp by Miss K. M. Richardson in 1938 (Fig. p. 586), disclosing use by the Roman engineers of the lower of the two platforms formed by the silted ditches of the Iron Age camp. At the N.E. corner, where the buried channel swings S. to follow thereafter the inner edge of the Iron Age outer ditch, the engineers may have contributed to the destruction of the rampart. The position

of the channel in relation to the E. defences is shown in a section drawing of the S. face of the railway cutting, by the railway surveyor (1855; in D.C.M.), and in a photograph published by Miss Richardson of the N. face cut back in 1918; the outer scarp, omitted (N. of the railway) from the latest edition of the O.S. plan, is the upper scarp of the aqueduct terrace, on the site of the Iron Age outer rampart levelled by the Roman engineers, who cast the excavated material into the silted Iron Age ditch.[1]

S. of the Roman(?) road, the aqueduct was traced by Coates in a scarp then apparent on the N.W. side of the combe, formerly Sheald's Bottom, now occupied by the W. army camp, and its channel was sectioned in 1956 in the N. and S. foundation trenches at the W. end of No. 22 Poundbury Crescent, 67969064 (Fig. p. 586; R.C.H.M. records). Swinging N.E. probably some 130 yds. short of Bridport Road, the further course to Dorchester may be assumed to coincide approximately with the top of the scarp marked on the O.S. as aqueduct, which in the tithe survey of Fordington was shown as a strip of pasture (Sheald's Wall Common) and headland, and then with Poundbury Road, to discharge into a reservoir somewhere in the vicinity of the W. gate. A 'wide ditch', with a Roman burial incorporated or cut down into its filling, was found in 1931, in the Corporation Yard, Poundbury Road, (68819069); this would be on the presumed line of the aqueduct, but although it was not cleared it was thought to run N. to S. Some 110 yds. to N. (68817: 90800) two slightly curving ditches with 'brown silt' at bottom were seen for a short distance in 1965 W. of the former tennis courts of the Women's Institute; 6 ft. wide and cut some 3 ft. into the Chalk, they ran parallel and 6 ft. apart in a south-easterly direction. A samian sherd was found in one. *See* Burials (223a, b). (Coates, Barnes, Dorset *Procs.* XXII (1901), 80–90; XXIII (1902), 1–li; Colley March, XXIV (1903), 80, 89–90; Foster, XLVI (1925), 1–13, with unpublished 6 in. maps in D.C.M.; Richardson, *Ant. J.* XX (1940), 429–48; *D.C.C.*, 25 Sept. 1902, 4; R.C.H.M. records. Other references are contained in the text; an unpublished paper by Foster, *The Roman Aqueduct at Dorchester* II (1928), in D.C.M., adds nothing significant.)

(b) Water conduit (Fig. p. 554), perhaps a spillway for the aqueduct although it is likely to have been tapped for domestic purposes, was sectioned in at least six places in Colliton Park in 1938. Its straight alignment of 341½°, with very regular W. side, was traced from a point (69029080) 34 yds. W. of the N. end of Colliton House for 90 yds. but was lost to N. where the surface of the Chalk was cut away. It pointed to the E. end of the S. range of the Roman house (182), but must be presumed to have changed its direction E. before reaching it. The drop in level was 1½ ft. (1 : 180); the height of channel bottom, presumably at road cutting 9 (69029081) where the conduit was best preserved, was 233 ft. above O.D. (information from W. Thorneycroft). Here the V-shaped trench, some 17 ft. wide after weathering, was dug nearly 10½ ft. into the

---

[1] Excavation in 1967 for a new building immediately outside the E. entrance of the hill-fort revealed the same close relationship between the channel and the inner lip of the Iron Age outer ditch (information, and photographs, from Mr. C. J. Green).

PLATE 227

DORCHESTER. (228) Maumbury Rings, Roman amphitheatre. Entrance.

Excavation drawing in pencil, *c.* 1910, by H. St. George Gray. (N. point added.) Scale: 1 in. = 8 ft.   (*Dorset County Museum*)

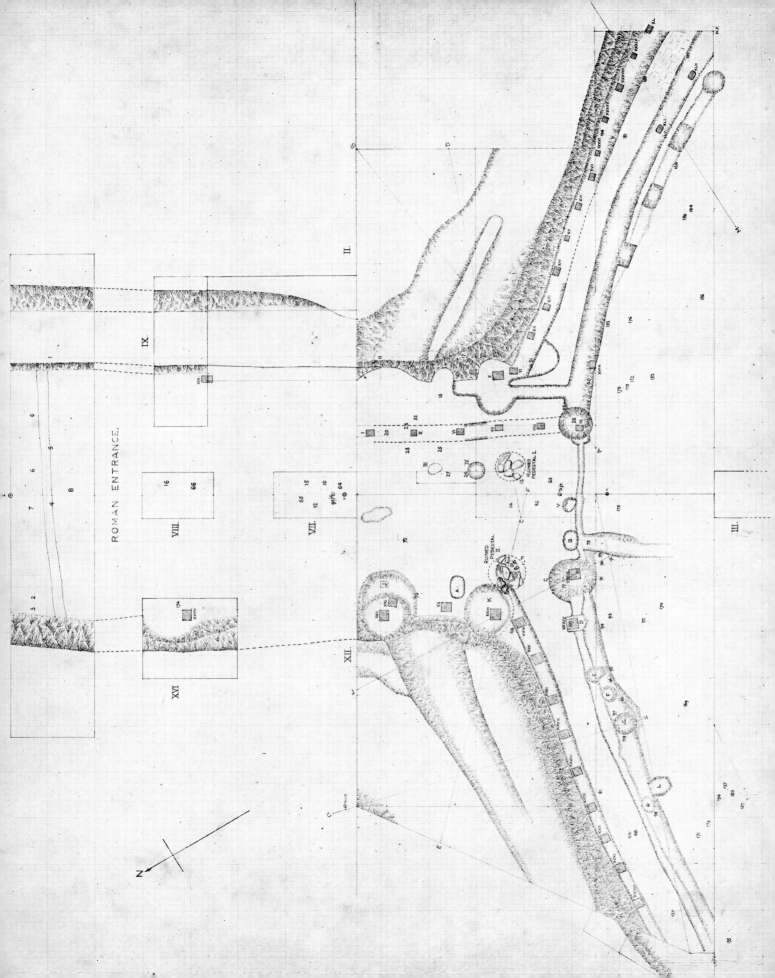

ROMAN ENTRANCE.

Chalk; the square-cut channel at its foot was paved with clay roof-tiles and walled with mortared limestone over a thin layer of clay which contained a slightly worn silver coin of Vespasian (A.D. 69–79). This channel was 2½ ft. wide between the walls and 1½ ft. high; ledges in the rock, level with the top, suggest that it was covered, and the trench was probably refilled; if left open, it must originally have been bridged at this point where it was crossed by a street (180). The filling dug out in 1938 seems, however, to have been associated with robbing of the masonry of the channel and subsequent weathering and filling with rubbish; in this condition late street metalling was laid across it.

The coin shows that the conduit was not made before c. A.D. 90. It was said to have been partly dismantled and filled by the end of the 2nd century, but, amongst much 2nd-century pottery, the conical flanged bowl[1] was present as low as layer 6 of the rubbish fill, and the 3rd-century forms with grooved rim[2] in the stony destruction debris of layer 7. A longer period of use is therefore likely, and the filling was certainly not complete before the 4th century, at which time the street (180) would seem to have been remade and a house (186) built or extended over the conduit and on the same alignment. (Dorset *Procs.* LX (1938), 64–5, pl. IX.)

(c) Other records of conduits or 'subways' in Dorchester are inadequate but ought not to be ignored. Under the County Museum, High West Street (69229076), an 'underground passage' cut into the Chalk was seen in 1880 running S.S.W., with mortared flint walls about 2 ft. high 'set back 6 in. on each side' (Moule). Almost due S. at the Devon and Cornwall Bank, South Street (69239059), a similar work without remains of walls was found in 1899, evidently running S. several feet beneath the remains of the mosaic (195); in 1898 a like feature was seen, parallel with the same street and evidently close to the mosaic (194c), in building Messrs. Duke's former offices on the site now occupied by Messrs. Woolworth (69229055). In High East Street, outside the King's Arms (69329074), some 10 ft. below the road, the top of a 'large brick arch . . . like the crown of an ancient arched drain' (D.C.M. accessions book, Sept. 1908) was seen in 1900; it was in a cutting about 5 ft. wide thought to come from N.W. To S., B. A. Hogg is said to have noted similar cuttings in two places, running S., in Charles Street and outside South Walk, but the latter would be in the Roman town ditch. A large cavity flanked by two smaller ones, said to lead to the town from the Castle site to N. and to have been found in 1720 in building the former Unitarian Chapel in Colliton Street (69189083), was evidently a work of different character from the foregoing. (Moule, 27–9; Dorset *Procs.* LXXVII (1955), 129.)

An arched passage apparently leading S. below the present concrete floor of Tilley's Garage, 26 Trinity Street (69139051), is said to have been found when a vehicle broke through about the same time as the discovery of the mosaic (192) in 1925. The materials are unknown. (Information, 1950, from the employee concerned.)

AMPHITHEATRE

(228) MAUMBURY RINGS (SY 68 NE, 690899; Fig. p. 591, Plate 227) lies S. of Dorchester immediately E. of the Weymouth road. It has long been recognized as the amphitheatre of *Durnovaria*, modified during the Civil War of the 17th century to form a strongpoint of the town defences. Its original construction, however, as a Neolithic henge monument incorporating unique features, remained undiscovered until the excavations of 1908–13.[1]

The earthwork lies on a gentle N.E. facing slope, almost at the summit (260 ft. above O.D.) of a low, rounded Chalk ridge running E.-W. between the River Frome on the N. and the South Winterborne on the S. It is circular in plan, except for an external bulge on the S.W. and is defined by a single surrounding bank with an extrance on the N.E. It has an average external diameter of 330 ft. and internal diameters of 160 ft. and 210 ft. The oval interior, about ½ acre in area, lies below the external ground level so that the bank now rises from 20 ft. to 30 ft. above the interior and from 8 ft. to 17 ft. above the exterior. The base of the bank varies in width from 80 ft. to 90 ft. and its flattish top widens from 7 ft., on either side of the entrance, to 16 ft. in the S.W. half of the earthwork, except at the bulge, where it narrows markedly. Extending from this point in either direction along the outer edge of the bank top is a low parapet up to 1 ft. high and 6 ft. across, which ends halfway towards the entrance on either side in low raised platforms occupying the full width of the top. The internal slope of the bank is interrupted by curving terraces beginning at ground level on either side of the entrance and continuing round to meet the long gentle slope which runs from the top of the bank at the bulge almost to the centre of the floor. They reach a maximum height and width of 16 ft. and 10 ft. respectively at points halfway along.

Maumbury Rings was excavated under the direction of H. St. George Gray between 1908 and 1913 and the results were published as a series of interim reports. The entrance and about half of the inner side of the bank were examined but no complete cutting was made through the bank. The surviving finds and records (one of the eleven pencil drawings is here reproduced as Plate 227) are in D.C.M. and the site is now under grass. (Dorset *Procs.* XXIX (1908), 256–72; XXX (1909), 215–35; XXXI (1910), 230–63; XXXIV (1913), 81–106; XXXV (1914), 88–118; *Antiquity* XIII (1939), 155–8.)

---

[1] Gillam's type 228 (*cf.* type 315), not now dated in the N. before the early 4th century; *Arch. Ael.* XXXV (1957).
[2] *Ibid.*, types 226–7, 314.

---

[1] A pre-Roman origin had been suspected by A. H. Allcroft, *Earthwork of England* (1908), 589.

The Neolithic Henge

This was of single entrance type (Class I),[1] the entrance corresponding to the present one, defined by a single bank with internal ditch formed by the coalescing mouths of a series of closely spaced shafts quarried deeply into the Chalk.

Two cuttings made into the bank as far as its central point, one from the exterior on the N.W. side, the other from the interior on the S.E., showed clearly the original ground surface 15 ft. below the bank top. No objects lay on it, but antler picks and fragments and a piece of carved chalk were found within the lower few feet of bank material. Except for a few bones of young pig and a burnt bone fragment, possibly of human skull, no other objects were found within the bank. Excavation photographs (*e.g.* Dorset *Procs.* xxxv (1914), Pl. V, facing p. 116), suggest that the bank was of two periods. In the first period, that of the henge, it was perhaps 11 ft. in height. It appears to have been heightened later by the addition of material to its crest and outer face while its inner face was in places cut back. These alterations probably took place in the Roman period.

The removal of nearly 12 ft. of material from the interior to reach a suitable floor for the Roman arena has largely destroyed the internal ditch, of which only the lower part still exists, no longer visible on the surface. Deep funnel-shaped pits or shafts were so arranged that their mouths must, originally, have coalesced to form a continuous but irregular ditch—in many cases the mouths were found to unite even below the level of the arena floor. Gray estimated that this ditch had averaged about 16 ft. in depth and 40 ft. across at the top. Over half of the apparent ditch bottom was examined mainly on the N. and E. Seventeen shafts were located in it, the centre of each lying on the arc of a true circle 169 ft. in diameter. Only seven shafts, Nos. 1, 6, 9, 10, 11, 14 and 15, were excavated to the bottom, and the elongated plan of some of the others (*e.g.* No. 4) suggests that full excavation would have shown them to have been divided into several pits.

The shafts varied in depth from $32\frac{3}{4}$ ft. to $36\frac{3}{4}$ ft. below the original surface, and in width at the mouth from an oval 14 ft. by 8 ft. to a circle 7 ft. in diameter. They tapered irregularly often to a diameter of 3 ft. or less at the bottom. The filling was a clean chalk rubble very loosely compacted, especially near the bottom, and only at the mouths had materials later been rammed in to provide a firm floor for the Roman amphitheatre. Finds were not numerous and came chiefly from the lower filling. Antler picks, some broken and charred, were most common but flints, including round scrapers and cores, and carved chalk objects—cups, phalli and scratched blocks—were also found. Shaft 6 yielded a sherd of cordoned pottery allied to Rinyo-Clacton ware. At one point the ditch had cut through an earlier hole, containing many well-struck flint flakes.

A group of sherds of coarse hand-made pottery, apparently of Iron Age 'A', was found in the upper filling of shaft No. 4.

The Roman Amphitheatre

The earthwork was adapted as an amphitheatre by the excavation of an approximately level floor of oval form nearly 10 ft. below the level of the natural Chalk, filling in the depressions left by the prehistoric ditch and shafts and cutting back the natural Chalk to a vertical face where necessary to form the arena wall (*podium*). The oval shape of the arena, $192\frac{1}{2}$ ft. by 158 ft. within the fenced passage, was achieved largely by encroaching on the entrance area outside the setting of shafts. It was then surfaced with gravel. Some of the excavated chalk was heaped on the existing bank, but the builders of the amphitheatre were apparently content to use the circular earthwork largely as it stood and did not follow the normal practice of building up a ramped auditorium (or *cavea*) against a high rear wall of masonry or brick.

A gangway for performers, 3 ft. to 6 ft. wide, between two palisades of stout squared posts set in trenches and presumably linked by fencing, followed the oval circumference of the arena, the outer palisade serving as a revetment to the arena wall. The gangway continued for some distance along the E. side of the single N.E. entrance (Plate 227); on the W. indications remained only of the revetment posts. In two places, W. of the entrance and at the centre of the E. side, series of horizontal wedge or keyhole-shaped slots, cut into the natural Chalk surface, may have held timbers to tie back the revetment posts. The arena was closed by a gate, 12 ft. wide, in the inner palisade, indicated by posts 6 ins. or 10 ins. square set in large circular pits, some $5\frac{1}{2}$ ft. behind which were two piles of stone, 9 ft. apart and about $2\frac{1}{2}$ft. in diameter, apparently of the 4th century and interpreted as rustic pedestals for monuments. At the S. end of the inclined chalk-cut entrance passage, which was about 22 ft. wide, two opposite pairs of posts 10 ins. square in shallow pits against the passage wall, three of which survived with indications of a fourth, may have carried a *cavea* gangway across the entrance.

Since the chalk face of the arena wall was at best only some 6 ft. high, against a safety minimum of 12 ft., earth and chalk rubble from the excavated arena must have been packed on the existing inner scarp behind the revetment, or some kind of staging erected for the front seats with its edge supported perhaps by one or both of the post-settings around the arena. The seating in general was probably cut in the scarp and revetted with timber or chalk. The *cavea* bank was not stripped for signs of such work. Access to the *cavea* could have been gained by steps cut in or placed against the outer scarp, as well as from the entrance passage within the outer gate, perhaps by two short footpaths recognized there on the chalk surface behind the arena wall.

At the S.W. end opposite the entrance a rectangular chamber about 18 ft. wide by about $14\frac{1}{2}$ ft. was cut back into the Chalk at arena level. A ramp led down from the crest of the bank to the top of the rear wall, $3\frac{1}{2}$ ft. high. The chamber, floored with gravel and perhaps roofed with clay tiles, was regarded as a den for wild beasts. Similar chambers were excavated midway along the E. and W. sides. Stout posts set in trenches against their side walls probably carried timber platforms or boxes accommodating officials and important spectators, although only the W. chamber showed post-holes of uprights to strengthen the front of the structure. The chambers below could have housed performers or served as shrines of appropriate deities such as Nemesis (as at Chester, *J.R.S.* LVII (1966),

---

[1] R. J. C. Atkinson, C. M. Piggott and N. K. Sandars, *Excavations at Dorchester, Oxon.*, 1st Report (1951), 99.

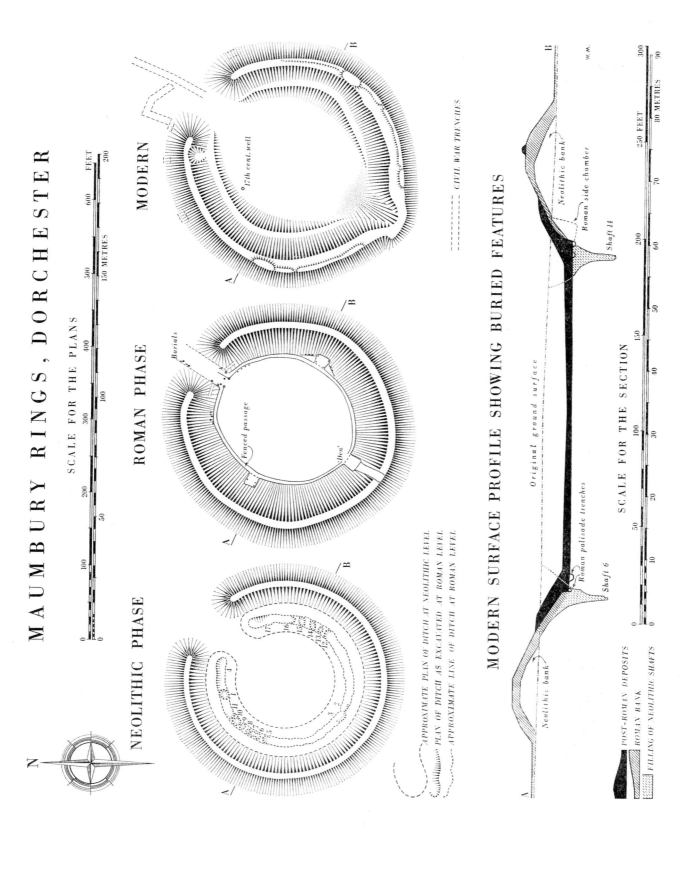

MAUMBURY RINGS, DORCHESTER

NEOLITHIC PHASE

ROMAN PHASE

MODERN

SCALE FOR THE PLANS

---- APPROXIMATE PLAN OF DITCH AT NEOLITHIC LEVEL.
------ PLAN OF DITCH AS EXCAVATED AT ROMAN LEVEL.
—— APPROXIMATE LINE OF DITCH AT ROMAN LEVEL.

----- CIVIL WAR TRENCHES

17th cent. well

Burials

Fenced passage

'Den'

MODERN SURFACE PROFILE SHOWING BURIED FEATURES

Original ground surface

Neolithic bank

Roman side chamber

Shaft 14

W.M.

Neolithic bank

Roman palisade trenches

Shaft 6

SCALE FOR THE SECTION

POST-ROMAN DEPOSITS
ROMAN BANK
FILLING OF NEOLITHIC SHAFTS

180). It is noteworthy in this connexion that both E. and W. chambers had rounded chalk-cut niches in their S. walls, respectively about 30 ins. and 15 ins. wide.

There is little evidence for dating, although an inhumation probably of the 2nd century, on the silt of the entrance passage, is certainly later than the construction (*see* Burials (220 h)). Objects on the arena floor and elsewhere suggest use in the 4th century.

The 17th-century Strongpoint

During the Civil War Maumbury was incorporated in the Dorchester defences and fortified by the Parliamentarians as an outwork guarding the Weymouth road. Work began on the fortifications in July 1642 (A. R. Bayley, *The Civil War in Dorset* (1910), 98, 99).

Excavation showed that parts of the earthworks belonged to this period, including the internal terraces and the S.W. bulge or gun-platform. 17th-century objects were found both in the make-up of the terraces and on the old surface covered by them. At the bulge, where the original bank had been removed in the Roman period, the present bank lay on a surface, scattered with 17th-century pottery, which sloped gently from a point level with the exterior almost to the centre of the arena. The low parapet and platforms, which occupy part of the bank top, are probably of Civil War date. Over 160 lead pistol bullets from the E. bank had presumably been fired at it in practice. A well 4 ft. in diameter and 27 ft. deep had been left unfinished near the N.W. edge of the arena.

A narrow-bottomed ditch between 6 ft. and 8 ft. wide and from 2½ ft. to 4 ft. deep was found at three different points along the outer foot of the bank on the N. The main bank had been considerably steepened by the construction of this ditch which was thought to be of Civil War date and may have

been an additional defence surrounding the entire earthwork. It ran at a higher level into a further short length of ditch 95 ft. long forming a further protection, angular in plan, immediately outside and N. of the entrance. This was V-shaped in profile, 9½ ft. wide and 6 ft. deep. The 17th-century remains, together with the apparently short period of use and deliberate in-filling, suggest that it was a Civil War construction.

A flat-bottomed trench led from the entrance of Maumbury towards the S. gate of Dorchester. Finds and limited usage again suggest that it was dug during the Civil War as a covered way linking the outwork with the town defences. It had been found earlier further N. on the sites of the County Police Headquarters and of Eldridge Pope's brewery (Dorset *Procs.* LXXIII (1951), 101; *see also* Burials (220 c)). It was steep-sided, about 5 ft. deep but deepening to 7 ft. immediately outside the earthwork before rising to meet the internal floor level. The width ranged from 8¼ ft. to 11½ ft. at the top and from 4¾ ft. to 6½ ft. across the bottom.

Subsequent changes at Maumbury have been mainly due to ploughing. In 1724 Stukeley recorded that 'the plough encroaches on the verge of the entrance every year' (*Itinerarium Curiosum* (2nd edn., 1776), 165). A marginal vignette on I. Taylor's Map of Dorset (1765) shows the interior under ridge and furrow. In 1705 Mary Channing was executed by burning in the arena and until 1766 the county gallows stood outside the Rings on the W. (Dorset *Procs.* XXIV (1903), 36; XXXII (1911), 62–3). In 1879 there was an unsuccessful excavation to find a large stone which had once stood W. of the entrance (Dorset *Procs.* XXI (1900), 107; XXX (1909), 259; Moule, 26). In 1895 'about a hundred loads of soil were hauled to the middle of Maumbury from Cedar Park, Dorchester—a place known to teem with Roman shards . . .,' (Dorset *Procs.* XXIX (1908), 263).

OTHER ROMAN MONUMENTS

(Within each parish the monuments are grouped as far as possible in accordance with their geographical setting.)

AFFPUDDLE

Remains of the Roman road from Old Sarum to Dorchester, to be described in *Dorset* V, may be seen descending to the ford at Ashley Barn.

ARNE

(49) WORGRET (SY 98 NW). *Occupation Debris* was found in 1952 and 1955 in a field W. of Cuckoo Pound Lane, on Valley Gravel, towards the crest of the ridge (91258695) and to the S.E. overlooking the flood-plain of the R. Frome (91488669). The pottery (in D.C.M.), ranging from the 1st or 2nd century to the 4th century, seems to be domestic waste. In an army camp here in 1915 a mass of pottery, untraced, was observed lying on 'river gravel' at a depth of 3 ft. and was thought to be derived from Romano-British pottery-kilns. (Dorset *Procs.* XXXVI (1915), xl–xli; LXXIV (1952), 96; LXXVII (1955), 151.)

The following sites (50–54) occupy sandy Bagshot Beds around Poole Harbour, largely heathland.

(50) STOBOROUGH (SY 98 NW). *Occupation Debris*, and a clay-lined vat or basin (Fig.), suggesting industrial activity throughout the Roman period, were found in 1952 on the N. side of Nutcrack Lane (92638638), and subsequently in fields to S. and W.

The 'vat' (in D.C.M.), roughly bell-shaped and about 3 ft. wide internally and 2 ft. deep, has a lining some 4 ins. or 5 ins. thick of puddled chalk faced with fire-hardened clay, a small eccentric sump-hole at bottom and remains of five vertical holes about 4 ins. deep in the flattened rim. The functions of a tongue of chalk about 9 ins. wide projecting obliquely from below the rim on the W. for some 3½ ft., and of two groups of stake-holes flanking the 'vat' in the underlying soil at a depth of 2 ft. 8 ins., are obscure. The 'vat' was constructed in a deposit of ash and burnt earth some 4 ft. to 5 ft. thick containing native Durotrigian and local romanized coarse pottery, much of it oxidized, not necessarily later than the early 2nd century A.D. Similar pottery in the ashy soil inside the 'vat', probably a deliberate filling, may have come from this deposit.[1] It has been suggested that it was a puddling-hole for preparing potter's clay. Neither kiln nor undoubted wasters have, however, been found.

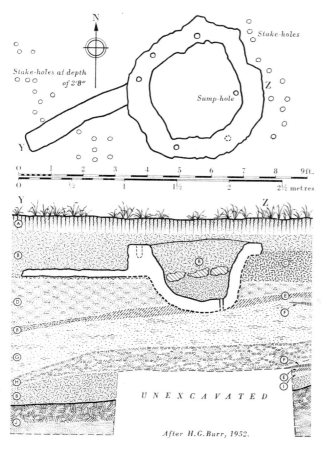

Arne (50). Stoborough, 'vat'. A topsoil; B grey or brown ashy earth; C grey ash; D red ashy earth; E red or orange ash; F dark earth; G ashy sand; H sandy ash; I sand; J alluvium.

In the W. half of the field (925863), S. of the lane, ploughing has revealed widespread pottery, some of the late 4th century. Test pits in paddocks further W. adjoining Stoborough village revealed what were said to be ash deposits, with pottery from Iron Age 'B' and 'C' to 4th-century Romano-British (92488633, 92468630, 92498630, 92498629, 92388627, 92508624). Further S. (92658614), beyond a brook, a bore-hole for clay revealed Romano-British pottery in 1962. (Dorset *Procs.* LXXIV (1952), 95–6; LXXVI (1954), 81–2.)

[1] Two vessels (D.C.M. 1957. 24. 2–3), said to come from the 'vat' are, however, not earlier than *c.* 200.

(51) RIDGE (SY 98 NW). *Occupation Debris* was found in 1953–4 in test pits in the field E. of Redcliff Farm, at the edge of the flood-plain of the Frome (93558672). Much ashy soil, in places 1 ft. to 2 ft. thick, was found with local coarse pottery dating from at least the 2nd to the 4th century A.D., including complete vessels (some, apparently wasters, in Christchurch Museum), a quern-stone and a coin of Septimius Severus (193–211). Pottery manufacture has been suggested here. Romano-British sherds (93288673) were also observed N.E. of the farm. (Dorset *Procs.* LXXVI (1954), 81; LXXXI (1959), 123; *Swanage Times*, 4 Nov., 30 Dec. 1953.)

(52) ARNE HEATH (SY 98 NE). *Occupation Debris* from salt-boiling and possibly also from pottery manufacture has been ploughed up in heathland afforestation N. of Bank Gate Cottages, a few feet above sea level some 300 yds. from the present shore of the Wareham Channel of Poole Harbour (95748723).

The remains comprise several concentrations of coarse-ware sherds (in D.C.M.), almost all oxidized and brittle, with much 'briquetage' associated, as elsewhere in Poole Harbour and the Isle of Purbeck, with crystallization of salt from brine (*see* Introduction, p. 526). The pottery ranges from the 1st or 2nd century to the 3rd or 4th century A.D.; the 'briquetage' includes fragments of large thin-walled containers, perhaps semicircular troughs, with knife-cut rims or edges, and perhaps one piece of a hand-moulded support. Shapeless fragments of fired clay, some with vitrified surface, may belong to associated structures. (Dorset *Procs.* LXXXIV (1962), 140.)

(53) BIG WOOD (SY 98 NE). *Occupation Debris* comes from rabbit-burrows in a shallow re-entrant below the 50 ft. contour W. of Big Wood (97608843). The pottery (in D.C.M.), of local Romano-British coarse ware not necessarily later than the 2nd century, is oxidized and said to be associated with red ashy soil. (Dorset *Procs.* LXXVI (1954), 81.)

(54) SHIPSTAL (SY 98 NE). *Occupation Debris* connected with the salt industry occurs in a strip at least 170 yds. long and 25 yds. wide at the edge of the scarp bordering the mud-flats of Poole Harbour S. of Shipstal Point (central point, 98198809).

Material excavated by H. P. Smith is untraced, but the few subsequent finds of pottery, mostly oxidized, suggest activity in the 1st or 2nd century, while small fragments of 'briquetage' are consistent with material from similar local saltings. Smith records, however, the characteristic hand-moulded clay supports for the brine containers, misinterpreting them as 'kiln rests', and also part of a floor of fired clay which he assigned to a pottery-kiln, but which was more probably a salter's hearth as at Warsash (Hampshire Field Club, *Procs.* XIII, pt. I (1935), 105–9) or Ingoldmells, Lincolnshire (*Ant. J.* XII (1932), 239–253). Objects found recently are in D.C.M. (Dorset *Procs.* LVI (1934), 16–17; LXXIV (1952), 96; LXXXIV (1962), 142; *J.R.S.* XXIV (1934), 216; H. P. Smith, *History of Poole*, I (1948), 88.)

BERE REGIS

The parish contains considerable remains of the Roman road from Old Sarum to Dorchester, to be described in *Dorset* V. Scattered sherds of Romano–

British pottery, some of the 4th century, have been found near Bere Down Buildings (84019723), and a coin of Domitian (81–96) and one of Septimius Severus (193–211) behind the N. rampart of Woodbury hill-fort (856649).

The following sites are on Upper Chalk downland, capped locally by Plateau Gravel.

(120) BAGWOOD (SY 89 NW, NE). *Floors, Wells, Pits* and *Occupation Debris* have been found about 250 ft. above sea level on Bere Down, in Bagwood Close and Coppice and for some 300 yds. W. of the latter, astride the Roman road between Badbury Rings (*Vindocladia?*) and Dorchester.

A well, supposed to lie some 40 yds. N. of the Roman road (85149714), was excavated in 1860 by William Shipp for the Dorset antiquary, Charles Warne, to a depth of 60 ft. to 70 ft. without reaching bottom. It was about 8 ft. in diameter and cut in chalk with the upper 10 ft. to 12 ft. revetted with regularly laid blocks of chalk and 'green sandstone' about 1 ft. square. The ashy filling contained much coarse pottery, some samian, nails and blocks of Kimmeridge shale.[1]

The topsoil of the close W. of the coppice, particularly S. of the line of the Roman road,[2] is noticeably dark, with Romano-British pottery, some of the 4th century; N. of the coppice there is debris from an ancient flint industry, but pottery is scarce, and signs of 'Celtic' fields peripheral to Ancient Field Groups (31) and (32) suggest that this area may have been cultivated during the life of the settlement.

In the W. part of the close, on the gentle northerly slope N. of the Roman road, excavations by Mr. G. Toms in 1962–6 revealed traces of an occupation floor (85109712) with clay roof-tiles, mortared flint and chalk, sandstone, daub, fragments of Kimmeridge shale including parts of incised tablets or panels, worked bones used for weaving, and much iron slag and clinker. This occupation, apparently of the mid or later 2nd century, overlay an earlier 2nd-century pit. Isolated post-holes, two gullies and several pits were found, one of them, refilled in the late 1st century, possibly for road-metal. A chalk-cut well, 3½ ft. in diameter and at least 70 ft. deep, contained six coins, the latest of Tetricus I (270–3), large quantities of pottery and daub with plank and wattle impressions, an extensive series of animal remains including bird, rodent and fish bones, and many objects including a Purbeck stone mortar, quern-stones, an ox-goad and a bill-hook.

Excavations at the S. side of the Roman road in the N.W. corner of the coppice (85169712) disclosed a gravelled area of the late 3rd or 4th century overlying natural gravel, covered with a layer of cobbles in which were a few isolated post-holes;

above this a 2 ft. deposit of burnt occupation debris, including daub and building rubble without roof-tiles, was dated to the 4th century by pottery and a small coin series ending with an issue of 341–6. W. of this point surface finds of the earlier 2nd century to the mid 4th century suggested occupation for at least 300 yds. along the Roman road, and a trial excavation at 84909700 revealed much 2nd and 3rd-century pottery S. of the road.

Warne's identification of the site with the *Ibernio* of the Ravenna Cosmography is without foundation (*cf. Archaeologia* XCIII (1949), 35), nor do any known features connect the site with an official posting-station (*mutatio*). (*Archaeologia* XXXIX (1863), 85–92, reprinted in Warne's *Ancient Dorset* (1872), 201–8; Hutchins I, 147–8; Dorset *Procs.* LXXXIV (1962), 103–6, 115; LXXXV (1963), 99–100; LXXXVI (1964), 110–2; LXXXVII (1965), 98–9; LXXXVIII (1966), 116–7.)

(121) MUDDOX BARROW COPPICE (SY 89 NE). *Occupation Debris* comes from Bere Down N.E. of the coppice some 250 ft. above sea level (85389688). It comprises a few Durotrigian or Romano-British sherds, found in a dark layer about 2 ft. below surface in laying water-pipes in the arable field some 400 yds. S.E. of the remains at Bagwood. (Dorset *Procs.* LXXIII (1951), 102–3.)

BINCOMBE

Remains of the Roman road from Dorchester to Radipole can be seen crossing Ridgeway Hill (*see* Roman Roads, p. 528). Samian ware and Romano-British coarse pottery have been found in Chalbury hill-fort at 69548379 and 69448396 (*Ant. J.* XXIII (1943), 103, 108). Scattered sherds, some of the 3rd or 4th century, occur on Bincombe Hill (688847) among 'Celtic' fields (*see* Ancient Field Group (8)).

(77) WEST HILL (SY 68 SE). An *Inhumation Burial* was found in 1943 during ploughing below the crest of the Chalk ridge (69968494). The adult skeleton, extended E.-W. with head to W., lay in a cist lined at the sides and covered with flat limestone slabs, the top about 1 ft. below surface. There were no associated objects, but analogous burials in Dorset, where datable, are of the Roman period. (Unpublished note and photographs by V. F. M. Oliver, in D.C.M.)

BROADMAYNE

A coin of Constantine I (not Constantius II as stated) of 324–30 comes from Broadmayne village (730865; Dorset *Procs.* LXXVII (1955), 152). Pits and debris indicating settlement into the 4th century have since been found in the village (726866; Dorset *Procs.* LXXXVIII (1966), 103).

CHALDON HERRING

A few Romano-British shale objects and sherds, one of New Forest ware, were found in 1958 E. of Holworth Farm (771832; Dorset *Procs.* LXXXI (1959), 132); Romano-British sherds also come from among 'Celtic'

---

[1] Another well, and remains possibly of a religious nature, were found by J. C. Mansel-Pleydell in 1888 in a 'neighbouring field' in Winterborne Kingston parish but beyond the area of the present volume. The site is unknown but was within a few hundred yards of the Roman road at Bagwood (*Ant. J.* XXXIII (1953), 74–5). A lead coffin found in 1858 is recorded by Ordnance Survey about ¼ mile to the E. (861971).

[2] Excavation here in 1966 revealed pits and traces of a chalk floor associated with a slot for a sleeper-beam of a timber building.

fields in the Warren (790805; *see* Ancient Field Group (15)).

CHICKERELL

(34) PUTTON BRICKYARDS (SY 68 SW). *Occupation Debris* and *Inhumation Burials* have been found in the brickfields on Oxford Clay (649800). Of two burials found in 1924, presumably extended, one had a coarse ware bowl (D.C.M. 1907.3.9) perhaps of the 3rd century;[1] 20 other skeletons were said to have been found in ploughing previously. Occupation debris was 1st and 2nd-century samian ware, coarse pottery including a 3rd-century sherd, and a small grotesque human face in Kimmeridge shale (1933.18.1). A burial (64838000) in a stone cist aligned N.-S. was destroyed in 1963, and three more in 1965, apparently in plain graves similarly orientated, with heads to N., one of them at 64828001. (Dorset *Procs.* XLVI (1925), xlvi, lxix; LVI (1934), 15; LXXXV (1963), 100–1; LXXXVII (1965), 115–8; *J.R.S.* XIV (1924), 235; XXI (1931), 241; *Bath Herald*, 13 Sept. 1924.)

(35) BUCKLAND RIPERS (SY 68 SW). *Inhumation Burials* have been found on the crest of the Langton ridge (Cornbrash) in the S.W. corner of the former parish of Buckland Ripers (631819).

According to Ellis several unaccompanied adult inhumations in covered slab-lined cists, with some charcoal and traces of burning on the stones, were exposed in quarrying 'Tatton Hill' in 1826 and subsequently reburied together. They were presumably extended. Hutchins adds that eight or ten were in cists, about 1 ft. below surface. In 1928 an unaccompanied adult skeleton extended E.-W. with head to W. was found at the same depth nearby (63178191) in a covered cist without end slabs, 6½ ft. long, 20 ins. wide at shoulders and 15 ins. at knees. The posture and type of grave are characteristic of the Roman period in the region. The cemetery apparently extends into Portesham parish (Portesham (63)). (G. A. Ellis, *History and Antiquities of Weymouth and Melcombe Regis* (1829), 254–6; Hutchins II, 492; Dorset *Procs.* L (1928), 122–4.)

CHURCH KNOWLE

Romano-British sherds and a piece of shale armlet were found in the ditch of a Bronze Age barrow (*see* Round Barrows, Church Knowle (41)) on the E. part of Knowle Hill (Dorset *Procs.* LXXVI (1954), 53, 55).

Sites (57–58) lie on the heathland of the Bagshot Beds.

(57) EAST CREECH (SY 98 SW). *Villa;* a tessellated pavement and other remains of buildings about 200 ft. above sea level were partly explored in the 19th century some 300 yds. N. of the Chalk downs.

The site, long under plough, is marked on O.S. by an antiquity symbol at 93538275.[2] A slight ridge, from which

the ground falls away in all directions save W., runs E. on the long axis of the field to some 15 yds. S. of the map symbol, and for the last 60 yds. the crest is slightly flattened, suggesting an artificial platform some 7 yds. wide, with some loose heathstone rubble in the E. end. Around the point marked by the symbol and to the N., much Romano-British material occurs over an area some 50 or 60 yds. square, especially about 93518279, consisting of heathstone, Purbeck limestone, clay roof and flue-tile fragments, wall-plaster, a few large red tile and limestone tesserae, pottery, and Kimmeridge shale waste. The adjoining marshy field to S. has banks and probably drainage ditches of doubtful age, but recent test-borings for clay are not thought to have revealed occupation.

After deep ploughing in 1869, internally-plastered walls were traced by the tenant, Mr. Pike, who found a Tuscan

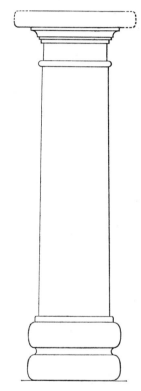

Church Knowle (57). Column. Drawn from photograph. (Approx. $\frac{1}{12}$)

column (*see* Fig.) about 4 ft. high, apparently of Purbeck stone.[1] A pavement with simple lattice design executed in coarse tesserae of red tile on a 'white' ground, and measuring about 16 ft. by at least 11 ft., was found in 1888, while Hutchins records 'many small thin triangular or kite-shaped stones of different dimensions having fine points and thin edges',

---

[1] The type (*cf. Arch. Ael.* XXXV (1957), 203, no. 226) may have a local origin in the later 2nd century.

[2] The symbol first appeared on O.S. 25 in. Dorset LVI.1 (1887), referring to 'Roman coins, pottery and other remains found A.D. 1885', and need not indicate the site of the structural remains found in 1869 and 1888.

[1] The column, not traced, was removed to Mr. Pike's house, 'Leymore', Parkstone. A drawing appeared in *Fresh Leaves and Green Pastures* and a photograph, on which the fig. is based, is in R.C.H.M. records.

suggesting *opus sectile*. A note in D.C.M. states that about 100 or 150 yds. N. of the pavement 'was found a basement, of stone, containing the lower courses of (apparently) a stoke hole, from whence issues a side channel, having a side branch, and showing evident marks of fire. This may be the basement of a hypocaust.' This feature, apparently 12 ft. square according to *The Builder*, may alternatively have been a corn-drying oven; its position is doubtful since a disused clay-pit already existed in the area specified.

Some tesserae are in Poole Museum. Recent surface finds (D.C.M. 1936.18; 1963.1) show occupation from at least 2nd to 4th century. Turned Kimmeridge shale armlet cores occur, and Hutchins records a vessel full of them from a neighbouring field. A shale industry is possible, and although some arable was probably available on the mixed downwashed soils at the foot of the Chalk ridge, the latter was never here occupied by 'Celtic' fields. (Hutchins I, Addenda (1874), 716; Warne, *Ancient Dorset* (1872), Appendix, 282; *D.C.C.*, 13 Dec. 1888; *The Builder* LV (1888), 478; Anon. (Mrs. J. E. Panton), *Fresh Leaves and Green Pastures* (1909), 234; photographs of pavement, R.C.H.M. records.)

(58) GREENSPECKS CLAY-PIT (SY 98 SW). A *Working-floor* and *Occupation Debris* found *c.* 1912 in clay-workings (92658270) some 350 yds. W. of East Creech Farm indicate existence of a workshop of the Kimmeridge shale industry, now perhaps wholly destroyed, which may have originated in Iron Age 'C'.

The material (in D.C.M. and the Furzebrook office of Pike Bros., Fayle and Co.) consists of shale waste, mainly trimmed discs and broken or unfinished armlets, some probably cut by iron tools, almost entirely of the hand-cutting industry elsewhere being replaced by the lathe in Iron Age 'C' and Roman times. An unusual conical object (D.C.M. 1912.37.2) and a circular plaque (1919.2.11) found with 'Roman pottery' are lathe products. Some indurated pieces of the working-floor, containing shale chips, flint flakes and sherds, are preserved at Furzebrook, with 1st-century native ware and sherds probably of the 3rd century presumably from this site. (Dorset *Procs.* LXX (1948), 43–4; LXXIII (1951), 89–91; LXXV (1953), 65, 69; D.C.M. Accessions Book, 17 Dec. 1913.)

(59) BARE CROSS (SY 98 SW). *Inhumation Burials* were found in 1859 on the crest of a saddle in the Purbeck Hills (Upper Chalk), 375 ft. above sea level. They were discovered in the road cutting and an adjoining chalk-pit, probably that at 93088210 behind a W.-facing cross-ridge dyke (*see* Dykes, Church Knowle (56a), Fig. opp. p. 509). Parallel chalk-cut graves 1 ft. or so apart, some 2 ft. deep and 20 ins. wide, lay E.-W. with head to W. Of six examined all were female or young people according to the anthropologist J. Thurnam; one, a woman of at least 40, lay E. of three individuals of about 12, 15, and 18 years. The regular disposition and presumably extended posture argue Roman date. (*Purbeck Papers* I (1859–60), 232–3.)

Sites (60–62) lie on the limestone uplands of the Purbeck and Portland Beds.

(60) BRADLE FARM (SY 98 SW). *Inhumation Burials* were found ¼ mile S. of the farmhouse on the N. slope some 300 ft. above sea level (*c.* 92958020). A covered cist of stone slabs, 11 ft.

long and 1½ ft. wide, found in 1888 1 ft. below surface, contained a central adult skeleton with head to E. and hobnails (in D.C.M.) at feet, with other bones beyond the head. A similar, smaller coffin-shaped cist was found *c.* 1876 about 100 yds. away in the same field. (*D.C.C.*, 17 May 1888; *Notes and Queries for Somerset and Dorset* I (1890), 47.)

(61) SMEDMORE HILL (SY 97 NW). *Occupation Debris* and waste from manufacture of shale armlets were found after pipe-laying in 1956 above the 500 ft. contour near earthworks of a settlement (Church Knowle (55)). The material, mainly from 93167955 about 70 yds. S.E. of the earthworks, consists of Iron Age 'A' ware, samian, 3rd or 4th-century coarse ware, several shale armlet cores of Calkin's classes A, C and D, and a flint lathe-tool. (Dorset *Procs.* LXXVIII (1956), 76; LXXXV (1963), 102–3.)

(62) WEST ORCHARD FARM (SY 97 NW). *Occupation Debris* comes from an undefined area (93657926) on both sides of the field wall some 200 yds. S.E. of Newfoundland copse, about 550 ft. above sea level. A trial excavation in 1956, N. of the wall, partly exposed a rough floor of limestone blocks of unknown date overlying an Iron Age 'A' deposit (93687925). Excavated material and surface finds include waste from manufacture of hand-cut shale armlets, much Iron Age 'A' pottery (some haematite-coated), sherds of Iron Age 'C' or early Roman date, and a 2nd-century enamelled brooch, but no demonstrably later material. Flint flakes and scrapers occur in the field to W. (Dorset *Procs.* LXXV (1953), 69; LXXVII (1955), 126–7; LXXXV (1963), 102.) Excavation S. of the field wall in 1967 revealed pits and further traces of flooring, and suggested two phases of Iron Age 'A' occupation associated with a hand-cut shale armlet industry. The later occupation, marked by Durotrigian pottery and other finds, some certainly of post-conquest date, was associated with waste from a similar shale industry perhaps using metal tools, and a few shale lathe-cores. There was evidence for a flint industry of Mesolithic character in the vicinity. (Dorset *Procs.*, LXXXIX (1967), 141–3.)

COOMBE KEYNES

(21) MANOR FARM (SY 88 NW). *Occupation Debris* comes from N.E. of Coombe Wood about 175 ft. above sea level on Upper Chalk near its junction with Reading Beds of the Frome valley (83688552). A silage pit in 1950 showed dark patches 3 ft. or 4 ft. below surface containing sherds of the 1st or 2nd to the 4th century. There are other remains nearby (*see* Wool (50)). (Dorset *Procs.* LXXII (1950), 82; LXXIII (1951), 85.)

CORFE CASTLE

Roman pottery and in some cases shale objects have come from the following sites not listed as monuments: (i) clay-pits S. of Norden Farm (Dorset *Procs.* LXXIII (1951), 88–9; *Ant. J.* XXXI (1951), 193–4); (ii) Challow Hill (Dorset *Procs.* LXXXVII (1965), 111; (iii) Town's End, SY 96308117 (Dorset *Procs.* LXXXVI (1964), 117); (iv) Lynch (*Purbeck Papers* III (1859–60), 220; Dorset *Procs.* LXXVII (1955), 150); (v) Chapman's Pool (Dorset *Procs.* XIII (1892), 183). For the Roman objects and intrusive inhumations probably of that age, in two barrows at Afflington, *see* Round Barrows, Corfe Castle (183–4); for two settlements, both probably of Roman date, associated with 'Celtic' fields, *see* Settlements, Corfe Castle (221–2).

Sites (224–230) occupy sandy Bagshot Beds, largely heathland, in and around Poole Harbour.

(224) GREEN ISLAND (SZ 08 NW). *Occupation Debris*, perhaps Iron Age 'A' to late Roman, with waste from Kimmeridge shale armlet manufacture, comes mainly from the N. half of the island below the 50 ft. contour.

Pottery including New Forest ware, and shale, were found before 1925 in the N.W. cliff scarp at 00588674, and above the W. cliff at 00458656. Test pits by H. P. Smith in 1951 near The Hermitage (00608664) and in five places N. and S.W. of the lagoon and two or three W. of the N. landing-stage, nearly all showed occupation remains, including Iron Age 'C' pottery, samian, and shale from both hand-cut and lathe-turned armlet industries; at The Hermitage, hand-cut waste showing use of iron tools occurred with 'C' sherds; iron slag was found on the E. shore N. of the lagoon and in one of the test pits S. of it. Subsequent excavation by Mr. J. B. Calkin near the N. shore (00608673) revealed an occupation layer with some Iron Age 'A' and 'B' pottery but mainly 'C'; a Hengistbury class H sherd[1] and fragments of amphorae suggesting a regional pre-Caesarian trade with the Continent; also shale workers' waste, mostly class A cores from turned armlets with a few hand-cut roughs, and worked flints, some approaching the standardized Romano-British type of lathe-tool. Oxidized sherds (in D.C.M.), some of the 3rd or 4th century, come from near the old landing-stage (00708679). Some of Smith's finds are in Poole Museum. (Dorset *Procs.* LXXV (1953), 53–4, 60, 64–6, 69; LXXXV (1963), 104–5; LXXXVIII (1966), 121; H. P. Smith, *History of Poole* I (1948), 89; O.S. Archaeology Division records.)

Buried remains, mostly below low water mark, of a stone-ramped causeway connecting the W. shore with the mainland some 200 yds. W. of Cleavel Point, save for a gap in the centre of the channel, were confirmed by excavation and diving in 1959. The causeway, undated, was probably surfaced with stone flags on a log corduroy laid axially (Dorset *Procs.* LXXXVIII (1966), 158–60.)

(225) FURZEY ISLAND (SZ 08 NW). *Occupation Debris* comes from two places in the low cliff face on the W. shore. A shallow earth-filled depression, unexcavated, some 3 ft. below surface and about 12 ft. wide in exposed section (00918694), yielded a small amount of native coarse pottery, not closely datable. Unworked shale fragments are said to occur. Some 200 yds. N.W., a narrow feature, perhaps a gully (00838710), had a similar sherd and a fragment possibly of Romano-British salting 'briquetage'. (Dorset *Procs.* LXXXV (1963), 104.)

(226) FITZWORTH (SY 98 NE). *Occupation Debris*, Iron Age and Roman, with remains of a hut and salters' waste, comes from a wide area in the N. of the low-lying Fitzworth peninsula.

Two oval areas of Romano-British domestic occupation with much shell refuse, each with adjacent working area, were examined in 1947 some 400 yds. N.E. of the farmhouse. The larger domestic area of some 50 yds. by 25 yds. (99228676) had pottery of the 2nd to 4th centuries A.D. and, on the W., remains perhaps of a round hut (99208676) about 20 ft. wide, with sandstone footings and central hearth; the smaller (99388670) had similar pottery and two coins of the later 3rd and early 4th centuries. The working areas (99268674, 99338668) showed no structural remains but much oxidized coarse pottery of the 1st century and later, unfired clay, and 'briquetage', mostly broken brine-containers and props, but including fire-bars possibly from pottery-kilns. Subsequent ploughing revealed similar material in the same field: burnt clay (99318677), sherds and 'briquetage' (99208682, 99178672, and especially 99298667). Romano-British sherds also come from the field to N.W. (99148687), near Iron Age 'A', 'B' and 'C' sherds exposed in a bomb-crater further W. (99038687). (Dorset *Procs.* LXX (1948), 42–3, 51, 57–8; LXXI (1949), 62–3; LXXXIV (1962), 137, 142.)

(227) OWER (SY 98 NE, SZ 08 NW). A *Pottery-kiln*, and *Occupation Debris* including salters' waste, have been found in low-lying arable fields in the N.E. part of the Ower peninsula where the South Deep approaches Cleavel Point.

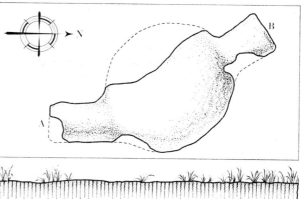

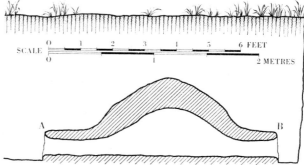

Corfe Castle (227). Pottery-kiln.

---

[1] *Cf.* J. P. Bushe-Fox, *Excavations at Hengistbury Head, Hampshire* (1915), 44–5; R. E. M. Wheeler and K. M. Richardson, *Hill-forts of Northern France* (1957), 58.

The pottery-kiln of 'horizontal-draught' type, excavated in 1951 underneath the low bank bordering the mud-flats of Poole Harbour (00048618), consisted of a 10 in. thick dome of fired clay, some 1½ ft. high and 4 ft. in diameter internally, on a level clay floor 2 ins. thick, with two flues sub-rectangular in cross-section, about 1 ft. wide and 6 ins. high, set against the S. and N.W. sides. The dome was broken into on W., probably to extract the load after firing, but does not seem to have possessed vents unless these had been plugged with clay.

Oxidized coarse ware sherds found close to the kiln include a type (*cf. Arch. Ael.* XXXV (1957), no. 314) hardly datable before *c.* 200 as well as others of Durotrigian origin. Excavation about 30 yds. S.W. (00018616) showed similar oxidized ware including a 3rd or 4th-century type (*cf. ibid.*, no. 228).

Salters' waste, consisting mainly of fragments of large thin-walled containers and hand-moulded props, abounds at the kiln site, and is associated with oxidized sherds in a thin layer below topsoil, visible in the scarp bordering the mud-flats for some 230 yds. (00198609 to 00008619) and reappearing further W. for about 50 yds. (99928618 to 99878618). Excavation showed 1st and 2nd-century occupation debris, including a shell midden, at two places, 116 yds. S. (00038606) and 250 yds. S.W. of the kiln (99898599), the latter with oxidized sherds, perhaps wasters. Romano-British sherds also come from ploughing near Newton Bay (99998595) and, with 'briquetage', from the field W. of the kiln (99888603). (Dorset *Procs.* LXXIII (1951), 91–2; LXXXIV (1962), 115–6, 141.)

(228) REMPSTONE (SY 98 SE). *Occupation Debris* comes from Rempstone Hall and neighbourhood.

The lower half of a rotary quern and part probably of an upper stone, both of heathstone, were found after ploughing in the field W. of the Hall, the former at about 99068249. A few Romano-British sherds have been found here; a waste core from a turned shale armlet comes from the stream in the grounds of the Hall (99168246). (Dorset *Procs.* LXXXV (1963), 103–4.)

A deposit of similar cores with a shale object 'like the bowl of a large glass or rummer . . .' was found in 1845 in draining a withy-bed, presumably that adjoining the main road at 995820, in which lies the Rempstone stone circle. This is probably to be identified with the conical object (D.C.M. 1908.28.1), apparently a waste product of the lathe, formerly said to come from Norden, Corfe Castle. (Devonshire Assoc. *Trans.* II (1867–8), 630; *W.A.M.* XLIV (1928), 113; *Purbeck Papers* I (1856–7), 86; Hutchins I, 563; Warne, *Ancient Dorset* (1872), Appendix, 229–30.)

(229) BRENSCOMBE FARM (SY 98 SE). *Villa*; remains of two mosaic pavements were found in 1961 and 1967 about 500 yds. N. of the foot of the Chalk downs some 150 ft. above sea level (97898272). The site is scheduled as an ancient monument.

The first fragment, 6 ins. below surface and orientated approximately N.E. to S.W., measures some 7 ft. by 3 ft. exclusive of remains of mortar bedding, and is of approximately ½ in. tesserae of chalk and brown ferruginous sandstone. The pattern, much disturbed, shows parallel brown and white bands of varying width with traces of a rectangular panel to S.W. within a chevron border. Excavation revealed spreads of stone debris, or rough cobbling, on all sides. A superior mosaic with a foliate scroll was partly exposed near by in 1967.

Surface debris includes pieces of Roman brick, roof and flue-tile, small red brick tesserae, a few sherds of samian ware and some coarse ware of the 3rd or 4th century. (Dorset *Procs.* LXXXIV (1962), 113–4; LXXXV (1963), 103; LXXXVIII (1966), 120; LXXXIX (1967), 144.)

(230) NORDEN (SY 98 SE). *Inhumation Burials, Floors* and *Occupation Debris*, including objects from a Kimmeridge shale industry, have been found above the 50 ft. contour in the Norden Clay Works, some 300 yds. N. of the Corfe gap in the Chalk range.

In and perhaps before 1882 several burials in 'stone coffins', probably slab cists, were found in the Matcham pits (957826), with remains thought to belong to a road at a depth of 18 ins., and, nearby, a 'fine collection of Roman pottery', mostly 'urn-shaped vessels, decorated with a lozenge pattern around the neck'. These vessels, preserved by Lord Eldon but not traced, were thought to indicate the proximity of a kiln.

Roman remains have been found recently between the clay-pits beside the Wareham road. N.E. of the road were surface finds (956827), remains of a stone-paved floor with pottery, some of the 4th century (95788261), a small cist containing Romano-British sherds (95648265), and, beyond the railway, a chalk and limestone floor at a depth of 2½ ft., associated with a coin and sherds of the 4th century (95948264). Finds S.W. of the road occurred between the mineral railway (95568266) and 'North Castle' (95788250). A deposit 1 ft. thick of chalk and limestone capped with small stone blocks, 1½ ft. below ground surface but rising N.W. in conformity with it, was exposed in 1964 in an excavation 3 ft. square (95558266). It was observed in a pipe-line trench for 6 yds. to 10 yds. S.E. until destroyed by a clay-pit, and is possibly a road, perhaps that claimed to have been found *c.* 1882. It overlay Roman material including a coarse ware sherd of the early 2nd century and part of an oblong shale plaque with incised geometric decoration (in Christchurch Museum). A piece of a carved shale table leg (in D.C.M.) and some 20 small siltstone cubes, perhaps unused tesserae, were unstratified except for a single cube below the deposit.

Cores from turned shale armlets are said to have been common at Norden; a few are in D.C.M. Also in D.C.M. are two more shale plaques, one circular, found before 1859 with a pair of bronze dividers in lowering the road N.W. of St. Edward's Bridge, and part of a carved table leg from a clay-pit near Hill Coppices (95068257; *Ant. J.* XXXI (1951), 193–4). These objects suggest a manufactory of furniture and other objects of shale besides armlets. (Dorset *Procs.* VIII (1887), xxxix–xl; XIII (1892), 188; LXXIII (1951), 86–9; LXXV (1953), 69; LXXVII (1955), 126, 150; LXXVIII (1956), 91; LXXXVI (1964), 116–7; LXXXVII (1965), 111–3; LXXXVIII (1966), 119; LXXXIX (1967), 145; *Purbeck Papers* I (1859–60), 225; II (1867), 53–4; Hutchins I (1861), 471; H. J. Moule, *Dorchester Antiquities* (2nd edn. 1906), 44.)

Sites (231) and (232) lie on Upper Chalk.

(231) CASTLE HILL (SY 98 SE). *Occupation Debris* has been

found on the N. and W. parts of the hill occupied by the castle. Sherds of 2nd-century samian and coarse ware, and small fragments seemingly of Roman flue-tile, come from excavations in the West Bailey (95838228); a few sherds of coarse ware are recorded from the surface of the scarp S. of the latter and at the outer base of the N.E. wall of the Inner Ward (95948233). (*Med. Arch.* IV (1960), 38; Dorset *Procs.* LXXXV (1963), 104.)

(232) WEST HILL (SY 98 SE). *Occupation Debris* comes from ploughing above the 300 ft. contour on the crest of the narrow ridge overlooking the Corfe gap (954823; Fig. p. 97). Romano-British sherds, some of the 3rd or 4th century, flint flakes, part of an unfinished hand-cut shale armlet, and 26 bronze coins (all of the 4th century down to Gratian (367-83) save two of the 2nd and 3rd centuries) have been found since 1952 on the crest of the hill. (Dorset *Procs.* LXXIV (1952), 93; LXXXI (1959), 108; LXXXVI (1964), 117; LXXXVIII (1966), 120.)

Sites (233) and (234) occupy loamy Wealden Beds.

(233) SANDYHILLS COPSE (SY 98 SE). *Occupation Debris* of Iron Age 'C' or early Roman date comes from ploughing W. of Sandyhills Copse and the adjacent part of Corfe Common, on and near the crest of a ridge some 150 ft. above sea level. A concentration of coarse ware sherds and some burnt and unburnt clay occurs close to the copse (96958157); a scatter of similar sherds, flint flakes and shale fragments has been found on the common about 100 yds. S.W. (96888149). A waste core from a hand-cut shale armlet comes from E. of the copse. The objects are in D.C.M. (Dorset *Procs.* LXXXIV (1962), 114-5.)

(234) BLASHENWELL (SY 98 SE). *Inhumation Burials, Floors* and *Occupation Debris* including waste from both hand-cut and lathe-turned shale armlet industries and ranging from Iron Age 'A' to Roman times, have been found in and near the old marl-pit (951805) in the calcareous tufa deposit N. of Blashenwell Farm. The site is about 150 ft. above sea level, close to the Purbeck marble outcrop.

The geology and ecology of the tufa, apparently deposited by the neighbouring stream draining from a synclinal trough in the Upper Purbeck Beds and containing a Mesolithic industry (*see* p. 511) have been much studied. Deposition of tufa ceased before the Roman period and it was overlaid by 1 ft. or more of topsoil containing Roman debris and a mixed Roman and post-Roman fauna indicating locally open conditions.

A contracted skeleton of a youth in a Purbeck stone cist was found in 1895 some 4 ft. deep in the tufa at the S. end of the pit (95188047). In 1908 another cist, with floor and cover slabs, containing an adult skeleton probably extended with head to N., was exposed but not cleared nearby in the S. face above the tufa a few feet from the road, while indications of at least two more graves were seen in the side of the road cutting. Some 6 ft. to 8 ft. W. of the cist a compact mass of unmortared herringbone masonry, some 2 ft. high and 4 ft. long or wide, appeared in the face, based in the tufa. In 1965

a tightly contracted inhumation facing E. with head N. was found between two end slabs, resting on undisturbed tufa at a depth of 2½ ft. A later pit, cutting through the grave but avoiding the burial, which was perhaps of the Early Bronze Age, contained a Romano-British sherd.

In 1936 Dr. W. H. C. Frend recorded 'floors of laid paving-stone, traces of hearths and a large amount of coarse pottery and "coal money"[1] ... brought to light through the construction of a farm road to the farmhouse'. In 1938 two vessels found near human vertebrae in topsoil at the roadside between the pit and the farmhouse were exhibited at the Institute of Archaeology, London;[2] one of these, in the Institute's collection, is of Iron Age 'C' or early Roman date. The site, now under plough, yields Iron Age 'A', 'C', and Romano-British pottery, flint and shale waste from a hand-cut armlet industry, and equivalent waste from manufacture of turned armlets, mainly in and near the S. end of the pit. Stone slabs may indicate a floor some 20 yds. S.W. (95168045). Photographs of the 1908 discoveries are in D.C.M. and R.C.H.M. records. Some remains were noted in 1965 a quarter of a mile N.N.W. (Dorset *Procs.* XVII (1896), 67-75; XXIX (1908), xl; LXX (1948), 43; LXXV (1953), 52, 69; LXXXVII (1965), 97-8; LXXXVIII (1966), 120; LXXXIX (1967), 145; W. H. C. Frend, 'Iron Age and Roman sites in Purbeck' (MS. in D.C.M., 1936), 13; *Procs. Geologists' Association* LXVI (1955), 87-8.)

Sites (235-239) are on the limestone plateau of the Purbeck and Portland Beds. For position of (237-9) *see* Fig. p. 631.

(235) ENCOMBE OBELISK (SY 97 NW). A *Building* and *Occupation Debris* including waste from the manufacture of turned shale armlets, were excavated in 1954 about 550 yds. W. of the obelisk, on the upper N. slope of a limestone ridge above the 500 ft. contour (94277898).

The building, aligned approximately N.-S. towards the S.W. corner of a 'Celtic' field (Ancient Field Group (21)), was

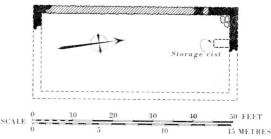

rectangular, 51 ft. by some 20 ft. to 25 ft., and probably thatched; its E. side was indicated approximately by surface debris and no internal partitions were observed. Surface rubble suggested that the building may have stood in a compound. The remaining walls, some 6 ins. high at most, below

[1] The local name for turned shale armlet cores.
[2] *Catalogue of an Exhibition of Recent Archaeological Discoveries* (Institute of Archaeology, University of London, 1938), 25. A note (in R.C.H.M. records) by the exhibitor, Henrietta Davies, shows part of a Durotrigian jar found there in 1936 'with 4 other pots, all within 12 ins.'

6 ins. of topsoil, were 2 ft. wide, of rubble faced with selected or roughly dressed limestone blocks, unmortared and resting on weathered Portland Stone brash. Some flagstones remained in the N.W. corner. A rectangular cist, about 4 ft. by 2 ft. and 1½ ft. deep, sunk from floor level beside the N. wall-footings, and floored and lined on the three outer sides with flagstones including reused roof-tiles, may have been an addition. It contained five prepared shale discs and 27 lathe-cores of Calkin's class C. Surface finds included similar cores and examples of classes A and B, flint lathe-tools and pottery of the 1st or 2nd century to the 4th century, as well as Iron Age 'A' sherds and a few rejects from a hand-cut armlet industry. (Dorset *Procs.* LXXV (1953), 54, 69; LXXVI (1954), 80–1; LXXXVIII (1966), 114–5, 120.)

(236) QUARRY WOOD, ENCOMBE (SY 97 NW). An *Inhumation Burial* was found *c.* 1788 in quarrying near the former Encombe Lodge. The skeleton, under 'two very large flat stones set up edgeways', was accompanied by an earthen vessel of about one gallon capacity filled to the brim with 'coal-money'; the quarry is evidently that at 949791 above the 400 ft. contour on the N.E. side of the North Gwyle. (*Purbeck Papers* I (1859–60), 226.)

(237) KINGSTON PLANTATION (SY 97 NE). *Occupation Debris* including Kimmeridge shale waste comes from ploughing on the plateau S. of the plantation, about 475 ft. above sea level (953788). The material includes samian ware, coarse ware of Iron Age 'C' or early Roman date and some of the 3rd or 4th century, shale armlet lathe-cores of Calkin's class C, and a few Iron Age 'A' sherds and rejects from a hand-cut shale armlet industry. (Dorset *Procs.* LXXV (1953), 69; LXXVI (1954), 80.)

(238) KINGSTON BARN (SY 97 NE). *Occupation Debris*, including an altar, has been found in arable about 450 ft. above sea level S. of Kingston Barn (963788). Samian sherds, coarse ware of the 1st or 2nd to the 4th century, fragments of shale, and a few large stones possibly from structures, come from W. of the footpath, with, at 96267894, a roughly made Roman altar of Purbeck stone some 14 ins. high (now in D.C.M.; Plate 228). Sherds of Iron Age 'A', and shale waste, occur in the field (962788) to W. (Dorset *Procs.* LXXIV (1952), 93; LXXVI (1954), 79; LXXXIII (1961), 85–6.)

(239) WESTHILL WOOD, ENCOMBE (SY 97 NE). *Occupation Debris* comes from ploughing above Westhill Wood near Hounstout Cliff, about 475 ft. above sea level (950778). The debris consists of samian ware, coarse pottery of the 1st or 2nd century to the 4th century, a coin of Carausius of *c.* 293, some clay roof-tile fragments, chert and flint flakes, and shale waste including a few cores from turned armlets. A mound (95067783), some 75 ft. in diameter and 2 ft. high, shows much limestone rubble. (Dorset *Procs.* LXXXI (1959), 108.)

(240) ELDON SEAT, ENCOMBE (SY 97 NW). *Huts* of Iron Age 'A', and *Occupation Debris* from Iron Age 'A' to the Roman period including waste from shale armlet industries, have been excavated near the Kimmeridge Clay cliffs W. of Freshwater Steps, about 250 ft. above sea level (939776).

Excavations by Prof. B. Cunliffe, in 1963–4, where an area with Iron Age and Roman surface debris is crossed by an E.-W. lynchet of Ancient Field Group (22), revealed remains of an early phase of Iron Age 'A' showing features derived from the Late Bronze Age, succeeded by a phase associated with haematite-coated pottery. A circular hut of the earlier phase, 22 ft. in diameter with post-holes and a S.E. porch, was associated with a paved area to S. overlying some earlier post-holes. A broadly contemporary hut to N. was of 24 ft. diameter with remains of a clay and earth floor, a clay hearth and a small adjacent clay oven partly lined with sherds. Between them slighter traces of a hut perhaps 17 ft. by 24 ft., floored with broken limestone and with a hearth of stone slabs capped with clay, belonged to the later phase. Debris from a hand-cut shale armlet industry was associated with both phases, but other objects suggest normal domestic activities such as spinning and weaving, especially in the second phase. The lynchet, apparently developing after this occupation had ceased, had Durotrigian sherds towards its base and early Roman above, doubtless derived from nearby occupation of Iron Age 'C' or early Roman date, with evidence for a lathe-turned armlet industry, which Austen also recorded in the vicinity in 1856.

Previous excavations here, including those of *c.* 1936 which are probably wrongly recorded as at 94097748 some 250 yds. nearer Freshwater Steps, were thought to indicate the presence of roughly cobbled floors and drystone walls. They produced abundant material like that found in 1963–4, with Romano-British sherds of the 1st or 2nd century and perhaps the early 3rd century. (J. H. Austen, *Purbeck Papers* I (1856–7), 90; Dorset *Procs.* LXXI (1949), 52; LXXV (1953), 69; LXXVII (1955), 150; LXXXIII (1961), 83–4; LXXXV (1963), 98–9; LXXXVI (1964), 109.)

CORFE MULLEN

Remains of the Roman road from Badbury Rings to Hamworthy can be seen on Barrow Hill and on much of the parish boundary with Poole further to the S. (*see* Roman Roads, p. 530). Romano-British sherds are recorded from a garden at Lamb's Green (99599871; Dorset *Procs.* LXV (1943), 58), an oven (99619885) to N. beside the Roman road and a pit (99729877) with early pottery to N.E. (*ibid.* LXXXVIII (1966), 115; *see* Fig. p. 530).

Sites (24) and (25) occupy the Plateau Gravel ridge overlooking the Stour valley to N.

(24) EAST END (SY 99 NE). A *Pottery-kiln*, *Pits*, *Ditches*, and *Occupation Debris* have been found about 200 ft. above sea level in the railway ballast pit beside the destroyed Roman road (992983).

A settlement, possibly established in Iron Age 'B' or 'C' and surviving at least to the mid 4th century, is indicated by storage and rubbish pits and alleged hut sites observed since 1927, a pottery-kiln, excavated in 1932, ascribed to *c.* A.D. 50–60 with contemporary pits and ditches, and possibly by a late Roman kiln. Early wares, including Continental imports, were sherds of Hengistbury class B, butt-beakers, Belgic platters, amphorae and S. Gaulish samian, with metallic-lustred ware of New

Forest type indicating the latest known occupation. Iron slag suggested smelting; milling on a commercial or military scale is implied by a piece of upper stone (*catillus*) of a Niedermendig lava donkey-mill (*see* Fig.) in Poole Museum.[1] One or possibly two pits lined with clay contained carbonized grain, mainly Spelt wheat.[2]

The stoke-hole of the kiln alone survived (99219830). Its filling and that of four pits and two ditches some 15 ft. long found within 20 yds. of it, yielded analogous sherds and an *as* of Caligula of A.D. 40. Kiln wares included ring-neck flagons, mortaria, and thin-walled romanized versions of Durotrigian cooking-pots probably unintentionally oxidized. Six oxidized vessels (four in B.M.), found together in two rows in 1929, were probably rejects from a late 3rd or 4th-century kiln producing cooking-pots and bowls of Gillam's types 147 and

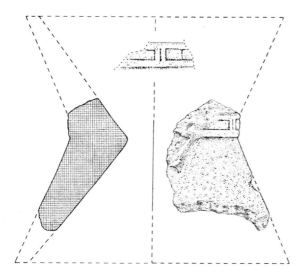

Corfe Mullen (24). Donkey-mill, upper stone. ($\frac{1}{12}$)

228 (*Arch. Ael.* XXXV (1957), 180–251). Objects are in B.M., D.C.M., Poole Museum and Christchurch Museum. (*Ant. J.* XV (1935), 42–55; Dorset *Procs.* LXV (1943), 57–8; *Procs. Bournemouth Natural Science Society* XLI (1951), 52–3; M. H. Callender, *Roman Amphorae* (1965), 156.)

(25) COGDEAN ELMS, EAST END (SY 99 NE). A *Cremation Burial* was found in 1865 in the old Corfe Mullen gravel pit, E. of the Roman road (995982). A Durotrigian bead-rim jar of Brailsford's class 4, containing burnt bones of an adult, a worn imitation *as* of Claudius I (41–54) and fragments of two glass phials distorted by fire, was found with amphora fragments 'in a gravel pit near the Cogdean Elms Inn, 1865' (B.M., Register of Antiquities, 1892.9–1.365–8). Several urns, undated, with charred bones, were found before 1847 appar-

---

ently in the same pit. (*Arch. J.* LXXXVII (1930), 286; *P.P.S.* XXIV (1958), 116; Dorset *Procs.* XI (1890), 22.)

DORCHESTER

For Roman remains, *see* pp. 531–92.

HOLME, EAST

Three coins, two of Constantine I (306–37), are recorded from gardens of Holme Priory, SY 897860 (*Swanage Times*, 17 Feb. 1954, and information from Mr. J. B. Calkin).

(13) SWANAGE RAILWAY BRIDGE (SY 98 NW). *Occupation Debris* has been found in cleaning the bed of the Frome S. of Worgret (90808616). Romano-British pottery, possibly derived from a site on the Valley Gravel terrace to N., was first noted in 1899. Recent finds of coarse pottery (in D.C.M.) include sherds of the 3rd or 4th century. (Dorset *Procs.* XX (1899), 149.)

KIMMERIDGE[1]

Sites (16–18) are on Kimmeridge Clay.

(16) METHERHILLS (SY 97 NW). An *Inhumation Burial* and *Occupation Debris* indicating manufacture of shale armlets come from a low hill S. of the village overlooking Kimmeridge Bay (913792).

An oval stone cist lined with water-worn boulders, apparently plastered and containing human remains with a rough hand-cut shale ring on either side of the skull, and in the same field a large hoard of turned shale armlet cores, were found before 1856. Subsequent examination by Warne showed similar cores to a depth of 18 ins. Excavation on the S. slope (91357917) in 1946 indicated shale-working in an oval area some 40 yds. long below the 200 ft. contour; the remains were flint lathe-tools and worked flakes, slabs of unworked shale, and Romano-British sherds including 4th-century ware. (*Purbeck Papers* I (1856–7), 89, 90; *Arch. J.* XVI (1859), 300; Warne, *Ancient Dorset* (1872), Appendix, 329; Dorset *Procs.* XIII (1892), 183; LXXV (1953), 52, 69.)

(17) KIMMERIDGE BAY (SY 97 NW). *Debris* from salt-boiling exists above high water mark near the site of the former pier below the Clavel Tower.

The remains consist of a deposit at least 4 ft. thick of burnt and unburnt shale and fine grey soil in the talus at the foot of the hill, about 8 ft. above high water mark, extending for some 25 yds. (90807872 to 90817870) and containing salt-boiling 'briquetage' and some vesicular slag; the deposit is cut through by remains of walls of relatively recent date. Burnt shale appears at a higher level some yards further S. The 'briquetage' includes hand-moulded supports and pieces of coarsely-gritted flat-bottomed containers about 1 in. thick. (Dorset *Procs.* LXXXIV (1962), 140, 142.)

(18) SWALLAND FARM (SY 97 NW). *Occupation Debris* associated with shale armlet industries, probably Iron Age and Roman, comes from 400 yds. S.W. of the farmhouse (92547798).

---

[1] The fragment, some 16 ins. square, belongs to a mill of Pompeian type. The *catillus* was perhaps 2¾ ft. high, with a simple moulding at the waist, below which a rough excrescence could be remains of a lug.

[2] J. Percival, *Wheat in Great Britain* (1948), 19; K. Jessen and H. Helbaek, *Cereals in Great Britain and Ireland in Prehistoric and Early Historic Times* (1944), 40–1.

[1] For the major site usually known as 'Kimmeridge' or 'Gaulter' *see* Steeple parish, Monument (31).

The site, about 650 yds. N.E. of Clavell's Hard where the 'blackstone' band of the Kimmeridge shale outcrops at the base of the cliff, yields shale waste from a hand-cut armlet industry probably of the Iron Age, and from a turned armlet industry of the Roman period. A few sherds, perhaps Iron Age 'A' and Romano-British, come from 150 yds. W.N.W. (92427804). (Dorset *Procs.* XIII (1892), 183; LXXV (1953), 69; LXXXV (1963), 99.)

KNIGHTON, WEST

Sites (26) and (27) are on the edge of Reading Beds overlying Upper Chalk.

(26) LITTLE MAYNE FARM (SY 78 NW). *Occupation Debris* has been found near the farmhouse (72308708). A late 1st-century samian cup and other Roman sherds (in D.C.M.) were found in 1930 and 1936 in tree-planting S.W. of the house above the 200 ft. contour (Dorset *Procs.* LXXIV (1952), 99).

(27) WEST KNIGHTON (SY 78 NW). *Occupation Debris* has been found S. of the village (73278735). A quern-stone of Wessex type and a sherd of Iron Age 'C' or Roman date come from trenching in 1941 in an army camp W. of the road to Broadmayne about 200 ft. above sea level (Dorset *Procs.* LXXIV (1952), 100).

LANGTON MATRAVERS

A few Romano-British sherds are recorded on the limestone ridge seawards of Spyway Barn, SY 995773, and on Wealden Beds near Windmill Barn, SZ 00928005 (Dorset *Procs.* LXXXV (1963), 102).

(42) WILKSWOOD (SY 97 NE). *Occupation Debris*, probably connected with the Purbeck marble industry and possibly with shale-working, has been found on Upper Purbeck Beds below 200 ft. on the N. slope of the limestone ridge (99377941).

The remains, excavated at the E. edge of a modern quarry in the Purbeck marble outcrop, consisted of debris apparently of a midden covering some 20 sq. yds., with scattered material for perhaps 100 yds. E. The bulk of the datable sherds, including samian, amphorae, colour-coated bowls and white flagons, as well as native wares, ranged from mid to late 1st century A.D., with a few pieces of Iron Age 'A' and late Roman ware. A sawn and polished piece of Purbeck marble, several worked and unworked fragments of shale, four turned armlets, and many flints including notched tools, suggest marble and shale-working, although characteristic armlet cores and lathe-tools are wanting. The site lies below remains of 'Celtic' fields of Ancient Field Group (28). (Dorset *Procs.* LXXV (1953), 52–3; LXXXI (1959), 121–2; *Archaeological News Letter* I, no. 11 (1949), 15.)

Sites (43–44) lie on Middle Purbeck limestone.

(43) ACTON (SY 97 NE). An *Inhumation Burial* and *Occupation Debris*, probably connected with shale armlet industries of the Iron Age and Roman period, have been found in quarrying about 400 ft. above sea level near Blacklands.

The occupation site (98957774), largely destroyed by earlier quarrying, was tested in 1945, yielding a few Iron Age 'A' sherds, burnt daub, sling-stones, several unfinished hand-cut

shale armlets and turned armlet cores of Calkin's class C, shale waste, and large concentrations of flint flakes including rough tools, at a depth of about 3 ft. (Dorset *Procs.* LXX (1948), 43; LXXV (1953), 69.)

The burial, some 500 yds. N. (989782), was extended with feet to S.E. in a covered stone cist without grave-goods, and is probably Romano-British (Dorset *Procs.* LXXI (1949), 66).

(44) PUTLAKE FARM (SZ 07 NW). *Inhumation Burials* and *Occupation Debris* have been found S. of the farmhouse above the 300 ft. contour.

A collapsed stone cist, with two pieces of a coarse ware mug, perhaps a local copy of a 2nd-century type, lying on the cover-stones, was found in making a silo in 1957 (00197837). Remains of two inhumations without cists were found nearby about 1 ft. below surface, one with bowl fragments of Brailsford's Durotrigian class 1 (cf. *P.P.S.* XXIV (1958), 103); more burials were suspected in the W. side of the silo. Surface debris in the field, including beach-pebbles (sling-stones?), shale, and Romano-British sherds, suggest nearby occupation. (Dorset *Procs.* LXXXI (1959), 122–3.)

Two Roman coin hoards contained in vessels are untraced. One came from an extension c. 1842 to Leeson House (004786); the other, including a coin of Constantine, was ploughed up at 'Langton' in 1817 (Hutchins I (1861), 560; D.C.M. Parishes Index).

LULWORTH, EAST

There are no known sites in the parish, but several discoveries suggest occupation near Arish Mell (SY 854803): a 4-lugged stone mortar (D.C.M. 0.231.1) 'from a barrow at Arish Mell'; a bronze trumpet-brooch (1934.7.2), found in 1932 at a depth of 18 ins. in laying electric cable 20 yds. from Maiden Plantation; and a rough quern-stone found near quantities of iron slag 'in breaking up a portion of the Down near Arishmill' (Warne, *C.T.D.* (1866), cpf, 26). A bronze mounting in the shape of a cockerel (1886.9.127) also comes from the parish.

LYTCHETT MINSTER

A few scraps of coarse ware, apparently Romano-British, occur in plough-soil within Bulbury Camp, where a hoard of Celtic metalwork probably dates from about the time of the Roman conquest (*see* Hill-forts, Lytchett Minster (30)).

MORDEN

(57) CHARBOROUGH PARK (SY 99 NW). *Occupation Debris* and *Inhumation Burials* have been found in the park. The former consisted of Romano-British sherds (not traced) found in 1956 in replacing a post in the deer-fence in High Wood about 150 yds. W. of Charborough Tower, on an outlier of Reading Beds over Upper Chalk about 300 ft. above sea level (92789752). The burials were found in the Chalk in making a plantation fence on the estate in 1864 about 100 yds. N. of a large barrow 'towards the west end of Charborough Down'; 14 to 16 skeletons, extended with feet to E., were placed

parallel 2 ft. apart in a line N.-S. (Dorset *Procs.* LXXXV (1963), 102; Hutchins III, 505-6.)

MORETON

(31) MORETON PARK (SY 88 NW). *Occupation Debris* comes from the lower N. slope of Fir Hill below the 100 ft. contour, on Valley Gravel. The remains consist of a few sherds of Iron Age 'C' or Romano-British coarse ware from plough-soil E. of the sunken fence (80808867). Four turned shale armlet cores of Calkin's class C are preserved at Moreton House, residue of a quantity 'found in an earthen pot in digging the ditch to the fence on the addition being made to the Fir hill on the west side in 1807'. (Dorset *Procs.* LXXXV (1963), 99; LXXXVII (1965), 111.)

OSMINGTON

Part of a hand-moulded clay prop (in D.C.M.) probably from salt-boiling, comes from an unrecorded site on the cliffs at Osmington (Dorset *Procs.* LXXXIV (1962), 115.)

(43) LANDSLIP (SY 78 SW). *Occupation Debris* comes from W. of Sandy Barrow close to the N. edge of the landslip, on the crest of the Upper Greensand ridge above the 300 ft. contour. The remains consist of a scatter of Romano-British sherds, with some perhaps of Iron Age 'A', found in 1962 in plough-soil for at least 100 yds. E. of the lane from Osmington (72778258 to 72908264). A few Romano-British sherds come from 250 yds. S., in the landslip (73908236). Other finds, not precisely located, include sherds probably of Iron Age 'A', and Romano-British ware, some of the 3rd or 4th century. Objects are in D.C.M. (Dorset *Procs.* LXXXIV (1962), 113; LXXXV (1963), 98-9.)

(44) RINGSTEAD (SY 78 SW). An *Inhumation Burial* was found in 1926 in a chalk-pit at Spring Bottom (74708210). A shallow grave in Lower Chalk contained an extended skeleton with a one-handled bead-rim beaker of Romano-British coarse ware; iron nails in two lines by the skeleton, some with traces of wood, suggest a coffin. Objects are in D.C.M. (MS. note in D.C.M.)

OWERMOIGNE

Native vessels, Iron Age 'C' or early Romano-British, were found outside and in the ditch of an enclosure at Bowley's Plantation (*see* Enclosures, Owermoigne (36)).

POOLE

Substantial remains of the Roman road from Badbury Rings to Hamworthy survive on the parish boundary with Corfe Mullen on the W., and further S. (*see* Roman Roads, p. 530). In addition to remains described below, intrusive inhumation burials, possibly Romano-British, have been found in a Bronze Age barrow near Cogdean Elms (*see* Round Barrows, Poole, Barrow Hill Group (P)). A beaker (in Poole Museum) and sherds, of New Forest ware, come from Branksea Avenue by

Poole Harbour (989902; H. P. Smith, *History of Poole* I (1948), 88-9); Romano-British pottery is reputed to have come from the Lake Clay-pits (981906), and coins and tesserae from a field near St. Michael's Church, Hamworthy (993911; H. P. Smith, *op. cit.*, 64, 75-6; Dorset *Procs.* XI (1890), 21). For a site of military character, lying mainly in the parish of Pamphill, *see* p. 529, and Fig. p. 530.

(402) HAMWORTHY (SZ 09 SW). *Pits, Ditches, Ovens* and *Occupation Debris* including salt-boilers' waste, of Iron Age and Roman date, have been found on Valley Gravel beside Holes Bay at Carter's Tile-Works, at or near the termination of the Roman road from Badbury Rings to the harbour (002904).

Excavation by H. P. Smith in 1926-33[1] and 1949, supplemented by information of discoveries made in extensions to the premises and gravel-digging, indicated occupation over at least 6 acres from the W. end of the Tile-Works to the gardens of Ivor Road. The site is now a store-yard behind recently reclaimed land. The main features were three oval pits, some 5 ft. in diameter and 8 ft. deep, twelve ditches, apparently some 2½ ft. wide by 6 ft. deep, and eight oval or circular dished areas (five on Smith's 1928 plan) about 9 ft. or 10 ft. in diameter, some with traces of hearths, regarded by him as hut-sites. Hearths were also found outside the latter. The ditches, mostly, it seems, U-shaped with vertical sides, appear to have been straight, discontinuous features between 40 ft. and at least 125 ft. long; most ran N.-S. with a few N.W.-S.E., but three, disposed radially, met in a 'silt-hole'. All were presumably for drainage, although one (Smith's T 4), 40 ft. long and presumably of normal depth, ended in an oven (Smith's 'pottery-kiln') described below, while another (T 9), of flask-shaped section, was filled with the local mottled red and white clay.

The pits and some of the ditches, reaching present water-table, and all the 'hut' areas, were filled with black earth containing most of the 'late Celtic' (Iron Age 'C') pottery. All were assigned to the pre-Roman phase, but at least one pit and one ditch, cut through the 'Early Iron Age stratum', appear to be of Roman date (Dorset *Procs.* LVI (1934), 20, plate II).

The dished areas, excavated some 10 ins. in the gravel, and perhaps working areas rather than hut-sites, were between 40 ft. and 50 ft. apart and adjacent to pits and ditches. One (H 3) had a circular hearth of clay and flints, with iron and iron slag nearby; another (H 5) had remains of a clay hearth overlying its black occupation soil. Both were sealed by compact shingle, containing Roman sherds, believed to belong to a branch of the Roman road, running E.S.E. parallel with the S. side of Messrs. Carter's premises (*see* Road II, p. 531).

Further structural evidence for the Roman phase is scanty, and only a few pieces of roof and flue-tile occurred. Two floors of 'coarse red tile' (broken brine-containers) were thought to belong to rectangular huts; one (RH) overlay a hearth of the pre-Roman phase. The circular clay oven at N.

---

[1] No details are available of excavations between 1928 and 1933 but they do not seem to have been extensive.

end of ditch 4, with base some 5 ft. below surface, is probably of Roman date. As preserved in the Old Town House, Poole, its internal diameter is 18 ins.; the walls, some 8 ins. thick, survive to 14 ins. high, and the slightly concave floor is 12 ins. thick. The damaged front suggests an aperture some 9 ins. wide. No trace of an upper floor survived, and its size, and the absence of wasters, preclude its use as a pottery-kiln. It was associated with hand-moulded clay supports and pieces of thick straight-sided containers with rounded corners, of gritty clay, which were generally widespread in the Roman stratum and in the upper filling of the ditches nearest Holes Bay. This 'briquetage' indicates a salt-boiling industry in this phase. Two or three oven bases were found together in 1949 to N. (00249045) with similar 'briquetage' and Romano-British sherds.

Many fragments of shale, a few unfinished hand-cut armlets and three lathe-turned armlet cores of Calkin's classes A and C, suggest shale industries in both phases, but specialized tools for shale-working are unrecorded among the many flints.

The pottery (in Poole Museum) comprises a little native Iron Age 'B' (Southern Third 'B') ware and much Iron Age 'C' and Romano-British pottery including New Forest and other 4th-century types. Five vessels of the 3rd or 4th century came from harbour mud at the new quay (01049002) in 1931. Extraneous pre-Roman wares include a few pieces of 'Glastonbury' ware and of 'graphite'-coated jars comparable with class H at Hengistbury Head, Hampshire, possibly from N. France.[1] Fragments of amphorae need not be earlier than the Roman conquest. The initial occupation need not be dated before the early 1st century B.C., although a coin of Tauromenium, Sicily, of the 3rd century B.C., found near the site, and a Siculo-Punic coin of the 4th century B.C. from the harbour shore, are local examples of a number of pre-Imperial coins from the Mediterranean occurring in the hinterland of Poole Harbour and thought to indicate pre-Roman trade.[2]

Imported early Roman wares include Gallo-Belgic *terra nigra* and *terra rubra*, ring-neck flagons, colour-coated beakers, and pre-Flavian samian. The only coins from the site are two of Claudius of A.D. 41–2. This material points to Claudian occupation, although the best evidence for a military stores base (cf. *Arch. J.* CXV (1959), 57) is the complete Niedermendig lava slave or donkey-mill from the site, in the British Museum,[3] with part of another at the Claudian site at Corfe Mullen (Corfe Mullen (24)) 5 miles N. on the same Roman road. (Dorset *Procs.* LII (1930), 96–130; LIV (1932), 5, 13–14; LVI (1934), 11–21; LXXI (1949), 66; LXXXIV (1962), 137, 142; H. P. Smith, *History of Poole* I (1948), 51–76.)

Sites (403–4) occupy sandy Bagshot Beds.

(403) TURLIN MOOR (SY 99 SE). *Occupation Debris* was found in 1963 in a housing estate in the N. part of the Hamworthy peninsula (978916). The material from drainage trenches comprises samian and Romano-British sherds, and some fragments resembling salt-boiling 'briquetage', in black soil some 2½ ft. below surface (Dorset *Procs.* LXXXVI (1964), 115–6).

---

[1] R. E. M. Wheeler and K. M. Richardson, *Hill-Forts of Northern France* (1957), 58.
[2] J. G. Milne, *Finds of Greek Coins in the British Isles* (1948), 18–32.
[3] *Guide to the Antiquities of Roman Britain* (1951), 46, fig. 21.

(404) STERTE (SZ 09 SW). *Occupation Debris* and a *Coin Hoard* have been found near the E. shore of Holes Bay, Poole Harbour (00939165).

The hoard (in Poole Museum), found in remains of a coarse ware jar 2 ft. below surface in laying water-mains in 1930, consists of 965 mid 3rd-century coins (964 *antoniniani*, 1 *as*) ending with Aurelian (270–5), and was doubtless part of the same Aurelianic hoard as were over 300 coins (not traced) discovered in a broken urn in the same meadow in 1833. Iron Age 'C' and Romano-British sherds have also been found. (Dorset *Procs.* LII (1930), 127–8; H. P. Smith, *History of Poole* I (1948), 87–8, 90–1; *Bournemouth Echo*, 12 Nov. 1930; *Num. Chron.* new ser. IX (1869), 283–5; 5th ser. XIII (1933), 229–32.)

The provenance of 34 *antoniniani* (in Poole Museum) stated to have been dug up as a hoard in 1936 in allotments at Baiter (018902) is doubtful (*Num. Chron.* 5th ser. XVIII (1938), 300; H. P. Smith, *op. cit.*, 91). The series resembles that of the Dorchester hoard found at the same time (Dorchester (194a)).

PORTESHAM

An intrusive burial of a child in a stone cist of Roman date came from a barrow on Ridge Hill in 1885 (*see* Round Barrows, Portesham (43)). 'Human remains found A.D. 1858' are recorded on O.S. maps near The Buildings (61168606); a group of undated inhumations in stone cists aligned N.W.–S.E. was found on Corton Farm in 1765 (Hutchins II, 761–2) and one on Corton Down (63668674) in 1936 (MS. note by C. D. Drew, in D.C.M.). Three cist burials extended with heads W., found in a landslip on the downs near Portesham, were described in Dorset *Procs.* XXIV (1903), xliv–v; another on an adjacent hill was thought Saxon.

(63) TATTON FARM (SY 68 SW). *Inhumation Burials* have been found on the Langton ridge (Cornbrash) S.E. of Langton Cross. Many burials in stone cists were ploughed up in 1883 on 'Tatton Hill' (approx. 629819) adjoining similar remains in Chickerell parish (Chickerell (35)), and skeletons found on Tatton Farm before 1845 probably come from the same cemetery. (Dorset *Procs.* L (1928), 123; *Gentleman's Magazine* (1845), pt. i, 79.)

(64) PORTESHAM WITHY BED (SY 58 NE). *Occupation Debris* was found c. 1901 at about 350 ft. above sea level 'exactly six furlongs due west of St. Peter's Church' (approx. 590859). The site, near the junction of Upper Greensand and Lower Chalk, occupied a shelf in the W. slope of a re-entrant valley, among 'Celtic' fields (*see* Ancient Field Group (4)). The remains, from foundations 1½ ft. deep for a gamekeeper's house, included flint and chert flakes and tools, and pottery, thought prehistoric to late Roman (Dorset *Procs.* XXXVII (1916), xxxix–xl; XXIV (1903), xlv).

PORTLAND

In addition to sites described below, a stone-lined well found 'a little to the south of the parish church' (St. George's, Reforne, SY 68657201) was said to have contained much Roman pottery (*J.B.A.A.* XXVIII

(1872), 32–3); a coin of Marcus Aurelius (161–80) was found at Portland Bill (67836874; Dorset *Procs.* LXXXIV (1962), 112); Roman coins and other objects, possibly from wrecks, have been found on Chesil Beach one mile from Portland (about 675744; *Num. Chron.* II (1840), 255–6). Of several unlocated graves (Dorset *Procs.* XXXIII (1912), X; Dorset Album I, part 1, in D.C.M.; *P.P.S.* XXIV (1958), 118), the most notable one contained a bronze collar, coarse ware jar, 2nd-century samian bowl and Late Bronze Age knife, in B.M. (*Guide to Early Iron Age Antiquities* (1925), 150–1; *P.P.S.* XXIV (1958), 118).

(99) NORTH COMMON (SY 67 SE). *Inhumation Burials* and *Occupation Debris* have been found in North or Verne Common, Castletown, on Kimmeridge Clay.

About 20 skeletons 'in a cramped or sitting posture', with limpet shells and pottery believed Roman, were found in making the old reservoir *c.* 1855 (68777429; C. King Warry, *Old Portland Traditions* (*c.* 1908), 35). Several cists containing skeletons, some E.-W., were found in drain-laying *c.* 1860; one, with sides and cover stones of Kimmeridge shale, had nails suggesting a wooden coffin. Two iron ingots (in Portland Museum),[1] two 2nd-century coins, a handled bead-rimmed beaker and enamelled disc-brooch (D.C.M. 1923.3.4 and 7) were amongst objects found nearby. (*Arch. J.* XXIII (1866), 75; XXV (1868), 52–3, 56–7; Royal Engineers' List, copy 1882 by Major Peck, in D.C.M.; R. Damon, *Geology of Weymouth* (2nd ed. 1884), 240–2; Dorset *Procs.* XLIV (1923), 35–6, 38, 46, 48.)

Six apparently adult inhumations were found in laying water-mains in 1950 in Zigzag (now Verne Common) Road on the steep slope E. of Victoria Gardens. Two, probably of the first half of the 2nd century A.D., lying N.-S. with heads N., 230 ft. above sea level (68747380), had been compressed into short stone cists 3 ft. 4 ins. and 3 ft. 9 ins. long. The northernmost had a coarse ware jar and dish (*cf. Arch. Ael.* XXXV (1957), types 123, 307); the other had one coarse ware vessel (stolen). A third cist, some 40 yds. S.W. (68727377), orientated N.E.-S.W. with head to N., was 6 ft. 5 ins. long and had nails indicating a wooden coffin. The fourth and fifth graves, at the foot of the road about 100 ft. above sea level (68487366), were damaged and of doubtful orientation. The northernmost was apparently in a full-length cist, with a Trajanic samian dish (form 18) of Secundus and a coarse ware jar of the same type as in grave 1; the fifth, in an unlined grave, had Trajanic samian dishes (forms 18/31 and Curle 11), and the base of a coarse ware jar. A sixth burial to N., E. of the Police Station (68517377), apparently without grave-goods, was in a diagonally tooled Portland stone sarcophagus with ridge-roofed lid (in Portland Museum), 6 ft. 4 ins. long by nearly 2 ft. wide overall. Objects are in D.C.M. and Portland Museum. (Dorset *Procs.* LXXII (1950), 83.)

(100) THE VERNE (SY 67 SE, 77 SW). *Inhumation Burials*

and *Occupation Debris* have been found in and near the Verne Citadel, now H.M. Prison, on Portland Stone some 400–450 ft. above sea level.

According to Hutchins several inhumations in covered stone cists were found in the landslip of 1734 on the shore between the 'old pier', probably King's Pier, and Portland Castle, probably about 700735 towards N. end of East Wear. Four inhumations in cists, one of which was at least partly of shale, were found in building the Citadel *c.* 1860, 4 ft. deep within the destroyed enclosure (68987354) to S.W. (*see* Enclosures, Portland (98)). Three (one perhaps of a child with head W.) lay E.-W.; one to W. lay N.-S. with head N. Sherds were also found. In the same works, at 'top of Verne Hill', a cist of Portland stone slabs contained three burials, one with a large urn containing some charcoal.

Another cist, of beach-derived Portland stone slabs, laid 3 ft. deep in a deposit of 'glacial drift earth',[1] was found in 1882 on the S.E. Glacis (about 695734), and perhaps two burials *c.* 1878, one in a cist, the other with part of a Celtic bronze mirror (C. Fox, *Archaeologia Cambrensis* C (1949), 40). Two Romano-British coarse ware dishes (not traced) and a jar (D.C.M. 1923.3.5) also came from the S.E. Glacis according to the R.E. List. Remains of two burials 10 ft. apart were found in making a football ground here in 1933, about 5 ft. below surface (69487336). One was in a stone cist; the other had two 'Romano-British food-vessels' by the skull (C. H. Wood-house). A circular drystone wall some 6 ft. in diameter and 5 ft. high, perhaps a 'beehive' chamber (*cf.* Monuments (101) and (105) below), was found *c.* 1860 near the S.E. Demi-bastion (about 695735), containing an ox-skull, bones and ashes. An undated shell-midden found before 1882 in glacial drift beside the road below the S.W. Glacis (about 691734) contained flint scrapers.

Objects from these works include a waste core from a turned shale armlet, a spiral bronze ring from a finger-bone, and a gold coin of Allen's Gallo-Belgic type F. Other finds from the area include a lidless diagonally-tooled Roman sarcophagus of Portland stone, 6 ft. 2 ins. by 2 ft. wide overall, preserved at the Governor's house, and, in D.C.M. and Portland Museum, Iron Age 'C' or early Romano-British vessels and sherds, samian ware, fragments of 4th-century colour-coated ware, Roman glass beads and part of an incised circular shale plaque. (Hutchins II, 826; *Arch. J.* XXIII (1866), 75–6; XXV (1868), 47–9, 53–6; Royal Engineers' List, copy 1882 by Major Peck, in D.C.M.; R. Damon, *Geology of Weymouth* (2nd ed. 1884), 240–2; Dorset *Procs.* XLIV (1923), 35–7, 47; Brig. C. H. Wood-house, MS. note, 1933, in D.C.M.)

Sites (101–105) occupied Lower Purbeck Beds now largely removed in quarrying.

(101) KING BARROW (SY 67 SE). *'Beehive' Chambers* and *Inhumation Burials* have been found in quarrying in King Barrow and Withies Croft E. of the Verne Yeates–Easton road some 400 ft. above sea level.

Between 1880 and 1884 over a dozen circular corbelled stone chambers or cists probably of Iron Age and Roman date,

---

[1] L. V. Grinsell, *Archaeology of Wessex* (1958), 137; D. F. Allen, *P.P.S.* XXXIII (1967), 314–5, 317, 335. The distribution of these objects is focused on the middle and lower Rhine.

---

[1] The deposit, not recorded by the Geological Survey, is noted in Dorset *Procs.* XIII (1892), 234.

in two cases interconnected, were found within an area of ½ mile in Weston's and Steward's quarries at King Barrow, mostly together. One of these is recorded by the Geological Survey (6-in. MS. sheet, Dorset LVIII SE, 1890) at 69207285. Slightly divergent descriptions by Damon and Holmes derive from the superintendent, A. M. Wallis. The chambers were normally some 9 ft. in diameter and 8 ft. high with extremes of 6 ft. by 4 ft. and 12 ft. by 8 ft.; holes dug in limestone rubble to an underlying clay seam were lined with flat stones, corbelled towards the top to a man-hole some 16 ins. in

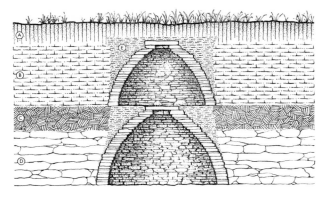

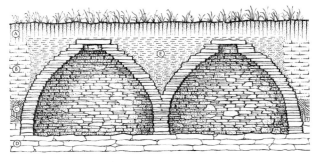

Ⓐ *Top soil*　Ⓑ *Rubble-stone*　Ⓒ *Clayey seam*　Ⓓ *'Slate'*　Ⓔ *Rubble fill*

Portland (101). 'Beehive' chambers. *After T. V. Holmes*

diameter normally with a slab cover at the base of the overlying humus. Some were seemingly corbelled from the base. Most stood alone, some 10 or 15 yds. apart, but two were superimposed with the entrance to the lower centrally in the floor of the upper chamber; another pair was joined at the base either directly (*see* Fig., after Holmes) or by a short lined tunnel (Damon). Domestic animal bones, limpet shells (in D.C.M.), round pebbles ('corn-crushers') from Chesil Beach, 'slingstones', flint flakes,[1] pieces of Kimmeridge shale and a bronze coin were said to have been found in these chambers, and in one was a quantity of carbonized grain.[2] Oblong cists

---

[1] A so-called flint 'celt' (D.C.M. 0.19.1) is a broken pebble of hornblende schist.

[2] Samples in D.C.M. and Portland Museum. Spelt, and small amounts of Hulled Barley, Oats and Chess, have been identified (H. Helbaek, *P.P.S.* XVIII (1952), 229).

found nearby are supposed to have contained human and animal bones, ornaments, an iron sword, sherds and quernstones, amongst which a rotary quern[1] and perforated whetstone of micaceous schist,[2] in D.C.M., are probably recognizable.

Two similar chambers were found here in 1885[3] and 1886, the former with stone 'spindle-whorl' and roughly-hollowed pebble 'mortar' outside. The other, containing a few 'slingstones' and limpet shells, was near a cist with two superimposed extended skeletons, the uppermost on right side with head E.; 2 in. iron nails suggested a wooden coffin. Each had a pot; the lower had two metal finger-rings, one with 'zigzag ornament'. Another chamber found *c.* 1890 was near a cist containing human bones and sherds, with two querns and hammer-stones nearby.

Other burials probably in stone cists were noted in quarries superintended by Wallis: a grave, 1888, with iron knife, two iron rings about 1½ ins. in diameter, three flint hammerstones, and three coarse ware vessels of the 3rd or 4th century (D.C.M. 0.208. 1–8; *cf. Arch. Ael.* XXXV (1957), types 65, 228)); three graves, *c.* 1890, two with an urn and one with a ring and beads; a grave with skeleton in 'crouching position' with two stone 'spindles', three large round stones, and a piece of worked shale. Two pear-shaped jars in Portland Museum, Iron Age 'C' or Roman, come from King Barrow Quarry, and a wheel-made jar of Romano-British grey ware and two 2nd-century dishes (D.C.M. 1889. 4. 1–3) are probably from the same site. (T. V. Holmes, *Procs. Geologists' Association* VIII (1883–4), 404–11; R. Damon, *Geology of Weymouth* (2nd ed. 1884), 164–6; MS. anon., 'Early Interments on Portland' (1886, in D.C.M.); Dorset *Procs.* XII (1891), xix, xxxii, 11; XLIV (1923), 47; H. J. Moule, MS. List of Roman Pottery in D.C.M.)

In Withies Croft Quarries to S., a stone cist found in 1868 contained a coarse ware beaker and bowl, probably of the 2nd century, and in 1879 a grave with skeleton and two jars was discovered in the 'Maggot quarries' (691726). A hoard of eleven 3rd-century radiate coins, in Portland Museum, came from the E. end of lawn 612 in Inmosthay Quarries (69007216) in 1896. (*Arch. J.* XXVII (1870), 217; *J.B.A.A.* XXVIII (1872), 34; *D.C.C.*, 29 May 1879; *Southern Times*, 20 Feb. 1897.)

(102) THE GROVE (SY 67 SE). *Inhumation Burials and Pits* were found in 1851 in the Breakwater Quarries (now playing-fields) opposite the Clifton Hotel near the Convict Prison (now H.M. Borstal Institution) some 350 ft. above sea level (about 697725).

Nearly 200 graves are said to have been found, mostly stone cists but including two diagonally-tooled Portland stone sarcophagi (at Borstal Institution) with 3 in. walls and ridge-roofed lids about 1 ft. high. The smaller (*see* Fig.) is 6 ft. 3 ins. long overall; the larger (Plate 229), 6 ft. 10 ins. by 2 ft., and 1 ft. 6 ins. high, had remains of two skeletons head to foot, apparently without grave-goods. A stone plinth (Plate 229; at Borstal Institution), 7 ft. by 4 ft. and some 6 ins. thick,

---

[1] *Antiquity* XI (1937), 141, no. 7.

[2] K. Kenyon, *Excavations at the Jewry Wall, Leicester* (1948), 232.

[3] A. M. Wallis, correspondence in D.C.M.(Box-file, Portland).

similarly tooled and perhaps for a sarcophagus, consisted of four pieces of unequal size with a semicircular channel at edge; it was laid in clay, or cement (G. Clifton). Some short cists with single cover-stones, in some cases with single slabs for sides, had skeletons with knees drawn up; others were extended in normal cists. A contemporary sketch by Poppleton

Portland (102). Sarcophagus.

indicates a width of 4 ft. 8 ins. for a 7 ft. 3 in. cist. The burials were from 1 yd. to 20 yds. apart, the orientation being unstated except that some in short cists had head to N. Primary sources state that vessels of black and dishes of red ware (in one case certainly samian with leaf-decorated rim) accompanied some of the skeletons; a skull of a calf and a quern-stone also came from graves. Roman coins and a pounding stone, and deep pits containing animal bones (some of birds), were found nearby. A later authority (Clifton) claims many double graves, metal equipment including javelin-head and shield fragment, round stones, ornaments and coins of Caligula (37–41), Hadrian (117–38), Constantine (306–37) and Julian (355–63). A Celtic mirror-handle (in Coburg Museum; *Archaeologia Cambrensis* c (1949), 29, 30) found in 1875, is probably from the area. (R. Poppleton and Jones, correspondence in D.C.M.; *D.C.C.*, 9 Oct. 1851; *Arch. J.* x (1853), 60–1; G. Clifton, *J.B.A.A.* XXVIII (1872), 204–5.)

(103) BROADCROFT QUARRIES (SY 67 SE). *Occupation Debris* has been found in S.E. extensions to the quarries, near Easton, above the 300 ft. contour.

Limited excavation in 1950–1 exposed an occupation deposit 1 ft. to 1½ ft. below surface at the then E. edge of the quarries (69857193). Remains included a few samian sherds, much Romano-British coarse ware, some of the 4th century, a shale spindle-whorl, a rotary quern-stone of Wessex type, two pebble hammer-stones, some 50 sling-stones, winkle, limpet and oyster-shells, and a coin of Victorinus (268–70). Amongst earlier finds to W. were a coin of Trajan (98–117), and, according to quarrymen, stone cist burials and a small covered cist filled with limpets. (Dorset *Procs.* LXXII (1950), 87–8; LXXIII (1951), 93–4.)

Human remains found 350 yds. S.S.W. in 1951 in a fissure (69737165) N. of Bumper's Lane, with bones of domestic animals, several limestone and quartzite pebble hammer-stones (one perforated), and flakes and cores of Portland chert, have been referred to the Bronze Age or earlier (Dorset *Procs.* LXXIV (1952), 39–47; LXXXIX (1967), 120), but such objects are matched at Iron Age and Roman sites in the Isle of Portland. A 'beehive' chamber, some 10 ft. deep, is said to have been destroyed in quarrying N. of the railway c. 1920. (Information from Mr. G. H. Lynham, Director of The Stone Firms Ltd.)

(104) BOTTOM COOMBE QUARRIES (SY 67 SE). An *Inhumation Burial* was found in the late 19th century some 250 ft. above

sea level in the quarries (693715) W. of Wakeham Street, Easton. The burial was in a stone 'coffin', probably a cist. Several Roman coins, 'republican' to 4th-century A.D., are said to have been found at the same time. (Information from the late J. Pearce, J.P.; Dorset *Procs.* XXXVIII (1917), xxvii.)

(105) COOMBEFIELD QUARRIES (SY 67 SE). *'Beehive' Chambers, Inhumation Burials*, and *Occupation Debris* have been found in the quarries (689706) at Weston some 200 ft. above sea level.

A corbelled stone 'beehive' chamber found in 1897, diameter about 5 ft., contained human remains according to B. M. Head. Some 2 yds. away, an oblong chamber with rounded corners, 7 ft. by 4½ ft. and 3 ft. high, lay N.N.W. to S.S.E., walled with Purbeck stone partly corbelled and closed with flat slabs; the filling, mainly of stones, included sherds, a crude stone 'mortar', a flint hammer-stone or 'pestle', flint flakes, 'slingstones', pebbles, charred wood, bones of ox and sheep, and shells of cockle and limpet. A covered cist of orthostats backed with horizontal slabs, similarly aligned but 50 yds. N.W., had contained a skeleton.

A stone-lined 'beehive' chamber, 4½ ft. high, diameter 5 ft., examined by E. Cunnington in 1898, had an arched passage or 'entrance' on the N. side, 8 ft. long with a circular hole 4½ ft. deep in its floor. The chamber contained a rough mortar of grey stone and an elongated pebble 'pestle' (in D.C.M.), and three sherds of black ware, of which two surviving are rims of hand-made jars of Iron Age 'B' or 'C' tradition (in D.C.M.; *see* Fig.)

Two photographs in D.C.M. depict additions to the series. One, given by Head in 1906, is of a corbelled 'beehive', diameter about 4 ft., probably the empty structure referred to in V.C.H.; the other, taken by H. Colley March, was of

Portland (105). Sherds. (¼)

a 'beehive' found in 1907, 4¾ ft. in diameter, with vertical walls surviving to 4½ ft. (Dorset *Procs.* XIX (1898), 128–9; XX (1899), 120–1; XXVIII (1907), lxxvii; XXIX (1908), cxvi; E. Cunnington, 'Memorandum of discovery of bee-hive building at Coombe Field Quarry' (MS. 1898, in D.C.M.); V.C.H., *Dorset* II (1908), 338.)

Sites (106–107) occupy Lower Purbeck Beds.

(106) AVALANCHE ROAD, SOUTHWELL (SY 67 SE). *Occupation Debris*, Iron Age 'A' to late Roman, comes from allotments and gardens adjoining St. Andrew's Church, about 175 ft. above sea level. The remains consist of sherds of Iron Age 'A' and Roman date, the latter including samian and 4th-century

ware, mainly from immediately S.E. of the church (68707016) and from the garden of 'Coombe Ridge' to N. (68717022), with scrapers and flakes of Portland chert. A quern-stone of Wessex type, a flint hammer-stone, and a three-lugged mortar of Purbeck burr-stone (D.C.M. 0.230.1), are also recorded. Eliot noted Roman pottery which he believed to be associated with traces of a circular embankment in the vicinity. (Dorset *Procs.* LXXXV (1963), 101; G. Eliot, *J.B.A.A.* XXVIII (1872), 33.)

(107) SWEET HILL, SOUTHWELL (SY 66 NE). *Inhumation Burials* some 400 yds. S.W. of Monument (106) were found in road-making in 1950 below the 200 ft. contour. A diagonally-tooled Portland stone sarcophagus with ridge-roofed lid (in Portland Museum), 7 ft. long by 2 ft. wide overall, freshly disturbed but containing hob-nails, was at 68386994, orientation unknown. Some 3 yds. S.E. an extended skeleton on axis of 140° with head S.E. and hob-nails at feet lay on loose stones over loamy subsoil, in a covered stone cist some 6 ft. long by 2 ft. wide overall, with slabs leaning outwards slightly. In the face of the cutting some 5 yds. N.W. of the sarcophagus, the corner of a destroyed cist, axis either 130° or 220°, had foot-bones, hob-nails, parts of a coarse ware jar of the 3rd or 4th century, and nails with adherent wood suggesting a wooden coffin. Objects are in D.C.M. (Dorset *Procs.* LXXII (1950), 83.)

POXWELL

Finds indicating an occupation site associated with Ancient Field Group (11) were made during excavation of strip lynchets in 1967 (SY 736840; Dorset *Procs.* LXXXIX (1967), 135–9).

STAFFORD, WEST

(25) CROFTS (SY 78 NW). *Inhumation Burials* were found *c.* 1850 above the 200 ft. contour on Upper Chalk (724890). Of two burials found near the 'skeleton of a horse' and other animal bones, about 20 yds. from a barrow (Round Barrows, Stafford, West, (18)) in the field called Crofts S. of Parsonage Plantation, one had a samian bowl (form 22) of the 1st century A.D. apparently placed between the legs; the other was near five vessels of Durotrigian coarse ware. The vessels are in D.C.M. (*Arch. J.* IX (1852), 93; Hutchins II, 517.)

STEEPLE

Sites (28–29) are on sandy Bagshot Beds.

(28) WEST CREECH (SY 88 SE). *Occupation Debris* comes from a low ridge about 150 ft. above sea level E. of North Hills Plantation (898827). The remains consist of a thin scatter of Romano-British pottery first noted in rabbit-holes in 1953, and subsequently after ploughing (Dorset *Procs.* LXXVI (1954), 86).

(29) CREECH GRANGE (SY 98 SW). *Occupation Debris* and some traces of structures have been found at the house, which lies at the N. foot of the Chalk range (911822).

Much black and red Romano-British pottery, some figured in *Purbeck Papers* and perhaps mainly of the 2nd and 3rd centuries, and a samian sherd stamped GENITORF, were recovered from black mould in alterations to the kitchen garden in 1858. Quern-stones, pieces of shale and waste cores from turned armlets were also found. Amongst a quantity of stones, three stone pillars, 2½ ft. high with the lower 6 ins. left rough, were unburnt but thought to be supports for a drying floor, and there were two or three perforated fragments of baked clay 1 in. to 1½ ins. thick. Evidence for a pottery-kiln is inconclusive. A Durotrigian bowl of Brailsford's class 1 is in D.C.M. Coarse ware sherds found in 1958, one from a flanged bowl of the 3rd or 4th century, came from building work in the N. side of the kitchen garden (91098236). (*Purbeck Papers* I (1859–60), 215–20, 225; *Arch. J.* XV (1858), 87; Dorset *Procs.* LXXXVI (1964), 116.)

(30) SMEDMORE HILL (SY 98 SW). *Inhumation Burials* have been found at the W. end of Smedmore Hill in or near the upper quarry in Lower Purbeck limestone, some 400 ft. above sea level.

Nine or ten burials, probably all extended in covered cists, have been found since 1944. Two side by side in the quarry (about 91908002) were of a young adult and a child, extended approximately N.-S. with heads N.; the longer cist had shale ends. Most of the others were exposed in the E. face of the sunken approach. One, extended W. by S. with head W., was at 91938007 near the entrance. Three were side by side some 18 yds. further S. at 91928005. Two of these, containing adults with heads W.S.W., were almost wholly of shale slabs; one of them, 6 ft. 4 ins. long, had no end slabs. The third, almost destroyed by 1958 but apparently on the same alignment, may have been one of two unexamined cists seen in 1952. Human bones were also observed in the W. face of the approach. In 1967 another cist largely of shale, with an adult burial aligned E.-W. (head), was found at the edge of the field to N. (91968012). (Dorset *Procs.* LXXIV (1952), 49–50; LXXXI (1959), 94–7; LXXXIX (1967), 145.)

(31) KIMMERIDGE BAY (SY 97 NW). *Inhumation Burials, Working-floors* and *Occupation Debris* indicating shale-working and salt-boiling from Iron Age 'A', have been found on Kimmeridge Clay in the cliff about 50 ft. above sea level W. of Gaulter Gap.

The cliff is being eroded and much material has been excavated from the site, by Miles, Austen and others, since 'coal-money' was first recorded here by Hutchins in 1768. The sequence of occupation has been determined by clearance of the cliff-face at seven points by Dr. Henrietta Davies and excavation of some 80 sq. yds. close to it by Mr. J. B. Calkin (90707917); the site extends some 240 yds. W. of the Gap (90787911 to 90607923) and perhaps for some 200 yds. inland.

An occupation stratum on virgin soil at a depth of about 3 ft. was associated with working-floors of a hand-cut shale armlet industry presumed to have obtained its raw material from the 'blackstone' or 'Kimmeridge coal' outcrop at Cuddle ½ mile S.E., and employing semi-standardized flint tools. Pottery refers it to an early phase of Iron Age 'A'. A sterile deposit above indicated a hiatus, followed by a lengthy further occupation in Iron Age 'A'; this was marked by haematite-coated pottery, in a loamy deposit some 15 ins. thick in part made up with beach-derived sand, and containing several thin lenses of burnt material, in two main horizons, including shale pebbles used as fuel. One of these burnt floors was at least 20 ft. by 12 ft. Short lengths of straight and curved drystone walls and pieces of burnt daub were interpreted as remains of huts at least once replaced, but similar structures at Gallows Gore (*see* Worth Matravers (40)) appear to be directly associated with shale-working. There was some evidence for continued production of shale armlets in this later phase. Pieces of small cylindrical jars of coarse reddish clay, apparently cut in half to form troughs with one open end and thought to relate to a salt-boiling industry, were mainly associated with the burnt layers. Pieces of small bowls of similar ware found in a heap of unburnt shale rarely occurred elsewhere in the deposit.

The upper level of some 12 ins. to 18 ins., below topsoil, contained Romano-British pottery of the 2nd to the 4th century, with some admixture of native types of perhaps earlier date. Beach-pebbles regarded as sling-stones and limpet shells occurred in all occupation phases. A drystone wall is recorded, but otherwise daub and groups of cobbles were the only evidence of structures in this phase. Abundant waste cores, mainly class C, often in small concentrated groups, and their associated debris including specialized flint tools knapped on the spot, point to a very considerable turned shale armlet industry, in which undecorated armlets of light-weight type were recognized.

A cist burial, dated to the end of the 3rd century or later by the only coin recorded from the site, was cut through the workshop floor at 90707917. This was of an elderly arthritic female, with the severed head and detached mandible placed beside the shins, and a shale spindle-whorl beside the left hand; the cist of limestone and shale slabs was orientated 30° W. of N. and had been filled deliberately with soil and a deposit of limpets and snails (*Helix aspersa*). A coin of Carausius (286–93) was in the grave-pit. On the capstones a secondary burial in nearly the same alignment was of another elderly female with detached mandible near the knees and shale spindle-whorl by the left hand.

Miles' excavation yielded much material including a mortar of 'granite', probably Purbeck marble, and a supposed bullock sacrifice in a pentagonal cist of shale slabs; his pieces of hand-moulded clay associated with burnt shale strongly suggest the props used in local saltings of the Roman period, not otherwise clearly attested here. Romano-British sherds and several armlet cores of classes A and C (in D.C.M.) were found by Dr. W. H. C. Frend some 200 yds. inland beside the stream N. of the cottages (90837930). Objects are in B.M., D.C.M., Christchurch Museum, and London University Institute of Archaeology. (Hutchins, in *Gentleman's Magazine* (1768), 111–2; Hutchins I, 556–7; W. A. Miles, *The Deverel Barrow* (1826), 39–44; J. H. Austen, *Purbeck Papers* I (1856–7), 82–97; *Arch. J.* XCIII (1936), 200–19; Dorset *Procs.* LXIX (1947), 33–41; LXX (1948), 29–59; LXXV (1953), 45–71; LXXXIV (1962), 139–41.)

STOKE, EAST

(51) ST. MARY'S CHURCH (SY 88 NE). *Occupation Debris* comes from the graveyard extension beside the R. Frome on Valley Gravel below the 50 ft. contour (87288702). Romano-British sherds and a piece of shale core from a turned armlet, in D.C.M., were found at a depth of 2 ft. to 3 ft. in digging a grave in 1932. (Dorset *Procs.* LXXIII (1951), 92.)

(52) RUSHTON COMMON (SY 88 NE). *Occupation Debris* comes from Valley Gravel and Alluvium about 15 ft. above sea level beside the Frome some 350 yds. S.W. of Holme Bridge (88788650). Romano-British coarse pottery including 4th-century types and many worked flints, in D.C.M., were found in the meadows in 1947, apparently on the flood-plain. (Dorset *Procs.* LXXI (1949), 65–6.)

(53) WEST HOLME (SY 88 NE). *Occupation Debris* comes from Bagshot Beds and Valley Gravel near the S. bank of the Frome, mainly below the 50 ft. contour. Romano-British coarse pottery, some in D.C.M., has been found on the surface and in test pits, on both sides of the road to Holme Bridge between about 88668600 and 89008637. (Dorset *Procs.* LXXIII (1951), 92.)

STUDLAND

Romano-British pottery is said to have been found on Brownsea Island in Poole Harbour (Dorset *Procs.* XXVI (1905), 187).

Sites (44–47) occupy sandy Bagshot Beds.

(44) KINGSWOOD FARM (SY 98 SE). A *Floor* and *Occupation Debris* have been found about 250 ft. above sea level on a S.E. slope at the foot of the Chalk downs. Deep ploughing c. 1953 disclosed remains of a rectangular floor of sandstone slabs at 99828201 with Romano-British sherds some 25 yds. to N.; no walls were noticed. (Information from Mr. Elford, Kingswood Farm.) Sherds (in D.C.M.) found in 1958 include one of the 3rd or 4th century.

(45) GODLINGSTON HEATH (SZ 08 SW). *Occupation Debris* including coarse 'briquetage' comes from an old sand or gravel pit E. of Thorny Barrow about 300 ft. above sea level. In the N. face of the pit, at a depth of about 2 ft., deposits of clay and sandy soil showing signs of burning were traced laterally for some 15 ft. in 1958 (01478212). Many fragments of reddish 'briquetage' of coarse sandy finger-marked clay, and Romano-British sherds, some oxidized, ranging from at least the 2nd to the 3rd century, come from these deposits and from the filling of old excavations in the sand some 20 yds. away in the S. face of the pit (01468210). Similar material occurs in rabbit-scrapes on the N. slope of the hill (01508213). The 'briquetage' consists mainly of short hand-moulded props with flat or grooved ends and pieces of large thin-walled containers, and compares closely with that from salt-boiling sites on the fringes of Poole Harbour. A large curved fragment of similar fired clay some 2 ins. thick may be part of an oven or kiln. (Dorset *Procs.* LXXXIV (1962), 141–2.)

(46) WOODHOUSE HILL (SZ 08 SW). *Buildings* and *Huts* in two groups, dating perhaps from just before the Roman conquest to the 4th century A.D., were excavated by Mr. N. H. Field in 1952–8 on the S. slopes of a spur of sandstone 200 ft. above sea level. Excavation between

the groups was insufficient to disprove presence of further buildings.

In the N. group (03128220) slight lines of stones and traces of post-holes suggested two rounded huts (D) and (E) perhaps of the mid 1st century A.D.; the western (D) of 16 ft. by 14 ft. was succeeded on the same site by a roughly rectangular hut (C), measuring 18 ft. by 14 ft., with a central hearth, paved threshold to N.E. and a clay 'shelf' 6 ins. high on W. A ditch to E., 3 ft. wide and 1½ ft. deep at N., increasing in size to S.,

interpreted as double entrances. Floors were largely of clay and earth. The E. building (A), perhaps with an eccentric line of posts bisecting the long axis, for which, however, the evidence is insecure, had a hearth W. of centre, clay platforms in N.W. and S.W. corners, and an internal gully with round sump E. of the S. entrance. Finds from (A) included a chalk loom-weight and shale spindle-whorls, also iron slag and parts of an iron cauldron from the E. part of the building. Five coins of 259–96 and coarse pottery indicated occupation in the 3rd and perhaps the first half of the 4th century. The W.

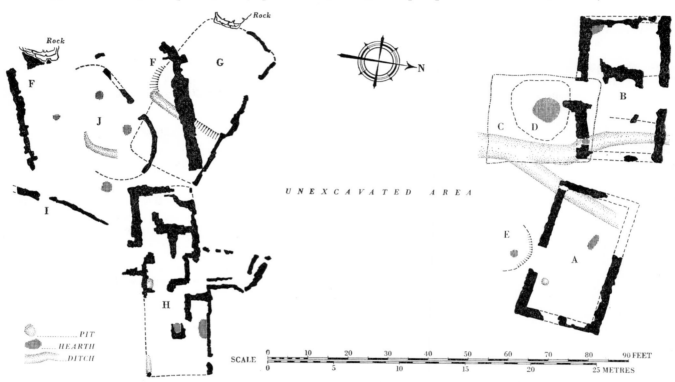

THE BUILDINGS ON WOODHOUSE HILL, STUDLAND

After N. H. Field.

was filled in when, according to the excavator, hut C was extended by the addition of sheds on all sides save the W. to measure 26 ft. by 23 ft. Finds on the 'shelf' included a samian platter of *c.* 65–80, a brooch, and a coin of Vespasian of A.D. 73; the date of abandonment seemed to be *c.* 85. Pieces of crucibles for copper-working were associated with huts (D) and (E).

N. of these remains were two rectangular buildings or 'cottages', nearly end to end on slightly different alignments, with unmortared sandstone and flint footings some 2 ft. to 3 ft. wide, probably for cob walls. Each building, terraced into the westerly hill-slope, measured 36½ ft. to 37 ft. by 21½ ft., with an entrance 4½ ft. to 5½ ft. wide in the S. wall, and, in the W. building (B), possibly a corresponding N. entrance, perhaps an addition. Gaps in the E. walls were

building (B) may have been divided into aisles by two rows of four or five posts, for which again the evidence is slight, and, by revetted changes of floor-level from W. to E., into three rooms, identified by the excavator as a dwelling-room with hearth in S.W. corner, byre and workshop respectively. A mass of stones 10 ft. long and 6 ft. wide, revetting the W. or dwelling-room, had two concavities in the E. side identified as heads of ox-stalls between N. and S. doorways. Evidence for an internal door between dwelling-room and 'byre' and a very low window in the adjacent S. wall is insecure. Most finds came from the E. end where there were a knife, a spike, and some slag. A coin of Allectus (293–6) below the floor and coarse pottery above it suggested construction and occupation in the 4th century.

In the S. group (03128217) five hearths and slight scatters

of stones were attributed to seven huts of which the most certain (J) was probably oval about 30 ft. long by 20 ft. and perhaps of *c.* A.D. 25–75. The finds of pottery and brooches from the other 'huts'[1] were of similar date, except at hut (I) probably of the 2nd to 3rd centuries. Two parallel lines of walling 34 ft. long and 44 ft. apart were attributed to a barn-like building (F), not earlier than *c.* 180 and perhaps of the 3rd century, but no firm traces of E. and W. walls were found. N. of (F), a line of flints and sandstone 24 ft. long and 1 ft. wide running N.W. to S.E., and a gully 2 ft. to 3 ft. wide and 1 ft. deep running at right angles to it, were ascribed to a rectangular building (G) with internal partition, preceding (F) and of later 1st century to early 3rd century.

More substantial remains (H) to E. consisted initially of a rectangular building, 26 ft. E.-W. by 16 ft., apparently of the late 3rd century, divided into two rooms of which the eastern was interpreted as a byre, with two ox-stalls as in (B) and with a 5 ft. wide door in its S. wall. An easterly extension marked, however, by little more than a N. wall 23 ft. long, was apparently added subsequently when the 'byre' of phase I was possibly adapted for living quarters or storage; the extension contained a substantial central clay hearth on a stone base 4½ ft. by 3 ft. and a walled recess to N. An irregular line of walling running N. and then N.W. for 19 ft. from the W. end of the extension was interpreted as a new byre of phase II. Pottery, mostly from a rubbish-pit in the S.E. corner of the original building, suggested occupation in the 4th century; iron spikes and nails, two turned shale armlet cores, a baked clay sling-stone with the impression of a grain of Spelt wheat, and animal bones, were also found. The nearest remains of 'Celtic' fields (Ancient Field Group (29)) are ½ m. to S. on Ballard Down. (Dorset *Procs.* LXXXVII (1965), 142–207.)

(47) St. Nicholas' Church (SZ 80 SW). *Inhumation Burials* have been found about 100 ft. above sea level in rebuilding the church and in digging graves in the churchyard extension to N. A number of burials in stone cists and a rotary quern were recorded by W. M. Hardy during renovations in 1881. Indications of others in the churchyard, not examined, were followed by the discovery in 1951 at a depth of some 3½ ft. of a covered cist of weathered Purbeck marble slabs aligned N.W.-S.E. (03638254), partly floored with limestones and containing remains of an extended skeleton probably of a female aged 30-40 with the severed head and detached mandible placed near the left foot at the N.W. end of the cist. The grave was not wholly cleared but a turned shale spindle-whorl was found in the pelvic region. Another cist of Purbeck marble was found a few yards to N. in 1955. (Dorset *Procs.* XII (1891), 177–8; LXXIV (1952), 51–4; LXXVII (1955), 126.)

Sturminster Marshall

The Roman road from Badbury to Dorchester, to be described in *Dorset* V, crosses the N.W. part of the parish and survives as an earthwork in Little Almer Wood. Other remains of doubtful location consist of a grave with hand-cut shale ring, in a railway cutting, and some eight pits exposed in a chalk-pit in the

'common-field', containing Romano-British pottery, bones, etc. (Dorset *Procs.* LXXXV (1963), 105; LXXXVI (1964), 115).

(47) Bailey Gate (SY 99 NW). *Occupation Debris* has been found W. of Church House in gravel pits over Upper Chalk on the 100 ft. ridge S. of the river Winterborne. Several pits containing Romano-British pottery were observed in 1936, presumably in the workings traceable on the brow of the hill (944992). Pottery found in 1935 presumably in the same workings is in Poole Museum. (Dorset *Procs.* LXXXV (1963), 105; *Bournemouth Daily Echo*, 11 Sept. 1937.)

Swanage

A coin probably of Antoninus Pius (138–61) comes from a field N. of Caldron Barn Farm, SZ 024795 (*Swanage Times*, 7 Oct. 1953), and an issue of A.D. 332 of Constantine I from Swanage beach, 03117896 (Dorset *Procs.* LXXXIV (1962), 116).

(91) Ballard Down (SZ 08 SW). *Inhumation Burials* were found in 1917 on Upper Chalk about 350 ft. above sea level on the S. slope about 100 yds. from the cliffs (03978123). A skeleton in a cist of Purbeck stone slabs was found, with remains of another nearby in a plain grave. (*Procs. Society of Antiquaries* XXX (1917–18), 236–7.)

(92) Ulwell Farm (SZ 08 SW). *Inhumation Burials* were found in 1949 about 150 ft. above sea level on Lower Greensand about 150 yds. N.N.W. of the farmhouse (02268092). Fragmentary remains of three skeletons close together were in cists of limestone slabs; one pierced slab was probably a Roman roof-tile. (Dorset *Procs.* LXXI (1949), 68; LXXXVIII (1966), 120–1.)

Sites (93–94) lie on Wealden Beds.

(93) Godlingston Farm (SZ 07 NW). *Occupation Debris* comes from an E.-W. ridge about 50 ft. above sea level some 600 yds. S.E. of the farmhouse. Three nearly complete Durotrigian jars were found in 1961 in trenching for drains near the stream (01917979). Excavation by Mr. J. B. Calkin revealed sherds of similar type at a depth of 5 ft. to 6 ft., and 3rd or 4th-century coarse ware has since been collected after ploughing. An area of dark earth with sherds and sling-stones was seen on the crest 185 yds. W. (01747975), and drain-trenching revealed widespread sherds, limestone fragments and peat deposits. Vessels and sherds are at Godlingston Farm and Christchurch Museum. (Dorset *Procs.* LXXXVI (1964), 118–9.)

(94) Swanage Bay (SZ 07 SW). *Inhumation Burials* were exposed in 1877 in a cliff fall about ½ m. N. of Swanage (about 031798). Of two covered and partly floored cists of stone slabs, about 3 ft. apart at a depth of 18 ins., one about 2½ ft. long contained fragmentary bones of a child, the other, some 3 ft. long, probably the same. Large nails in both graves, one with oak (?) fibres, suggested wooden coffins perhaps of boards 2 ins. thick. One cist contained one or two sherds of black ware. The remains were near the 'North Ledge', presumably the Tanville Ledges offshore near Highcliffe Road, New Swanage. Objects, untraced, were formerly in Mowlem

---

[1] K, L, M, N, O, in same area (not shown in Fig.).

Institute, Swanage. (*The Times*, 23 Aug. 1877; C. E. Robinson, *A Royal Warren: Picturesque Rambles in the Isle of Purbeck* (1882), 101.)

Sites (95–98) lie on Middle Purbeck limestone.

(95) HERSTON (SZ 07 NW). *Inhumation Burials*, and *Occupation Debris* from Iron Age 'A' to late Roman times, have been found in quarrying the N. slopes about 250 ft. above sea level (about 021783).

The site, perhaps all now destroyed, yielded haematite-coated and other Iron Age 'A' sherds, Iron Age 'C' and Roman sherds, a few hand-cut shale armlet roughs and class A and C cores from turned armlets. Of two pits examined in 1931, one contained Iron Age 'C' pottery. Several extended burials in stone cists side by side are referable to the Roman period. Some pottery is in Poole Museum. A cist with adult inhumation was found in this area *c.* 1860. (Dorset *Procs.* LXX (1948), 42, 50; LXXV (1953), 69; *Swanage Times*, 7 Oct. 1953, 17 Feb. 1954; W. M. Hardy, *Old Swanage* (1908), 12.)

(96) ATLANTIC ROAD (SZ 07 NW). An *Inhumation Burial* was found in 1953 below the 200 ft. contour in building a house about 100 yds. S.S.W. of the Cottage Hospital (02807834).

The extended skeleton, evidently, from some 3 dozen 2½ in. nails, in a wooden coffin, lay with head S.E. at a depth of 4 ft. in an unusual cist consisting of two 1½ ft. high drystone walls nearly 2½ ft. apart and over 6 ft. long, capped with a double layer of local 'blue rag' slabs. The remains were of a male of about 50 years with exceptionally thick skull; the filling contained a brooch of the mid 2nd century, in private hands. The cranium is in Christchurch Museum. (*Swanage Times*, 30 Sept. 1953; Dorset *Procs.* LXXVI (1954), 76–7.) A circle of burials, undated, was reported 500 yds. to N. (*ibid.*, LXXXVII (1965), 112–13).

(97) BON ACCORD ROAD (SZ 07 NW). *Occupation Debris* was found *c.* 1904 above the 200 ft. contour in levelling the Durlston Court School playing-field (02907810). Sherds identified as Romano-British, flints, and coins, one certainly Roman, were found with indications of hearths. (W. M. Hardy, *Old Swanage* (1908), 11–13.)

(98) DURLSTON CLIFF (SZ 07 NW). *Inhumation Burials* were found in 1904 some 200 ft. above sea level in building 'The View', now 'Durlston Cliff', in La Belle Vue Road a few yards from the cliff edge (03437813). Of eight skeletons found close together by the builder, W. M. Hardy, four were extended with feet to E. in plain graves; four were in covered stone cists, one of these, about 2½ ft. by 2 ft., containing two skeletons 'in a bent attitude' with feet to S. Two coarse ware sherds, one with handle, were apparently associated with cist graves. (W. M. Hardy, *Old Swanage* (1908), 11–12; *Swanage Times*, 7 Oct. 1953.)

TYNEHAM

Sites (39–40) occupy Wealden Beds.

(39) TYNEHAM VILLAGE (SY 88 SE). *Occupation Debris* and *Inhumation Burials* have been found near the head of Tyneham Gwyle about 150 ft. above sea level. Bones, samian ware and sherds thought Romano-British were found in 1860 in the diverted stream bed (88148031). A human skeleton was found

in a nearby garden, and burials in cists of shale slabs were found in removing the S. porch of St. Mary's Church (88148039). Seven interments and a separately buried skull found in a sandy mound (87948030) near the Rectory, one with a vessel of 'black unbaked clay' near the head, were probably of Iron Age 'C' or Roman date. (Hutchins I, 628; locations from O.S. 6 in. map.) *See also* p. 454.

(40) WORBARROW BAY (SY 87 NE, 88 SE). *Inhumation Burials*, and *Occupation Debris* perhaps Iron Age to late Roman, with evidence for shale-working and perhaps Purbeck marble and salt industries, have been found on the cliffs N. of Tyneham Gwyle above the 100 ft. contour and near the Purbeck marble outcrop at Worbarrow Tout.

Remains, consisting of a layer of large stones at a depth of about 1½ ft. with darker soil above and many sherds, shale fragments and flint flakes, are visible in the cliff face for some 125 yds. (86938003 to 87017995) and may extend for some 30 yds. inland. Excavation in 1937 by Dr. W. H. C. Frend in an area over 20 yds. N.-S. (apparently about 87008000) revealed the layer of stones, including Purbeck marble from the beach, at a depth of 1½ ft. to 2 ft., in one place near the cliff edge acting as foundation for a floor of chalk blocks. Little was found on or above this layer, but black earth up to 1½ ft. thick below it contained charcoal, clay daub, much pottery, sling-stones, spindle-whorls of pot and shale, and a bronze plaque with repoussé decoration near a depression or pit in the cliff face. Other finds indicated shale-working on the site and perhaps also Purbeck marble and salt-boiling industries nearby. Evidence for the shale industry were pieces of shale, flint flakes with worn points, an armlet fragment and turned cores of classes A, B, C and D, and a deposit of 72 cores beneath a stone slab with an iron knife and arrow-head. Amongst stones used for the rough flooring were a quern-stone, a loom-weight of Purbeck marble, and part of an unfinished lugged mortar of Purbeck marble 'burr-stone'. A few pieces of salt-boiling 'briquetage' come from the site, and a coin of Commodus (180–92) from the cliffs.

The pottery including Durotrigian types is mainly of the 1st and 2nd centuries with some strays of Iron Age 'B' and perhaps 'A', but 2nd-century samian sherds were found in several places on or above natural subsoil. Common later types were rare, but an otherwise similar range of pottery collected by the excavator from the combe some 130 yds. E. (87118001) included conical flanged bowls of the 3rd or 4th century and a piece of salting 'briquetage'. Colour-coated pottery of this date came from the stream about 250 yds. S.E. (87207990).

Warne describes similar features in excavations in 1842, noting charred wheat in several places, mainly below the stone layer. The earliest accounts, by Miles and Pennie, substantiate but add few acceptable details except an inhumation in a covered stone cist. Another, all or partly of shale (D.C.M. Accessions Book, 20 Feb. 1908) was found in 1908. Objects are in D.C.M. (Dorset *Procs.* LXXI (1949), 51–2; LXXV (1953), 69; LXXXIX (1967), 146; W. H. C. Frend, 'Iron Age and Roman Sites in Purbeck' (MS. in D.C.M., 1936), 8–12; W. A. Miles, *The Deverel Barrow* (1826), 34–9; J. F. Pennie, *Tale of a Modern*

Genius II (1827), 336–41; J. H. Austen, *Purbeck Papers* I (1856–7), 82; Warne, *Ancient Dorset* (1872), 327–9.)

Sites (41–42) lie on Kimmeridge Clay.

(41) HOBARROW BAY (SY 87 NE). An *Inhumation Burial* and *Occupation Debris* from a salt-boiling industry come from a mound at the cliff edge below the 100 ft. contour ½ m. S.S.W. of South Egliston (89547909), and about 300 yds. S.E. of the 'blackstone' outcrop of the Kimmeridge Shale at cliff-top in Brandy Bay.

The mound, on an E. slope and partly sectioned by the cliff, is now some 75 ft. in diameter and 8 ft. high, with indications that the deposits composing it fill a hollow of unknown depth. A roughly circular dished area of some 120 ft. diameter extending from its N. and W. base and yielding pottery and salting 'briquetage', may indicate its extent before exploitation for use as marl.

Excavation by Miles to a stated depth of 20 ft. to 30 ft. revealed pottery, 'briquetage', objects of iron, shale, bone and horn, animal bones, shells, clinker, and beds of clay, ashes and burnt shale to a depth of 20 ft. if not throughout. A covered stone cist at 5 ft. contained an inhumation; another at 12 ft., below human bones, had ashes and snail shells; a third of shale, slightly lower, contained shale ash. In the centre, at unspecified depth, a stone wall about 3 ft. thick, with 'divisional slabs' set off it, ran N.E. A lathe-turned shale armlet core of Calkin's class A occurred at 12 ft. and another apparently of class B at 20 ft.

There have been small excavations in the mound by the Rev. A. J. Watson, Dr. W. H. C. Frend and Mr. J. B. Calkin, and objects have been collected by Dr. Henrietta Davies and R.C.H.M. Frend found a deep layer of shale ash, clinker and 'briquetage' below 1½ ft. of shaly clay topsoil, and observed heaps of 'briquetage' alternating with layers of shale ash in the cliff section, the thickest of which was 10 ft.

The material from the above sources (in D.C.M. and London University Institute of Archaeology) consists mainly of 'briquetage', some pottery, a broken hand-cut shale armlet rough and several turned armlet cores of classes A and C. The clinker may derive from high combustion of shale, here clearly used as fuel in salt-boiling. The 'briquetage' of this industry consists of many roughly hand-moulded clay supports with flat or grooved ends, complete examples ranging from 3 ins. to 7½ ins. long; a few small irregular squeezed lumps; many fragments of thick straight-sided containers of pebbly clay with rounded corners; a few pieces of thinner-walled vessels of doubtful shape, some with knife-cut rims or edges, and several bun-shaped pads. The pottery, mainly Durotrigian coarse ware, suggests occupation beginning in Iron Age 'C' or early Roman times but includes a few Iron Age 'A' and late Roman sherds. (W. A. Miles, *The Deverel Barrow* (1826), 51–3; *Purbeck Papers* I (1859–60), 217; Hutchins I, 627; W. H. C. Frend, 'Iron Age and Roman Sites in Purbeck' (MS. in D.C.M., 1936), 5–6; Dorset *Procs.* LXX (1948), 56, 58; LXXI (1949), 52–3; LXXV (1953), 69; LXXXIV (1962), 140–2.)

(42) CHARNEL (SY 87 NE). *Occupation Debris*, probably from

a salt-boiling industry, comes from two mounds at the cliff edge about 50 ft. above sea level ½ m. S. of South Egliston.

A roughly circular mound some 12 ft. high and 30 yds. in diameter, with a lower extension some 15 yds. wide running N. for about 15 yds., stands at the cliff edge (89867893) some 50 yds. E. of the Egliston Gwyle stream. It seems to consist largely of unburnt shale, but construction of a concrete pill-box has thrown up burnt shale and several fragments of pebbly 'briquetage' (in D.C.M.). About 45 yds. N.E. (89897897) a mound some 5 ft. high and 19 yds. N.-S. by 15 yds. E.-W. seems to consist of unburnt shale. (Dorset *Procs.* LXXXIX (1967), 146.)

(43) BRANDY BAY (SY 87 NE). *Occupation Debris*, some probably from salt-boiling, comes from two adjacent sites on the cliffs below Tyneham Cap, near the junction of Portland Sands with Kimmeridge Clay.

Dr. W. H. C. Frend's note of Iron Age 'C' and Romano-British pottery at a site (89397961) comparable with that at Hobarrow Bay (41) is confirmed by a few scraps of burnt shale and reddish flint-gritted ware of fabric resembling salting 'briquetage' found in 1958 about 70 yds. S.W. some 300 ft. above sea level (89347956). Romano-British sherds and one probably of Iron Age 'A' come from the cliff edge 220 yds. S.W. (89217941). Stone cobbles and Iron Age 'A' sherds noted by Frend in the cliff face between Tyneham Cap and Broad Bench are unlocated. Objects are in D.C.M. (W. H. C. Frend, 'Iron Age and Roman Sites in Purbeck' (MS. in D.C.M., 1936), 4, 6; Dorset *Procs.* LXXI (1949), 53; LXXXIX (1967), 146.)

Sites (44–45) are unlocated.

(44) POVINGTON FARM (SY 88 SE). *Occupation Debris* from a lathe-turned shale armlet industry has been found on the farm N. of the Chalk range, presumably on London Clay or Bagshot Beds.

Following an earlier discovery of large quantities of waste cores from turned shale armlets in draining an irregular undulating field said to have foundations below surface, excavation by J. H. Austen in 1856 and 1859 produced from an area of some 2 sq. yds. of black earth about 700 cores of five varieties including Calkin's classes A, B, C and D, some with incompletely detached rings, and many broken armlets. Circular blanks, shale chips and flint tools were found, and a hand-cut shale dish or lamp-stand (in D.C.M.); 'black Roman pottery' occurred. Finds were made over an area of about ½ acre. (*Purbeck Papers* I (1856–60), 90–1, 221–3; *Arch. J.* XVI (1859), 299–300; Hutchins I, 560–2; Dorset *Procs.* LXXV (1953), 67, 69.)

(45) EGLISTON MEAD (SY 88 SE). *Occupation Debris* from a lathe-turned shale armlet industry has been found in a field called Egliston Mead near Tyneham village, probably on Wealden Beds. In 1856 J. H. Austen examined part of a site thought to cover an acre; many turned armlet cores of Calkin's class A were found scattered in black earth, with a piece of an armlet and a few sherds. The site, about a mile inland from Worbarrow Bay, is possibly Chapel Close (89508050, 'Egglestone Little Mead' on the Tithe Map, 1840)

or its neighbour 'Egglestone Great Mead' to W. (*Purbeck Papers* I (1856–7), 91; Dorset *Procs.* LXXV (1953), 69.)

WAREHAM LADY ST. MARY

(85) WAREHAM (SY 98 NW). *Occupation Debris*, Iron Age 'A' to late Roman has been found at several points within or near the post-Roman town walls, notably in the N.W. and S.E. quarters. The site is Valley Gravel some 25 ft. above sea level between the rivers Frome and Piddle (Fig. p. 323).

Two Iron Age pits about 5¾ ft. in diameter and 5½ ft. deep were found in the old ground surface under the W. walls in excavations in 1952 (91978747; a on Fig. p. 323); they contained Iron Age 'A', 'B' and perhaps 'C' pottery and were overlaid with deposits including burnt material. Similar sherds and much Romano-British pottery, some of the late 4th century, were found in the rampart, derived from the old ground surface; Romano-British sherds were found in a like situation to S. in 1940 (92048731; b).

At 20 West Walls in 1953 H. G. Burr found traces of occupation probably of the 4th century, and below it part of a clay floor and two post-holes. Underneath this floor a pit contained early Romano-British sherds (92058748; c). Another pit or ditch was found opposite (92078749; d) with Iron Age 'C' or early Romano-British pottery and worked shale. A complete 4th-century jar was found *c.* 1936 at c, and in 1940 two similar vessels, a quern and a stone bowl or mortar, were found nearby at 9 Tinker's Lane (92028751; e). A group of small pots reported from the electricity transformer station adjoining these discoveries (92028743; f) may have been Roman or Saxon. Numerous Roman coins are reported from gardens inside the N.W. angle of the walls (g), whence came Romano-British sherds in 1947. Two coins of Constantius II (324–61) were found *c.* 1935 at the junction of Mill Lane and Cow Lane (92208746; h), and pottery, some certainly Romano-British, had been found in Mill Lane in 1898–9; sherds from here, including Durotrigian ware, are in D.C.M. Finds made in 1896 on the site of All Saints' Church (92288749; i) included samian and glass beads.

In the N.E. quarter the chief find was a group of three almost intact but worn samian bowls, in the Royal Albert Museum, Exeter, from the Folly (about 92258778; j); one was by the Antonine potter Mainacnus. Some 40 coins, probably a hoard, were found *c.* 1850 in lowering the hill at the N. end of North Street (k); Romano-British sherds have also been found in the garden of 45 East Street (92528746; l).

Most of the finds still preserved were made *c.* 1889–90 in the cemetery extension E. of St. Mary's Church (92588718; m). They include Claudian to Antonine samian, much coarse ware, and coins of Augustus (issue of 29–27 B.C.) and Constantine I (306–37). Large stones, a well, burnt human bones and charcoal were also found, not necessarily Roman. A coin of Constantine, of A.D. 330–5, comes from the Priory grounds (92508715; n), and at 21 South Street (92388727; o) were found four coins unusual in that, with a worn, probably Constantinian issue, were three Persian coins of the 2nd and 3rd centuries A.D. Finds from unspecified gardens near the E. rampart included 3rd and 4th-century coins and a lead statuette of a negro athlete, lost but of doubtful authenticity.

The only certain Roman finds from the S.W. quarter were a coin of Antoninus Pius (138–61) from West Street, sherds and a coin of Constantine I from S. of Castle Close (92178711; p), and sherds, possibly Roman, from gardens at West Port, perhaps extra-mural. Unprovenanced discoveries include a bronze *patera* handle, a Purbeck stone mortar, and part of an incised shale plaque.

These finds indicate occupation of relatively humble character, established in Iron Age 'A' and continuing throughout the Roman period, over much of the area within the later walls. The inscriptions in St. Mary's Church, cut on Roman architectural fragments of unknown derivation (*see* p. xlix), may imply continuity of occupation into post-Roman times. Objects are in St. Mary's Church, D.C.M., and Exeter Museum. (Dorset *Procs.* XX (1899), 148–60; LXXVI (1954), 82–5; *Med. Arch.* III (1959), 120–38.)

WAREHAM ST. MARTIN

(17) SWINEHAM (SY 98 NW). *Occupation Debris* comes from a field 600 yds. E. of Swineham Farm on Valley Gravel at the neck of an alluvial peninsula in Poole Harbour. Coarse pottery ranging from perhaps the 1st to the 4th century was found at least down to the water-table at a depth of about 3 ft., mostly in what may have been a shallow ditch cut into natural sand (94228799). Many sherds occur in upcast from dyke-scouring between 94238801 and 94208808. (Dorset *Procs.* LXXVII (1955), 127.)

WEYMOUTH

A 4th-century coin hoard believed to come from the area is described in *Num. Chron.* 6th ser. IX (1949), 252–3. Several objects in the British Museum (Durden Collection), believed to come from Greenhill (SY 683802), include a Celtic bronze collar and tankard handle, and a Roman legionary belt-plate (*Arch. J.* CXV (1958), 95); there is, however, another Green Hill W. of Monument (449) below. Three Romano-British vessels come from an unspecified site or sites in the Dorchester road and a coin of Trajan (98–117) from 'Monksdene' therein (68038203; Dorset *Procs.* XLIV (1923), 40, 41). Shale objects and part of a quern, in B.M. (Durden Collection) and D.C.M., come from Ferry Bridge, Wyke Regis (666762), but there is no confirmation of a Roman building said to have been found there *c.* 1900 (Dorset *Procs.* XII (1891), 33; XXXI (1910), xxix).

Sites (437–438) lie on Cornbrash.

(437) RADIPOLE, SPA HILL (SY 68 SE). *Occupation Debris* and *Inhumation Burials* have been found at about 100 ft. on the ridge at the N. end of Radipole Lake.

Part of a concrete floor was found in 1937 by the N.E. corner of 112 Spa Road (66938128), with a 1st-century brooch, sherds of samian and coarse ware, some of the 4th century, and three coins including an issue of 367–75 of

Gratian. Sherds and an imitation *as* of Claudius I (41–54) come from gardens to E.N.E. (66978142), and a bronze key from Icen Road to E. Objects are in D.C.M. and private possession.

Over seven skeletons, some at random, three extended E.-W. and one N.-S., were found nearby by J. Medhurst *c.* 1844, near the road at the crest of the hill (about 66918127), accompanied by black ware urns and samian. Remains of a Roman 'causeway', pitched stones, sherds, ashes, bones and shells were found in an extensive area of made soil and, in adjoining fields, debris including Roman tile and coins. A shale plaque, samian dish and grey ware jar, said to have been found at Radipole in 1869, are in B.M. (Medhurst Collection). Further burials on the crest of Spa Hill, found with a samian dish and black ware jar, were destroyed in 1886.

A cylindrical amphora stamped P. towards the base, in D.C.M. and dating probably before *c.* A.D. 50 (M. H. Callender, *Roman Amphorae* (1965), 199–200), was found *c.* 1890 in mid-channel silt between the Backwater dam and the Gasworks tunnel (about 67687906). 'Roman ware, Roman bricks, ridge and flat tiles, remnants of Kimmeridge Coal urns, coins, pottery, etc.' had been found earlier in the Backwater near the Gasworks (Notes by E. Jackson Brown, 1835–45, extracted by V. L. Oliver, in D.C.M.), and a flanged coarse ware bowl of the 3rd or 4th century, in D.C.M., came from the N. end of Radipole Lake, about 670805 (A. D. Passmore, letter 24 Apr. 1934, in D.C.M.). Two amphorae were recovered from Weymouth Bay (1880, in D.C.M.) and Portland Harbour (1914–18, D.C.M. correspondence, 1920).

The evidence is insufficient to determine the site of the port installations served by the Roman road from Dorchester (p. 528), although the remains at Spa Hill lie on its projected alignment. Some remains of the road were claimed by Ellis at the foot of the hill. (*Gentleman's Magazine* (1844), pt. ii, 636; (1845), pt. i, 79; Dorset *Procs.* XI (1890), 88–90; XLIV (1923), 41–3, 54–5; LXXIII (1951), 96–9; LXXVI (1954), 97–8; Warne, *Ancient Dorset* (1872), 187.)

(438) RADIPOLE LANE (SY 68 SE). An *Inhumation Burial* and *Occupation Debris* have been found about 100 ft. above sea level in the South Hill Estate at the E. end of the Chickerell ridge. A contracted inhumation probably not earlier than the 3rd or 4th century A.D. was found in 1935 near the hill-crest (66338100), lying E.-W. with head W. in a scoop at the base of a shallow pit. A stone cist, apparently empty, was found earlier about 100 ft. to N. near a coarse ware jar probably of the 2nd century. Romano-British sherds were seen in builders' excavations here, and in the field to E., on the crest and S. slope. Objects are in D.C.M. (Dorset *Procs.* LXXIII (1951), 95–6.)

Sites (439–445) lie on Corallian Beds.

(439) NEWBERRY ROAD, WEYMOUTH (SY 67 NE). A *Villa* is probably indicated by a mosaic or mosaics found in 1835 and 1902 on the lower S.-facing slope of a re-entrant in Nothe Clay about 25 ft. above the sea which lies 200 yds. to E.

The corner of a mosaic floor removed to D.C.M. in 1902 was found E. of the road, about 67987839, and was probably distinct from a 'Roman tessellated pavement' found nearby

in 1835 perhaps under Spring Terrace, 67977837. The surviving pattern of five colours, $10\frac{1}{2}$ ft. by 5 ft., is unusual. A coarse border of two red lines on a white ground encloses a finer triple border consisting of black and white chevrons, guilloche in black, white, brown and red, and chequers in white, red, grey and brown. Remains of a centre panel consist of a white ground divided apparently into triangular spaces by three oblique lines of guilloche. A small grey-edged square at the base of the best preserved triangle was of variously coloured tesserae set lozenge-wise, of which only the white are present. The adjoining triangle, in which the white ground tesserae are set lozenge-wise, may have contained a curvilinear pattern. The only find recorded was a Saxon *sceatta* allegedly on the floor. (Dorset *Procs.* XLIV (1923), 39–40; LXXXV (1963), 96–8.)

(440) CLEARMOUNT, RODWELL (SY 67 NE). *Inhumation Burials* were found *c.* 1864 in the railway cutting about 100 ft. above sea level.

A 'Roman burial place' was cut through at Rodwell in constructing the Weymouth and Portland Railway, opened in 1865. Two vessels in B.M., not closely dated, were found 'in a railway cutting at Clearmount', presumably E. of Clearmount Road (about 675779), while Lock's *Guide* states that 'during the excavation for Rodwell station' (674783) 'pieces of Roman pottery and some Roman coins were unearthed, as well as the bones of a man, horse and dog.' A Roman bronze spoon came from the garden of 'Faircross' (669783). (Dorset *Procs.* XLIV (1923), 42–3; *Procs. Society of Antiquaries* III (1865), 93; *Pictorial and Descriptive Guide to Weymouth* (Ward, Lock & Co., 10th edn.), 53.)

(441) WYKE REGIS RESERVOIR (SY 67 NE). *Inhumation Burials* have been found above the 200 ft. contour E. of All Saints' Church.

Of two burials, each with a pot, found in 1858 in the glebe allotments about 30 yds. E. of the graveyard (about 66307784), one was contracted E.-W., head E., in a 4 ft. long cist with single stone slabs for sides and a shale(?) cover, and had a Durotrigian bowl of Brailsford's class I by the shoulder; there were remains probably of two additional stone cists. A bead-rimmed jar containing a samian cup (form 27) of *c.* 60–80 and a coin, untraced, allegedly of Faustina I (*c.* 139–45), came from construction *c.* 1900 of the older part of the reservoir, about 66367788. In 1936, following discovery in the adjoining new reservoir of three or four burials, one at least in a stone cist, a skeleton in a shallow grave containing six or seven iron nails was excavated some 20 yds. from the roadside (66417791); it was extended E.-W., head E., on its right side with knees slightly flexed. A handled beaker of black coarse ware of the later 3rd or 4th century was recovered in fragments from the grave. Two Roman coins and several sherds are recorded from the allotment gardens to W. Objects are in D.C.M. (*Arch. J.* CXVI (1959), 201–2; *J.B.A.A.* XV (1859), 283; Dorset *Procs.* XXXI (1910), xxix; LXXI (1949), 70–2; *Dorset Daily Echo* 28 Oct. 1936.)

(442) OVERLANDS, WYKE REGIS (SY 67 NE). An *Inhumation Burial* and *Occupation Debris* were found in 1937 in drainage trenches on the housing estate near Camp Road, about $\frac{1}{4}$ m. W. of Monument (441) and some 200 ft. above sea level.

A cist 4 ft. by 2 ft., with single stone slabs for sides and cover, contained a contracted adult skeleton on its left side, head W., with a coarse ware jar probably of the 3rd century in front of the face and a few sherds and winkle shells in the filling. The site, 'Overlands' in the local newspaper and North Road in D.C.M. records, was probably on the knoll where the latter joins Overlands Road, about 65837792. A Durotrigian bowl of Brailsford's class 1a and a small handled cup of black ware, both whole, probably indicate other burials. A 'hearth', limpet and winkle shells, including a thick deposit of the latter, suggest domestic occupation, and many Roman coins were said to have been found in ploughing. Vessels and bones are in D.C.M. (D.C.M. correspondence, 17 July, 20 Aug. 1937; *Dorset Daily Echo* 3 July 1937.)

Roman remains including bricks and burnt stones are said to have been found at Barrow (658776) to S. (E. Jackson Brown, MS. notes 1835–45, extracted by V. L. Oliver, in D.C.M.).

(443) BROADWEY (SY 68 SE). An *Inhumation Burial* was found beside the Weymouth road *c.* 1844. The remains, apparently of a young person, were found 'in the Roman grave by the side of the Roman road, four miles south of Dorchester' (F. T. Buckland, *Curiosities of Natural History* 2nd ser. (1860), 112). 'Portions of a Roman cinerary urn' were found at St. Nicholas' Church in 1862 in digging Dr. Puckett's grave (66808354; Hutchins II, 490), and a Durotrigian bowl, in D.C.M., comes from the 'lower end of the railway cutting'. (Dorset *Procs.* XLIV (1923), 43.)

(444) SOUTH DOWN FARM, LODMOOR (SY 68 SE). An *Inhumation Burial* and *Occupation Debris* were found in 1934 in making a road E. of the farmhouse about 100 ft. above sea level (about 68738189). A skeleton, found at a depth of about 7 ft. by the builder, Mr. A. C. Whettam, but removed before examination, was believed by V. L. Oliver and C. D. Drew to have been buried at the bottom of a shallow domestic pit containing burnt material, oyster shells, sherds and iron nails. (V. L. Oliver, MS. notes in D.C.M., 1934; information from Mr. A. C. Whettam.)

(445) JORDAN HILL, PRESTON (SY 68 SE). A *Building* (*Temple*?) and *Cemetery* have been found on the hill-crest about 150 ft. above sea level overlooking Weymouth Bay. The building was excavated by J. Medhurst in 1843, and by C. S. Prideaux and C. D. Drew in 1931–2; the exposed foundations (69898207) are in the care of the Ministry of Public Building and Works. The cemetery to N. and N.E. was investigated by Medhurst in 1845–6.

The *Building* was some 25 ft. square internally with walls 3 ft. 8 ins. wide on foundations 9½ ft. wide. Both stone and clay roofing tiles were found. A thin concrete surround on all sides was at least 11 ft. wide on S. and 9 ft. on W. Observers in 1843, perhaps misled by two offsets in the foundations, noted traces of steps at the centre of the S. wall, and bases of four small columns *in situ* 4 ft. from it;[1] a limestone base and a Purbeck marble Tuscan capital (Fig.) for a column or columns about

---

[1] Harford placed them on the E. side.

5 ft. high, in D.C.M., were found loose near the N. wall. An oblong shaft 4 ft. by 3 ft. and 12 ft. deep lay within the S.E. angle, largely under the line of the wall footings; the sides were lined with roofing slabs set in clay, and the filling consisted of 16 layers of ash and charcoal alternating with double layers of roofing slabs arranged in superimposed pairs,

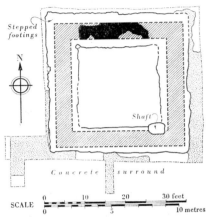

Weymouth (445). Jordan Hill, temple (?)

between each of which were bones of a single bird and a small bronze coin. At the bottom a stone cist contained two urns, a sword, spear-head, knife, steelyard, bucket-handle, crook and other iron objects; a similar cist half-way down enclosed urns, a sword and a spear-head. The bird bones were identified as of buzzard, raven, starling and crow, and one coin as of Theodosius I (379–95). There were also bones of a hare.

The building was set, apparently centrally, in an outer square enclosure, not confirmed in 1931–2, with walls 5 ft. thick and dimensions variously given as 280 ft. square, 110 ft. or 37 yds. square. Within this were found many animal remains, especially horns of oxen, pottery, and about 300 coins all apparently of the late Empire including one of Arcadius (383–408). In later excavations and consolidation 177 coins

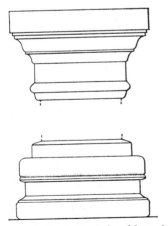

Weymouth (445). Capital and base. ($\frac{1}{12}$)

WHITCOMBE. (26) Rider, stone relief sculpture, from Whitcombe Hill.

DORCHESTER. Antefix (p. 538),
ht. 6 ins.

ditto. (217a) Glazed jar, ht. $5\frac{1}{3}$ ins.

CORFE CASTLE. (238) Altar of Purbeck stone, ht.
$14\frac{1}{3}$ ins., from Kingston Barn.

MISCELLANEA, now in Dorset County Museum.

PLATE 229

ROMAN

DORCHESTER. (225e) Sarcophagi from Poundbury, one with 'gypsum' burial (*Phot.: D.C.M.*); sarcophagi now in Dorset County Museum.

PORTLAND. (102) Stone plinth and sarcophagus, from The Grove, now at H.M. Borstal Institution.

PLATE 230

ROMAN

(216c): Necklace, shale bracelets and spindle whorls. (⅔).

(194) Coin hoard, as found in Building (a).

(*Phot.: D.C.M.*)

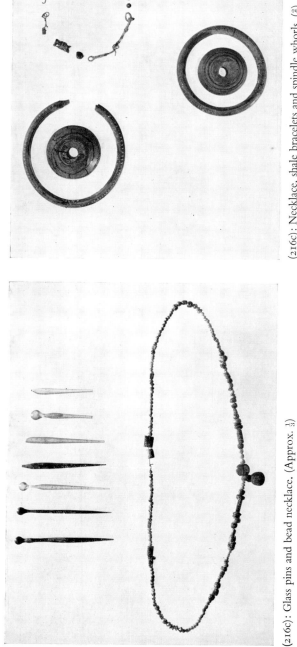

(216c): Glass pins and bead necklace. (Approx. ⅔).

(216d): Snaffle bit and bronze rings. (Approx. ⅔).

DORCHESTER. Finds from burials, and coin hoard, now in Dorset County Museum.

Settlement on Little Hogleaze, Frampton, from E.

'Celtic' fields and later ridge and furrow on Westminstone Down, Compton Valence, from N.

WESTMINSTONE—TOWN HILL (Group 1).   (*Phots.: Min. of Defence, Air Force Dept.*)

'Celtic' fields in Valley of Stones, looking N.E. from Crow Hill.

Valley of Stones, with sarsen enclosure (Little Bredy 7a), from S.E.

LITTLE BREDY, WINTERBOURNE STEEPLETON (Group 3).

PLATE 233   ANCIENT FIELD GROUPS, etc.

PORTESHAM WITHY BED (Group 4). 'Celtic' fields, with strip lynchets (Portesham 32a), from S.E.

RINGS HILL—POVINGTON HILL Group 17). 'Celtic' fields on Whiteway Hill, Tyneham, from N.

(*Phots.: Min. of Defence, Air Force Dept.*)

Ground view of 'Celtic' fields and settlement site (b) in Vicarage Bottom.

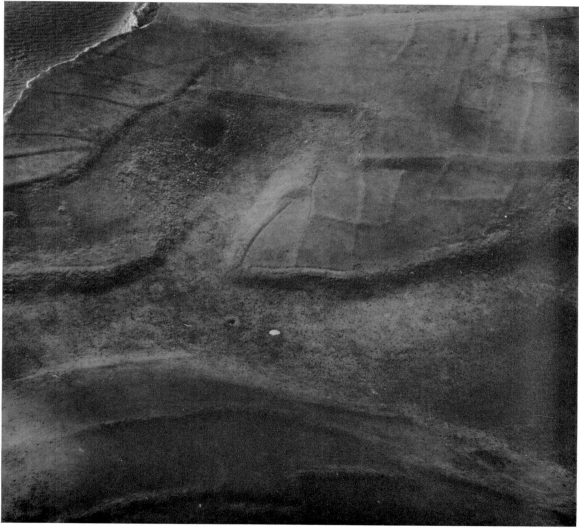

Aerial view.

CHALDON HERRING, etc. (Group 15). Chaldon Herring Warren, from E. (*Air phot.: Min. of Defence, Air Force Dept.*)

PLATE 235   ANCIENT FIELD GROUP, etc.

Ground view, from S.W., showing 'Celtic' fields on W. side of spur.

Aerial view, from N., showing 'Celtic' fields, settlements (Corfe Castle 221–2) and later ridge and furrow.

KINGSTON DOWN (Group 23).   (*Air phot.: Min. of Defence, Air Force Dept.*)

were found on the site, 61 of them certainly of the period 388–95, amongst them a bronze Durotrigian coin and examples from Vespasian (69–79) to Arcadius. Of two coin hoards discovered on the hill, one in 1812 consisted of several hundred silver coins, mostly it seems of 244–68; the other (69808201), found in 1928, was of over 4,400 bronze coins ranging from Postumus (259–68) to Honorius (393–423) but mostly issued after 379.

The *Cemetery*, perhaps pre-Roman in origin, lay N. and N.E. and extended at least 300 yds. over an area where Roman material occurs on the surface. The most reliable account is probably that of T. W. Wake Smart in Warne's *Ancient Dorset*. About 80 inhumation burials of adults and children were found in an area of about one acre, variously orientated and often flexed, and sometimes in groups of up to six individuals. Some were in stone cists and one grave was paved with chalk tesserae; nails indicated that some had been in wooden coffins. Low drystone walls, one of crescent-shape 21 ft. long, apparently demarcated burial plots and sometimes had burials in their structure (Shipp (in Hutchins) states that the cemetery was within a parallelogram 500 ft. across with a low thick wall). Near the burials were (i) several floors of white clay, one seemingly of 18 ft. by 12 ft. with stone walls; (ii) clay-lined hollows containing ashes, animal bones and sherds, several apparently provided with stone-lined drains; (iii) two stone cists containing burnt shale and calcined animal bones; (iv) several stone piles on which rested animal bones or vessels containing them. Some burials had single pots or groups; in one group of nine vessels, three (a samian dish, a black ware imitation of samian form 37, and a handled cup of black ware) stood on an engraved oblong plaque or tray of shale placed at the shoulder, with five black ware bowls ranged around it, and a bottle of yellowish ware at the knees. Another imitation of samian form 37 was made of shale. Some 80 vessels survive (mostly in D.C.M. and B.M.) out of perhaps 125 listed as from Jordan Hill in sale catalogues of the Medhurst Collection (Sotheby's, 1 July 1879; C. T. Jefferies, Bristol, 1893), including many Durotrigian jars, bowls and handled mugs, some samian ware, imitation samian in black fabrics, a Gallo-Belgic *terra rubra* bowl and *terra nigra* platters, and two lead-glazed beakers. Although sherds of late Romano-British ware were found, most of the whole vessels may be attributed to the cemetery and assigned to the second half of the 1st century A.D., with some few of the 2nd century or later. A bronze armlet, finger-rings and sandal-nails accompanied burials, also iron arrow-heads, an iron sword, styli, and bone weaving-combs.

Other objects from the cemetery area, not necessarily with burials and in some cases suggesting domestic or industrial occupation, included iron spear-heads, saddle and rotary quern-stones, chert and flint balls, a shale armlet and lathe-turned armlet cores, a Durotrigian silver coin and three of the 3rd and 4th centuries, sherds including painted ware of New Forest type, and many pieces of angular supports resembling salt-boiling 'briquetage'. Less precisely attributed objects from Jordan Hill are four more whole or partial shale plaques or trays with engraved decoration, a carved shale slab, a shale tablet with a stylized lion in relief from a site yielding bronze coins and sherds, Iron Age swan-necked and ring-headed pins (*Arch. J.* XCI (1934), 288–9), La Tène I and III and Roman

brooches, and a bronze Roman mirror-handle (*Archaeologia Cambrensis* C (1949), 32).

The date and purpose of the Jordan Hill building are uncertain. The coins and pottery point to intensive occupation in the 4th and early 5th century but do not exclude an earlier date of construction; although it appears likely that the Theodosian shaft predated the building, or was a foundation deposit, their relationship cannot now be established. The building has usually been regarded as the cella of a temple perhaps with portico, surrounded by a *temenos*. The columns, and the shaft which seems clearly to be of ritual character as at Ashill (V.C.H. *Norfolk* I (1901), 295–6), would support this ascription, although use as a signal station has been suggested (Dorset *Procs.* LVII (1935), 140). Objects from the site are in B.M., D.C.M., Pitt-Rivers Museum (Oxford), Taunton, Bristol, and Warrington Museums. (*Gentleman's Magazine* (1844), pt. i, 185–6; (1844), pt. ii, 413, 635–6; H. C. Harford, *Essay on Roman Remains near Weymouth*, read to Soc. Antiquaries, 21 Mar. 1844 (privately printed); *Abstracts of Procs. Ashmolean Society* II (1843–55), 55; Hutchins I, 562; II, 838–9; Warne, *Ancient Dorset* (1872), 224–34, Appendix 297–8; William Shipp MS. II (in D.C.M.), 59–66; Warne, MS. 'Illustrations to the History of Dorset' (in D.C.M.), 179, 248, 256, 272, 392; Dorset *Procs.* LIII (1931), 265–76; LIV (1932), 15–21. *Coins:* G. A. Ellis, *History and Antiquities of Weymouth and Melcombe Regis* (1829), 3, 253–4; Warne, *C.T.D.*, mopr, 60; Dorset *Procs.* LI (1929), 158–82; LVII (1935), 140–2; *Num. Chron.* XI (1931), 14–27. *Other objects: Purbeck Papers* I (1859–60), 228–9; Dorset *Procs.* XLIV (1923), 48–53; *Catalogue of Roman Pottery in the B.M.* (1908), 10, 127, 418, 420; *Guide to the Antiquities of Roman Britain* (B.M., 1922), 70–1, 114–5; (1951), 29–30, 36, 56); *Later Prehistoric Antiquities of the British Isles* (B.M., 1953), 56, 72.)

(446) BOWLEAZE COVE, PRESTON (SY 78 SW). *Occupation Debris, Floors,* and an *Inhumation Burial* have been found near the mouth of the River Jordan on Early Holocene Loam over Oxford Clay and in landslips on Furzy Cliff to the W. on Nothe Grit over Oxford Clay.

An occupation layer probably of the 4th century A.D. some 6 ins. to 8 ins. thick, containing animal bones, Romano-British tile fragments and sherds ranging from at least the 2nd century onwards, is sectioned some 9 ins. below surface in a low scarp above foreshore W. of the stream; it extends for some 60 yds. from 70198195 to 70248194, and perhaps eastwards towards the stream (J. N. Carreck). A floor of fine pebbles on a double course of large beach stones, and fragments of amphorae, were observed in 1935, and in 1945–9 traces of ditches running seawards. Romano-British sherds come from the stream 100 yds. N.E. (70328201). Piles of a supposed Roman landing stage are said to have been found by J. Medhurst c. 1845.

About 1 ft. below surface in the upper face of Furzy Cliff to W.N.W., some 60 ft. above sea level (70148196), a roughly mortared 'floor' some 9 ins. thick, of oolite, chert and shingle, extends in section for about 22 ft. between rough settings or curbs of heavier stones. The feature slopes gently eastwards in conformity with ground surface; a thin stony layer continues its line to E. for about 24 ft., the last 12 ft. or so overlying a mass of 'cannon-ball' concretions which, though occurring

O

naturally in bands in the Nothe Grit, appear here to have been deliberately pitched. Romano-British sherds and tile fragments occur above and immediately below the 'floor'; a Durotrigian silver coin of late 1st century B.C. was also found. Objects are in D.C.M. (Dorset *Procs.* LXX (1948), 63–4; LXXIII (1951), 97; LXXXIV (1962), 112; J. N. Carreck, *Procs. Geologists' Association* LXVI (1955), 74–100; K. C. C. Selby, D.C.M. Correspondence, No. 609, 17 May 1935.)

A grave found 'in the cliff near Jordan gate' between 1835 and 1845, probably in the landslips at Furzy Cliff, contained a skeleton with a 'hollow gold' finger-ring with glass intaglio, a model bronze battle-axe, and a silver coin of Ptolemy of *c.* 285 B.C. The coin, now lost, was evidently of Ptolemy I or II, but the reset intaglio is Graeco-Roman of the 1st century B.C. or later. Objects are in private possession. (E. Jackson Brown, MS. notes, 1835–45, extracted by V. L. Oliver, in D.C.M.)

Sites (447–448) lie on Kimmeridge Clay.

(447) PRESTON (SY 78 SW). A *Villa* discovered by J. Medhurst in 1844 below the 50 ft. contour on the W. slope of the Jordan valley, ½ m. N.N.E. of Monument (445), was partly explored by him and T. Baker following diversion of the stream through the site in 1852, and again by Baker in 1871, and by C. D. Drew in 1932. The principal remains, a mosaic scheduled as an Ancient Monument, were concealed beneath a concrete floor in 1946 following extensive dilapidation (70298270).

The mosaic (Plate 225), occupying a room 21 ft. square, appears to have been at the N.W. angle of two ranges running due E. and S. respectively. A border of coarse white tesserae with red band, and an inner border of finer white tesserae with black band, enclosed an oblong guilloche-framed panel in black, white and red, of perhaps 18 ft. by 12 ft. apparently with long axis E.–W. This panel consisted of two end-panels with running leaf scrolls flanking a square panel cut off at the corners to form an octagon containing a rosette in a central square; the spandrels were filled with frets and triangles. The design was apparently symmetrical except perhaps for maladjustment of central square to octagon shown in the D.C.M. version of Crickmay's drawing on which the illustration is based. The materials were said to be Kimmeridge shale, Purbeck stone, and tile.

The floor, some parts of which including a corner were damaged, was not completely exposed until 1871, when some of the surrounding area was examined. There were no remains to N., but Baker found 'a room at the south-west with very rough tesserae, the court paved with stone at the centre, and a room to the south-east about twelve feet square, also roughly paved with tesserae'. His account refers to a wall 63 ft. 8 ins. long, and perhaps to three other rooms, one 12 ft. by 11½ ft. and two of unascertained dimensions. Small tiles 8 ins. square of chalk and shale (some of the latter in D.C.M.) were said to come from the villa.

Drew disclosed S. and E. wall foundations of the mosaic chamber partly under those of the protective building erected by Baker, and two parallel walls running E. in alignment

with this chamber, forming a N. range at least 98 ft. long until cut by the stream. Of Drew's parallel walls, the N., consisting of a single diagonally pitched limestone course, lay throughout beneath the modern yard wall and was probably Baker's long wall; the S. wall, 2 ft. 4 ins. wide at base, was of two courses pitched in clay with a single mortared course set back above. The area between had a well-worn floor of limestone slabs of Roman date, in part over-riding and hence later than the wall foundations, occasional patches of ash where paving was missing, and at the E. end (70318270) a stokehole and rectangular oven or furnace, 2½ ft. by 1¾ ft., apparently contemporary with the floor. A table-leg of Kimmeridge shale (further discussed in *Antiquity* XXIV (1950), 25–8) was found below a floor-slab. Foundations and loose red and white tesserae were found in a test pit across the stream to S. (70328269), and three test pits 10 yds. to 20 yds. S.W. of the mosaic suggested a W. range running N.–S. Finds included painted wall-plaster, clay and stone roof-tiles, coins of Carausius (286–93) and Constans (issue of 335–41), and pottery mainly of the 3rd or 4th century including ware of New Forest type, in D.C.M. Part of an antefix of red clay (in D.C.M.), similar to those from Dorchester but not from the same mould, may come from the site (*see* p. 538).

Medhurst is believed to have found traces of structures elsewhere in the meadows between Jordan Hill and the village of Preston, and Romano-British pottery is said to have been found in the churchyard (70578296). (*Gentleman's Magazine* (1844), pt. i, 186–7; (1844), pt. ii, 636; Warne, *Ancient Dorset* (1872), 224, 235, Appendix, 297; T. Baker, *J.B.A.A.* XXVIII (1872), 94–6, plate facing 292; *D.C.C.*, 24 Aug. 1872, 13; Dorset *Procs.* X (1889), xxviii–xxx; XXI (1900), 265–6; XLIV (1923), 49–50; LIV (1932), 21–34.)

(448) SUTTON POYNTZ, WATERWORKS (SY 78 SW). *Inhumation Burials* and *Occupation Debris* were found E. of the Waterworks in 1939 in building a house 'Watermeadow', on a S.-facing slope below the 100 ft. contour. Two burials lying E.–W. on right side with legs flexed, were found at 70678393 in a drain-trench running S. from the S.W. corner of the garage forming the W. end of the house. One, 34 ft. from the corner with head E., had a bead-rimmed bowl of Brailsford's class 2 near the head, with sherds and shale fragments and two bronze brooches, one a plate brooch of the second half of the 1st century A.D., in the grave filling. The other, at 30 ft., with head W., had a bead-rimmed vessel by the head and hob-nails at the feet; the grave filling contained sherds and a bronze needle. A third burial, unexcavated, was found in the inspection pit at the S.W. corner of the garage. Romano-British sherds, some of the 3rd or 4th century, come from the garden N. of the house. A bronze brooch, a coin of Antoninus Pius (138–61) and 4th-century sherds came from the house foundations. Objects and sketch plan are in D.C.M.

A handled jug was found before 1898 at the Waterworks, and a black ware tazza at the Rimbury reservoir ½ m. S.W. (699833; Dorset *Procs.* XLIV (1923), 53).

(449) SUTTON POYNTZ, PLAISTERS LANE (SY 78 SW). *Occupation Debris*, a *Hut*, and *Inhumation Burials* were found in 1931–6 in the garden of 'Wyndings' at the

junction of Upper Greensand and Kimmeridge Clay on a S.-facing slope below the 200 ft. contour.

Rough limestone paving was found in excavations N. of the house by J. F. C. Kimber in 1935–6, over an area at least 60 ft. E.-W. by 40 ft. (70198424), with traces at E. of an oblong hut some 17 ft. by 15 ft. overall with drystone wall, enclosing an approximately central stone-lined oven 2 ft. wide internally. Limestone slabs suggesting a structure had been found previously under an extension on the N. side of the house, and a pit, a rotary quern-stone and pottery including a complete native imitation of a samian form 30 bowl (in D.C.M.) on the site of the tennis court to N.W. Finds from the site range from 1st to 4th century, including samian and New Forest type ware, several complete Durotrigian vessels and later cooking-pots, fragments of two shale plaques or trays (one engraved) and of three lugged mortars of Purbeck marble. In addition to two human skeletons (one of a child), found earlier in the garden, a contracted inhumation was excavated in 1936 W. of the house (70178423); it lay E.-W. with head E. beside which was a pedestalled Durotrigian bowl of Brailsford's class 2. (Finds and unpublished notes in possession of Mrs. J. F. C. Kimber; *J.R.S.* XXI (1931), 241; XXVII (1938), 194; Dorset *Procs.* LXXXVI (1964), 114–5.)

WHITCOMBE

(26) WHITCOMBE HILL (SY 78 NW). *Building Remains, Pits, Ditches, Inhumation Burials* and a stone *Relief* (Plate 228) have been found E. of Cole Hill Wood near the crest of a ridge of Upper Chalk 250 ft. above sea level.

Surface debris seen after the relief was ploughed up in 1963 consisted of pottery sherds ranging from the 1st or 2nd to the 4th century A.D., clay roof-tiles and large worn paving slabs of limestone. Excavation in 1965 revealed (i) remains of a rectangular building (71138807) approximately 27 ft. by 22 ft. on a north-easterly alignment, with a floor of chalk and earth and robbed walls with traces of internal painted wall-plaster *in situ*; (ii) some 25 yds. to W. (71118807) flint foundations 1¾ ft. wide of a wall running on a different north-easterly alignment, flanked on both sides by remains of a chalk and earth floor with three infant burials; (iii) 45 yds. S.W. of (i), three contracted inhumations, one male and one female, buried on the right side in hollows in the chalk (71008803). These last were variously aligned N.W.-S.E. (head), S.W.-N.E. (head), and E.-W. (head); the man was buried with two Durotrigian vessels, possibly pre-Roman, the women with joints of pig, sheep and horse, and in one case an amber-coloured glass ring bead.

Further excavation in 1966–7 indicated a native Durotrigian settlement of pre-Roman origin with chalk-cut storage pits and ditches, some of which had been made up with chalk at the sides where they had cut through older pit-fillings. Of nine more inhumations, mostly in shallow scooped graves, at least seven were contracted on the right side with heads in easterly directions. One adult male wore an iron bracelet; two others had a pair of Durotrigian pots, while two seem to have been unaccompanied except, in one case, by bones indicating food offerings such as occurred in several of the graves. A girl

aged about 16, one of two burials in rectangular graves, had a necklace of ten glass, one paste and two wooden beads, and two Durotrigian and two samian vessels (forms Déch. 67 and Ritt. 12) dating the interment to *c.* A.D. 90 at earliest. A male of about 27, with indications perhaps of a wound in the right shoulder, was unique in the region in being buried with iron weapons as well as ornaments. These had consisted of a sword 2½ ft. long, lying by the right side in a bronze-mounted wooden scabbard probably attached by two rings to a belt or baldric, a spear perhaps grasped in the right hand, and a hammer-like weapon with chalk pommel in the left. A bronze brooch of La Tène II type lay above the right shoulder and a bronze ring with stud on the breast probably to fasten clothing or a baldric. This burial must be presumed prior to the Roman conquest.

The relief, apparently found near wall (ii), is of local Portland limestone, 8 ins. thick and 2 ft. 3½ ins. wide with a 3 in. plain border, and is now 1 ft. 11 ins. high having lost top and bottom portions. It depicts a bearded horseman with bare head turned to face the onlooker, wearing a flowing cloak curving in folds behind him over a belted tunic. The rider carries in his right hand a thick lance held at a forward slant and bears a round shield on his crooked left arm. A baldric, presumably to support a sword (not shown) at the left side, passes over a pad on the right shoulder. The horse, a stallion with short mane, drooping tail and prominent eye and nostril, walks to the right; it is harnessed with a neck rein, breast and crupper straps with two pendant straps or tassels, and has a rectangular saddle cloth and a saddle with raised front or saddle tree curving over the rider's thigh.

The sculpture, perhaps of the later 2nd or 3rd century, may be either a tombstone of an auxiliary cavalryman or a dedication possibly to a Thraco-Danubian hero-god regarded as a protector of hunters and a saviour in the struggle against forces of evil. Its probable date, and the lack of other evidence for a military site, favours the second interpretation. Coins suggest occupation of the site into the late 4th century at least. The relief and other finds are in D.C.M.(*J.R.S.* LIV (1964), 172; Dorset *Procs.* LXXXVI (1964), 103–4; LXXXVII (1965), 96; LXXXVIII (1966), 113; LXXXIX (1967), 126–7; *cf.* E. Will, *Le Relief Cultuel Greco-Romain* (1955), 56 ff.; G. I. Kazarow, *Die Denkmäler des Thrakischen Reitergottes in Bulgarien*, 2 vols. (1938); D. Tudor, 'I cavalieri Danubiani', *Ephemeris Dacoromana* VII (1937), 189–356.)

An inhumation burial, apparently contracted but of unknown date, was found at a depth of 3 ft. about ½ m. to N.E. in making the loop road round Whitcombe Hill (*D.C.C.*, 19 May 1836).

WINFRITH NEWBURGH

Two bronze penannular brooches, one of Iron Age and one of Romano-British type, and other objects, in D.C.M., come from an unlocated site in Sleight Bottom, N. of Randall's Farm (SY 805819).

WINTERBORNE MONKTON

An inhumation burial in a stone cist probably of this period was found in 1862 near the top of the large

Bronze Age bell barrow N. of Maiden Castle (SY 66698928; *see* Round Barrows, Winterborne Monkton (6)). A coin of Constans (333–50) was found near the Roman road (680880; note in Haverfield Library, Ashmolean Museum).

WINTERBORNE ST. MARTIN

For Roman occupation at Maiden Castle, including a late 4th-century temple, *see* Hill-forts, Winterborne St. Martin (142). Two intrusive inhumation burials in stone cists probably of Roman date were found in Clandon Barrow, 65648900, and about ten without cists in a barrow to S.E., 65748894 (*see* Round Barrows, Winterborne St. Martin (134–5)).

(146) MANOR FARM (SY 68 NW). An *Inhumation Burial* was found in 1950 in ploughing Middle Eweleaze below the crest of a spur of Upper Chalk above the 400 ft. contour (64658724). The burial lay in a stone cist about 7 ft. long E.-W. Some 20 round flint nodules, a sherd of Iron Age 'C' and two of mediaeval type were found on the site, and some Roman and mediaeval sherds occur in ploughsoil 100 yds. N. where traces of scarps may belong to destroyed 'Celtic' fields peripheral to Ancient Field Group (6). (Dorset *Procs.* LXXII (1950), 90.)

WOODSFORD

Two Romano-British shale spindle-whorls and a flint tool come from the area of the mediaeval settlement, Woodsford (4), SY 760905 (Warne, *Ancient Dorset* (1872), 19).

WOOL

A bronze coin of the 2nd century A.D. (in D.C.M.) comes from a garden in Wool village beside the Lulworth road (SY 846862).

(50) BURTON CROSS (SY 88 NW). *Occupation Debris* was found in 1959 in laying an effluent pipe-line for the Atomic Energy Authority on a gentle S.-facing slope on Reading Beds about 200 ft. above sea level.

A layer of large flints 20 ft. across, and traces probably of horizontal beams about 6 ins. wide, lay about 30 yds. apart on natural sandy subsoil (83628562). An extensive layer of dark soil above contained pottery ranging from late 1st to 4th century, two 2nd-century coins, clay daub and cement-like material, possibly derived from a main building or buildings to N.E. where surface finds include fragments of clay roof-tile. A crop-mark adjoining the latter apparently indicates a rectangular ditched enclosure some 100 ft. by over 120 ft. long cut by the Winfrith Newburgh parish boundary (83728577). Worked flints and sherds, one probably of Iron Age 'A', were also found in the pipe-line trench to W. (83378578). (Dorset *Procs.* LXXXIV (1962), 125–30; *see also* Coombe Keynes (21) above.)

(51) BOVINGTON CAMP (SY 88 NW). A Durotrigian pot, probably from an *Inhumation Burial*, was found in 1962 at about 150 ft. on the crest of the low ridge of Bagshot Beds occupied by the permanent military camp (83218911). The vessel, a bowl of Brailsford's Durotrigian class 2 (in D.C.M.), was found in pieces about 3 ft. below the surface in laying electric cable to the junior ranks' club. (Dorset *Procs.* LXXXVII (1965), 110–11.)

WORTH MATRAVERS

Romano-British sherds have been reported from an unconfirmed site in a quarry on the Upper Purbeck marble of Primrose Hill about SY 98827948 (Dorset *Procs.* LXXIV (1952), 93). Burials in stone cists are said to have been found in the churchyard, 97287744 (*Purbeck Papers* I (1855), 34). A recently discovered site at Dunshay (98347974) near the Purbeck marble outcrop is described in Dorset *Procs.* LXXXVIII (1966), 120.

Sites (39–41) lie on the centre of a ridge of Middle Purbeck limestone about 450 ft. above sea level. The first two, wholly or largely destroyed, are about ½ m. W. of surviving 'Celtic' fields (Ancient Field Group (28)).

(39) GALLOWS GORE, WEST (SY 97 NE). *Inhumation Burials, Pits, Hut-floors,* and *Occupation Debris,* Iron Age 'A' to late Roman, with waste from shale armlet manufacture, have been found since 1931 over an area of 220 yds. by 100 yds. in Lander's quarry S. of Downshay Wood (97827901).

A child's skeleton perhaps in a wooden coffin, with objects including a brooch of *c.* 50–80, was enclosed in a covered cist of two slabs in the N.E. sector of the site. An unlined grave of two females extended E.-W. with heads at opposite ends was found 12 yds. to S. One elderly with three Durotrigian bowls of Brailsford's class 1 by the body and a native copy of a Gallo-Belgic butt-beaker of perhaps the mid 1st century A.D. in fragments over the head; nearby were two inhumations, one extended in a cist E.-W. Of two more to W. in plain graves, one had legs flexed.

Of 14 pits examined, six were of Iron Age 'A' and two of 'C' or early Roman date; one of the latter, stone-lined, was possibly a well. The others were Roman or undated. Two areas, one oval with central hearth, sling-stones and a crude flint industry, were probably hut-floors of an early phase of Iron Age 'A'; a third was a working-floor with debris of a hand-cut shale armlet industry and 'A' pottery. Thereafter occupation was apparently continuous into the late 4th century A.D., although Iron Age 'B' elements were confined to stray sherds. The Roman phase was marked by storage-pits, the well (?), fragments of burnt clay daub, and a few short lengths of drystone wall thought to be of the 2nd century or later near which were floor-slabs and stone roof-tiles; there were also two rectangular storage cists, one of reused roof-tiles containing three jugs of perhaps the mid 2nd century, and three shale-working floors with ribbed and light-weight plain armlets, class C armlet cores and flint lathe-tools. Miscellaneous finds included Iron Age loomweights, weaving combs, spindle-whorls, Romano-British brooches of the 1st and 2nd centuries, coins of the 3rd and 4th centuries, a pierced shale slab (in D.C.M., possibly a window-shutter), and fragments of crude pottery containers perhaps connected with trade in salt. Objects are in B.M., D.C.M., Christchurch Museum and Poole Museum. (Dorset *Procs.* LX (1938), 66–72; LXIX (1947), 42–4; LXX (1948), 29–59; LXXV (1953), 52, 69; LXXXIV (1962), 115; *Swanage Times* 20 Jan., 1954; information from Mr. J. B. Calkin.)

(40) GALLOWS GORE, EAST (SY 97 NE). An *Inhumation Burial, Walls,* and *Occupation Debris,* Iron Age 'A' to late Roman, with waste from shale armlet manufacture, have been found since 1931 in Lander's quarry (98177895) N.W. of Gallows Gore Cottages, some 400 yds. E. of (39).

Excavations in the small area remaining unquarried revealed an identical sequence of occupation to that of (39), but without evidence for a pre-Roman shale workshop. No structural features of Iron Age 'A' or 'C' were found, although burnt clay daub and evidence perhaps for leather-working occurred in the 'C' or early Roman level. A thin scatter of flagstones marked the base of Romano-British occupation of perhaps the 2nd to the 4th century. At one point five stone blocks some 6 ft. apart, the largest 2 ft. square and 5 ins. high, were associated with concentrations of shale-workers' debris including worked flints and lathe-tools, shale armlet fragments, and turned cores of class C with a few of class A. These were possibly bases for individual lathes belonging to the primary industry here. Two short lengths of drystone wall here may have served a similar purpose; one of them overlay shale debris of the primary phase. Elsewhere a small storage cist with a paved area adjoining a short length of drystone wall was probably of the 3rd or 4th century. The inhumation, S. of the road (98227875), was of a child in a covered cist of two slabs with a hand-made vessel probably of Iron Age 'A'. Objects are in Christchurch Museum, B.M., and in the possession of Mr. J. B. Calkin. (Dorset *Procs.* LXIX (1947), 42; LXX (1948), 40–1; LXXV (1953), 45–71; *Trans. S.E. Union of Scientific Societies* XL (1935), 30; information from Mr. J. B. Calkin.)

(41) COMPACT FARM (SY 97 NE). *Occupation Debris,* Iron Age 'A' to late Roman, with waste from shale armlet manufacture, comes from about ¼ m. N.E. of St. Nicholas' Church. Excavation for a silage pit (97427782) revealed a black layer containing fragments of turned shale armlets and waste cores of class C, specialized flint lathe-tools and other objects, with Iron Age sherds on natural limestone beneath. Unstratified finds here and for about 100 yds. N. included Iron Age 'A' sherds, rough-outs for hand-cut shale armlets, part of a turned shale bowl, a bronze signet-ring, and sherds of at least the 2nd to the 4th century A.D. Some objects are in D.C.M. and Christchurch Museum. (Dorset *Procs.* LXXV (1953), 54, 59, 69; LXXVI (1954), 77; LXXXII (1960), 86; LXXXVI (1964), 118.)

Sites (42–43) lie on Lower Purbeck limestone.

(42) WESTON FARM (SY 97 NE). *Occupation Debris* was found in 1958 on a S.-facing ridge about 350 ft. above sea level (96977730), following examination of soil from the site dumped near (41). The objects (in D.C.M.) were sherds of hand-made pottery probably of Iron Age 'A' and pieces of worked shale including a waste disc for a hand-cut armlet, and Romano-British sherds of 1st to 4th century. (Dorset *Procs.* LXXXVI (1964), 118.)

(43) ST. ALBAN'S or ST. ALDHELM'S HEAD (SY 97 NE). *Occupation Debris* comes from the ridge about 350 ft. above sea level E. of the quarry (96587609).

A thin scatter of debris over an area of about ½ acre included sherds of hand-made pottery probably of Iron Age 'A', samian and Romano-British coarse pottery of perhaps the 1st to the 4th century, a coin of Gallienus (253–68) and five turned shale armlet cores of class C (in possession of Mr. P. A. Brown). A barrow excavated in 1850, 300 yds. S.W. at the angle of a 'Celtic' field of Ancient Field Group (24), had near the top coarse pottery, fragments of shale including a waste core from a turned armlet, and a samian sherd with five coins ranging from *c.* 98–273 (*see* Round Barrows, Worth Matravers (34)). Stone settings possibly indicating cist burials have been noted in the area. (Dorset *Procs.* LXXVIII (1956), 76–7; *Purbeck Papers* I (1855), 34, 37–8.)

ANCIENT FIELDS

Ancient fields are described in groups, numbered generally from E. to W., independently of the parish arrangements; for ease of reference the groups are given topographical names, although these cannot always be precise. These groups consist mainly of 'Celtic' fields but include later field remains where the two are so intermingled as to make separate description difficult; strip lynchets and broad ridge-and-furrow will otherwise be found in the parish inventories. Other earthworks similarly intermingled or of uncertain nature, sometimes possible settlements, are described with the fields and usually identified by letters in parentheses. The first three groups include remains within the bounds of *Dorset* I and parish monument numbers used in that volume have been retained; settlements and other sites omitted from that volume will be described in *addenda* to *Dorset* I which are reserved for inclusion in the last Inventory of the Dorset series.

The term 'Celtic' fields is used to indicate all fields of regular shape laid out before the Saxon Conquest.[1] Their remains cover an area of 4,000 acres in South-East Dorset (Fig. opp. p. 634). Most are on chalk and limestone but some are on the Clay-with-Flints often capping the chalk hills or on sandy and gravelly areas adjoining chalk soils (Groups 25 and 26). They occur on slopes of up to 25° facing all directions, on valley bottoms and on the summits of ridges, at heights from below 100 ft. to more than 750 ft. above sea level. The remains described below are, however, only what is left of much more extensive tracts of 'Celtic' fields. How great an area they formerly covered is unknown, since they only survive on land which was largely uncultivated in later periods. The boundaries of the groups are thus generally determined by later destruction, and some (13, 15 and 29) once extended over land now eroded by the sea.

There are many traces of later ploughing over areas of 'Celtic' fields, whether in the form of strip lynchets,[2] as in Group (19), or broad ridge-and-furrow (Group 1), both mediaeval in form, or of 18th and 19th-century 'narrow rig'. In Group (4) narrow rig overlies both 'Celtic' fields and strip lynchets. In addition to this ploughing which, if it had continued long enough, would have destroyed the earlier remains completely, these fields have been damaged by quarrying for flints, as in Groups (11) and (15), or by landslips and weathering on exposed and steep slopes (Groups 17, 18, 29). Because of this widespread destruction any conclusions based on the distribution of the surviving fragments must be severely limited. In the only extensive stretch of undisturbed land suitable for cultivation, the Purbeck Hills, original gaps between areas of 'Celtic' fields can, however, be observed. The existence of an Iron Age settlement, probably pastoral (Church Knowle (54)), may account for one such gap.

The fields are usually defined by lynchets, *i.e.* scarps built up or steepened by cultivation processes, ranging in height from 1 ft. to 10 ft. or more. A lynchet 35 ft. high in Group (14) includes natural slope as well as the scarp resulting from ploughing. Slight banks are found where lynchet formation does not take place, that is, where field sides run directly uphill (Group 17), or on flat ground. Relatively massive stony banks on a limestone plateau in Group (23) suggest former walls.

The fields range in shape from squares to rectangles six times as long as they are broad, and in size from $\frac{1}{8}$ acre to $1\frac{1}{2}$ acres. There is an unusual triangular field in Group (5). On Ballard Down (Group 29) are many small fields, frequently with sides of 23 yds. to 26 yds., while some fields in Group (8) are long and narrow, 100 yds. by 21 yds. In Group (15) there are over fifty fields with a proportion of roughly two to

---

[1] For a fuller study of both 'Celtic' fields and the forms of strip ploughing that followed *see* H. C. Bowen, *Ancient Fields* (1961).
[2] Evidence was discovered in 1967 for Romano-British settlement on 'Celtic' fields, under strip lynchets in Poxwell at SY 736840 (Dorset *Procs.*, forthcoming).

one and a size not far removed from the Roman measure of two square *actus* (240 by 120 Roman feet or 78 yds. by 39 yds.).

The development of the groups is often complex but certain patterns can be seen within them. The long axes of fields may run in the same direction over large areas despite the existence of valleys (Group 3); a notably regular pattern may appear to replace one less regular (Group 17); fragmentary remains on steep S. slopes in three Groups (17, 18 and 29) may represent sporadic development or the effects of weathering; an arrangement of field angles staggered on the downhill side is common, and was perhaps intended to facilitate access from one level to another over a field side rather than over its steeper lower edge.

Settlements which are certainly associated and contemporary with the 'Celtic' fields during their latest period of widespread use appear to belong to the Roman period. In Group (17), however, the fields are apparently associated with the occupation of the Iron Age hill-fort of Flower's Barrow and in Group (3) the settlement remains seem from their form to be pre-Roman. In several groups, notably (1), double-lynchet tracks ran through the fields from settlements or past them. In Group (23) boundaries between the farm land of contemporary settlements can seemingly be traced and can perhaps be recognised elsewhere (Groups 3, 15, 27). There is not enough evidence, however, to assess the area attributed to any settlement.

Two Neolithic long barrows, Bere Regis (66) and Portesham (33), were used as field boundaries in Groups (30) and (5). Bronze Age round barrows, whether singly or in groups, were generally respected by the farmers cultivating 'Celtic' fields so that a group would be left on an island of unploughed ground (Group 3) or a barrow be left near the angle or side of a field.

Other dating evidence for the fields is scanty. In Group (3) their relationship to a linear ditch, probably of the Bronze Age, suggests origins in that period. A Late Bronze Age hoard found in the area of Group (15) may have been hidden in a field lynchet. Iron Age pottery has occasionally been found in the fields but Romano-British pottery is much more common. The Roman road running W. from Dorchester and the aqueduct serving the Roman town probably cut across 'Celtic' fields (Group 2). There is no evidence of continuous use of the surviving fields in the post-Roman periods, but mediaeval farmers sometimes incorporated certain of the scarps bounding 'Celtic' fields in their strip lynchets, while ploughing over others (Group 19). In Group (15) the parish boundary between Chaldon Herring and West Lulworth partly follows the line of a division between blocks of 'Celtic' fields.

GROUP (1): WESTMINSTONE TO TOWN HILL (SY 59 SE, 69 SW; 600920–628920; Fig. opposite). 'Celtic' fields are virtually continuous over about 900 acres, mostly Upper Chalk but with a capping of pebbly clay and sand on the main ridge top, in the S. of Frampton and Compton Valence[1] parishes and the N. of Winterbourne Abbas parish. They were formerly more extensive and have mostly been overlaid by or integrated into a later pattern of broad ridge-and-furrow some of which has, in turn, been ploughed in narrow rig. This broad ridge-and-furrow on the downland probably represents a temporary or sporadic extension of cultivation beyond the limits of the permanent arable in the mediaeval period or, possibly, later. Modern ploughing is completing the work of destruction throughout the whole group. The remains have been further disturbed by numerous small quarries and chalk pits, now disused. Two settlements in Frampton, (a) on Little Hogleaze (613922) (Plate 231) and (b) above West Hill Bottom

(605928), Romano-British at least in their final phases, are contemporary with the 'Celtic' fields as is a system of tracks probably linked to the Roman road running W. from Dorchester on a line near that of the present ridgeway road.

(i) *Westminstone Down* (Plate 231). 'Celtic' fields, mostly overlain by broad ridge-and-furrow on the gentle slopes of the higher ground, cover 60 acres in the S.E. of Compton Valence parish. Surviving fields have sides 40 yds. to 50 yds. long and are bounded by lynchets up to 10 ft. high or by low, flinty boundary banks. A track running from the line of the Roman road towards settlement (a) apparently formed a boundary to the S.

(ii) *West Hill Bottom and Little Hogleaze*, at W. of Frampton parish. 'Celtic' fields of $\frac{1}{2}$ to $\frac{4}{5}$ acre in size, where complete, are overlain by disturbed broad ridge-and-furrow. Tracks 4 yds. to 7 yds. wide, mostly of double-lynchet form, run into settlements (a) and (b). It is possible that the latter was developed on old fields and certainly both settlements seem to have extended on to former fields.

(iii) *Town Hill and Great Hogleaze*. 'Celtic' fields with lynchets up to 7 ft. high are overlain in an area of at least 60 acres by broad ridge-and-furrow. The fields often have

---

[1] Frampton and Compton Valence are in the area covered by *Dorset* I.

staggered angles but an almost continuous run of lynchets from settlement (a) to 621929 suggests a boundary. Two complete 'Celtic' fields near the centre of the area measured only 25 yds. square but others, to the N., have been thrown together to form long fields. Enclosure Frampton (20) has no demonstrable link with the fields but is probably prehistoric. Curving scarps in a copse at 621927 suggest the possibility of contemporary settlement.

(iv) *Eweleaze to Higher Ground.* 'Celtic' fields, disturbed by later ploughing, stretched S. from Pigeon House Cottage, near which there are remains of strip lynchets, to Higher Ground where, after a wide gap with no sign of ridging, they are overlain by broad ridge-and-furrow, and at the S.E. further overlain by narrow rig. A hollow-way (?), Frampton (21), and a faint track which joins it from the S.E., as well as a continuation W. of both, apparently belong to a phase of 'Celtic' fields which end against them. The deep hollowing of the track is unusual in a 'Celtic' field system and is probably due to subsequent wear or to the utilisation of a ditch line.

(v) *Winterbourne Abbas, S. of the Roman road.* Fragmentary traces of 'Celtic' fields extend for about 1 mile. Around 603919 they are apparently overlain by broad ridge-and-furrow which perhaps continued S. to meet the strip lynchets of the open-field system (*see* Winterbourne Abbas (12)). An undated enclosure (Winterbourne Abbas (55), Fig. p. 507), was built over 'Celtic' fields, but its relationship to the ridge-and-furrow was not clear. On the N., on the approximate line of the Roman road and traceable for over a mile, is a track with a bank on the N. separating it from the modern road. It is defined on the S. by a low scarp from which 'Celtic' lynchets occasionally run. (R.A.F. V.A.P. CPE/UK 2431: 3141–3.)

GROUP (2): BRADFORD PEVERELL[1] AND WINTERBORNE MONKTON (SY 69 SE; 662917–667902; Fig. p. 494). Traces of 'Celtic' fields, mutilated by a system of strip fields and modern ploughing, cover some 300 acres on Fordington Down but formerly extended in all directions. Two Romano-British settlements at 667907 and 666910, now destroyed, lay within the fields (Dorset *Procs.*, LXXVIII (1956), 80–1). Most of the fields are N. of the Roman road W. from Dorchester which appears, together with the Roman aqueduct at the S.W. of Fordington Bottom, to have cut across 'Celtic' fields. Only a few scarps survive S. of the road in Winterborne Monkton. (R.A.F. V.A.P. CPE/UK 1934: 5087–9 and 2088.)

GROUP (3): LITTLE BREDY[2] AND WINTERBOURNE STEEPLETON (SY 58 NE, 68 NW; 595872–613893; Fig. opposite, Plate 232). 'Celtic' field remains, some very well preserved, cover about 450 acres between Little Bredy Farm, Black Down Barn, Sheep Down and Loscombe. Similar remains continue W. and S.W., and probably a further 100 acres of remains have been destroyed within the area. Strip lynchets run into the 'Celtic' fields from W. and N.E. while broad ridge-and-furrow, partly defaced by later narrow rig, crosses them at the extreme W. just off the plan.

---

[1] Bradford Peverell is in the area covered by *Dorset* I.
[2] Little Bredy is in the area covered by *Dorset* I.

The geology is complex. Much of the area is Upper Chalk but the Valley of Stones, named after a spread of sarsens, is partly covered by Clay-with-Flints and Bagshot Beds while the high ground of Black Down bears red sandy clay with cobbles. N. of this a mixture of gravels and sands is interspersed with patches of chalk. With the exception of Black Down and the Valley of Stones most of the area is arable.

The long axes of the 'Celtic' fields run predominantly N.W. to S.E., partly because they were laid out up and down the slopes of the valleys which here generally run S.W. to N.E. The fields lay across hilltops, valley bottoms and slopes on all aspects. Despite the abundance of sarsens no field sides are visibly marked by them but some lynchets probably incorporate walls for marking out fields. Occasionally field sides running up and down slopes are marked by low banks.

The following monuments are apparently contemporary with some phase of the 'Celtic' fields: Winterbourne Steepleton (64) settlement, (66) dyke; Little Bredy (6) enclosure, (7a, b) sarsen-walled enclosures; also hut circle (a) and settlement (b). Platforms (e, f) are of uncertain date. Enclosures Little Bredy (5a, b) and Winterbourne Steepleton (63) are almost certainly later than the 'Celtic' fields. The long barrow Winterbourne Steepleton (13) and round barrow (15) were incorporated into the pattern of fields but not ploughed over in antiquity. Round barrows are, however, mostly grouped in areas apparently never cultivated as 'Celtic' fields, as on Sheep Down and S. of settlement Winterbourne Steepleton (64). The round barrows in square enclosures, Winterbourne Steepleton (24–6), are arguably later than the early 'Celtic' fields.

(i) *Little Bredy Farm.* S. of the farm, near the W. end of the Group, a complex of slight ditched banks, probably relatively recent, cuts across 'Celtic' field lynchets. A probable hut circle (a) with a floor 14 ft. across lies beneath the end of a 'Celtic' field lynchet at 59438800. Further slight banks, again comparatively recent, divide the hilltop and overlie 'Celtic' field remains on the spur top N. of the farm. Four earthen circles here (Little Bredy (15), *see Dorset* I) are almost certainly of recent origin, possibly the remains of landscaping associated with Bride Head to the N. On the shoulder of the hill $\frac{1}{4}$ mile E. of Little Bredy Farm at 59758820 is a small settlement (b), probably pre-Roman, comprising four or five hut circles set immediately below well-developed lynchets at the edge of largely destroyed 'Celtic' fields. Strip lynchets occur N., W. and E. of the farm indicating the former extent of the open fields of Little Bredy.

(ii) *Crow Hill and the Valley of Stones* (Little Bredy (17)). On the E. shoulder of the heavily ploughed summit of Crow Hill are two possible hut platforms (c) and (d), the latter set into the top of a 'Celtic' field lynchet. The large valley-bottom enclosure Little Bredy (5a) was apparently built over 'Celtic' field remains, already reploughed. Enclosure (5b), also on the valley floor, may be connected with two unusual long narrow plots set within 'Celtic' field boundaries above it. Immediately W. a flat floor, 18 ft. square with a gap towards (5b), has been cut into the face of a lynchet.

In the Valley of Stones at least seventeen complete 'Celtic' fields may be traced, ranging in area from ½ acre to 1¼ acres. Five are nearly square and eight are about twice as long as they are broad. Nine fields have sides about 50 yds. long, the remainder vary from 33 yds. to 125 yds. The fields are rarely found on slopes of more than about 10° and are bounded mostly by lynchets, up to 12 ft. high, but occasionally by low banks. At the foot of the W. side of the valley is a band of sarsens, the product of clearance, against which lynchets have formed.

A D-shaped, sarsen-walled enclosure (Little Bredy (7a)), in the valley bottom, possibly the site of a dwelling or of a pound, was apparently built at the edge of a small 'Celtic' field which continued in cultivation. A short distance to the S.W. is a triangular platform (e), 38 ft. by 30 ft., at the angle of a 'Celtic' field, while to the N.E. is a rectangular platform (f), about 42 ft. by 30 ft. On the valley floor 530 yds. N.N.E. of (7a) is a much smaller and less well-marked sarsen enclosure (7b).

(iii) *Black Down.* The ground above 600 ft. was apparently not much ploughed in the 'Celtic' field phase, but is greatly disturbed. At (g) a bank appears to run N.N.E. among deep-cut hollow-ways while a slighter bank runs N.W. at right angles to it. 100 yds. farther S. a terrace-way runs approximately N. to S. for 150 yds. above well-developed 'Celtic' fields. On the N. edge of Black Down a dyke (Winterbourne Steepleton (66)) runs W. across the parish boundary with Little Bredy into the head of a small combe where it turns S. and ends abruptly below a field angle. Several shallow scoops (h) on the slope N.W. of this recall those at the Iron Age settlement on Knowle Hill (*see* Settlements, Church Knowle (54)). 'Celtic' fields run up to the dyke on the N. side and an enclosure (Little Bredy (6)) is attached to it.

(iv) *Sheep Down and Cowleaze.* The slight bank (j) with a ditch on the S., running N.W. for some 450 yds. across Sheep Down, was possibly an original boundary between 'Celtic' fields and the unploughed area containing barrows. Cowleaze was mostly covered with 'Celtic' fields, later overlaid by recent banks forming enclosures, and by strip fields. The latest phase of ploughing has often formed secondary lynchet lines under the 'Celtic' field boundaries giving a false impression of double-lynchet tracks. Some of the better preserved fields lie on the E. slopes of the narrow combe running S.W. from Loscombe Plantation. (R.A.F. V.A.P. CPE/UK 1934: 1069–71, 3095–100.)

GROUP (4): PORTESHAM WITHY BED, N. of (SY 58 NE; 593863; Plates 140, 233). 'Celtic' fields, partly overlain by strip lynchets, and strip lynchets which probably obliterate 'Celtic' fields, almost all ploughed over in narrow rig, cover a re-entrant valley of about 30 acres. Other strip lynchets lie immediately N., W., and E. of the Withy Bed (*see* Portesham (32a)), and there are traces of scarped fields, almost destroyed, extending on higher ground W. and E. from the valley. A

terraceway climbs the steep natural scarp N. from the Withy Bed where finds of pottery, iron, bronze, bone and flint (Dorset *Procs.* XXXVII (1916), xxxix), now lost, suggest Romano-British and earlier occupation.

Only one certainly complete 'Celtic' field, of about ⅓ acre, is detectable at the head of the valley on the W. side, where 'Celtic' field traces generally survive. The strip lynchets are confined to the valley floor and E. side where the treads are generally flat and the risers pronounced, indicating long usage. Some are high up the steep valley side on ledges. They appear to mark the limit of an open field extending from Portesham village. The narrow rig around 590860, which is set against a slope of 16½°, cuts across the end of a strip lynchet (*cf.* H. C. Bowen, *Ancient Fields* (1961), plate IIb). (R.A.F. V.A.P. CPE/UK 2431: 3288–90.)

GROUP (5): BENECKE WOOD, S. of (SY 68 NW; 609867–618868), in Portesham parish, comprises about 30 acres of disturbed 'Celtic' fields on the N.-facing slope and floor of a dry valley in the Upper Chalk, partly capped by Clay-with-Flints. Other certain but very slight traces appear N., W. and E. To the N., scarps almost ploughed-out can be seen on the chalk but not on the gravels of the Bagshot Beds just beyond, where enclosure Portesham (57) lies. To the W., on Portesham Hill, the Hell Stone long barrow (33) has been used as a 'Celtic' field boundary, and S. of it strip lynchets run into 'Celtic' fields. To the E. and S.E., in and near Hell Bottom, a few 'Celtic' field scarps survive around Bench (623865), partly overlain by strip fields, and S.W. of Shilvinghampton Barn (about 627861).

In the main field area a triangular 'Celtic' field, 150 yds. by 130 yds. by 80 yds., lies on the fairly steep valley side under a double lynchet track following the S. shoulder. It is 1¼ acres in area with lynchets up to 10 ft. high. The only other measurable fields, with low lynchets, are 67 yds. by 33 yds. (R.A.F. V.A.P. CPE/UK 1934: 1066–9.)

GROUP (6): SHORN HILL TO RIDGE HILL (SY 68 NW, NE; 631876–657869; Fig. p. 626), in Winterborne St. Martin and Portesham parishes, includes 'Celtic' fields and undated long fields. Broken remains of 'Celtic' fields cover at least 200 acres of the spurs and re-entrants N. of the Ridgeway and 20 acres immediately S. of it, about 647865. The most prominent, though very incomplete in plan and not illustrated, are at the extreme E., N. of Ridge Hill, covering 12 acres around 655868. Fragments extend N. of these on the spur top and in the valley W. of it leading to Ashton Cottages. Most are on chalk but some, S. of Shorn Hill, are on a sandy wash and pebble capping. There are only two complete fields, each of about ¼ acre, but original field sides are between 30 yds. and 60 yds. long. Lynchets are up to 8 ft. high, N. of Ridge Hill, on a maximum slope of 15°. Subsequent cultivation has flattened many former field divisions and in places has left 'Celtic' lynchets in continuous lines along the contours giving a misleading effect of strip fields, as on the S.E. side of Great Hill. A slight boundary bank and ditch, of mediaeval or later date, runs N. from a round barrow (Winterborne St. Martin (58)).

N.W. of Shorn Hill and S.W. of Great Hill are long narrow fields, apparently later than the normal 'Celtic' fields but bounded by contour lynchets or, up and down hill, by low flinty banks. In places they may have utilised the lynchets of previous fields as boundaries. Complete fields are usually 26 yds. or 37 yds. wide and from 100 yds. to 160 yds. long. On Great Hill faint traces of slight banked fields of similar type have been much disturbed by narrow rig ploughing. In proportion and form these long fields are akin to 'Celtic' long

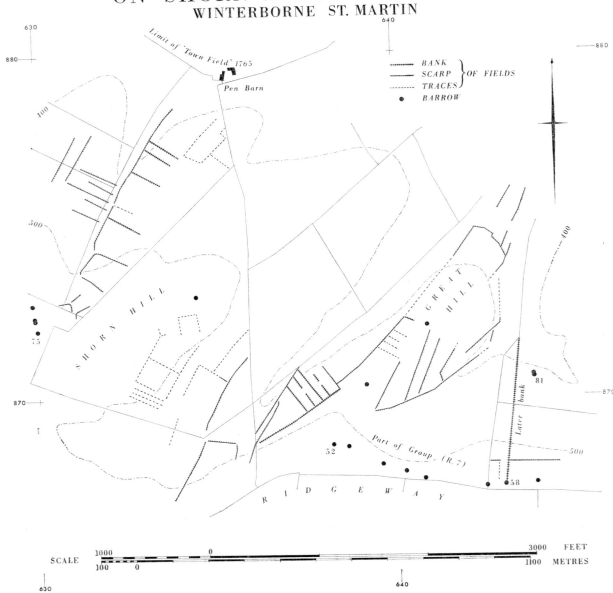

ANCIENT FIELD GROUP (6)
ON SHORN AND GREAT HILLS
WINTERBORNE ST. MARTIN

fields, elsewhere thought to be Romano-British, but some doubt arises from their extent and from the absence of a known Romano-British settlement. There are relatively recent downland fields of this form (*e.g.* near Stratton, around 652950), while mediaeval cultivation of the downland is attested for Winterborne Asshe (Ashton, Inquisitions *post mortem*, P.R.O., C. 142/216/29). By 1765 some of the enclosed strips of Winterborne St. Martin resembled in plan these long fields (*cf.* Isaac Taylor's map of Town Field Farm in D.C.R.O.). (R.A.F. V.A.P. CPE/UK 1934: 1063–66 and 3092–94.)

GROUP (7): BINCOMBE TUNNEL (SY 68 NE; 673855), in Bincombe and Weymouth parishes. 'Celtic' fields are clearly seen only N.E. of the S. tunnel entrance on the S. shoulder of the chalk ridge about 400 ft. above O.D. (Fig. p. 24). Two complete fields are 88 yds. by 40 yds. Lynchets are generally about 3 ft. high, occasionally 5 ft. Very faint remains over about 20 acres continue N. over the crest. One air photograph, by Major G. W. G. Allen (Ashmolean Museum, No. 154), shows round barrows (Weymouth (416–18)) at 'Celtic' field angles. (R.A.F. V.A.P. CPE/UK 1821: 6447–9.)

GROUP (8): BINCOMBE HILL (SY 68 SE; 687847–691847), in Bincombe parish. Traces of 'Celtic' fields over 15 acres mostly on the crest and S. shoulder of Bincombe Hill include, towards the W., three long fields with lynchets about 1½ ft. high on a slope steepening to 11°. Two are 100 yds. by 21 yds. and one about 120 yds. by 30 yds. Ploughing at some uncertain period has almost destroyed fields S. of the line of barrows and removed the E. ditch of round barrow Bincombe (46). 'Celtic' fields once continued N. into the area of Bincombe 'North Field' (*see* Fig. p. 24) where relatively recent

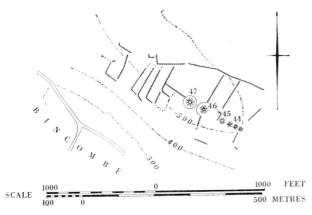

SCALE

Group (8) on Bincombe Hill, with S.E. part of Barrow Group (R.10).

ploughing has obliterated almost all earlier field traces. Sherds of Romano-British coarse ware were found mostly N. of the barrows. (R.A.F. V.A.P. CPE/UK 1821: 6445–6.)

GROUP (9): WHITCOMBE, S. of (SY 78 NW; 712870), in Whitcombe parish. Remains of 'Celtic' fields survive over 12 acres of ground falling gently N., the former Eweleaze. Where

still unploughed, lynchets are up to 6 ft. high, some cut by quarries. There are further traces N.E. (on 'New Ground' of a late 18th-century Lulworth Castle estate map, in D.C.R.O.) and the faintest traces suggest a former spread towards the Ridgeway. (R.A.F. V.A.P. CPE/UK 1934: 1054–5.)

GROUP (10): WEST HILL (SY 78 SW; 703845–710848), in the N.E. of Weymouth parish, comprises incomplete 'Celtic' field remains over about 11 acres between 350 ft. and 450 ft. above O.D. on a S.-facing spur and above the valley head E. of it, where round barrows Weymouth (419) and (420) are at 'Celtic' field angles. Re-ploughing at some unknown date has broken down former field divisions. (R.A.F. V.A.P. CPE/UK 1821: 6442–4.)

GROUP (11): POXWELL AND MOIGNS DOWN (SY 78 SW, SE; 744836–756835) in Poxwell, Watercombe and Owermoigne parishes. Remains of 'Celtic' fields survive over about 30 acres on, and N. of, the limestone ridge from E. of Poxwell Lodge to Moigns Down and on a chalk spur N. of it. Only two complete 'Celtic' fields survive N. of Moigns Down. The area has been much disturbed by quarrying and mediaeval and later cultivation.

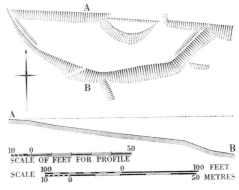

SCALE OF FEET FOR PROFILE

SCALE

Group (11). Platform (a) on Moigns Down.

N. of the ridge, partly in Poxwell and partly in Watercombe, are fields marked by low N.-S. lynchets crossing the valley bottom. These were covered with narrow rig and probably represent much altered 'Celtic' fields. S. of them, on the N. slope of the ridge, disturbed terraces appear to be the remains of strip lynchets. A trackway, 12 ft. wide, associated with the remains of 'Celtic' fields, followed the N. shoulder of the ridge from 74408355 eastwards into Owermoigne parish where it joined the N. edge of a possible settlement area related to a platform (a) (753835; Fig. *above*) on the S. shoulder of the ridge. This platform, ⅕ acre in area, is bounded on the S. by a low bank above scarps up to 6 ft. high from the angles of which 'Celtic' fields appear to have been laid off. A lynchet above the N. side of the platform is due to subsequent ploughing of the ridge top. (R.A.F. V.A.P. CPE/UK 1821: 4440–3.)

GROUP (12): RINGSTEAD BARN (SY 78 SW, SE; 744829–754824), in Osmington parish. Traces of 'Celtic' fields between 250 ft. and 400 ft. above O.D. cover 40 acres of the gentle N.-facing slope at the extreme N.E. of Spring Bottom Hill, mostly on Wealden Beds with bands of greensand and gault. Lynchets are generally about 3 ft. high but up to 10 ft. towards the S. Four round barrows (Osmington (38–41)) on the ridge crest, only 11 yds. to 14 yds. from the southernmost lynchet line, lie on ground that was perhaps never ploughed in antiquity. The area, though adjacent to Up Ringstead, was presumably pasture for W. Ringstead, of which the strip fields (Osmington (28)) are due S. (R.A.F. V.A.P. CPE/UK 1821: 4441–3.)

GROUP (13): RINGSTEAD BAY (SY 78 SE; 766817–768814), Owermoigne. Remains of 'Celtic' fields cover 14 acres of the bottom and N.-facing slope, rising to a cliff edge, of a narrow combe, and formerly extended N. and S. The inner edges of some fields, with lynchets up to 6 ft. high, are preserved on the cliff edge. (R.A.F. V.A.P. CPE/UK 1821: 2442–3.)

GROUP (14): BRIMSTONE BOTTOM (SY 78 SE; 770825–775826), Owermoigne and Chaldon Herring. Fragmentary and partly quarried 'Celtic' fields covered about 20 acres between 300 ft. and 400 ft. above O.D., on chalk, along the steep N.-facing slope above Brimstone Bottom. Surviving lynchets are high, one scarp reaching 35 ft. (R.A.F. V.A.P. CPE/UK 1821: 4439–41.)

GROUP (15): CHALDON HERRING, WEST LULWORTH AND WINFRITH NEWBURGH (SY 78 SE, 88 SW; 784808–786819–823828–808803; Plate 234), includes about 850 acres of 'Celtic' fields. Traces of others, almost destroyed by mediaeval and later ploughing, occur to the E., around Hambury Tout (815805), and between blocks (i–iii) below, suggesting that they were formerly continuous. All the remains lie between 100 ft. and 500 ft. above O.D. on chalk, 'angular flint gravel', slurry (in the combe bottoms), or sands and clays of the Reading Beds. Lynchets up to 12 ft. high indicate long cultivation and there is also evidence, especially in block (i), for change and development within the 'Celtic' field phase. Major boundary lines appear in block (iii) and in block (i), which is the most extensive and has a large number of complete fields. Strip lynchets from Chaldon Herring (24), and Winfrith Newburgh (30), lie partly on 'Celtic' fields at the limits of the open fields. There are no certain settlements but a number of possible areas of settlement are suggested in blocks (i) and (iii). The Late Bronze Age 'Lulworth hoard' was found somewhere in block (ii) during flint quarrying. The so-called 'flint-filled hollows' which occur within all blocks are probably the remains of such quarrying, frequently into lynchets and sometimes into piles of flint at field angles. Other evidence of relatively recent activity is marked by narrow rig, by brick and rubble foundations on the site of Warren House (79238106), and by tile,

brick and glazed pottery at the head of Vicarage Bottom.

(i) *Chaldon Herring Warren, Newlands Warren (W. Lulworth) and Chaldon Down* (Fig. opposite). Three main combes— Middle, Vicarage and Scratchy Bottoms—have floors sloping gently back from cliff edges to heads which rise steeply towards the E.-W. coastal ridgeway, beyond which narrow dry valleys run N. from Chaldon Down. 'Celtic' fields are continuous for 500 acres over bottoms, sides and intervening ridges and formerly continued seaward, where land has been lost by erosion. N. of the ridgeway they have mostly been heavily ploughed.

Lynchets are mostly 2 ft. to 4 ft. high but occasionally reach as much as 12 ft., as in Middle Bottom. There are 63 complete fields around Vicarage and Scratchy Bottoms with mean dimensions of 85 yds. by 45 yds. (just over $\frac{3}{4}$ acre). On the ridge N. of (a) eight long fields average 103 yds. by 27 yds. Barrows Chaldon Herring (38) and (39) are probably at the angles of fields, the N.-S. banks of which have been flattened. A line of very small fields, including some of $\frac{1}{8}$ acre, survives S.E. of the block at 808805. The maximum field slope is 16°. Boundary lines are indicated by continuous runs of lynchets S. to N., one on the high ground between Middle and Vicarage Bottoms and another between Vicarage and Scratchy Bottoms which for 300 yds. is followed by the present parish boundary.

There has been some strip cultivation in the E. part of Newlands Warren (about 806805), narrow rig ploughing W. of the site of Warren House, in Scratchy Bottom and E. of it, and recent cultivation over fields just S. of the ridgeway. 'Flint-filled hollows' are prominent in Middle and Vicarage Bottoms.

Settlement sites are nowhere clear but possibly existed at:

(a) (793806) on the sheltered E. shoulder of a narrow col between Middle and Vicarage Bottoms where ill-defined platforms and scoops lie over 2 acres on a gentle slope. The area is bounded on the W. by a terraceway, on the N. by a faint terrace and on the S. by 'Celtic' fields.

(b) (795806; Plate 234), 200 yds. E. of (a), a very shallow 'angle-ditch', with outer bank, 270 ft. by 230 ft., partly encloses 'Celtic' fields on a slope of 16°. A platform 18 ft. square lies above the W. end of the ditch on the shoulder of a re-entrant gully. These features are undated, but a comparable angle-ditch over 'Celtic' fields in Nether Cerne (5), *Dorset* I, lay in an area of Romano-British settlement.

(c) (80108085) at the head of Scratchy Bottom is a quarried-out, roughly flat, trapezoidal floor, with sides between 15 ft. and 76 ft. long. It lies clear of, and 20 ft. below, a 'Celtic' field lynchet and is approached by a narrow track from the S.W.

(d) (80558065), E. of Scratchy Bottom, a pentagonal area of $\frac{1}{7}$ acre is outlined by 'Celtic' field fragments.

Surface finds from Scratchy Bottom and from N.W. of Vicarage Bottom include Romano-British, Iron Age 'C' and possibly earlier sherds.

(ii) *Sleight Bottom, Winfrith Newburgh.* 'Celtic' field lynchets, some massive but all very disturbed, cover about 70 acres of a dry valley. Strip lynchets just N. and very faint traces of strip cultivation immediately E. suggest that some extension of such cultivation may have created the curving lynchets and broken-down field divisions at the N. of the block. Flint pits have been quarried into lynchets crossing the valley floor. The 'Lulworth hoard' of Late Bronze Age bronzes (actually from Winfrith Newburgh parish) was found in 1903 during flint quarrying near 805824 (*Ant.J.* xv (1935), 449–51) and so had possibly been hidden in a lynchet.

(iii) *Daggers Gate and Marley Bottom.* 'Celtic' field remains, in the combe and on the downland to either side, are continuous for over 270 acres, from 814811, N. of Daggers Gate, to 813832 in Marley Bottom, S. of Winfrith Newburgh. They include many high lynchets, but complete original fields have all been broken down. Some field banks are packed with flint and in the combe bottom E. from 813827 there is a series of small, often circular, quarries dug into the lynchets. Most of the downland was arable on the Tithe Maps but this cannot be associated certainly with surviving narrow rig.

A track, partly double-lyncheted with tread 16 ft. wide and lower scarp 8 ft. high, runs S.E. for 600 yds. from 818829 on the E. of the block. There are faint indications of another track approaching the possible settlement area (e). A continuous boundary line, formed by a massive but ploughed-down scarp, runs S. for ½ mile from about 809827, S.W. of Marley Wood.

(e) *Settlement* is suggested at 815818, where surviving fields on the S.-facing slope of a dry valley are different in shape and size from most of those around. Above them to the S.W., air photographs show enclosures, one with a curved side skirted by a track from the W., on relatively flat ground. The whole covers about 3 acres. (R.A.F. V.A.P. CPE/UK 1821: 2434–41.)

GROUP (16): BINDON HILL (SY 88 SW; 82408040–82908033), W. Lulworth. Fragmentary 'Celtic' fields on the N. slope of Bindon Hill, near its W. end, lie over about 10 acres between 300 ft. and 500 ft. above O.D. Others probably extended S. to lower ground where faint traces appear under the remains of strip cultivation around 831805. The fields only reach the earthwork on the hill-top (*see* Hill-forts, W. Lulworth (53)) at their S.E. limit and seem to be unconnected with it. Lynchets are up to 10 ft. high on a slope of about 10°. (R.A.F. V.A.P. CPE/UK 1821: 5432–4.)

GROUP (17): RINGS HILL TO POVINGTON HILL (SY 88 SE; 859807–885812), in East Lulworth and Tyneham parishes. 'Celtic' fields appear on about 100 acres of the N. slope of the W. end of the Purbeck Hills. In addition, isolated and slight scarps occur on the corresponding S. slope. Almost all are in an area generally inaccessible and very disturbed so that, although extensive, the pattern cannot be worked out in detail. Ploughing of the hill-top, marked in places by narrow rig, has destroyed all but a few lynchets there. The fields are of two types and in two blocks.

(i) *Flower's Barrow*, immediately N.W. and N.E. of (*see* Hill-forts, E. Lulworth (40), Plate 215). On a slope of up to 23° are 30 acres with squarish, small fields (some of about ⅓ acre), some irregular, marked by lynchets between about 4 ft. and 10 ft. high and arranged along base-lines which mostly

follow the contour. Two 'base-lines' appear to meet Flower's Barrow, one at the N.W. angle, the other at the N.E. angle of the first-phase hill-fort. The fields also extended N. and E. from this latter point to well below the natural shoulder of the ridge.

(ii) *Whiteway and Povington Hills.* Fields over 20 acres are arranged in regular manner with parallel base-lines 20–40 yds. apart, up and down the slope (Fig. in pocket, Part 2; Plate 233). These are marked by slight banks or lynchets about 1 ft. high, in places running unbroken for at least 170 yds. Apart from some very slight cross-divisions there are some higher lynchets. These may belong partly to earlier fields, since there are indications that this regular pattern has been imposed on fields of the type of block (i). One such field is just outside this block, at 873811. Traces of irregular fields are more clear further E., on Povington Hill, extending over 25 acres but with suggestions of the regular, banked type inserted among them. (R.A.F. V.A.P. CPE/UK 1821: 2421–5; 5425–8.)

GROUP (18): W. CREECH AND GRANGE HILL (SY 88 SE, 98 SW; 893818–905816), in Steeple parish. Very faint and disturbed traces of 'Celtic' fields occur as banks or slight scarps for about a mile along the ridge of the Purbeck Hills, N. of it at the W. end of this area, and S. of it at the E. There are no complete fields. Lynchets are generally low. Fragmentary low banks, some ditched, of uncertain date, run against the S. slope at up to 24°. (R.A.F. V.A.P. CPE/UK 1821: 2419–20.)

GROUP (19): TYNEHAM COAST (SY 87 NE, 88 SE; 871796–891799; Fig. in pocket, Pt. 2; Plate 197), consists of 'Celtic' field fragments, mostly overlain and disturbed by strip lynchets, some unusually irregular, over 5 acres of the N.-facing slope of the limestone ridge about 500 yds. S. of Tyneham village. Only at about 87807975, N.E. of Gold Down on a slope of 24°, are the fields not overlain. Lynchets are, rarely, up to 12 ft. high, as immediately S. of Tyneham Great Wood, where a 'Celtic' field angle and side, much rounded by strip ploughing, are particularly prominent. Very faint traces indicate former extensions of the 'Celtic' fields E. along the ridge as well as N. on to lower ground. (*Cf.* Tyneham (7, 9d), mediaeval remains.) (R.A.F. V.A.P. CPE/UK 1821: 5423–4 (part reproduced as Plate 197).)

GROUP (20): SMEDMORE HILL (SY 97 NW; 925798–936795), in Church Knowle and Steeple parishes, between 500 ft. and 600 ft. above O.D. Traces of 'Celtic' fields can be detected over some 80 acres in an area rich in Iron Age and Romano-British settlement remains. An almost certain relationship is only now visible around settlement Church Knowle (55), *q.v.* Strip lynchets (*see* Church Knowle (32)) and later narrow rig have contributed largely to the destruction of the fields.

GROUP (21): ENCOMBE OBELISK (SY 97 NW; 942790–948790), Corfe Castle. Very disturbed 'Celtic' fields cover some 40 acres between about 400 ft. and 500 ft. above O.D. on the summit and gentle N. slopes of a W.–E. spur about ¼ mile N. of Encombe. On the S. the remains are bounded by a sharp edge above a steep natural slope on which there are no fields; to the N. their limit is not clear. The earliest surface finds are Iron Age 'A', but a Romano-British building (Roman section,

Corfe Castle (235)) was discovered amongst the fields at the S.W. In the only complete field, about 50 yds. square, a small mound (94397913) was seen under the plough to consist of Portland stone blocks associated with burnt clay and Romano-British pottery, including samian ware. The Romano-British building lay 200 yds. S.W. of this. 'Celtic' fields near it are 20 yds. to 25 yds. wide and probably represent continued cultivation. (R.A.F. V.A.P. CPE/UK 1821: 3407–9.)

GROUP (22): ENCOMBE BIG WOOD (SY 97 NW; 941778), Corfe Castle. Remains of 'Celtic' fields with lynchets up to 3 ft. high cover a small area immediately S. of Big Wood, ⅔ mile S. of Group (21), but formerly extended in all directions. One lynchet, crossing a settlement site to the S. (Roman section, Corfe Castle (240)), seems to have accumulated in the later Iron Age and early Romano-British period (Dorset *Procs.* LXXXV (1963), 98–9; LXXXVI (1964), 109). (R.A.F. V.A.P. CPE/UK 1821: 3407–8.)

GROUP (23): KINGSTON DOWN (SY 97 NE; 957781; Fig. p. 631, Plate 235), Corfe Castle and Worth Matravers. 'Celtic' fields, many fragmentary, cover about 150 acres of plateau and valley S. of Kingston and formerly extended in all directions except, possibly, S.; an isolated block survives at 972781, N. of Worth Matravers village (Fig. p. 414). They lie between 200 ft. and 450 ft. above O.D. on Portland Stone, Sand and Clay. The best preserved, though disturbed, are on the top and W. side of the plateau spur 1 mile S. of Kingston village, beyond the limits of the open fields. Here they are associated with two neighbouring settlements (Corfe Castle (221–2), Figs. p. 510). Three other settlement sites (Roman section, Corfe Castle (237–9)) lie in areas of destroyed fields peripheral to the group. Surface finds indicate an Iron Age or Romano-British date.

Settlement features and fields are generally marked on the spur top by stone-packed banks and lynchets. The banks, possibly tumbled walls, are up to 2 ft. high and 12 ft. wide. Curved sides suggest settlement features extending into the fields and make it difficult to see the bounds of the settlements. The enclosure with bowed sides (a), 340 yds. S.S.W. of the nucleus of (221), is apparently separated from it by fields and is itself closer to a narrow, rather broken, terraced area (b), which runs across the 'funnel' end of a track from settlement (222). Excluding this area, (221) covered nearly 6 acres and (222) nearly 5 acres.

Two contemporary tracks lead from (222): the track just mentioned, 6 ft. wide and mostly of double-lynchet form with scarps up to 4 ft. high above and below, and a terraceway, 15 ft. wide, running S.W. diagonally downhill for 250 yds. before disappearing in an area of landslip.

A continuous run of field sides, with lynchets dropping as much as 4½ ft. E., extends N. from the bend in the double-lynchet track past the nucleus of settlement (221) and may have been a boundary separating its territory from that of (222) (*cf.* H. C. Bowen, *Ancient Fields* (1961), 35–6 and plate III).

Ridge-and-furrow up to 11 yds. wide, as well as traces of narrow rig, covers large areas N.E. of the group. It is also clear in the 'Celtic' fields, as N.W. of settlement (221) where sides appear to have been removed to form long fields. The more extensive destruction on the E. half of the spur top has left no sign of ridge-and-furrow. Elsewhere, re-ploughing is occasionally marked by secondary lynchets, as at 96117803 in Worth Matravers parish where the 'Celtic' fields have been generally much altered.

Some thirteen fields appear to be undisturbed. Five, on the main spur top, are all less than twice as long as broad and from under ½ acre to nearly 1 acre in area. A number of broken fields have sides the lengths of which are multiples of 40 yds. On the W. side of the spur, where fields lie on the maximum slope of about 21°, eight fields include four between ¼ acre and ½ acre and none more than ¾ acre.

GROUP (24): ST. ALDHELM'S HEAD (SY 97 NE; 959768–965754), Worth Matravers. 'Celtic' fields, variously preserved and in places overlain by strip fields, are found over about 60 acres N. and N.E. of St. Aldhelm's Head between 200 ft. and 400 ft. above O.D. (Fig. p. 414). Romano-British debris occurs nearby (*see* Roman section, Worth Matravers (43)). There are two relatively well preserved blocks.

(i) *Pier Bottom*. E.N.E. from 959759, lynchets cross the valley floor, terraceways not necessarily contemporary run along the foot of the valley sides above them to both N. and S., and other fields lie on the shoulders. One of these has a round barrow, Worth Matravers (34), containing secondary Romano-British material, at its S.E. angle and a N.W. side which curves along the contour.

(ii) *St. Aldhelm's Chapel*, E. of. 'Celtic' fields bounded by lynchets about 1½ ft. high and stone banks, recently exposed by ploughing, lie on a slope of up to 7° in an area that could not be adequately examined. Apart from the spread banks there was no scatter of stones on the fields. On pasture S. of this, about 96557545, disturbed lynchets are up to 7 ft. high on maximum slope of 15°.

Traces of strip fields are best seen on air photographs but remains of strip lynchets occur at 964759, S.E. of barrow (34). The name 'Middle Plains' shown near here on the Tithe Map may be connected with strip cultivation. (R.A.F. V.A.P. CPE/UK 1821: 1396–7.)

GROUP (25): CORFE COMMON (SY 98 SE; 955809–960810; Fig. p. 97), Corfe Castle. Remains of 'Celtic' fields cover 15 acres of sandy Wealden Beds on a maximum S. slope of 10°. A block of at least six fields lies relatively well-preserved at about 95758086 within a total area of some 2 acres. Lynchets are up to 8 ft. high. There is no ascertainable relationship with the barrows of Group (K). (R.A.F. V.A.P. CPE/UK 1821: 2409–10.)

GROUP (26): SANDYHILLS (SY 98 SE; 967815–974809), Corfe Castle. Traces of 'Celtic' fields are traceable over at least 70 acres of undulating sandy ground (Wealden Beds), much-ploughed, on the E. of Corfe Common just above the 100 ft.

SETTLEMENTS AND 'CELTIC' FIELDS
KINGSTON DOWN, CORFE CASTLE
ANCIENT FIELD GROUP (23)

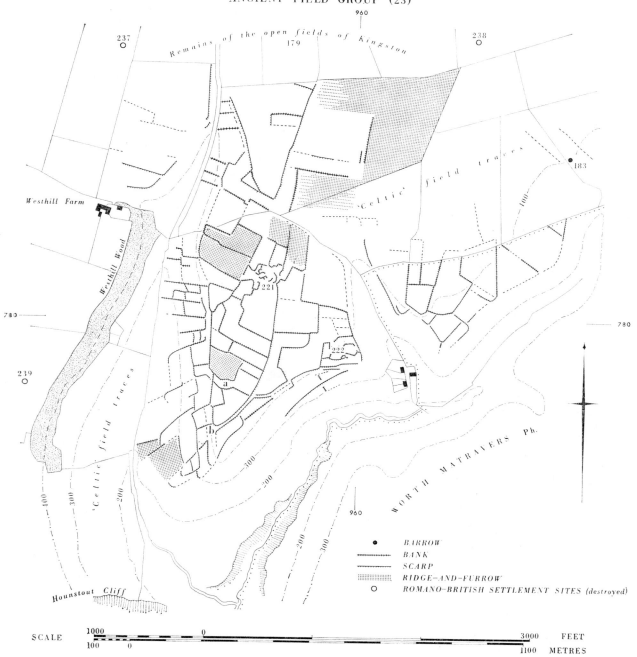

BARROW
BANK
SCARP
RIDGE—AND—FURROW
ROMANO—BRITISH SETTLEMENT SITES (destroyed)

SCALE

1000   0   3000   FEET

100   0   1100 METRES

contour. Lynchets are up to 2 ft. high. A staggered angle survives by round barrow Corfe Castle (196), but there are no complete fields. An Iron Age 'C' or Romano-British site (Roman section, Corfe Castle (233)) is adjacent but not demonstrably related. (R.A.F. V.A.P. CPE/UK 1821: 2406–7.)

GROUP (27): CHALLOW HILL (SY 98 SE; 962824–969823; Fig. p. 97), Corfe Castle. Traces of 'Celtic' fields cover about 34 acres, between 200 ft. and 300 ft. above O.D., of the W. brow, domed summit and N. slope of the chalk ridge which continues the Purbeck Hills E. from the Corfe Gap (Plate 81). The E. end of the group appears to be marked by a lynchet line 1 ft. to 4 ft. high crossing the ridge at about 969823. To the E. there are no signs of 'Celtic' fields until Ballard Down, Group (29), 3½ miles on. Fields are marked by banks, some confused by narrow rig, and lynchets up to 8 ft. high, though generally much lower. Only two complete fields survive, each about 60 yds. by 67 yds., immediately S. of Rollington Wood. (R.A.F. V.A.P. CPE/UK 1821: 2406–7.)

GROUP (28): MOUNT MISERY (SY 97 NE; 989791–994789–992793), Langton Matravers. Very broken 'Celtic' fields cover about 20 acres on the gentle N. slope from the limestone ridge between 350 ft. and 220 ft. above O.D. Lynchets are up to 6 ft. high. Narrow rig and former village closes add to disturbance by quarrying and ploughing. The Wilkswood Romano-British site (Roman section, Langton Matravers (42)) lay beyond the surviving fields at the foot of the slope. (R.A.F. V.A.P. CPE/UK 1821: 5403.)

GROUP (29): BALLARD DOWN (SZ 08 SW), in the parishes of Studland and Swanage. 'Celtic' fields, some with the remains of mediaeval and later ploughing, survive on Ballard Down and behind Handfast Point. The remains are in disconnected blocks, totalling about 65 acres, which may once have joined. Some have disappeared into the sea near Handfast Point. Most are fragmentary but (iii), now destroyed, was notable for its well-preserved small, almost square, fields. All the 'Celtic' fields are separated from the Romano-British buildings at Woodhouse Hill (Roman section, Studland (46)), by the mediaeval open fields.

(i) *N. slope of Ballard Down*, W. end (019813–031813). Traces of 'Celtic' fields cover about 18 acres on a slope of up to 15°. Only one complete field survives, measuring 46 yds. by 35 yds., above a lynchet 10 ft. high. A negative lynchet 2 ft. high runs along the slope only 12 yds. below the undisturbed edge of Ulwell Barrow, Studland (29), suggesting the upper limit of the fields at this point.

(ii) *S. slope of Ballard Down* (030812–035811). The only remains are low scarps on each side of a natural gully, the ground sloping at 25°.

(iii) *N. slope of Ballard Down*, centre (035815–039814). 'Celtic' fields covered 12 acres on a maximum slope of 19° and formerly extended in all directions. Where the fields were not square, the long axes were generally up-and-down. Areas were from ⅙ acre to ½ acre, thirteen sides being between 23 yds. and 26 yds. Lynchets were up to 8 ft. high. A double-lynchet

track running diagonally S.W. up the hill was blocked at the top by a scarp 2 ft. high apparently forming the lower side of a 'Celtic' field. (See H. C. Bowen, *Ancient Fields*, fig. 3B.)

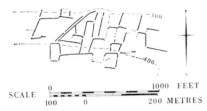

Ancient Field Group (29), area (iii).

(iv) *Handfast Point*, W. and S. of (050820–055825). On ground falling gently to the N., 'Celtic' fields, some crossed by strip fields, lay over about 34 acres between 60 ft. and 160 ft. above O.D. and formerly continued in all directions. The N.E. of the area was known as 'Cliff Fields' on the Tithe Map. Clay-with-Flints and sand lie patchily on the chalk here. Lynchets are up to 4 ft. high. The inner sides of 'Celtic' fields lie on the cliff edge in the area of St. Lucas Leap. (R.A.F. V.A.P. CPE/UK 1893: 3305; 4300–2.)

GROUP (30): ROKE DOWN AND BERE DOWN WEST (SY 89 NW; 813964–831974), Bere Regis. 'Celtic' fields, mostly broken and in parts overlain by strip ploughing, cover 220 acres between 160 ft. and 320 ft. above O.D. on the sides and floor of a shallow valley running S.E.–N.W. The subsoil is chalk with some clay and pebble capping. Lynchets are generally very well developed but only survive clearly at the N.E. of the group and near a probable settlement (a) at the S.W. Fields have been carefully fitted around a long barrow, Bere Regis (66), and a number of round barrows, all at or near field angles. The parish boundary which forms the W. limit of the group generally lies on a bank (see Dykes, Bere Regis (119)), which is interrupted by the track W. from (a). 160 yds. S.E. of Roke Barn, about 821963, is a low banked circle about 18 ft. across, without entrance, and probably modern.

(i) *Roke Down*. S.E. of the former Roke Barn, lynchets are in places up to 21 ft. high, though most are levelled. Strip ploughing is apparent and immediately S.E. of Roke Barn is marked by ridge-and-furrow 15 yds. to 17 yds. broad and up to 1 ft. high. At 81559625 is a probable settlement area, (a), of about 1½ acres, on the sheltered N. brow of an E.–W. ridge with 'Celtic' fields above and below. It consists of an almost flat strip of ground 50 ft. to 100 ft. wide with occasional low and poorly defined platforms along it, which stretches for 750 ft. on the S. side of a scarped track, now partly hollowed, up to 21 ft. wide. This track terminates at the E. end of the supposed settlement where there are two ill-marked curved platforms set into the hillside below another platform measuring about 70 ft. by 24 ft.

(ii) *Bere Down*. At the W. end of the Down, on ground

sloping gently S.W., lynchets are frequently about 4 ft. high, though all ploughed over, and no complete fields survive. Long barrow (66), the ditches of which cannot be seen, appears to have been used as a 'Celtic' field side (R.A.F. V.A.P. CPE/UK 1934: 4117–9.)

GROUP (31): ELDERTON CLUMP (SY 89 NW; 843974–846973), Bere Regis and Winterborne Kingston.[1] 'Celtic' fields, now almost destroyed, occur over 12 acres between 250 ft. and 350 ft. above O.D., S. and W. of the Clump, and formerly extended in all directions. The chalk here is capped with clay, pebbles and a deep loamy soil. There is a probable settlement in the area (cf. Hutchins I, 147) but the only earthwork to suggest it is a fragment of double-lynchet track 10 ft. wide, which runs into Elderton Clump from the direction of round barrow, Bere Regis (110), S.W. of it, at a field angle. Coarse pottery in the Iron Age 'A' tradition and some Romano-British sherds, including New Forest ware, were found with iron slag, burnt clay and daub in the ploughed scarp, 10 ft. high, at the

---

[1] Winterborne Kingston is in the area to be covered in *Dorset* III.

foot of the slope 130 yds. W. of the clump. (R.A.F. V.A.P. CPE/UK 1934: 2121–2.)

GROUP (32): BERE DOWN (SY 89 NW; 845969), Bere Regis. Remains of 'Celtic' fields, with lynchets up to 12 ft. high, occur over 20 acres between 200 ft. and 300 ft. above O.D., N. and S. of a small dry combe where the Roman road from Badbury Rings to Dorchester probably cut across them. They formerly extended in all directions and almost certainly joined Group (31). A lynchet lies against round barrow Bere Regis (112). A 'settlement' marked on some maps immediately S. of the Roman road at 84559684 is a quarry area. (R.A.F. V.A.P. CPE/UK 1934: 4122.)

GROUP (33): BLOXWORTH DOWN (SY 89 NE; 875958–879962), Bloxworth. Remains of 'Celtic' fields with lynchets up to 5 ft. high cover 50 acres between 150 ft. and 240 ft. above O.D., mostly on moderate W. and N. slopes. A probable double-lynchet track is traceable for $\frac{1}{4}$ mile running N. from under a 'Celtic' field angle at 87589580 to just W. of round barrow, Bloxworth (36) (cf. Hutchins I, 184). (R.A.F. V.A.P. CPE/UK 1934: 4127.)

P

DISTRIBUTION MAPS

Distribution maps of BARROWS and of IRON AGE AND ROMAN SITES in South-east Dorset, to a uniform scale of ½ in. to 1 m., will be found opposite. A third map in the series, showing MEDIAEVAL SETTLEMENTS, is included with the Sectional Preface in Part 1 (opp. p. xxxvi).

Note. The only sites marked in the areas shown on the maps peripheral to S.E. Dorset as defined in this Inventory are those which cannot be dissociated from monuments included in *Dorset* II.

GLOSSARY
OF THE MEANING ATTACHED TO THE TECHNICAL TERMS USED IN THE INVENTORY

ABACUS—The uppermost member of a capital.

ACANTHUS—A plant represented in Classical and Renaissance ornament, used particularly in the Corinthian and Composite Orders.

ACCESSORY VESSEL—A miniature urn accompanying a cinerary urn and often of similar shape.

ACHIEVEMENT—In heraldry, the shield accompanied by the helm, crest, mantling, supporters, etc. In the plural the term is also applied to the insignia of honour carried at the funerals and suspended over the monuments of important persons, comprising helmet and crest, shield, tabard, sword, gauntlets and spurs, banners and pennons.

ACROTERIA—In Classical architecture, blocks on the apex and lower ends of a pediment, often carved with honeysuckle or palmette ornament.

AEDICULE—A small temple or similar shrine, or a miniature representation of the same. A surround to a doorway, niche or window having a pediment or canopy resting on pillars and suggestive of a small and exquisite building.

AGGER—In Roman engineering, the bank formed by spoil thrown up in digging the *fossa*; in particular, the earthen ridge (*agger viae* or *dorsum*) of a road.

ALTAR-TOMB—A modern term for a tomb of stone or marble resembling, but not used as, an altar.

AMPHORA-AE—A large two-handled jar with narrow neck and pointed or rounded base, used for the transport and storage of wines, oils etc.

ANTA-AE—In Classical architecture, a pilaster terminating a range of columns in the manner of a respond, with base and capital differing from those of the columns. *In antis*—Placed in a line between paired anta-responds.

ANTEFIX—In Classical architecture, an ornamental plaque for roof-decoration, usually made of clay and attached before firing to a length of *imbrex* (*q.v.*) for use at the eaves.

ANTHEMION—Honeysuckle or palmette ornament in Classical architecture.

'ANTIQUE' WORK—Renaissance ornament evoking particular compositions in the Classical decorative repertory.

ANTONINE—Of the reigns of Antoninus Pius, Marcus Aurelius and Commodus, A.D. 138–92.

ANTONINIANUS-I—A Roman base silver or silver-washed coin tariffed probably at 2 *denarii*, first issued by Caracalla (M. Aurelius Antoninus) in A.D. 214-5, and portraying the emperor with a radiate crown. The claim to this name is uncertain.

APRON—A panel, plain or decorative, below an architectural feature, usually a window, or composition, such as a funeral monument.

APSE—A projection from the wall of a church, hall or other building, semicircular or polygonal on plan, usually covered with a semi-dome or vault.

ARABESQUE—A kind of highly stylised fret-ornament in low relief, common in Moorish architecture, and found in 16th and 17th-century work in England.

ARCADE—A range of arches carried on piers or columns. *Blind arcade*, a series of arches, frequently interlaced, carried on shafts or pilasters against a solid wall.

ARCH—The following are some of the more usual forms:-
Equilateral—A pointed arch struck with radii equal to the span.
Flat or *straight*—Having the soffit horizontal.
Four-centred, depressed, Tudor—A pointed arch of four arcs, the two outer and lower arcs struck from centres on the springing line and the two inner and upper arcs from centres below the springing line. Sometimes the two upper arcs are replaced by straight lines.
Lancet—A pointed arch struck with radii greater than the span.
Nodding—An ogee arch curving also forward from the plane of the wall-face.
Ogee—A pointed arch of four or more arcs, the two uppermost being reversed, *i.e.*, convex instead of concave to the base line.
Pointed or *two-centred*—Two arcs struck from centres on the springing line, and meeting at the apex with a point.
Relieving—An arch, generally of rough construction, placed in the wall above the true arch or head of an opening to relieve it of most of the superincumbent weight.
Segmental—A single arc struck from a centre below the springing line.
Segmental-pointed—A pointed arch, struck from two centres below the springing line.
Skew—Spanning between responds not diametrically opposite.
Squinch—*See* SQUINCH.
Stilted—An arch with its springing line raised above the level of the imposts.
Three-centred, elliptical—Formed with three arcs, the middle or uppermost struck from a centre below the springing line.

ARCHITRAVE—The lowest member of an entablature (*q.v.*); often adapted as a moulded enrichment of the jambs and head of a doorway or window-opening.

ARCHIVOLT—In Classical architecture, the moulding round an arch.

ARMET—A close-helmet. Restricted in modern usage to the type in use in the 15th century with hinged cheek-pieces overlapping on the chin.

ARMORICA—The ancient region of N.W. Gaul now called Brittany.

ARRIS—The sharp edge formed by the meeting of two surfaces. *On arris*—Set diagonally.

AS-ASSES—The ancient unit of Roman base metal currency; in Imperial times a copper or bronze coin rather less than half the size of a *sestertius*.

ASHLAR—Masonry wrought to an even face and square edges.

AUMBRY—Cupboard in a church for housing the sacred vessels.

AVENTAIL or CAMAIL—A tippet of mail attached to the bascinet to protect the throat and neck, and falling to the shoulders.

BADGE—In heraldry, a device used as a cognisance, as distinct from a coat-of-arms or a charge.

BAILEY—The enclosure of a castle.

BALL-FLOWER—In architecture, a decoration, peculiar to the first quarter of the 14th century, consisting of a globular flower of three petals enclosing a small ball.

BALLISTA-AE—A large spring-operated weapon with half-tubular barrel, propelling balls or bolts.

BALUSTER—A vertical support to a rail.

BARGE-BOARD—A board, often carved, fixed to the edge of a gabled roof, a short distance from the face of the wall.

BARONET'S BADGE—In heraldry, an escutcheon argent with the Red Hand of Ulster, borne upon a baronet's shield.

BAROQUE—A style of architecture and decoration emerging in the 17th century which uses the repertory of classical forms with great freedom to emphasize the unity and pictorial character of its effects. The term is also applied to sculpture and painting of a comparable character.

BARREL-VAULTING—*See* VAULTING.

BARROW—A burial mound.
  Bank—A long barrow of exceptional length, uniform in height and with parallel sides.
  Chambered—A type of prehistoric barrow, more often long than round, containing a chamber or series of chambers, usually of stone, in which burials were deposited, often at intervals of time.
  Long—An elongated burial mound of the Neolithic period.
  Round—A circular burial mound, usually of the Bronze Age. For explanation of different types of round barrow, see *S. E. Dorset*, Part 3, p. 422.

BASCINET—Steel headpiece, egg-shaped with pointed apex, usually worn with an aventail, and fitted with a vizor.

BASTION—A projection from the general outline of a fortress or work from which the garrison is able so see, and defend by a flanking fire, the ground before the ramparts.

BASTION-TRACE FORT—A 17th-century type of fort with projecting angles or bastions.

BATTLEMENTED—*See* EMBATTLED.

BAY or BOW-WINDOW—Window in an angular or curved projection.

BAYS—The main vertical divisions of a building or feature. The divisions of a roof, marked by its main trusses.

BEADING—A small round moulding.

BEAKER—A large drinking vessel, usually further defined by shape and fabric; *butt beaker*, shaped like a butt or barrel. In particular, a pottery jar characteristic of a culture introduced into Britain towards the end of the Neolithic period, hence *Beaker culture* or *Beaker people*.
  Bell or '*B*'—The type which most closely resembles widespread Continental prototypes and which first appears here soon after 2000 B.C.
  Long-necked or '*A*'—An insular development first appearing *c.* 1800 B.C.

BEAVER—A defence for the lower part of the face.

BELGIC—Of the Belgae, *i.e.* of people from N.E. Gaul first settled in southern Britain before Caesar's invasions and already politically dominant in much of the region before the Roman conquest.

BENEFACTOR'S TABLE—Tablet or panel recording a benefaction.

BERM—A ledge between a mound or bank and its associated ditch.

BILLET—In architecture, an ornament used in the 11th and 12th centuries consisting of short attached cylinders or rectangles with spaces between.

BOLLECTION-MOULDING—A bold moulding of double curvature raised above the general plane of its setting.

BOND, ENGLISH or FLEMISH—*See* BRICKWORK.

BOSS—A projecting square or round ornament, covering the intersections of the ribs in a vault, panelled ceiling or roof, etc.

BOX-TILE—*See* FLUE-TILE.

BOXED RAMPART—A type of defence, often found in early Iron Age hill-forts, comprising a wall of rubble and earth retained within vertical timber frames and backed by a sloping ramp. The wall was separated from its ditch by a narrow platform or berm and was probably surmounted by a protected walk.

BRACE—In roof construction, a subsidiary timber inserted to strengthen the framing of a truss. *Wind brace*, a subsidiary timber inserted between the purlins and principals of a roof to increase resistance to wind-pressure. *Sling brace*, in barn roofs, a timber framed between wall-post and principal-rafter and supporting the end of a short horizontal member suggestive of a truncated tie-beam.

BRATTISHING—Ornamental cresting on the top of a screen, cornice, etc.

BRESSUMMER—A spanning beam forming the direct support of an upper wall or timber-framing.

BRICKWORK—*English Bond*—A method of laying bricks so that alternate courses on the face of the wall are composed of headers or stretchers only.
  English Garden Wall Bond—Bricks laid with three courses of stretchers to one of headers.
  Flemish Bond—A method of laying bricks so that alternate headers and stretchers appear in each course on the face of the wall; successively with more than one stretcher, *open Flemish bond*.
  Header—A brick laid so that the end only appears on the face of the wall.
  Stretcher—A brick laid so that one side only appears on the face of the wall.
  Tumbled—In a gable, triangular areas of brickwork laid at right angles to the pitch.

BRIQUETAGE—Fragments of coarse brick-like fired clay containers and props used in the manufacture of common salt in prehistoric and Roman times.

BROACH—*See* SPIRE.

BROACH-STOP—A half-pyramidal stop against a chamfer to effect the change from chamfer to right angle.

BRONZE AGE—The period when bronze was used for weapons and tools, in Britain dated roughly as follows: Early Bronze Age, 1650 to 1350 B.C.; Middle Bronze Age, 1350 to 800 B.C.; Late Bronze Age, 800 to 500 B.C.

BUTTRESS-ES—A mass of masonry or brickwork projecting from or built against a wall to give additional strength.
  Angle—Two meeting, or nearly meeting, at an angle of 90° at the corner of a building.
  Clasping—One that clasps or encases an angle.
  Diagonal—One placed against the right angle formed by two walls, and more or less equiangular with both.
  Flying—An arch or half-arch transmitting the thrust of a vault or roof from the upper part of a wall to an outer support.

CABLE-MOULDING—A moulding carved in the form of a rope or cable.

CAMAIL—*See* AVENTAIL.

CAMBERED—Curved so that the middle is higher than the ends or sides.

CANONS (of a bell)—The metal loops by which a bell is hung.

CANOPY—A projection or hood over a door, window, etc., or the covering over a tomb or niche.

CANTHARUS-I—A wide-bellied drinking vessel with two handles.

CAPSTONE—A large slab of stone forming the roof of a chamber within a chambered tomb.

CARDO-INES—In Roman land division, the boundary line drawn from N. to S., at right angles to the *decumanus*; *cardo maximus*, the principal *cardo* of a series. The terms *cardo* and *decumanus* are commonly applied, with some ancient authority, to the elements of a grid street plan.

CARSTONE—A dark brown ferruginous gritstone from the Bagshot Bed heathland or from near Swanage.

CARTOUCHE—In Renaissance ornament, a tablet imitating a scroll with ends rolled up, used ornamentally or bearing an inscription or arms.

CARYATID—Sculptured female form used as column or support.

CASEMENT—A wide hollow moulding in window-jambs etc. The hinged part of a window.

CASTOR WARE— *See* NENE VALLEY WARE.

CAUSEWAYED CAMP—A Neolithic enclosure bounded by a bank or banks each with external ditch interrupted at intervals by 'causeways' or lengths of undisturbed ground.

CELLA—The part of a Roman temple where the image of a god stood.

'CELTIC' FIELDS—Small, rectangular fields, usually bounded by lynchets, originating in the Bronze Age but widespread in Romano-British times, especially in the south of England.

CHALCOLITHIC—A cultural phase marked by the first use of copper tools in a predominantly stone age society, in Britain dating roughly from 1800 to 1650 B.C.

CHALICE—The name used in the Inventory to distinguish the pre-Reformation type of Communion cup with a shallow bowl from the post-Reformation cup with a deeper bowl.

CHAMFER—The small plane formed when the sharp edge or arris of stone or wood is cut away, usually at an angle of 45°; when the plane is concave it is termed a *hollow chamfer*, and when the plane is sunk a *sunk chamfer*.

CHANTRY CHAPEL—A chapel built for the purposes of a chantry (a foundation, usually supporting a priest, for the celebration of masses for the souls of the founder and such others as he may direct).

CHAPE—The metal plate or mounting which covers the point of a scabbard or sheath.

CHARGE—In heraldry, the representation of an object or device upon the field.

CHEQUER or CHESSBOARD PATTERN—In mosaic, an arrangement of alternately coloured squares.

CHEVAUX-DE-FRISE—Iron spikes, originally set in timber to repel cavalry, now usually along the tops of walls to protect property.

CHEVRON—In architecture, a decorative form resembling a V and often used in a consecutive series.
Chevron pattern—In mosaic, a series of triangles arranged like teeth.

CHIP-CARVING—Architectural enrichment of sunk triangular form resembling chip-carved woodwork.

CINQUEFOIL—A heraldic flower of five petals. *See also* FOIL.

CIST—A cavity, normally a grave, lined with slabs of stone or other material, or cut into rock.

CIVITAS-ATES—A self-governing municipal community in the Roman world; strictly *civitas peregrina*, a self-governing community of provincials without Roman or Latin citizenship, centred on a town and ranking below the chartered *coloniae* and *municipia*.

CLAUDIAN—Of the period from the Roman conquest to the death of Claudius, A.D. 43–54.

CLEARSTOREY—An upper storey, pierced by windows, in the main walls of a church. The same term is applicable in a domestic building.

CLOSE—Enclosure. In earthworks, an area enclosed by banks.

CLOSE-HELMET—A helmet fitted with vizor etc., completely enclosing the head and face.

CLUNCH—Hard stratum of the Lower Chalk used as a material for building and sculpture.

COAL MONEY—An antiquarian term, derived from local usage, for the waste discs resulting from the turning of armlets of Kimmeridge shale in ancient times.

COARSE WARE—Roman pottery other than lead-glazed wares and *samian* or allied varieties of *terra sigillata*.

COB—A building material consisting of clay mixed with fine gravel and straw.

COFFERS—Sunk panels in ceilings, vaults, domes and arch-soffits.

COIF—Small close hood, covering head only.

COLLAR-BEAM—In a roof, a horizontal beam framed to and serving to tie together a pair of rafters some distance above the wall-plate level.

COLONIA-AE—Originally a chartered land settlement of Roman citizens, especially discharged legionaries, usually associated with a newly-founded town. Later a title signifying the grant of colonial status, the highest grade of civic dignity, to an existing town.

COLOUR-COATED WARE—*See* SLIP-COATED WARE.

CONSOLE—A bracket with a compound-curved outline.

CONSTANTINIAN—Of the reign of Constantine I, A.D. 306–37; the term may be used in a wider sense for the dynasty or House of Constantine from his accession in 306 to the death of Constantius II in 361.

CONTRACTED or CROUCHED POSTURE—Descriptive of a skeleton with knees drawn up towards the chest, as a foetus.

COPE—A processional and choir vestment shaped like a cloak, and fastened across the chest by a band or brooch; worn by clerks of most grades.

COPED SLAB—A slab of which the upper face is ridged down the middle, sometimes hipped at each end.

COPS, ELBOW—A modern term for elbow defences of leather or plate, *see* COUTER. *Knee-cops*—In modern usage applied to the leather or plate defences of the knees at all dates, *see* POLEYN.

CORBEL—A projecting stone or piece of timber for the support of a superincumbent weight. *Corbel-table*—A row of corbels, usually carved, and supporting a projection.

CORNICE—A crowning projection. In Classical architecture, the crowning or upper portion of the entablature; *block cornice*, with shaped blocks regularly spaced beneath the projection, closer than modillions, wider than dentils.

CORONA—The square projection in the upper part of a Classical cornice with vertical face and wide soffit.

COUNTERSCARP—*See* SCARP.

COUTER—Elbow defence of leather or plate.

COVE—A concave under-surface of the nature of a hollow moulding but on a larger scale.

COVER-PATEN—A cover to a communion cup, used as a paten.

CRENELLES—The openings in an embattled parapet.

CREST, CRESTING—A device worn upon the helm or helmet. An ornamental finish along the top of a screen etc.

CROCKETS—Carvings projecting at regular intervals from the vertical or sloping sides of parts of a building, such as spires, canopies, pinnacles, hood-moulds, etc.

CROMLECH—A Welsh word, once widely used, for *dolmen*.

CROP-MARKS—Marks, best seen from the air, caused by differences in the growth of crops overlying archaeological features and so revealing the presence of such features.

CROSIER or PASTORAL STAFF—A tall staff ending in an ornamental crook carried as a mark of authority by archbishops, bishops, and heads of monastic houses, including abbesses and prioresses.

CROSS—In its simplest form in heraldry, a pale combined with a fesse, as the St. George's Cross; of many other varieties the following are the most common:-
Crosslet—With a smaller arm crossing each main arm.
Saltire (or *St. Andrew's*)—An X-shaped cross.
Tau (or *Anthony*)—In the form of a T.
Trefly—With the arms terminating in trefoils.

CROSSING—In a cruciform building, the space about the intersection of the axes of the main range and the transepts.

CROSS-RIDGE DYKE—A bank and ditch, sometimes a ditch between two banks, crossing a ridge or spur; often Iron Age.

CROSS WING—In a house, a range at the end of, and at right angles to, the main range.

CROWN POST—In a roof truss, the central post between tie beam and collar.

CRUCK TRUSS— *See under* ROOFS.

CULTURE—In archaeology, an aggregation of associated traits exemplified by material remains (of implements, dwellings, etc.) and believed to indicate a people with a distinctive tradition.

CURSUS—A Neolithic ritual monument comprising a pair of parallel banks with external ditches, rarely more than 300 ft. apart, from 500 ft. to as much as 6 miles in length; the banks and ditches are usually returned at right angles to enclose the ends.

CURTAIN—The connecting wall between the towers or bastions of a castle.

CUSHION-CAPITAL—A capital cut from a cube with its lower angles rounded off to adapt it to a circular shaft.

CUSPS (*cusping, sub-cusps*)—The projecting points forming the foils in Gothic windows, arches, panels, etc.; they were frequently ornamented at the ends (*cusp-points*) with leaves, flowers, berries, etc.

CYMA—A moulding with a wave-like outline consisting of two contrary curves.

DADO—The separate protective or decorative treatment applied to the lower parts of wall-surfaces to a height, normally, of 3 ft. to 4 ft. *Dado-rail*, the moulding or capping at the top of the dado.

DECUMANUS-I—In Roman land division, the boundary line drawn from E. to W.; *decumanus maximus*, the principal *decumanus* of a series. *See* CARDO.

DECURION—A member of the senate (*ordo*) of a *civitas*.

DENARIUS-II—The standard Roman silver or base silver coin until the 3rd century A.D., worth 16 *asses* or 4 *sestertii*.

DENTILS—The small rectangular tooth-like blocks used decoratively in Classical cornices. In mosaic, an analogous ornament forming a simple type of *fret*.

DETENT (of Crossbow)—The small knotched nut of bone which detains the string when the bow is spanned.

DEVEREL-RIMBURY—The name given to a Middle Bronze Age culture flourishing in southern England between *c.* 1250 and 1000 B.C. and characterised by *barrel*, *bucket* and *globular urns*. It takes its name from two sites in Dorset, the Deverel Barrow, Milborne St. Andrew (30) (*Dorset* III), and the Rimbury Urnfield, Weymouth (435).

DEXTER—In heraldry, the right-hand side of a shield as held.

DIAPER—All-over decoration of surfaces with squares, diamonds, and other patterns.

DIE—The part of a pedestal between the base and the cornice.

DISC-BROOCH—A class of *plate-brooch* with a disc-shaped front, often ornamented or enamelled.

DOG-LEGGED STAIRCASE—*See* STAIRCASES.

DOG-TOOTH ORNAMENT—A typical 13th-century carved ornament consisting of a series of pyramidal flowers of four petals; used to enrich hollow mouldings.

DOLMEN—A group of large stones representing the chamber, either intact or collapsed, of a prehistoric chambered tomb from which the mound or cairn has been removed.

DONKEY-MILL or SLAVE-MILL—A mill consisting of a large pair of stones and requiring animals or slaves as motive power. The conical lower stone (*meta*) carried a spindle supporting the upper stone (*catillus*), which consisted of a hollow double or single cone.

DORMER—A sleeping recess contrived as a projection from the slope of a roof and having a roof of its own, usually unfenestrated but occasionally with small lights in the cheeks.

DORMER-WINDOW—A vertical window on the slope of a roof and having a roof of its own.

DORSUM—*See* AGGER.

DORTER—A monastic dormitory.

DOUBLE LYNCHET TRACK—A trackway running through fields on a slope and bounded and defined by lynchets, one rising from the uphill side and the other falling from the downhill side; often associated with 'Celtic' fields.

DOUBLE-OGEE—*See* OGEE.

DOVETAIL—A carpenter's joint for two boards, one with a series of projecting pieces resembling doves' tails fitting into the other with similar hollows.

DRAWBAR—A wooden or metal bar for securing a door, being drawn from a tunnel-like housing in one jamb to engage in a socket in the opposite jamb.

DRESSINGS—The stone or brickwork used about an angle, window or other feature when worked to a finished face, whether smooth, tooled or rubbed, moulded or sculptured.

EMBATTLED—In architecture, a parapet with *merlons* separated by *embrasures* or *crenelles*.

EMBRASURES—The opening or sinkings in embattled parapets, or the recesses for windows, doorways, etc.

EMMER—A species of wheat, *Triticum dicoccum*.

END SCRAPER— A type of flint artifact used widely during the Neolithic and Bronze Ages probably for domestic purposes, *e.g.* the dressing of skins.

ENTABLATURE—In Classical or Renaissance architecture, the moulded horizontal superstructure of a wall, colonnade or opening. A full entablature consists of an *architrave, frieze*, and *cornice*.

ENTASIS—The convexity or swell designed to correct the optical illusion of concavity in the sides of a column or spire effecting straight profiles.

ESCUTCHEON—*See* SCUTCHEON.

EXTENDED POSTURE—Descriptive of a skeleton, usually on its back, with legs straight or almost straight.

FAIENCE (Ancient)—A composition consisting mainly of powdered quartz covered with an opaque blue or, more rarely, green vitreous glaze. It first appears in Britain about 1400 B.C. in the form of small beads of Egyptian origin.

FAN-VAULTING—*See* VAULTING.

FASCIA—A plain or moulded facing board.

FIBULA-AE—A brooch, especially one of safety-pin form with sprung or hinged pin and catch.

FINIAL—A formal bunch of foliage or similar ornament at the top of a pinnacle, gable, canopy, etc.

FLAVIAN—Of the reigns of Vespasian and his sons, Titus and Domitian, A.D. 69–96.

FLEXED POSTURE—Descriptive of a skeleton, usually lying on its side, with legs drawn up to a right angle, or less, with the spine.

FLINT CORE, FLAKE, BLADE—A *core* represents the remains of a block of flint from which *flakes*, for the manufacture of artifacts, have been removed by striking. In the process numerous waste flakes too were produced. Cores were sometimes fashioned into implements. A *blade* is a long narrow piece of flint struck from a core.

FLUE-TILE—A tile shaped like a box open at both ends, used in *hypocaust* flues.

FOIL (*trefoil, quatrefoil, cinquefoil, multifoil,* etc.)—A leaf-shaped space defined by the curves formed by the cusping in an opening or panel.

FOLIATED (of a capital, corbel, etc.)—Carved with leaf ornament.

FOOD-VESSEL—A pottery vessel of the Early and Middle Bronze Age, developed in the main from *Beaker* pottery and frequently found in association with burials. Its name contrasts with 'drinking vessel', a term once commonly applied to *Beaker* pottery.

FOSSA-AE—A ditch or trench.

FOUR-CENTRED ARCH—*See* ARCH.

FRATER—The refectory or dining-hall of a monastery.

FRET—In heraldry, a charge formed of a voided lozenge interlaced with two narrow pieces in saltire. *Fretty*—Three or more narrow bends and as many bends sinister interlaced in a lattice pattern. In mosaic, a pattern of lines, usually straight, joined at right angles.

FRIEZE—The middle division in an *entablature*, between the *architrave* and the *cornice*; generally any band of ornament or colour immediately below a cornice.

FUNERAL-ARMOUR—*See under* ACHIEVEMENTS.

FURLONG—Area of the common field containing a number of adjacent strips running in the same direction.

GABLE—The wall at the end of a ridged roof, generally triangular, sometimes semicircular, and sometimes with an outline of various curves, then called *curvilinear* or *Dutch*. A *stepped* gable has an outline suggestive of a flight of steps.

GADROONED—Enriched with a series of convex ridges, the converse of fluting, and forming an ornamental edge or band.

GALLETING—The technique of facing wide mortar joints with small pebbles, stone chips or flint flakes.

GALLO-BELGIC—Of the region, N. and E. of the Seine and Marne, incorporated in the Roman province of Gallia Belgica.

GARDEROBE—Wardrobe. Antiquarian usage applies it to a latrine or privy chamber.

GARGOYLE—A carved projecting figure pierced or channelled to carry off the rain-water from the roof of a building.

GAUGING—In brickwork, bringing every brick exactly to a certain form by cutting and rubbing. Specially made soft bricks are used for the purpose.

GLACIS—In military engineering, a natural or artificial slope beyond an outer defensive ditch, concealing the latter without affording a covered approach to an attacker. The term is also used by archaeologists for an unbroken slope from the top of a rampart to the bottom of its ditch, in contrast to *boxed rampart* and *berm* construction.

GLASTONBURY WARE—Hand-made pottery incised or tooled with curvilinear, hatched, and sometimes rectilinear decoration, characteristic of the later phases of the Iron Age in the S.W. of Britain, especially at the settlements of Glastonbury and Meare.

GLEVUM WARE—A wheel-thrown, largely hand-burnished, buff or orange-red pottery made at or near Gloucester (*Glevum*) in the 1st and 2nd centuries A.D., probably at first in legionary kilns.

GNOMON—The rod of a sundial, showing the time by its shadow.

GORGET—The plate-armour protecting the neck.

GORGONEION—A representation of the head of a Gorgon.

GRAFFITO-I—A scratched or scrawled inscription or design.

'GRAPHITE'-COATED WARE—Pottery with a grey lustrous surface resembling shading with a 'lead' pencil; in particular a ware (Hengistbury class H) found in a late Iron Age context at coastal sites in southern Britain and comparable with pottery found in Brittany.

GRISAILLE—Painting, decorative or on glass, in greyish tints.

GROINING, GROINED VAULT—*See* VAULTING.

GUIGE—Suspension strap of a shield.

GUILLOCHE PATTERN—A geometrical ornament consisting of two or more intertwining wavy bands. In mosaic, three or four-strand guilloche is alternatively called *plait*.

GUTTAE—Small stud-like projections under the triglyphs and mutules of the Doric entablature.

HAEMATITE WARE—A type of highly burnished pottery produced mainly during the earlier phases of the Iron Age and characterised by an iron-rich slip-coating turned red or reddish-brown in firing.

HALL—The principal room of a mediaeval house, often open to the roof.

HAMMER-BEAMS—Horizontal brackets of a roof projecting at wall-plate level, and resembling the two ends of a tie-beam with its middle part cut away; they are supported by braces, and help to diminish lateral pressure by reducing the span. Sometimes there is a second and even a third upper series of these brackets.

HATCHMENT—Now used for the square or lozenge-shaped tablet displaying the armorial bearings, usually painted, of a deceased person, first hung outside his house and then laid up in the church.

HAUBERK—Shirt of mail.

HEATHSTONE—*See* CARSTONE.

HELM—Complete barrel or dome-shaped head-defence of plate. No longer used in warfare after the middle of the 14th century; it continued in use in the tilt-yard into the 16th century.

HELMET—A light head-piece. *See* ARMET, CLOSE-HELMET, POT, SALLET.

HENGE or HENGE MONUMENT—A ceremonial circle formed by a bank with a ditch, usually internal, and with one or two, opposed, entrances; the interior often contained circular or other arrangements of stones or posts. Originated in the late Neolithic period.

HENGISTBURY CLASS B WARE—Pottery ornamented with raised bands, or cordons, and with a form of base often including a raised boss, or *omphalos*; found especially at Hengistbury Head, Hampshire, and comparable with pottery of the mid 1st century B.C. at the hill-fort of Le Petit Celland, Normandy; *Class H Ware, see* 'GRAPHITE'-COATED WARE.

HEXASTYLE—A portico having six columns.

HILL-FORT—A defensive enclosure fortified with rampart and ditch, single or multiple, and usually placed on more or less dominant ground; datable to some phase of the Iron Age.

HIPPED ROOF—A roof with sloped instead of vertical ends. *Half-hipped*, a roof the ends of which are partly vertical and partly sloped.

HOLLOW WAY—A sunk track caused by wear or by earth building up on either side.

HOOD-MOULD (*label, drip-stone*)—A projecting moulding on the face of a wall above an arch, doorway or window; it may follow the form of the arch or be square in outline.

HORNWORK—A short curving bank, or bank and ditch, thrown out to protect an approach or entrance to a defensive earthwork such as a hill-fort.

HOUSES—See *S.E. Dorset*, Part 1, pp. lxi–lxiv.

HUT CIRCLE—Footings or other remains of the walls of a circular dwelling, usually prehistoric.

HYPOCAUST—In Roman buildings, a low basement over which a fireproof floor is supported on small pillars (*pilae*) or walls, constructed for the circulation of hot air to warm the room above.

IMBREX-ICES—A long half-tubular Roman tile, normally of fired clay, used to cover the flanges of adjacent rectangular roof-tiles (*tegulae*), or to cap a roof-ridge.

IMPALED—In heraldry, applied to the marshalling side by side on one shield of the arms of a husband and wife, or of a dignity and its holder.

IMPOST—The projection, often moulded, at the springing of an arch, upon which the arch appears to rest.

INCENSE CUP—A tiny ritual or symbolic vessel often found in association with urn burials of the Early Bronze Age, and particularly of the Wessex culture.

INDENT—The sinking in a slab for a monumental brass.

INFULAE—The tasseled labels or strings of a mitre.

INSULA-AE—A term used by archaeologists for the areas, usually rectangular or approximately so, enclosed by the street system of a Roman town; in Roman town-planning, strictly a unified block of buildings with a central courtyard reached through entrances from the streets.

INTAGLIO—A design cut into any substance, resulting in the pattern being sunk below the surface of the material.

INTERVALLUM—In a Roman camp or fort, the perimeter space between the rampart and internal buildings, usually containing the *intervallum road*.

IRON AGE—The prehistoric period in which iron was used for weapons and tools, dating in Britain from before 500 B.C. to the Roman Conquest, A.D. 43.

JAMBS—The sides of an archway, doorway, window, or other opening. In armour, (*greaves*) plate-defences for the legs below the knees.

JETTY—The projection of the upper storey of a building beyond the plane of a lower storey.

JOGGLING—The method of cutting the adjoining faces of the voussoirs of an arch with rebated, zigzagged or wavy surfaces to provide a better key.

JUPON—Close-fitting surcoat, worn over armour *c.* 1350 to *c.* 1410; sometimes called a *gipon* or *coat armour*.

KEYSTONE—The middle stone of an arch.

KIMMERIDGE SHALE—A form of bituminous oil-shale outcropping in the sea cliffs of the Isle of Purbeck and prized in prehistoric and, more particularly, Romano-British times, when it was used for furniture, armlets, etc.

KING-POST—The middle vertical post rising to the ridge in a roof-truss. *See under* ROOFS.

KNEELER—The stone at the foot of a gable.

KNOT—In mosaic, a simple device consisting of two oblong links intertwined at right angles; *endless knot* or *interlace*, a development of the device, resembling matting or basket-work.

LABEL—*See* HOOD-MOULD.

LANCET—A long, narrow window with a pointed head, typical of the 13th century.

LA TENE—A continental Iron Age culture named after a Swiss lake site; elements of it first appear in Britain about 400 B.C.

LATTICE PATTERN—A pattern of cross lines, set square or diagonally.

LENTEN VEIL—A hanging suspended before the altar during Lent and taken down on the Wednesday or Thursday before Easter.

LIERNE-VAULTING—*See* VAULTING.

LIGULA—A spoon with diminutive bowl for extracting and dropping aromatic essences; a special type has a curved prong at the other end of the stem.

LINENFOLD PANELLING—Panelling ornamented with a conventional representation of folded linen.

LINKED-TRIANGLE PATTERN—In mosaic, a series of triangles arranged apex to base.

LINTEL—The horizontal beam or stone bridging an opening.

LOCKER—A small cupboard formed in a wall. *See also* AUMBRY.

LOOP—A small narrow light, often unglazed.

LOUVRE—A lantern-like structure surmounting the roof of a hall or other building, with openings, for ventilation or the escape of smoke, usually crossed by sloping slats (called *louvre-boards*) to exclude rain. Louvre-boards are also used in church belfries, instead of glazing, to allow the bells to be heard.

LYNCHET—A cultivation scarp, usually produced by ploughing, in which the *positive* element represents the accumulation of plough-soil from uphill, and the *negative* element the portion cut away by the plough and moved downhill. *See* 'CELTIC' FIELDS and STRIP LYNCHETS.

MANDORLA—A glory in the form of an oval surround. *See also* VESICA PISCIS.

MANNERIST—A use of the repertory of revived antique forms in an arbitrary way.

MANSARD—*See under* ROOFS.

MANTLE or MANTLING—In heraldry, a cloth hung over the hinder part of the helm; the edges were often fantastically dagged and slit.

MARGINAL PANES—Narrow borders in the glazing of a window.

'MATHEMATICAL' TILES—Special-purpose tiles hung vertically on battens to simulate brickwork.

MEDALLION—In mosaic, a small circular panel, sometimes within an octagonal frame, used repetitively, or singly as a centre piece.

MENHIR—An obsolete term for a single standing stone.

MERLON—The solid part of an embattled parapet between the embrasures.

MESOLITHIC—Middle Stone Age; a phase extending in Britain from about 12000 B.C. to 3400 B.C.

METOPES—The panels, often carved, filling the spaces between the triglyphs of the Doric entablature.

MICROLITHS—Very small flint artifacts characteristic of the Mesolithic phase.

MILL-RIND—The iron socket in the centre of a mill-stone.

MINIM—An unofficial Roman coin of very small size.

MISERICORDE—A bracket, often elaborately carved, on the underside of the hinged seat of a choir-stall. When the seat is turned up the bracket comes into position to support the occupant during long periods of standing. In monastic planning, a small hall, generally attached to the Infirmary, in which meat and better food than normal were provided.

MODILLIONS—Brackets under the cornice in Classical architecture.

MORTARIUM-A—In Roman pottery, a stout bowl with heavy rim and spout, internally grit-studded (or, in some early types, grooved) to assist the grating or trituration of food; perhaps also for curdling and cheese-making.

MOSAIC PAVEMENT—A patterned floor made of differently coloured pieces of stone, tile, glass etc., most commonly in *opus tessellatum* (*see* TESSELLATED PAVEMENT).

MOTTE—In earthworks, a steep mound, flat-topped, forming the main feature of an 11th or 12th-century castle; originally often surmounted by a timber tower; associated with a BAILEY (*q.v.*).

MULLION—A vertical post, standard, or upright dividing an opening into lights.

MULTIVALLATE—With multiple banks and ditches.

MUNICIPIUM-A—A self-governing town with a charter of Roman type, the free inhabitants possessing Latin or, less commonly, Roman citizenship.

MUNTIN—In panelling, an intermediate upright, butting into or stopping against the rails.

MUTULES—Shallow blocks under the corona of the cornice in Classical architecture.

NAIL-HEAD—Architectural enrichment of small pyramidal form used extensively in 12th-century work.

NARROW RIG—A form of ridge-and-furrow with ridges up to 5 yds. across, dated mostly to the 18th and 19th centuries.

NECKING or NECK-MOULDING—The narrow moulding at the lower edge of a capital.

NENE VALLEY or CASTOR WARE—Pottery manufactured in the Nene Valley near Peterborough, widely distributed in Roman Britain from *c.* A.D. 175 to the late 4th century; in particular, brown, red, or black glossy slip-coated table wares, early examples of which include 'hunt-cups', with trailed decoration 'en barbotine', best distinguishable from similar products of Colchester kilns by their white or cream body.

NEOLITHIC—New, or later, Stone Age, at present taken to date in Britain from about 3400 B.C. to 1800 B.C.

Neronian—Of the reign of Nero, A.D. 54–68.

New Forest Ware—Pottery made in New Forest kilns in the 3rd and 4th centuries A.D.; in particular the more widely distributed and distinctive varieties: (i) 'imitation samian' red slip-coated soft ware, (ii) cream or 'parchment'-coloured gritty ware with painted decoration, (iii) purple metallic-lustred hard grey ware, often with white painted decoration.

Newel—The central post in a circular or winding staircase; also the principal posts at the foot and the angles of a dog-legged or well-staircase.

Nodding Arch—See under Arch.

Octastyle—Of a portico, having eight columns.

Ogee—A compound curve of two parts, one convex, the other concave; a double-ogee moulding is formed by two ogees meeting at their convex ends.

Ogival Dagger—A type of Early Bronze Age dagger, characteristic of the Wessex culture, with a blade of ogival outline and with a raised midrib; attachment to the grip is by rivets.

Open Fields—Large, unenclosed fields of mediaeval and later date, usually held in common and cultivated on a strip system.

Opus Sectile—A form of mosaic employing thin slabs cut into patterns.

Orders of Arches—Receding concentric rings of voussoirs.

Orders of Architecture—In Classical or Renaissance architecture, the five systems of columnar architecture, known as Tuscan, Doric, Ionic, Corinthian and Composite. Colossal Order, one in which the columns or pilasters embrace more than one storey of the building.

Oriel-window—A projecting bay-window carried upon corbels or brackets. In great houses a special usage is for the large projecting windows generally lighting the Hall dais.

Orthostat—A standing stone.

Oversailing Course—A brick or stone course projecting beyond the one below it.

Ovolo Moulding—A Classical moulding forming a quarter round or semi-ellipse in section.

Palimpsest—Of a brass, reused by engraving the back of an older engraved plate. Of a wall-painting, superimposed on an earlier painting.

Pall—In ecclesiastical vestments, a narrow strip of lambswool, having an open loop in the middle, and weighted ends; it is ornamented with a number of crosses and forms the distinctive mark of an archbishop; it is worn round the neck, above the other vestments.

Palladian Window—A three-light window with a tall round-headed middle light and shorter lights on either side, the side lights with flanking pilasters and small entablatures forming the imposts to the arch over the centre light.

Park Pale—A fence round a park; mediaeval park pales usually survive as banks with inner ditches.

Parlour—In a monastery, a passage-way, usually though the east range of the cloister, the talking place. The principal private room in 15th-century and later houses.

Pastoral Staff—See Crosier.

Paten—A plate for holding the Bread at the celebration of the Holy Communion.

Patera-ae—A broad flat dish or saucer. A flat ornament applied to a frieze, moulding, or cornice; in Gothic work it commonly takes the form of a four-lobed leaf or flower.

Pediment—A low-pitched gable used in Classical and Renaissance architecture above a portico, at the end of a building, or above doors, windows, niches, etc.; sometimes the gable angle is omitted, forming a broken pediment, or the horizontal members are omitted, forming an open pediment. A curved gable-form is sometimes used in this way.

Pegging—In timber-framing, dowelling with headless wooden pegs; hence pegs and pegholes.

Pelican in Piety—A pelican shown, according to the mediaeval legend, feeding her young upon the drops of blood she pecks from her breast.

Pelta-ae—A device, common in mosaic, based on the crescentic Amazonian shield of this name. Running pelta, a repetitive pattern made up of opposed peltae. Voluted or spiral pelta, one with attached scrolls or spiral tendrils.

Penannular—Of brooches, armlets, etc., in the form of a ring, but not completely closed.

Peristalith—A setting of standing stones skirting a burial mound.

Peterborough—A type-site of the Neolithic period which gives its name to pottery and a culture dating from c. 2700 B.C. to 1600 B.C. Peterborough pottery may be divided chronologically into Ebbsfleet (earliest), Mortlake and Fengate types.

Phallus-i—The male organ; ancient representations were prized for their supposed talismanic qualities.

Piscina—A basin for washing the sacred vessels and provided with a drain, generally set in or against the wall to the S. of the altar, but sometimes sunk in the pavement.

Plat-band—A flat projecting horizontal band of masonry or brick-work across the face of a building, as distinct from a moulded string.

Plate-brooch—A class of brooch with a flat front instead of a bow, generally enamelled and of varied form (crescentic, zoomorphic, swastika-shaped, etc.).

Plinth—The projecting base of a wall or column, generally chamfered or moulded at the top.

Podium—In Classical architecture, a basis, usually solid, supporting a temple or other superstructure.

Poleyn—Knee defence of leather or plate.

Poppy-head—The ornament at the heads of bench-standards or desks in churches; generally carved with foliage and flowers, somewhat resembling a fleur-de-lis.

Portcullis—A movable gate, rising and falling in vertical grooves in the jambs of a doorway.

Portico—A covered entrance to a building, colonnaded, either constituting the whole front of the building or forming an important feature.

Pot—Colloquial term for an open helmet in the 17th century.

Presbytery—The part of a church in which is placed the high altar, E. of the choir.

Pretence—In heraldry, a scutcheon 'of pretence' or 'in pretence' is a shield bearing the wife's arms placed by the husband of an heiress upon the centre of his own shield.

Primary Burial—The original burial, usually in, or beneath, a barrow.

Principals—The main as opposed to the common rafters of a roof.

Pulpitum—A screen in a monastic church, dividing the monastic choir from the nave.

Pulvinated Frieze—In Classical and Renaissance architecture, a frieze having a convex or bulging section.

Purlin—In roof construction, a horizontal timber carried by the principal rafters of a truss, and forming an intermediate support for the common rafters.

Quarry-ies—In leaded glazing, small panes of glass, generally diamond-shaped or square.

Quarry Ditch—A ditch, usually of irregular shape, formed by coalescent quarry pits often dug behind the inner rampart of a hill-fort to provide material for strengthening the same.

QUARTERED or QUARTERLY—In heraldry, applied to a shield divided chequerwise into four or more spaces, or 'quarters'; when there are more than four 'quarters' the number is specified. Usually the arms in the quarters diagonally opposite to each other are alike, but sometimes four or more different coats of arms are marshalled thus chequerwise on one shield.

QUEEN-POSTS—See under ROOFS.

QUERN—*Rotary*, a hand mill for grinding corn, consisting of two circular stones, the lower socketed or perforated for a pivot, the upper perforated as a hopper.
Saddle, primitive form of hand mill, consisting of a bed-stone, slightly hollowed on its upper surface, and a large oval stone or pebble for a muller.
Wessex or *Beehive*, a rotary quern of thick beehive shape with steeply-sloping milling surfaces, in use from the later Iron Age into Roman times.

QUOINS—The dressed stones at the angle of a building, or distinctive brickwork in this position.

RADIATE COIN—A Roman base metal coin, often copied locally, exemplifying the decline in weight and quality, after the middle of the 3rd century A.D., of the coin commonly known as the *antoninianus*.

RAFTERS—Inclined timbers supporting a roof-covering. *See also under* ROOFS.

RAIL—A horizontal member in the framing of a door, screen, or panel.

REAR-ARCH—The arch on the inside of a wall spanning a doorway or window-opening.

REBATE—A continuous rectangular notch cut on an edge.

REELS—Ornament resembling a line of bobbins, used in Classical architecture.

RELIQUARY—A small box or other receptacle for relics.

REREDORTER—A monastic latrine.

REREDOS—A screen of stone or wood at the back of an altar, usually enriched.

RESPONDS—The half-columns or piers at the ends of an arcade or abutting a single arch.

REVEAL—The internal side surface of a recess, especially of a doorway, or window opening.

RIDGE-AND-FURROW—Remains of former cultivation of mediaeval and later date; initially strips of tilled land, usually 3 to 12 yds. wide, thrown into ridges by the action of ploughing, leaving furrows between them.

RINYO-CLACTON—A type of late Neolithic pottery, taking its name from sites in Orkney and Essex, and characterised by grooved and/or applied decoration.

RISER—The vertical piece connecting two treads in a flight of stairs. Hence, by analogy, the steep unploughed face of a strip lynchet.

ROCOCO—The latest (18th-century) phase of Baroque, especially in Northern Europe, in which effects of elegance and vivacity are obtained by the use of a decorative repertory further removed from antique architectural forms than that in the earlier phases and often assymmetrically disposed.

ROLL-MOULDING or BOWTELL—A continuous prominent convex moulding.

ROOD—(*Rood beam, Rood screen, Rood loft*)—A cross or crucifix. The Rood, generally in carved wood and often accompanied by the figures of Mary the Virgin and St. John, was normally set up at the E. end of the nave of a church upon the loft or bressumer of a Rood screen or on a special *Rood beam* spanning from wall to wall. Some were painted on the wall over the chancel arch or on a boarded tympanum. Only fragmentary mediaeval Roods survive. More recent Roods are often suspended from the soffit of the chancel arch. *Rood screen*, the partition across the E. end of the nave, at the entrance to the chancel; sometimes it was contrived right across an aisled church. Mediaeval examples survive with

ROOD—*Continued*
lofts, approached by stairs contrived in the flanking walls, on which were the Rood and perhaps an altar with candlesticks; the lofts could also be used as music galleries.

ROOFS—*Collar-beam*—A principal-rafter roof with horizontal timbers ('collar beams') connecting the principals at a level, or levels, above the wall plates; *arch-braced collar beam*, with arched stiffening members ('braces') between the principals and collars.
Cruck—Having a truss with principals springing from below the level of the wall plates. The timbers are usually curved, but examples with straight timbers are recorded. *Raised crucks*, with the principals rising from a level well above ground. *Upper crucks*, with the principals rising off the cross beams carrying an upper floor.
Hammer-beam—Short cantilever members ('hammer beams') in place of tie beams, braced from a level below the wall plates, form the basis of construction.
King-post—In which posts ('king posts') standing on tie beams or collar beams directly support the ridge.
Mansard—Characterised in exterior appearance by two pitches, the lower steeper than the upper.
Principal-rafter—With sloping timbers ('principal rafters') of greater scantling than the common rafters placed at intervals along the roof and framed to form trusses; normally called by the name of the connecting member used in the truss, *tie-beam* or *collar-beam*.
Queen-post—With two vertical or nearly vertical posts ('queen posts') standing on the tie beam of a truss and supporting a collar beam or the principal rafters.
Scissors-truss—As *Trussed-rafter*, but with crossed braces instead of collars.
Tie-beam—A principal-rafter roof with the truss comprising a simple triangulation of a horizontal beam ('tie beam') linking the lower ends of the pair of principals to prevent their spread.
Trussed-rafter—In which each pair of common rafters (all the timbers in the slopes being common rafters of uniform size) is connected by a collar beam, often braced. At intervals pairs of the rafters may be tenoned into a tie beam.

ROPING—Ornament resembling a rope or cable.

ROUGH-CAST—Of pottery, decorated with particles of dried clay or similar material dusted over the surface, generally under a *slip-coating*.

ROUNDEL—A circular unit of decorative or figure composition.

RUBBLE—Wall of rough unsquared stones or flints.
Coursed—Rubble walling with the stones or flints very roughly dressed and levelled up in courses some 1 ft. to 1½ ft. in height.
Regular Coursed—In which the stones or flints are laid in distinct courses and kept to a uniform height in each course.

RUPILATION—See RUSTICATION.

RUSTICATION—Primarily, masonry in which only the margins of the stones are worked; also used for any masonry where the joints are emphasised by mouldings, grooves, etc.; rusticated columns are those in which the shafts are interrupted by square blocks of stone or broad projecting bands. *Rupilation*—Masonry faced to resemble a waterworn rock surface.

SACRISTY—A room generally in immediate connection with a church, in which the holy vessels and other valuables are kept.

SALLET—A light helmet. The form varied but, in English representations, it is usually characterised by a short tail. Often fitted with a vizor worn in conjunction with a beaver.

SALTIRE—See under CROSS.

SAMIAN WARE—Red-gloss table ware manufactured from the early 1st century to the mid 3rd century A.D., mainly in southern, central and eastern Gaul, but rarely imported into Britain after the end of the 2nd century. The alternative name, *terra sigillata*, includes other varieties of red-gloss ware occasionally found in Britain, such as Arretine ware.

SCALLOPED CAPITAL—A development of the cushion-capital in which the single cushion is elaborated into a series of truncated cones.

SCARP—A short, abrupt slope, generally artificial. In fortification, a defensive slope away from the defenders; particularly the inner slope of a defensive ditch, of which the opposite, outer, slope is the *counterscarp*. *Counterscarp bank*, a small bank raised immediately beyond the counterscarp (or ultimate counterscarp in multi-vallation). *See also* LYNCHET.

SCEATTA—A coin or denomination of money mentioned in Anglo-Saxon documents.

SCREEN—In secular buildings, the partition separating the main space of a hall from the service end. *Screens passage*, the space at the service end of a hall between the screen and the end wall; *screens* is sometimes used to describe the whole arrangement of screen and screens-passage. *See also under* ROOD.

SCUTCHEON or ESCUTCHEON—A shield; a charge in heraldry. Also a metal plate pierced for the spindle of a handle or for a keyhole.

SECONDARY BURIAL—A burial additional to and later than a *primary burial*.

SEDILIA (sing. *sedile*)—The seats in a church S. of the altar, used by the ministers during the Mass.

SELION—The land between two furrows in an open field.

SESTERTIUS-II—A large Roman coin of brass or similar alloy, worth 4 *asses*.

SEXPARTITE VAULT—*See* VAULTING.

SHAFT—A slender column.

SHAFTED JAMBS—Jambs containing one or more shafts either engaged or detached.

SHERD—A scrap or broken piece of pottery.

SILIQUA-AE—A silver coin of the late Roman Empire, probably introduced by Diocletian.

SILL—The lower horizontal member of a window or door-frame; the stone, tile or wood base below a window or door-frame, usually with a weathered surface projecting beyond the wall-face to throw off water. In timber-framed walls, the lower horizontal member into which the studs are tenoned.

SINISTER—In heraldry, the left-hand side of a shield as held.

SITULATE—Resembling the Italian high-shouldered bronze bucket (*situla*); a term used of pottery vessels with straight tapering sides, high shoulders and short everted necks, characteristic of the earlier phases of the Iron Age in Britain.

SLAVE-MILL—*See* DONKEY-MILL.

SLING-BRACE—See *S.E. Dorset*, Part 1, p. lxvii.

SLIP-COATED WARE—Pottery coated with slip (clay wash), applied before firing. The slip was often prepared to produce a glossy or distinctively coloured finish, as in Rhenish imports of Claudian and later date, and Nene Valley and New Forest wares.

SLIP-TILES—Tiles moulded with a design in intaglio which was then filled in, before burning, with clay of a different colour.

SNECKS—In masonry, small stones filling gaps or making up courses in ashlar or squared rubble walling.

SOFFIT—The underside of an arch, staircase, lintel, cornice, canopy, etc.

SOFFIT-CUSPS—Cusps springing from the flat soffit of an arched head, and not from its chamfered sides or edges.

SOIL-MARKS—Marks on cultivated ground, usually most clearly observed from the air, differing in colour from the surrounding soil and produced by the presence of features such as ploughed-out banks, roads and walls, and buried ditches and pits.

SPANDREL—The space between the outside curve of an arch and the surrounding rectangular framework or moulding, or the space between the outside curves of two adjoining arches and a moulding above. In mosaic etc., a space between an outside curve or curves and a surrounding rectilinear frame.

SPELT—A species of wheat, *Triticum spelta*.

SPINDLE-WHORL—A rounded weight, perforated to fit the spindle used with a distaff in spinning wool or flax.

SPIRE, BROACH SPIRE, NEEDLE SPIRE—The tall pointed termination forming the roof of a tower or turret. A *Broach spire* rises from the sides of a tower generally without parapets, the angles of the tower being surmounted by half-pyramids ('broaches') against the facets of the spire to effect the change from the square to the polygon. A *Needle spire* is small and narrow and rises from the middle of the tower roof well within the parapet.

SPLAY—A sloping face making an angle of more than a right angle with another face, as in internal window-jambs etc.

SPRINGING LINE—The level at which an arch springs from its supports.

SPURS—*Prick*—in the form of a plain goad, an early type.
Rowel—with spiked wheel, came into general use about 1325.

SQUINCH—An arch thrown across the angle between two walls to support a superstructure, such as the base of a stone spire.

SQUINT—A piercing through a wall to allow a view of an altar from places whence it could otherwise not be seen.

STAGES—The divisions (*e.g.* of a tower) marked by horizontal string-courses externally.

STAIRCASE—*Close-string*—one having a raking member into which the treads and risers are housed.
Open-string—one having the raking member cut to the shape of the treads and risers.
Dog-legged—having adjoining flights running in opposite directions with a common newel.
Well—having stairs rising round a central opening more or less as wide as it is long.

STANCHION—An upright iron bar in a screen, window, etc.

STATER—A Celtic gold or silver coin based originally on the gold stater of Philip II of Macedon.

STOPS—Blocks terminating mouldings or chamfers in stone or wood; stones at the ends of labels, string-courses, etc., against which the mouldings finish, frequently carved to represent shields, foliage, human or grotesque masks; also, plain or decorative, used at the ends of a moulding or a chamfer to form the transition thence to the square.

STORAGE-PIT—A type of pit believed to have been used for storing produce, particularly corn, usually of cylindrical or 'beehive' shape and from about 4 ft. to 8 ft. deep and 3 ft. to 8 ft. across; first known in Britain during the Iron Age, and often found on settlement sites.

STOUP—A receptacle, normally by the doorway of a church, to contain holy water; those remaining are usually in the form of a deeply-dished stone set in a niche or on a pillar.

STRAIGHT JOINT—An unbonded junction between two structures.

STRING or STRING COURSE—A projecting horizontal band in a wall, usually moulded.

STRIP FIELDS—Cultivations of mediaeval or later date, usually part of the open fields, represented by broad ridge-and-furrow and/or strip lynchets.

STRIP LYNCHETS—Long, narrow cultivation terraces, usually open-ended, with *risers* (lynchets) above and below the cultivated *treads*. They appear to originate in the post-Roman period and represent strip cultivation on a hill side.

STRUT—A timber forming a sloping support to a beam etc.

STUDS—The common posts or uprights in timber-framed walls.

STYLE—The vertical members of a frame into which are tenoned the ends of the rails or horizontal pieces.

STYLOBATE—The podium or architectural base of a temple or other Classical building.

STYLUS or STILUS—An implement with a point and flat base for writing and erasure on waxed tablets.

SURCOAT—Coat, usually sleeveless, worn over armour.

SURPLICE—A white linen vestment with wide hanging sleeves.

SWAG—An ornament; a festoon suspended from both ends and carved to represent cloth or flowers or fruit.

TABARD—Short loose surcoat, open at the sides, with short tab-like sleeves, sometimes worn with armour, and painted or embroidered with arms; distinctive garment of a herald.

TAS-DE-CHARGE—The lower courses of a vault or arch, laid in horizontal courses and bonded into the wall, forming a solid mass; as they project forward they lessen the span.

TAZZA-E—A term, proper to Italian Renaissance vessels of open form with stem and foot, applied to Belgic and Roman pottery vessels of similar form.

TEMENOS—The sacred precinct containing the altar and temple of a god.

TERMINAL FIGURE—The upper part of a carved human figure growing out of a column, post, or pilaster diminishing to the base.

TERRA NIGRA and TERRA RUBRA—Black-surfaced and red-surfaced Gallo-Belgic pottery of good, close body, inspired by Italian and Romano-Gaulish red-gloss wares, and consisting mainly of cups and plates. It was imported into Britain both before and after A.D. 43.

TERRACE-WAY—A trackway in the form of a terrace, following the side of a slope.

TESSELLATED PAVEMENT—A floor of small cubes (*tessellae* or *tesserae*) of stone, tile, etc., often arranged as a mosaic of coloured patterns.

TESSERA-AE—A small cube of stone, tile, glass, etc., used in tessellated paving. In modern usage, although not without ancient precedent, the term replaces the more correct diminutive *tessella*.

TETRASTYLE—Of a portico, having four columns.

THUMB-GAUGING—Ornamental finish to a ridge-tile, made with the thumb before the tile is baked.

TIE BEAM—The horizontal transverse beam in a roof, tying together the feet of pairs of rafters to counteract outward thrust.

TIMBER-FRAMED BUILDING—A building of which the walls are built of open timbers and the interstices filled in with brickwork or lath and plaster ('wattle and daub'), the whole often covered with plaster or boarding. Boarding may obviate the need for filling.

TOOLING—Dressing or finishing a masonry surface with an axe or other tool, usually in parallel lines. (A change from diagonal tooling to vertical has been noted at Wells Cathedral *c.* 1210 (*Arch. Jour.* LXXXV).)

TOOTHING—*See* TUSKING.

TORUS—In Classical architecture, a convex moulding, generally a semicircle in section.

TOUCH—A soft black marble, quarried near Tournai and used in monumental art.

TRABEATION—The use of horizontal beams in building construction; descriptive in the Inventory of conspicuous cased ceiling-beams.

TRACERY—The ornamental work in the head of window, screen, panel, etc., formed by the curving and interlacing of bars of stone or wood, grouped together, generally over two or more lights or bays.

TRAJANIC—Of the reign of Trajan, A.D. 97–117.

TRANSOM—An intermediate horizontal bar of stone or wood across a window-opening.

TREAD—The horizontal platform of a step or stair. Hence, by analogy, the cultivated part of a strip lynchet above the riser.

TRELLIS—Lattice-work of light wood or metal bars.

TREPANNING—The removal of a circular piece of bone from the skull.

TRIBUNE—*See* TRIFORIUM.

TRIFORIUM—In larger churches, an arcaded wall-passage at about mid wall height, between the aisle arcades and the clearstorey. A large gallery the full width of the aisle below is termed a *Tribune*.

TRIGLYPHS—Blocks with vertical channels, placed at intervals along the frieze of the Doric entablature.

TROMPE L'OEIL—In painting, marquetry, etc., deceptively three-dimensional effect produced on the flat.

TRUSS—A number of timbers framed together to bridge a space, to be self-supporting, and to carry other timbers. The *trusses* of a roof are generally named after a peculiar feature in their construction, such as *King-post, Queen-post, Hammer-beam, Cruck,* see under ROOFS.

TUFA (Calcareous)—Spongy deposit formed by the action of water on limestone and resembling volcanic lava. Often used in vaulting on account of its lightness.

TUSKING—Bricks or stones in alternate courses left projecting beyond the wall-face of a building to facilitate the bonding-in of an extension. Also *Toothing*.

TYMPANUM—The triangular or semicircular field in the face of a pediment or in the head of an arch.

UNIVALLATE—With single bank and ditch.

URN—*Barrel*—A pottery vessel of the Middle/Late Bronze Age characterised by a convex body, a more or less concave neck and a flat or internally bevelled rim, often with applied decoration, especially on the shoulders.

Biconical—A pottery vessel of the Middle Bronze Age, in form reminiscent of two truncated cones set vertically base to base; in Dorset apparently derived from Cornish biconical urns of the Early Bronze Age.

Bucket—A pottery vessel of the Middle/Late Bronze Age, with sides tapering like those of a bucket but often incurving at the top.

Cinerary—A pottery vessel containing the remains of human cremation.

Collared or *Overhanging-Rim*—A type of pottery vessel with a deep rim, frequently found in association with cremation burials. It first appears in the Early Bronze Age (*c.* 1550 B.C.) and is largely a development of Late Peterborough (Fengate) pottery.

Globular—A type of pottery vessel of the Middle/Late Bronze Age, probably of foreign derivation and regarded as intrusive into southern England. It is characterised by a spherical body with a constriction above leading to a more or less vertical neck.

VALLUM-A—In Roman fortification, an earthern wall or rampart usually set with palisades.

VASE SUPPORT—A type of small pottery vessel of unknown use, often perforated with triangular slits; it is found in later Neolithic contexts in N. France and the *incense cups* of the Wessex culture appear to be related to it.

VAULTING—An arched ceiling or roof of stone or brick, sometimes imitated in wood and plaster. *Barrel-vaulting* is a continuous vault unbroken in its length by cross-vaults. A *groined vault* (or *cross-vaulting*) results from the intersection of simple vaulting surfaces. A *ribbed vault* is a framework of arched ribs carrying the covering over the spaces, or cells, between them. One bay of vaulting, divided into four quarters or compartments, is termed *quadripartite*; sometimes the bay is divided transversely into two subsidiary bays; the vaulting bay is thus divided into six compartments, and is termed *sexpartite*. Increased elaboration is given by *tiercerons*, secondary ribs springing from the wall-supports and rising to a point other than the centre, and *liernes*, tertiary ribs that do not spring from the wall-supports but cross from main rib to main rib. In *fan-vaulting* numerous ribs rise from the springing in equal curves, diverging equally in all directions, giving fan-like effects when seen from below.

VENETIAN WINDOW—*See* PALLADIAN.

VENTAIL—*See* VIZOR.

VESICA PISCIS—A pointed oval frame generally used in mediaeval art to enclose a figure of Christ enthroned. *Also* MANDORLA (*q.v.*).

VEXILLUM—A scarf on a pastoral staff.

VICE—A small circular stair.

VILLA—In early context, a relatively highly romanised dwelling in the country, forming the centre of an estate most often concerned principally with farming.

VIZOR—A defence for the eyes, sometimes for the whole face. The close-helmet of the 16th century was fitted with a vizor consisting of three separate plates: the vizor proper, the ventail or upper beaver covering the face, and the chin-piece or lower beaver.

VOLUTE—An ornament in the form of a spiral scroll, e.g. in the Ionic capital.

VOUSSOIRS—The stones forming an arch.

WALL PLATE—A timber laid lengthwise on the wall to receive the ends of the rafters and joists. In timber-framing, the studs are tenoned into it.

WASTER—Of pottery etc., an object spoilt or flawed in manufacture.

WAVE-MOULDING—A compound moulding formed by a convex curve between two concave curves.

WEATHERBOARDING—Horizontal planks nailed to the uprights of timber-framed buildings and made to overlap; the planks are generally wedge-shaped in section, the upper edge being the thinner.

WEATHERING (to sills, tops of buttresses, etc.)—A sloping surface for casting off water.

WEEPERS—Small upright figures, generally of relatives of the deceased, placed in niches or panels round the sides of mediaeval tombs; occasionally also represented on brasses.

WELL-STAIRCASE—See STAIRCASES.

WESSEX CULTURE—An Early Bronze Age culture, largely confined to the Wessex area, known almost entirely from burials in round barrows associated with exotic grave goods of gold, amber, faience, etc.

WIMPLE—Scarf covering the chin and throat.

WINDMILL HILL—A causewayed camp in Wiltshire and a type-site of the earlier Neolithic (3400 B.C. to 2500 B.C.) in Britain, giving its name to a culture and to a pottery tradition characterised by several regional types (Hembury, Abingdon, Whitehawk, etc.).

WOODMAN or WOODHOUSE—A wild man of the woods, generally represented naked and hairy.

WREATH PATTERN—In mosaic, a symmetrical wreath-like arrangement of overlapping loops with central tongues.

ABBREVIATIONS

USED IN THE TEXT OF THE INVENTORY

Abercromby — J. Abercromby, *Bronze Age Pottery*, 2 vols. (1912).

A.B.M.E. — L. V. Grinsell, *The Ancient Burial Mounds of England*, 2nd ed. (1953).

Ant. J. — *Antiquaries' Journal.*

ApSimon — A. M. ApSimon, 'Dagger Graves in the Wessex Bronze Age', Institute of Archaeology, University of London, *Tenth Annual Report* (1954), 37–62.

Arch. Ael. — *Archaeologia Aeliana.*

Arch. Camb. — *Archaeologia Cambrensis.*

Arch. J. — *Archaeological Journal.*

Arkell — W. J. Arkell, *The Geology of the Country around Weymouth, Swanage, Corfe and Lulworth*, Geological Survey Memoir (1947).

B.M. — British Museum.

Butler and Smith — J. J. Butler and I. F. Smith, 'Razors and Urns of the British Middle Bronze Age', Institute of Archaeology, University of London, *Twelfth Annual Report* (1956), 20–52.

Coker — *Survey of Dorsetshire* (1732); attributed to John Coker but probably by Thomas Gerard of Trent, *c.* 1625.

C.T.D., mopr, cpf & tovp — C. Warne, *Celtic Tumuli of Dorset* (1866). Three sections, separately paginated: 'My own personal researches'; 'Communications from personal friends'; 'Tumuli opened at various periods'.

Cunnington MS — E. Cunnington, MS notes (*c.* 1890), in Dorset County Museum (in part summarized in Dorset *Procs.* XXXVII (1916), 40–7).

D.C.C. — *Dorset County Chronicle.*

D.C.M. — Dorset County Museum, Dorchester.

D.C.R.O. — Dorset County Record Office.

D.N.H.A.S. — Dorset Natural History and Archaeological Society. See also Dorset *Procs.* below.

Dorset I, III, IV, V — Volumes of the Dorset *Inventory*: vol. I, *West Dorset* (1952); vols. III, *Central Dorset*, IV, *North Dorset* and V, *East Dorset* (forthcoming).

Dorset Album — Volumes of MSS., photographs and cuttings, in D.C.M., now partly broken up.

Dorset Barrows — L. V. Grinsell, *Dorset Barrows* (1959).

Dorset *Procs.* — *Proceedings of the Dorset Natural History and Archaeological Society* (formerly the Dorset Natural History and Antiquarian Field Club).

Durden Catalogue — G. Payne, *Catalogue of the Museum of Local Antiquities Collected by Mr. Henry Durden of Blandford* (1891).

Fägersten — A. Fägersten, *Place-Names of Dorset* (Uppsala, 1933).

Hutchins — J. Hutchins, *History of Dorset*, 2 vols. (1774). Third edn., ed. W. Shipp, 4 vols. (1861–70). All references are to 3rd edn., unless otherwise stated.

J.B.A.A. — *Journal of the British Archaeological Association.*

J.R.S. — *Journal of Roman Studies.*

LVG — L. V. Grinsell. Used as prefix to the barrow numbers in his *Dorset Barrows* (see above).

Med. Arch. — *Medieval Archaeology.*

Moule — H. J. Moule, *Dorchester Antiquities* (1901); references are to 2nd edn. (1906).

Moule MS — MS attached to O.S. 25-in. plan of Dorchester in D.C.M.

Num. Chron. — *Numismatic Chronicle.*

O.A.P.   Oblique air photograph.

O.S. 1811   Ordnance Survey one-inch map, first
                   edition (Dorset area), 1811.

P.C.T.E.W.   G. E. Daniel, *The Prehistoric Cham-
                   ber Tombs of England and Wales*
                   (1950).

P.P.S.   *Proceedings of the Prehistoric Society.*

P.R.O.   Public Record Office.

Purbeck Papers   J. H. Austen, *Purbeck Papers*, 2 vols.
                   (1856–69).

Raven   J. J. Raven, *Church Bells of Dorset*
                   (Dorchester, 1906).

Taylor's Map   Map of the County of Dorset, by
                   Isaac Taylor, 1765, reprinted.

V.A.P.   Vertical air photograph.

V.C.H.   Victoria County History.

Walters   H. B. Walters, 'Dorset Church Bells'
                   in Dorset *Procs.* LX (1939), 97–120.

W.A.M.   *Wiltshire Archaeological and Natural
                   History Magazine.*

Wessex inter-   Reference no. from S. Piggott, 'Register
ment no.   of Grave-Groups of the Wessex Culture
                   in the Wessex Area', *P.P.S.* IV (1938),
                   102–6.

LIST OF BLAZONS

OF UNIDENTIFIED ARMS IN *DORSET* II

For the ARMORIAL INDEX of the whole county see *Dorset* V.

1. *A fesse between six roses.* Bere Regis (1), p. 18.
2. *Sable, a fesse or between three cinquefoils (?) argent.* Corfe Castle (1), p. 54.
3. *Ermine, a lion rampant crowned, impaling (?).* Turners Puddle (1), p. 298.
4. *Ermine, a lion rampant, over all two barrulets.* Winterborne Came (1), p. 383.
5. *Argent, two bars gules, in chief three mullets gules.* Winterborne Came (1), p. 383.

INDEX

Numbers in brackets refer to the serial numbers of the monuments in each parish; where, in Parts 1 and 2, these are sufficient to enable the reference to be found, no page number is given. Page numbers are given for references not covered by a monument number, for references in monument entries extending to more than one page, and for references in Part 3. The letters a and b denoting left and right-hand columns are added where necessary. Numbers printed in bold type indicate that there is a line drawing to illustrate the text.

Pages 1 – 188, Affpuddle – Owermoigne, are in Part 1; pages 189 – 417, Poole – Winterbourne Steepleton, are in Part 2; pages 418 – 633 are in Part 3.

Q

649

Floyer—*continued*

Anna, 1774, monument, Weymouth (334), 366b.

John, house altered by, Stafford, West, (5), 266a.

Sarah, 1733, monument, Weymouth (334), 366b.

Follies, Landmarks, etc.

See also **Parks and Garden Buildings.**

ARCH, 18TH-CENTURY, Steeple (4), 271b, Pl. 58.

OBELISKS

18TH-CENTURY: Dorchester (11); Moreton (6), inscriptions from, Moreton (2).

19TH-CENTURY: Corfe Castle (11), 81a; Portland (11) (landmark).

TOWERS

18TH/19TH-CENTURY, Morden (3), 164b, 170a, Pl. 111.

19TH-CENTURY: Kimmeridge (2), Pl. 58; Portesham (3).

Folly Pier, Portland, 247b.

Fonblanque, Elizabeth, 1844, monument, Osmington (1), 179b.

Font Covers

15TH-CENTURY, Winterborne St. Martin (1), 392b.

17TH-CENTURY, Poole (6), 199a.

19TH-CENTURY: Arne (1), 9b; Poole (1), 193b, Pl. 9.

Fonts: lii.

11TH-CENTURY, Chaldon Herring (1), 34a.

12TH-CENTURY: Affpuddle (1), 3b; Bere Regis (1), 16b, Pl. 8; Chickerell (1), 38b; Dorchester (1), 106b; Kimmeridge (1); Morden (1), 161a; Studland (1), 279a; Sturminster Marshall (2), 286a; Wareham Lady St. Mary (1) (lead), 307b, Pls. 167–8; Weymouth (3) (291); Winterborne St. Martin (1), 392b; Winterbourne Steepleton (1), 395a.

12TH/13TH-CENTURY: Osmington (1), 179b; Weymouth (302), 362a; Winterbourne Abbas (1), 381b.

13TH-CENTURY: Bincombe (1), 22b; Bloxworth (1), 26a; Coombe Keynes (I), 50a; Langton Matravers (I); Poole (6), 199a; Portesham (I), 241b; Steeple (I), 269b; Stoke, East, (I), 274b; Sturminster Marshall (2), 286a; Warmwell (1), 327b; Weymouth (322), 364a; Whitcombe (1), 375b.

14TH-CENTURY: Arne (1), 9b; Winterborne Came (1), 383b; Winterborne Monkton (1), 391a.

15TH-CENTURY: Broadmayne (1), 31a; Corfe Castle (1), 54a; Corfe Mullen (1), 102a; Dorchester (4), 112a; Lulworth, East, (1), 145a; Lytchett Minster (1), 158a; Sturminster Marshall (1), 285a; Weymouth (334), 366a; Wool (1), 403a, Pl. 8.

c. 1500, Lytchett Matravers (1), 155b, Pl. 8.

MEDIAEVAL: Chickerell (2), 39b; Moreton (1) (fragment), 175a; Poole (5a); Stafford, West, (1), 265a.

17TH-CENTURY: Dorchester (4), 112b; Wareham Lady St. Mary (1) 308a, (2) 313b.

18TH-CENTURY: Owermoigne (1); Portland (1), 249a; Swanage (2), Pl. 9.

19TH-CENTURY: Dorchester (1), 106b; Lytchett Minster (1), 158b; Moreton (1), 175a; Poole (1) 193b, Pl. 9, (11) Pl. 9; Portland (4), 250a; Steeple (2), 270a; Wool (2), 404a; Worth Matravers (1), 411b.

Fookes

C. B., *see* **Architects and Surveyors.**

Thomas, 1701, and John Thomas, 1728, table-tomb, Weymouth (302), 362a.

Fooks

Katherine, 1714, wife of John, headstone, Osmington (1), 180a.

Fawn and, *see* **Builders and Contractors.**

Foot, George, 1693, headstone, Kimmeridge (1), 133b.

Forbes, Charles, M.P., monument erected by, Weymouth (369), 372b.

Ford

Hannah Frances, 1820, monument, Weymouth (369), 372a.

John, and Elizabeth his wife, 1797, also Elias Dugdale, 1797, floor-slab, Wareham Lady St. Mary (1), 309a.

Fordington, Dorchester, 105b, 129–131; village plan, **114**; buildings, Dorchester (4) (139–65); mediaeval fields, (166–7); barrows near, 444b; Roman finds, (210) 569–70, (216) 573–5.

  ,,   **Bottom,** Bradford Peverell, aqueduct in, Dorchester (227a), 588, Pl. 221.

  ,,   **Down,** Bradford Peverell, Ancient Field Group (2), 624.

  ,,   **Field,** Winterborne Monkton, barrow in, 465b.

  ,.   **House,** Dorchester (139).

Ford's Barn, Chaldon Herring (18).

Forest Hill Cottage, Lytchett Minster (16).

Forseth, Robert, 1717, floor-slab, Winterbourne Abbas (1), 382a.

Fortunes Well and Fortuneswell, Portland, 247a; church, (4), 249; houses, etc., Portland (15–51).

Fossil, Chaldon Herring, 33b.

Foster, Julia Harriet, daughter of Rev. Joseph, 1849, monument, Winterborne Monkton (1), 391a.

Fountain, with 18th-century figures, Morden (3), 170a.

Four Barrow Hill Barrow Group (AK), Winterborne St. Martin, 430, 469.

Fowler, William, *see* **Builders and Contractors.**

Fox, Rev. Thomas, paten given by, Stoke, East, (1), 274b.

  ,,   **Barrow,** Bere Regis (71), 436.

  ,,   **Inn,** *see* **Inns.**

Foxhills Dairy, Lytchett Matravers (32).

Frampton

Arms of, Moreton (1), 174b, 175a; rebus of, 174b.

Diaries (yearbooks), building records in: Affpuddle, 2a; Moreton, 174a, 175b.

Family, 174a, Moreton (5).

James (Jamys Framton), 1523, brass, Moreton (1), 175a.

James, of Buckland Ripers, bequest to church, 1655, Chickerell (2).

James, of Corfe Castle Corporation, 57a.

James, 1784, monument, Moreton (1), 175a; church rebuilt by, 174a; initials inscribed, 174b; bridge built by, (4); obelisk in memory of, (6); aisle owned by, Turners Puddle (1), 298a.

James, 1818, eldest son of James and Harriot, monument, Moreton (1), 175a.

Harriot, 1844, daughter of Henry Thomas, Earl of Ilchester, and wife of James, monument, Moreton (1), 175b.

Mary (Houlton), 1762, 1st wife of James, monument, Moreton (1) 175a, Pl. 113.

Mary, 1846, daughter of James and Phillis, monument, Moreton (1), 175a; initials inscribed, 174b.

Phillis (Byam), 1829, 2nd wife of James, monument, Moreton (1), 175a.

Robert, house built by, Moreton (5), 175b.

William, and Judith (Arnold) his wife, monument erected 1755, Moreton (1) 175a.

Frampton (*Dorset* I): Roman mosaic, 569b; Roman aqueduct, Dorchester (227a), 585; Ancient Field Group (1), 623–4, Pl. 231; settlements, 623, Pl. 231; enclosure, Frampton (20) 624a.

France, Royal arms of, Poole (30), 212a.

Franciscans, *see* **Religious Foundations.**

Franklin, Maria, *see* **Henning,** Rev. Robert.

Freke

Mary, 1712, table-tomb, Weymouth (334), 366b.

Robert, 1699, table-tomb, Weymouth (334) 366b.

Friar Waddon, Portesham, xxxvii, 240b; buildings at, Portesham (29), Pl. 147.

  ,, ,,   **Hill,** Portesham: Barrow Group (Q), 430, 450; barrows (50–1), 450; dyke (62), 518.

Frome Billet, manor of, Stafford, West, 263b, 264a, 266a.

  ,,   **Hill,** barrow on, Stafford, West, (20), 451.

  ,,   **House,** former, Stafford, West, (5), 265b.

Fry, William and Eliza, children of George and Elinor, floor-slab, Corfe Castle (1), 54b.

Fryer Mayne, Knighton, West, 136a; manor house (2), 137; deserted village (19), 138; round barrow (21), 445.

Furmedge, John, 1849, and Ann his wife, 1858, table-tomb, Weymouth (291).

Furniture

BOOKCASES, 19TH-CENTURY: Moreton (5), 177a; Stafford, West, (5), 267a.

CHAIRS

17TH-CENTURY: Affpuddle (1), 3b; Arne (1), 9b; Church Knowle (1), 43a; Dorchester (10), 115a; Morden (2), 161b; Poole (6) 199a, (8) 201b; Sturminster Marshall (1), 284b; Wareham Lady St. Mary (1) 307b, (2) 313b; Weymouth (10), 338b; Winfrith Newburgh (1), 378a.

c. 1700, Morden (1), 160b.

19TH-CENTURY: Poole (1), 193b; Winterborne Came (1), 383b, Pl. 9.